Ethics for Life

A Text with Readings

Seventh Edition

JUDITH A. BOSS, PhD

D1597564

McGraw Hill Education

ETHICS FOR LIFE: A TEXT WITH READINGS

Published by McGraw-Hill Education, 2 Penn Plaza, New York, NY 10121. Copyright 2019 by McGraw-Hill Education. All rights reserved. Printed in the United States of America. No part of this publication may be reproduced or distributed in any form or by any means, or stored in a database or retrieval system, without the prior written consent of McGraw-Hill Education, including, but not limited to, in any network or other electronic storage or transmission, or broadcast for distance learning.

Some ancillaries, including electronic and print components, may not be available to customers outside the United States.

This book is printed on acid-free paper.

1 2 3 4 5 6 7 8 9 LCR 21 20 19 18

ISBN 978-1-260-09158-8
MHID 1-260-09158-9

Cover Image: ©Design Pics/Natural Selection John Reddy

mheducation.com/highered

To My Interns

Contents

Section II Ethical Relativism   113

Section III   Morality as Universal   207

Preface

Aristotle wrote that "the ultimate purpose in studying ethics is not as it is in other inquiries, the attainment of theoretical knowledge; we are not conducting this inquiry in order to know what virtue is, but in order to become good, else there would be no advantage in studying it." *Ethics for Life* is a multicultural and interdisciplinary introductory ethics textbook that provides students with an ethics curriculum that has been shown to significantly improve students' ability to make real-life moral decisions.[1]

One of the frustrations in teaching ethics is getting students to integrate moral theory into their lives. Developing a meaningful philosophy of life, at one time the highest priority among entering college freshmen, has declined rapidly in the past thirty years as a motive for attending college. Criminal activities—including sexual assault, hate crimes, burglary, drug dealing, and murder—remain a problem on many college campuses. On the other hand, while the number has leveled off in the past few years, more college students are engaging in community service since 2001.[2] In addition, today's college students are increasingly committed to political activism and civic involvement.[3] Despite their good intentions, the moral reasoning of 20 percent of college students is at the level of that of a junior high student. By the time they graduate from college, 90 percent of students will not have made the transition from cultural relativism (in which morality is equated with cultural norms and laws) to independent principled reasoning.

How can ethics teachers provide students with the skills necessary to make better moral decisions in their lives? Traditional ethics courses, which restrict the study of ethics to the purely theoretical realm and avoid any attempt to make students better people, have been found to have little or no impact on students' ability to engage in moral reasoning outside the classroom.[4] While students are able to memorize theories and lines of reasoning long enough to pass the final exam, there is little true understanding and carryover into their moral reasoning outside the classroom. When confronted with real-life moral issues, most students simply revert back to their earlier forms of reasoning based on cultural norms or self-interest.

In the 1970s and 1980s, some professors who were dissatisfied with the traditional theory-laden ethics course replaced it with the values-clarification or value-neutral approach. This approach involves "nonjudgmental" and "nondirective" discussions of popular moral issues where students are encouraged to express their own opinions without fear of criticism or judgment. Unfortunately, the values-clarification approach has been found to have no positive effect on students' moral development and may even inhibit moral growth by sending the message that morality is all relative and hence anything goes as long as it feels good.

These findings have prompted researchers and instructors to look for new approaches to ethics education. *Ethics for Life* provides a curriculum that combines traditional ethics theory with a pedagogy based on the latest research on how to enhance moral development in college students. This approach has been found effective in improving students' moral judgment, moral behavior, and self-esteem.[5]

Objective

The primary objective of *Ethics for Life* is to provide a text that is solidly based in the latest research on moral development of college students, while at the same time providing students with a broad overview of the major world moral philosophies and case studies based on real-life issues.

Interdisciplinary and Multicultural Approach

One of the main obstacles students face in taking an ethics course is its perceived lack of relevance to their lives. Most ethics students are not philosophy majors. Ethics courses also tend to attract a widely diverse group of students, many of whom do not personally relate to the traditional European approach to moral philosophy. *Ethics for Life* includes coverage of, to name only a few, Buddhist ethics, Native American philosophy, ecofeminism, Confucianism, the utilitarian philosophy of Mo Tzu, feminist care ethics, and liberation ethics. The inclusion of moral philosophies from all over the world and from both women and men makes the book more appealing to nontraditional students, and it helps students move beyond the implicit cultural relativism in most ethics textbooks that privileges traditional Western male approaches to ethics.

Moral theory does not occur in isolation nor is morality practiced within a social vacuum. While the primary focus of this text is philosophical ethics, *Ethics for Life* adopts a more holistic approach. The book is presented in a historical and interdisciplinary context and includes extensive material from anthropology and sociology, political science, religion, psychology, and literature.

Because many students taking an ethics course are weak in critical thinking skills, Chapter 2 on moral reasoning includes sections on constructing moral arguments, resolving moral dilemmas, avoiding logical fallacies, and the relation between moral analysis and practice.

A Developmental Pedagogy

There is a saying that if students cannot learn the way we teach them, we have to teach them the way they learn. In creating ethics curriculums that promote moral development, one of the approaches that has held out the most promise is the use of a cognitive-developmental approach to ethics education combined with experiential education, generally in the form of community service and the discussion of real-life moral dilemmas.

Ethics for Life is organized using a developmental or progressive approach. This approach has been shown to have a higher success rate than the more traditional or values-clarification approaches to teaching ethics in terms of helping students move beyond ethical relativism and become principled moral reasoners.

Most ethics textbooks focus only briefly on ethical relativism. However, more than 90 percent of college students are ethical relativists. Rather than talk over students' heads, *Ethics for Life* starts at their level by including material on ethical relativism. The chapters in the book are arranged in the same order that these stages appear in a person's actual moral development. Only later are the students introduced to in-depth discussions of more advanced theories such as deontology, rights ethics, and virtue ethics.

Rather than lecturing from a higher stage of development (the traditional moral-indoctrination approach) or ignoring differences (the values-clarification approach), this approach entails building a bridge to the students and then guiding them across that bridge toward a higher stage of moral development and respectfully engaging them by challenging them to question their own assumptions. This process is also known as a cognitive apprenticeship whereby the teacher or mentor (the "expert") teaches the student (the "novice") a new skill by collaborating with him or her on a task—in this case the application of moral theory to hypothetical and real-life issues.[6] Respectful engagement also requires that the teacher takes an active role in the dialogue, including challenging students rather than creating an atmosphere of passive indifference and superficial tolerance.

To avoid reinforcing the belief that morality is all a matter of personal opinion and the mistaken impression that most moral decisions involve moral dilemmas, the case studies used in the first part of the book present situations where what is morally right and wrong seems clear-cut. This helps students sort out the relevant moral principles so that they later have a solid foundation for resolving more difficult moral dilemmas.

The book makes extensive use of exercises throughout each chapter. The purpose of the exercises is to encourage students to relate the theories in the text to real-life events and issues as well as to their own moral development. In addition to case studies that relate to students' own experience, case studies and personal reflection exercises are chosen with an eye to expanding students' concept of moral community. This is accomplished through the use of readings, case studies, and reflective exercises that focus on multicultural issues and problems of racism, sexism, classism, and nationalism. In addition, each chapter features pictures along with discussion questions related to issues raised in the chapter.

Also important for moral development is the integration of students' experiences by means of readings in developmental psychology and discussions of the personal meaning and relevance of these experiences to their own personal development. Chapter 3 provides an in-depth discussion of the latest research on moral development. Students are also encouraged throughout the text to relate the material to their own experience and their own moral growth.

McGraw-Hill Connect® is a highly reliable, easy-to-use homework and learning management solution that utilizes learning science and award-winning adaptive tools to improve student results.

Homework and Adaptive Learning

- Connect's assignments help students contextualize what they've learned through application, so they can better understand the material and think critically.

- Connect will create a personalized study path customized to individual student needs through SmartBook®.

- SmartBook helps students study more efficiently by delivering an interactive reading experience through adaptive highlighting and review.

Connect's Impact on Retention Rates, Pass Rates, and Average Exam Scores

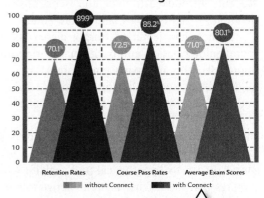

Over **7 billion questions** have been answered, making McGraw-Hill Education products more intelligent, reliable, and precise.

Using **Connect** improves retention rates by **19.8** percentage points, passing rates by **12.7** percentage points, and exam scores by **9.1** percentage points.

73% of instructors who use **Connect** require it; instructor satisfaction **increases** by 28% when **Connect** is required.

Quality Content and Learning Resources

- Connect content is authored by the world's best subject matter experts, and is available to your class through a simple and intuitive interface.

- The Connect eBook makes it easy for students to access their reading material on smartphones and tablets. They can study on the go and don't need internet access to use the eBook as a reference, with full functionality.

- Multimedia content such as videos, simulations, and games drive student engagement and critical thinking skills.

Robust Analytics and Reporting

©Hero Images/Getty Images

- Connect Insight® generates easy-to-read reports on individual students, the class as a whole, and on specific assignments.

- The Connect Insight dashboard delivers data on performance, study behavior, and effort. Instructors can quickly identify students who struggle and focus on material that the class has yet to master.

- Connect automatically grades assignments and quizzes, providing easy-to-read reports on individual and class performance.

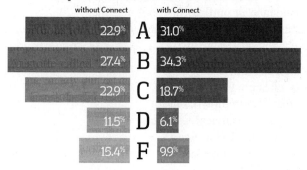

Impact on Final Course Grade Distribution

without Connect		with Connect
22.9%	A	31.0%
27.4%	B	34.3%
22.9%	C	18.7%
11.5%	D	6.1%
15.4%	F	9.9%

More students earn
As and **Bs** when they
use **Connect.**

Trusted Service and Support

- Connect integrates with your LMS to provide single sign-on and automatic syncing of grades. Integration with Blackboard®, D2L®, and Canvas also provides automatic syncing of the course calendar and assignment-level linking.

- Connect offers comprehensive service, support, and training throughout every phase of your implementation.

- If you're looking for some guidance on how to use Connect, or want to learn tips and tricks from super users, you can find tutorials as you work. Our Digital Faculty Consultants and Student Ambassadors offer insight into how to achieve the results you want with Connect.

Instructor's Manual

An online Instructor's Manual provides summaries of the chapters and readings, helpful teaching tips, and a bank of test questions for each chapter. Please contact your local McGraw-Hill sales representative for more details.

Ethics for Life is set up so it can be used with or without a community service component. Studies show that participation in community service as part of an ethics class has a positive effect on students' self-esteem and level of empathy as well as their ability to engage in moral reasoning. Community service gives them an opportunity to integrate what they are learning in class into real-life situations. To assist in this goal, exercises are provided in each chapter to help students relate classroom theory to their community service. These exercises are marked with asterisks.

Acknowledgments

My deepest gratitude goes to my students, who, through their interest and feedback, provided invaluable guidance in putting this book together.

I would also like to thank the reviewers for their critical comments and encouragement:

Dr. Irene A. Wolf, Penn State University
Earl Kumfer, University of Saint Francis
Jeff Kautz, Catawba Valley Community College
Weston Jorde, Dakota County Technical College
Elysa Koppelman White, Oakland University
Robert F O'Connor, Texas State University
Peter Kanetis, College of DuPage
Dr. Sarah Lublink, Florida Southwestern State College
Donald Becker, Austin Community College
Guy Rohrbaugh, Auburn University
Bob Fischer, Texas State University
Rev. Dr. Ryan M. Lozano, Alamo Colleges–Central Texas Technology Center

Thanks to my writing interns from the University of Rhode Island, including Dustin Jordan, for their help in putting together the sixth as well as previous editions. In addition, I would like to express my appreciation to the library staffs and other faculty at the University of Rhode Island, Brown University, and Roger Williams University Law School for assisting me with my research and for providing a supportive work space. Last, but certainly not least, my deepest appreciation and admiration goes out to my editorial team, Portfolio Manager Jamie Laferrera and Product Developers Erika Lo and Sarah Paratore, for their unflagging enthusiasm, encouragement, and patience.

Notes

1. Judith A. Boss, "Adopting an Aristotelian Approach to Teaching College Ethics," *Philosophy and Community Service Learning* (Washington, DC: Association for the Advancement of Higher Education, 1997); and Judith A. Boss, "The Effect of Community Service Work on the Moral Development of College Ethics Students," *Journal of Moral Education*, 23 (1994): 183–198.
2. U. S. Bureau of Labor Statistics, "Volunteering in the United States, 2015," http://www.bls,gov/news.release/volun.nr0.htm
3. Cooperative Institute Research Program, *The American College Freshman Norms for Fall 2015*, Higher Education Research Institute, University of California, January 2016.
4. James Rest, "Why Does College Promote Development in Moral Judgment?" *Journal of Moral Education* 17, no. 3 (1988): 183–184.
5. Boss, "The Effect of Community Service Work on the Moral Development of College Ethics Students."
6. See William Damon, *Greater Expectations* (New York: The Free Press, 1995). See also Chapter 7, for a discussion of this method of moral education.

The Study of Ethics

Many college ethics students want to skip ethical theory and immediately begin with discussions of compelling moral issues. However, productive discussion of issues requires first establishing a solid foundation in the nuances of ethical theory and moral reasoning.

As a philosophical discipline, ethics is the study of the values and guidelines by which we live as well as the justification of these values and guidelines. The first chapter, "Ethics: An Overview," begins with an introduction to ethics and a brief discussion of different types of ethical theories. It also addresses some of the fundamental philosophical questions that underlie ethics, including questions about human nature, free will versus determinism, moral knowledge, and the nature of philosophical inquiry.

The second chapter, "Moral Reasoning," provides the reader with the skills necessary to analyze and evaluate different moral theories and lines of reasoning. Developing critical thinking skills enables students to make better moral judgments and makes them less likely to be taken in by faulty reasoning.

As people develop morally, they tend to be less likely to fall for faulty reasoning and more likely to be satisfied with their moral decisions. The third chapter, "Conscience and Moral Reasoning," looks at some of the theories of moral development. The study of moral development not only enhances our own moral development, it also helps us place the various types of ethical theory and own style of moral decision making in context.

Ethics education is making a comeback. As such, speculations about what morality is are bombarding us from all sides. This is exciting: We are challenged to be on our toes and to sharpen our analytical skills in order to discern which theories are workable and which ones we need to discard. By figuring out what doesn't work, we can learn a lot. We may not have come up with the perfect theory by the end of this course, but we will have a much better sense of how to make satisfactory moral decisions.

CHAPTER 1

Ethics
An Overview

*The ultimate purpose in studying ethics is not as it is in other
inquiries, the attainment of theoretical knowledge; we are not
conducting this inquiry in order to know what virtue is, but in order
to become good, else there would be no advantage in studying it.*
  —ARISTOTLE, *Nicomachean Ethics*, Bk. 2, Ch. 2

It's the beginning of a new semester. Tomorrow morning is your first ethics
class. You signed up for the class only because it was required. "What a waste
of time," you grumble as you climb into bed. "What's the point in studying
ethics? It doesn't have anything to do with real life. I wish there was no such
thing as ethics or morality."

The next morning you wake up and wearily grope your way to the bathroom.
As you open the door, you find to your dismay that your roommate has left the
bathroom in a total mess. Your roommate's clothes are soaking in cold slimy
water in the sink and bathtub, and the toilet is caked with grime. Annoyed, you
return to your room and shake your roommate's shoulder: "Come on, get up.
You promised to clean the bathroom yesterday."

"So what?" your roommate replies. "I don't have to keep my promises if I
don't feel like it." And with that, your roommate rolls over and, looking quite
peaceful, goes back to sleep.

You are now feeling very annoyed, but you manage to get ready for class,
although not in time to have breakfast. You arrive at class right on time; however, the teacher hasn't turned up. You take a seat next to another student who
lives in your dormitory. But instead of returning your greeting, he grabs your
book bag and heads toward the door. "Stop!" you protest. "That's mine. You
can't take that."

He looks at you like you're nuts. "Why not?"

"Because it doesn't belong to you," you reply indignantly. "It's stealing!"

At which he laughs, "You're not making any sense."

"You have no right . . . ," you add.

The thief rolls his eyes: "Didn't you hear the latest news? Ethics, morality—
they no longer exist. Isn't that great news! Now we can do whatever we like!
And no one can pass judgment on anything we do, including you!"

You wait another twenty minutes for the teacher to show up; then you decide to head over to the cafeteria to get some breakfast. However, the dining staff didn't bother to report to work either. The back door has been smashed open, and trays of donuts and fruit have been taken out onto the quad, where a group of administrators and faculty members, including your ethics teacher, are squabbling over the booty. You step up onto a chair that has been tossed out on the curb, to get a better look, when someone comes rushing up from behind and knocks you down.

As you fall, you hear a sickening snap and feel a stabbing pain in your knee. You cry out in agony. Then, you recognize the person who knocked you over. It's the dean of your college. You plead for her to call for help. But she only pushes you out of her way and hurries on toward the skirmish on the quad. Off in the distance, you hear another cry for help as two men drag a terrified woman into the bushes. No one tries to stop them. A few people stop and peer at you out of curiosity before moving on. Most just stare blankly at you as they walk past. No one offers to help. And why should they? Sympathy and compassion no longer exist. The duty not to cause harm to others or to help those in need no longer exists. No one has any rights that we have to respect anymore. No more stupid obligations, such as sharing with others or keeping our commitments, to prevent us from doing what we enjoy.

As you begin to lose consciousness, you start having second thoughts about the importance of ethics and morality in your life. At that moment, your alarm clock goes off. You get out of bed and wearily grope your way to the bathroom. As you open the door, you realize that your roommate has left the bathroom in a total mess. Annoyed, you return to your room and shake your roommate's shoulder: "Come on, get up. You promised to clean the bathroom yesterday."

"Oh, no," your roommate groans. "I'm sorry, I forgot all about it." After a short pause, your roommate rolls out of bed, complaining under her breath, "I can't think of anything else I'd less rather do." You breathe a sigh of relief and go to the kitchenette to make yourself some breakfast while your roommate begrudgingly cleans the bathroom.

SELF-EVALUATION QUESTIONNAIRE*

Rate yourself on the following scale from 1 (strongly disagree) to 5 (strongly agree)

Culture determines what is moral and immoral.	1	2	3	4	5
There are no right or wrong answers. Everyone has a right to his or her own opinion.	1	2	3	4	5
I tend to stick to my position on an issue even when others try to change my mind.	1	2	3	4	5
It is important that we obey the law, even though we may disagree with it.	1	2	3	4	5
People ought to do what best serves their interests.	1	2	3	4	5
There are universal moral principles that hold for all people, regardless of their culture.	1	2	3	4	5

(continued)

Religion is the source of morality.	1	2	3	4	5
I would refuse to comply if an authority figure ordered me to do something that might cause me to hurt someone else.	1	2	3	4	5
I tend to sacrifice my needs for those of others.	1	2	3	4	5

* Explanations for each item on this scale can be found in the instructor's manual and online at www .mhhe.com/bossef17e.

What Is Ethics?

Ethics is a lot like air: It is pretty much invisible. In fact, for many centuries, people did not realize that such a substance as air even existed. So too we often fail to recognize the existence of ethics or morality until someone fails to heed it.

The term **ethics** has several meanings. It is often used to refer to a set of standards of right and wrong established by a particular group and imposed on members of that group as a means of regulating and setting limits on their behavior. This use of the word *ethics* reflects its etymology, which goes back to the Greek word *ethos*, meaning "cultural custom or habit." The word *moral* is derived from the Latin word *moralis*, which also means "custom." Although some philosophers distinguish between the terms *ethical* and *moral*, others, including the author of this text, use the two terms interchangeably.

The identification of ethics and morality with cultural norms or customs reflects the fact that most adults tend to identify morality with cultural customs. Philosophical ethics, also known as *moral philosophy*, goes beyond this limited concept of right and wrong. Ethics, as a philosophical discipline, includes the study of the values and guidelines by which we live and the *justification* for these values and guidelines. Rather than simply accepting the customs or guidelines used by one particular group or culture, philosophical ethics analyzes and evaluates these guidelines in light of accepted universal principles and concerns.

More important, ethics is a way of life. In this sense, ethics involves active engagement in the pursuit of the good life—a life consistent with a coherent set of moral values. According to Aristotle, one of the leading Western moral philosophers, the pursuit of the good life is our most important activity as humans. Indeed, studies have found that even criminals believe morality is important—at least for others. Although criminals may not always act on their moral beliefs, they still expect others to do so. Almost all criminals, when asked, state that they do not want their children to engage in immoral behavior and would get angry if one of their children committed a crime.[1]

Aristotle believed that "the moral activities are human *par excellence*."[2] Because morality is the most fundamental expression of our human nature, it is through being moral that we are the happiest. According to Aristotle, it is

Connections

What is the role of habituation and self-development in Confucian ethics? *See Chapter 10, pages 324-325.*

through the repeated performance of good actions that we become moral (and happier) people. He referred to the repeated practice of moral actions as **habituation**. The idea that practicing good actions is more important for ethics education than merely studying theory is also found in other philosophies, such as Buddhism.

[A] man becomes just by the performance of the just . . . actions; nor is there the smallest likelihood of a man's becoming good by any other course of conduct.

—ARISTOTLE, *Nicomachean Ethics*, Bk. 2, Ch. 4

At the age of seventeen, Aristotle became a student at Plato's Academy in Athens, where he remained until Plato's death twenty years later. The Academy was founded by Plato in 388 B.C.E. and lasted over nine hundred years; it is reputed to be Europe's first university.[3] Plato's famous Academy was not like universities today, with organized classes, degrees, and specialized faculty. Instead, it was more of a fellowship of intellectuals interested in Athenian culture and the opportunity to listen to and exchange ideas with the great philosopher Plato.

Aristotle later opened his own school, the Lyceum, in Athens. The Lyceum contained a garden known as "the walk," where Aristotle supposedly had the habit of walking while teaching his students. In 323 B.C.E., Aristotle was accused of impiety for teaching his students to continually question the accepted ideas

The philosopher Plato (c. 427-347 B.C.E.) with his disciple Aristotle (384-322 B.C.E.) at the Academy in Athens. The Academy is reputed to be Europe's first university.
©Bettmann/Getty Images

and norms of the time. Several years earlier, in 399 B.C.E., the Athenians had sentenced Plato's teacher, Socrates, to death on similar charges. Aristotle fled to Euboea rather than take a chance that "the Athenians should sin a second time against philosophy." He died in Babylon a year later.

Exercises

1. Complete the Self-Evaluation Questionnaire on pages 4–5. Relate your answers to your ideas regarding the ultimate source of morality. Discuss how this influences what criteria you use in making moral decisions in your life. Use specific examples to illustrate your answer.

2. One way to define what we mean by "moral" is to look at the lives of those whom we regard to be good people, as Aristotle looked up to Plato. Do you have a hero? If so, who is your hero and why?

3. Do all actions have a moral dimension? If not, why do some actions involve moral judgments while others are morally neutral? Explain using specific examples.

4. Discuss ways in which participation in an academic community has encouraged you, as it did Aristotle, to critically analyze your ideas and assumptions about morality and moral issues.

5. Do you agree with Aristotle that practicing moral virtues and behavior is more important for ethics education than the study of moral theory? How might his approach be integrated into a college ethics course?

Normative and Theoretical Ethics

> . . . *a complete moral philosophy would tell us how and why we should act and feel toward others in relationships of shifting and varying power asymmetry and shifting and varying intimacy.*
>
> —ANNETTE BAIER, *Ethics* (1986), p. 252

There are two traditional subdivisions of ethics: (1) theoretical ethics or metaethics and (2) normative ethics. **Theoretical ethics** is concerned with appraising the logical foundations and internal consistencies of ethical systems. Theoretical ethics is also known as **metaethics**; the prefix *meta* comes from the Greek word meaning "about" or "above." **Normative ethics**, on the other hand, gives us guidelines or norms, such as "do not lie" or "do no harm," regarding which actions are right and which are wrong. In other words, theoretical ethics, or metaethics, studies *why* we should act and feel a certain way; normative ethics tells us *how* we should act in particular situations.

Normative ethics affects our lives at all levels: personal, interpersonal, social (both locally and globally), and environmental. Normative ethics gives us practical hands-on guidelines or norms that we can apply to real-life situations.

Because of this, it is sometimes referred to as *applied ethics.* A professional code of ethics is an example of a set of practical moral guidelines.

Moral guidelines are not simply a list of dos and don'ts that others impose upon us, however. As adults, it is not enough just to do as we are told. We expect to be given good reasons for acting certain ways or taking certain positions on moral issues.

Theoretical ethics operates at a more fundamental level than normative ethics. Theoretical ethics takes, as its starting point, the most basic insights regarding morality. Moral norms and guidelines need to be grounded in theoretical ethics; otherwise, morality becomes arbitrary. In this text, we will concern ourselves primarily with the theoretical underpinnings of ethics.

Metaethical theories can be divided into cognitive and noncognitive theories. **Noncognitive theories**, such as **emotivism**, claim that there are no moral truths and that moral statements are neither true nor false but simply expressions or outbursts of feelings. If moral statements are neither true nor false, there is no such thing as objective moral truths.

Cognitive theories, on the other hand, maintain that moral statements can be either true or false. Cognitive theories can be further subdivided into relativist and universalist theories (Table 1.1). **Relativist theories** state that morality is different for different people. In contrast, **universalist theories** maintain that objective moral truths exist that are true for all humans, regardless of their personal beliefs or cultural norms.

TABLE 1.1   Metaethical Theories

NONCOGNITIVE	COGNITIVE		
Emotivism	**Relativist Theories**	**Universalist Theories**	
	Ethical Subjectivism	Ethical Egoism	Deontology
	Cultural Relativism	Utilitarianism	Virtue Ethics
	Divine Command	Natural Law Ethics	Rights Ethics

Relativist Theories

Connections

What is the role of opinion in ethical subjectivism? *See Chapter 4, pages 115-116.*

According to the **relativist theories**, there are no independent moral values. Instead, morality is *created* by humans. Because morality is invented or created by humans, it can vary from time to time and from person to person. **Ethical subjectivism**, the first type of relativist theory, maintains that moral right or wrong is relative to the individual person and that moral truth is a matter of individual opinion or feeling. Unlike reason, **opinion** is based only on feeling rather than analysis or facts. In ethical subjectivism, there can be as many systems of morality as there are people in the world. Many college students—especially freshmen—maintain that morality is relative to each individual. We'll be studying this theory in more depth in Chapter 4.

> Moral values are not absolute but relative to the emotions they express.
>
> —Edward Westermarck (sociologist)

Connections

How does acceptance of cultural relativism affect how we treat people who are different from us or are from other cultures? *See Chapter 6, pages 182-189.*

Cultural relativists, on the other hand, argue that morality is created collectively by groups of humans and that it differs from society to society. Each society has its own moral norms, which are binding on the people who belong to that society. Each society also defines who is and who is not a member of the moral community. With cultural relativism, each circle or moral system represents a different culture. The majority of Americans believe that morality is culturally relative (see Chapters 3 and 6).

> We recognize that morality differs in every society, and is a convenient term for socially approved habits.
>
> —Ruth Benedict (anthropologist)

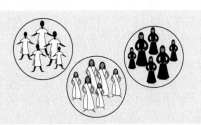

A third type of relativist theory is **divine command theory**. According to this theory, what is moral is relative to God. There are no universal moral principles that are binding on all people. Instead, morality is dependent on God's will and may differ from person to person or from religion to religion. We'll be examining this theory in depth in Chapter 5.

Ethical subjectivism, cultural relativism, and divine command theory are mutually exclusive theories. When theories are mutually exclusive, a person cannot consistently hold more than one of the theories to be true at the same time. For example, either morality is created by the *individual* and the opinion of the individual always takes precedence over that of the collective, or else morality is relative to one's *culture* and the moral rule of the culture always takes precedence over that of the individual.

Universalist Theories

Universalist theories, the second group of cognitive theories, maintain that there are universal moral values that apply to *all* humans and, in some cases, extend beyond the human community. Morality is *discovered*, rather than created, by humans. The basic standards of right and wrong are derived from principles that exist independently of an individual's or a society's opinion.

Do not do to others as you would not wish done to yourself.

—Confucius (philosopher)

Act only on that maxim through which you can at the same time will that it should be a universal law.

—Immanuel Kant (philosopher)

Connections

How did a belief in ethical relativism contribute to the rise of Nazism and the internment of Jews? *See Chapter 6, pages 194-196.*

Unlike relativist theories, most universalist theories include all humans in their moral community rather than only those living in their society, as often happens in cultural relativist theories. The **moral community** is composed of all those beings who have moral worth or value in themselves. Because members of the moral community have moral value, they deserve the protection of the community, and they deserve to be treated with respect and dignity. Universalist theories can be represented by one circle that includes individuals from all cultures.

Universalist ethics, also known as *moral objectivism*, is not the same as moral absolutism. **Absolutists** believe that there are moral norms or principles that should always be obeyed. Some people—though not most—who subscribe to universalist moral theories may be absolutists when it comes to certain moral principles.

There is a great deal of overlap between the different universalist theories. Instead of being mutually exclusive, like ethical subjectivism, cultural relativism, and divine command theory, universalist theories, for the most part, emphasize one particular aspect of morality rather than providing a comprehensive picture. Almost all ethicists include aspects of more than one of these theories in their moral philosophy. The different universalist theories are covered in Chapters 7-12.

Ethics, as a branch of philosophy, however, begins in wonder—not theory. Theories, by their very nature, oversimplify. A theory is merely a convenient tool for expressing an idea. Some theories are better than others for explaining certain phenomena and providing solutions to both old and new problems. When studying the different moral philosophers, we must be careful not to pigeonhole their ideas into rigid theoretical boundaries.

Theories are like telescopes. They zoom in on certain key points rather than elucidate the total extent of thinking about ethics. Because morality covers such a broad scope of issues, different philosophers tend to focus on different aspects of morality. Problems arise when they claim that their insight is the complete picture—that morality is merely consequences or merely duty or merely having good intentions. Morality is not a simple concept that can be captured in a nice tidy theory; it is a multifaceted phenomenon.

![feather icon]

Exercises

*1. Choose a moral issue from your life as a college student. Discuss how this issue affects decisions in your life in terms of the norms you adopt to guide your behavior. If you are doing community service, relate your answer to your service learning.

2. Discuss which of the ethical theories you would most likely use in judging the morality of the different people—including the messy roommate, the thieving classmate, the tardy professor, and the uncaring dean—in this chapter's opening scenario. To what moral theories, universalist or relativist, did the subject of the scenario appeal?

3. Looking back at the scenario at the beginning of this chapter, what ethical theory is the roommate promoting? Discuss some of the problems with the roommate's approach to ethics. Use examples from your own experience to illustrate your answer.

Philosophy and the Search for Wisdom

To do philosophy is to explore one's own temperament, and yet at the same time to attempt to discover the truth.

—IRIS MURDOCH

In most North American and Western European universities, ethics is taught as a course in a philosophy department. Although some aspects of the study of ethics extend beyond the purview of philosophy, philosophical inquiry is at the heart of the ethical enterprise.

The word **philosophy** comes from the Greek words *philos*, meaning "lover," and *sophos*, meaning "wisdom." To be a lover (*philos*) entails not only having a positive attitude toward the object of our affection (wisdom, in this case) but also taking action and actively pursuing that object. This interplay of attitude and action is reflected in the study of ethics. Ethics education also goes beyond theory by challenging us to live consistently with our moral values.

Philosophy arises out of a natural sense of wonder and what many philosophers regard as a basic human need to find higher meaning and value in our lives. As small children, we wondered and asked countless questions about the world around us. Indeed, child psychologists note that curiosity and ethical concerns about justice and sharing emerge spontaneously in children sometime between the ages of eighteen and thirty-six months, regardless of their culture and without prompting from adults.[4]

---

* An asterisk indicates that the exercise is appropriate for students who are doing community service learning as part of the course.

We all share a common humanity, but how we proceed in our quest for wisdom and the good life will vary to some extent from person to person and from culture to culture because we all have different personalities and different experiences. This does not imply, however, that wisdom is relative. Rather, it suggests that there are several paths to wisdom, just as there can be several paths to the top of a mountain.

Becoming Autonomous

In seeking answers to questions about the meaning of life and the nature of moral goodness, the philosopher goes beyond conventional answers. Rather than relying on public opinion or what others say, it is up to each of us to critically examine and analyze our reasons for holding particular views. In this way, the study of philosophy encourages us to become more autonomous.

Connections

What is the relationship between autonomous moral reasoning and stage of moral reasoning? *See Chapter 3, page 78.*

The word *autonomous* comes from the Greek words *auto* ("self") and *nomos* ("law"). In other words, an **autonomous moral agent** is an independent, self-governing thinker. A **heteronomous moral agent**, in contrast, is a person who uncritically accepts answers and laws imposed by others. The prefix *hetero-* means "other."

Because philosophy encourages people to question the deeply held beliefs of their society, most people, as Socrates discovered, resist philosophical inquiry. Socrates, who is known as the Father of Western Philosophy, was born in Athens, Greece, in 469 B.C.E. At that time, Athens was a flourishing city-state and a democracy. Socrates never wrote any books or papers on philosophy. What we know of him comes primarily from the writings of his student, Plato. Like most of the early philosophers, Socrates was not a career philosopher; he most likely made his living as a stonemason or artisan. His real love was philosophy, however. As Socrates got older, he began hanging out more at the market and other places where people congregated, talking to the populace and questioning conventional answers to issues regarding justice and virtue.

According to Socrates, wisdom is important for achieving happiness and inner harmony as well as the intellectual and moral improvement of community. His approach to philosophy, known as the **Socratic method**, consists of a didactic dialogue using questions and answers. The Socratic method is one of the most popular and productive methods used in philosophy.

The road to wisdom, Socrates believed, begins with the realization that we are ignorant. In his search for wisdom, Socrates would stop people on the street to ask them questions about things they thought they already knew. In doing this, he hoped to show people that there was a difference between *truth* and what they *felt* to be true (their opinions). By exposing the ignorance of those who considered themselves wise, Socrates taught people to not simply accept the prevailing views but to question their own views and those of their society in a never-ending search for truth and wisdom.

Not everyone appreciated having their views challenged by Socrates. People in positions of power were especially threatened and outraged by Socrates's habit of asking people to question existing laws and customs and encouraging

"The Death of Socrates," by Jacques-Louis David. Socrates (469–399 B.C.E.). Socrates remained true to his principles right up to the moment of his death.
©Universal Images Group/Getty Images

them to think in new ways. At the age of seventy, Socrates was arrested and charged with blasphemy and corrupting the youth of Athens. He was found guilty and was sentenced to death by drinking poison hemlock.

Even as Socrates faced death, he did not cease being a philosopher. At his trial, Socrates is reputed to have said the following in a speech in his own defense before the 501 members of the jury:

> I shall never stop practicing philosophy and exhorting you and elucidating the truth for everyone that I meet. I shall go on saying . . . Are you not ashamed that you give your attention to acquiring as much money as possible, and similarly with reputation and honor, and give no attention or thought to truth and understanding and the perfection of your soul?
>
> And if any of you disputes this . . . I shall question him and examine him and test him . . . I shall do this to everyone that I meet.[5]

Self-Realization

Some of the most important philosophical questions are those regarding the meaning and goals of our lives. What kind of person do I want to be? How do I achieve that goal? Many philosophers define their life goal in terms of **self-realization**—also known as *self-actualization* and *enlightenment*. Self-realization is closely linked to the idea of moral virtue. According to psychologist Abraham Maslow, self-actualized people are autonomous: They do not depend on the opinions of others when deciding what to do and what to believe. Philosophers such as Socrates and Buddha exemplified what Maslow meant by a self-realized person.[6]

Self-realization is an ongoing process. People who are self-actualized devote their lives to the search for ultimate values. People who are not honest with themselves will have a difficult time making good life choices. Being honest involves the courage to be different and to work hard at being the best one can be at whatever one does. People who are lacking in authenticity or sincerity blame others for their own unhappiness, giving in to what French philosopher Simone de Beauvoir (1908–1986) called "the temptations of the easy way."[7]

Connections

Do we have a moral duty to engage in self-improvement? *See Chapter 10, page 318.*

People who are self-actualized, in contrast, are flexible and even welcome having their views challenged. Like true philosophers, they are open to new ways of looking at the world. They are willing to analyze and, if necessary, change their views—even if this means taking an unpopular stand. This process involves actively working to recognize and overcome barriers to new ways of thinking; chief among these is cultural conditioning.

Skepticism

Philosophers try to approach the world with an open mind. They question their own beliefs and those of other people, no matter how obviously true a particular belief may seem. Rather than accepting established belief systems uncritically, philosophers first reflect on and analyze them. By refusing to accept beliefs until they can be justified, philosophers adopt an attitude of skepticism, or doubt, as their starting point.

Skepticism, unlike cynicism, is grounded in wonder. The skeptic is always curious and open-minded, with an eye to the truth. Cynicism sometimes masquerades as philosophy; however, it is very different. **Cynicism** is closed-minded and mocks the possibility of truth, especially in ideas that go against the mainstream. Cynicism denies rather than analyzes.

The first [rule for seeking truth] was to accept nothing as true which I did not clearly recognize to be so: that is to say, carefully to avoid precipitation and prejudice in judgments, and to accept in them nothing more than what was presented to my mind so clearly and distinctly that I could have no occasion to doubt it.

—René Descartes, *Discourse on the Method of Rightly Conducting the*

Reason and Seeking Truth in the Sciences (1637)

Plato's "Allegory of the Cave"

Plato's "Allegory of the Cave" has been used to illustrate the nature of philosophical thought. In the reading from his *Republic*, Plato compared us to prisoners who have been chained and left in a cave since childhood. Our heads are held fast in place, so we face the back wall. When people and animals pass by the entrance of the cave, we see them only as shadows on the back wall. We hear the sounds of the outside world only as echoes.

Now, suppose that one of the prisoners has been unchained and turns to face the entrance of the cave. At first, the prisoner is frightened and blinded by the light. At this point, most people will try to return to the comfort of the cave. But if our prisoner is forced or cajoled out of the cave into the light, his eyes will begin to adjust. Once the prisoner is out in the light and freed of the shackles of everyday opinion, he begins to see and learn about wonderful truths that he never before imagined.

After a period of study, he feels the urge to return to his fellow prisoners and share his knowledge with them. Each step back into the cave, however, is painful. He is ridiculed for his beliefs. At this point, the budding philosopher has three options: (1) He can leave the cave again and return to the light. In this case, his newfound wisdom will become irrelevant to the world of human experience. (2) He can give up the wisdom he has acquired and return to his old beliefs. By doing so, he gives in to public opinion rather than risk being unpopular. Or (3) he can remain in the cave and persist in his quest to share his wisdom with others. This last option, according to Plato, is the path of the true philosopher.[†]

Plato believed that truth was embodied in changeless universal forms that could be discerned by the use of reason. Other philosophers see truth, rather than being static and absolute, as dynamic and as constantly revealing itself to us. Pre-Socratic philosopher Heraclitus (c. 535–475 B.C.E.) taught that an essential feature of reality is that it is ceaselessly changing, like a flowing river. Just as you cannot step into the same river twice, permanence is an illusion. Everything is in flux. And Zen Buddhists speak of truth as being found in "the continued or repeated unfolding of the one big mind."

Connections

What role does sympathy play in Plato's moral philosophy? *See Chapter 12, pages 405–406.*

Some people believe that morality demands a sort of rigid, absolutist attitude and that a person should stick to his or her principles no matter what. However, if we believe that truth is constantly revealing itself to us—whether through reason, experience, or intuition—we must always be open to dialogue with each other and with the world at large. If we think at some point that we have found truth and, therefore, close our minds, we have ceased to think like a philosopher. We will lose our sense of wonder and become rigid and self-righteous.

For a philosopher to stop seeking truth is like a dancer freezing in one position because he thinks he has found the ultimate dance step or an artist stopping painting because she thinks she has created the perfect work of art. Similarly, to cease wondering is to cease thinking like a philosopher. To cease thinking like a philosopher is to give up the quest for the good life.

[†] To read the complete text of Plato's "Allegory of the Cave," go to http://classics.mit.edu/Plato/Republic.html

Exercises

1. What is the difference between wisdom and knowledge? Which are you acquiring at college? How does one actively seek wisdom or live wisely? What is the connection between wisdom and morality?

2. Critically analyze whether Socrates did the right thing in sticking to his principles during his trial (see pages 12–13). Discuss a time when you did what you believed was right even though it ran counter to cultural norms. How did you justify your actions?

3. According to Socrates, the first step on the path to wisdom is to "know thyself." Discuss the following questions in light of this mandate.

   a. What is my goal or plan of life?

   b. What sort of person do I want to be?

   c. How close am I to my goal?

   *d. For those of who are doing community service, how does your service fit in with or assist you in clarifying and achieving your life goals?

4. Do you agree that self-actualization is linked to virtue and to happiness? Explain. To what extent are you a self-actualized person? What barriers are holding you back from achieving self-actualization? What can you do to remove some of those barriers?

5. German philosopher Friedrich Nietzsche asked us to imagine what sort of life we would create for ourselves if we knew that it would be repeated over and over again for the rest of eternity. This is known as the theory of *eternal recurrence.* Nietzsche described it as follows:

   > *What if, some day or night a demon were to . . . say to you: This life as you now live it and have lived it, you will have to live once more and innumerable times more; and there will be nothing new in it, but every pain and every joy and every thought and sign and everything unutterably small or great in your life will have to return to you, all in the same succession and sequence—even this spider and this moonlight between the trees, and even this moment and I myself. The eternal hourglass of existence is turned upside down again and again, and you with it, speck of dust!*

   > *Would you not throw yourself down and gnash your teeth and curse the demon who spoke thus? . . . Or how well disposed would you have to become to yourself and to life to crave nothing more fervently than this ultimate eternal confirmation and seal?*[8]

   How would you answer Nietzsche's questions? Are you satisfied with the life you are now creating for yourself? If not, what could you do to make it a better life, one that you would want to repeat over and over.

6. Discuss your own life in terms of Plato's "Allegory of the Cave." Where are you now in your journey? Explain.

Metaphysics and the Study of Human Nature

In every writer on philosophy there is a concealed metaphysic, usually unconscious; even if his subject is metaphysics, he is almost certain to have an uncritically believed system which underlies his specific arguments.

—BERTRAND RUSSELL, *The Philosophy of John Dewey*

Ethical theories do not stand on their own but are grounded in other philosophical presumptions about such matters as the role of humans in the universe, the existence of free will, and the nature of knowledge. **Metaphysics** is the branch of philosophy concerned with the study of the nature of reality, including what it means to be human.

Our concept of human nature influences our concept of how we ought to live. Are humans basically selfish? Or are we basically altruistic? What is the relationship between humans and the rest of nature? Do we have free will? Or is all of our behavior subject to the laws of physics?

Metaphysical assumptions about the nature of reality are not simply abstract theories; they can have a profound effect on both ethical theory and normative ethics. Metaphysical assumptions play a pivotal role, for better or for worse, in structuring relations among humans and between humans and the rest of the world.

Connections
What is the theory of psychological egoism and how does it differ from ethical egoism? *See Chapter 7, pages 212-216.*

Metaphysical Dualism

According to **metaphysical dualists**, reality is made up of two distinct and separate substances: the material or physical body and the nonmaterial mind, which is also referred to as the soul or spirit. The body, being material, is subject to causal laws. The mind, in contrast, has free will because it is nonmaterial and rational. Some philosophers believe that only humans have a mind, and hence, only humans have moral value. The belief that adult humans are the central or most significant reality of the universe is known as **anthropocentrism**.

According to most dualists, humans express their nature or essence through reason, which is the activity of the nonmaterial mind. Only through reason can we understand moral truth and achieve the good life. Dualistic philosophies tend to support a hierarchical worldview and a morality based on the exclusion of some beings from the moral community—particularly nonhuman animals and humans who are regarded as not fully rational. Aristotle writes:

> *For living is apparently shared with plants, but what we are looking for is the special function of a human being: hence we should set aside the life of nutrition and growth. The life next in order is some sort of life of sense-perception; but this too is apparently shared, with horses, oxen and every animal. The remaining possibility, then, is some sort of life of action on the part of the soul that has reason.*

> *. . . the human function is the soul's activity that expresses reason. . . . The excellent man's function is to do this finely and well. Each function is completed well when its completion*

expresses the proper virtue. Therefore, the human good turns out to be the soul's proper function.

—ARISTOTLE, *Nicomachean Ethics*, Bk. 1, Ch. 1

Ecofeminist Karen Warren argues that the domination of women and the domination of nature that typify Western dualism are inexorably connected.[9] Both, she claims, are based on a hierarchical and dualistic metaphysics and a "logic of domination" that assumes that certain beings (whether human or non-human) are morally superior and that those who are superior have a right to dominate those who are subordinate.

Connections

Do we have a moral duty to respect the environment? *See Chapter 5, page 155.*

Hindu metaethics, like Western dualism, at one time supported a hierarchical view of reality.[10] This hierarchy manifested itself primarily within the caste system that was believed to reflect the natural order of the universe. In India, the Hindu caste system and the hierarchical metaphysics upon which it was based were challenged by Mohandas Gandhi (1869-1948). He denounced the caste system as "evil" and "an ineffaceable blot that Hinduism today carries with it."[11] Gandhi's demand for change was strongly influenced by the teachings of another Indian philosopher, Siddhartha Gautama (563-c. 483 B.C.E.), better known as Buddha or the "Enlightened One."

One of the main problems with dualism is coming up with an explanation of how two apparently completely different substances—mind and body—are able to interact with each other, especially on a causal level. Because of the mind-body problem, many philosophers have rejected dualism.[12]

Metaphysical Materialism

There are many variations of nondualistic or one-substance theories. One of the more popular is **metaphysical materialism**. In this worldview, physical matter is the only substance. While materialists do not have to deal with the mind-body problem, they have a difficult time explaining the phenomenon of consciousness and intention. Because metaphysical materialists reject, or consider irrelevant, abstract concepts such as mind or soul, morality must be explained in terms of physical matter.

Connections

Is war inevitable? *See Chapter 7, pages 212-213.*

Sociobiology is based on the assumption of metaphysical materialism. As a branch of biology, sociobiology applies evolutionary theory to the social sciences—including questions of moral behavior. Sociobiologist Edward O. Wilson claims that morality is based on biological requirements and drives.[13] Human behavior is governed by the same innate **epigenetic rules** as other animals.

According to sociobiologists, human social behavior, like that of other social animals, is primarily oriented toward the propagation of the species. This goal is achieved through inborn cooperative behavior that sociobiologists call **biological altruism**. Biological altruism accounts for the great sacrifices we are willing to make to help those who *share our genes*. We will be looking more at the concept of biological altruism in Chapter 7 on ethical egoism.

One of the problems with basing ethics on metaphysical materialism is that it gives us no guidance in a situation where two epigenetic rules, such as egoism and altruism, are in conflict. For this and other reasons, the majority of philosophers, although not denying that biology is important, reject biology as the *basis* for morality.

Buddhism and the Unity of All Reality

Buddha, like Socrates, did not leave behind any writings. What we know of his philosophy comes from the writings of his disciples. Leading a moral or right lifestyle is central to Buddha's philosophy. Buddha rejected metaphysical dualism, emphasizing the unity of all reality rather than differences.

According to Buddha, the natural order is a dynamic web of interactions that condition or influence, instead of determining, our actions. Mind and body are not separate substances but are a manifestation of one substance or the "One." Because all reality is interconnected, Buddhism opposes the taking of life and encourages a simple lifestyle in harmony with and respectful of other humans and of nature in general.

Like Buddhists, the Lele, a Bantu-speaking tribe living in the Democratic Republic of Congo, believe that the world is a single system of interrelationships among humans, animals, and spirits. Avoiding behavior such as sorcery that disrupts this delicate balance of interrelationships is key to the moral life.[14] Some Native American philosophies also stress the interrelatedness of all beings; they do not divide the world into animate and inanimate objects but rather see everything, including the earth itself, as having a self-conscious life.[15] This metaphysical view of reality is reflected in a moral philosophy based on respect for all beings and on not taking more than one needs.

Key Concepts in Metaphysics

Metaphysics   The study of the nature of reality.

Anthropocentrism   The belief that humans are the most important reality in the universe.

Metaphysical Dualism   The theory that reality is made up of two distinct substances—mind and matter.

Metaphysical Materialism   The theory that reality is made up of one substance—matter.

Determinism   The theory that all events are governed by causal laws; there is no free will.

Determinism versus Free Will

Another question raised by metaphysics is whether humans have free will. The theory of **determinism** states that all events are governed by causal laws: There is no free will. Humans are governed by causal laws as are all other physical objects and beings. According to strict determinism, if we had complete knowledge, we could predict future events with 100 percent certainty. The emphasis in the West on the scientific method as the source of truth has contributed to the trend in the West to describe human behavior in purely scientific terms.[16]

> I do not at all believe in human freedom in the philosophical sense. Everybody acts
> not only under external compulsion but also in accordance with inner necessity.
>
> —ALBERT EINSTEIN

Connections

How do behaviorists explain the existence of conscience? *See Chapter 3, page 78.*

Psychoanalyst Sigmund Freud (1856–1939) claimed that humans are governed by powerful unconscious forces and that even our most noble accomplishments are the result of prior events and instincts. **Behaviorists** such as John Watson (1878–1958) and B. F. Skinner (1904–1990) also believed that human behavior is determined by past events in our lives. They argued that, rather than the unconscious controlling our actions, so-called mental states are really a function of the physical body. Rather than being free, autonomous agents, we are the products of past conditioning and are elaborately programmed computers—an assembled organic machine ready to run.

Existentialism goes to the opposite extreme. According to existentialists, we are defined only by our freedom. Existentialist Jean-Paul Sartre (1905–1980) argued that "there is no human nature, since there is no God to conceive it. . . . Man [therefore] is condemned to be free."[17] As radically free beings, we each have the responsibility to create our own essence, including choosing the moral principles upon which we act. Because we are free and not restricted by a fixed essence, when we make a moral choice, we can be held completely accountable for our actions and choices.

Buddhist philosophers also disagree with determinism, although they acknowledge that we are influenced by outside circumstances beyond our control.[18] This is reflected in the concept of karma in Eastern philosophy. Karma is sometimes misinterpreted as determinism. However, **karma** is an ethical principle or universal force that holds each of us responsible for our actions and the consequences of our actions, not only in this lifetime but in subsequent lifetimes. Rather than our being predetermined by our past karma, karma provides guidance toward liberation from our past harmful actions and illusions and toward moral perfection. In Chapters 11 and 12, we will learn about the influence of this metaphysical view on Buddhist ethics.

Connections

What are the implications of determinism for moral responsibility? *See Chapter 3, page 80.*

Determinism and Excuses

The determinism versus free will debate has important implications for ethics. In particular, it raises serious questions about to what extent we can hold people morally responsible for their actions. Making excuses for our actions is as old as humankind: Adam excused his behavior by blaming Eve for the apple incident. Eve in turn blamed the serpent.

    The trend toward seeing forces outside our control as responsible for our actions has contributed to relabeling behaviors such as alcoholism and pedophilia as illnesses or disabilities rather than moral weaknesses. The belief that human behavior is determined has also influenced how we treat people who commit crimes. In his book *The Abuse Excuse*, criminal defense attorney Alan Dershowitz examined dozens of excuses that lawyers have used successfully in court to enable people to "get away with murder"[19] and to avoid taking responsibility for their actions. Excuses such as "battered woman syndrome," "Super Bowl Sunday syndrome," "adopted child syndrome," "black rage syndrome," "the Twinkies defense," and "pornography made me do it syndrome" have all

Jerry Sandusky, former Penn State University football coach, 2011. In June 2012 Sandusky was found guilty of 45 counts of child sexual abuse involving boys who were part of a charitable football program serving underprivileged and at-risk youth. During the trial, it was revealed that college administrators and head coach Joe Paterno had known about the sexual abuse since 2001 but had chosen not to go public with the allegations. Their excuse for not reporting the abuse to authorities? They didn't want to damage the reputation of Penn State's football program. Sandusky is currently serving a life sentence in prison.
©ASSOCIATED PRESS

Connections

Can cultural relativism be used to excuse behavior that harms others? *See Chapter 6, pages 168-169.*

been used in court cases. In 1978, former San Francisco supervisor Dan White entered City Hall carrying a loaded gun. He shot and killed Mayor George Moscone along with supervisor and gay rights activist Harvey Milk. The claim at White's trial that his diet of junk food may have caused an imbalance in his brain came to be known as the "Twinkie Defense." Excuses may also be used by people who collude in covering up another's misdeeds or crimes, as happened in the case of former Penn State University football coach, Jerry Sandusky (see Analyzing Images, page 21).

Analyzing Images

1. Group loyalty can result in a person failing to report a crime or misdeed. For example, the majority of fraternity men who witness a rape by a brother refuse to disclose the information to authorities. Think of a time when you or a friend withheld information about an offense you witnessed. What was your excuse for not reporting the incident? Discuss the moral implications of your decision.

2. Dozens of women came forth recently with allegations of rape and sexual misconduct against members of Congress and other high profile men. In several of these cases the women were paid off with money from a congressional or corporate slush fund in exchange for their silence. Discuss whether the people who were complicit in the cover-up should be held morally responsible for their actions and, if so, should they be punished.

3. Should people who sexually abuse children be held responsible for their actions or are pedophiles simply a product of their biology and culture? Critically analyze how both an existentialist and a behaviorist would answer this question.

When, if ever, are we responsible for our actions? At one extreme, the existentialists claim that we are completely responsible and that there are no excuses. At the other extreme are those, such as the behaviorists, who say that free will is an illusion. Most philosophers accept a position somewhere in the middle, arguing that although we are the products of our biology and our culture, we are also creators of our culture and our destiny.

Exercises

*1. Discuss how your concept of reality and human nature influences the way you think about morality. For example, are humans made of two distinct substances—mind and body? Or are we made of the same substance as the rest of reality as metaphysical materialists and Buddhists claim? Use specific examples to illustrate your answer. If you are doing community service work, relate your answer to your service.

2. Do you agree with Karen Warren's theory that sexism and naturalism are linked? What is the relationship of sexism and naturalism to anthropocentric metaphysics? How does this affect how you define your moral community? Discuss how Aristotle might have responded to Warren's theory.

3. Warren talks about the importance of using the first-person narrative to raise philosophical questions that more abstract methods of philosophy might overlook.

   a. Find a comfortable spot outside or by a window. Putting on the mantle of a metaphysical dualist, look at others, including humans of a different ethnic background or gender, nonhuman animals, plants, and inanimate objects. After five minutes, or however long you need, write down your thoughts and feelings regarding the different beings you see and their moral worth.

   b. Repeat this exercise, putting on the mantle of a nondualist, such as Buddha or Warren.

   c. Again, repeat the exercise, now looking at the world through the eyes of a metaphysical materialist such as B. F. Skinner.

      When you have finished the exercise, compare and contrast your experiences. Discuss how adopting the different metaphysical viewpoints affects how you see others and how you view your place in the world.

4. Alan Dershowitz argues that the current vogue of making excuses for violent actions threatens the democratic ideal of individual freedom. Do you agree with him? If we are merely products of our environment, should we be held morally responsible for their actions? Discuss your answer in light of the determinism versus free will debate as well as your own personal experience.

5. Because medical resources are limited for such things as organ transplants, we must decide how they should be allocated. If a person knowingly engages in behavior that could jeopardize his or her health, should this be taken into consideration when allocating scarce resources? For example, baseball superstar Mickey Mantle received a liver transplant, even though the damage to his liver was mainly the result of his years of heavy drinking. Mantle died shortly after receiving the transplant. Was it right to give him the liver? Or should someone else who needed a new liver because of an inherited liver disease have been given priority over Mantle? How does your position in the determinism versus free will debate influence your answers to these questions?

*6. Discuss how our current policies toward vulnerable populations such as the homeless, children, prisoners, and families living in poverty are influenced by a philosophical view of human behavior as free or determined. If you are doing community service work, illustrate your answer using examples from your service.

Moral Knowledge: Can Moral Beliefs Be True?

Opinion is that exercise of the human will which helps us to make a decision without information.

—JOHN ERSKINE, *The Complete Life* (1943)

In the 1991 movie *Terminator 2*, the "terminator," an android played by Arnold Schwarzenegger, is about to kill two unarmed men who are harassing his friend John Connor. Connor jumps in, just in the nick of time, and pushes the terminator's gun aside:

Connor: You were going to kill that guy!

Terminator: Of course. I'm a terminator.

Connor: Listen to me very carefully. You're not a terminator anymore. You just can't go around killing people.

Terminator: Why?

Connor: What do you mean "why"!? 'Cause you can't!

Terminator: Why?

Connor: Because you just can't.

In this passage, John Connor is making two important points. First, morality transcends our nature. We cannot use the excuse "but it's my nature" to justify our hurtful actions. Morality, including the principle of **nonmaleficence**, or "do no harm," is binding on everyone. The terminator is by nature a killer, but this does not mean that he *ought* to kill. Morality creates in us obligation to refrain from carrying out certain harmful actions in a way that our nature or natural tendencies may not. Second, basic moral knowledge, according to Connor, is self-evident. We may need to justify our behavior, but we do not have to justify the general moral principles that inform our moral decisions.

Connections

Does the principle of nonmaleficence apply universally under all circumstances? *See Chapter 8, page 256* and *Chapter 10, pages 331* and *335-336.*

Of course, not everyone would agree with John Connor that the principle of nonmaleficence entails that it is *always* morally wrong to kill unarmed people. Disagreement or uncertainty, however, does not negate the existence of moral knowledge. We also disagree about empirical facts, such as the age of our planet, the cause of Alzheimer's disease, whether people in comas can feel pain, and whether it is going to rain on the weekend. When we disagree about an important moral issue, we don't generally shrug off the disagreement as a matter of personal opinion. Instead, we try to come up with good reasons for accepting a particular position or course of action. We also expect others to do the same. In other words, most people believe that moral knowledge is possible and that it can help us in making decisions about moral issues.

Even the most egoistic people generally accept a sort of **moral minimalism**. That is, they believe that there are certain minimal morality requirements that include, for example, refraining from torturing and murdering innocent, helpless people.

Epistemology and Sources of Knowledge

Epistemology is the branch of philosophy concerned with the study of knowledge—including moral knowledge. As such, epistemology deals with questions about the nature and limits of knowledge and how knowledge can be validated. There are many ways of knowing: Intuition, reason, feeling, and experience are all potential sources of knowledge.

Many Western philosophers, like Plato, believe that reason is the primary source of moral knowledge. **Reason** can be defined as "the power of understanding the connection between the general and the particular."[20] **Rationalism** is the epistemological theory that most human knowledge comes through reason rather than through the physical senses.

Other Western philosophers, such as Bentham, Ross, and Hume, and many non-Western philosophers have challenged the dependence on reason that characterizes much of Western philosophy. They suggest that we discover moral truths primarily through intuition rather than reason. **Intuition** is immediate or self-evident knowledge, as opposed to knowledge inferred from other truths. Intuitive truths do not need any proof. Utilitarians, for example, claim that we intuitively know that pain is a moral evil (see Chapter 8). Confucians maintain that we intuitively know that benevolence is good. Rights ethicists claim that we intuitively know that all people are created equal (see Chapter 10).

Cognitive-developmental psychologist Lawrence Kohlberg (1927–1987) believed that certain morally relevant concepts, such as altruism and cooperation, are built into us (or at least *almost* all of us). According to Kohlberg, these intuitive notions are part of humans' fundamental structure for interpreting the social world, and as such, they may not be fully articulated.[21] In other words, we may *know* what is right but not be able to explain why it is right.

Connections
What is Kohlberg's stage theory of moral development? *See Chapter 3, pages 91–92.*

The difficulty with using intuition as a source of moral knowledge is that these so-called intuitive truths are not always self-evident to everyone. White supremacists, for example, do not agree that all people are created equal. On the other hand, the fact that some people do not accept certain moral intuitions does not make these moral intuitions false or nonexistent any more than the deafness of some people means that Beethoven's symphonies do not exist.

A similar problem exists with grounding moral knowledge in religious faith. Since knowledge gained by faith is not objectively verifiable, we have no criteria for judging the morality of the actions of someone such as a Muslim extremist who, for example, commits an act of terrorism in the name of their faith. Most religious ethicists, such as Thomas Aquinas, overcome this problem by grounding morality not in faith but in objective and universally applicable moral principles based on reason.

Key Concepts in Epistemology

Epistemology   The study of the nature and limits of knowledge.

Rationalism   The theory that most human knowledge comes through reason.

Empiricism   The theory that most human knowledge comes through experience or the five senses.

Intuition   Immediate or self-evident knowledge.

Emotivism   The position that moral judgments are simply expressions of individuals' emotions.

The Role of Experience

Experience is also a source of moral knowledge. Aristotle emphasized reason as the most important source of moral knowledge, yet he also taught that ethics education needs an experiential component to lead to genuine knowledge. Some philosophers carry the experiential component of moral knowledge even further. **Empiricism** claims that all, or at least most, human knowledge comes through the five senses.

Positivism, which was popular in the first half of the twentieth century, represents an attempt to justify the study of philosophy by aligning it with science and empiricism. Positivists believe that moral judgments are simply expressions of individuals' emotions; this is known as **emotivism.** Because statements of moral judgment don't seem to convey any information about the physical world, they are meaningless. Emotivists such as Alfred J. Ayer (1910–1989) concluded that these moral judgments are merely subjective expressions of feeling or commands to arouse feelings and stimulate action and, as such, are devoid of any truth value.

He writes:

> We begin by admitting that the
> fundamental ethical concepts are
> unanalysable . . . that they are mere
> pseudo-concepts. The presence of an
> ethical symbol in a proportion adds
> nothing to its factual content.[22]

The statement "torturing children is wrong," in the context of emotivism, is neither true nor false. It is nothing more than the expression of a negative emotion or feeling toward torturing children—much like saying "yuck" when tasting a food that disagrees with one's palate. Someone's preference for torturing young children and another person's preference for a particular flavor of ice cream are both morally neutral.

This alliance between ethics and science (as interpreted by the positivists) proved fatal to ethics. If science is the only source of knowledge, then moral statements such as "killing unarmed people is wrong" and "torturing children is wrong" are meaningless because they do not appear to correspond to anything in the physical world, as do statements such as "tigers have stripes" or "it was sunny at the beach yesterday."

Emotivism was never widely accepted as a moral theory. The horrors of the Nazi Holocaust forced some emotivists to reevaluate their moral theory and to commit themselves to the position that some actions such as genocide, terrorism, and torturing children are immoral regardless of how one feels about it.

Philosopher Sandra Harding (b. 1935) also maintains that experience is an important component of knowledge; however, she disagrees with the emotivists that moral knowledge is impossible. Moral knowledge, she claims, is radically interdependent with our interests, our cultural institutions, our relationships, and our life experiences.[23] To rely solely on abstract reasoning, she argues, ignores other ways of experiencing the world and moral values within the world. Instead, knowing cannot be separated from our gender and position in society. Moral knowledge and moral decision making lie within the tension between the universal and the particular in our individual experiences. By emphasizing the importance of experience, feminist epistemology reminds us that we must listen to everyone's voice before forming an adequate moral theory—not just the voice of those, such as "privileged White males."[24] This concern with experience has led to an increased emphasis on multiculturalism in contemporary college education.

Exercises

1. Referring to the different epistemological theories, discuss how you would respond to someone who thinks that torturing infants is either morally right or, in the case of the positivists, morally neutral.

2. Discuss Alfred Ayer's claim, in the selection from his essay "Emotivism," that moral judgments are nothing more than expressions of feeling and have no validity. If morality is simply an expression of feeling, is there any such thing as moral responsibility? Are Gandhi and Hitler morally equivalent? Support your answer.

3. Sandra Harding suggests that there may be different ways of knowing moral truths for different groups. Do you agree with her? Are there certain basic moral truths that transcend our particular experiences? Relate your answer to the current conflict between terrorists and anti-terrorist government forces in Syria and the Middle East.

Summary

1. *Ethics* is concerned with the study of right and wrong and how to live the good life.

2. The two main subdivisions of ethics are theoretical and normative ethics. Theoretical ethics, or *metaethics*, is concerned with appraising the logical foundations of ethical systems. *Normative ethics* gives us practical guidelines for deciding which actions are right or wrong.

3. There are two types of *ethical theories. Noncognitive theories*, such as emotivism, claim that moral statements are neither true nor false. *Cognitive theories* claim that moral statements can be true or false. Cognitive theories can be further subdivided into relativist theories and universalist theories. *Relativist theories* maintain that right and wrong are creations of either individuals or groups of humans. *Universalist theories* claim that there are universal moral values that apply to all humans.

4. *Philosophy* is, literally, the "love of wisdom."

5. The *Socratic method* involves a dialogue in which a teacher questions people about things they thought they already knew.

6. Wisdom begins in self-knowledge, which in turn leads to *self-realization* or self-actualization.

7. True philosophers approach the world with an open mind. They begin the process of inquiry by adopting an initial position of *skepticism* or doubt.

8. Plato's "Allegory of the Cave" defines the task of the philosopher: moving out of our conventional mode of thinking (the darkness of the cave) into the light of truth. This experience of truth should in turn be shared with others who are still living in darkness.

9. *Metaphysics* is the philosophical study of the nature of reality, including human nature.

10. *Metaphysical dualism* claims that reality is made up of two distinct substances: physical matter and nonmaterial mind. *Metaphysical materialism*, in contrast, claims that physical matter is the only substance.

11. Buddhist metaphysics maintains that reality is a unity and manifestation of one substance.

12. *Sociobiologists* claim that morality is genetically programmed into humans and other animals. *Behaviorists*, on the other hand, claim that morality is shaped by our environment.

13. *Determinism* claims that all events, including human actions, are caused by previous events (predetermined) and that *free will* is an illusion. If there is no free will, then of course there is no such thing as moral responsibility.

14. *Epistemology* is the study of knowledge. Most traditional Western philosophies emphasize reason as the primary source of moral knowledge; most non-Western and feminist philosophies emphasize intuition or sentiment.

15. *Emotivism* is the theory that moral statements are meaningless because they do not correspond to anything in the physical world. Emotivism arose from an attempt by the *positivists* to scientifically legitimate the study of philosophy.

Notes

1. James Q. Wilson, *The Moral Sense* (New York: Free Press, 1993), p. 11.
2. Aristotle, *Nicomachean Ethics*, trans. J. A. K. Thomson (Baltimore, MD: Penguin, 1953), p. 305.
3. Anthony Flew, *A Dictionary of Philosophy* (New York: St. Martin's Press, 1979), p. 3.
4. For more information on the emergence of a moral sense in children, read James Q. Wilson, *The Moral Sense* (New York: Free Press, 1993). Also see Chapter 3 in this textbook.
5. This speech was reputedly recorded by Plato, Socrates's disciple, in the dialogue entitled "Apology." Most of what we know about Socrates comes from the dialogues of Plato.
6. Abraham Maslow, "Self-Actualization and Beyond," *The Farther Reaches of Human Nature* (New York: Viking, 1971), pp. 41-53.

7. Simone de Beauvoir, *The Second Sex*, trans. H. M. Parshley (New York: Vintage, 1974), p. 728.

8. Friedrich Nietzsche, *The Gay Science*, trans. Walter Kaufman, *The Portable Nietzsche* (New York: Penguin, 1976), p. 341.

9. Karen J. Warren, "The Power and Promise of Ecological Feminism," in *Environmental Ethics*, ed. Susan J. Armstrong and Richard G. Botzler (New York: McGraw-Hill, 1993), pp. 434–444.

10. Cows are considered sacred not because of a belief that all animals have moral values but because humans can be reincarnated as cows.

11. C. F. Andrews, *Mahatma Gandhi's Ideas, Including Selections from His Writings* (New York: Macmillan, 1930), pp. 109–110.

12. For a more in-depth discussion of the mind-body problem, see Rene Descartes, *Meditations on First Philosophy*, Meditation VI (1641); Gilbert Ryle, *The Concept of Mind* (1992); and/or John R. Searle, *The Rediscovery of the Mind* (1992).

13. For more on sociobiology, read Edward O. Wilson, *On Human Nature* (Cambridge, MA: Harvard University Press, 1978); and Michael Ruse, *The Darwinian Paradigm: Essays on Its History, Philosophy and Religious Implications* (London: Routledge & Kegan Paul, 1989).

14. Mary Douglas, "Animals in Lele Religious Thought," *Africa* 27 (1957): 51–56.

15. See Annie L. Booth and Harvey M. Jacobs, "Ties That Bind: Native American Beliefs as a Foundation for Environmental Consciousness," in *Environmental Ethics*, ed. Susan J. Armstrong and Richard G. Botzler (New York: McGraw-Hill, 1993), pp. 519–526.

16. For a more in-depth discussion of the determinism versus free-will debate, see Thomas Hobbes, *The Questions Concerning Liberty, Necessity, and Chance* (1656); Gerald Dworkin, *Determinism, Free Will and Moral Responsibility* (Englewood Cliffs, NJ: Prentice-Hall, 1970); and Robert Nozick, "Choice and Indeterminism," in *Philosophical Explanations* (Cambridge, MA: Harvard Univ. Press, 1981), pp. 294–305.

17. Jean-Paul Sartre, *Existentialism and Human Emotions* (New York: Philosophical Library, 1957), pp. 15, 23. This brings up a question that Sartre does not adequately address—how other animals can have an essence or nature, if God is required for a human essence or nature to exist.

18. For more on this subject, see Charles Wei-hsun Fu and Sandra A. Wawrytko, eds., *Buddhist Ethics and Modern Society* (New York: Greenwood Press, 1991).

19. Alan M. Dershowitz, *The Abuse Excuse and Other Cop-Outs, Sob Stories and Evasions of Responsibility* (Boston, MA: Little, Brown, 1994).

20. Immanuel Kant, *Education*, trans. Annette Churton (Ann Arbor: University of Michigan Press, 1960).

21. Lawrence Kohlberg, *The Psychology of Moral Development*, vol. 2 (San Francisco, CA: Harper & Row, 1984).

22. A. J. Ayer, *Language, Truth and Logic*, 2nd ed. (London: Victor Gollancz), p. 103.

23. Sandra Harding, ed., *Discovering Reality: Feminist Perspectives on Epistemology, Metaphysics, Methodology and Philosophy of Science* (Dordrecht, Netherlands: D. Reidel, 1983).

24. Ibid.

CHAPTER 2

Moral Reasoning

In a republican nation, whose citizens are to be led by reason and persuasion and not by force, the art of reasoning becomes of the first importance.
    —THOMAS JEFFERSON

In 1960, Stanley Milgram of Yale University placed an advertisement in the newspaper asking for men to participate in a scientific study on memory and learning. The participants were told that the purpose of the experiment was to study the effects of punishment (electric shock) on learning. In fact, the real purpose of the study was to see how far people were willing to go in obeying an authority figure. Although no shock was actually being delivered, the "learner"—an actor—responded with (apparently) increasing anguish as the shocks being delivered by the participant supposedly increased in intensity whenever he gave a wrong answer. Despite repeated pleas from the learner to stop the experiment, two-thirds of the participants administered the requested 450 volts—enough to kill some people—simply because an authority figure told them to continue.* Were these results simply a fluke?

Several years later, Stanford University conducted a prison simulation experiment that involved twenty-one male student volunteers who were judged to be stable, mature, and socially well-developed. The volunteers were randomly assigned the role of guard or prisoner. The basement of one of the buildings at Stanford was converted to resemble a prison. Great care was taken to make the prison situation as realistic as possible. The "guards" and "prisoners" wore appropriate uniforms for their roles. The guards were expected to turn up for work, and the prisoners remained confined to prison twenty-four hours a day. As the experiment progressed, the guards became increasingly aggressive and authoritarian, and the prisoners become more and more passive and dispirited. After six days, the experiment had to be called off because of the atrocious and immoral behavior that the guards were exhibiting toward the prisoners.

What would you have done had you been a subject in the Milgram or the Stanford Prison experiment? Most of us like to think we have the resources to

---

*The video "Obedience" is available on the Milgram experiment.

At a September 2017 rally President Trump, instead of directly addressing North Korea's nuclear ambitions, resorted to the ad hominem fallacy by referring to North Korean leader Kim Jong Un as "little rocket man." Kim Jong Un returned the insult by calling Trump a "mentally deranged U.S. dotard.
©YONHAP/EPA-EFE/REX/Shutterstock *(left)*; ©SHAWN THEW/EPA-EFE/REX/Shutterstock *(right)*

resist authority or resist getting swept up in cultural roles that allow us to demean and even kill other people. But do we? Milgram writes:

> Ordinary people, simply doing their jobs and without any particular hostility on their part, can become agents in a terrible destructive process. Moreover, even when the destructive effects of their work become patently clear, and they are asked to carry out actions incompatible with fundamental standards of the majority, relatively few people have the resources needed to resist authority.[1]

What are some of the resources we need to resist authority figures, or even our peers, when they urge us to commit or turn a blind eye to immoral acts? Good moral reasoning skills are certainly one of these resources. Unlike those who obeyed, those who refused to continue in the Milgram study were able to give well-thought-out reasons for why they should stop. In this chapter we'll learn how to critically analyze moral arguments and how to recognize and overcome faulty reasoning and barriers in our own thinking.

Connections
Which logical fallacy might we be committing when we uncritically follow those in positions of authority? *See Chapter 2, page 55.*

The Three Levels of Thinking

By sharpening our analytical skills, we can become more independent in our thinking and less susceptible to worldviews that foster narrow-mindedness. The thinking process used in philosophical inquiry can be broken down into three tiers or levels: experience, interpretation, and analysis. Keep in mind that this division is artificial and merely one of emphasis. We never have *pure* experience or engage in *pure* analysis. All three levels overlap and interact with one another (Figure 2.1). Experience provides the material for interpretation and analysis; analysis, in the end, returns to experience. If the results of our analysis are inconsistent with our experience, then we need to start over and fine-tune our analysis so that it takes into account all relevant experience. Analysis also returns to experience in the form of action or *praxis.*

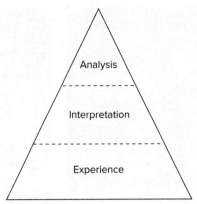

FIGURE 2.1   The Three Levels of Thinking

Experience

Experience is the first level of thinking. Experience goes beyond the five senses: We notice certain events happening, we observe different feelings within ourselves, we have certain intuitions, and we receive information about the world by reading or hearing about the experiences of others. Experience forms the foundation of the philosophical enterprise. Without experience, there can be no thought.

At this level of thinking, we simply *describe* our experiences. We do not, at least in theory, interpret or pass judgment on our experience. Figure 2.2 shows examples of statements at the level of experience:

FIGURE 2.2   Statements at the Experience Level

Interpretation

Interpretation involves trying to make sense of our experience. This level of thinking includes individual interpretations of experience as well as collective or cultural interpretations. Some of our interpretations may be well-informed; others may be based merely on our opinions or personal feelings. Upon analysis, an opinion may just happen to be true. Even opinions that make good sense and win the approval of others are still only opinions if we cannot support them with good reasons or factual evidence. Figure 2.3 provides some examples of statements at the level of interpretation.

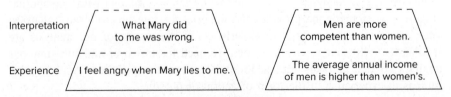

FIGURE 2.3   Statements at the Interpretation Level

The interpretations of our experiences taken together form our **worldview**. Most of us like to think that we came up with our worldviews regarding morality on our own. In reality, our worldviews are strongly influenced by our upbringing and by cultural norms. Our experience contributes to our worldview, and our worldview also shapes how we experience the world. For example, in a study on stereotyping, college students were shown a picture of a White thug beating up a Black man in a business suit. When students were later asked to describe what they saw, the majority reported that they saw a Black thug beating up a White businessman! By not analyzing our worldview, we can get caught up in a sort of self-fulfilling prophecy, or vicious cycle, where our worldview is verified by our "experience" and our experience, in turn, further confirms our distorted worldview.

Analysis

People often blend fact and opinion. It is important, therefore, to learn to distinguish between the two. By learning how to critically analyze our worldview, we can break the vicious cycle we just described. **Analysis** of moral issues draws on the findings of other disciplines such as psychology, sociology, and the natural sciences; it also involves an examination of our worldviews in light of fundamental moral intuitions, moral sentiments, and collective insights.

Analysis demands that we raise our level of consciousness and refuse to accept narrow interpretations of our experience. As such, analysis often begins with questions about the assumptions underlying our interpretations. Figure 2.4 includes examples of statements at the analysis level.

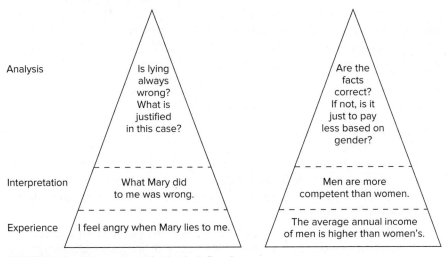

FIGURE 2.4   Statements at the Analysis Level

The process of moving from experience to interpretation to analysis and from there back to experience again is ongoing. Analysis is most productive when it is done collectively because people bring with them different

Connections

At what level of thinking are cultural relativists and how does this affect their moral decision making? *See Chapter 6, pages 166–167.*

experiences. At the same time, we cannot simply accept other people's interpretations of their experiences at face value.

Because we are social beings who do not exist apart from a culture and a particular cultural worldview, it is all too easy for us to be lured into accepting cultural interpretations of reality as truth. Even well-trained philosophers can become captivated by the prevailing cultural worldview or the traditional philosophical interpretations of their professional colleagues.

When we succumb to the temptation to follow public opinion or accept traditional assumptions without question, we become maintainers of the status quo. As such, we may even become part of the problem. Analysis that ignores certain relevant aspects of experience can become distorted. The complicity of philosophers such as Martin Heidegger (1889–1976) in destructive ideologies like Nazism and the promotion of sexism, elitism and religious intolerance in the name of philosophy are all instances of a philosopher accepting a prevailing worldview as truth without bothering to analyze it thoroughly.

Connections

How do cultural relativists define who is in the moral community? *See Chapter 6, pages 182–184.*

Some liberation ethicists claim that certain groups of traditionally disempowered people, such as African Americans, women, and economically disadvantaged people, have **epistemological privilege**. Those who do not benefit from or are harmed by conventional interpretations of reality, it is argued, are the least likely to buy into or defend the interpretations that oppress them. Being the least biased in favor of traditional interpretations, they also have the least resistance to analyzing them. This is a reversal of the conventional wisdom that favors insight and the logical, abstract thinking processes used by well-educated White males.

Whether or not being disempowered or disadvantaged gives one an epistemological advantage is up for debate. However, we do know that engaging in dialogue with people from diverse backgrounds, rather than only with people who are like us—whether we are socially and economically advantaged or disadvantaged—can help us make more effective moral decisions.[2] For more on conditions that promote moral development see Chapter 3.

Exercises

1. Select a simple experience, such as a man holding a door open for a woman or a student giving a dollar to a beggar on the street. In groups, discuss different interpretations of the experience, being careful not to let prejudice distort your interpretation.

2. Use the three-tiered model of thinking to discuss the following experiences. The interpretations you list do not have to be ones that you personally accept; you might also want to write down some interpretations that are common in our culture. Discuss how your interpretation of this experience has shaped your past experience and actions and how analyzing this issue might affect future actions regarding the issue.

a. Although Blacks represent only 13.3 percent of the U.S. population, they make up 37.8 percent of the prison inmates.[3]

b. In 2016, only 50 percent of Americans between the ages of 18 and 29 voted in the presidential election, well below the 55 percent for all voters. In addition, voter turnout was the lowest in 20 years.

c. More than half of the agricultural workers in the United States are undocumented immigrants.

d. Marijuana use has been decriminalized in Canada but possession for recreational use is still a crime in most U.S. states.

e. Men are much more likely than women to hold high-ranking faculty positions in science departments at Ivy League colleges in the United States.

3. Choose an experience from your life. Analyze this experience using the three-tiered model.

*4. Discuss the claim that people who have the least power in a society—those who see the world from "below"—are epistemologically privileged. If you are doing community service with a group of people such as the homeless, the economically disadvantaged, or elderly people in nursing homes, use examples from this experience to illustrate your answer. Explain.

Moral Analysis and Praxis

The following story, which is attributed to Buddha, illustrates what is meant by praxis in moral philosophy: A group of people came across a man dying from a wound from a poison arrow. Instead of trying to save the man, the crowd stood around debating about where the arrow had come from, who had fired it, and the angle of the trajectory. Meanwhile, the man dies. The proper goal of the philosopher, according to Buddha, is to save the dying man, not to stand around engaging in speculation.

Western philosophical methodology has traditionally focused primarily on one mode of analysis—abstract, logical reasoning—and downplayed praxis. Although logical reasoning is very important in moral philosophy, it represents only one aspect of what is meant by analysis in moral philosophy.

Feminist Methodology and Praxis in Ethical Analysis

In an article entitled "Shifting Perspective: A New Approach to Ethics," Canadian philosopher Sheila Mullett outlines a process for ethical analysis based on what she calls a feminist methodology. Mullett's approach to ethical analysis involves three steps or dimensions:

1. The first dimension, **moral sensitivity**, grows out of a collective consciousness raising. Until we develop an awareness of the experience of violence,

Connections

What role does moral sensitivity play in women's moral development?

See Chapter 3, page 95.

victimization, and pain that surrounds us, we will continue to inadvertently perpetuate it. Only through actually experiencing—directly or indirectly—"this consciousness of pain," Mullett argues, "can we begin to cultivate a new attitude towards the social arrangements which contribute to suffering."[4] College community service learning programs have the potential to enhance our moral sensitivity.

2. The second dimension is **ontological shock. Ontology** is the philosophical study of "being" or the nature of being. Ontological shock is something that shakes us to the very core of our being, thus forcing us to call into question our cherished worldview or interpretations of our experiences. Simply being aware of the injustices and pain in the world are not sufficient to motivate us to do this. When we experience ontological shock, the worldview that we once took for granted is displaced, thereby forcing us to reanalyze our old assumptions. Freshmen who have never lived away from home often experience ontological shock when they go away to college and come into contact with different ideas and values.

3. The third dimension of analysis is **praxis**. Praxis refers to the practice of a particular art or skill. In ethics, praxis requires informed social action. True philosophical analysis always returns with an altered and heightened consciousness to the world of particular experiences. For example, the September 11, 2001, terrorist attacks on the World Trade Center, which created ontological shock among Americans, were followed by an increase in altruistic behavior among New Yorkers.

Connections

Do we behave altruistically simply out of self-interest?

See Chapter 7, pages 213-214.

Liberation Ethics and Social Action

Liberation ethicist Paulo Freire, in his book *The Pedagogy of the Oppressed*, writes: "This shift in consciousness includes a search for collective actions that can transform the existing unjust social structures. . . ."[5] Authentic thinking, thinking that is concerned about reality, does not take place in ivory tower isolation."[6] Indeed, genuine praxis demands a shift away from the manner in which an individual routinely sees the world to viewing the world through the eyes of the collective "we." For example, there was an increase in hostility against Muslim-Americans following 9/11 and, more recently, the Boston Marathon shootings in 2013. This type of thinking is due in part to an error or bias in human thinking, known as the "one of them/one of us" error, in which we divide the world into the "good guys" (us) and the "bad guys" (them). Hispanic immigrants, especially those who are in the country illegally, also tend to be relegated to the "them" category. Praxis requires that we become aware of this tendency and work to overcome it by treating all people with proper respect.

Analysis, in this broader sense, is interactive, interdisciplinary, and directed toward praxis or social action. This approach is not only richer and more inclusive but also more effective for promoting moral growth. Praxis demands that we cultivate our own moral character. Until we overcome our own narrow interpretations of the world and incorporate these changes into our personal life, it is unlikely that we will be able to sustain our involvement in praxis.

Thought without practice is empty, practice without thought is blind.

—KWAME NKRUMAH, former president of Ghana

Exercises

1. Relate the notion of ontological shock to a time when your worldview was shaken. How did you respond to the shock? Did it make you more morally sensitive and more likely to act upon your moral beliefs? Explain.

2. The civil rights movement in the United States in the 1960s involved the application of moral analysis to praxis. Malcolm X (1925–1965) wrote the following about the importance of taking action in the ongoing struggle against racism:

   > I believe in political action, yes. Any kind of political action. I believe in action period. Whatever kind of action is necessary. When you hear me say "by any means necessary," I mean exactly that. I believe in anything that is necessary to correct unjust conditions—political, economic, social, physical, anything that's necessary. I believe in it as long as it's intelligently directed and designed to get results.[7]

   What do you think Malcolm X meant when he said "by any means necessary"? Relate his comments to the concept of praxis.

3. Who is your hero (your hero can be a real or fictional person)? Is your hero more willing than the average person to engage in serious analysis of his or her own cultural worldviews? More likely to engage in praxis than most people? Explain, using examples to illustrate your answer.

*4. Discuss your choice of community service in terms of the three levels of thinking and the concept of praxis. Relate your service learning as well to Mullett's three dimensions of ethical analysis.

Overcoming Resistance

Nothing strong, nothing new, nothing urgent penetrates man's mind without crossing resistance.

—HENRI DE LUBAC, *Paradoxes* (1969)

Most of us hate to be proved wrong. When a particular paradigm becomes thoroughly entrenched in our worldview, we may begin to see it as fact rather than an interpretation of experience, especially if we benefit by that particular worldview. For example, when slavery was legal, it was seen as a natural part of the world order by those who benefited from it. Few White people bothered to analyze or even to question the morality of the practice. Even President Abraham Lincoln did not always support the abolition of slavery in his public statements. In his first inaugural speech, Lincoln reassured the Southern voters that "I have no purpose, directly or indirectly, to interfere with the institution of slavery in the States where it exists. I believe I have no lawful right to do so, and I have no inclination to do so."[8] Fortunately, Lincoln had the moral courage to reevaluate his position on slavery.

To avoid having our worldview challenged, we may use a type of defense mechanism known as resistance. **Defense mechanisms** are psychological tools, which we usually learn at an early age, for coping with difficult situations. Defense mechanisms can be divided into two main types: (1) coping and (2) resistance.

Healthy Defense Mechanisms

Coping, or healthy defense mechanisms, allows us to work through challenges to our worldview and to adjust our life in ways that maintain our integrity. Healthy ways of coping include logical analysis, objectivity, tolerance of ambiguity, empathy, and suppression of harmful emotional responses.

Immature Defense Mechanisms

Resistance, in contrast, involves the use of immature defense mechanisms that are rigid, impulsive, maladaptive, and nonanalytical. Isolation, rationalization, and denial are all examples of immature defense mechanisms.[9] Everyone uses defense mechanisms at times to keep from feeling overwhelmed. Children from abusive backgrounds often find it necessary to construct rigid defenses to avoid being crushed by their circumstances. The problem arises, though, when people carry these once-appropriate defense mechanisms into their adult life. When resistance becomes a habitual way of responding to issues, it acts as a barrier to critical analysis of interpretations or worldview (Figure 2.5).

Connections

What are the stages of moral development? *See Chapter 3, pages 90-94.*

The use of immature defense mechanisms or resistance impedes our moral development. Daniel Hart and Susan Chmiel, in a study of the influence of defense mechanisms on moral reasoning, found a strong relationship between the use of immature defense mechanisms in adolescence and lower levels of moral development in adulthood.[10] The habitual use of resistance entails avoiding experiences and ideas that challenge our worldview. This, in itself, can create both anxiety and boredom. Resistance can also numb us to the needs of others, immobilize us in the face of moral outrage, and prevent us from devising a plan of action.

Rather than being prisoners of our past, we can take steps to overcome immature defense mechanisms, including recognizing which ones we use, that stand in the way of our making effective moral decisions in our lives. In

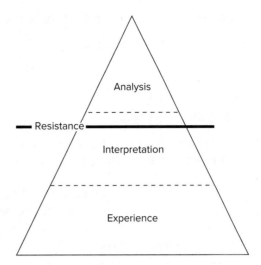

FIGURE 2.5 Resistance as a Defense
Mechanism

identifying our resistance, we may find that we rely primarily on one type of resistance, or we may have a repertoire of several types depending on the situation. The following are a few of the types of resistance that people are prone to use when their moral views are challenged.

Ignorance There are situations where we are ignorant simply because the information is not available. Sometimes, however, we avoid learning about particular issues because we just do not want to know. Some people think that not knowing excuses them from having to think about the issue or take a stand. As a result, problems such as global conflicts and poverty continue to get worse. Ignorance is regarded as a vice and a hindrance to the good life in virtually all world

©YAY Media AS/Alamy Stock Photo

philosophies. Socrates is reputed to have said, "The unexamined life is not worth living." Confucius taught that "ignorance is the night of the mind." "Ignorance," writes Hindu Yogi Swami Prabhavananda, "creates all the other obstacles."[11]

Analyzing Images

1. Has there ever been a time when you've preferred ignorance to being informed? Compare the outcome of your experience to that of the businessmen in the cartoon above.

2. Some people accuse college students of taking the attitude that "ignorance is bliss" when it comes to public life and policies. Do you agree? Support your answer. Relate your answer to the issue of low-voter turnout among young people in national elections.

Avoidance   Rather than seeking out people who have different points of view, we may avoid certain people and situations and instead hang out only with people who agree with us. Some people who hold very strong opinions about certain moral issues, yet are insecure in the face of challenges to their position, only read literature or watch news shows that support their opinion and only attend social and political events, meetings, or rallies attended by people who agree with them, a phenomenon known as *confirmation bias*. More and more Americans over the past three decades or four have been choosing to live in communities of like-minded people and to watch television news shows that support their views.[12] The tendency to avoid controversial situations or people with opinions unlike our own can lead to a serious lack of communication and even hostility between people who hold widely opposing points of view.

Denial   Andrè Trocme, a leader in the French Resistance in World War II, defined denial as "a willingness to be self-deceived."[13] During World War II, most Germans tacitly supported the war effort by denying the cruelty of the Nazi policies. Similarly, parents may be in denial regarding their children's destructive lifestyles until it is too late. Mothers in incestuous families may fail to take action to halt the sexual abuse, not because they don't care about their children but because they have convinced themselves that such a terrible thing could not really be happening. Denial is also common in people who are addicted to alcohol or drugs. Denial keeps people from acknowledging and working on solutions to these pressing moral problems.

Anger   We cannot always avoid people who disagree with us. Some people respond by getting angry when they are confronted with a challenge to their views. Anger may be expressed overtly by physical violence or threats, or it may be expressed more subtly in angry phrases such as "don't force your views on me," an expression that implies, ironically, that the person challenging another's views is somehow threatening his or her autonomy. During a March 2016 Trump rally in Chicago, fights broke out between Trump supporters and anti-Trump protesters resulting in several injuries and five arrests. The rally was canceled as a result. Anger as a form of resistance is most effective in thwarting disagreement when backed by a large group of supporters or when a person has greater social, political, or physical power.

Not all anger involves resistance. We may feel anger or moral indignation when we hear that one of our favorite professors was denied tenure because he is Arab. Rather than acting as a barrier to analysis, this type of anger may motivate us to correct this injustice by writing a well-argued letter of protest to the local newspaper. We'll look more into the role of moral sentiments in Chapter 3.

Clichés   "Don't force your views on me." "It's all relative." "To each his own." "Things always work out for the best." "I have a right to my own opinion." Hannah Arendt wrote that when Nazi war criminal Adolf Eichmann was challenged to analyze the contradictions of his society, he became "genuinely incapable of uttering a single sentence that was not a cliché."[14] Used sparingly, clichés can be useful for illustrating a point; however, the habitual use of clichés in responding to challenges to our worldview keeps us from thinking seriously about issues.

Connections
Why was Eichmann a "good" citizen from the point of view of a cultural relativist? *See Chapter 6, page 196.*

Conformity/Superficial Tolerance   Many people are afraid that they will not be accepted by their peers if they disagree with them. Even though they may actually disagree, they go along with the group rather than risk rejection. For example, suppose that someone at a party makes an offensive ethnic or sexist joke. Rather than speaking up or leaving the room, some people will either laugh or say nothing, thus tolerating and perpetuating the bigotry.

> Many people fear nothing more terribly than to take a position which stands out sharply and clearly from prevailing opinion. The tendency of most is to adopt a view that is so ambiguous that it will include everything, and so popular that it will include everyone.
>
> —Martin Luther King Jr.

Some people who engage in superficial tolerance really do not have a point of view of their own. The expression "I can see both sides of the issue" often masks a reluctance to analyze the various and often contradictory sides of a moral issue. Italian poet Dante (1265–1321) had a dim view of people who use this sort of resistance. In his *Divine Comedy*, he reserved "the darkest places in Hell" for those who decide to remain neutral when confronted with a moral conflict.

"I'm Struggling"   During the Nazi occupation of France in World War II, the 3,500 people of the village of Le Chambon-sur-Lignon provided refuge for Jews who were fleeing the Nazis. In doing this, the villagers took tremendous risks. When Pierre Sauvage, who directed *Weapons of the Spirit*—a documentary about the resistance movement of Le Chambon—was asked years later why the people of Le Chambon acted, while others were still struggling about what to do, Sauvage replied: "Those who struggle don't act; those who act don't struggle." It is appropriate to wrestle with moral issues before reaching at least a tentative stand; but for some people, the struggle is used to avoid taking a stand while still creating an appearance of being concerned.

Distractions   The use of distractions is a popular means of blocking out conflicting thoughts. Some people hate silence and being alone with their thoughts. They turn on the television or have loud music playing whenever they are home alone. Or they use alcohol, drugs, food, partying, work, talking on their cell phones, logging onto the Internet, or shopping for things they don't really need as a means of keeping their mind off of their problems. Indeed, some enterprising people have become wealthy marketing distractions to the public.

Mental hindrances, according to Buddhist teaching, keep us from having clear understanding. For this reason, most Eastern philosophies emphasize the importance of stillness and quiet contemplation for achieving wisdom. Putting aside resistance often means experiencing uncomfortable feelings and ideas that we have been defending ourselves against. Because giving up old ways of thinking can be both painful and confusing, people will rarely change without being challenged through *knowledge perturbation*, also known as **cognitive dissonance**. Knowledge perturbation occurs when our worldview is called into question, thus throwing us into a state of ontological shock. Socrates was a master at knowledge perturbation. It is also practiced by some Eastern philosophers and masters.

Connections

Why was Socrates put to death by the state? *See Chapter 1, page 7.*

Types of Resistance

Resistance is the habitual use of immature defense mechanisms when our worldviews are challenged.

Ignorance   Not learning about a particular issue because we don't want to know.

Avoidance   Staying away from people and situations that challenge our worldviews.

Denial   Refusing to acknowledge problems and issues.

Anger   Using threats or violence to keep others from challenging our views.

Clichés   Responding with trite sayings or expressions when our views are challenged.

Conformity/Superficial Tolerance   Agreeing simply for the sake of agreeing.

"I'm Struggling"   Wrestling with an issue as a substitute for taking a stand.

Distractions   Turning to diversions to keep from thinking about troubling issues.

Philosophy is a social pursuit. Both the Socratic method and the traditional master–disciple relationship used in Eastern philosophy provide a supportive context in which the student can engage in self-examination. An experienced teacher or supportive friends can help us identify and work through our resistance by challenging us and offering constructive criticism.

Doublethink

Because most people resist analyzing their worldviews, they may unwittingly get caught up in *doublethink*, a term coined by author George Orwell. **Doublethink** involves holding two contradictory views at the same time and believing both to be true. Orwell's novel *1984* was written in 1948, in part, as a warning that, unless we recognize the insidious role of doublethink in our society, we will continue to head down the path toward destruction.

In Allan Bloom's book on U.S. colleges and universities, *The Closing of the American Mind*, the author claims that most students believe morality is relative and that there are no universal moral values. At the same time, however, these students profess to believe that human equality and tolerance are universal moral values!

> There is one thing a professor can be absolutely certain of: almost every student entering the university believes, or says he believes, that truth is relative. . . . Students nowadays are unified only in their relativism and in their allegiance to equality. . . . The danger they have been taught to fear from absolutism is not error but intolerance. . . . The point is not to correct the mistake and be really right; rather it is not to think you are right at all.

Connections
What are the moral issues in the debate over animal rights? *See Chapter 11, pages 383.*

Doublethink often takes the form of supporting double standards. For example, surveys indicate that most college students believe that women should be the primary caregivers of children, but these students will just as vehemently argue that they believe in equality and freedom of choice for all humans in regard to lifestyle and career. Many people also claim that they believe in animal rights. They point out that they are morally opposed to hunting or to the mistreatment of pets. Yet, they have no qualms about eating meat or wearing animal products (leather shoes or fur coats).

Sometimes, doublethink involves a conflict between our expressed worldview and our actual actions. In 2006, students at Boston College were up in arms when Bush's secretary of state, Condoleezza Rice, was invited to speak at graduation and receive an honorary degree. Student groups called for the invitation to speak to be revoked because the Bush administration had such a bad record when it came to the issue of freedom of speech. In other words, the students demanded that Rice's freedom to speak at graduation be squelched in order to demonstrate their support of freedom of speech!

To use another example, most teachers, even those who claim to be ardent feminists, treat their female students differently than their male students. They call on the boys more often, praise their accomplishments more often, and are more tolerant of their disruptive behavior.[15] Yet, when teachers are told this, the great majority will deny that it happens in their classroom. When teachers are shown videotapes of their classes, most are shocked at the extent to which they ignore the girls in the classroom and downplay their abilities.

In other words, doublethink often goes unnoticed. For this reason, it is important to be on the alert for doublethink in our lives. This involves learning what type of resistance we are most likely to use when our views are challenged. It may seem that, by avoiding conflict, life will be more tranquil; in fact, habitual resistance takes a lot of energy. When we shut out ideas and experiences that conflict with our cherished worldview, we also shut out much of life's richness.

Exercises

1. Name some of your healthy coping mechanisms. What can you do to strengthen these?

2. What type of resistance are you most likely to use when one of your cherished worldviews is challenged? Illustrate your answer with a specific example of a time you used this type of resistance during a discussion about a moral issue. What can you do to make yourself less prone to use this type of resistance?

3. Relate Orwell's concept of doublethink to a specific current political issue or foreign policy and to your own thinking on these issues and policies.

4. Studies focusing on the college experience have found that college freshmen are particularly influenced by peer opinion. Do you think that you were more of a conformist when you first entered college? How did this tendency to conform affect your views on morality?

5. Do you agree with Allan Bloom that the morality espoused by most students involves doublethink? Why or why not? What about the belief that morality is relative? How might this theory itself involve doublethink?

*6. If you are doing community service, has it helped you to strengthen your healthy coping mechanisms and to overcome your immature coping mechanisms (resistance)? If so, give specific examples.

The Role of *Is* and *Ought* Statements in Ethics

Descriptive Statements

Descriptive statements tell us what *is*. Descriptive statements are either true or false. As Detective Joe Friday, of the old *Dragnet* television series, used to say, "Just the facts, ma'am." Here are some examples of a descriptive statement:

> I saw a man pulling a screaming woman into the bushes outside the Classroom Building at 8:54 A.M.

> At 11:17 P.M. last night, my roommate said to me, "I promise to clean the bathroom before I go to bed."

This morning I saw Gloria coming out of John's room.

The average temperature of Narragansett Bay has increased by 3°F in the past fifty years.

Prescriptive Statements

Prescriptive statements deal with values. They tell us what *ought to be:*

We *ought* to tell the truth to Detective Friday about what happened on campus this morning.

It is wrong to (that is, we *ought* not to) hurt other people for our own amusement.

People *ought* to keep their promises.

We *ought* to cut down on our use of fossil fuels, which contribute to global warming.

Moral values are only one type of value. *Nonmoral values* include good health; aesthetic values; social values such as power, fame, and popularity; economic values; and political values such as national integrity and solidarity. Only moral values carry the force of the *ought*. Although it would be awfully nice to be healthy, wealthy, popular, and a straight A student, moral values, by their very nature, demand that we give them precedence over nonmoral values when they conflict.

Unlike science, which is descriptive, ethics is primarily *prescriptive* with descriptive statements playing a supportive role. When making moral decisions, we use descriptive statements about the world and about human nature, along with prescriptive statements about moral values. It is important for making an informed moral decision that we first get our facts straight. For example, in the current debate over same-sex marriage, has legalizing same-sex marriage weakened traditional marriage, as critics claim it will do?

The social sciences are important to ethics because they systematically test our ideas about human nature and society. Our ideas may be useless, and even harmful, if they are not grounded in reality. For example, many moral philosophers in the past have operated on the assumption that women are not as capable of rationality as are men. Domination of women by men was morally justified on the grounds that women needed the guidance and protection of men. Good intentions alone, in other words, are insufficient to guide our moral decision making.

Connections

How can the utilitarian calculus help us make better moral decisions? *See Chapter 8, pages 249-252.*

The road to Hell is paved with good intentions.

—old English proverb

To use another example, until relatively recently, many physicians lied to patients who were dying. Physicians justified the practice based on their limited experience with a few distressed patients. When properly controlled studies were carried out regarding the effects of knowing the truth, it was discovered that people with terminal cancer actually did better and lived longer if they knew the truth about their condition.[16]

Ethics goes beyond science and observation, however. We cannot go directly from a descriptive statement about how things are to a statement about how things ought to be. For example, most patients with terminal cancer do better if they know they are dying, but this does not mean that we *ought* to tell Juan, who is depressed and suicidal, that he has cancer. Similarly, social scientists have found that individuals are more likely to help those who are most like them, but we cannot decide, based on this description alone, that Professor Smith, who is blond and blue-eyed, *ought* to offer tutoring only to her blond and blue-eyed students. Instead, moral judgments and values—such as "do not lie," "be fair," and "do no harm"—need to be brought into the picture when we are making a decision about the right course of action.

Exercises

1. Looking back at the scenario at the beginning of Chapter 1, construct an imaginary dialogue between yourself and the student who took your book bag. You are trying to convince the student to return your book bag. Which statements in the conversation are descriptive and which are prescriptive? Discuss how these two types of statements support each other.

2. Do you think it is morally acceptable for Professor Smith to give preferential treatment to her blond, blue-eyed students? Would it make any difference if she believed it was right? What if her intentions were "good"? For example, suppose that she genuinely believed that only blue-eyed people had intellectual potential and that it was unfair to give non-blue-eyed people the false hope (by providing tutoring) that they might be able to succeed in college. Support your answers.

3. Make a list of general guidelines that you use in making moral decisions. Where did you get these guidelines? Compare your list with those of other students in the class. To what extent do the lists correspond to each other? Is there a general theme or themes underlying your list of guidelines? If so, what are these themes?

4. Some people claim that *knowing* what is right is harder than *doing* what is right. Others say just the opposite: that doing what you know to be right is harder. Which do you find harder? Explain why using specific examples.

5. Discuss a time when you put, or were tempted to put, nonmoral values over moral values. How did you resolve the conflict? Were you satisfied with how you resolved the conflict? Explain.

Recognizing and Constructing Moral Arguments

The very first lesson that we have a right to demand that logic shall teach us is how to make our ideas clear; and a most important one it is, depreciated only by minds who stand in need of it.

—CHARLES SANDERS PEIRCE

Logic

Logic, the study of correct and incorrect reasoning, provides us with the methods and skills to formulate sound moral arguments and to distinguish good arguments from poor arguments. Logic enables us to analyze the logical consistencies and inconsistencies of the different ethical theories. Logic also helps us to make better moral decisions. Without correct reasoning, even a person with good intentions can end up causing more harm than good. Although people may be motivated to do what is right, they cannot always figure out *what* is the best course of action to accomplish this goal.

In addition, there may be times when we know that a person's argument is faulty, but we refrain from speaking out because we cannot figure out exactly what is wrong with the argument. When this happens, we are more likely to back down on our own position or even adopt the other person's and possibly do something that we may later regret. When individuals fail to take appropriate moral action or make a moral decision that they later regret, we call it a **moral tragedy**. A knowledge of logic helps us to break through patterns of resistance—our own and those of others—and thus avoid moral tragedies.

Connections

Why is cultural relativism based on faulty logic? *See Chapter 6, pages 197–200.*

Recognizing Moral Arguments

The Components of an Argument   To distinguish between correct and incorrect reasoning, we need to be able to recognize arguments. An **argument** is made up of two or more propositions; one of these is claimed to follow from or be supported by the others. A **proposition** is a statement that expresses a complete thought. It can be either true or false. The **conclusion** is the proposition that is affirmed or denied on the basis of other propositions in the argument. The **premise** is a proposition that supports or gives reasons for accepting the conclusion. An argument can have one or many premises.

In an argument, we move from the premise(s) to the conclusion through a process known as *inference:*

$$\text{Premise(s)} \longrightarrow \text{Inference} \longrightarrow \text{Conclusion}$$

There are two types of logical arguments: inductive and deductive. In a **deductive argument**, the conclusion *necessarily* follows from the premises *if* the premises are true and the reasoning process is valid. For example:

> All killing of unarmed people is morally wrong. Capital punishment involves the killing of unarmed people. Therefore, capital punishment is morally wrong.

In the above argument, we must accept the conclusion as true, if we accept the premises. Of course, not everyone accepts the first premise.

With an **inductive argument**, the conclusion *probably* follows from the premises but we can't be 100 percent sure. The stronger and more complete the premises, the stronger the argument. For example:

> Murder rates are not significantly lower in states that have capital punishment.
> Therefore, capital punishment is probably not an effective deterrent against murder.

In the above example, we cannot accept the conclusion as necessarily true because there may be other factors at work that influence the murder rate.

Ethical arguments usually contain both descriptive and prescriptive statements or propositions. A proposition in a moral argument can also be a lexical definition of a key term. The proposition "lying is any intentionally deceptive message that is stated" gives us a lexical definition of *lying.* We determine the truth or falsehood of a lexical definition by looking up the term in a dictionary.

Different sentences can express the same proposition. For example, the statements "torturing children is wrong," "it is wrong to torture children," and "Kinder zu quälen ist unmoralisch" are the same proposition because they all express the same thought. Several propositions can be found in one sentence. French philosopher René Descartes's famous *cogito* argument can be summarized in one sentence, "I think, therefore I am," which contains two propositions: "I think" and "I am."

Tips for Recognizing and Breaking down Arguments

- The entire argument may appear in either one sentence or several sentences.
- The conclusion can appear anywhere in the argument.
- Identify the conclusion first. Ask yourself: What is this person trying to prove?
- The conclusion is often, though not always, preceded by words or phrases known as conclusion indicators, such as

therefore	which shows that
hence	for these reasons
thus	consequently

- The premises are often, though not always, preceded by words or phrases known as premise indicators, such as

because	may be inferred that
for	the reason is that
since	as shown by

- Underline, or highlight, the conclusion and the premises.

Premise and Conclusion Indicators   Some arguments contain terms known as *premise indicators* and *conclusion indicators* that can help us identify the conclusion and the premises. Words such as *because, since*, and *for* can serve as premise indicators. The words *therefore, thus, hence, so, as*, and *consequently* are examples of conclusion indicators. Indicators signal that a premise or conclusion follows. In the argument "I think, therefore I am," the word *therefore* tells us that the conclusion is "I am."

The bad news is that not all arguments contain indicators. In addition, words such as *since, for, therefore, because*, and *as* can serve as premise or conclusion indicators in one context but not in another context. For example, *because* and *therefore* can be used in explanations. In the statement "Ying stole the food because his children were starving," we are not trying to prove that Ying stole the food; rather, we are explaining why he stole the food.

Breaking Down Arguments   When breaking down an argument into its components, if there are no premise or conclusion indicators, it is usually easiest to identify the conclusion first. To do this, we should ask ourselves: What is the argument trying to prove? Let's look at the following inductive argument from an article by Dr. Joseph Collins entitled "Should Doctors Tell the Truth?"

> Every physician should cultivate lying as a fine art. . . . Many experiences show that patients do not want the truth about their maladies, and that it is prejudicial to their well-being to know it.[17]

There are three separate propositions in this argument.

> 1. [*Every physician should cultivate lying as a fine art*] 2. [*Many experiences show that patients do not want the truth about their maladies*] and 3. [(many experiences show) *that it is prejudicial to their well-being to know it* (the truth).]

If you cannot identify the conclusion and there are no conclusion or premise indicators, try inserting a conclusion indicator, such as *therefore*, before the proposition that you suspect might be the conclusion. Or try inserting a premise indicator, such as *because*, before the proposition(s) that you think might be the premise(s). If the argument is not essentially changed by the addition of an indicator, this means that it is in the right place.

> 1. [*Every physician should cultivate the fine art of lying*] <u>because</u> 2. [*Many experiences show that patients do not want the truth about their maladies*] and <u>because</u> 3. [(many experiences show) *that it is prejudicial to their well-being to know it* (the truth).]

In the preceding argument, the first proposition is the conclusion, and propositions 2 and 3 are the supporting premises. The first premise (proposition 2) is a descriptive statement about an **empirical** fact. In this case, we might want to find out how many patients were surveyed and whether the sample was representative. The second premise (proposition 3) is also a descriptive proposition. The claim is that knowing the truth will bring harm to the patient in the form of anguish and earlier death.

Connections
Is lying always wrong? *See Chapter 10, pages 326–327.*

If the premises are found to be false or logically unrelated to the conclusion, as they are in this argument, then we have a poor argument. However, this does not necessarily mean that the conclusion itself is false or worthless: It is simply unsubstantiated.

Some arguments have unstated premises. It is sometimes assumed that certain beliefs are so generally accepted that there is no need to state them. In the preceding argument, there is an unstated third premise regarding a moral principle, the *principle of nonmaleficence*, also known as the "do no harm" principle.

You may be surprised to learn that premises about general moral principles or sentiments are often the least controversial of the premises—an observation that runs contrary to the popular belief that morality is relative and varies from individual to individual.

Rhetoric   Many people mistake rhetoric for logical argument. **Rhetoric**, also known as *the art of persuasion*, is often used by politicians as a means of promoting a particular worldview rather than analyzing it. In logical arguments, we end with the conclusion. Rhetoric, in contrast, begins with a conclusion or position. The rhetorician then presents only those claims that support his or her particular position. The purpose of rhetoric is to win over your opponents through the power of persuasive speech; the purpose of argumentation is to discover the truth. Some people are so emotionally invested in certain opinions on moral issues that they may unknowingly manipulate their arguments to "prove" a conclusion that does not logically follow from the premise(s).

Constructing Moral Arguments

When constructing an argument about a moral issue, we begin by making a list of premises. *Never* begin by first stating your position or opinion and then seeking only evidence that supports your particular position in an attempt to persuade those who disagree with you to come around to your way of thinking and to dismiss any conflicting views.

When coming up with premises, it is generally most productive to work with others, especially those who disagree with us. According to Socrates, it is through the process of dialogue that we can test our views and, ideally, come closer to discovering the truth. The following is a summary of the steps for constructing an argument:

1. *Develop a list of premises.* In a good argument, the premises will be relatively uncontroversial and acceptable to all, or most, reasonable people. Much of the disagreement in moral arguments, as we noted earlier, stems not from disagreement about basic moral principles but from disagreement about empirical facts or the definitions of ambiguous key terms. It is important to be able to identify relevant moral principles and ideals; in addition, good moral reasoning depends on first getting the facts straight rather than relying on unsupported assumptions or opinions. Any ambiguous key terms should be clearly defined and used in a consistent manner throughout your argument.

2. *Eliminate irrelevant or weak premises.* After coming up with a list of premises, go back and eliminate any that are weak or irrelevant. Resist the temptation to eliminate premises that do not mesh with your particular opinion regarding the moral issue. Also make sure that there are no obvious gaps in the list of premises and no fallacies. We will learn how to recognize some of the more common fallacies later in this chapter.

3. *Come to a conclusion.* The last step in constructing a moral argument is drawing the conclusion. The conclusion should take into account the information in the premises but should not state more than what is contained therein. Conclusions that are too broad include more than the premises say; conclusions that are too narrow ignore certain premises.

4. *Try out the argument on others.* The next step is to try out your argument. When doing this, be careful not to slip into rhetoric. Remember, the mark of a good philosopher is to be open-minded.

5. *Revise your argument if necessary.* The final step in constructing an argument is to revise it in light of feedback and additional information you receive. This may involve changing or modifying your conclusion. If your argument is weak, you should be open to revising it.

Five Steps for Constructing Moral Arguments

1. Develop a list of premises.

2. Eliminate irrelevant or weak premises.

3. Come to a conclusion.

4. Try out your argument on others.

5. Revise your argument if necessary.

Exercises

1. Break down the following arguments into their premises and conclusions. In each of the arguments, ask yourself whether there are other premises that might strengthen the argument. Also, think of premises that might be unstated but simply assumed in each of the arguments.

   a. Racism and sexism are wrong because all people deserve equal respect.

   b. It is immoral to use rabbits in cosmetic experiments because causing pain is immoral, and animals such as rabbits are capable of feeling pain.

   c. People need to pass a driving test to get a license to drive a car. People should also have to take a test and get a license before they can become a parent. After all, parenting is a greater responsibility and requires more skill than driving.

   d. Embryos are not persons with moral rights. Furthermore, the embryos used in stem cell research are going to be discarded anyway. Because we have a moral obligation to help people suffering from disease and the use of stem cell research has the potential to help many of these people, stem cell research should be legal.

   e. We have an obligation to become the best person we can. One of the primary purposes of education is to make us better people. Therefore, colleges should seriously consider having a community service requirement for graduation, since community service has been shown to increase students' self-esteem and facilitate their moral development.

2. Choose one or more of the following controversial moral issues:

   a. Reinstating military conscription for men and women between the ages of eighteen and forty-five

   b. Capital punishment

   c. Giving legal status to illegal immigrants who came here with their parents as children.

   d. Abortion for sex selection

   e. Legalization of marijuana

   f. Using unmanned drones for assassination

   g. Lowering the drinking age to 18

   h. The high cost of college tuition

   Working in small groups, construct an argument using the five steps listed on page 51.

3. Look back at the argument you constructed in the previous exercise. To what extent were you tempted to engage in rhetoric instead of logical analysis by using only those statements that supported your particular opinion on the topic? Did working in a group make it easier for you to avoid rhetoric? Explain.

Avoiding Informal Fallacies

> *. . . arguments, like men, are often pretenders.*

> —PLATO

Connections

On what grounds does W.D. Ross argue that moral duties are prima facie rather than absolute? *See Chapter 10, pages 331–332.*

Most moral arguments are inductive, in part because most moral principles and rights are *prima facie*; that is, they are binding unless they conflict with a pressing moral duty or right. There are several ways in which an inductive argument can be weak or invalid. For example, the premises may be weak or false. When an inductive argument is psychologically or emotionally persuasive but logically incorrect, it contains what logicians call an **informal fallacy**. We are more likely to use fallacies when we are unsure of our position. The use of fallacies may be effective in the short run, but thoughtful people will eventually begin to question the reasoning behind the fallacious argument. Being able to recognize and identify fallacies makes us less likely to fall victim to them or to use them unintentionally in an argument.

In this section, we will look at some of the fallacies that are most likely to appear in moral arguments. As you read through the following descriptions of these fallacies, consider which fallacy or fallacies you are most likely to fall victim to or to use in an argument regarding a moral issue.

Fallacy of Equivocation

Some words or terms—such as *right, duty,* or *relativism*—have several definitions. Most often, the context in which a particular word or phrase is used lets us know which definition is intended; however, this is not always the case. When the meaning of a particular term is unclear from its context, we refer to it as an *ambiguous* term. The **fallacy of equivocation** occurs when an ambiguous word changes meaning in the course of an argument. For example:

> *Hans:* All people have a right to a minimal level of health care.
>
> *Beth:* That's not true. Our constitution says nothing about people having a right to health care; therefore, as taxpayers we have no obligation to provide it.

In this argument, Hans and Beth are using differing meanings of the word *right. Webster's Encyclopedic Unabridged Dictionary* gives sixty-two different meanings of *right*! By taking a closer look at their respective arguments, we can see that Hans is most likely talking about rights in terms of moral or human rights, while Beth is using the term to refer to legal rights. Their first task in resolving their disagreement is to agree on which definition of *right* they will use.

Stephen Colbert, host of *The Late Show* on CBS, frequently makes use of this fallacy as in the following example from the April 29, 2006, White House Correspondents' Association dinner in which he equivocates on the word *stand*:

Connections
What is the difference between a legal right and a moral right? *See Chapter 11, page 358.*

> I stand by this man [President George W. Bush]. I stand by this man because he stands for things. Not only for things, he stands on things. Things like aircraft carriers and rubble and recently flooded city squares. And that sends a strong message: that no matter what happens to America, she will always rebound—with the most powerfully staged photo ops in the world.

Appeal to Force

This fallacy occurs when we use or threaten to use force—whether physical, psychological, or legal—in an attempt to coerce another person to accept our conclusion. The phrase "might is right" summarizes the reasoning (or lack thereof) behind **appeal to force**. This fallacy is illustrated in the following argument:

> Don't disagree with me because if you do I'll slap your #@& face. Don't forget who's paying your tuition. I'll show you who's in charge around here!

Although most people would not be taken in by such overt threats of violence, others such as children may actually come to believe that might does make right. At other times, the intimidation is more subtle. There may be an implied threat to withdraw affection or favors if the other person does not come around to our way of thinking. However, there is no logical connection between being right and having the power to hurt someone else.

This is a particularly dangerous fallacy, not only because it can lead to injury or even death, but because we are taken in by it more often than most of us like to admit. People who have financial, social, or political power over others may come to believe that they deserve their privileged status. This is particularly troublesome when people who lack power start to agree with their oppressors and become resigned to or even blame themselves for their own oppression and inferior status. The disempowered person may also internalize the message that "might is right" and, in turn, attempt to impose his or her views on others by using force against those who are even more socially disenfranchised.

Abusive Fallacy

This fallacy occurs when we disagree with someone's conclusion, but instead of addressing their argument, we turn and attack or slur the character of the person(s) who made the argument. By doing so, we attempt to evoke a feeling of disapproval toward the person, so that disapproval of the person overflows into disapproval of the person's argument. The **abusive fallacy** is also known as the **ad hominem fallacy**.

> *Lila:* I think abortion is morally wrong.
>
> *Chloe:* You pro-lifers are just a bunch of narrow-minded, anti-choice, religious fanatics who think they have a right to force their religious morality on others.
>
> *Lila:* Oh, yeah? Well you pro-choice people are nothing but a bunch of selfish baby-killers who are out to destroy the family and all it stands for!

In the preceding conversation, the issue of the morality of abortion has been completely sidetracked. Instead, Lila and Chloe got caught up in slandering the character of the people who hold the opposing view. When we call people "narrowminded," "idiots," "fanatics," or "selfish baby-killers," we are dismissing their views without ever analyzing them. (See photo on page 59.)

Virtually all great thinkers and reformers, because they challenge us to rethink our cherished worldviews, have had detractors who have tried to discredit their ideas through character assassination. What distinguishes great thinkers is their ability to remain focused and not be distracted by critics' use of fallacies against them. Elizabeth Cady Stanton and Lucretia Mott, for example, first met in 1840 at the World Anti-Slavery Society convention in London, where their husbands were attending as delegates.[18] The women delegates from the United States were denied seats at the convention because of the strenuous objections of some male delegates from the United States. Mott, in response, demanded that she be treated with the same respect accorded any man—White or Black. During these discussions, Stanton, who was then a young newlywed, marveled at the way Mott, a woman of forty-seven, held her own in the argument, "skillfully parried all their attacks . . . turning the laugh on them, and then by her earnestness and dignity silencing their ridicule and jeers."[19] This meeting and Mott's refusal to back down in the face of ridicule and attacks upon her character led to the first women's rights meeting in U.S. history.

Connections

According to feminist care ethics, how do women usually make moral decisions? *See Chapter 3, pages 95-96.*

Circumstantial Fallacy

The **circumstantial fallacy** occurs when we argue that our opponent should accept a certain position because of special circumstances, such as his or her lifestyle or membership in a particular group based on race, ethnicity, gender, nationality, or religion. This fallacy, like the previous one, is a type of ad hominem fallacy because it entails attacking one's opponent rather than addressing his or her argument. Here is one example:

> Granted, you may be a vegetarian, but you certainly can't argue against the killing of animals. After all, you do wear leather shoes and use products that were tested on animals.

As in the preceding example, someone can use animal products and still argue against the very practice in which they engage. Likewise, parents who are heavy drinkers or smokers, can give their children sound arguments regarding the evils of alcohol and drug abuse. Being a hypocrite or engaging in doublethink does not invalidate their arguments against alcohol and drug abuse.

Appeal to Inappropriate Authority

In an argument, it is appropriate to use the testimony of someone who is an expert in the field or area that is being debated. We commit a fallacy, however, when we **appeal to inappropriate authority**, to an expert or authority in a field other than the one under debate. The assumption that someone who is an authority in one field must also be knowledgeable in all other fields is sometimes called the "halo effect." Here's an example:

> My priest says that genetic engineering and cloning are dangerous. Therefore, all experimentation in this field should be stopped immediately.

In this example, the person cited as providing support for the conclusion ("all experimentation in this field should be stopped immediately") is not an expert in the medical field; he is simply someone who is admired as an expert in his particular field of theology. Titles such as Doctor, Professor, President, and Lieutenant and the visual impact of uniforms such as white lab coats and police or military uniforms all increase our perception of a person's authority. We tend to believe and obey these authority figures even when they overextend their authority to the point where it would be appropriate to question their authority.

Popular Appeal

This fallacy occurs when we appeal to popular opinion to gain support for our conclusion. **Popular appeal** can take several different forms. The most common one in moral arguments is the bandwagon approach, when a certain conclusion is assumed to be right because "everyone" is doing it or "everyone" believes it. The following is an example:

> In 2009, Boston University student Joel Tenenbaum was ordered by the courts to pay $675,000 in damages for illegally downloading music from the Internet. When he was asked by a CNN news reporter if he thought what he had done was wrong, he replied he did not because "everyone in my generation is doing this." Therefore, he concluded what he did was "perfectly acceptable."

Connections

Why are cultural relativists most likely to fall for the fallacies of appeal to authority and popular appeal? *See Chapter 6, pages 166-167.*

Tenebaum's conclusion, unfortunately, was based on the fallacious assumption that the majority of us, or at least the majority in his generation, know what is right.

This fallacy is also committed when we use polls to support the correctness of our positions on issues such as abortion or gun control. The conclusion is based upon the assumption that the majority of us know what is right. One of the dangers of living in a democracy is what philosopher John Stuart Mill (1806-1873) referred to as the "tyranny of the majority." Historian Alexis de Tocqueville, after visiting the United States in 1826, made the observation that, although democracy liberates us from tradition, the great democratic danger is enslavement to public opinion.[20] Studies show the majority of U.S. citizens define morality in terms of what the majority believe to be right and wrong. Young people often simply accept the norms of their peer group; adults are more likely to uncritically adopt the established norms of the wider community or nation. However, a particular position or conclusion is not necessarily correct just because most people agree with it. After all, the majority of people once believed that the earth is flat and slavery is natural.

Connections

At what stage of moral development are most high school and college students? *See Chapter 3, pages 90-93.*

Hasty Generalization

When used properly, generalization can be a valuable tool for gathering information in both the physical and social sciences. The fallacy of **hasty generalization** occurs when we use only unusual or atypical cases to support our conclusion. In doing so, we hastily generalize to a rule or conclusion that fits only these unusual cases rather than the whole group. For example, early doctors such as Joseph Collins hastily generalized from their experience with a few patients with terminal cancer to the faulty conclusion that no one with a terminal condition really wants to know the truth about their condition (see pages 45-46).

Unusual cases ⎯⎯⎯⎯⎯⎯⎯⎯⎯⎯⟶ Odd rule about a whole group
(Premises)   (Hasty generalization)   (Conclusion)

Connections

In what ways does cultural relativism contribute to stereotyping and a "we/them" mentality? *See Chapter 6, pages 182-186.*

Stereotypes and *prejudices* are often based upon hasty generalizations. A woman who has been abused by her father or boyfriend may hastily generalize from her limited experience to the conclusion that all men are abusers. Negative stereotypes can lead to an unconscious devaluation of whole groups of people, particularly when not much interaction exists between the different cultural groups. During wartime, governments may intentionally create negative stereotypes of the enemy, thus justifying the dehumanization and destruction of that enemy.

More recently, stereotypes of Muslims as radical extremists and President Trumps' call for a ban on immigration from certain Muslim countries have contributed to the belief that many, if not most, Muslims are terrorists or terrorist sympathizers. In fact, according to a senior political scientist at the Rand Institute, less than 1 percent of Muslims are at risk of becoming radical.[21]

Fallacy of Accident

This fallacy occurs when we apply a rule that is generally accepted as valid to a particular case whose exceptional or accidental circumstances render the rule inappropriate. The **fallacy of accident** is the opposite of hasty generalization. In this fallacy, we start with the rule and apply it to an unusual or accidental case or circumstance:

Good rule ————————————————⟶ Exceptional or accidental cases
(Premise)   (Inappropriate application of rule)   (Conclusion)

The vast majority of rules have exceptions. However, rather than spelling out all the circumstances that might produce an exception, people are expected to use their powers of discernment and reason to decide when a rule should be applied and when it is inappropriate.

Following is an example of a person taking a rule to be absolutely binding that was never intended to be so:

> Going through a red light is illegal. Therefore, Wanda should be given a ticket for going through that red light on the way to the hospital with her dying child.

Almost everyone would accept the rule "stop at red lights" to be a reasonable law. This law is good for *most* cases, but that does not mean it is appropriate in all cases. In the preceding case, preventing the child's death—the moral duty of nonmaleficence—should take precedence over obeying the law about stopping at red lights. Indeed, a police officer who pulled Wanda over and gave her a ticket would be considered overly rigid in interpreting the law as well as remiss in his or her moral duties. Like legal rules, moral rules can also have exceptions:

> You should keep your promises. You promised to pay back the money I loaned you today. So give it to me—I need it to buy the last few parts for my bomb.

As with the law to stop at red lights, most of us consider "keep your promises" to be a good moral rule. However, circumstances can render a normally good moral rule inappropriate. In the above example, the moral duty not to abet a malevolent action is more important than the duty to fulfill one's promise to pay back the money on time.

A rule that is universally accepted as a good rule need not be absolute. We need to consider the context in which the rule is being considered. People who rigidly apply moral rules regardless of the circumstances are known as **absolutists**. Some people, in their rejection of absolutism, swing to the opposite extreme, moral relativism. They believe that, because moral rules have exceptions, all rules should be thrown out. Indeed, many college freshmen respond to the plethora of ideas that they encounter and the realization that rules are not absolute by subscribing to moral relativism.

Connections

On what grounds does deontologist W.D. Ross reject the idea of moral duties as absolute? *See Chapter 10, page 331.*

Fallacy of Ignorance

Ignorance, in this fallacy, does not indicate that we are stupid. It simply means that we are ignorant of how to go about proving something. The **fallacy of ignorance** is committed whenever it is argued that our conclusion is true simply because it has not been proven false or that it is false because it has not been proven true. However, our being ignorant of how to prove the existence of something such as UFOs or free will does not mean that they do not exist. When we lack proof of a particular phenomenon, the most that we can logically conclude is that we do not *know* whether or not it exists.

> *Kwesi:* God is clearly the creator of the moral order. Ethicists have been unable to come up with any other explanation of the source of universal moral principles.

> *Mercedes:* You're mistaken. The fact that no one can come up with a proof regarding the source of universal moral principles just goes to prove that there are no universal moral principles and that morality is really just a matter of personal opinion.

In this example, both speakers are guilty of using the fallacy of ignorance. Kwesi makes the claim that his conclusion must be true because his opponent cannot prove it false. Mercedes, on the other hand, commits the fallacy of ignorance when she counters with the argument that, if we cannot identify the source of universal moral principles, then they don't exist.

The ultimate source of universal moral principles has been a source of puzzlement to many ethicists. This does not mean, however, that universal moral principles do not exist. We also don't know the source of the laws of physics, but this ignorance on our part does not prove that the laws of physics don't exist, nor does it diminish the hold that the laws of physics have upon us as physical beings.

Begging the Question

Begging the question is also known as *circular reasoning.* This fallacy occurs when a premise and conclusion are actually rewordings of the same proposition. In other words, when making the argument, we assume the truth of our conclusion rather than offering proof for it as illustrated below:

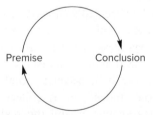

Premise   Conclusion

The premise may simply be just a definition or synonym of a key term in the conclusion. At first glance, it may appear to us that the person using this fallacy has an airtight argument because the premise seems to support the conclusion so perfectly. However, upon closer inspection, it will become clear that this is so because, despite differences in language, the premise and conclusion both express the same idea and, in fact, are the same proposition as in the following example:

Connections

Why does psychological egoism commit the fallacy of begging the question? *See Chapter 7, page 215.*

> Voluntary euthanasia is morally acceptable because people have the right to choose when and how they will end their lives.

The conclusion of this argument is a rewording of the premise. Rather than offering proof that voluntary euthanasia is morally acceptable, the premise *assumes* that it is morally acceptable. If we reverse the conclusion and the premise, we are left with exactly the same argument: "Voluntary euthanasia is morally acceptable; *therefore*, people have the right to choose when and how they will end their lives."

This fallacy can be very frustrating if we fail to recognize it because there seems to be no way to disprove the person's position. The best way to recognize this fallacy is to reverse the premise and conclusion. If this can be done without changing the essence of the argument, then chances are the argument contains the fallacy of begging the question.

Antiabortion and pro-abortion rights students confronting each other at a rally in San Francisco. Arguments over abortion often contain fallacies including the abusive fallacy and name-calling.
©Jeff Chiu/AP Photo

Discussion Questions

1. Is the fetus a "person" or a human being? The controversy over abortion stems, in part, from an equivocation on the term *person*. Discuss how someone who

is antiabortion and someone who is pro-abortion rights might each define "person" and how their definitions influence their position on abortion.

2. Supporters of legalized abortion may argue that it is unfair that a woman is forced to bring up a child she did not want. Discuss how this argument is based on the fallacy of irrelevant conclusion. Give examples of other fallacies that may occur in a discussion on the morality of abortion.

3. Have a debate in class on the issue of abortion without using fallacies. Afterward, discuss how avoiding fallacious reasoning helped clarify the issue for you.

Irrelevant Conclusion

In one sense, all the conclusions in fallacious arguments are logically irrelevant. However, in the **fallacy of irrelevant conclusion**, the conclusions are irrelevant in a particular way. This fallacy is committed when we support or reject a conclusion using premises that are, in fact, directed at a different conclusion. In other words, we change the topic to a related but different subject that we feel more comfortable discussing.

Sometimes, people will avoid a specific topic that makes them feel uncomfortable by changing the topic to something more general or less controversial. At the January 12, 2017, Senate Armed Services Committee meeting regarding his nomination as Trump's Secretary of Defense, General James Mattis was asked if ". . . openly gay service members are undermining U.S. Forces." Rather than answer the question directly, Mattis replied that he believes "the U.S. must stay focused on a military that is so lethal that it would be the worse day for enemies in the field." Thus, Mattis avoided directly answering the question about gays in the military by changing the topic to a less controversial issue.

Irrelevant conclusion in a moral argument can also take the form of changing the topic from what one *ought* to do (a prescriptive question) to what one *would* do (a descriptive question). In one study, 20 percent of the teenagers interviewed did not seem to understand questions about "what ought (or should) you do?" They chose to reframe them instead as "what would you do?"[22]

> *Rosa:* Don't you think that it was wrong for Michael to copy the test answers from the person sitting next to him?
>
> *Katrina:* Oh, I don't know about that. If I had been in his situation, I probably would have done the same thing.

In this example, Katrina answers Rosa as though the question was about what she *would* do rather than what she thinks a person *ought* to do in a similar situation. In doing so, Katrina changes the topic. To say that a student probably *would* cheat on a test, if they had the opportunity, is not the same as saying that they *ought* to cheat on the test. Indeed, we often do things that we know we ought not do.

Naturalistic Fallacy

The **naturalistic fallacy** is a specific type of irrelevant conclusion. We commit this fallacy when we go from an *is* to an *ought* statement. We cannot assume, because something *is* natural, that it is morally acceptable or *ought to be* that way. Homosexual relations have been condemned as immoral on the grounds that homosexual relations are unnatural because they cannot lead to procreation—the "natural" result of sex. The following example illustrates that nature is certainly not the sole determinant of what is good.

> Only women are physically capable of bearing and nursing children. Therefore, women ought to be the primary caregivers of children.

While it may be true that women are physically capable of bearing and nursing children, and men are not (what *is*), this does not mean that women have a moral obligation to be the primary caregivers of children (what *ought to be*). On the other hand, nature sets the limits on what ought to be. We cannot argue that men ought to share equally in the bearing of children because men, by nature, are incapable of bearing children!

People who use the naturalistic fallacy may refer to the natural activities of other animals to support their position. However, the fact that other animals eat meat, that they sometimes kill and eat their young, or that most animals have several sexual partners (and a few even eat their partner after mating!) does not imply that it is morally acceptable for humans to do so. The morality of these behaviors must be evaluated on grounds other than that it is natural.

Thirteen Informal Fallacies

Informal fallacies are psychologically persuasive but incorrect arguments.

Equivocation   A key term shifts meaning during the course of an argument.

Appeal to force   Force, threat of force, or intimidation is used to coerce our opponents into accepting our conclusion.

Abusive   We attack our opponent's character rather than address his or her conclusion.

Circumstantial   We argue that our opponent should accept a particular position because of his or her lifestyle or membership in a particular group.

Appeal to inappropriate authority   The testimony of someone who is an authority in a different field is used as support for our conclusion.

Popular appeal   The opinion of the majority is used as support for our conclusion.

Hasty generalization   Our conclusion is based on atypical cases.

Accident   We apply a generally accepted rule to an atypical case where the rule is inappropriate.

Ignorance   We argue that a certain position is true because it hasn't been proven false or that it is false because it hasn't been proven true.

Begging the question The premise and conclusion are different wordings of the same proposition.

Irrelevant conclusion Our argument is directed at a conclusion different from the one under discussion.

Naturalistic We argue from what *is* natural to what *ought* to be the case.

Appeal to tradition We argue that something is moral because it is traditional.

Appeal to Tradition

This fallacy also goes from an *is* to an *ought* statement. Whereas the naturalistic fallacy points to what is natural, this fallacy appeals to tradition or cultural norms as a reason for a certain practice. The following argument is based on the 1857 U.S. Supreme Court *Dred Scott* case (see pages 184–185 for a selection from the ruling).

> The Negro has never been recognized as a person in this country or by the U.S. Constitution. Therefore, slavery should remain legal.

People who use **appeal to tradition** may argue, as in this example, that a certain practice is moral because it is constitutional. However, the U.S. Constitution is a legal rather than a moral document. Our constitution has allowed slavery and prevented women from voting, but this does not necessarily mean that these traditions are or were moral. On the contrary, the provisions of the constitution itself should be judged in the light of moral principles.

The fallacy of appeal to tradition is used primarily by cultural relativists to legitimate the status quo. Once a practice becomes a tradition, people begin to accept it as normal and natural, even in the face of overwhelming evidence that it harms people. Our current attachment to armed conflicts as a means of resolving international disputes is a good example of how appeal to tradition inhibits us from thinking of creative alternatives. The traditions of other countries, such as lack of legal and social protection for women and children, have also been used as excuses for exploiting people living in those cultures.

Connections

On what grounds do rights ethicists argue that moral rights are universal rather than cultural creations? *See Chapter 11, pages 372–373.*

Exercises

1. Identify the fallacy in each of the following arguments.

   a. Human activities are not the primary cause of global warming. No scientists have come up with any definitive proof that human activities are the cause.

   b. Capital punishment is morally acceptable because murderers should be put to death.

   c. Euthanasia is wrong because it interferes with the natural dying process. We should wait until it is our time to die.

d. I'm not surprised you're arguing that hate speech should not be banned on college campuses. After all, you're one of the most hateful, racist, and insensitive people I've ever met. Why, you couldn't care less about the effect of hate speech on its intended victims.

e. I support racial profiling and the questioning of all Arabs and Muslims by security officials in airports. Remember, it was Arabs who blew up the Twin Trade Towers. They just can't be trusted.

f. Why all this concern about the way women are treated in Afghanistan? After all, women in this country still suffer from discrimination in the workplace.

g. My parents used to get into arguments all the time, and they ended up getting divorced. Logic teaches people how to make arguments. Therefore, if you want a happy marriage, you should stay away from logic.

h. "The bullying and humiliation of detainees at Abu Ghraib is," as George W. Bush said, 'a strain on our country's honor and our country's reputation.' . . . But let us also recognize what this scandal is not. There is a large difference between forcing prisoners to strip and submit to hazing at Abu Ghraib prison and the sort of things routinely done there under Saddam Hussein. This is a county where mass tortures, mass murders and mass graves were, until the arrival of the U.S. Army, a way of life."[23]

i. It is morally wrong to cause pain to another person. Therefore, dentists are immoral people.

j. My philosophy professor doesn't think that the loss of animal and plant species due to the destruction of rain forests is going to permanently upset the balance of nature. Therefore, it is morally acceptable to continue clearing rain forests for cattle grazing.

k. So you're going to argue in class that alcohol should be banned on campus. Well, this is the last time we're going to ask you to go out with us on the weekend.

l. How can you be in favor of human cloning? After all, you're a Catholic and the church supports a ban on all human cloning.

m. Science has not been able to explain every movement from single cell organism to human beings. Therefore, the theory of evolution is false.

2. Which fallacy are you most likely to use in a discussion about a moral issue? Give an example of a time you used this fallacy. Which fallacy are you most likely to fall for in a discussion about a moral issue? Give an example of a time this fallacy was used on you. Discuss strategies you might use to make yourself less prone to using or falling for these particular fallacies.

3. Consider the argument that you constructed in exercise 2 on pages 51–52. Are there any fallacies in your argument? If necessary, rework the argument so it is fallacy-free.

4. How might you have responded had you been a subject in Milgram's study (see page 30) and wanted to stop but the experimenter said that "you must continue"? Think of a time when you went along with an authority figure, even though you knew what they were doing was wrong. Discuss some strategies you could use to make yourself less prone to falling for appeal to authority.

5. The Bill of Rights was put forth to protect minorities or dissenters from the "tyranny of the majority." Should those in the minority be protected from the dictates of the majority? Or should the will of the majority always prevail in a democratic nation? Support your answers. (For a copy of the full text of the Bill of Rights and the other amendments to the U.S. Constitution, go to www.archives.gov/exhibits/charters/constitution_transcript.html.)

6. Discuss some of the common stereotypes of groups found on your campus. Are these based on hasty generalization? How do these stereotypes harm or diminish the autonomy of the people being stereotyped? What effect do the stereotypes of your group have on your life. Are there steps you and others on your campus could take to overcome these stereotypes?

*7. Contact with diverse groups of people has been found to decrease a person's tendency to stereotype or prejudge people. If you are doing community service work, discuss how, if at all, your work has helped you overcome negative stereotypes about people such as senior citizens and the homeless.

Resolving Moral Dilemmas

Moral conflicts are neither systematically avoidable, nor all soluble without remainder.
—Bernard Williams, *Problems of Self* (1973), p. 82

In the movie *Sophie's Choice*, a guard in the Nazi internment camp tells Sophie, who is standing in a line with her two children, to make a choice: She can choose to have one of her children killed and save the other, or she can choose not to choose, in which case both children will be killed. The choice facing her is especially agonizing because she is not sure if the guard is serious or if he is only playing a cruel mind game.

What Is a Moral Dilemma?

Situations in which we have a conflict between moral values are known as **moral dilemmas**. We do *not* have a moral dilemma when the conflict is between moral values and nonmoral values such as economic success or popularity. In a moral dilemma, no matter what solution we choose, it will involve doing something wrong in order to do what is right. Solutions to moral dilemmas are not right or wrong, only better or worse. In deciding what to do, like Sophie, the best we can hope for is to find the solution that causes the least harm.

The great majority of moral decisions are straightforward. Moral decision making is such a normal part of our everyday life that we generally don't give it a second thought. We don't struggle about whether we should run down a pedestrian, even though he or she is jaywalking. Instead, we stop or at least try to avoid hitting the person. We don't kill a person, even though we may want to, because he irritates us. Nor do we clobber the person sitting next to us in class and take her textbook simply because we forgot ours. We wait our turn,

The economic recession of 2007 to 2009 left almost 600,000 Americans homeless, many of them veterans and children.[24]
©Con Tanasiuk/Design Pics

learn to share, apologize if we hurt someone, refrain from stealing, and for the most part, get along with others without having to think too much about it.

Sometimes, however, we encounter a situation where the right thing to do is not so clear-cut. Most of us have struggled with moral dilemmas at one time or another. We may be torn between our loyalty to a friend and telling the truth—particularly when it involves bad news. Or we may have to decide whether to get out of a relationship with an abusive spouse or partner.

Discussion Questions

1. A person on the street who appears to be homeless asks you for money. Working in small groups and using the steps for resolving a moral dilemma listed on pages 66-67 come up with a plan of action.

2. Homelessness has also grown among college students due in part to rising tuition and housing costs. Many of these homeless students keep their situation secret for fear of being stigmatized. You have just discovered that one of the students in your class is living out of her car. When you approach her about it, she becomes flustered and denies it. What should you do?

Most people try not to let troublesome problems get out of hand, but this can occur if we do not have the requisite skills for resolving moral dilemmas when they first arise. Even worse, we may not recognize a situation as a moral dilemma. Because of resistance or inability to resolve moral dilemmas, problems can accumulate and worsen until we find ourselves in a crisis.

Practice at resolving moral dilemmas has been found to be an effective means of improving our skill at moral reasoning in real-life situations. Dilemmas, by their very nature, demand that we sort out and take a closer look at moral values and learn how they are relevant to making decisions about our lives. In a study of moral reasoning and the college experience, discussion of real-life dilemmas was found to be more effective in promoting moral reasoning than the acquisition of knowledge in specific content areas, such as the study of different ethical theories.[25]

Steps for Resolving Moral Dilemmas

Resolving a moral dilemma is similar to constructing an argument. It begins with the collection of relevant facts and moral principles and ends with a proposed solution or conclusion. As with moral argumentation, it is important to resist the temptation to start with a "solution" and then rationalize it by selecting only the facts and principles that support it.

Steps for Resolving a Moral Dilemma

1. Describe the facts.
2. List the relevant moral principles and concerns.
3. List and evaluate possible courses of action.
4. Devise a plan of action.
5. Carry out the plan of action.

Describe the Facts   The first step in resolving a moral dilemma is to come up with a clear description of the case. Avoid the use of emotional or biased language. This description of the facts, which can be as short as a paragraph or two, is similar to the descriptive premises in an argument. When putting together this description, facts may come to light that we did not initially realize were relevant. In the process, we may discover that what at first appeared to be a moral dilemma was not a dilemma after all. For example, as we noted earlier, doctors who used to routinely lie to cancer patients realized that lying in general was wrong, but they also believed that the conflicting moral principle of "do no harm" was more compelling. However, once they found out that telling the truth was actually more beneficial to their patients, the conflict between the two principles disappeared.

List Relevant Moral Principles and Sentiments   The next step is to identify the relevant moral principles and sentiments. In the physician–patient relationship the duty to tell the truth, have sympathy for the patient, remain loyal, and do no harm were all relevant in the preceding case about physicians. Our relationships with the people involved and our individual temperaments and circumstances all affect how much weight we give to each of the conflicting moral values.

List Possible Courses of Action   Once the first two steps are complete, begin listing possible alternative courses of action. This is a time to brainstorm. List any possible actions that come to mind. Some ideas that seem silly at first may work well in combination with others.

Devise a Plan of Action   Because none of the solutions will be completely satisfactory in the case of a moral dilemma, the proposed course of action needs to be examined to determine which actions or combination of actions takes into account the greatest number of important moral concerns. Highlight the courses of action that seem the best and delete the others. Your final plan of action can include a combination of some of the alternative courses of action, just in case your first plan doesn't work.

Carry Out the Plan of Action   Finally, as with any type of moral reasoning, you must put the chosen plan of action into effect. Even the best-thought-out plan is useless if it's not carried out. Moral reasoning that is unrelated to action or praxis becomes a mere academic exercise.

In working toward a resolution of a real-life moral dilemma keep in mind that human judgment is fallible. Not all facts can be known at the onset. For example, we may not know if a person in a coma wants heroic measures performed on him or her. In the decision about whether or not to remove the feeding tube from Terri Schiavo, who was in a persistent vegetative state from 1990 to 2005, it was unclear whether she would have wanted it removed or even if she was brain-dead with no hope of recovery.[26]

Nor can we accurately predict the consequences of all our actions, let alone the actions and choices of others. In addition, some of our premises or assumptions may later prove to be false, or new facts may come to light. Thus, we can only do our best with the facts at hand. We also need to be pragmatic. Lofty moral solutions, such as free college tuition for everyone, may seem ideal on paper but may not be practical or may meet with too much resistance. Thus, we need to ask ourselves which course of action is most likely to work given the particular circumstances.

Exercises

1. Think of a time when a decision you made, or failed to make, resulted in a moral tragedy. How might you have avoided that moral tragedy? Discuss how knowing how to break down and construct arguments may have been helpful to you in making better moral decisions in your life. Be specific.

2. Choose one or more of the following real-life dilemmas and resolve it using the method outlined in the previous section.

a. On May 19, 1894, the yacht *Mignonette* sailed from England for Sydney, Australia. There were four persons aboard: Dudley, the captain; Stephens, the mate; Brooks, a seaman; and Parker, a seventeen-year-old cabin boy and apprentice seaman. The yacht capsized in the South Atlantic during a storm, but the crew managed to put out in a thirteen-foot lifeboat. They drifted for twenty days in the open boat. During this time, they had no fresh water except rainwater and, for the last twelve days, no food. They were weak and facing starvation. The captain called them together to make a decision about their fate. What should they do?

b. Prosenjit Poddar, a student at the University of California, Berkeley, fell in love with a fellow student, Tatiana Tarasoff, whom he met at folk dancing classes. When Tatiana rejected him, he fell into a deep depression. He decided to seek treatment at the Cowell Memorial Hospital, which was affiliated with the university. During his course of treatment, he confided to a hospital psychologist, Dr. Moore, that he was going to kill a girl after she returned from spending the summer in Brazil. Although he didn't name the girl, it was clear that he was referring to Tatiana. What should Dr. Moore do?

c. You live in the Arctic. Every fall and spring, you need to move camp to find enough food. Winter is coming, and it is time to move camp and head south with your family. Your family consists of your spouse, your three children (ages six to twelve), and your aged father. Your father, who was once a proud seal hunter, is now blind and in poor health. The journey would be very hard on him, and he may not survive it. Also, he would slow down the progress of the group, and it is likely that you would not be able to reach your winter camp in time to avoid the first winter storms and starvation. What should you do? (For more on this particular case, see pages 173–174.)

d. You are a member of the National Guard and have been told to evacuate people from an area that is predicted to be hit by a potentially devastating hurricane. You approach a family with three young children living in a high-risk area. The parents refuse to evacuate, saying that they rode out the last hurricane and survived and plan to do the same this time. One of the children is frightened and wants to go with you. The parents say no, the family belongs together. What should you do?

*e. You are answering a hotline for the local women's resource center as part of a community service project. An eighteen-year-old high school junior calls and asks if she can get into a shelter. She tells you that she has run away from home because she is afraid her father will beat her when he finds out about her poor grades. She gives you permission to call her father and tell him she is okay, as long as you promise not to tell him where she is. As it happens, her father is head of the psychology department at your university, and you need a recommendation from him to get into graduate school. What should you do?

*3. Choose an unresolved moral dilemma from your personal life or from your community service. Using the method outlined in this chapter, find a solution to your dilemma. Carry out your proposed solution. Report on the results of your decision.

A Final Word

> *Between us and the universe there are no "rules of the game." The important thing is that our judgments should be right, not that they should observe a logical etiquette.*
>
> —WILLIAM JAMES (1842–1910)

Logic or moral reasoning is a tool rather than an end in itself. Moral reasoning is only one of the components of moral development. Moral sentiments like sympathy and intuitive truths are also important for ethical decision making. Indeed, just as a person who is deficient in moral reasoning can make decisions that he or she later comes to regret, so too can people who are rational but lack sympathy inadvertently behave in cruel and unfeeling ways.

Summary

1. The thinking process used in moral reasoning can be divided into three levels. The first level is *experience*. The second level involves *interpretation* of these experiences. The third level of the thinking process is *analysis* of the interpretations. Analysis includes logical reasoning as well as examination of these interpretations in light of moral intuitions and sentiments, consciousness raising, and collective insights.

2. Sheila Mullett outlines three dimensions in the process of ethical analysis. The first is the development of *moral sensitivity* through collective consciousness raising. The second dimension is *ontological shock*, or awareness of the pain and injustice in the world. The third dimension is *praxis*, or informed social action.

3. *Resistance* is a type of immature defense mechanism that acts as a barrier to critical analysis of our interpretations of the world. Ignorance, avoidance, anger, conformity, and the use of clichés or distractions are all examples of resistance.

4. *Descriptive statements* are about what *is*. *Prescriptive statements* are about what *ought* to be. Moral statements are prescriptive.

5. *Doublethink* involves simultaneously holding two contradictory views and believing both to be true.

6. A *moral tragedy* occurs when we fail to take appropriate moral action or when we make a moral decision that we later regret.

7. An *argument* is made up of propositions. *Propositions* are statements that express a complete thought. They can be either true or false. The *conclusion* in an argument is a proposition that is supported by one or more propositions known as *premises*. In an argument, we move from the premises to the conclusion by the use of *inference*.

8. *Premise indicators* are words such as *because* and *since* that signal a premise follows. *Conclusion indicators* are words such as *therefore* and *thus* that signal a conclusion follows. Not all arguments contain indicators.

9. When *constructing arguments* in moral discourse, we first create a list of premises and from there move to our conclusion.

10. *Rhetoric* involves the use of persuasion to get others to accept our position.

11. A *fallacy* is a type of argument that is psychologically persuasive but incorrect. Many different types of fallacies can occur within a moral argument. (See page 61).

12. *A moral dilemma* is a situation with conflicting moral values. In resolving a moral dilemma, we should (1) describe the facts, (2) list the relevant moral principles and sentiments, (3) make a list of possible courses of action, (4) come up with a plan of action, and (5) carry out the chosen plan of action.

13. *Logic* or *moral reasoning* is a tool and only one aspect of morality.

Notes

1. Stanley Milgram, *Obedience to Authority* (New York: Harper & Row, 1974), p. 6.
2. W. Pitt Derryberry and Stephen J. Thoma, "The Friendship Effect: Its Role in the Development of Moral Thinking in Students," *About Campus*, (May–June 2000): 13-18.
3. Federal Bureau of Prisons, 2016, http://www.bop.gov/about/statistics/statistics_inmate_race.jsp
4. "Shifting Perspectives: A New Approach to Ethics," in *Feminist Perspectives: Philosophical Essays on Methods and Morals*, eds. Lorraine Code, Sheila Mullett, and Christine Overall (Toronto: University of Toronto Press, 1988), p. 115.
5. Paulo Freire, *The Pedagogy of the Oppressed* (New York: Continuum Press, 1983), p. 120.
6. Ibid., p. 64.
7. Malcolm X, *By Any Means Necessary: Speeches, Interviews and a Letter by Malcolm X*, ed. George Breitman (New York: Pathfinder, 1970).
8. Abraham Lincoln, "First Inaugural Address," 1861.
9. Norma Haan, "Proposed Model of Ego Functioning: Coping and Defense Mechanisms in Relationship to IQ Change," *Psychological Monographs* 77, pt. 571 (1963): 8.
10. Daniel Hart and Susan Chmiel, "Influence of Defense Mechanisms on Moral Judgement Development: A Longitudinal Study," *Developmental Psychology* 28, no. 4 (1992): 722-729.
11. Swami Prabhavananda and Christopher Isherwood, *How to Know God: The Yoga Aphorisms of Patanjali* (Hollywood: Vendanta, 1969), p. 1.
12. Lauren Howe, "The Big Sort: When Personal Preferences Build Political Partisanship," http//:www.civilpolitics.org/2010/n/the-big-sort.
13. Quoted in Sara Ruddick's *Maternal Thinking* (Boston, MA: Beacon Press, 1989), p. 230.
14. Hannah Arendt, *Eichmann in Jerusalem: A Report on the Banality of Evil* (New York: Penguin, 1977), p. 44.
15. Peggy Orenstein, *Schoolgirls: Young Women, Self-Esteem, and the Confidence Gap* (Doubleday, American Association of University Women, 1994). See also Dale Baker, "Teaching for Gender Differences, 2012," www.narst.org/publications/research/gender.ctm.
16. For more on this, read Joseph Collins, "Should Doctors Tell the Truth?" *Harper's Monthly* 155 (August 1927): 320-326; and Donald Oken, "What to Tell Cancer Patients: A Study of Medical Attitudes," *Journal of the AMA* 175 (1961): 1120-1128.
17. Collins, pp. 320-326.
18. Alice S. Rossi, ed., *The Feminist Papers: From Adams to de Beauvoir* (New York: Columbia University Press, 1973), p. 242.
19. Lloyd Hare, *The Greatest American Woman: Lucretia Mott* (New York: American Historical Society, 1937), p. 193.
20. Alexis de Tocqueville, *Democracy in America* (New York: McGraw-Hill, 1981).

21. Alexander LaCasse, "How many Muslim Extremists Are There? Just the Facts, Please," *Christian Science Monitor*, January 13, 2015.
22. Tom Kitwood, *Concern for Others: A New Psychology of Conscience and Morality* (London: Routledge & Kegan Paul, 1990), p. 227.
23. Philip Terzian, "A Self-Inflicted Wound," *Providence Sunday Journal*, May 9, 2004, p. 19.
24. The National Alliance to End Homelessness, "The State of Homelessness in America 2016".
25. James Rest, "Why Does College Promote Development in Moral Judgment?" *Journal of Moral Education* 17, no. 3 (1988): 183–194.
26. From "The Battle over Terri Schiavo," *AOL News*, March 27, 2005.

CHAPTER 3

Conscience and Moral Development

Let a man not do what his own sense of righteousness tells him not

to do, and let him not desire what his sense of righteousness tells

him not to desire;—to act thus is all he has to do.
    —MENCIUS, *The Book of Mencius,* 7A17

A woman was near death from a rare form of cancer, and there was only one drug that doctors thought could save her. "It was a form of radium that was recently discovered by a druggist in her town. The drug was expensive to make, but the druggist was charging [$2,000] ten times what the drug cost to make...The sick woman's husband, Heinz, went to everyone he knew to borrow the money, but he could only get together about $1,000... He told the druggist that his wife was dying, and asked him to sell it cheaper or let him pay later. But the druggist said, 'No, I discovered the drug and I'm going to make money from it.' So Heinz got desperate and began to think about breaking into the man's store and stealing the drug for his wife."

"Should Heinz steal the drug?"[1] What would you do in a situation like this? Different people answer this question quite differently, depending on the strength of their conscience and the level of their moral development. In this chapter, we'll learn about the factors that shape our conscience and the role of a well-developed conscience in making moral decisions. We'll also be looking at theories on moral development and the different components, such as reason and sympathy, which contribute to our moral behavior. Finally, we'll examine strategies for enhancing our moral development, so we can make better moral decisions—ones we are less likely to regret later.

Ethics and Human Development

Immanuel Kant once said that the basic questions of philosophy—including the question "What ought I to do?"—are all fundamentally related to anthropology, or "What is man?"[2] The study of moral development takes place at this juncture of philosophical theory and the social sciences. Any adequate theory of morality must take into consideration the relevant facts about human nature and human behavior.

If we agree with Aristotle (see pages 5-6) that the primary reason for studying ethics is to make us better people, then an examination of our development must be part of that process. Most of us know what is good, at least in principle. The difficulties arise in living what we know and in the application of general moral knowledge to particular contexts. Self-knowledge can help us toward this goal. By learning about the psychological mechanisms that govern our moral development, we can actually advance our moral growth.

One of the assumptions underlying developmental theories is that humans have an innate desire to grow and to fulfill their potential. The belief that human nature strives toward the good life is consistent with the philosophies of Kant and Aristotle as well as many non-Western philosophies such as Confucianism and Buddhism. Cognitive-development theorists also claim that people who live up to their potential and lead morally good lives are happier, experience greater inner peace and harmony, and are more satisfied with their moral decisions.

Connections

According to Aristotle, what is the most important human activity? *See Chapter 1, pages 5-6.*

SELF-EVALUATION QUESTIONNAIRE*

Jennifer, a college junior, is taking five courses and doing an internship while trying to maintain her 4.0 GPA, so she can get into a good law school and become a civil rights lawyer. After staying up all night to complete a fifteen-page term paper, Jennifer realizes that she forgot to write a four-page response paper due for an English literature class she's taking. Strapped for time and not wanting to damage her grade in the course, she remembers another student in her class telling her about a Web site that sells essays. She goes to the Web site and finds an essay that fits the assignment. Should Jennifer buy the paper and turn it in as her own?

Looking at the following list determine which considerations are most important to you in deciding what to do, with (1) being not important at all to (5) being very important.[3]

a) Whether the campus rules against plagiarism should be respected. 1 2 3 4 5

b) What is the risk that Jennifer will get caught? 1 2 3 4 5

c) Is it fair to the other students applying to law school if Jennifer isn't caught and gets accepted instead of them because she turned in a plagiarized essay? 1 2 3 4 5

d) Other students in the class are plagiarizing so why shouldn't Jennifer? 1 2 3 4 5

e) Will turning in the paper from the Internet be best for her future career? 1 2 3 4 5

f) Is she violating the rights of the professor and other students in the class by turning in the essay? 1 2 3 4 5

g) Did the professor bring this on himself by placing too many demands on his students? 1 2 3 4 5

h) Is there a way Jen can maintain her grade average without cheating and possibly lowering the grades of other students?

---

*The stage represented by each consideration can be found at the end of the chapter.

Exercises

1. Working in small groups, discuss how you would respond to the opening scenario if you were in Heinz's situation. Identify two or three factors that are most important to you in making your decision.

2. What do you think or feel when you hear the word *conscience*? Take a few minutes to draw a picture of your conscience or make a list of words describing your conscience.

Conscience: Culturally Relative or Universal?

Some good must come by clinging to the right. Conscience is a man's compass, and though the needle sometimes deviates, though one perceives irregularities in directing one's course by it, still one must try to follow its direction.

—VINCENT VAN GOGH, *Dear Theo: An Autobiography of Vincent van Gogh*

For most people, a well-developed conscience is the essence of the moral life. What seems to differentiate the saint from the sociopath is not so much the norms of their culture, their religious affiliation, or their power to impose their desires upon others; rather, it is the vitality and strength of their conscience. Conscience is clearly assumed to be guiding the majority of our actions. Acts of violence and degradation are newsworthy precisely *because* they are so unusual.

Connections

How does a cultural relativist explain conscience? *See Chapter 6, page 166.*

Despite the centrality of the concept of conscience in our lives, the concept itself has received little direct attention from philosophers and psychologists. The English word **conscience** comes from the Latin words *com* ("with") and *scire* ("to know"). Conscience, in other words, provides us with *knowledge* about what is right and wrong. However, it is more than just a passive source of knowledge. Conscience involves reason and critical thinking; it also involves feelings. Conscience not only *motivates* us; it *demands* that we act in accord with it.

Many religious people view the conscience as divine guidance or the voice of God speaking through our hearts. In Islam, conscience is a "spiritual quality that differentiates between right and wrong." Conscience inspires us by making us feel good when we do the right thing.[4] In Judaism, worshipping and following one's conscience are inseparable: "When our conscience is not at one with the actions of our body, then our worship of our Creator is imperfect."[5] The Ethiopian *Book of the Philosophers* compares conscience to an inner light in the soul that not only bears the fruit of love for one another but also gives us the "wisdom that distinguishes what should be."[6] The comparison of conscience with light or energy is found in many other philosophies.

Psychologist Carl Jung believed that morality is a basic law of consciousness. As such, conscience involves both our conscious and unconscious thought processes, including our dreams. The Hindu Upanishads locate the conscience in the deepest levels of the mind, beyond ordinary reasoning. Meditation, consequently, is an important tool for getting in touch with our conscience. Kant also believed that the good will—the expression of our true conscience—has its source beyond ordinary reason,[7] though it may be affirmed by "ordinary rational knowledge."

Plato defined conscience as an activity of the soul that directs us toward the good. Acting in accordance with conscience or reason is thus essential to our functioning as human beings. A human without a conscience, according to Plato, is not a person and lacks moral standing in the community. In his *Republic*, Plato makes a provision for the execution of these people or those "whose souls are incurably evil."[8]

Sometimes, other messages get confused with those from our true conscience. Those who are heteronomous moral reasoners or cultural relativists, in particular, may describe their conscience as a voice coming from outside of them—from God, or their parents, or society. One of the popular images associated with conscience is that of a little angel on one shoulder, whispering into one ear, while on the other shoulder perches a little demon gleefully telling us to do the exact opposite. German philosopher Friedrich Nietzsche (1844-1900), in his book *Beyond Good and Evil*, refers to this heteronomous "morality" that is shaped by and caters to outside forces as "herd [or] slave morality."[9]

This image of conscience as both good and evil captures one of the paradoxes of conscience. Although the basic structure of our conscience may be innate, like language, the specifics are culturally shaped. This, combined with our social nature and desire to be liked by others, leaves the uncritical or unanalytical conscience vulnerable to public opinion and outside forces that want to control us in the name of morality. Thus, we cannot rely on conscience alone to be our moral guide. Instead, we need to hone our analytical skills and learn how to be more discerning.

There are three main forces that contribute to the shaping of our conscience: (1) heredity or biological factors, (2) learning or environmental factors, and (3) conscious moral direction.

Heredity or Biological Factors

Altruistic Behavior Confucian philosopher Mencius believed that human nature is basically good. People, he pointed out, will rush to save a child, not because they think about it first or because they expect a reward, but out of an innate feeling of benevolence that is essential to humans. Professor of public policy James Q. Wilson refers to this predisposition as the "moral sense." He writes:

> What is striking about the newer findings of child psychologists is that the emergence of a moral sense occurs before the child has acquired much in the way of language. The rudiments of moral action—a regard for the well-being of others and anxiety at having failed to perform according to a standard—are present well before anything like morality could occur.[10]

Along similar lines, sociobiologists, such as E. O. Wilson, speak of an "altruism gene" that genetically predisposes us to care for and help others. Aristotle refers to this aspect of our conscience as "natural virtue." According to

Connections

Who, according to Kant, are people of good will? *See Chapter 10, page 318.*

Connections

What is the difference between an autonomous and a heteronomous moral reasoner? *See Chapter 1, page 12.*

psychologist Robert Katz, the capacity for altruistic behavior or sympathy seems to be inborn.[11] Sympathy is visible as early as ten months after birth, when a baby gets upset in response to another baby's distress.[12]

Studies also show that the level of an individual's sympathy and generosity tends to remain relatively stable over the years, suggesting that this capacity is to a large extent part of our innate disposition.[13] In some children, the capacity for sympathy is strong, but in others it is weak or nonexistent. Florence Nightingale "was so ready with her sympathy for all who suffered or were in trouble," even as a teenager, that people referred to her as an "angel in the homes of the poor."[14] Frederick Douglass, as a child of six, was already deeply troubled by the injustices of slavery. Yet he displayed an inordinate sympathy and love for those who profited by the system.[15] Sociopaths, in contrast, seem incapable of empathy no matter how loving their home environments.[16]

Justice as fairness appears at an early age—even though the recognition of the duty of fairness is initially limited to issues regarding the child's own fair treatment and an adult's duty to treat him or her fairly. Even very young children will protest their unfair treatment despite their parents' or society's attempts to impose "unjust" cultural norms upon them. This suggests that a basic sense of justice is also, to some extent, inborn rather than learned.

Connections

Why are socio-paths like ethical subjec-tivists? *See Chapter 4, pages 125-126.*

The Frontal Lobes   The frontal lobe cortex in the brain plays a key role in moral decision making. Most of the work in this area has been with *sociopaths*—people who lack a conscience or moral sense. A study of prisoners found that, when sociopaths were compared to nonsociopathic criminals, the former had specific deficits associated with frontal lobe functioning.[17]

Sociopaths are generally intelligent, rational, and outwardly normal. However, they have a deficit in the affective, or emotional, side of their brain. They can mimic emotions such as sympathy, guilt, and moral indignation, but apparently they do not actually feel them. They can lie, cheat, maim, and even kill without feeling the slightest remorse.

Research of the brain has found that damage to the prefrontal cortex makes people less susceptible to guilt and impairs empathy and concern for others. This deficit is reflected in dysfunctional social behavior and poor social decision making.[18] One of the most fascinating scientific studies of the relation between the brain and morality was carried out by a team on the skull of Phineas Gage.[19] In 1848, Phineas P. Gage was drilling holes and blasting rock to make room for a railway track in Vermont, when one of the explosives accidentally went off. The impact sent a long metal rod through his skull just behind his left eye. The rod passed through the frontal lobes of his brain and landed several yards away. (See image on page 77.)

After Gage recovered from the accident, his intellectual and motor skills were found to be unaffected; however, he no longer seemed to be capable of making moral decisions. Before the accident, Gage had been well liked, responsible, and hardworking, whereas afterward he was untrustworthy, obscene, and unable to make the simplest moral decisions. This and similar studies of people with frontal lobe damage have led scientists to the conclusion that this part of our brain plays a critical role in our moral behavior.

Although natural moral dispositions are apparently present at the time of birth in most people, this is not enough to ensure the development of moral character. Without community and nurture, a moral capacity cannot develop.

Learning or Environmental Factors

Our conscience is also shaped through the interactions of our natural moral disposition with our early experiences and our environment (family, religion, nation). While culture is not the source of our basic moral sense, it helps establish the boundaries and guidelines within which our moral sentiments and principles express themselves. Sometimes, however, cultural norms run contrary to the basic demands of morality. In these cases, our conscience helps us discern which cultural norms are consistent with the demands of morality.

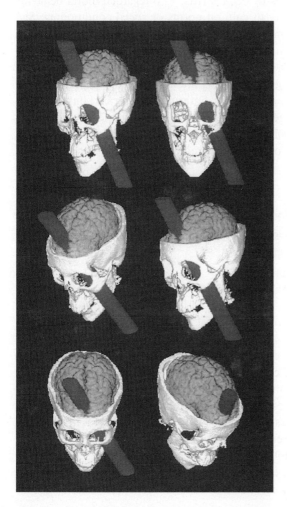

Computer images of the skull of Phineas P. Gage showing the most likely path of the rod that passed through the frontal lobes of his brain. Following his injury, Gage became obscene and incapable of making moral decisions.
©Patrick Landmann/Science Source

Analyzing Images

1. If our ability to engage in moral reasoning is dependent on our brain, should people such as Gage, and other criminals whose frontal lobes are damaged or abnormal, be held morally responsible or punished for their harmful actions? If not, how should we respond to people who seem to lack a moral sense and hurt others without compunction?

2. We expect people to behave morally. Think of a situation where you've been surprised because someone seemed to lack a sense of morality. What was your reaction to this person? If you cannot come up with a real-life scenario, role play a situation in small groups, then discuss your reactions to the role play.

Connections

In what ways can a belief that morality is culturally relative contribute to intolerance and even war? *See Chapter 6, pages 199-200.*

The view of so-called conscience as purely a product of our environment was reinforced in the early 1900s by behaviorists, who regarded moral behavior as nothing more than conformity to cultural norms or social conditioning. Sigmund Freud also regarded "conscience," or **superego**, as a product of our environment. Although Freud maintained that the conscience, or superego, is necessary for life within society, he also argued that it could become oppressive and that people with the strongest superegos are also the most repressed. The Freudian concept of conscience as an internalized tyrant imposed on us by our parents and by society has dominated much of the contemporary literature on the subject. The belief that morality is wholly a product of learning and our environment is no longer accepted by most ethicists and psychologists.

Three Factors Contributing to Conscience

- Heredity or biological factors
- Learning or environmental factors
- Conscious moral direction

Conscious Moral Direction

Autonomous Moral Reasoning   Although innate and external forces can influence our conscience, the exercise of the conscience demands active participation on our part through the use of conscious and responsible deliberation. Autonomous moral reasoners are also more likely to act on the courage of their convictions. During a 2016 Black Lives Matter Protest in Baton Rouge, Louisiana, an unnamed protester planted herself in front of the police and refused to move. Such acts of peaceful protest exemplify autonomous moral reasoning. Unlike the protester in the photo on the following page, most Americans who oppose racism and social injustice do not engage in praxis—that is, their moral beliefs did not lead to informed social action.

A protester confronts police with her act of moral courage and peaceful resistance during a 2016 Black Lives Matter demonstration in Baton Rouge, Louisiana.
©Jonathan Bachman/Reuters

Most people like to think of themselves as autonomous moral reasoners. Collective morality, however, exerts a greater influence over us than most of us realize, as demonstrated by the Holocaust and by slavery here in the United States. Many people back down when cultural norms and other nonmoral values, such as job security or popularity, conflict with their conscience. We readily internalize cultural norms such as "Muslims are bad" or "homosexuals are perverts." Because of our readiness to uncritically accept cultural norms, it is important for us to develop autonomy through conscious moral direction.

Connections

Why is autonomy important for moral dignity? *See Chapter 10, page 315.*

Nature prepares in us the ground for their [moral virtues] reception, but their complete formation is the product of habit.

—ARISTOTLE, *Nicomachean Ethics*, Bk. 1, Ch. 1

Aristotle emphasized the importance of **habituation**—practicing virtuous behavior. Confucian philosophy also teaches that, although inborn moral sentiments are important, only through conscious reflection can we achieve perfect goodness. The ability to engage in conscious moral direction—to be a morally mature person—entails accepting responsibility for our actions rather than simply reacting to our environment. One of the basic assumptions of moral philosophy is that humans have free will and can, at least to some extent, overcome negative influences in our lives.

Connections

What is determinism and what is the implication of determinism in regard to moral responsibility? *See Chapter 1, pages 19-20.*

Determinism and Moral Responsibility   Determinists, as we noted in Chapter 1, claim that there is no such thing as conscious moral direction. We are nothing more than products of our environment or our genetic inheritance; therefore, we are no more to blame for our behavior than a computer would be.

Some defense lawyers try to excuse their clients' criminal actions by claiming that they were determined by prior—usually childhood—traumas. Forty-five-year-old Willie Bosket lives in New York's Woodbourne Correction Center in a specially-built Plexiglas cell. When Willie was nine, he was sent to reform school. At the age of fifteen, he murdered two people on a New York City subway. Willie says it is wrong to hold him responsible for his actions and that he is, to use his own words, "a monster created by the system." His biographer, Fox Butterfield,[20] also argues that Bosket is the product of a three-hundred-year tradition of violence that began with a brutal system of slavery and culminated in out-of-control urban youth violence and poverty.

In extremely oppressive societies, to do what we know is right can cost us our lives. Sometimes our options are so limited—especially if we are a member of a marginalized group—that it is difficult to act autonomously. Failure to acknowledge the restrictions that social norms place upon people is one of the main criticisms of moral philosophers who regard people as completely autonomous and self-sufficient beings. On the other hand, even though our options may be limited, this does not justify harming others. Indeed, it is a tribute to the power of the human conscience that so many people from terribly cruel and oppressive backgrounds do not choose to travel the path of Willie Bosket.

A Delicate Balance

As beings who are both free and embedded in society, we live under the constant tension of balancing our social nature and our freedom. We cannot, nor would we want to, deny the role that society plays in shaping our conscience. However, nor do we want our identity and our conscience to be absorbed by society. On the other hand, we are not simply passive computers receiving direct instructions from our conscience. The exercise of the conscience involves willpower or action on our part. Because conscience is much more than gut feelings or a list of instructions about how to behave, to make use of it, we also need to develop our powers of discernment and to cultivate our moral sentiments.

Exercises

*1. Discuss how your conscience influences your moral decisions. For example, did it influence your choice of a community service site, or perhaps your decision not to cheat on a test or to steal from the bookstore, or a decision to refrain from hurting someone who was really irritating you, or to help someone in need?

2. Friedrich Nietzsche wrote:

> Being nationalistic in the sense in which it is now demanded by public opinion would, it seems to me, be for us who are more spiritual not mere insipidity but dishonesty, a deliberate deadening of our better will and conscience.[21]

> Discuss how nationalism in our own culture promotes what Nietzsche calls a "herd morality" and discourages independent moral thinking.

*3. Do you agree with Mencius that we are born with a moral sense? If you are doing community service with young children, illustrate your answer with examples.

4. Does your conscience sometimes demand that you act contrary to the cultural norms? If so, where do you think these demands come from? Explain, using examples.

5. Should insensitive people be held to a lower moral standard than people who are naturally empathetic? Discuss whether students who have an underdeveloped sense of justice and empathy for others should receive a lighter punishment than those who "should have known better." Support your position.

6. Attorney Alan Dershowitz argues that the black rage excuse, such as that used by Bosket's lawyer, is an "insult to millions of law-abiding African Americans." The vast majority of African Americans, Dershowitz points out, do not use "the mistreatment they suffered as an excuse to mistreat others."[22] Similarly, most battered women, another excuse that has been used in criminal trials, do not turn around and kill their abusers. Discuss Dershowitz's argument that excuses such as "black rage" and the "battered woman syndrome" should not be used to exonerate people from crimes they committed.

7. Discuss a time when you went along with the crowd—either actively or as a passive bystander—even though you knew that what they were doing was morally wrong. How did you feel afterward? What thoughts went through your mind? Relate your answer to the concept of conscience.

8. Discuss the following quote from Hillary Clinton's book *It Takes a Village* (1996): "Nothing is more important to our shared future than the well-being of our children. For children are at our core—not only as vulnerable beings in need

---

*An asterisk indicates that the exercise is appropriate for students who are doing community service learning as part of the course.

of love and care but as a moral touchstone amidst the complexity and contentiousness of modern life. Just as it takes a village [community] to raise a child, it takes children to raise up a village to become all it should be."[23]

The Affective and Cognitive Sides of the Conscience

The bodhisattva is one who possesses the dual nature of wisdom (prajna) and compassion (karuna), which are, in many respects, two aspects of the same reality of a perfected being.

—KENNETH INADA, "The Buddhist Perspective on Human Rights" (1982)

Connections

Why does Noddings emphasize sentiment and caring over reason and duty? See Chapter 12, pages 406–409.

Conscience can be broken down into two elements: (1) affective (moral senti-ments/emotions) and (2) cognitive (moral reasoning). This division is artificial and is primarily a tool for trying to better understand how our conscience works. Our affective or emotional side almost always contains a cognitive aspect, and our reasoning is almost always informed to some extent by our feelings. Tradi-tional Western epistemology favors reason as the source of moral knowledge. However, many Eastern philosophers, as well as some Western philosophers such as David Hume and Nel Noddings, maintain that moral sentiments are important sources of moral knowledge and that reason and sentiment, rather than being opposed, complement one another.

Moral Sentiments/Emotions: The Affective Element of Conscience

Moral Sentiments are emotions that move us to feel moral approval or disap-proval. These sentiments include, among others, sympathy, "helper's high," indignation or resentment, and guilt.

Sympathy and Compassion   **Sympathy** is "the capacity for and inclination to imagine the feelings of others."[24] Sympathy expresses itself as both tenderness and joy at another's happiness and sadness or indignation at another's misfor-tune or mistreatment. Through sympathy, we move beyond our own small world by feeling for and establishing connections with each other. Without sympathy, true intimacy and a genuine sense of community would be impossible. To many moral philosophers, sympathy is the greatest virtue and the cultivation of sympa-thy and compassion our primary moral duty.

Compassion, a more active form of sympathy, is the combination of sympa-thy with praxis or social action. The moral principle of universal compassion and love is found in moral teachings throughout the world: In Buddhism, it is known as **metta**. In Indian philosophy, universal compassion is called **ahimsa**. In Christianity, it is called **agape**.

You have heard that it was said, "You shall love your neighbor and hate your enemy." But I say to you, Love your enemies and pray for those who persecute you. . . .

If you love those who love you, what reward have you? Do not even the tax collectors do that? And if you greet only your brothers, what more are you doing than others? Do not even pagans do that? You, therefore, must be [morally] perfect, as your heavenly Father is perfect.

—MATTHEW 5:43–44; 46–48

Like most sentiments, sympathy must be nurtured to develop properly and to flourish. However, sympathy by itself, without moral reasoning, could even lead us to behave immorally or to uncritically fall for unscrupulous people's plays for our sympathy. As humans, we seem to have a strong natural urge to be among people who are like us and to distrust people who are different. It is, therefore, easy for us to sympathize with those who are like us at the expense of those who are different. For example, most Americans felt great sympathy for those who lost their lives or loved ones in the September 11, 2001, terrorist attacks on the Twin Towers. However, there is little outpouring of sympathy for the thousands of civilians in Iraq and Afghanistan, Pakistan, and Yemen who have been killed in the "war on terror." Conscious moral direction requires us to grow beyond our natural tendency to sympathize only with those who resemble us.

"Helper's High" According to Plato, we behave justly not only because it is the right thing to do but because of the positive effect it has upon us.[25] Feminist care ethicist Nel Noddings likewise notes that caring for others is often accompanied by a sense of joy.[26] The association of morality with happiness and a sense of well-being is found in moral philosophies throughout the world. Buddhist ethics teaches that joy comes only through the desire to help others.[27] When we help others, we generally come away from the experience feeling better about ourselves and energized by the experience. Our conscience, in other words, "strokes" us when we act in accordance with it. Psychologists call this feeling **helper's high**.

There is considerable medical evidence that doing good for others has more than just psychological benefits. According to the Institute for the Advancement of Health, community service work has a positive effect on our overall sense of physical and emotional well-being. Hans Seyle, author of *The Stress of Life*, suggests that people engage in altruistic projects as a means of reducing stress. The helper's high that accompanies volunteer work results from an increase in endorphins—morphinelike chemicals that occur naturally in the body. The release of endorphins, in turn, is followed by a longer period of increased relaxation and improved self-esteem.[28]

Connections

On what grounds did Kant argue that feelings are insufficient as a foundation for morality? *See Chapter 10, page 313.*

Is an action moral if it is done simply so that we can feel better about ourselves? Most philosophers would say no. Conscience and morality are far more complex. Unlike true moral acts, helping others just to experience helper's high does not stem from a respect for others and the moral law but from self-interest. While feeling good about what we are doing can make helping others easier, feeling good in itself is not usually enough to sustain our good actions.

Moral Outrage   Not all moral sentiments or emotions make us feel warm and fuzzy. Moral outrage occurs when we witness a violation or transgression of the boundaries of moral decency. As such, moral outrage is oriented toward justice and motivates us to correct the situation by demanding that justice be done. Moral outrage can take two forms. The first, **resentment**, is the anger we feel when we have been personally injured. **Moral indignation** is the anger we feel at the sight of others being harmed.

Moral outrage in the form of resentment appears very early in childhood, when children believe that they have been treated unfairly. Moral indignation appears later, as our sense of moral community expands to include others besides ourselves. In each case, moral outrage involves passing judgment upon someone else's behavior. This involves the use of the cognitive side of our conscience in conjunction with the affective.

Connections

Why is proper self-esteem important for leading a moral life? *See Chapter 10, pages 318-320, and Chapter 12, page 408.*

Just as moral indignation is the appropriate response in the face of the abuse and oppression suffered by others, so too is resentment appropriate in the face of one's own abuse and oppression. Resentment is a "form of personal protest which expresses our respect for self, for others, and for morality."[29] By sending a message to the abuser that we will not tolerate such treatment, resentment serves to affirm our moral worth and to protect us from future abuse. Indeed, philosopher Immanuel Kant and the feminist care ethicists regard the cultivation of proper self-esteem as one of our primary moral duties.

To put aside resentment or moral indignation and forgive in the face of ongoing abuse serves to absolve oppressors of any need to change their behavior. People who never feel resentment or moral outrage—such as servile people—also do not acknowledge injustice. Instead, they believe that they, or other groups who are being oppressed, deserve to be harmed or treated with contempt.

. . . people who are not angered by the right things, or in the right way, or at the right times, or towards the right people, all seem to be foolish. . . . Since he is not angered, he does not seem to be the sort to defend himself; and such willingness to accept insults to oneself or to overlook insults to one's family and friends is slavish.

—ARISTOTLE, *Nichomachean Ethics*, Bk. 4, Ch. 5, 1126a

Rosa Parks (1913-2005), American civil rights activist. Parks was arrested in 1955 after refusing to give up her seat to a white man on a bus in Montgomery, Alabama.
©Bettmann/Getty Images

Moral outrage fosters community by encouraging victims and their sympathizers to work toward justice and moral reform. On December 1, 1955, Rosa Parks, an African American woman living in the South, refused to stifle her moral outrage. After a long, tiring day at work, she climbed aboard a crowded bus and sat down in the middle section since there were no seats in the back of the bus where African Americans were supposed to sit. A few stops later, a White man got on the bus. The bus driver ordered Parks to give up her seat; she refused. The White people on the bus were horrified at her impertinence. How dare she think she was above the law! The bus driver threatened to call the police, to which she replied, "You may do that." Her defiant action, her resentment at her disrespectful treatment, and her demand that she be treated with dignity acted as a catalyst in the civil rights movement. The ensuing case went all the way to the U.S. Supreme Court, which ruled that segregation on public transportation was unconstitutional.

Like sympathy, moral outrage can be a powerful motivation. A study of why some people go to the aid of a crime victim, while others do not, found that the people who intervened were also the quickest to anger. Most said they acted reflexively, without rational deliberation or reflection upon their sympathy for the victim.

Connections

In what ways has a belief in ethical subjectivism reinforced the Kitty Genovese syndrome? *See Chapter 4, pages 129-130.*

One might wonder whether the Kitty Genovese syndrome—when people passively stand by and watch with indifference as another person is beaten, raped, or even killed (see page 127)—is, at least in part, the product of years of learning to stifle our moral outrage. In our "live and let live" society, righteous anger is frowned on and passing judgment on others is considered disrespectful and even arrogant. "Who are *you* to pass judgment?" we are admonished. Given this nonjudgmental atmosphere, it is not surprising that the moral outrage that often accompanies moral judgment is often regarded as a bad feeling that we should work to get beyond.

The world needs anger. The world often continues to allow evil because it isn't angry enough.

—BEDE JARRETT (historian)

The effects of suppressed or misdirected moral outrage are now becoming apparent in our culture. Friedrich Nietzsche used the term **ressentiment** to describe this phenomenon. Ressentiment occurs when we suppress or redirect our resentment. Resentment, denied its proper expression, degenerates into ressentiment, which eventually leads to a "self-poisoning of the mind" by saturating the entire personality with repressed feelings of "revenge, hatred, malice, envy, the impulse to detract, and spite."[30] This, in turn, leads not only to self-blame and self-loathing but often to the search for a scapegoat. Our scapegoats are often members of even more oppressed groups. Moral outrage can become destructive when it drifts from its cognitive mooring in justice. Women who continue to live with an abusive husband are far more likely to beat their children than they are if they leave the abusive husband.[31]

Guilt   **Guilt** is a moral sentiment that occurs when we violate a moral norm. As a culture, we have a love/hate relationship with guilt. We generally regard a person who feels no guilt—such as sociopath Hannibal "the Cannibal" Lector in the 1991 movie *Silence of the Lambs*—as either inhuman or a monster. At the same time, guilt is often regarded as a barrier to freedom and human liberation. This is due, in part, to the Freudian psychoanalytical view of guilt as a symptom of neurosis and, hence, in need of a cure.

Moral Sentiments/Emotions

- **Sympathy**   The capacity to imagine the feelings of others.
- **Helper's high**   The positive effect we experience when helping others.
- **Moral outrage**   The anger felt when we witness a violation of a moral decency.
- **Moral indignation**   The anger we feel at the sight of others being harmed.
- **Resentment**   The anger we feel at being personally injured by someone.
- **Guilt**   The feeling that arises when we violate a moral norm.

It is also due to a confusion of guilt with shame. The word *guilt* is frequently used broadly to include shame as well; however, it is important to distinguish between the two. Teenagers who are gay or lesbian, for example, can develop a deep sense of shame for not living up to their family's and church's expectations, but they do not generally feel moral guilt. **Shame**, which is heteronomous and associated with Freud's superego, is aroused as a result of a violation of social norms. Shame leaves us feeling inadequate, embarrassed, and humiliated before others.

In contrast, feelings of guilt result from the violation of a moral norm. Most adults, as cultural relativists, have learned to include the two feelings—shame and guilt—under one rubric; however, studies show that children as young as seven are able to distinguish between the shame that often accompanies the breaking of a nonmoral social custom and the guilt that occurs as the result of transgressing a moral norm.[32]

Guilt not only demands that we accept moral responsibility for our actions but that we make reparation to those we have harmed and, if necessary, change ourselves to make a repeat of the harmful behavior less likely. However unpleasant guilt may be, it seems to be important to our well-being. Our whole autonomic nervous system is disrupted when we experience feelings of guilt. Both pain and guilt act as damage control. Physical pain occurs when we damage our bodies, as a signal for us to take steps to fix the damage or remove the cause of the harm. In the same manner, guilt lets us know when something is morally wrong so that we can take steps to correct the situation.

> A guilty conscience is a form of punishment for wrongdoing which any normal wrong-doer cannot escape and so it is better to stop doing wrong and do good.
>
> —Ewe proverb of Africa

Guilt also motivates us to avoid harming ourselves and others. Rather than being a private experience with no social consequences, guilt is very important in maintaining relationships.[33] Guilt motivates us to pay attention to other people. Studies show that adults with the strongest conscience and the strongest sense of guilt have the strongest affiliations with others. Guilt also serves to equalize power in a relationship since misuse of power leads to feelings of guilt. In addition, guilt motivates us to restore a damaged relationship by making up for the harms that we have done to the relationship.[34]

Moral Reasoning: The Cognitive Element of Conscience

The cognitive side of our conscience is involved in making rational judgments about what we *ought* to do. If we neglect to develop the critical cognitive side of our conscience, our moral sentiments may get us into trouble. Moral

Connections
Why are sociopaths dangerous? *See Chapter 4, pages 125-126.*

Connections
What is the prima facie duty of reparation? *See Chapter 10, page 334.*

Connections
Why are good reasoning skills important in moral decision making? *See Chapter 2, pages 30-34.*

sentiments by themselves are uncritical. People who are uncritically sympathetic, as we noted earlier, make easy targets for those who would take advantage of their kindness. Other people feel overwhelmed with guilt but are unable to discern why or to devise a plan of action to remedy the situation that gave rise to the guilt.

Studies suggest that moral reasoning is not something that must be taught or that develops only when children have achieved a certain level of rationality.[35] About half of the children between eighteen and thirty-six months of age will spontaneously—without any prompting from an adult—offer to share things such as food or a toy with another person. According to psychologist William Damon, by the age of four, children are "already in possession of active, flourishing conceptions of fairness."[36] This phenomenon has been observed cross-culturally: It is found in North American babies and the infants of African Bushmen.[37]

People with bad consciences always fear the judgment of children.

—MARY MCCARTHY, *On the Contrary*

Although many young children possess a concept of fairness, they tend to engage in moral judgments in an egocentric manner. Most young children are concerned only with how others' actions affect them and are less concerned with how their own actions affect others. As we grow older, our sense of fairness and justice, like our feelings of sympathy, extends to encompass a wider and wider moral community.

A well-developed conscience demands that we treat ourselves and others with respect. When we behave in ways that violate basic moral principles, the cognitive side of our conscience asks us to justify our actions. To say that we felt like hurting someone else or enjoyed inflicting harm does not satisfy our conscience. Instead, we must offer justifications based on higher moral claims.

An uncritical conscience is likely to resort to **rationalization**, which involves the use of rhetoric, fallacies, and resistance rather than logical analysis. People who rationalize their harmful actions suffer from what is known as weakness of the will or a weak conscience. Weak-willed people place nonmoral values such as popularity or economic success above moral values.

The affective and cognitive elements of conscience are inseparable. The critical importance of moral sentiments for moral reasoning is particularly evident with sociopaths. Sociopaths are quite capable of complex reasoning; however, because they lack the ability to sympathize with others, they are apparently incapable of using their cognitive abilities in the service of morality.

Conscience not only has a powerful influence in shaping both our conduct and our character; it is also an essential part of who we are as individuals. Acting in good conscience seems to be necessary for maintaining our

Connections

What are some of the more common types of resistance? *See Chapter 2, pages 37–42.*

sense of personal integrity. Our conscience compels us to question cultural norms that urge us to be insincere or to pretend that we are someone we are not. To be at odds with our conscience is to be out of harmony with our very being.

Exercises

*1. Psychologists have found that one of the best means of cultivating our feelings of sympathy is to place ourselves in situations where we come face-to-face with people who are different from us. Discuss ways, if any, in which your community service work has affected the development of your capacity to sympathize with others.

2. Some parents shield their children from experiences that set them apart from the group. But should they? Thinking back to your own childhood, what experiences contributed most to the development of your sympathy for others? Explain.

*3. In an interview conducted shortly after the death of Jerry Garcia, the lead guitarist for the Grateful Dead, Carlos Santana said of Garcia's life: "You can only get high serving people." Discuss this statement in light of your own experience.

   How does helper's high sustain or motivate you in your community service? Is service a moral action if it is done only to make ourselves feel better? Why or why not?

4. Think of a time when you, like Rosa Parks (see page 85), witnessed an action that was legal, but that you thought was immoral. On what grounds did you regard the action as immoral? How did you react? Discuss also how we might distinguish between anger that is based on moral outrage and destructive or vicious anger.

5. Jesus taught that we should "turn the other cheek" and "love our enemies." Discuss this in light of the quotation from Aristotle regarding the moral value of moral indignation in the face of our mistreatment. Do the teachings of Jesus preclude resentment and indignation? Support your answer.

6. Cultural relativists tend to confuse shame with guilt. Discuss examples of both from your own experience. Compare and contrast the two experiences.

7. How do you respond to guilt? Discuss the types of defenses, especially immature defenses or resistance, that you sometimes use when you feel guilty. Discuss also how might you substitute mature defense mechanisms for resistance.

8. Gandhi and Martin Luther King Jr. argued that violence can never be justified by moral outrage. Instead, we need to use our moral reasoning to devise non-violent strategies for responding to violence. Do you agree? Support your answer.

Lawrence Kohlberg: The Stage Theory of Moral Development

Moral thought, then, seems to behave like all other kinds of thought. Progress through the moral levels and stages is characterized by increasing differentiation and increasing integration, and hence is the same kind of progress that scientific theory represents.

—LAWRENCE KOHLBERG, *The Philosophy of Moral Development* (1971)

Swiss psychologist Jean Piaget (1896–1980) was one of the first to systematically study moral reasoning in children. Children, he noticed, go through distinct stages in their moral development. The first stage he labeled the *stage of heteronomy*. This stage is based on a "morality of constraint." The second stage, the *stage of autonomy*, is based on a "morality of cooperation."[38] Although Piaget regarded moral development as part of human nature, he also believed that interrelationships between the individual and society are essential to nurture the development of a sense of moral duty.

Connections

How do behaviorists explain moral behavior? *See Chapter 1, page 20.*

Because of the domination of modern psychology by behaviorism—whose corollary in moral philosophy is cultural relativism—Piaget's research on moral development received little attention until relatively recently. In the 1970s, the work of Harvard psychologist Lawrence Kohlberg (1927–1987) caught the public's attention. Kohlberg was influenced primarily by Piaget, as well as Socrates, Immanuel Kant, and John Rawls—all philosophers whose works, he believed, exemplified a high stage of moral reasoning.

Kohlberg's Stages

Lawrence Kohlberg's ideas about moral development became popular in the wake of the Vietnam War protests and the civil rights movement, both of which gave rise to dissatisfaction with cultural relativism. The analytical movement in moral philosophy had culminated in the theory of emotivism, which disconnects morality from the real world. Kohlberg wanted to return to a synthetic approach in which theory and practical experience came together.

According to Kohlberg, although the specific content of moral codes can vary depending on a person's culture, the difference is only on the surface. The conceptual structures from which these specific codes are formulated are innate and universal.

Kohlberg and his colleagues believed that humans, with the exception of sociopaths and other severely impaired people, have an inherent potential for growth from the lower (earlier) to higher (later) stages of moral development. These stages are transcultural and represent "transformations in the organization of thought, rather than increasing knowledge of cultural values."[39] Each stage, according to him, is distinct and reflects a level of moral judgment that is more complex than that of the preceding stage.[40] Gains that are made in moral judgment tend to be retained. The lower stages are not so much replaced by higher stages as incorporated into them—much like elementary school arithmetic becomes part of our way of understanding calculus.

Kohlberg identified three levels of moral development, each with two distinct stages (Table 3.1). In the preconventional stages, moral duty and moral community are defined primarily in egocentric terms. Young children are preconventional reasoners. The majority of adults in the United States are in the conventional stages of moral reasoning. They are heteronomous cultural relativists who look to outside sources—their peers or cultural norms—for moral guidance. Less than 10 percent of American adults ever reach the postconventional stages of autonomous moral reasoning.

While the so-called higher stages come later than the lower stages in human development, this in itself does not prove that the higher stages are morally better. Kohlberg was well aware that we cannot logically draw a conclusion regarding what *ought* to be from what *is*. To do so is to commit the naturalistic fallacy (see pages 60–61). Instead, he argued, higher stages are preferable because people at these stages are more satisfied with their moral decisions. People, in general, *prefer* a solution to a moral problem that uses the highest stage of moral reasoning conceptually available to them.[41] People who operate at a higher stage of moral reasoning are less likely to make moral decisions that they will later regret.

Connections

What logical fallacies are cultural relativists most likely to commit? *See Chapter 2, pages 52-60.*

TABLE 3.1 Kohlberg's Stages of Moral Development

STAGE	DESCRIPTION
Preconventional	
1. Punishment and obedience	Avoid punishment; submit to authority. Fear of punishment is the primary motive.
2. Egoist	Satisfy one's own needs; only consider the needs of others if it benefits you: "You scratch my back, I'll scratch yours."
Conventional	
3. Good boy/nice girl	Please and help others; concern for maintaining good relationships and earning others' approval; conformity to peer and group norms.
4. Society maintaining	Respect authority and social rules; maintain the existing social order.
Postconventional	
5. Social contract or legalistic	Obey useful, albeit arbitrary, social rules; appeal to social consensus and majority rule as long as minimal basic rights are safeguarded. The U.S. Constitution is written using this stage of reasoning.
6. Conscience and universal principles	Autonomously recognize universal rules, such as justice and equality, that are rational and logically consistent and reflect a respect for equal human rights and the dignity of each individual.

Based on Barbara Panzi and Timothy McMahon, "Ethical Decision-Making: Developmental Theory and Practice," speech delivered at the National Association of Student Personnel Administrators, Denver, March 1989.

Kohlberg also pointed out that *moral philosophers* believe that the principled reasoning that characterizes the higher stages is more desirable than the cultural relativism of the conventional stages or the egoism of the preconventional stages. Most of the world's moral philosophers maintain that autonomous moral reasoning, universality and impartiality, compassion and a concern for justice, and mutual respect are the hallmarks of sound moral reasoning.

Because each new stage of moral development integrates the components of the previous stage, later stages provide us with better tools for resolving crises. In addition, our concept of the moral community also becomes more inclusive as we mature, going from the self-centered egoism of the young child to universal respect for all beings.

A person will prefer his or her current stage of moral development until it is, in turn, replaced by a newly comprehended stage. Each stage represents an equilibrium point, so a person will generally remain in that stage until sufficient cognitive or social disequilibrium has occurred. People move beyond their current stage when they encounter a crisis that their current mode of thinking is unable to satisfactorily resolve.

Until the age of forty-three, Aung San Suu Kyi (1945–) had been leading a quiet life in England as a housewife and academic before she was transformed into a powerful and charismatic leader of the Burmese people. While living in England, she had heard about the political unrest and shooting of demonstrators. However, not until Suu Kyi returned to Burma in 1988 and came face-to-face with the crisis facing her people was she transformed. "Overnight, Aung San Suu Kyi became the leading representative of the movement for freedom and democracy." After spending fifteen of the years between 1989 and 2010 under house arrest, she is now a free woman and was elected to the Burmese parliament in 2012.[42]

Gains made in moral development affect a person's real-life behavior.[43] Level of moral reasoning is positively correlated with honesty and altruistic behavior— what Piaget called *practical morality*. A study of eighty-six subjects found that only 9 percent of people at stage 2 (egoist) and 38 percent of people at Kohlberg's stage 4 (society maintaining/cultural relativist) would offer help to someone lying on a sidewalk who appeared to be suffering from drug side effects; yet all of the subjects at stage 6 (conscience and universal moral principles) offered their assistance.[44] Higher stages of moral reasoning are also positively correlated with higher scores on other components of moral behavior and on developmental scales such as ego development, self-esteem, and mental health.

Cross-Cultural Findings

Studies from more than forty Western and non-Western countries support Kohlberg's theory that stages of moral development are universal. Cross-cultural findings also lend support to the claim that some cultures are more prone to promote virtue in their citizens. When matched by age and education, people in the United States score lower in measures of moral development than people from Iceland or Canada but higher than people living in Taiwan.

Subcultures and institutions also influence a person's stage of moral reasoning. One of the greatest frustrations of our current prison system is that criminals often come out in worse shape than when they entered prison. Prisoners interact with the guards primarily in terms of stage 1 behavior—avoiding coercion and punishment. However, with each other, the prisoners are primarily in stage 2, acting out of mutual self-benefit but without any genuine respect for one another. In other words, prison life tends to mold prisoners into a morality that is lower than their "private best."[45]

Colleges and Moral Development

Most high school students and college freshmen use primarily stage 3 moral reasoning; as such, they tend to be very conformist and easily influenced by their peer culture. This phenomenon in college students has been dubbed the "freshman personality."[46] On a more hopeful note, formal education has been found to be an important factor in promoting moral development, probably because it challenges students to analyze their worldviews. When young people leave their family of origin and enter college, they often experience a crisis. Events that conflict with our cherished worldviews—such as encountering people from different backgrounds and learning new ideas—can precipitate disequilibrium.

During the transition from conventional to postconventional moral reasoning, students are often torn between the rejection of moral values as relative and the reluctance to commit to universal moral principles. College students frequently respond, at least initially, to this unsettling experience by becoming more conforming to their peer culture. This conflict can also manifest itself in hedonistic disregard for any moral values—either relative or universal. The movement from conventional to postconventional moral reasoning involves a paradigm shift or change in our worldview. Educator and philosopher Dwight Boyd refers to the condition in which students are struggling with the transition from conventional to principled moral reasoning as "sophomoritis."[47]

Unfortunately, most college students do not complete the transition to postconventional moral reasoning. A college education instead tends to push students into a higher level of *conventional* reasoning. In other words, a traditional college education can make students less reliant on the opinions of their peers; however, the tradeoff is that they conform more to wider societal norms rather than becoming more autonomous in their thinking.

Criticisms of Kohlberg's Stages

Kohlberg has been criticized for inadvertently reflecting the biases of U.S. culture. For example, he did not find much change in level of moral development after the age of twenty-five. However, most of his subjects were students; very few were over the age of forty or fifty, a time of life that is revered in many non-Western cultures for its moral wisdom.

Perhaps the most telling criticism of Kohlberg's theory is that, at least when it was initially formulated, it failed to take into account women's moral development. Before the late 1970s, researchers in both medicine and psychology routinely used only male subjects, based on the assumption that men were generic humans and that generalizations about women could legitimately be made from studies done only on men. In keeping with this thinking, the subjects in Kohlberg's initial studies were all male. Adding insult to injury, Kohlberg even drew the conclusion on the basis of his all-male research that men operate at a significantly higher level of moral reasoning than do women.

Exercises

1. Do you agree with Kohlberg's claim that we have an intrinsic drive toward inner growth? Or do people, as the expression goes, "never change"? Illustrate your answer using examples from your own life.

2. Has the strategy you use for making moral decisions changed since you were a child? Since you started college? If so, explain how it has changed? Do you think the strategy you use now is better or more effective than your earlier strategies? Explain.

3. Referring to your responses to the Self-Evaluation Questionnaire on page 73, as well as to your response to the scenario at the beginning of this chapter about Heinz, discuss your responses to the two cases in light of Kohlberg's stages of moral reasoning. Has learning about the stages of moral development changed how you would respond and, if so, why and in what direction?

4. Discuss some of the forces in our culture that discourage people from developing past the conventional stage but encourage us to develop beyond the preconventional stages.

   What changes in U.S. public policy, including our public education system, would you suggest that might make this culture more conducive to moral development? For those of you live or who have lived in different cultures, discuss how these cultures encourage or inhibit moral development.

5. Studies have found that, in the United States, professional education in fields such as business and teaching actually tends to inhibit moral development.[48] A liberal arts education, on the other hand, tends to enhance moral development. Why might this be so? Discuss how professional education might be changed to encourage moral development.

6. Given that the average criminal is at the same level of moral reasoning as a junior high school student, is it fair that criminals are held responsible for their actions while youth who commit the same crimes get lighter sentences or are excused on the grounds that they are not mature enough to make moral decisions? To what extent should a person's level of moral reasoning be taken into account when holding someone culpable for his or her antisocial actions?

Carol Gilligan: The Care Perspective

The elusive mystery of women's development lies in its recognition of the continuing importance of attachment in the human life-cycle . . . while the [masculine] development litany intones the celebration of separation, autonomy, individuation, and natural rights. . . .
—CAROL GILLIGAN, *In a Different Voice* (1982), p. 23

Women and the Care Perspective

The neglect of many philosophers and psychologists to take women's perspectives into account has created the false impression that women are morally deficient compared to men. Carol Gilligan, who had studied with Kohlberg, decided it was time to correct this. In her interviews with women and through her study of women in literature, she concluded that women's moral development tends to follow a different path than men's. Men tend to be duty and principle oriented; women are more context oriented and tend to view the world in a more emotional and personal way. Women's moral judgment, Gilligan found, is characterized by a concern for themselves and others, accepting and maintaining responsibility within relationships, attachment, and self-sacrifice. She named this the "care perspective," in contrast to Kohlberg's "justice perspective."[49]

In her research with women, Gilligan postulated three stages of moral development (Table 3.2). Although Gilligan and Kohlberg emphasize different aspects of moral development, their stages are roughly parallel. Gender can influence how our moral development unfolds, but the basic paradigms or ground plans that inform our moral development are similar. For example, the preconventional stage in both Gilligan's and Kohlberg's theories includes egoists and ethical subjectivists. Similarly, people at the conventional stage are heteronomous cultural relativists who look to their culture for moral guidance.

The different descriptions of the conventional stage are not surprising, given the different ways in which men and women are socialized in our culture. Men, for the most part, are socialized to be the upholders of law and order and to believe that maleness carries certain privileges. Women, on the other hand, are taught that being a good woman involves self-sacrifice and putting the welfare of others first.

TABLE 3.2 Gilligan's Stages of Moral Reasoning in Women

STAGE	DESCRIPTION	MORAL COMMUNITY
Preconventional	Self-centered	Viewing one's own needs as all that matters
Conventional	Self-sacrificing	Viewing others' needs as more important
Postconventional	Mature care ethics	Able to balance one's own needs and the needs of others

Malala Yousafzai (b. 1997) became the youngest person ever to be awarded the Nobel Peace Prize. An outspoken advocate of education for girls and women, Malala was shot three times (once in the head) by a Taliban assassin as she was boarding her school bus in Pakistan. Unable to return to Pakistan because of an order by the Taliban to kill her, she and her family remained in England where, after her recovery, she continued her advocacy work. Thanks to her efforts, Pakistan ratified its first Right to Education Bill in 2015.
©Simon Davis/DFID

Discussion Questions

1. Discuss ways in which Malala exemplifies Gilligan's mature care ethics.
2. Think of a cause that you feel strongly about. To what extent would you take action to support the cause or bring about a change? Discuss your actions, or lack thereof, in light of Gilligan's and Kohlberg's stages of moral reasoning.

In both Kohlberg's and Gilligan's theories, the postconventional stage is represented by autonomous moral reasoning: The person looks to transcultural values—whether in the form of principles of justice and respect or moral sentiments such as compassion and empathy. The transition to the postconventional stage for women, according to Gilligan, involves realizing that any individual woman has as much moral value as the next person. Kohlberg emphasized cognitive disequilibrium as playing a key role in pushing people into a higher stage of moral development; Gilligan and many other feminist ethicists place more importance on *social disequilibrium* as the "gate" to moral development.[50]

Connections

How does cultural relativism shape women's idea of what it means to be virtuous? *See Chapter 6, pages 182-184.*

Women and Self-Sacrifice

Because of women's inferior social status in many cultures, their socialization generally involves internalizing the message that they should nurture and care for the needs of others. Failure to recognize their own equal worth as humans can be costly for women. In situations of famine, for example, women starve to death at a higher rate than men do. When there is not enough for everyone, women will often engage in deliberate self-deprivation, offering men the best food at the expense of their own nutritional needs.[51]

Placing other's needs before their own can leave women who are at the self-sacrificing stage of moral development vulnerable to the cycle of domination and domestic violence in which abused women discount their own moral worth and remain with or return to their abuser. Younger women are especially at risk. About one-quarter or more of college women have been victims of dating or domestic violence.

Put it down in capital letters: SELF-DEVELOPMENT IS A HIGHER DUTY THAN SELF-SACRIFICE. The thing which most retards and militates against women's self-development is self-sacrifice.

—Elizabeth Cady Stanton to a reporter[52]

The identification of the "good" woman with habitual deference to others' needs and wishes can be destructive not only to women's self-esteem but to their ability to have a genuine caring relationship. In Amy Tan's novel *The Joy Luck Club*, Rose Hsu Jordan, the American-born daughter of An-Mei Hsu, does everything she can to be the perfect wife to her American husband, Ted Jordan. She sacrifices her own dreams of a career and always defers to her husband's wishes—even when he asks for her opinion—until she is no longer able to make decisions for herself:

> I thought about things, the pros and the cons. But in the end I would be so con-
> fused, because I never believed there was ever any one right answer, yet there were
> many wrong ones. So whenever I said, "You decide," or "I don't care," or "Either
> way is fine with me," Ted would say in his impatient voice, "No, you decide. You
> can't have it both ways, none of the responsibility, none of the blame."[53]

Ted, an autonomous moral reasoner, wants a wife who can think for herself. When he asks Rose for a divorce, she is stunned. Her perfect world is shattered, and she experiences social dissonance.

Only by going through the agony of the separation and hearing her mother tell the story of her own mother's marriage in China to an abusive husband does Rose finally come to realize that she does have choices. By learning to say no to her husband and to express her anger at being betrayed, Rose is finally able to make the transition to mature care ethics and, in the end, establish a relationship with Ted that is based on mutual care and respect rather than self-imposed servility.

Synthesizing the Justice and Care Perspectives

Some studies support Gilligan's theory,[54] but others have found gender differences in moral reasoning to be insignificant.[55] In later studies, Gilligan and others found that both the justice and care perspectives are present in most people's thinking, although each of us tends to favor one perspective over the other. Although women are more likely to prefer the care perspective, some women have a strong justice orientation, while some men, including many philosophers, are very empathetic and care oriented. Buddhist ethics likewise emphasizes compassion and community over abstract reason.

The strength inherent in the mature care perspective is that it calls attention to our attachment to each other and to the particular needs and circumstances of individuals. On the other hand, by focusing on the individual and on relationships, care ethics tends to ignore wider issues of equality.

Reason instructs us in the several tendencies of actions, and humanity (sympathy)

makes a distinction in favor of those which are useful and beneficial.

—DAVID HUME, *Enquiry Concerning the Principles of Morality* (1751)

The justice perspective, in contrast, focuses on justice, overcoming oppression, and the ideal of equality for all people. This more detached focus can occur, however, at the expense of attention to individual needs. Gilligan and Kohlberg came to agree in their later work that the most adequate moral orientation takes both the justice and care perspectives into consideration; the two perspectives, rather than being mutually exclusive, complement and enrich each other.[56]

Exercises

1. Which of these two approaches, Gilligan's care perspective or Kohlberg's justice perspective, do you use most in your own moral reasoning? Illustrate your answer with specific examples. What might you do to strengthen whichever of the two perspectives is weaker?

2. Gilligan argues that our "depictions of adult development" tend to discourage moral maturity. Aging is frequently associated in our culture with deterioration rather than growth. Discuss whether our present youth-oriented society, our fear of aging, and degradation of older people discourage moral maturity.

*3. If you are doing community service work, how has it helped to strengthen your moral reasoning? On which of the two perspectives, care or justice, has it had the greatest impact? Explain using specific examples.

*4. People sometimes justify their failure to confront others who are behaving in a morally immature manner on the grounds that criticism would not make a difference. However, research on moral development indicates that social and cognitive dissonance—where a person's views are challenged—contributes to that person's moral development. Given this, do we have a moral obligation to confront others or share our stories of moral struggle and growth with others, as An-Mei Hsu, Rose's mother, did in *The Joy Luck Club*? Explain.

Discuss a time when hearing someone else's story changed your way of thinking and helped you to grow morally—whether this occurred during your community service work, through a personal encounter with a teacher or friend, or even as a result of a movie that you saw or a novel that you read.

The Four Components of Moral Behavior

There is widespread agreement that there are more components to morality than just moral judgment. The trick, however, is to identify what else there is in morality, and how all these pieces fit together.

—JAMES REST, *Moral Development in the Professions* (1994), p. 22

Most studies have found that the stages of moral reasoning are positively correlated to moral behavior;[57] however, other studies have found no statistically significant correlation.[58] These findings suggest that moral reasoning is not the only determinant or component of moral behavior. Proficiency in making moral judgments does not in itself guarantee that one will act morally. For example, we may fail to act morally because of fear or pressure from peers or authority figures even when we know what is right, as happened in the Milgram experiment. Moral behavior, in other words, is a complex phenomenon that cannot be represented as a single variable.

> **Connections**
>
> What is the role of sympathy and moral sensitivity in feminist care ethics? *See Chapter 12, pages 408-409.*

Psychologist James Rest identified four components of moral behavior: (1) moral sensitivity, (2) moral reasoning or judgment, (3) moral motivation, and (4) moral character. A deficiency in any of these components can result in a failure to act morally.

Moral Sensitivity

Moral sensitivity is the awareness of how our actions affect others. It involves the ability to empathize and imagine ourselves in another person's shoes. Problems such as poverty, social isolation, and homelessness exist, in part, because we simply don't see the problem. Research in developmental neuroscience has found that moral sensitivity and concern for the well-being of others usually emerges between the ages of six and twelve months, and that moral sensitivity is as important, or more important than conscious cognitive processes in moral behavior.[59]

In 2012, former Rutgers' college student Dharun Ravi was found guilty for using a Webcam to spy on his gay roommate, Tyler Clementi, during a sexual encounter. Clementi committed suicide after finding out he had been watched. During the trial Ravi showed no remorse. Only later, after he was found guilty, did he issue a formal apology to Clementi's family. Ravi served only 20 days of his 30 day sentence. Ravi appealed the decision. In 2016, his conviction was overturned by a New Jersey appeal court.
©AP Photo/Mel Evans

Analyzing Images

1. Ravi's lawyers argued that Ravi was not motivated by bias based on sexual orientation. Given that this is true, is the claim that he was not motivated by bias or hatred morally relevant when it comes to assigning guilt? Support your answer.

2. Imagine you had been one of the friends with whom Ravi shared the Webcam video. Roleplay the scenario. Afterwards discuss how each of you reacted and what would have been the morally appropriate response.

3. As part of his sentence Ravi was ordered by the court to do 300 hours of community service. Discuss the pros and cons of assigning offenders community service.

There are striking differences in people's sensitivity to the needs and welfare of others. People such as Mother Teresa, for example, are highly sensitive to the suffering of others. People who are morally sensitive are more likely to extend a helping hand and to engage in community service. In addition, they are more likely to feel guilty when they harm another person or to feel moral indignation in the face of injustice. Morally sensitive people also do better academically and make better roommates in college.[60]

People who are deficient in moral sensitivity may fail to act morally simply because it did not occur to them to do so. They may make offensive comments, not out of malice, but because they are unaware of the effect of their comments on others. Insensitivity to others' suffering can present itself as unrealistic optimism and minimizing of other people's distress. Making statements such as "don't worry" or "things always work out for the best" to someone who has suffered a terrible misfortune can add further to their despair and isolation. Morally insensitive people may even take pride in the fact that others' bigoted comments or behavior do not bother them and accuse those who do react with resentment or indignation of being "overly sensitive."

During the 1991 U.S. Senate Judiciary Committee hearing regarding Anita Hill's allegations that Supreme Court nominee Clarence Thomas sexually harassed her, many people expressed surprise that the senators were so poorly informed and morally insensitive regarding the problem of sexual harassment in the workplace. "The insensitivity and lack of comprehension about the complex psychology of sexual harassment displayed by the senators questioning the witnesses in the Clarence Thomas hearing," wrote one lawyer in her commentary on the case, "was, in a word, unbelievable."[61]

Moral sensitivity can be enhanced by experiences that provide opportunities to see the world from other people's perspectives.[62] The perception of a person in distress can trigger empathy; hearing other people's stories can also contribute to one's consciousness raising. Only when we are painfully sensitive to actual suffering can we begin to move toward changing the social conditions that perpetuate injustice and suffering. Indeed, one of the strengths of feminist care ethics is its recognition of the importance of cultivating moral sensitivity.

Moral Reasoning or Judgment

Despite the focus on reason as the highest attribute of humans, recent studies of moral behavior indicate that **moral reasoning** is insufficient in itself to bring about moral action. On the other hand, without first engaging in critical judgment, our well-intentioned actions can hurt innocent people and lead to moral tragedies. Moral judgment that is not tempered with moral sensitivity can lead to behavior that is rigid and unfeeling. Loyalty to one's peer group or country, when not balanced by feelings of sympathy for people outside one's community, can lead to blind obedience as happened in Nazi Germany.

People who are deficient in moral reasoning do not recognize the different moral values and principles involved in making a moral decision and thus tend to come up with simplistic solutions. For example, not revealing the name of a fraternity brother who raped a woman may be justified in the name of loyalty, or lying about an affair on the grounds of sparing another person's feelings. These people often fail to see the full repercussions of their decisions and become easily baffled in situations where they are presented with conflicting values.

People who are competent moral reasoners, in contrast, make more satisfactory moral decisions from both their own point of view and that of moral philosophers. People whose capacity for moral reasoning is well developed are more fulfilled by their careers, are more likely to pursue further education, are more involved in their communities, and have higher self-esteem.[63]

Real-life exposure to ideas that do not fit in with our more simplistic ideas seems to be a condition for the development of moral reasoning. Practice in

Connections

How does an understanding of logic make it less likely that we will get caught up in a moral tragedy? *See Chapter 2, page 47.*

Connections

What is the five-step method for resolving moral dilemmas? *See Chapter 2, pages 66-67.*

resolving moral dilemmas, the acquisition of proficiency in logic, and the study of ethical theory also contribute to the development of this component. These strategies have been found to be particularly effective when combined with a study of the stages of moral development.[64]

Moral Motivation

Political philosopher Edmund Burke once wrote that the only thing necessary for evil to triumph is for good men to do nothing. Many otherwise good people know what is right and are sensitive to the moral issues involved; however, they lack the motivation to put this knowledge into action or praxis. This happened in the case of the college administrators at Penn State who knew that Sandusky was sexually molesting young boys, but failed to report it to outside authorities. (See Analyzing Images, page 22.) People who fail to act on what they know is right are known as weak-willed.

Moral motivation entails putting moral values above competing nonmoral values. Nationalistic and economic values as well as concerns about popularity can all take precedence over what we clearly recognize to be the morally right action. Dysfunctional families, for example, often place a higher value on the appearance of harmony—what others will think—than on the welfare of the individual members of the family.

Connections

What do most college students mean when they say "morality is all relative"? *See Chapter 4, page 120.*

In a survey of 62,000 undergraduates, two-thirds admitted to some form of academic cheating, including Internet plagiarism and cheating on tests.[65] Although some students justify their dishonesty by stating that morality is relative, the majority acknowledge that what they did was wrong. So why did they cheat? Because most of them regard good grades and/or getting into a reputable graduate school as more important than honesty.

The motivation to behave morally is intimately tied in with how we define ourselves. Social reformers such as Martin Luther King Jr. and Henry David Thoreau were highly motivated morally. Socrates also made it clear, during his trial, that doing the right thing was more important to him than any nonmoral values such as money, reputation, or even life itself. Unlike these men, though, most people allow themselves to be defined by others. People who define themselves primarily in terms of their social/economic status, academic accomplishments, or popularity with their peers may fail to act morally, even when they know what is right and are sensitive to the suffering of others.

Men pride themselves that they have a kind heart because they wish that every one might be happy; but merely to wish is not the sign of a kind heart; we are kind-hearted only in so far as we actually contribute to the happiness of others: that alone betokens a kind heart.

—IMMANUEL KANT, *Lectures on Ethics* (1775-1780)

Group mores can also weaken our motivation to do what we know is right because group behavior is more often motivated by nonmoral values than is individual behavior. Social activist and theologian Reinhold Niebuhr (1892– 1971) wrote the following about the My Lai massacre during the Vietnam War:

> . . . individual American soldiers murdered non-combatant women and children. They did so, not primarily because their moral judgment that such action was morally right was immature, or because, as individuals, they were "sick" in some sense, but because they participated in what was essentially a group action taken on the basis of group norms. . . . In short, the My Lai massacre was more a function of the group "moral atmosphere" that prevailed in that place at that time than of the stage of moral development [reasoning] of the individuals present.[66]

Similarly, Lynndie England at her court martial for charges related to the 2004 Abu Ghraib prison abuse scandal stated in her defense: "I chose to do what my friends wanted me to."[67] Her plea was rejected by the judge.

People who are highly motivated morally are more likely to act on their beliefs about what is right. Dentists who score high on a measure of moral motivation, for example, are far more likely than other dentists to treat a patient who has tested positive for HIV and to agree that the profession has a responsibility to treat patients known to be infected with other blood-borne diseases.[68]

Improvement in this component of morality involves knowing how to recognize different types of values—moral and nonmoral. Practice in exercising our moral judgment can strengthen moral motivation. Moral motivation can also be enhanced by meeting role models who are happy and successful and concerned about moral issues, as "active moral agents in a wider social world."[69]

Moral Character

The last component of moral behavior is **moral character**. Moral character is related to integrity. A person of high moral character has integrated the other three components of moral behavior into his or her personality. Moral character predisposes us to act morally. It includes personality traits such as ego strength, high self-esteem, courage, assertiveness, perseverance, and strength of convictions.[70] During World War II, when the Nazis first introduced the idea of requiring Jews to wear the yellow star of David, the king of Denmark, a man of high principles, announced that he would be the first to wear one. The people of Denmark quickly followed suit. Without the cooperation of the Danish people, the Nazis were unable to tell which of the Danes were Jews and which were non-Jews, thus making deportation of Jews almost impossible. Indeed, it was said that Nazi officials who had lived in Denmark for years were noticeably affected by this experience and could no longer be trusted to carry out Nazi policy.

The moral courage and fortitude of Tibet's exiled Dalai Lama (b. 1935) has held his country together during the more than fifty years of Chinese occupation.

Dalai Lama
©Panom/Shutterstock

Rather than losing heart or resorting to violence, he has sought dialogue with China's leaders. Instead of demanding political independence, the Dalai Lama, as a person of high moral character, places a higher value on preserving the moral integrity of his people and feels concern for all people everywhere, even those who are oppressing him. In 1989, the Dalai Lama was the recipient of the Nobel Peace Prize. In 2006 the U.S. Congress voted to award the Dalai Lama the Congressional Gold Medal, the nation's highest civilian honor, in recognition of his advocacy of religious harmony, nonviolence, and human rights throughout the world.

[The Dalai Lama] has used human compassion, courage and conviction as his tools in carving a path for peace....In doing so, he has been a shining light to all those fighting for freedom around the world.

–Senator Dianne Feinstein, co-sponsor of the bill to award the

Congressional Gold Medal to the Dalai Lama (2006)

People who have strong moral character are better at regulating their own behavior and are less likely to be distracted by short-term rewards. They will persevere in accomplishing their goals, even in the face of strong pressures to do otherwise. People who are deficient in moral character, on the other hand, are easily distracted and cannot be depended upon. Because they lack the courage of their convictions, they are liable to back down when the going gets rough.

Moral sensitivity, moral reasoning, moral motivation, and moral character all have an important influence on our moral behavior. These four components do not work independently of one another. Rather, they "comprise a *logical* analysis of what it takes to behave morally."[71] The failure to act morally can occur because of a deficiency in any one of these components.

Exercises

1. If morality is simply a matter of personal feeling, a person who is morally insensitive will have fewer moral obligations to others than a person who is morally sensitive. If a person does not feel bad about harming another person, or even realize he or she is causing the other person to suffer, did that person do anything morally wrong? Is insensitivity a legitimate reason for excusing such behavior? Relate your answer to experiences you have had with people who were lacking in moral sensitivity.

2. People who make offensive comments are sometimes unaware of the effects of their comments on others. Break up into groups and choose one of the following scenarios. Discuss ways in which we might tactfully and sensitively point out someone's insensitive behavior.

   a. You are at a party when someone makes a joke that is racist (or sexist or homophobic).

   b. You're feeling depressed because your beloved dog just died and you don't feel up to going out to a party with your roommate. When you tell your roommate, he rolls his eyes and says in an annoyed tone, "Get over it; it's just a dog."

   c. A student in your calculus class is having trouble understanding an assignment. She asks the professor to explain the assignment. He replies that she shouldn't worry her pretty little head about such matters but should instead ask one of the men in the class to help her with her homework.

3. Moral tragedies occur because people are deficient in at least one of the components of moral behavior. Think of a time when you made a moral decision that you later came to regret. How did a deficiency in one (or more) of the four components contribute to your poor decision?

4. You are taking an exam when you notice that the student beside you, who is pretending to check an e-mail message, is actually reading her class notes on her cell phone. The teacher has not noticed what is happening. What should you do? Analyze the other student's behavior as well as your response in light of the four components of moral behavior.

5. David Callahan, author of *The Cheating Culture*, writes, "The rational incentives to cheat for college students have grown dramatically, even as the strength of character needed to resist those temptations has weakened somewhat."[72] What steps might be taken to make it easier for college students to engage in moral behavior when they face the temptation to cheat? Support your answer using specific examples.

6. Discuss your own moral development in light of the four components of moral behavior. Illustrate each component using specific examples. Which components are the strongest and which are the weakest? What can you do to strengthen the weaker components?

*7. Has your community service work contributed to the development of any of the four components of moral behavior? Illustrate your answer with specific examples from your community service.

Moral Maturity: Moving Beyond Ethical Relativism

One day we will learn that the heart can never be totally right if the head is totally wrong. Only through the bringing together of head and heart—intelligence and goodness— shall man rise to a fulfillment of his true nature. . . .

—MARTIN LUTHER KING JR., *The Strength to Love* (1963), p. 45

Why should we be concerned about our moral development? If we are happy with the way we are, what is wrong with staying in the conventional stage of moral reasoning? After all, the American norm—the American way of life—has served most of us well so far.

The problem with being a cultural relativist or conventional moral reasoner is that, when cultural norms change, the cultural relativist—for better or for worse—just changes along with them. Most of us are convinced that something as horrendous as the Holocaust could never happen here, but Stanley Milgram's studies of obedience tell a different story. His study, described in Chapter 2, exposed the willingness of many, if not most, adults in the United States to uncritically follow the norms or commands of those in authority, even when they believed that they may have killed another person by doing so.[73]

Connections

What is the connection between stage of moral development and obedience to authority? *See Chapter 2, page 31.*

Moral development involves more than just improving our moral reasoning and logic skills. In Milgram's study, most of the subjects who continued to deliver the shocks realized what they were doing was wrong. However, they were insufficiently motivated to act on their moral beliefs and/or lacked enough empathy for the apparent suffering of the subject receiving the shocks.

Our moral development, how we interact with others, and our self-actualization are all intimately connected. The higher our level of moral development, the more consistent our behavior will be with our beliefs and our conscience. Morally good people not only sympathize with those who are suffering but, when feasible, take active steps to alleviate that suffering and to restore justice and a sense of community. They are willing to speak out on behalf of themselves and others when they witness an injustice and will take effective and well-thought-out action to correct that injustice.

Moral maturity involves overcoming resistance and rigidity in one's thinking and one's perception of the world. The ability to be flexible in our thinking involves both the recognition that there is more than one way to approach a given problem and the ability to effectively integrate the various components of moral development. In the next section, we are going to examine three different theories that claim morality is relative. While each of these theories is flawed, it is important that we understand them since moral maturity requires that we first reject these lower, relativist stages before we can move on to a higher stage.

Exercises

1. Briefly describe your character or personality. Now describe yourself as the person you would like to be. Compare the two descriptions. Which description of you has the stronger moral character? What steps can you take to strengthen your moral character?

2. Has your college experience enhanced your moral development? If so, discuss what experiences have had both positive and negative impacts on your moral development.

*3. How do public figures who have reached a high stage of moral reasoning affect the moral development of others in their culture? Are there any public figures, or people you have met through your community service work, that you admire as highly moral people? Discuss the influence, if any, these people have had on your own moral development.

Summary

1. *Conscience* provides knowledge about right and wrong, motivates us to do what is right, and demands that we act in accord with it.

2. There are three main forces that shape our conscience: heredity, learning or environmental factors, and conscious moral direction.

3. Heredity or biological factors include natural virtues such as sympathy and a sense of justice. The frontal lobes of the brain appear to play a critical role in conscience.

4. Learning or environmental factors that shape our conscience include our cultural norms, our family, and our experiences. Cultural relativists, behaviorists, and Freudians maintain that morality is the result of environmental forces.

5. Conscious moral direction involves active deliberation and accepting responsibility for our moral decisions. Most philosophers contend that the development of conscious moral direction is necessary for becoming a truly moral person and a person of integrity.

6. Conscience involves both *moral sentiments* and *reason.*

7. The *affective* element of conscience includes moral sentiments or feelings such as sympathy, "helper's high," moral outrage, and guilt.

8. The *cognitive* element of conscience involves making rational moral judgments.

9. The affective and cognitive elements of the conscience work together.

10. Jean Piaget noted that children go through distinct stages of moral development. The first stage he labeled the stage of heteronomy. The second stage he called the stage of autonomy.

11. The cognitive-development approach to moral development is based on the following assumptions and findings:

- Certain concepts, such as moral excellence, are fundamental to all humans.
- Humans have an intrinsic potential and drive to grow from lower to higher stages of moral development.
- Each stage of moral development involves a structurally different mode, or paradigm, for making moral decisions.
- Stages of moral development are universal and transcultural.
- People progress through the stages sequentially; they do not skip stages.
- Gains made in moral development tend to be retained.
- People tend to prefer the highest stage of moral development that is conceptually available to them.
- It is more desirable to reason at a higher stage.

12. Lawrence Kohlberg identifies three levels of moral development, each having two stages. The preconventional level includes punishment and obedience and the egoist stages; the conventional level includes the good boy/nice girl and the culture-maintaining stages; the postconventional level includes social contract reasoning and principled moral reasoning. Only about 10 percent of U.S. adults ever reach the postconventional stage of moral reasoning.

13. Although college tends to move students into a higher stage of moral reasoning, most college students do not successfully make the transition into the postconventional stage.

14. Culture and profession have an impact on one's level of moral reasoning.

15. Carol Gilligan argues that women, in general, are more likely to use a *care perspective* and that men are more likely to use a *justice perspective* in their moral reasoning.

16. Gilligan postulates three stages of moral reasoning: preconventional or self-centered, conventional or self-sacrificing, and postconventional or mature care ethics.

17. Gilligan and Kohlberg later came to agree that moral maturity involves a synthesis of both care and justice perspectives.

18. James Rest identifies four components of moral behavior:

- *Moral sensitivity* is the awareness of how our actions affect others.
- *Moral reasoning* or judgment involves the ability to make critical judgments regarding moral values and various courses of action.
- *Moral motivation* entails placing moral values above competing nonmoral values.
- *Moral character* involves having certain personality traits, such as courage, perseverance, and high self-esteem, that predispose us to act morally.

19. Working on our moral development is important because, otherwise, we are likely to simply follow cultural norms, even when they are destructive.

Notes

1. This case is from James Rest, *Defining Issues Test*, University of Minnesota, 1979.
2. From Kant's unpublished handbook to his lectures on ethics, as quoted by Martin Buber in *Between Man and Man* (New York: Macmillan, 1965), p. 119.
3. For the above case, the basis of each decision is: (a) maintain norms (conventional), (b) appeal to personal interests (preconventional), (c) appeal to moral ideals and principles (postconventional), (d) maintaining norms (conventional), (e) appeal to personal interests (preconventional), (f) appeal to moral ideals and principles (postconventional), and (g) appeal to peer norms (conventional).
4. Maqsood Jafri, "Islamic Concept of Conscience," Islamic Research Foundation International, Inc., www.irfi.org.
5. Eleventh-century scholar Bahya ben Joseph ibn Paquda, as quoted in Daniel Bonevac, William Boon, and Stephen Phillips, *Beyond the Western Tradition* (Mountain View, CA: Mayfield, 1992), p. 107.
6. Quoted in Bonevac, Boon, and Phillips, *Beyond the Western Tradition*, p. 29.
7. Immanuel Kant, *The Moral Law: Groundwork of the Metaphysic of Morals*, trans. H. J. Paton (New York: Routledge & Kegan Paul, 1991), pp. 60–61.
8. Plato, *Republic* 3, trans. G. M. A. Grube (Indianapolis, IN: Hackett, 1992), p. 410a.
9. Friedrich Nietzsche, *Beyond Good and Evil*, trans. R. J. Hollingdale (New York: Penguin, 1990), pp. 120–121.
10. James A Wilson, *The Moral Sense* (New York: Free Press Paperbacks, 1993), p. 130.
11. Robert Katz, *Empathy: Its Nature and Uses* (New York: Free Press, 1963), p. 11.
12. Martin L. Hoffman, "The Contribution of Empathy to Justice and Moral Judgment," in *Empathy and Its Development*, ed. Nancy Eisenberg and Janet Strayer (New York: Cambridge University Press, 1987), pp. 47–80.
13. Nancy Eisenberg and Paul A. Mussen, *The Roots of Prosocial Behavior in Children* (Cambridge, England: Cambridge University Press, 1989).
14. Sarah A. Tooley, *The Life of Florence Nightingale* (New York: Macmillan, 1905), pp. 39–40.
15. Frederick Douglass, *Life and Times of Frederick Douglass* (New York: Citadel Press, 1984).
16. For more on sociopaths, see Robert D. Hare, *Without a Conscience* (New York: Guildford Press, 1993), or Martha Stout, *The Sociopath Next Door* (New York: Broadway Books, 2005).
17. Patricia B. Sutker, C. E. Moan, and Albert N. Allain, "Assessment of Cognitive Control in Psychopathic and Normal Prisoners," *Journal of Behavioral Assessment* 5 (1983): 275–287.
18. Ian Krajbich, Ralph Adolphs, Daniel Tranel, Natalie L. Denburg, and Colin F. Camerer, "Economic Games Quantify Diminished Sense of Guilt in Patients with Damage to the Prefrontal Cortex," *The Journal of Neuroscience*, 29, no. 7 (February 18, 2009): 2188–2192.
19. Hanna Damasio et al., "The Return of Phineas Gage: Clues about the Brain from the Skull of a Famous Patient," *Science* 264 (May 1994): 1103–1105.
20. Fox Butterfield, *All God's Children* (New York: Knopf, 1995).
21. Friedrich Nietzsche, "Letters," *The Portable Nietzsche*, trans. William Kaufman (New York: Penguin, 1954), p. 442.
22. Alan Dershowitz, *The Abuse Excuse* (Boston, MA: Little, Brown, 1994).
23. Hillary Rodham Clinton, *It Takes a Village and Other Lessons Children Teach Us* (New York: Simon & Schuster, 1996). Excerpted in *Newsweek*, January 15, 1996, p. 33.
24. James Q. Wilson, *The Moral Sense* (New York: Free Press, 1993), p. 32.
25. Plato, *Republic 2.*
26. Nel Noddings, *Caring: A Feminine Approach to Ethics and Moral Education* (Berkeley: University of California Press, 1984).

27. Sogyal Rinpoche, *The Tibetan Book of Living and Dying* (San Francisco, CA: HarperCollins 1992), p. 94.
28. Hans Seyle, *The Stress of Life* (New York: McGraw-Hill, 1956).
29. Jeffrie Murphy, "Forgiveness and Resentment," in *Minnesota Studies in Philosophy: Social and Political Philosophy*, vol. 7, ed. Peter A. French, Theodore E. Uehling Jr., and Howard K. Wettstein (Minneapolis: University of Minnesota Press, 1982), p. 507.
30. Max Scheler, *Ressentiment*, ed. Lewis A. Coser, trans. William W. Holdheim (New York: Free Press, 1969), pp. 45–46.
31. Lewis Okun, *Woman Abuse* (Albany, NY: SUNY Press, 1986), p. 59. See also Lenore E. Walker, *The Battered Woman Syndrome* (New York: Springer-Verlag, 1984).
32. Tamara J. Ferguson, Hedy Stegge, and Ilse Damhuis, "Children's Understanding of Guilt and Shame," *Child Development* 62, no. 4 (1991): 827–839.
33. For more on this topic, read William Damon, *Greater Expectations* (New York: Free Press, 1995); Jerome Kagan and S. Lamb, eds., *The Emergence of Moral Concepts in Young Children* (Chicago, IL: University of Chicago Press, 1987); E. H. Erikson, *Childhood and Society* (New York: Norton, 1950); William Damon, *The Moral Child* (New York: Free Press, 1988); and Jean Piaget, *The Moral Judgment of Children* (London: Routledge & Kegan Paul, 1932).
34. "Feeling Guilty May Even Be Good for You," *Providence Sunday Journal*, May 15, 1994, p. D4.
35. James Q. Wilson, *The Moral Sense* (New York: Free Press, 1993), pp. 104–105.
36. Damon, *The Moral Child*, p. 36.
37. Richard L. Lee, *The !Kung San: Men, Women and Work in a Foraging Society* (Cambridge, MA: Harvard University Press, 1979).
38. Piaget, *The Moral Judgment*, p. 171.
39. Elliot Turiel, "Conflict and Transition in Adolescent Moral Development," *Child Development* 45 (1974): 15.
40. Lawrence Kohlberg, *Essays in Moral Development, Vol. II. The Psychology of Moral Development* (San Francisco, CA: Harper & Row, 1984).
41. James Rest, Elliot Turiel, and Lawrence Kohlberg, "Level of Moral Development as a Determinant of Preference and Comprehension of Moral Judgment Made by Others," *Journal of Personality* 37 (1969): 738–748.
42. David Wallechinsky, "How One Woman Became the Voice of Her People," *Parade Magazine*, January 19, 1997, p. 5.
43. James Rest, "Research on Moral Development: Implications for Training Counseling Psychologists," *The Counseling Psychologist* 12, no. 2 (1984): 19–29.
44. T. M. Kitwood, *Concern for Others: A New Psychology of Conscience and Morality* (London: Routledge & Kegan Paul, 1990), pp. 146–147.
45. Lawrence Kohlberg, P. Scharf, and J. Hickey, "The Justice Structure of the Prison: A Theory and Intervention," *Prison Journal* 51 (1972): 3–14.
46. N. Sanford, ed., *College and Character* (New York: Wiley, 1964).
47. Dwight R. Boyd, "The Condition of Sophomoritis and Its Educational Cure," *Journal of Moral Education* 10, no. 1 (1980): 24–39.
48. James R. Rest and Darcia Narváez, eds., *Moral Development in the Professions: Psychology and Applied Ethics* (Hillsdale, NJ: Erlbaum, 1994).
49. Carol Gilligan, *In a Different Voice: Psychological Theory and Women's Development* (Cambridge, MA: Harvard university Press, 1993).
50. Norma Haan, *On Moral Grounds: The Search for Practical Morality* (New York: New York University Press, 1985). See also L. Walker, "Experiential and Cognitive Sources of Moral Development in Adulthood," *Human Development* 12 (1986): 113–124.
51. Lisa Leghorn and Mary Roodkowsky, *Who Really Starves? Women and World Hunger* (New York: Friendship Press, 1977).
52. Quoted in Carol Gilligan, *In a Different Voice* (Cambridge, MA: Harvard University Press, 1982), p. 129.
53. Amy Tan, *The Joy Luck Club* (New York: Putnam's, 1989), pp. 119–120.
54. See G. R. Donenberg and L. Hoffman, "Gender Differences in Moral Development," *Sex Roles* 18, nos. 11–12 (1988): 701–717; Carol Gilligan and Jane Attanucci, "Two Moral Orientations," *Merrill-Palmer Quarterly* 34, no. 3 (1988): 223–237; Nancy Stiller and Linda Forrest,

"An Extension of Gilligan and Lyon's Investigation of Morality: Gender Differences in College Students," *Journal of College Student Development* 31, no. 1 (1990): 54–63; Gunnar Jorgensen, "Kohlberg and Gilligan: Duet or Duo?" *Journal of Moral Education* 35, no. 2 (June 2006): 179–196; and Mohammad J. Abdolmohammadi and C. Richard Baker, "The Relationship between Moral Reasoning and Plagiarism in Accounting Courses: A Replication Study," *Issues in Accounting Education* 22, no. 1 (2007): 45–55.

55. See B. Sichel, "Women's Moral Development in Search of Philosophical Assumptions," *Journal of Moral Education* 14, no. 3 (1985): 149–161.

56. Gilligan and Attanucci, "Two Moral Orientations," p. 225.

57. R. Blotner and D. J. Bearison, "Developmental Consistencies in Socio-Moral Knowledge: Justice Reasoning and Altruistic Behavior," *Merrill-Palmer Quarterly* 30, no. 4 (October 1984): 349–357.

58. Augusto Blasi, "Moral Cognition and Moral Action: A Theoretical Perspective," *Developmental Review* 3 (1983): 178–210.

59. Jean Decety, Kalina J. Michalska, and Katherine D. Kinzler, "The Developmental Neuroscience of Moral Sensitivity," *Emotional Review* 3, no. 3 (July 2011): 305–307.

60. Beth Teitell, "Feeling Guilty? Good!" *Boston Sunday Herald*, March 13, 1994, pp. 1, 14.

61. Anne C. Levy, "The Anita Hill-Clarence Thomas Hearings," *Wisconsin Law Review* 1106 (1991).

62. A. F. Smith, "Lawrence Kohlberg's Cognitive Stage Theory of the Development of Moral Judgment," *New Directions for Student Services* 4 (1978): 53–67.

63. James Rest, "Background: Theory and Research," in *Moral Development in the Professions*, ed. Rest and Narváez, (Lawrence Erlbaum Associates Publishers, Hillsdale, NJ, 1994), p. 15.

64. James Rest, *Advances in Research and Theory* (New York: Praeger, 1986).

65. Jonathan D. Glater, "Colleges Chase as Cheats Shift to Higher Tech," *New York Times*, May 18, 2006, p. Al.

66. A. Higgins, C. Power, and Lawrence Kohlberg, "The Relationship of Moral Atmosphere to Judgments of Responsibility," in *Morality, Moral Behaviour and Moral Development*, ed. W. M. Kurtines and J. L. Gewitz (New York: Wiley, 1984), p. 75.

67. "Perspectives," *Newsweek*, January 2, 2006, p. 117.

68. Muriel J. Bebeau, "Influencing the Moral Dimensions of Dental Practice," in *Moral Development in the Professions*, ed. Rest and Narváez, (Lawrence Erlbaum Associates Publishers, Hillsdale, NJ, 1994), pp. 121–146.

69. Rest, "Research on Moral Development," p. 26.

70. Barbara Panzl and Timothy McMahon, "Ethical Decision Making: Developmental Theory and Practice," speech delivered at the National Association of Student Personnel Administrators, Denver, March 1989.

71. James R. Rest, "Theory and Research," in *Moral Development in the Professions*, ed. Rest and Narváez, (Lawrence Erlbaum Associates Publishers, Hillsdale, NJ, 1994), p. 24.

72. David Callahan, *The Cheating Culture: Why Americans Are Doing Wrong to Get Ahead* (New York: Harcourt, 2004).

73. Stanley Milgram, *Obedience to Authority* (New York: Harper & Row, 1974), p. 6.

---

*Stages for the Self-Evaluation Questionnaire on page 73:

a) Conventional, b) Preconventional, c) Conventional, d) Preconventional, e) Conventional, f) Postconventional, g) Conventional, h) Postconventional

Ethical Relativism

Except for those rare individuals who have led a completely cloistered life, we have all experienced moral disagreement in some form or another, whether on a personal or a cultural level. You may believe in abortion rights; your best friend may be pro-life. The majority of people in the United States are in favor of capital punishment, yet capital punishment is considered immoral in just about every other Western nation. Why the disagreement? Who is right and who is wrong?

Our inquiry will begin with a look at **ethical relativism**. According to ethical relativists, ethical values are created by, or are relative to, the people who hold the beliefs. Chapter 4 examines ethical subjectivism, also known as individual relativism. This theory states that morality is simply the expression of individual opinions or feelings. Chapter 5 briefly examines the divine command theory and American civil religion.

Finally, we'll be studying cultural relativism. According to cultural relativists, societal norms, rather than the opinions of isolated individuals, form the basis of morality. Because most American adults subscribe to cultural relativism, we'll be spending a large part of this section on this theory. Moral theories do not exist in isolation. Each of these theories has broad implications not only for how we define morality but also for how we define moral community and, consequently, how we treat one another.

The relativist theories contain several weaknesses and logical inconsistencies. Being able to recognize the problems with these theories enables us to put them behind us and move on to the theories, which we'll be covering in Section III, that provide better guidance in making satisfactory moral decisions.

CHAPTER 4

Ethical Subjectivism
Morality Is Just a Matter of Personal Feeling

Morality is a private choice.
   —CRAIG PRICE (convicted serial killer)

Ryan, a college sophomore, has just found out in the course of giving blood to the Red Cross that he is HIV positive—that is, he is infected with the AIDS virus. Naturally, he is upset as a result of this news. Sarah, a classmate who has a crush on Ryan, notices that he is feeling down; after class, she tells him that her parents are out of town and invites him over to her house—for the night if he wishes. Ryan does not want to be alone tonight and would find spending it with Sarah greatly comforting. They have not had a sexual relationship yet. Ryan has not told Sarah about the results of his blood test, nor does he intend to. Furthermore, he has no intention of using a condom, since he feels that it interferes with the pleasure of the act.

That afternoon Ryan tells you, his friend, of his test results and of Sarah's invitation to spend the night at her house. When you express concern that he is putting Sarah at risk for contracting HIV, he accuses you of trying to force your morals on him. "Moral judgments," Ryan says, "are purely subjective—a private choice. It's up to each individual to decide what personally feels good or right for him. And spending the night with Sarah feels right for me."

About one in four students will contract an STD in college. Many withhold their STD status from others, including potential partners.[1] Should informing a partner be a private, personal choice as Ryan claims? Or, are there moral considerations beyond what a person feels is right for him or her?

In this chapter, we'll be studying a theory known as ethical subjectivism. We'll end by examining some of the harmful implications of this "to each his own" philosophy when it comes to making real-life moral decisions and policy.

What Is Ethical Subjectivism?

Ethical subjectivism, also known as **individual relativism**, makes the claim that people can *never* be mistaken about what is morally right or wrong because there are no objective or universal moral standards or truths; instead, there are only opinions. An **opinion** expresses what a person believes. It does not have to be backed up by reasons or facts. What is right or wrong for one particular individual is a matter of personal taste, rather like our preference for particular foods or music. What is right for you may be wrong for another depending on each of your respective feelings or opinions. I may like broccoli; you might think it is quite disgusting. Along similar lines, you may feel that you should inform a sexual partner if you are HIV positive. Ryan's preference is not to say anything. No one is right or wrong; it's all a matter of personal opinion.

Do not confuse ethical subjectivism with the obviously true and therefore trivial statement that "whatever a person believes is right for him or her is what that person believes is right for him or her." Subjectivism goes beyond this by claiming that sincerely believing or feeling that something is right *makes* it right (or true) for that person.

Using the Buddhist analogy of the blind men and the elephant, in which each blind man comes up with a different and seemingly incompatible description of the elephant (see image on page 117), the ethical subjectivist would conclude that there is no such animal as an elephant. The "elephant," instead, is simply a creation of each person's imagination or feelings. "Elephant" is whatever you believe it to be—a winnowing basket, a granary, a post, a plow pole, or perhaps a column.

Now just as an "elephantness subjectivist" might argue that there are no objective standards by which to judge or make sense of the various descriptions of the elephant, so too do ethical subjectivists argue that there are no absolute standards by which to judge a person's moral preferences. If a person sincerely believes something to be morally correct for him or her, then this in itself causes it to be morally true.

For example, no one could rightfully accuse former Louisiana state senator and white supremacist David Duke of being insincere. As a defender of the Nazi ideology, Duke has expressed admiration for Nazi war criminals Rudolf Hess and Dr. Josef Mengele who performed experiments on twins at Auschwitz. As a member of the Ku Klux Klan (KKK), Duke also believes that blacks have "inherited tendencies . . . to act in anti-social ways." Not surprisingly, Duke opposed Obama's presidential candidacy referring to Obama as an anti-White, black racist.[2] It is irrelevant whether Duke can support his claim. What is important to an ethical subjectivist is simply that he personally believes something to be true. Political analyst George Will writes that, as a true believer, "his [Duke's] reputation is supposedly redeemed, at least a little bit, by 'sincerity,' considered inherently virtuous in an age so committed to subjectivism that it firmly believes only in believing."[3] David Duke ran for U.S. Senate in 2016 on the promise to defend the rights of European Americans. He lost the election.

The great majority of moral philosophers disagree with ethical subjectivism. They maintain that there are fundamental moral standards by which we can judge people like David Duke and our friend Ryan from the opening scenario. Philosopher Renford Bambrough, for example, claims that almost all of us would agree that it would be immoral to perform a painful operation on a small child without an anesthetic because we intuitively know that torturing children is wrong. There is no need to prove to someone that torturing children is wrong; it is self-evident.

IT'S AN ELEPHANT!!

In the Buddhist fable of the blind men and the elephant, each of the blind men came up with a different and incompatible description of an elephant. When considering differences in people's beliefs about morality, can we conclude that there is no objective elephant that exists independently of people's opinions about it?

Now, an ethical subjectivist would disagree with Bambrough's position. If Dr. Josef Mengele felt good about seeing Jewish children in extreme pain, operating without an anesthetic would then be the morally correct action for him and for other surgeons with similar feelings. Similarly, persecuting Jews and Blacks is the morally correct action for Duke because he believes it is right. In fact, if we want to carry ethical subjectivism to its logical conclusion, it may even be immoral for Duke to *refrain* from doing so.

In his reading at the end of this chapter, James Rachels uses the contemporary issue of homosexuality to explore the implications of ethical subjectivism. He concludes that, if we accept ethical subjectivism, a person who says homosexuality is morally wrong is not stating an objective fact about the morality of homosexuality but is simply expressing his or her feelings about it.

The statements "it is good to torture children," "homosexuality is immoral," and "it is right to persecute Jews and Blacks" are no different to ethical subjectivists than statements such as "I enjoy walking on the beach." Therefore, it makes no more sense to use reason to convince someone who feels that it is right to torture children that he does not actually enjoy torturing children than it does to try to convince our beachcomber that she does not enjoy walking on the beach.

Similarly, if Rutgers student Dharun Ravi*, whose gay roommate Tyler Clementi committed suicide after discovering that Ravi had videotaped him during a sexual encounter with another man, felt like videotaping and taunting

Connections

What is moral sensitivity and is the concept compatible with ethical subjectivism? *See Chapter 3, pages 99-101.*

*See *Analyzing Images*, Chapter 3, page 100.

Clementi, then he was perfectly in his rights to do so. The fact that Clementi committed suicide is irrelevant when it comes to determining the morality of Ravi's actions. The only relevant criteria was did Ravi feel what he did was morally justified? Personal tastes or feelings are the only standard. If it feels right, do it. There are no universal moral truths, only individual moral preferences or truths based on each person's own opinion and feelings.

Exercises

1. Are there moral truths such as it is wrong to torture children that do not require proof? Are there any other self-evident moral truths? If these moral truths are self-evident, how would you respond to someone who believes that it is morally acceptable to torture children or to treat other humans as morally inferior or even indispensable, as in the case of the Jews in Nazi Germany?

2. Khalil Sumpter, a high school sophomore in Brooklyn, New York, was afraid that two other students were planning to beat him up. These two students, Ian, a senior, and Tyrone, a junior, had had a falling-out with Khalil that had escalated into picking on Khalil and making threats against him. So, Khalil brought a .38 caliber pistol to school one morning, and he shot and killed both Ian and Tyrone at point-blank range in the school hallway.[4]

   Discuss whether this shooting was morally justified. Would it have made a difference if Khalil had shot Ian and Tyrone simply because he felt like it or because he didn't like the way they dressed? Discuss how an ethical subjectivist might respond to this case.

3. Discuss what you might have said to Ravi had he offered to share the video of his roommate with you. Discuss also how an ethical subjectivist would have responded and why. Are you satisfied with the response of the ethical subjectivist? Explain.

4. Make a list of general guidelines that you use to make moral decisions, including those you used to determine the morality of Khalil Sumpter's actions in the previous exercise. Where did you get these guidelines? How relevant were your personal feelings in coming up with these guidelines?

What Ethical Subjectivism Is Not

> *What we mainly need to notice here is that this exaltation of individual freedom apparently is itself a moral judgement, and that the arguments supporting it are moral arguments.*
>
> —MARY MIDGLEY, *Can't We Make Moral Judgements?* (1993), p. 17

Ethical subjectivism is a relatively straightforward theory, but despite its simplicity, it is often confused with other positions—a confusion that may account for its popularity among some people.

In his article "Student Relativism" at the end of this chapter, Stephen Satris argues that the relativism of most college students is not intended as a philosophical theory but rather as an "invincible suit of armor" to "prevent or close off dialogue and thought." In other words, the ethical subjectivism that is being promulgated by many students serves primarily as a type of resistance or immature defense mechanism rather than as a serious moral theory.

Tolerance: "Live and Let Live"

Many people confuse ethical subjectivism with an ethics of tolerance and respect for others' lifestyles—an ethics that is often summed up by the phrase "live and let live." Ethical subjectivism has been used, incorrectly, to support conclusions such as "People ought to tolerate (respect) other people's feelings and lifestyles." However, relativist premises cannot support a conclusion containing a universal moral principle. Consider the following two premises:

Premise 1: Individuals ought to do what feels right for them.

Premise 2: I feel that tolerance is right for me.

The conclusion "People ought to tolerate (respect) other people's feelings and lifestyles" does not follow from these two premises because it says more than is contained in the premises. The only conclusion that follows from these two premises is that "I ought to tolerate other people's feelings and lifestyles." We cannot conclude anything about what other people ought to do because premise 2 refers only to my feelings. If a person, such as a Nazi or a member of the al-Qaeda, does not want to be tolerant of others who are different, then this person has no moral obligation to tolerate others' opinions—or their existence, for that matter.

Tolerance is a universal moral principle. The statement "live and let live" implies a universal duty to respect others, regardless of how we personally feel toward them. According to ethical subjectivism, though, universal moral duties do not exist. If an ethical subjectivist does not feel that others are worthy of respect or simply dislikes them, then that person doesn't have to respect others or refrain from harming them.

Some people also confuse ethical subjectivism with the obviously true observation that individuals *do* hold different views about what is morally right and morally wrong. In the presence of moral disagreement, when asked if a particular person is right, some people will reply, "Well, they believe they are right." When people say this, they are changing the topic from what a person *ought* to do to what a person believes *is* the case—thus committing the fallacy of irrelevant conclusion.

Ethical subjectivism is a moral theory and, as such, it is prescriptive—that is, it is about what a person *ought* to do. The statement that a person believes something to be right, on the other hand, is descriptive. Ethical subjectivism, however, goes beyond the merely descriptive by claiming that sincerely believing or feeling that something is right *makes* it right (or true) for that person. By doing this, critics argue that ethical subjectivism fails to recognize the distinction between descriptive and prescriptive statements.

Connections

How can we distinguish a good argument from a poor argument? *See Chapter 2, pages 47–50.*

Connections

What is the difference between a descriptive and a prescriptive statement? *See Chapter 2, page 48.*

In July 2012, in one of the deadliest mass shootings in U.S. history, twenty-four-year-old James Holmes, a former graduate student in neuroscience, killed twelve and injured fifty-eight people at the midnight showing of the Batman movie, "The Dark Knight Rises," at a Colorado theater. ©Pool/Getty Images

Analyzing Images

1. Discuss what an ethical subjectivist would say about the morality of Holmes' actions. Support your answer.

2. Imagine that Holmes had come to you several days before the rampage and told you what he had planned. He said he felt good about doing it and asked you, as an ethics student, if that made it right and if he should go ahead with his plans. Discuss how you would respond to Holmes and why. Is your response consistent with ethical subjectivism? If not, explain on what grounds you disagree with the morality of his plan.

Moral Uncertainty

Ethical subjectivism is not the same as moral uncertainty. A friend may tell you that she saw the boyfriend of one of your mutual friends holding hands with another woman in a restaurant. What should she do? "Well," you reply, "there seems to be no clearly right answer to this." So, you advise your friend: "In this situation, do what you feel is right." But saying this does not necessarily mean that morality is relative. Rather, we are most likely to give this advice when we trust someone to make a morally acceptable decision. If your friend was wielding a gun and was on the verge of killing the seemingly unfaithful boyfriend, you probably would not tell her to do whatever feels right for her. Similarly, most people would not tell James Holmes (pictured above), who carried out a deadly shooting rampage in a Colorado theater, to do whatever felt right for him. Indeed, to do so could make us morally and perhaps legally complicit in the murders. In other words, don't confuse trusting someone's moral judgment in a particular situation with ethical subjectivism.

It is also logically inconsistent, as Rachels points out in his reading at the end of this chapter, to claim that morality is a matter of opinion in one case but not in another. If all moral values are a matter of individual preference, as the ethical subjectivist claims, then morality is relative in *all* situations.

Disagreement about moral values, in itself, does not imply that objective moral truths do not exist. Some scientists believe that there is a black hole at the center of every galaxy; others disagree. However, disagreement about black holes does not mean that *both* groups of scientists are correct in their claims. Similarly, the existence of disagreement about the morality of torturing children does not mean that both positions are morally correct.

Some people also confuse ethical subjectivism with the metaphysical position that humans have free will and are ultimately responsible for their own moral decisions. An ethical subjectivist does not necessarily believe that humans have free will, simply that a person's feelings and opinions are the source of moral truth. Indeed, moral responsibility, in terms of assigning moral blame or praise, becomes a moot issue with ethical subjectivists because there are no objective standards against which to measure the morality of a person's actions; ethical subjectivism therefore precludes passing judgment on other people's actions.

Ethical subjectivism is also sometimes mistaken for ethical skepticism or emotivism. There are, however, important differences among these three theories (Table 4.1). Both ethical skepticism and emotivism deny knowledge of

Connections

What is the distinction between an opinion and a fact? *See Chapter 1, page 8.*

Connections

What are the implications for moral responsibility of the free will versus determinism debate? *See Chapter 1, pages 19–20.*

TABLE 4.1 Summary of the Three Theories

	ETHICAL SKEPTICISM	EMOTIVISM	ETHICAL SUBJECTIVISM
Premises	People disagree about what is morally right and wrong.	People disagree about what is morally right and wrong.	People disagree about what is morally right and wrong.
	People do not agree on a set of objective standards for resolving moral differences.	People do not agree on a set of objective standards for resolving moral differences.	People do not agree on a set of objective standards for resolving moral differences.
	There is no convincing evidence that such moral standards exist.	There is no convincing evidence that such moral standards exist.	There is no convincing evidence that such moral standards exist.
		All moral statements are expressions of a person's feelings.	All moral statements are personal opinions.
		Opinions are neither true nor false.	Moral truths exist, but are not based on universal standards.
Conclusions	*Therefore:* We cannot know with certainty whether or not objective moral standards exist.	*Therefore:* All moral statements are meaningless.	*Therefore:* Individual feelings must provide the standard of moral truth.

moral truth. Ethical subjectivism, on the other hand, claims that there are moral truths but that these vary from person to person.

Ethical Skepticism

Ethical subjectivists and ethical skeptics accept different epistemological positions regarding moral knowledge. Ethical subjectivism states that we *can* know moral truths. **Ethical skepticism**, rather than denying the existence of universal moral principles, states that it is difficult, if not impossible, to know whether moral truths exist or what these truths are: Maybe there *are* universal moral standards, maybe not; we just don't know. Agnosticism, for example, is a type of religious skepticism. An agnostic believes that we have no way of knowing whether or not God exists. This uncertainty, however, does not imply that God does *not* exist; the most we can say is that we do not know. Similarly, an ethical skeptic maintains that the existence of moral truths cannot be proved. Ethical subjectivism, on the other hand, claims that universal moral truths do not exist but moral truths *do exist* for each individual.

Connections

What event contributed to emotivism falling out of favor among moral philosophers? *See Chapter 1, page 26.*

Emotivism

Emotivism goes beyond the uncertainty of ethical skepticism by stating that there are no moral truths. Because we cannot quantify or verify moral statements as we can scientific statements, emotivists conclude that there are no moral truths, only moral feelings or opinions. Like emotivism, ethical subjectivism also claims that morality is a matter of personal opinion; however, unlike emotivism (which denies the existence of moral facts), ethical subjectivism accepts as a premise that there *are* moral facts or truths. These moral facts, however, are based on each individual's feelings about a particular action or group of people.

Exercises

1. Mohandas Gandhi once wrote: "The golden rule of conduct, therefore, is mutual tolerance, seeing that we will never all think alike and we shall see Truth in fragments and from different angles of vision. Conscience is not the same thing for all. Whilst there, it is a good guide for individual conduct, imposition of that conduct upon all will be an insufferable interference with everybody's freedom of conscience."[5]

   How would an ethical subjectivist respond to Gandhi's words? Is Gandhi arguing from a position of ethical subjectivism or ethical objectivism? Support your answer.

2. Evaluate the different arguments put forth by ethical skepticism, emotivism, and ethical subjectivism (see Table 4.1). Discuss the strengths and weaknesses of

each of these three arguments. Are any of the premises questionable or weak? Are there any premises that you would add? Do fallacies exist in any of the arguments? If so, what are they?

*3. If you are doing or have done community service, what were your reasons for doing it? What do you do when you feel like not going to your site? Do you have a moral obligation not to turn up on those days? Discuss your answer in light of the theory of ethical subjectivism.

The Roots of Ethical Subjectivism in Romantic Sentimentalism

Nature made man happy and good, and society deprives him and makes him miserable.
—JEAN-JACQUES ROUSSEAU, *Émile* (1762), p. 253

Ethical subjectivism is, for the most part, a Western phenomenon and an outgrowth of the romantic sentimentalism that thrived from the late eighteenth through the mid-nineteenth century. Romantic sentimentalism, which emphasizes the inner person, is based upon the assumption that humans are by nature good. Unlike Enlightenment philosophers who regarded reason as the path to truth, romantic sentimentalists such as philosopher Jean-Jacques Rousseau believed in the "law of the heart." According to the law of the heart, we can discover true goodness by retreating to pure inner feelings. Only in this radical subjectivism does true moral goodness abide.

Connections

What was the Enlightenment period in Western philosophy? *See Chapter 10, page 312.*

Jean-Jacques Rousseau's Law of the Heart

Jean-Jacques Rousseau (1712–1778) was born in Geneva, Switzerland. His mother died when he was an infant. When Rousseau was ten, his father wounded a man in a duel, and fearful of being arrested, he fled Geneva, leaving his family behind. Despite these setbacks, Rousseau recalled his childhood as one of idyllic innocence, free of societal restraints. This recollection had a profound influence on the development of his moral philosophy.

Rousseau believed in the natural goodness of people and that virtue and society stand in opposition. In his book *Émile*, Rousseau argued that the negative influence of society that manipulates and thwarts nature could be remedied by early education. Education should be mainly concerned with removing the obstacles to a child's natural development and innate goodness. Feelings alone, Rousseau argued, not society or abstract principles, inform us of what is right and wrong. Society forces upon us masks of hypocrisy and deceit. The purpose of moral education, therefore, is not to train people to fit into society; rather, it is to help

*An asterisk in front of an exercise indicates that the exercise is appropriate for students who are doing community service learning as part of the course.

us remove these socially imposed masks to reveal the authentic openness and innocence that is our true essence. (For the complete text of Rousseau's *Emile*, go to www.ilt.columbia.edu/pedagogies/rousseau/Contents2.html)

Rousseau was not, strictly speaking, an ethical subjectivist. Even though he did believe that we can usually rely on our feelings for moral guidance, because humans are innately good, he also recognized that it is not feelings per se that are the ultimate source of morality as our natural goodness and feelings can be distorted by society. Nevertheless, Rousseau's romantic sentimentalism has been used to support ethical subjectivism.

Mary Wollstonecraft's Critique of Romantic Sentimentalism and Ethical Subjectivism

English philosopher Mary Wollstonecraft (1759-1797) wrote *A Vindication of the Rights of Woman* (1791) partly in response to Rousseau's belief that men and women are by nature different. (For the complete text, go to http://feminism.eserver.org/wollstonecraft-vindication.txt.) Wollstonecraft was an avid opponent of ethical subjectivism and disagreed with Rousseau's exaltation of feeling and sentiment over reason. Like men, she argued, women's "first duty is to themselves as rational creatures." Because of the prevailing belief that women lacked the capacity to reason, women were denied the educational opportunities to develop their intellectual potential.

Connections

Do men and women have different approaches to moral decision making? *See Chapter 3, pages 95-96.*

Wollstonecraft argued that men and women are intellectual and moral equals. Because women's nature is essentially the same as men's, Wollstonecraft advocated coeducation, a radical concept that was ridiculed by the male thinkers of her time. Furthermore, she maintained that to claim that there are two different moral systems—one for men and one for women—is to make a mockery of the concept of virtue. "How can women be just or generous, when they are the slaves of injustice?" she asked.[6] Moral truths, such as human equality, must therefore be the same for everyone.

Wollstonecraft argued that romantic sentimentalism, with its focus on inner feelings at the expense of reason, provides an incomplete description of morality. Moral development does not thrive on the free expression of opinions or feelings, as Rousseau claimed, but rather seems to flourish when our ideas and worldviews are challenged rather than uncritically affirmed. Our feelings or sentiments are often good guides for making moral decisions; however, they can sometimes lead us astray and contribute to bigotry and oppressive social structures. According to Wollstonecraft, because of this, our feelings and ideas about what is moral should also be held up to the light of reason.

Romantic Sentimentalism, Ethical Subjectivism, and Sociopathy

Romantic sentimentalism has failed partly because incorporating the "law of the heart" into a moral theory involves a contradiction. Like Rousseau, romantic sentimentalists expect others to share their sentiments. Rousseau seemed to believe that, with the proper upbringing, everyone will share the same moral sentiments, including sympathy, compassion, generosity, and forgiveness. This expectation involves doublethink, however. Given the obviously true observation that people do have different opinions about right and wrong, who are we to say that the feelings of those who disagree with us, even if they are influenced by social values, are any less valid for them than our feelings are for us?

Sociopaths feel no guilt at killing and may even feel pleasure in the control that comes from killing another person. During the 1970s, serial killer and one-time law student Ted Bundy brutally raped and murdered an estimated thirty to one hundred women, including several college students, before he was finally caught and put to death by the state of Florida in 1989. In the following statement purportedly made by Bundy to one of his surviving victims, Bundy uses ethical subjectivism to justify his actions.

Connections

What role does biology play in sociopathy? *See Chapter 3, page 78.*

> . . . then I learned that all moral judgments are "value judgments," that all value judgments are subjective, and that none can be proved to be either "right" or "wrong." . . . Nor is there any "reason" to obey the law for anyone, like myself, who has the boldness and daring—the strength of character—to throw off its shackles. . . . I discovered that to become truly free, truly unfettered, I had to become truly uninhibited. And I quickly discovered that the greatest obstacle to my freedom, the greatest block and limitation to it, consists in the insupportable "value judgment" that I was bound to respect the rights of others. I asked myself, who were these "others"? Other human beings, with human rights? Why is it more wrong to kill a human animal than any other animal, a pig or a sheep or a steer? Is your life more to you than a hog's life to a hog? Why should I be willing to sacrifice my pleasure more for the one than the other? Surely, you would not, in this age of scientific enlightenment, declare that God or nature has marked some pleasures as "moral" or "good" and others as "immoral" or "bad"? In any case, let me assure you, my dear young lady, that there is absolutely no comparison between the pleasure I might take in eating ham and the pleasure I anticipate in raping and murdering you. That is the honest conclusion to which my education has led me—after the most conscientious examination of my spontaneous and uninhibited self.[7]

Ethical subjectivism, by its very definition, cannot provide or even acknowledge universal moral standards, even those based on so-called natural moral sentiments, because it denies that universal moral standards exist. Instead, romantic ethical subjectivists are isolated in their own inner feelings—they are torn between the desire to see certain sentiments universalized and the contradiction involved in expecting people to acknowledge universal moral values.

Are Personal Feelings Alone a Reliable Moral Guide?

The belief that we are all good by nature but corrupted by society is called into question by the phenomenon of the sociopathic or antisocial personality.[8] Ironically, the sociopath, people such as Ted Bundy and Dr. Hannibal Lector, is perhaps the person who is most like Rousseau's "natural" person, as opposed

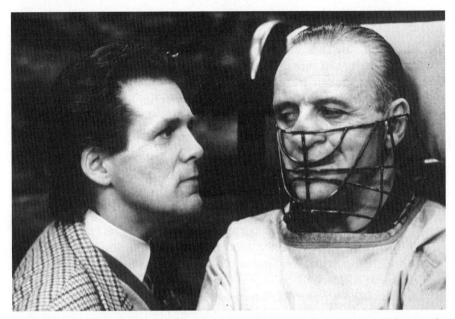

Dr. Hannibal "the Cannibal" Lector (played by Anthony Hopkins) with the prison psychologist in the 1991 movie The Silence of the Lambs. As a sociopath, Hannibal Lector exemplifies the ethical subjectivist—a person who listens only to his or her inner feelings without any regard for social norms.
©Orion/Kobal/REX/Shutterstock

Connections

How do reason and sentiment work together in making moral decisions? *See Chapter 3, pages 82–89; and Chapter 11, page 125.*

to someone who has been oversocialized and corrupted by society. Sociopaths seem oblivious to any attempts to indoctrinate them with social values. They have no concern for the social good or the welfare of others and experience no guilt if they hurt or even kill another human. Sociopaths are radically isolated, on a psychic level, from the rest of society; they listen only to their own inner feelings and have no desire that their feelings and beliefs be universalized as moral principles. Indeed, it is because of their consistent ethical subjectivism that sociopaths are so dangerous and socially disruptive.

Despite the logical inconsistencies in the assumptions underlying romantic sentimentalism, the theory should not be discarded wholesale. Its insistence on innate moral sentiments as the heart of morality, rather than abstract reasoning, provides a much-needed balance to the rationalism that dominates so much of Western ethics. Rousseau's idea that education should aim to nurture a person's natural moral development has also influenced theories of moral development.

Exercises

1. Discuss the statement purportedly made by Ted Bundy on page 125. How would you respond to Bundy's argument?

2. Martha Stout in her book *The Sociopath Next Door* notes that the prevalence of sociopathy, which is currently 4 percent, or one out of every twenty-five

people, is increasing in the American population. She conjectures that this is in part because our culture reinforces the me-first and self-serving behaviors associated with sociopathy.[9] Discuss how our educational system and culture might reinforce the types of justifications used by people such as Bundy.

3. Discuss Wollstonecraft's critique of Rousseau's romantic sentimentalism and her argument that moral education should be based on reason and universal moral principles rather than natural feelings.

4. What events in your childhood had the greatest influence on your moral development? Were these events part of your natural unfolding or did they come from outside ethics instruction and examples of moral behavior by parents, teachers, etc.? Explain.

The Kitty Genovese Syndrome

It is tempting to deny the existence of evil since denying it obviates the need to fight it.
—ALEXIS CARREL, *Reflections on Life*

Non-resistance to evil which takes the form of paying no attention to it is a way of promoting it.
—JOHN DEWEY, *Human Nature and Conduct* (1922)

Ethical theories do not exist in abstraction. Ethical theories inform and motivate our real-life decisions and actions. They shape the way we define ourselves, as well as our community and our ideas of community responsibility. In ethics education, romantic sentimentalism usually takes the form of the **values clarification** or value-neutral approach, where students are encouraged to express their opinions without fear of censorship or judgment. Values are considered something one clarifies rather than discovers. Moral truths are based on inner feelings rather than on a shared objective reality. Any opinion is just as valid as any other.

Unfortunately, this popular approach to moral education has been shown to have no effect on a student's actual moral development and, in fact, can even retard its development. Ethical subjectivism, by retreating into pure inner or subjective feelings, neglects to take into account the social context that gives moral sentiments their value in the first place. To remove morality from the social realm is to condone isolation and apathy in the face of others' pain.

Some social commentators believe that the prevalence of ethical subjectivism in our society may contribute to what has come to be known as the "Kitty Genovese syndrome." The Kitty Genovese syndrome is characterized by an attitude of moral indifference to another person's distress.

In 1964, twenty-eight-year-old Kitty Genovese was murdered outside her New York apartment building. Her killer left twice when other people in the building turned on their lights. Yet, during the half hour that elapsed during the attack, none of Kitty's neighbors, who heard her repeated cries for help, even bothered to call the police. The third time the killer returned to the scene, he finished her off.

Connections
What did those who studied the Genovese case conclude is our primary motivation when it comes to making moral decisions? *See Chapter 6, page 199.*

No one came to the aid of a seriously injured man lying in a busy street in Harford, Connecticut, after he was struck by a hit-and-run driver in May 2008. The victim, Angel Torres, later died from the injuries he sustained.
©Hartford Police Dept

Analyzing Images

1. Think of a time when you failed to come to someone's assistance, like the people in this photo, or failed to speak out against an injustice. How did you justify your failure to act? Discuss whether the failure to act in this case was morally justified. Support your answer. Discuss also how an ethical subjectivist would answer this question.

2. How did you react when you first saw this photograph? Relate your answer to the four components of moral development covered on pages 99–104. Discuss how an ethical subjectivist might try to explain the presence of moral sentiments, especially in those people who initially ignored the dying man but later came to regret their inaction.

In 1995, thirty-three-year-old Deletha Word jumped to her death from the Belle Isle Bridge in Detroit to escape her attacker—a nineteen-year-old man who savagely beat her after a fender bender accident. Dozens of spectators stood by and watched, some even cheering on the attacker. One man, who arrived at the scene just after Word had gone off the bridge, jumped into the river and tried, unsuccessfully, to save her. He later told a reporter that the crowd was "standing around like people taking an interest in sports."[10]

How would ethical subjectivists respond to these two preceding events? To be consistent, they would have to reply that, if the people in the crowds watching Genovese and Word being bludgeoned to death felt like simply standing around, then that was the right thing for them to do. Only personal feelings matter in ethical subjectivism. If Martell Welch, Word's attacker, felt that it was morally acceptable to beat another motorist to death for nicking a fender, then it was morally right, and perhaps even obligatory, for him to do so. As for the man who tried to save Word, of course this was the right thing for him to do, but it would have been wrong for the others.

With ethical subjectivism, there are no objective values regarding helping others or refraining from harming or even killing others. There are only individual opinions or feelings on the issue. Beating someone to death may be wrong for you, but it may be right for me. Calling the police may be right for you, but cheering on the assailant or ignoring a dying person's cries for help might be morally right for me. After all, morality is just a matter of personal opinion.

Exercises

1. Have you ever had a class where the teacher used the values clarification approach? If not try to imagine a situation where this approach is used and you are free to hold whatever position you want without fear of judgment. Discuss whether this experience, real or imagined, enhanced your ability to engage in moral reasoning or if it reinforced the belief that morality is all subjective.

2. In the Deletha Word case, discuss whether the actions of the people who cheered on her attacker were any more or less moral than those of the man who tried to save her. Discuss also how an ethical subjectivist would answer this question. If you disagree with the ethical subjectivist, on what grounds do you disagree? Explain.

Critique of Ethical Subjectivism

> *The campaign against [objective] "moral judgement" seems often to spring from, and to rely on, strong and confidently held moral positions. . . .*
>
> —MARY MIDGLEY, *Can't We Make Moral Judgements?* (1993), p. 14

1. *Ethical subjectivism incorrectly assumes that moral disagreement necessarily implies that there are no universal moral standards.* According to ethical subjectivists, it makes no more sense to try to convince someone who enjoys torturing children that what he or she is doing is wrong than to try to convince a chocoholic that he or she doesn't really like chocolate.

But these two situations are not comparable. It does not make sense to try to convince a chocolate lover that she really hates chocolate because love and hate, at least when it comes to food, are contradictory feelings. In contrast, most ethicists *do* believe that it makes good sense to try to convince people that they *ought* not torture children, even though they may believe it is right to do so. We might, for example, cite the principle of nonmaleficence (do no harm) or respect for the rights of others. Or we could appeal to their sense of compassion. In each of these instances, we do this because we have the expectation that the person we are trying to convince acknowledges the same basic moral values that we do.

In fact, the majority of people who commit heinous acts, with the notable exception of sociopaths, justify their actions by referring to generally accepted moral principles and sentiments. For example, most child abusers agree that it is wrong to initiate sex with a child or to beat a child for no good reason. Rather than deny the existence of moral standards such as nonmaleficence, liberty rights, and compassion, abusers will often justify their actions by claiming that the child seduced them or actually enjoyed the sexual encounter. A father who beats his children may justify it on the grounds that the children brought the beating upon themselves because of their "naughty" behavior or that he was beating the child for the good of the child, as a form of discipline. Thus, what is often interpreted as disagreement about basic moral principles is instead disagreement about the application of these principles in particular situations.

2. *Ethical subjectivism is based on the incorrect assumption that we cannot be mistaken in our moral beliefs.* However, people often pass judgment on their own past feelings and on actions that were based upon those feelings. When our tastes change, such as our taste for a particular kind of food, we do not regard our former tastes as wrong—just different. As a child, I disliked broccoli; now, it is one of my favorite foods. In contrast, when our moral views change, we do regard our former views as mistaken.

A true ethical subjectivist would not acknowledge the idea of mistaken beliefs. According to ethical subjectivists, to claim upon further reflection that we were wrong for lying to a friend in the past is as absurd as claiming that we were mistaken about disliking broccoli as a child.

3. *We do pass judgment on our feelings and actions.* We may feel a strong desire to punch out someone who annoys us or to ram into a motorist who has cut us off in traffic. Most of us, however, do not try to beat someone to death simply because he or she accidentally dented our fender. Instead, we refrain from doing so, even when we have a powerful urge to strike out, because we realize that acting on these feelings is wrong. If morality is the same as feeling, then it makes no sense to restrain ourselves from acting on our feelings. To restrain ourselves only makes sense if we are using moral criteria or principles that are *independent of our feelings.*

4. *In real life, we regard acting on certain feelings and desires as immoral.* Although moral evaluation can take a person's feelings into account, for the

most part we judge an action to be moral or immoral independently of the agent's feelings. When we passed judgment on Hitler's actions, for example, we did not ask how he felt about killing Jews. Nor did we judge his actions to be moral because he personally believed that he was doing the right thing. Rather than consider terrorists, the Nazis, sociopaths, child molesters, and serial killers as highly moral people just because they acted on their deeply held inner feelings, we generally regard their actions as even more immoral and horrific precisely *because* they believed what they did was morally acceptable.

5. *Ethical subjectivism is disastrous for the weak and defenseless.* People's desires frequently clash. Feeling that something is right does not necessarily mean that we will have the power or opportunity to act upon that feeling. The strong are able to fulfill their desires at the expense of the weak, while those who lack power often have no choice but to suppress their desires. Furthermore, if we accept ethical subjectivism, there is no such thing as a victim because there is no universal moral principle that says we must respect other people's "right" to put their desires into action. Rather than encouraging tolerance, acts such as slavery, rape, child abuse, and genocide can all be justified under ethical subjectivism.

Almost all moral theories contain at least a grain of truth, but a problem arises when theorists mistake this grain of truth for the whole truth. Ethical subjectivists, for example, are correct in noting that morality begins with the individual experience and that these experiences are sometimes at variance with one another.

But moral experience and moral growth do not end with our limited individual experience. Nor are we as humans infallible in discerning the moral voice within us. There seem to be other voices, from both within and without, that compete with our conscience or sense of morality. For us to develop morally, our sense of what is right and wrong must be nurtured, as well as challenged, by our community. Like the blind men and the elephant, ethical subjectivism does not see beyond our private feelings. Rather than engaging people in dialogue to see whether there is a common thread to our experiences, ethical subjectivists see us only as isolated individuals. Philosopher Mary Midgley rejects all forms of ethical relativism as illogical. Regarding ethical subjectivism she writes:

> The humbug lies in pretending that both the world and our own lives are now—in this modern age—so well designed that neither we nor anybody else has any obligation to do what they don't wish to. . . .
>
> What this means is that morality has not been put out of date in the simple way that has always looked so attractive—by making life so good that morals are not needed. Angels, it may reasonably be supposed, do not need a morality, because they never wish to do anything but what they ought to do. In such a situation, duty and obligation lose their meaning. But that situation is not ours.[11]

Connections

What is conscience? See *Chapter 3, pages 74–75.*

Connections

On what grounds does Midgley reject cultural relativism as well as ethical subjectivism? See *Chapter 6, page 204.*

Ethical subjectivism, if taken seriously, is a dangerous theory. It not only isolates the individual but permits people to exploit and hurt others without ever having to justify their actions or stand in judgment.

Exercises

*1. Ethical subjectivism is more popular among people who are members of traditionally powerful socioeconomic groups and thus have the opportunity to act on their feelings and desires. How do the people you work with in your community service feel about this theory? Do they agree or disagree with it? What reasons do they give for agreeing or disagreeing with ethical subjectivism?

 2. Discuss how you would respond to each of the people in the following case studies. Relate your answers to how an ethical subjectivist might view these cases. How do your answers differ from those of an ethical subjectivist?

   a. Ben Jones, one of your fraternity brothers, is bored with college. He is delighted when he is approached by a terrorist cell and asked to help in a plot to blow up some major nuclear research facilities in the United States. You, by chance, discover Ben's plan. What should you do? How would an ethical subjectivist respond to Ben's plan?

   b. Jeff, who lives in your dormitory, is already selling drugs on campus but would like to expand his market. He has heard that drug use among children is increasing, and he would like to cash in on the market by selling cocaine to the children at a local elementary school. He doesn't particularly like children, and he also has no qualms about selling drugs to young children. He tells you of his plan. How do you respond?

   c. Chris is doing community service work at a nursing home. She started working there as part of a class requirement, but because Chris enjoys working with elderly people, she is considering continuing to volunteer there throughout the summer. Chris's friend, Sandy, volunteers at the same nursing home. Like Chris, she also plans to continue volunteering since she finds it easy to steal from the elderly people while they are sleeping. How would you respond when Chris and Sandy tell you their plans?

   d. Some parents bear children specifically to use them to make kiddy porn films, a very profitable business. Discuss whether the parents' apparently sincere belief that this practice is morally acceptable (as these parents claim) makes this morally acceptable and perhaps even morally obligatory for them.

Summary

1. *Ethical subjectivism* states that what is morally right and wrong is simply a matter of personal opinion. What may be right for you may be wrong for me depending on our respective feelings.

2. An *opinion* is a statement that expresses how a person feels.

3. Ethical subjectivism is not an ethics of tolerance for individual differences. *Tolerance* is a universal moral principle, and ethical subjectivists reject the existence of universal moral principles.

4. Ethical subjectivism is not the same as observing that people do disagree on moral issues. The existence of disagreement, in itself, does not imply that there is no objective truth.

5. *Emotivism* states that all moral statements are meaningless and that there are no universal standards of moral truth; ethical subjectivism states that individual feelings provide the standards of moral truth.

6. *Ethical skepticism* states that we cannot know with certainty that there *are* objective moral truths; ethical subjectivism claims that there are no objective moral truths.

7. *Romantic sentimentalism* emphasizes the inner person and the innate goodness of people. Jean-Jacques Rousseau's ethical subjectivism was based on romantic sentimentalism.

8. The *values-clarification* or *values-neutral approach* in ethics education is based on the assumptions underlying romantic sentimentalism and ethical subjectivism.

9. A *sociopath* is a person without a conscience who acts solely on his or her feelings without concern for universal moral principles and sentiments. As such, sociopaths are true ethical subjectivists.

10. Mary Wollstonecraft disagreed with Rousseau's romantic sentimentalism. She argued that reason is more important to morality than individual feelings and that there *are* universal moral principles.

11. The *Kitty Genovese syndrome* involves the failure of people to help another person in distress. Some people suggest that the popularity of ethical subjectivism in our society has contributed to the breakdown of concern for others.

12. Ethical subjectivism not only contains logical inconsistencies as a moral theory but also justifies domination of the weak by the strong and leads to the breakdown of community.

The Basic Idea of Ethical Subjectivism

James Rachels

In 2001 there was a mayoral election in New York, and when it came time for the city's Gay Pride Day parade, every single Democratic and Republican candidate showed up to march. Matt Foreman, the executive director of a gay rights organization, described all the candidates as "good on our issues." He said, "In other parts of the country, the positions taken here would be extremely unpopular, if not deadly, at the polls." The national Republican Party apparently agrees; at the urging of religious conservatives, it has made opposition to gay rights a part of its agenda.

What do people around the country actually think? Since 1982, the Gallup Poll has been asking Americans, "Do you feel that homosexuality should be considered an acceptable alternative lifestyle or not?" In 1982, only 34% said it should be; by 2008, the number had risen to 57%. The Gallup Poll has also been asking people whether they personally believe homosexual relations to be morally acceptable or morally wrong. In 2001, 53%–40% called homosexual relations "morally wrong"; in 2008, the public was divided 48%–48%.

People on both sides have strong feelings. The late Reverend Jerry Falwell spoke for many when he said in a television interview, "Homosexuality is immoral. The so-called 'gay rights' are not rights at all, because immorality is not right." Falwell was a Baptist. The Catholic view is more nuanced, but it agrees that gay sex is impermissible. Gays and lesbians, according to the *Catechism of the Catholic Church*, "do not choose their homosexual condition" and "must be accepted with respect, compassion, and sensitivity. Every sign of unjust discrimination in their regard should be avoided."

Nonetheless, "homosexual acts are intrinsically disordered" and "under no circumstances can they be approved." Therefore, to lead virtuous lives, homosexuals must not act on their desires.

What attitude should we take? We might say that homosexuality is immoral, or we might say it is acceptable. But there is a third alternative. We might say:

People have different opinions, but where morality is concerned, there are no "facts," and no one is "right." People just feel differently, and that's all there is to it.

This is the basic thought behind Ethical Subjectivism. Ethical Subjectivism is the idea that our moral opinions are based on our feelings and nothing more. On this view, there is no such thing as "objective" right or wrong. It is a fact that some people are homosexual and some are heterosexual; but it is not a fact that one is good and the other is bad. So, when someone such as Falwell says that homosexuality is wrong, he is not stating a fact about homosexuality. Instead, he is merely saying something about his feelings.

Of course, Ethical Subjectivism is not merely an idea about the evaluation of homosexuality. It applies to all moral matters. To take a different example, it is a fact that the Nazis exterminated millions of innocent people; but according to Ethical Subjectivism, it is not a fact that what they did was evil. When we say that their actions were evil, we are only saying that we have negative feelings toward them. The same applies to any moral judgment whatever.

James Rachels, *The Elements of Moral Philosophy*, 6th ed. by Stuart Rachels. Copyright © 2010 by The McGraw-Hill Companies, Inc. Reprinted with permission.

Student Relativism

Stephen A. Satris

In this paper I offer an analysis of, and suggest some methods for dealing with, a quite particular and peculiar problem in teaching philosophy. It is, perhaps, not a problem essential to the discipline or to its teaching, but it is nevertheless one of the most serious, pervasive, and frustrating problems confronting most philosophy teachers today. I speak of the problem of student relativism—or, SR for short.

I

What is SR? It is a phenomenon or perhaps a cluster of phenomena manifested in statements such as the following.

> There is really nothing true or false—or nothing really good or bad—it's all relative. One person has an opinion or feeling, and another person has a different one. What is true for one person might not be true for another. After all, who's to say? Everybody has their own feelings.*

Quite a number of variations on these statements are open. One has only to replace *good or bad* by *right or wrong*, *feelings* by *values*, or *true* by *good*, in order to see the possibilities.

My suggestion, then, is that SR is not relativism, if by relativism one means a philosophical position characterized by holding that truth in some arena or field of inquiry (such as morality, science, religion)—or perhaps truth in all fields—is relative to the beliefs of individuals or social groups. Bluntly stated, my thesis is that SR is not the

same as some such philosophical position because it is simply not a position at all. To have a position (and especially a philosophical position) it is necessary in some sense to engage with questions and issues. A position is something that one arrives at or achieves with respect to those questions or issues. But it is the mark of SR that it does not engage with questions or issues, but aims to avoid them. . . .

Particular care must be taken to remember that those who seem to express a liberal attitude are not necessarily liberals. The point again is one of nondisclosure rather than the profession of principles such as those of liberalism or tolerance. This became clearer in my own class when we began to discuss human sexuality. Here, for example, most of the same students who evinced SR were the strongest homophobes. Those who insisted that human excellence lay in doing what feels right to or for one's own self were among the least tolerant of non-standard sexual relationships. . . . It became increasingly plausible to believe that the liberalism and tolerance that might seem to be (perhaps the best) part of SR are really demands or pleas that the hearer be liberal or tolerant toward the (still mysteriously undisclosed but usually disappointingly conventional) opinions, values, feeling, etc. of the speaker.

Here, SR is primarily a method of protection, a suit of armor, which can be applied to one's own opinions, whatever they may be—but not necessarily to the

---

Stephen A. Satris, "Student Relativism," *Teaching Philosophy* 9 (Sept. 1986) (3): 193-200. Some notes have been omitted. Reprinted with permission from the publisher.

---

*These expressions and their variants appear both singly and in clusters. The ungrammatical "their" is characteristic.

opinions of others. "Who's to say?" is not an expression of one's own intellectual humility, broadmindedness, or unwillingness to condemn others. Rather, it is an expression of the idea that no one step forward and judge (and possibly criticize) one's own opinions. One would not like that. One says it is impossible. One's own opinions are proper and acceptable just by virtue of their being "felt" as one's own. No further scrutiny, judgment, or improvement is to be allowed or tolerated.[†] . . .

If SR is an eraser, then the hand that reaches for the eraser must somehow be stayed. The suit of armor—really emperor's clothing—must be recognized for what it is. The chanting of SR must be stopped, its spell broken. One must be brought to realize that one is in a real world, not a fantasyland of platitudes and complacency.

[†] With the forthrightness made possible by anonymity, the author of a collegiate graffito I recently saw wrote: "Kill anyone who makes me question my values."

Discussion Questions

1. Do you agree with Satris regarding student relativism? Why or why not? Relate your answer to the concept of resistance discussed in Chapter 2.

2. Using the example of homosexuality in Rachel's reading, discuss the morality of homosexuality in class (or you can choose another issue such as abortion or capital punishment). Note to what extent students adopt the view of "student relativism" when discussing this issue.

3. According to a 2017 Gallup Poll, 64% of Americans support same-sex marriage, up from 48% in 2008 and 44% in 2001. Discuss how an ethical subjectivist might explain this change. Are you satisfied with their explanation? Why or why not?

4. In his book *Why Can't Johnny Tell Right From Wrong?*, Professor William Kirkpatrick writes that our schools are failing to teach young people right from wrong.[12] He cites a national study of sixth to ninth graders that found a majority of boys, as well as many girls, considered rape to be acceptable in certain circumstances. Do you think it is the role of schools to teach moral education? Why or why not? Support your answer.

Notes

1. Frank Elaridi, "College Students Overshare STDs," *Campus Times*, March 30, 2012.
2. David Duke, "Why I Oppose Obama as President of the United States," February 28, 2008, http://www.davidduke.com.
3. George Will, "The Bad Seed of Our Politics," *Newsweek*, October 8, 1990, p. 80.
4. Case cited in Daniel Goldman, *Emotional Literacy: A Field Report* (Kalamazoo, MI: Fetzer Institute, 1994), p. 1.

5. Mohandas Gandhi, *All Men Are Brothers* (New York: Columbia University Press, 1958), p. 143.
6. Mary Wollstonecraft, *A Vindication of the Rights of Woman* (New York: Norton, 1988), p. 189.
7. Harry V. Jaffa, "Homosexuality and Natural Law," Center for the Study of Natural Law, www.claremont.org/publications/homosexuality.com. Jaffa believed Bundy was a closet homosexual and that contributed to his hatred of and urge to kill women.
8. Hervey M. Cleckley, *The Mask of Sanity* (St. Louis, MO: Mosby, 1976).
9. Martha Stout, *The Sociopath Next Door* (New York: Broadway Books, 2005), p. 9.
10. Myron Stokes and David Zeman, "The Shame of a City," *Newsweek*, September 4, 1995, p. 26.
11. Mary Midgley, *Can We Make Moral Judgements?* (New York: St. Martins Press, 1993), pp. 154–155.
12. William Kirkpatrick, *Why Can't Johnny Tell right from Wrong?* (New York: Simon & Schuster, 1992).

CHAPTER 5

Divine Command Theory and Civil Religion

The God of the Bible . . . is a God who not only governs history, but who orientates it in the direction of establishment of justice and right. . . . He is a God who takes sides with the poor and liberates them from slavery and oppression. His might is at the service of justice. His power is expressed in the defense of the rights of the poor.
    —GUSTAVO GUTIERREZ, *The Power of the Poor in History* (1993)[1]

The religious perspective is the conviction that the values one holds are grounded in the inherent structure of reality, that between the way one ought to live and the way things really are there is an unbreakable connection.
    —CLIFFORD GEERTZ, *Islam Observed* (1968)[2]

On September 11, 2001, a group of terrorists affiliated with al-Qaeda flew two hijacked planes into the Twin Towers of the World Trade Center of New York City killing almost three thousand people, including the terrorists and passengers aboard the planes. What motivated the terrorists to carry out the slaughter of thousands of apparently innocent people? Among the pages of directions found in a bag belonging to one of the terrorists was the statement: "You're doing a job which is loved by God, and you will end your day in heaven where you will join the virgins." In the mind of the terrorist, his action was morally correct and perhaps even obligatory based on a divine command.

The association between morality and what God supposedly commands is not limited to terrorists. Divine command was also invoked by President George W. Bush in his response to the radical Islamic terrorists and, in his decision to run for president. Bush believed that he was given a divine mandate to carry out God's will. "I feel like God wants me to run for president," he told Texas evangelist James Robinson regarding his running for a second term. "I can't explain it, but I sense my country is going to need me . . . I know it won't be easy on me or my family, but God wants me to do it."[3]

How should we respond if someone, whether a terrorist or the president of the United States, justifies the morality of his actions based on a divine command? What is the connection, if any, between morality and religion? In this chapter, we will also be studying the relationship between religion and morality. In this chapter, we will be examining theories that claim that morality is relative to God's commands, whether for an individual (divine command theory) or a culture (American civil religion). According to divine command theory, something is morally right for an individual simply because God commands it. There are not independent criteria for judging the morality of an action. American civil religion is similar to cultural relativism in that God's commands are relative to a particular culture.

Religion and Morality

The term *religion* is notoriously ambiguous. Some people use the term broadly to refer to any set of beliefs concerning the nature, cause, and purpose of the universe. Others use it more narrowly to refer to a set of institutionalized beliefs about God. In this text, we use the narrower definition of **religion** as an institutionalized system of beliefs and values shared by a group and grounded in faith and the worship of a supreme transcendent being(s). Although occasionally referred to as nontheistic religions, Eastern philosophies such as Buddhism and Confucianism, which address questions of the meaning of life and what makes a life valuable, are more akin to philosophies such as those of Plato, Aristotle, and Kant.

During religious worship, people praise that which has the highest worth or value.[4] God is worshipped because God represents perfect goodness. By imitating God, believers express their morality. Worshipping reaffirms these moral values.

The concept of God in Judaism, Christianity, and Islam is so intimately connected to the concept of moral goodness that the moral code is incorporated right into the doctrine of these religions. The study of sacred scriptures is important, in part, because it teaches right from wrong. However, this by itself does not imply that religion or scripture is the only source of moral guidance or that morality is relative to religion. In the Jewish religion, Roman Catholicism, and mainstream Protestant religions, the basic moral principles are also held to be universal and discoverable through other means such as the use of reason or intuition.

In contrast, some Muslims and fundamentalist Christians maintain that ethics rather than being universal and the same for all people, is inseparable from and relative to religion. An action is right simply because God commands it. The sovereignty of Allah is the starting point of Islamic political philosophy and law.[5] In some Muslim countries, such as Saudi Arabia and Morocco, the law of the sacred texts—the Qur'an—is the law of the land and applies to everyone living in that country. Humans are not expected to discern right from wrong but to submit unquestioningly to God's will.

Connections

On what grounds do Buddhists extend moral rights to all living beings? *See Chapter 11, pages 384-385.*

Connections

In what ways are Confucian ethics similar to Kantian deontology? *See Chapter 10, pages 324-326.*

The authority rests with none but Allah. He commands you not to surrender to any one save Him. This is the right way (of life).

—Qur'an[6]

Religion also plays a prominent role in American politics. While the U.S. Constitution guarantees separation of church and state, the United States is unusual among Western nations in its willingness to blend religion and politics.[7] According to a 2014 Pew Research Center poll, 53 percent of Americans, more than in Canada or any European country, believe it is "necessary to believe in God to be moral."[8]

There are two different theories regarding the relationship between morality and religion. Divine command theory claims that morality is dependent on or relative to God's commands and, therefore, can change from time to time and person to person. Civil religion, which blends religion and cultural relativism, is a variant of divine command theory. It claims that God's commands are relative to a particular nation or culture. Natural law theory, in contrast, maintains that morality is based on universal, unchanging principles and that God commands or approves something because it is right prior to the command. We'll be looking at natural law theory in more depth in Chapter 9.

Exercises

1. Discuss how your religious beliefs, or lack thereof, have shaped your morality. Is there a difference between religious and secular morality in your life? If so, what are the differences? If there are differences, how do you resolve a conflict between religious and secular morality?

2. When religious people use the words *right* and *wrong*, are they using these words in a different sense than someone who is an agnostic or an atheist? Discuss the differences and similarities.

3. If you believe that religious morality is different from secular morality, what role should religious morality play in forming public policy? Is religious morality, if it is irrelevant to our public life, morality at all? Support your answers.

The Divine Command Theory

There is no Good save obedient behavior, save the obedient will. But this obedience is rendered not to a law or a principle which can be known beforehand, but only to the free, sovereign will of God. The Good consists in always doing what God wills at any particular moment.

—EMIL BRUNNER, *The Divine Imperative* (1947)

In Plato's *Euthyphro*, Socrates asked: "Do the gods love holiness because it is holy, or is it holy because the gods love it?" The **divine command theory** claims the latter: Something is holy or moral because God loves it (see excerpts from *Euthyphro* at end of this chapter).

Divine command theory, as we noted earlier, is a type of ethical relativism. According to this theory, morality is dependent on or relative to God. Morality does not exist independently of God's will. Just as morality for the cultural relativist is relative to cultural norms and commands, for the divine command theorist morality is relative to what God commands or wills whether it is an act of charity or an act of terrorism. There are no independent, universal moral standards by which to judge God's commands. No other justification is necessary for an action to be right other than that God commanded it.

The divine command theory could be compared to a parental command theory. Our parents tell us to do something that may seem unfair by our standards. So we ask, "Why?" The reply is, "Because I said so!" And that's the end of the conversation. Your parents' saying so makes it right. Similarly, with the

Connections

What is ethical relativism and what are the different types of ethical relativism? *See Chapter 4, page 115.*

TOLES © 1995 The Washington Post. Reprinted with permission of UNIVERSAL UCLICK. All rights reserved.

divine command theory, God does not have to give any reasons. God's command is right simply by virtue of God having commanded it.

Thus, to say that God is good is not to attribute any particular characteristic to God. To say that God is perfectly good is simply to say that "what God wills, God wills." God's reasons are ultimately unknowable to humans, and therefore, we must accept God's commands—whatever they are—on faith. To question God's commands or to demand independent nonreligious reasons for accepting a divine command shows lack of faith.

In divine command theory, God's commands are meant for a particular person or group of people at a particular time. Do *not* confuse divine command theory with the biblical Ten Commandments or Decalogue, which were meant to be universal moral laws that apply to all people at all times. The Muslim Qur'an also contains a universal moral code similar to the Decalogue that is a universal "message to all the worlds" (81:27).

Abraham and his son Isaac. As a test of his faith and obedience, God commanded Abraham to sacrifice Isaac.
©DEA/A. DAGLI ORTI/ Getty Images

Discussion Questions

1. Was Abraham morally correct in his willingness to obey God's command to kill his son? Was it morally relevant that God spared Isaac at the last moment? Explain.

2. How would you respond if your roommate told you that God a) commanded him or her to join the Peace Corps after graduation, or b) to join al-Qaeda? If your response was different in the two cases, explain why. Relate your answer to divine command theory.

The biblical story of Abraham and Isaac, in which God orders Abraham to take his son Isaac onto the mountain and sacrifice him, is sometimes used as an example of the divine command theory.[9] According to this interpretation, Abraham did not question God's command, because God, being omnipotent and the source of all morality, can change the moral rules at any time simply by an act of will. Abraham's righteousness stemmed from his unquestioning obedience to the will of God.

According to Dostoyevsky, if morality is reducible to or relative to the will of God, then without God, there can be no morality. However, the divine command theory does not offer a much better alternative to Dostoyevsky's bleak prognosis for a godless world. If God does exist, and if morality is dependent on God's will, then morality is arbitrary. Anything is permissible *as long as God wills or commands it.*

Connections

How do natural law ethicists interpret the story of Abraham and Isaac? *See Chapter 9, page 284.*

Other Examples of Divine Commands

Abraham was not the last parent to claim that God commanded them to kill their child. Some murder defendants, especially those in insanity cases, claim they were acting on a divine command. In 2001, Texas housewife Andrea Yates drowned her five children, ranging in age from six months to seven years, to save them from Satan. Her reason—that God commanded her to do so—was the same as that which motivated Abraham. Did God command her to kill her children? How are we to know what was in the mind of God? To dismiss her claim as a symptom of a deranged mind is to sidestep the whole issue of faith and its relation to morality. After all, we do not regard Abraham as deranged but as a righteous man of great faith, yet he was also willing to kill his son for God.

In the same year, on September 11, radical Muslims hijacked two passenger planes and flew them into the twin towers of the World Trade Center in New York City killing almost three thousand people. In correspondence found later, the terrorists justified their action on the grounds that God commanded them to do it. As believers in divine command theory, this alone made their actions on 9/11 morally right, or even imperative, in their eyes.

If God doesn't exist, everything is permissible.

—FYODOR DOSTOYEVSKY, *The Brothers Karamazov* (1880)

If we respond by arguing that God would not command these people to do such terrible things, we are implying that there are independent moral standards that we can use to appraise the morality of God's commands. If this is the case, then we should judge Abraham to be immoral because it is generally believed that parents have a moral duty to protect their children. The fact that God substituted a lamb at the last minute and saved Isaac from death does not negate

Abraham's willingness to kill his son. Similarly, if we accept divine command theory, then we have to accept the terrorists' actions on 9/11 as morally justified.

Key Claims of Divine Command Theory

- God is perfectly good and just.
- Morality is dependent on and relative to God's will.
- God's commands to particular people and groups override generally accepted moral principles when there is a conflict.

How should we respond if someone claims that they are acting on a divine command? Should we simply accept their word for it? What if their claims come into conflict? In the following section, we'll examine these and other questions.

Exercises

1. Imagine that Abraham and Andrea Yates have told you that God has commanded them to kill their children. Assuming that neither of them has yet carried out the act, discuss how you would respond to them.

2. Philosopher Philip Quinn argues, regarding God's command that Abraham kill his son Isaac, that "few people, if any at all, have actually been given such harsh commands [therefore] there is no reason for a divine command theorist to believe, or for others to fear, that widespread slaughter of the innocent will be prescribed or in any way encouraged." Discuss Quinn's statement in light of the terrorist attacks of September 11.

3. Discuss whether divine command theory is compatible with democracy and the rule of the people, or if theocracy (a form of government in which God is recognized as the supreme rule) is a more appropriate form of government. Support you answer.

Critique of Divine Command Theory

The primary concern with divine command theory is its apparent arbitrariness since there are no objective criteria for us to use to determine whether a particular claim or action was actually based on God's command.

1. *Morality is independent of God's commands.* Unlike Dostoyevsky, philosopher Kai Nielsen says that, as far as morality is concerned, it does not really matter whether God is dead or alive.[10] The divine command theory, Nielsen

argues, is logically unsound. If morality is dependent on or relative to God's will, then morality is arbitrary. Anything—rape, murder, genocide, killing one's own children—is permissible as long as God wills or commands it.

God cannot be used as a fundamental criterion for moral goodness, nor is God necessary for morality. Instead, the claim that what God wills is good *is dependent on a previous belief that there exists a being worthy of worship*. Thus, rather than God being the foundation of morality, a belief in God is dependent on our *already* having a concept of moral goodness by which to judge God's worthiness.

Morality represents what people already believe to be moral *independently* of their belief in God. For example, most people would reject a voiced command to kill their children as not being the voice of God. In other words, we do not depend on religion but rather on nonreligious criteria to discern right from wrong. We accept the ethical teachings in the scriptures as the revealed word of God *because* they are consistent with what we already believe to be moral. Although a moral code is incorporated into the doctrine of most religions, moral controversies can be resolved without appealing to religion.

2. *There are no criteria for determining whether God actually issued a particular command.* Because divine commands are issued to particular individuals or groups rather than being grounded in universal principles, we are left with no rational or objective means of determining if a person or group such as the September 11 terrorists actually were commanded by God or if they were mistaken or delusional.

We cannot even look to universal moral principles, including those contained in scripture such as the Bible or the Qur'an, since universal moral principles are prima facie and can be overridden by a divine command. For example, the Qur'an states that ". . . anyone who murders any person who had not committed murder or horrendous crimes it shall be as if he murdered all the people" (5:32). This moral precept is violated when terrorists and suicide bombers, apparently acting under a divine command, endanger the lives of innocent civilians, just as Abraham violated God's rule in Genesis 9:6 not to shed human blood when he prepared to kill his son. However much we may admire Abraham and despise the terrorists, in both cases we're left with no criteria for judging whether or not they were acting under an actual divine command.

3. *The theory provides no objective criteria for determining which claim to accept if two particular groups or individuals present conflicting claims based on divine commands.* Because divine commands can be particular rather than universal, they may come into conflict. When there is disagreement, there is no method of resolving the dispute or deciding if God actually issued one or both of the conflicting commands.

This brings us back to a problem inherent in all types of ethical relativism: Relativistic theories do not allow for rational discussion of what is the right thing to do, thus contributing to a rigid "either you're with us or against us" mentality.

4. *The theory is based on the assumption of the existence of a just, loving, and infallible personal God.* While this premise may be true, it has not been proven by divine command theorists. Not everyone believes in this concept of God. In many cultures and belief systems, the debate over the relationship between such a god and morality makes little sense.

Furthermore, even if we do believe that a particular command is an expression of God's or a god's will, this does not imply we are morally obligated to obey. In Hinduism, for example, the gods are not fallible and do not always act in a morally exemplary manner or give good advice to humans. Other belief systems are based on nature or ancestor worship. Yet people in these and other non-theist cultures, for the most part, have a concept of the moral and act in accordance with fundamental moral principles.

I can't combine faith in God with Auschwitz. Either there is no God, or I don't belong to him.

—Milan Machovec (Polish Marxist philosopher)[11]

5. *The existence of a perfectly good God who is the source of all morality seems inconsistent with the presence of so much suffering and evil in the world.*[12] If God is perfectly good and commands only that which is moral, why does God allow so much pain and suffering in the world? In addition to suffering caused by other people's actions, each year natural disasters, including hurricanes fires, droughts, genetic disorders, and disease, are a cause of suffering and death for millions. Indeed, the presence of so much apparently senseless suffering and evil in the world is one of the primary reasons people lose faith in God.

In a variation of philosopher Gottfried Leibniz's (1646–1716) "best of all possible worlds" theme, theologian John Hick attempts to resolve the problem by arguing that the purpose of suffering is the perfection of our souls. Thus, the problem of evil disappears in what he calls a "vale of soul making." Under this view, September 11, tragic as it may have seemed, actually brought about more good than harm by providing people with an opportunity for moving toward moral perfection. Is he right? In his address on the fifth anniversary of September 11, former president George W. Bush told the nation: "On 9/11, our Nation saw the face of evil. Yet on that awful day, we also witnessed something distinctly American: Ordinary citizens rising to the occasion, and responding with extraordinary acts of courage." Indeed, many people observed how much nicer people in New York City seemed to be to each other following the terrorist attacks.

On September 11, 2001, radical Islamic terrorists hijacked two passenger planes and flew them into the twin towers in New York City, killing almost three thousand people.
©Sean Adair/Reuters

Analyzing Images

1. Would God command people to engage in mass murder? If not, what is the source of morality and is God, if there is a God, bound by moral laws that exist independently of "His" commands? Support your answers.

2. Anwar Aulaqi, allegedly the spiritual advisor to the terrorists of September 11, 2001, said that "telling people to give their [lives] for their faith is not an unusual idea. That's the same thing as telling marines in this country [the United States] *semper fidelis* [always faithful]." Critically analyze Aulaqi's analogy.

Nevertheless, the anguish of those who survived these tragedies and the death of thousands of innocent people just to benefit others hardly seems a befitting action of a perfectly loving God. Hick is aware that evil and suffering can lead to bitterness, fear, mental and emotional breakdown, and even death. Because of this, he argues, the business of soul-making and striving after moral perfection must continue in the afterlife.

In summary, divine command theory offers little guidance when it comes to everyday morality or determining whether a particular command is in fact from God. On the other hand, these problems do not disprove the theory. We

Connections

What is the fallacy of ignorance? *See Chapter 2, page 58.*

cannot logically disprove divine command theory. For us to respond in turn that, without proof, the theory is false would be to fall prey to the fallacy of ignorance. The most we can conclude is that we do not know if divine command theory is a correct interpretation of morality. This being said, the best approach when confronted with someone or a group who claims to be acting on God's command is probably skepticism, especially if the purported command conflicts with fundamental, universal moral principles.

Exercises

1. Fyodor Dostoyevsky in *The Brothers Karamazov* (1880) writes, "If God doesn't exist, everything is permissible." Discuss his claim that morality is dependent on the existence of God. Discuss what, if anything, would be different about your moral beliefs and behavior if God did not exist.

2. You are attending a graduation ceremony where a high-ranking government official is the keynote speaker. In the middle of the ceremony, a young man from the audience jumps up and reveals a bomb strapped to his body. He declares that God has commanded him to blow up the auditorium and everyone in it. However, just before he pulls the cord to set off the bomb, he turns to you and asks how he can be absolutely sure this is what is commanded and also whether he has a moral obligation to follow God's command in this case. Discuss how you might answer his questions.

3. Discuss whether divine command theory, with its presumption of a good and just God, adequately addresses the problem of evil in the world.

Civil Religion, Society, and National Morality

No people can be bound to acknowledge and adore the Invisible Hand which conducts the affairs of man more than those of the United States. Every step by which we have advanced to the character of an independent nation seems to have been distinguished by some token providential agency.

—George Washington's "First Inaugural Address" (April 30, 1789)

Civil religion claims that morality, at least to some extent, is relative to a particular culture or nation. Religion, like cultural norms, can offer powerful external motivations for behaving morally. We are expected to behave morally because it pleases God. Eternal damnation awaits those who fail to heed religion's moral commands; prison or social ostracism awaits those who break cultural norms. Those who are obedient to their religion's moral code can look forward to eternal salvation and reward; similarly, those who adhere to social norms get their rewards, such as social approval and economic prosperity, here in this life. The melding of these two sets of sanctions—religious and cultural—can make civil religion a powerful force in our lives.

Religion as the Worship of Society

French sociologist and philosopher Émile Durkheim (1858-1917) argued, in *The Elementary Forms of the Religious Life*, that God stands in the same relationship to worshippers as society does to its individual members. God is the symbol of society, and each society creates God in its own image. God thus becomes a symbol of cultural unity. Religion is the worship of society, thereby acting as a mechanism for justifying the moral norms of a particular culture. By sacralizing cultural norms and values, religion gives these cultural norms a transcendent moral authority that they would otherwise lack. In this sense, it is similar to cultural relativism.

Unlike Durkheim, who admired how religion united people around a common set of values, Karl Marx denounced religion as a destructive force. He argued that religious institutions, rather than uniting people in a common interest, exist primarily for the purpose of maintaining the status quo and legitimizing the interests of the ruling class by deifying their norms. According to Marx, religion, rather than motivating us to work toward a more just society, serves as the "opium of the people" by lulling us into a sense of false security. Religion also prevents those who are oppressed from overthrowing their oppressors by extolling meekness and submissiveness.

Connections

What type of society did Marx envision as being the most moral? *See Chapter 11, pages 365-367.*

Religion is the sigh of the oppressed creature, the heart of a heartless world, just as it is the spirit of spiritless conditions. It is the opium of the people.

–Karl Marx

U.S. sociologist Robert Bellah (1927-2013), in his essay "Civil Religion in America," maintained that Christianity and Judaism are no longer the dominant religions in the United States; a new form of religion has emerged which he called *American civil religion*. Bellah suggested that the primary role of civil religion is the creation of a sense of cultural or national identity and purpose. He defined **civil religion** as an institutionalized set of beliefs, symbols, and rituals that provide a religious dimension to a nation's collective life. These principles come from God and represent a "higher standard" by which the experiences of a nation are interpreted and judged.[13] Civil religion played an important role in Egyptian civilization as well as in the Roman Empire with its pantheon of gods and goddesses.

[God] is actively interested and involved in history, with a special concern for America.

–Robert Bellah, "Civil Religion in America" (1967)

American flags are found inside many, if not most, American churches—a tribute to the power of American civil religion in the United States. Many religious organizations also celebrate national holidays ("holy" days) during religious services.
©Todd Korol/Getty Images

American Civil Religion: One Nation under God

American civil religion provides the nation with a set of moral principles as well as a divine purpose to act as a beacon of liberty and freedom for the rest of the world. Sociologist Robert Bellah wrote: "God is actively interested and involved in history, with a special concern for America." Although some of it is selectively taken from the Judeo-Christian tradition, American civil religion is not the same. For example, the Bible says nothing about democracy. American civil religion is also very specific when it comes to America's mission and moral authority in the world.

Connections

How do American civil religion and cultural relativism reinforce each other? *See Chapter 6, pages 185-186.*

Civil religion has been part of American politics since the nation's inception. The Declaration of Independence makes reference to God as the Supreme Judge, and "our firm reliance on the protection of divine Providence." Life, liberty, and the pursuit of happiness are taken to be inalienable rights "endowed by their creator" who takes a special interest in the American democratic experiment. This new democratic social order is identified with God's divine plan for human progression toward moral perfection. Hence, Americans distrust of non-democratic nations. The belief that the United States was established as a special nation under God has exerted a powerful influence on Americans' beliefs regarding their role in world affairs. (See selection from Robert Bellah at the end of the chapter.)

American civil religion expresses itself in symbols such as the American flag, the national anthem, war memorials, national holidays (holy days), and documents that outline our special status and mission as a "chosen" nation, such as the U.S. Constitution. In addition, references to God appear in the Pledge of Allegiance, on our money, and in oaths for public office.

Our ultimate moral obligation as a nation and as American citizens is to carry out God's will on earth. In his 2017 inaugural speech, President Donald Trump invoked God's name, stating that "most importantly we will be protected by God."

The intensity of American civil religion fluctuates over time. It is most powerful when the nation or national ideals are threatened. Accordingly, wars or "operations" to spread God's "plan for humanity, including bringing democracy to tribal areas of the world," are often couched in terms of a holy war—of good against evil. America's prosperity and status as a major world power are regarded as evidence of God's favor. American civil religion is expressed in semisacred national holidays, such as Memorial Day and Veteran's day, and the reverence shown for the American flag, as well as in movies and even cartoon figures such as Captain America.

In American democracy, although sovereignty officially resides in the people, it is implicitly understood that the ultimate sovereignty rests with God and that our country's actions are judged by a higher law. If the majority of citizens or elected officials make a decision that the president, as "head" of American civil religion, deems to be at odds with God's plan, then he can refuse to go along with the majority. This happened when Abraham Lincoln issued the Emancipation Proclamation (1863). The proclamation was grounded, not in the will of the majority, but in Lincoln's belief that slavery was an offense in the eyes of God and that the Civil War may have been punishment from God. The suspicion of socialism and the belief that capitalism, though never mentioned in the Bible, is God's plan also draws support from American civil religion.

The Dangers of Civil Religion

At its best, American civil religion is grounded in a natural law theory and natural rights ethics that hold a nation accountable under a higher moral law. In this capacity, civil religion provides a powerful motivation for mobilizing citizens to rally behind a higher moral ideal.

There is an ever-present danger, however, that civil religion may become unanchored from its roots in universal moral principles and a transcendent reality and instead identify national interests with God's plan for humanity. When this happens, civil religion becomes supplanted by cultural relativism, which we'll be studying in the following chapter. By sacralizing cultural norms and values, civil religion gives them a transcendent authority that they would otherwise lack. Rather than looking to natural law to judge a nation, the nation itself becomes the object of worship, and any dissent or moral criticism is oppressed in the name of patriotic duty.

Connections

What is religiously based natural law theory and how does it differ from civil religion? *See Chapter 9, pages 283-284.*

The belief that America itself is the higher power, a belief often couched in terms of American exceptionalism, can lead to arrogance as well as the implicit assumption that the people of nations we invade in order to spread the God-given principles of liberty and democracy will welcome us as liberators. Those who don't rally behind our cause or who resist our divine mission are, by definition, evil, or at least morally deficient. Alex de Tocqueville, in his book *Democracy in America* (1826), noted:

> For the last 50 years no pains have been spared to convince the inhabitants of the United States that they are the only religious, enlightened, and free people. They perceive that, for the present, their own democratic institutions prosper, while those of other countries fail; hence they conceive a high opinion of their superiority and are not very remote from believing themselves to be a distinct species of mankind.

Connections

What is Manifest Destiny and how was it morally justified? *See Chapter 6, page 174.*

When a nation comes to regard itself as the higher power—what Bellah terms the "idolatrous worship of the state"—the creative tension between civil religion and cultural relativism is lost. The worship of national interests—such as expansionism and the spread of capitalism and representative democracy—guides the nation's public policy rather than an understanding of the nation's purpose in light of a higher, transcendent reality. For example, the protest of Native Americans over the laying of the Keystone XL pipeline on or adjacent to their native lands has been dismissed by many politicians and capitalists in the name of progress.

In addition to justifying Manifest Destiny and our otherwise unconscionable treatment of Native Americans, civil religion was used to rationalize slavery. In American slavery, "men convinced themselves that a system which was so economically profitable must be morally justifiable. They formulated elaborate theories of racial superiority. Their rationalizations clothed obvious wrongs in the beautiful garments of righteousness. . . . Religion and Bible were cited to crystallize the status quo."[14]

Connections

What, according to King, is the relationship between religion and the state? *See Chapter 9, pages 294–295.*

When a person or group struggles to bring American civil religion back to its roots in universal moral principles, the creative tension may manifest in civil disobedience. Civil rights leaders such as Harriet Beecher Stowe, Elizabeth Cady Stanton, and Martin Luther King Jr. called upon the moral principles embodied in documents such as the U.S. Constitution. In the March on Washington for Jobs and Freedom (August 1963), Martin Luther King Jr. delivered the following speech:

> I have a dream that one day this nation will rise up and live out the true meaning of its creed—we hold these truths to be self-evident that all men are created equal. . . . this will be the day when all of God's children will be able to sing with new meaning "My country 'tis of thee, sweet land of liberty, of thee I sing. Land where my fathers died, land of the Pilgrims' pride, from every mountainside let freedom ring!"

Civil religion is also at risk for abdicating to divine command theory. This is most likely to happen during times of crisis when people are unsure of how to react and a powerful national leader claims to have knowledge of God's divine plan for the world. However, since divine commands do not need justification, there is no way of determining whether the commands actually come from God. Thus, rather than holding our national leaders to a higher moral law, divine command theory discourages critical analysis of their motives. When civil religion mutates into divine command theory, the use of unprovoked military force and the violation of human rights can be justified as God's way.

Although civil religion can stray from its roots in universal moral principle, in its truest form it can act as a powerful incentive to justice. The moral ideals of the Declaration of Independence, the Bill of Rights, and the Fourteenth Amendment of the U.S. Constitution have never been fully realized in this country. While these documents may not be sacred and are certainly not perfect, to their credit, the founders of this country sought to discern natural laws and incorporate them into our nation's thinking.

Exercises

1. Roger Williams, cofounder of Rhode Island, opposed the mixing of religion and politics, arguing that government corrupts religion and religion corrupts government. Discuss his claim and whether his concern applies to civil religion.

2. Discuss the influence of civil religion in the United States on Americans' concept of morality. Use specific examples to support your answers.

3. Discuss ways in which cultural relativism and civil religion may have influenced our current interpretation of our "mission" in the world. What is your moral obligation, as a citizen, when you have reason to believe that civil religion is being misused to support unjust public policies?

4. Although there have been presidents such as Lincoln who never belonged to a church, there has never been a president who was not a believer in God. To what extent did the religious beliefs of the candidates in the 2016 presidential election influence your view of their moral integrity? Would it be possible for an atheist or an agnostic to be elected president of the United States? Support your answers.

Religion and the Moral Community

God created man in his own image, in the image of God he created them; male and female he created them. And God blessed them and God said to them, "Be fruitful and multiply, and fill the earth and subdue it: and have dominion over the fish of the sea and over the birds of the air and over every living thing that moves upon the earth."

—GENESIS 1:27–28

Then I was standing on the highest mountain of them all, round beneath me was the whole hoop of the world. . . . I was seeing in the sacred manner of the shape of all things of the spirit and the shapes as they must live together like one being. And I say that the sacred hoop of my people was one of many hoops that make one circle, wide as daylight and starlight. . . . And I saw that it was holy.

—BLACK ELK, *The Sacred Hoop*

The assumptions of different religious traditions regarding the nature and purpose of humans in this world have a profound influence on our definition of moral community. Just as cultural relativism defines moral community in cultural terms, religious ethics tends to define moral community in relation to God, or at least that community's concept of God. The more a being is like God, the greater that being's moral value.

The teachings of the scriptures in Western religion not only affirm human dignity but also imply a special moral bond between God and humans and a special role for humans in creation. Because humans are created in the image of God and bear the greatest likeness to God, humans have the highest moral value. Other creatures, in contrast, exist only to satisfy the needs of humans.

Religion, Sexism, and Racism

Religious morality that has been tailored to support certain cultural beliefs can lead to the subjugation of those with less power in a society. Besides placing humans above other animals, religion has been used (or as some might argue, "misused") to support a hierarchy of moral values within humanity based on racial differences and the "different natures" of males and females. Theology, as thus interpreted, has been used to legitimate discrimination against women. Women's essential nature "is seen as having less of the divine image and more of the physical nature."[15] Carol Christ, in her essay "Why Women Need a Goddess," argues that patriarchal religions centering on the worship of a male God create an atmosphere and worldview "that keep women in a state of psychological dependence on men and male authority, while at the same time legitimating the political and social authority of fathers and sons in the institutions of society."[16] This, in turn, has led to unjust social structures and the marginalization of women in society. Indeed, it was not until 2016 when a woman—Hillary Clinton—was nominated as the presidential candidate of a major party.

Connections

What is liberation ethics and why does it reject civil religion based on the prevailing cultural norms? *See Chapter 11, pages 367-368.*

Theologian James Cone points out that the portrayal of God as a White man has also had a demoralizing effect on the psyche of African Americans. Given this, it is not surprising that less than 11 percent of American churches are racially integrated.[17] Cone rejects the "white American 'Christianity' that is built on racism," calling for the dissolution of current Christianity and its God and a "reevaluation of all values."[18] By calling for a reevaluation of traditional Christian values, Cone asks for a recognition of our common humanity and a rejection of our racist and hierarchical concept of the moral community that rotates around a white-skinned God.

Native American Attitudes

For many of the 2.5 million Native Americans, the whole earth is sacred and contained within the moral community. Their concept of moral community has led to antagonism and conflict between them and the European Christians who settled here—particularly around the concept of private ownership of land. Because the earth is sacred or has intrinsic moral value, in many Native American philosophies, it cannot be owned or sold. To do so is to treat the environment as having only instrumental value.

During his life, Black Elk (1863–1950), a Sioux holy man and philosopher, saw his people all but destroyed by European settlers. As a child, Black Elk began having visions calling him to bring his people back into the sacred hoop where they could be happy and prosperous again. The medicine man told Black Elk that he must enact his vision of a more inclusive moral community for the people on earth.

His journey took him to Pine Ridge, South Dakota, where in December 1890, the starving Sioux had gathered to surrender. Instead of accepting the surrender, twenty-five White soldiers killed almost three hundred Native Americans that day at Wounded Knee. Black Elk managed to escape into the Badlands. He eventually returned to Pine Ridge, where he lived the rest of his life with his broken dreams. In the 1930s, Black Elk's visions were written down by John Neihardt. His book, *Black Elk Speaks*, is widely acclaimed as one of the greatest books about Native American life, moral values, and religion.

Much of contemporary Native American religion is a countercultural movement against the traditional Judeo-Christian depiction of the moral community. As Amanda Porterfield writes:

> The universally agreed-upon tenets of American Indian spirituality include con-
> demnation of American exploitation of nature and mistreatment of Indians, regard
> to precolonial America as a sacred place where nature and humanity lived in
> plentiful harmony, certainty that American Indian attitudes are opposite to those
> of American culture and morally superior on every count, and an underlying belief
> that American Indian attitudes toward nature are a means of revitalizing American
> culture.[19]

The American Indian Religious Freedom Act of 1978 served as an acknowledgment by the U.S. Congress that certain places are sacred space to many Native American tribes. Although all of the earth and those upon it are sacred, a sacred space has special spiritual power or significance—it is a place where human beings experience a strong sense of being connected to the universe. The notion of sacred spaces in nature is also found in many other religions. For example, in Japan, Mount Fuji is considered a shrine; Ayers Rock is a sacred space for Australian aborigines.

The traditional Judeo-Christian concept of moral community, in contrast, places humans outside of and above nature. Environmental ethicist Lynn White writes that "by destroying pagan animism, Christianity made it possible

Connections

What are the four common moral values shared by Native Americans? *See Chapter 6, page 183.*

to exploit nature in a mood of indifference to the feelings of natural objects."[20] The destructive effects of the exclusion of nonhuman animals and the environment from our moral community have only recently begun to be realized.

Eagle Man, an Oglala Sioux lawyer and writer, warns us that "the plight of the non-Indian world is that it has lost respect for Mother Earth, from whom and where we all come."[21] The environmental destruction and pollution we are now experiencing, he says, are a warning from Mother Earth that we must change our attitudes and lifestyle. This change, however, can only come through a radical paradigm shift regarding our definition of the moral community.

Exercises

1. Draw a mandala of the moral community of your religion or one of the major religions in your country. What criteria are used for the inclusion and exclusion of different beings? How are these criteria justified? How does the mandala of the religion's moral community resemble and differ from that of the moral community in the United States?

2. The belief that we are all children of God has been a powerful force for motivating people to respect the dignity and rights of other humans and to work toward social justice for all humans. Is the belief that humans are a special creation necessary to motivate people to respect others? Would a belief in the equal dignity of all living beings, such as that espoused by many Native American and Eastern philosophers, weaken the moral value of humans? Support your answers.

*3. Discuss how religious depictions of God affect a society's concept of the moral community. Relate your answer to your community service work. Do you agree with the solutions proposed by James Cone and Carol Christ?

4. Discuss Lynn White's claim that the anthropocentric moral community supported by Christianity has been the primary culprit in our current ecological crisis. Relate your answer to the philosophy espoused by Black Elk and Eagle Man. Discuss how adopting their philosophy would change your lifestyle.

5. Discuss how American civil religion shapes our views of the moral community and the social hierarchy.

6. Discuss whether religious beliefs and values, including those of American civil religion, are adequate for addressing the moral issues involved in climate change and environmental degradation. To what extent do your religious beliefs, or lack thereof, affect how you think about our moral obligation to other animals and to the environment? Use specific examples to illustrate your answer.

---

*An asterisk indicates that the exercise is appropriate for students who are doing community service learning as part of the course.

Does Morality Need Religion?

The love of other human beings and the ethical life in general are autonomous in that they justify themselves, requiring no support from religion. But there is a religious dimension to life and it has its effect on the whole life. On the religious view it is God's concern, as it were, how man behaves towards his fellow and the love of the neighbor is the love of God.

—LOUIS JACOBS, "The Relationship Between Religion and Ethics in Jewish Thought" (1996)[22]

Religion has been credited with inspiring people—such as Susan B. Anthony, Martin Luther King Jr., and Mother Teresa—to reach a higher moral standard than that required by everyday life. Morality that is beyond what is normally expected of an individual is known as **supererogatory**. Acts such as giving away one's belongings to the poor or risking one's life in the name of a moral cause are examples of supererogatory actions. Some religious ethicists claim that it is faith in God that inspires people to engage in supererogatory actions. The belief that God is the creator of moral law, they argue, gives morality its authority and motivates the believer to behave in accordance with moral law even when it conflicts with human laws.

There is no shortage of examples of social reform movements and courageous acts of civil disobedience that have been inspired largely by faith in God. On the other hand, belief in God does not seem necessary to motivate someone to place morality above human law and to engage in supererogatory moral acts. Some natural law ethicists do not believe in God, thinking it unnecessary to postulate a God to justify the existence of a natural (moral) law.

Gandhi did not believe in a personal God. For Thoreau, discovery of the natural law came through the individual's dialogue with nature rather than with God. Yet, this lack of faith did not weaken the commitment of these two men to the moral law. The nineteenth-century feminist movement had religious underpinnings; the current women's liberation movement, in contrast, has been, for the most part, a secular movement. The animal liberation movement and environmental movements have also, for the most part, eschewed religion and adopted philosophical ethics as the basis of their moral beliefs.

Also, there is no shortage of atrocities committed in the name of religion and God. Slavery in the South was supported by the majority of White Christians at the time as morally acceptable and part of God's natural law. Herbert Spencer's contention that civilized Christians are more peaceful than their "primitive" non-Christian counterparts is hard to substantiate in the light of the many wartime atrocities and acts of terrorism committed in the name of God. The Crusades of 1095–1272, which were carried out in the name of God and the Christian faith, and the Inquisition that followed the Crusades cost countless lives and created untold misery.

On an individual level, religious people are no more likely to engage in acts of moral heroism than are nonreligious people. Surveys of Americans, including

Connections

What is natural law theory and how does it differ from divine command theory? *See Chapter 9, pages 281-282.*

Connections

How was Spencer's reinterpretation of Darwinism used to justify imposing Western-Christian values on other cultures? *See Chapter 6, pages 176-177.*

those who claim that religion is very important to them, show that religion has little effect on people's everyday moral values or on their ideas of social morality.[23] Even being a member of the clergy does not guarantee exemplary moral behavior.[24]

Spirituality versus Religiosity

Discussions of morality and religion should be separate from discussions of the role of spirituality in morality. In Western thought, spirituality is generally associated with being religious. In Eastern philosophies, spirituality is not associated with being religious—at least in the Western sense of being religious. Religion is a social phenomenon involving the institutionalization of a particular set of beliefs about a transcendent God. **Spirituality**, on the other hand, is an inner attitude of reverence or deep respect for the ultimate moral worth or sacredness of oneself and others, independently of a belief in a transcendent God or any particular religious or cultural doctrine.

Some religions encourage spirituality; others do not. Some people who are nonreligious or even antireligious regard themselves as highly spiritual. Gandhi, as we already noted, did not believe in a personal God. Yet, he was a highly spiritual person who believed in the power of the soul-force. Gandhi maintained that it is the soul-force that gives people the moral strength to persevere in nonviolent action and to love our oppressors and to engage in nonviolent action to overthrow unjust social structures and to overcome evil.

Being religious, in other words, does not ensure moral behavior. Indeed, studies show that church members, as a group, are *more racially prejudiced* than nonmembers. (For example, the Ku Klux Klan considers itself a Christian organization.) On the other hand, studies have also found that the most active members of the church are the least prejudiced of both church members and nonmembers.

Psychologist Gordon Allport explained this discrepancy by making a distinction between intrinsically religious people and extrinsically religious people.[25] *Intrinsically religious people* join churches because faith is meaningful to them as an end in itself. Because of this, they are more likely to be active in their church. Intrinsically religious people, studies find, are also more autonomous and *committed at the moral level* and are more likely to reject or protest cultural norms when these conflict with universal moral principles.

Extrinsically religious people, on the other hand, join churches because of the secular benefits, such as social status. Although they are likely to be "indiscriminately proreligious," their religious faith does not usually translate into being a "nuclear church member." These are the heteronomous moral reasoners who uncritically accept the tenets of civil religion—including its narrow view of moral community.

In a study of the differences between people who helped to rescue Jews during World War II and those who did not, it was found that religious affiliation was not a major factor. However, one's *interpretation of the nature of their religious commitment* was important. Rescuers were more likely to define their moral community more broadly to include all of humanity, whereas nonrescuers were more likely to use narrower cultural definitions of moral community.[26] Truly moral people, unlike heteronomous moral reasoners, strive to live the good life and to be a good kind of person—compassionate and just—not because God or their religion orders them to do so but because it is the right thing to do.

Morality Is Independent of Religion

Most philosophers and theologians agree that morality exists independently of religion. Although religious beliefs may strengthen moral conviction in intrinsically religious people, such as Martin Luther King Jr., religious ethics is not fundamentally different from philosophical ethics. When people who are religious use the terms *right* and *wrong*, they usually mean the same thing as someone who is not religious.

Religious differences tend to fall away in most serious discussions of moral issues, such as slavery and abortion, not because religion isn't important to the participants but because moral disputes can be discussed and even resolved without bringing religion into the equation. For example, many people initially regarded the protest against slavery as a religious issue. Most of the early petitions to Congress regarding slavery were presented by members of the Society of Friends (Quakers) and were, for the most part, dismissed by Congress as the "mere rant and rhapsody of meddling fanatics"[27] trying to force their religious views on Southerners. People living in the South resented the "very indecent attack on the character" of the slave states and slave owners by these religious fanatics. As the debate over slavery moved further into the public arena in the 1840s and 1850s, however, the discussion shifted from religious differences to the moral issues involved.

When debating moral issues that are associated with the doctrinal positions of specific religious groups, we must take care not to commit the circumstantial fallacy by assuming that a person must hold one particular view simply because he or she is a member of a particular religion. The current abortion debate, for example, is regarded by some people as a specifically Catholic issue; however, the debate can be carried on without any reference to religion. Some religions take an official stand regarding different moral issues—such as slavery, war, abortion, and pacifism—but this does not imply that these issues are specifically religious rather than moral issues. In debating these and similar issues, we must be careful to separate the moral issues involved from religious doctrine.

Connections

What is the circumstantial fallacy and when are we most likely to use it? *See Chapter 2, pages 54-55.*

Religious ethics that are not securely moored in autonomous universal ethics, but rather demand uncritical acceptance of official doctrines, promote heteronomous moral reasoning. It is easy for religious ethics, once set adrift, to become grounded on the rocky shores of cultural relativism. When this happens, religion can become a destructive force by sanctifying cultural customs that are unjust and limiting one's conception of the moral community.

Exercises

1. Can science and our everyday existence give our life meaning? Or do you agree that without God there is no purpose or meaning in life and, consequently, no reason we should be moral? Support your answer.

2. In his book *God and Human Anguish*, theologian Paul Schilling writes:

   > Whether or not he recognizes his situation, [the atheist] is confronted by the problem of good, which is at least as difficult for him as the pervasiveness of evil is for the theist. In a godless universe, how are we to account for the manifest fact that high values are sought for and realized? How can we reconcile with an absurd, meaningless cosmos that cares nothing for human striving, the patent reality in human experience of the pursuit and discovery of truth, the creation and appreciation of beauty, and the quiet strength of self-sacrificial love?[28]

   How would you respond to Schilling's questions? Support your answers.

3. What is the difference between religious faith and spirituality? Is spirituality necessary for moral autonomy? Why or why not? Does spirituality play a role in your moral life? If so, what role does it play?

4. Think of some religious people you know—either personally or as public figures—who have committed acts that are highly immoral. Discuss ways in which these people are either intrinsically or extrinsically motivated.

5. Choose a controversial issue, such as same-sex marriage or abortion, that is sometimes regarded as a religious issue. Can the debate over the morality of this issue be carried on without using religious doctrine? If not, what happens when a religious principle seems to conflict with a moral principle? Or is such a conflict even possible? Explain.

Summary

1. *Religion* is an institutionalized system of beliefs and values shared by a group and grounded in faith and the worship of a supreme transcendent being(s). *Worship* involves lifting up and praising that which has the highest worth. God is worshipped because he represents perfect goodness and the highest values.

2. In some religions, morality is dependent on religion.

3. The *divine command theory* states that an act is moral because God commands it.

4. *Natural law theory* states that morality is autonomous; that is, it is independent of religion and God's commands.

5. The actions of groups such as the 9/11 terrorists are examples of divine command theory.

6. Divine command theory is problematic in that there are no independent criteria for determining if an action carried out by someone was actually commanded by God.

7. Émile Durkheim argued that God is the symbol of society and that religion is the worship of society.

8. David Hume and Karl Marx regarded traditional religion as destructive to morality.

9. Sociologist Robert Bellah suggested that the primary role of modern religion is to create a sense of national unity. *American civil religion*, he argued, is the dominant religion in the United States.

10. The traditional Western religious concept of God is *anthropocentric, patriarchal,* and *racially biased*. Several philosophers, such as Rosemary Radford Ruether, Carol Christ, James Cone, Black Elk, and Eagle Man, suggest that we need to move beyond a definition of moral community that is based on Judeo-Christian concepts of moral worth.

11. A *supererogatory* action is one that is above and beyond everyday morality. There is no evidence that religious people are more likely to engage in supererogatory acts.

 # Euthyphro

Plato

SOCRATES: Then tell me. How do you define the holy [moral] and the unholy [immoral]?

EUTHYPHRO: Well then, I say that the holy is what I am doing, prosecuting the wrongdoer who commits a murder or a sacrilegious robbery, or sins in any point like that, whether it be your father, or your mother, or whoever it may be. And not to prosecute would be unholy. . . .

SOCRATES: . . . my friend, you were not explicit enough before when I put the question. What is holiness? You merely said that what you are now doing is a holy deed—namely, prosecuting your father on a charge of murder.

EUTHYPHRO: And, Socrates, I told the truth.

SOCRATES: Possibly. But, Euthyphro, there are many other things that you will say are holy.

EUTHYPHRO: Because they are.

SOCRATES: Well, bear in mind that what I asked of you was not to tell me one or two out of all the numerous actions that are holy; I wanted you to tell me what is the essential form of holiness which makes all holy actions holy. I believe you held that there is one ideal form by which unholy things are all unholy, and by which all holy things are holy. Do you remember that?

EUTHYPHRO: I do.

SOCRATES: Well then, tell me what, precisely, this ideal is, so that, with my eye on it, and using it as a standard, I can say that any action done by you or anybody else is holy if it resembles this ideal, or, if it does not, can deny that it is holy.

EUTHYPHRO: Well then, what is pleasing to the gods is holy, and what is not pleasing to them is unholy.

SOCRATES: Perfect Euthyphro! Now you give me just the answer that I asked for. Meanwhile, whether it is right I do not know, but obviously you will go on to prove your statement true.

EUTHYPHRO: Indeed I will.

Socrates has now received an answer to his question. Euthyphro has finally proposed necessary and sufficient conditions for something's being holy. Socrates proceeds to test this proposal by trying to determine whether the conditions identified really are necessary and sufficient.

SOCRATES: Come now, let us scrutinize what we are saying. What is pleasing to the gods, and the man that pleases them, are holy; what is hateful to the gods, and the man they hate, unholy. But the holy and unholy are not the same; the holy is directly opposite to the unholy. Isn't it so?

EUTHYPHRO: It is. . . .

SOCRATES: Accordingly, my noble Euthyphro, by your account some gods take one thing to be right, and others take another and similarly with the honorable and the base, and good and bad. They would hardly be at variance with each other, if they did not differ on these questions. Would they?

EUTHYPHRO: You are right.

SOCRATES: And what each one of them thinks noble, good and just, is what he loves and the opposite is what he hates?

EUTHYPHRO: Yes, certainly.

SOCRATES: But it is the same things, so you say, that some of them think right, and others wrong, and through disputing about these they are at variance, and make war on one another. Isn't it so?

EUTHYPHRO: Yes it is.

SOCRATES: Accordingly, so it would seem the same things will be hated by the gods and loved by them; the same things would alike displease and please them.

EUTHYPHRO: It would seem so.

SOCRATES: And so, according to this argument, the same things, Euthyphro, will be holy and unholy.

EUTHYPHRO: That may be.

SOCRATES: In that case, admirable friend, you have not answered what I asked you. I did not ask you to tell me what at once is holy and unholy, but it seems that what is pleasing to the gods is also hateful to them. Thus, Euthyphro, it would not be strange at all if what you now are doing in punishing your father were pleasing to Zeus, but hateful to Cronus and Uranus, and welcome to Hephaestus, but odious to Hera, and if any other of the gods disagree about the matter, satisfactory to some of them and odious to others.

Reprinted from *Plato on the Trial and Death of Socrates: Euthyphro, Apology, Crito, Phaedo*, translated by Lane Cooper. Copyright © 1941 by Lane Cooper. Renewed copyright © 1968. Used by permission of the publisher, Cornell University Press.

A second reading is available online at www.mhhe.com/bossef17e. This reading is titled "Civil Religion in America" by Robert N. Bellah. Go to the website and read the article before answering the following questions.

Discussion Questions

1. Critically analyze Socrates' objection to Euthyphro's definition of "holy" [moral] as that which is "pleasing to the gods." Discuss also how Bellah might respond to Euthyphro.

2. Bellah maintains that Christianity and Judaism are no longer the dominant religions in the United States; rather, it is American civil religion. Do you agree? Discuss the implications of this for the prophetic role of religion in calling political leaders to be morally accountable.

3. American exceptionalism—the belief that the United States is unique and superior to other nations—is one of the key concepts in American cultural identity. Discuss this concept in light of Bellah's description of American civil religion. Is it American exceptionalism consistent with the idea of American civil religion being based on a universal morality; or, is American exceptionalism an example of civil religion as a type of ethical relativism? Use examples to support your answer.

Notes

1. Gustavo Gutierrez, *The Power of the Poor in History*, trans. Robert R. Barr (Maryknoll, NY: Orbis Books, 1993), p. 7.
2. Clifford Geertz, *Islam Observed* (Chicago, IL: University of Chicago Press, 1968), p. 97.
3. David Domke, "Divine Dictates?" *Baltimore Sun*, February 6, 2005; Paul Harris, "Bush Says God Chose Him to Lead His Nation," *The Observer* (British), November 2, 2003, http://observer.guardian.co.uk/international/story/0,6903,1075950,00.html.
4. Keith A. Roberts, *Religion in Sociological Perspective* (Homewood, IL: Dorsey Press, 1984), p. 62.
5. Abul A'la Mawdudi, *The Islamic Law and Constitution*, trans. Khurshid Ahmad (Chicago, IL: Kazi, 1955), p. 132.
6. Qur'an, 12:40. As quoted in Abul A'la Mawdudi, *The Islamic Law*, p. 132.
7. "Poll: Religious Devotion High in U.S.," *USA Today*, June 6, 2005.
8. "Belief in God Essential to Morality." Pew Research Center: Global Attitudes and Trends, May 27, 2014.
9. Genesis 22:1-19. *The New Oxford Annotated Bible* (New York: Oxford University Press, 1977), pp. 25-26.
10. Kai Nielsen, "God and the Good: Does Morality Need Religion?" *Theology Today* 21, no. 1 (April 1964).
11. Quoted in S. Paul Schilling, *God and Human Anguish* (Nashville, TN: Abingdon, 1977), p. 34.
12. An excellent book that explores the problem of God and the existence of moral evil is Eli Wiesel's *Night* about the Holocaust and his experience in the Nazi death camps.
13. Robert Bellah, "Civil Religion in America," *Daedalus* 96, no. 1 (Winter 1967): 1-21. To read the article online, go to: www.robertbellah.com/articles_5.htm.
14. Martin Luther King Jr., *The Strength to Love* (1963), p. 41.
15. Rosemary Radford Ruether, *Sexism and God-Talk* (Boston, MA: Beacon Press, 1983), p. 94.
16. Carol P. Christ and Judith Plaskow, eds., *Woman spirit Rising: A Feminist Reader in Religion* (San Francisco, CA: Harper & Row, 1979), p. 274.
17. Nadra Kareen Nittle, "5 Ways to Make Your Racially Segregated Church More Diverse," *About News*, June 30, 2016, http://racerelations.about.com/od/diversitymatters. See also "Why Many Americans Prefer Their Sundays Segregated," August 4, 2008, http://us.cnn.com/2008/LIVING/wayof life/08/04/segregated.sundays/index.html.
18. James H. Cone, *Black Theology and Black Power* (New York: Seabury Press, 1969), p. 127.
19. Amanda Porterfield, "American Indian Spirituality as a Countercultural Movement," in *Religion in Native North America*, ed. Christopher Vecsey (Moscow: Univ. of Idaho Press, 1990), p. 154.
20. Lynn White, "The Historic Roots of Our Ecological Crisis," *Science* 155 (1976): 1203.

21. Eagle Man, "We Are All Related," in *Mother Earth Spirituality: Native American Paths to Healing Ourselves and Our World*, ed. Ed McGaa (San Francisco, CA: Harper & Row, 1990), p. 203.

22. Louis Jacobs, "The Relationship between Religion and Ethics in Jewish Thought," in *Moral Issues: Philosophical and Religious Perspectives*, ed. Gabriel Palmer-Fernandez (Upper Saddle River, NJ: Prentice-Hall, 1996), p. 35.

23. Roberts, *Religion*, p. 62.

24. Andrew M. Greeley, *Fall from Grace* (New York: Putnam, 1993), p. 45.

25. Quoted in Roberts, pp. 326–329.

26. Samuel P. Oliner and Pearl M. Oliner, *The Altruistic Personality: Rescuers of Jews in Nazi Europe* (New York: Free Press, 1988), p. 156.

27. Speech of Representative Smith, *Annals of Congress*, 1st Congress, 2nd session, I, p. 730.

28. Schilling, *God and Human Anguish*, p. 37.

CHAPTER 6

Cultural Relativism
Is Morality Dependent on Culture?

For if anyone, no matter who, were given the opportunity of choosing
from amongst all the nations of the world the set of beliefs which he
thought best, he would inevitably, after careful consideration of their
relative merits, choose that of his own country. Everyone without
exception believes his own native customs . . . to be the best.
    —HERODOTUS, *The Histories* (c. 500 B.C.E.)[1]

The morality of a group at a time is the sum of the taboos and
prescriptions in the folkways by which right conduct is defined.
    —WILLIAM GRAHAM SUMNER, *Folkways* (1906)

According to Sharia Muslim tradition, a wife is obliged to fulfill the sexual desires of her husband. In 2009, a Sharia state law was passed in Afghanistan stating that a husband had a right to demand sex from his wife every four days unless she was ill or would be harmed by sexual intercourse. The law, which states that "Obedience, readiness for intercourse and not leaving the house without the permission of the husband are the duties of the wife," applies only to Shiite Muslims—about 15 percent of the population of Afghanistan.

The law created contention both in Afghanistan and abroad. The three hundred protestors who turned out to demonstrate against the new law were pelted with stones by some one thousand Afghanis who supported the law. The law has been denounced by the United Nations Development Fund for Women as legalizing the rape of a wife by her husband. Other Western leaders and feminist groups have also spoken out against it. President Donald Trump has taken a stand against this practice among Muslims living in the United States on the grounds that it contradicts the freedoms guaranteed in the U.S. Constitution.

Backers of the law in Afghanistan denounce these Westerners as meddling in their affairs. "We don't want foreigners interfering in our lives," says Mariam Safadi, a twenty-four-year-old woman who is engaged to be married and who defends the law.[2]

On what grounds could people outside, or even within Afghanistan, call this law immoral? The majority of American adults believe that morality is synonymous with cultural tradition and laws, a position known as cultural relativism. If this is the case, then we should be able to determine if a particular practice is moral simply by establishing if it is legal or part of a culture's tradition. If this is the case, then this Sharia law is moral by definition, at least in Muslim countries where it is legal, while those who oppose it are voicing support of immoral behavior. In this chapter, we'll be studying cultural relativism and engage with people from different cultures as well as our own culture.

What Is Cultural Relativism?

Like ethical subjectivism, **cultural relativism** looks to people for standards of right and wrong. Subjectivists claim that individuals create their own moral standards; cultural relativists argue that moral standards and values are created by groups of people or cultures. Public opinion, rather than private opinion, determines what is right and wrong. There are no objective universal moral standards that hold true for all people in all cultures. Morality, instead, is regarded as nothing more than socially approved customs. Conscience, like Freud's superego, is simply the product of cultural conditioning.

Connections

According to both Freud and Skinner, what is the role of culture in shaping our conscience? *See Chapter 1, page 20.*

Cultural relativists point out that something regarded as morally wrong in one culture may be morally praiseworthy in another culture. Headhunting, for example, flourished in certain cultures well into the twentieth century and was even considered a courageous act.[3] In some cultures, a young man could not marry until he had taken his first head. However, a young man in the United States who tried to impress his girlfriend's family by displaying his collection of shrunken heads would be quickly locked up and labeled not only morally deviant but mentally ill as well. Similarly, being a suicide bomber is considered an honorable act in some Middle Eastern cultures. In addition to the glory and recognition the bomber receives, these cultures may even provide the family of the deceased bomber with substantial rewards. In our culture, on the other hand, a suicide bomber would be considered deviant and mentally unstable.

The great diversity of marriage habits has also been used to illustrate differences in cultural values. Polygamy is morally acceptable in some African and Asian cultures. In Muslim cultures, the number of wives is limited to four. In other cultures, the limit is set only by the husband's ability to support a large household. In our culture, polygamy is illegal.

Connections

How does cultural relativism commit the fallacies of popular appeal and appeal to tradition? *See Chapter 2, pages 55-56 and 62.*

Cultural variations in norms also exist within different historic time frames. One hundred years ago, serial polygamy, where marriages end in divorce and are followed by a new marriage, was not morally acceptable in North America; now it is. Two hundred years ago, slave ownership was morally acceptable and even a status symbol in some parts of the United States; now slavery is considered highly immoral. To know what is right or wrong, we need only ask what the norms and customs of our culture or society are at this point in history.

In 1996, only 27 percent of Americans supported same-sex marriage.[4] Indeed, former President Obama opposed it, stating in 2008, "I believe marriage is between a man and a woman. I am not in favor of gay marriage." Now, thirty years later, 61 percent of Americans support same-sex marriage, including Obama. Why the shift? Cultural relativists would say because several years ago same-sex marriage was immoral; now it is moral. But this doesn't explain how and why such a shift could occur.

To use a another example, polygamy is considered morally wrong in this country by the great majority of Americans. Whether or not people can offer independent arguments for their opposition is irrelevant. Only cultural norms count. Polygamy, on the other hand, is perfectly acceptable in other cultures while same-sex marriage is regarded with moral repugnance. Neither position is inherently right or wrong according to the cultural relativist; it's simply a matter of cultural custom. (See Analyzing Images, page 179.)

Because morality is nothing more than custom, we have no grounds for judging the moral practices of another culture or another time in our own culture whether these practices be same-sex marriage, polygamy, or slavery. If two cultures disagree about what is morally right and there is no disagreement about the facts or definitions of key terms, then there is no rational means for reaching agreement. Cultural relativists do not argue merely that *some* moral values are relative to the culture. Rather, they maintain that *all* moral values are nothing more than cultural customs.

Exercises

1. Discuss how we should respond, if at all, to customs and laws in other countries—such as the Afghani law discussed in the opening scenario—that clash with our own cultural beliefs about morality. On what grounds, if any, can we criticize a particular practice in another culture if the majority of people in that culture support it? Support your answer.

2. France has placed a ban on Muslim women wearing veils or headscarves in public. Writer Myria Francois criticizes the ban as a "warped form of European cultural relativism. It's just the French way, you see."[5] Quebec, Canada also has prohibitions against Muslim women wearing veils. Should citizens and immigrants be compelled to conform to the laws and customs of their adopted nation? Support your answer.

3. Name some customs or ideals in our culture that reflect moral values. Name some customs or ideals that reflect nonmoral values. What criteria can we use to distinguish between these two types of values?

4. Make a list of some of the primary moral values in our culture. Now make a list of some of your own moral values. Are the two lists in agreement? If not, how might you explain the disagreement?

5. Psychologist Lawrence Kohlberg found that most college students—despite their theoretical allegiance to ethical subjectivism—are cultural relativists when it comes to making real-life moral decisions. As cultural relativists, they are dependent on the opinions of their peers. Right and wrong are defined primarily in terms of prevailing norms and values. To what extent are the moral values you listed for yourself in exercise 4 the same as those of your peers? Discuss possible problems of relying on cultural norms and peer opinion for your moral values.

Observers at a Ku Klux Klan lynching, Indiana, 1930.
©Popperfoto/Getty Images

Analyzing Images

1. Would the Klan's values and activities be morally admirable if the majority of Americans believed in them today as they did when this photo was taken? Discuss whether the people participating in the lynching should be excused since discrimination against Blacks was the norm at the time this photo was taken.

2. Schools and neighborhoods today are more segregated than they were fifty years ago.[6] To what extent do students of diverse racial backgrounds come from different neighborhoods and hang out in separate groups at your college? Does this seem "normal" to you (as did the lynching to the people in the photo)? Discuss your reaction to the presence of segregation.

What Cultural Relativism Is Not

Cultural Diversity should be distinguished from both cultural absolutism and cultural relativism. Not all cultural values are benign.

—"Cultural Diversity Policy," University of Melbourne, Australia, 2002

Excusing

Cultural relativism is *not* the same as excusing certain cultural practices, such as slavery or infanticide, on the grounds that the people of that culture sincerely believe that what they are or were doing is morally acceptable. *Excusing* entails granting an exemption or pardon from *wrongdoing*. A person or group of people can be excused for several reasons or either they were not aware at the time that what they were doing was wrong; they were misinformed about the nature and consequences of their actions; they had no control over the situation; or they have made appropriate amends for their wrongdoing.

For example, cultures where headhunting was practiced generally believed that the soul matter was concentrated in the head. By preserving or eating the brain of the enemy, the soul matter of their own group was increased, and the power of the enemy was proportionally weakened. Consequently, headhunting was regarded as important to the survival of the culture. These cultures have since come to understand that this belief was mistaken. Thus, rather than condemn the headhunters for their past actions, we may *excuse* the behavior on the grounds that their actions were based on misinformation or incorrect beliefs.

Cultural relativists, in contrast, claim that these practices were actually morally right for the members of that culture. They would see no reason to excuse these behaviors. And in the case of slavery, if anyone needed to be excused, it would be the abolitionists, who acted against cultural values.

In the United States up until the middle of the twentieth century, Blacks were considered to be inferior and discrimination against Blacks was legal as well as the norm. This norm was epitomized by the activities of the Ku Klux Klan. The Ku Klux Klan was founded in the South in 1866 and officially disbanded in 1869. It was reorganized in 1915. By the 1920s, the Ku Klux Klan had 5 million members and had expanded its reign of terror to the Northern states as well. The Klan harassed Blacks and even lynched them while ordinary White citizens simply looked on. (See Analyzing Images box page 168). Some observers even brought their children and picnic lunches to the lynchings. Today, there are only five to eight thousand members of the Klan according to the Southern Poverty Center. Racial discrimination, though still a prevalent in our culture, is illegal and, we have even had an African American president. On the other hand, discrimination against Arab Americans and Muslims has increased following the attacks on the World Trade Center in 2001.

Connections

How can the fallacy of hasty generalization reinforce prejudice and intolerance? *See Chapter 2, page 56.*

Respect for Cultural Diversity

Cultural relativism is *not* the same as respect for cultural diversity. Cultural relativism is sometimes mistakenly advocated on the grounds that it promotes tolerance and respect for cultural diversity. One often hears the admonishment not to be judgmental or to impose our values on people from other cultural backgrounds. Instead, we are advised to be tolerant of others' customs and value systems. However, this is based on a misunderstanding of cultural relativism since this very tolerance precludes us from passing judgment on repressive customs that violate human rights and dignity.

> The idea of cultural relativism is nothing but an excuse to violate human rights.
>
> —SHIRIN EBADI, Iranian lawyer, human rights activist, and 2003 Nobel Peace Prize winner

The UNESCO Universal Declaration on Cultural Diversity rejects cultural relativism that, in the name of cultural diversity, tolerates cultural practices contrary to the basic principles of human rights and dignity. Instead, the fundamental and universal moral principle of mutual respect for the dignity of individuals and their right to self-determination needs to be part of any definition of cultural diversity. In addition, respect for cultural diversity must include the maintenance of harmony between cultures or different cultural groups within a society to ensure that being a member of a particular culture does not disadvantage anyone. At the same time, respect does not extend to tolerance of oppression and inequality within any culture. A culture that violates the fundamental rights of its own citizens should not be respected in the name of cultural diversity, but should be challenged by the international community.

By advocating tolerance and respect for cultural diversity and expecting others to do the same, we acknowledge the existence of universal, transcultural moral standards such as respect and tolerance. However, cultural relativists cannot both deny the existence of universal moral standards and also defend the existence of these standards without engaging in doublethink. Our culture may value tolerance. However, if other cultures value intolerance of diverse lifestyles and points of view, cultural relativists have no grounds for passing judgment on these cultures.

Connections

According to natural law ethicists, when is civil disobedience morally justified? *See Chapter 9, pages 291–296.*

In 2012, blind Chinese dissident and activist Chen Guangcheng, who was arrested for his outspoken opposition to China's one-child policy, escaped home detention and fled to the U.S. embassy in Beijing. (See Analyzing Images, page 171.) The action of the United States in offering him asylum touched off a diplomatic crisis. In offering him asylum, the United States rejected cultural relativism and instead appealed to the rights of self-determination and freedom of speech, both universal moral principles, which they believed should apply to people in all cultures.

Cultural Relativism versus "American Values"

A cultural relativist may hold similar beliefs to those who believe in universal, transcultural moral standards. For example, cultural relativists in the United States generally believe in human equality and universal human rights.

However, their belief in equality and universal human rights is based upon the view that these are "American values." As such, the concept of equal human rights is seen as a *creation of Western culture*. Thinkers such as Jefferson and Locke, in contrast, claimed that the principle of equal human rights is not a creation of one culture or even of Western culture in general but is *universal* and *self-evident to all humans*, whether they be Englishmen, Muslims, or Australian aborigines.

Protest in support of blind dissident and lawyer Chen Guangcheng. Guangcheng was arrested by the Chinese government for his outspoken opposition to forced abortions and sterilizations. In 2012, after nineteen months of house arrest, he managed to scale the wall surrounding his house and fled to the American embassy in Beijing where he sought refuge. The Americans finally agreed to let him come to the United States, even though he had violated the laws of China. He currently lives in New York City where he continues his work as a human rights advocate.
©Photo by State Department/Handout/Corbis via Getty Images

Analyzing Images

1. If cultural relativism is correct and morality is simply the customs and laws of a particular culture, then Guangcheng's action in protesting the laws of his culture was immoral. If you think Guangcheng behaved morally, critically evaluate on what grounds you judged the morality of his actions.

2. Did the United States behave immorally in giving Guangcheng sanctuary? Support your answer. Discuss what you would have done if you have been working at the American embassy in Beijing when Guangcheng came there to seek refuge. Support your decision.

Exercises

1. The following opinion was posted on a **PBS** Web site following a documentary on George Wallace (1919–1998), white supremacist, segregationist, and four-time governor of Alabama:

    George Wallace was one of the greatest politicians ever. He said what the people wanted to hear. Wallace was not a bad man. If he was, then what about the tens of millions of people who voted for him through the years.

Do you agree with the writer's reasoning? Why or why not? Discuss how a cultural relativist would most likely respond to the quote.

2. Reflect on how much our country has changed regarding racial discrimination and segregation. Use specific examples from your own experience. Discuss how a cultural relativist might explain this change.

3. Define "cultural diversity" or look up the definition of "cultural diversity" in your college student handbook. Discuss whether the definition is consistent with cultural relativism or if it rejects cultural relativism.

4. Can asylum for Chen Guangcheng or other people fleeing customs or laws in their culture be morally justified under cultural relativism? Support your answer.

5. Write down three "American" moral values. Do you regard these values as specifically American or as universal moral values? Support your answer.

Distinguishing between Cultural and Sociological Relativism

It is often said that one cannot derive an "ought" from an "is." . . . Put in more contempo-
rary terminology, no set of descriptive statements can entail an evaluative statement with-
out the addition of at least an evaluative premise. To believe otherwise is to commit the
naturalistic fallacy.

—JOHN SEARLE, *Speech Acts*, p. 51

Connections

What is the difference between a descriptive statement and a prescriptive statement? *See Chapter 2, pages 44-45.*

Cultural relativism is not the same as sociological relativism. Cultural relativism is a theory of *philosophical ethics*. As such, it is concerned with what *ought* to be. Sociological relativism, in contrast, is a theory in *descriptive ethics*, a branch of sociology that is concerned with what *is*. **Descriptive ethics** aims to discover and describe the moral beliefs of a given society. **Sociological relativism** is simply the *observation* that there is disagreement among cultures regarding moral values. Unlike cultural relativism, which is prescriptive, sociological relativism makes no judgments about the moral rightness or wrongness of different cultural standards.

Sociological relativism does not draw any conclusions about the correctness of moral standards. It leaves open the possibility that one society could be mistaken about its moral beliefs and that there might be universal, transcultural moral standards against which to judge conflicting cultural standards. Cultural relativists, in contrast, claim that differences in moral practices necessarily imply that there are no universal moral standards by which to judge a society.

Connections

What is the naturalistic fallacy? *See Chapter 2, pages 61-62.*

However, disagreement regarding moral practices among cultures can stem from a variety of factors, some of which are situational. Just as scientists using the same aeronautic principles can come up with different designs for a flying machine based on the needs of the various people who will be using it, so too people from different cultures may disagree about the application of different moral principles, while agreeing on the principles themselves. To argue that just because something *is* a certain way that is how it *ought* to be is to commit the naturalistic fallacy.

A parallel can also be found in the field of linguistics. According to one school of thought, the grammatical structures found in language are relative to each culture. This theory, like cultural relativism, gained popularity for a while in light of the tremendous cultural diversity in languages found by anthropologists. Most contemporary linguists now maintain that universal grammatical structures underlie *all* human languages. On the surface each culture's language, like a culture's moral practices and values, appears to be completely different from all others. Deeper analysis of the various human languages, however, reveals a deep grammatical or linguistic structure that is independent of culture and appears to be common to all human languages.[7]

Likewise, deeper analysis of the moral practices among cultures also reveals similarities in the fundamental moral principles. American anthropologist Clyde Kluckhohn (1905–1960) claimed that there are basic universal, transcultural moral standards that are recognized in all cultures and are binding upon all members of a culture's moral community. The existence of cross-cultural values does not, in itself, disprove cultural relativism; however, the presence of these apparently universally accepted values does strengthen the argument against cultural relativism. "In no human group," Kluckhohn notes, "is indiscriminate lying, cheating or stealing approved."[8] Incest, too, is prohibited or strictly controlled in all cultures. Every culture makes some provision for mating and the rearing of children. Random violence against other members of the community is also prohibited in all cultures. For example, in headhunting cultures, only people outside the cultural community were targeted as victims.[9]

Connections

On what grounds does anthropologist Ruth Benedict argue that morality is relative to each culture rather than universal? *See Chapter 6, pages 203-204.*

The following description of the Kabloona, an Eskimo culture living in the Canadian arctic, was published in 1941 by Gontran de Poncins:

> One observer was told of an Eskimo who was getting ready to move camp and was concerned about what to do with his blind and aged father, who was a burden to the family. One day the old man expressed a desire to go seal hunting again, something he had not done for many years. His son readily assented to this suggestion, and the old man was dressed warmly and given his weapons. He was then led out to the seal grounds and was walked into a hole in the ice into which he disappeared.[10]

This description is an example of *sociological relativism*. It does not contain any value judgments upon the morality of the act. A cultural relativist would go beyond the merely descriptive and say that, because the customs are different, the two cultures—ours and the Kabloona—have different basic moral standards. However, should we accept this conclusion?

On the surface, it appears that our moral standards are different and even in conflict with those of the Kabloona. In the United States, if we walked our elderly parents into a hole in the ice, we would surely be regarded as highly immoral! But is this the only possible interpretation of the experience? Perhaps this was the aberrant act of one deranged son, perhaps a son who had never resolved his childhood Oedipus complex. If so, then maybe Kabloona values are not so different from ours. However, as we read on, we discover that this was a custom of the Kabloona culture at that time. What the son did was considered morally acceptable by his culture. His father probably did the same thing to *his* father, and his son will probably do it to him when he is old and sick.

It may be tempting at this point to throw up our hands and accept cultural relativism. But let's not give up our quest for a common moral understanding so easily. Let's push on with our analysis. As we noted earlier, situational factors play an important role in shaping how a culture translates fundamental universal moral standards into particular cultural values and practices: What is the Kabloona culture like? Is it sedentary or nomadic? What are their religious beliefs and family customs? How does their environment determine their needs and shape the way they honor moral standards? How does our situation in the United States differ from that of the Kabloona?

As modern Americans, we can care for our elderly parents at home. If caring for an elderly and ailing parent becomes too burdensome for the family, we can place him or her in a nursing home. If our family does not have the resources to pay for a nursing home, public funds can be used to cover the cost.

Now compare our situation to that of the Kabloona. At the time of de Poncins, the Kabloona were nomadic people living in a cold and hostile environment. "Home" did not mean a permanent structure with a spare bedroom for grandma or grandpa. There were no adult day-care centers, home-care nurses, or nursing homes. None of these alternatives were available to the Kabloona. As nomadic people, their lives were dependent on moving camp regularly to follow the seal herds, their primary source of food. To take a blind and ailing parent on one of these treks could have resulted in the starvation not only of the parent but of the rest of the family as well. It is now apparent that much of what initially appeared to be disagreement about basic moral standards may instead be the result of situational differences. It is interesting that this practice ceased among the Kabloona once they had permanent settlements.

Differences in moral practices may also be due to differences in factual and/or religious beliefs, rather than different fundamental moral standards. Tolerance and respect for other cultures have not always been moral norms in the United States. During the early and mid-nineteenth century, the doctrine of Manifest Destiny was used to justify the United States' expansionist policy and the takeover of lands belonging to Mexico and to Native Americans. "The right to our Manifest Destiny to overspread and to possess the whole continent," wrote a nineteenth-century journalist, "[is a right] which Providence has given us for the development of the great experiment of Liberty and federated self-government entrusted us."[11] Some groups opposed expansionism as immoral and racist, but these groups were small and found little support.

Connections

What is the position of the United Nations regarding the existence of universal human rights? *See Chapter 11, page 374.*

Factual beliefs can also influence how moral principles are translated into cultural norms. For example, the belief that women are inherently seductive "informs" (albeit incorrectly) public policy and the requirement in some countries that women wear veils in public.

Very few ethicists believe that morality is completely independent of its particular context. As moral decision makers, we live in a world of particulars. Social settings, individual circumstances, cultural values, environmental conditions, and factual and religious beliefs vary from culture to culture. Acknowledging the influences of these factors in shaping the moral practices and values of a culture does not imply that there are no underlying basic universal moral standards. Universal moral standards, rather than determining the exact content of a culture's moral values and customs, provide general guidelines and set limits upon the values and customs that are morally acceptable within their particular context.

Exercises

1. Discuss some examples of sociological relativism, such as variations in marriage practices. What are the common underlying moral principles?

2. In the case of the Kabloona, can you think of any other relevant moral principles or sentiments? Was walking the aging father into a hole in the ice the morally best option for the Kabloona? Discuss your answers using the procedure for resolving moral dilemmas discussed in Chapter 2 on pages 64–67.

3. Although same-sex marriage is now legal in all fifty states, about 32 percent of Americans are still opposed to it.[12] Discuss arguments for and against legalizing same-sex marriage in the United States. Which of the premises in your arguments are based on cultural traditions and practices? Is the fact that Americans are divided over same-sex marriage morally relevant? Support your answers.

4. Being a suicide bomber is considered an honorable act in some Middle Eastern cultures; however, it is considered immoral in the United States. Discuss whether this difference is due primarily to fundamentally different moral values or to situational differences or to differences in factual and religious beliefs.

*5. Community service that puts us in contact with people who hold different values or worldviews from those we've come to accept as normal creates cognitive dissonance. Discuss a situation in your community service when this occurred. What were the conflicting values? How did you react when you encountered values that were at odds with your own? Could you resolve or make sense of this difference in values? Explain.

---

*An asterisk indicates that the exercise is appropriate for students who are doing community service learning as part of the course.

Social Darwinian Ethics: The Concept of Moral Progress

> *The leading moral laws are seen to follow as corollaries from the definition of complete life carried on under social conditions . . . in civilized societies more than in savage societies . . . the justice is greater.*
>
> —HERBERT SPENCER, *The Principles of Ethics* (1897), p. 35

> *[The savage] has no moral feelings of any kind, sort, or description; and his "mission" may be summed up as simply diabolical.*
>
> —CHARLES DICKENS, "The Noble Savage"[13]

Two events in the late nineteenth century led to a dramatic rise in the popularity of cultural relativism among intellectuals. The first was the publication of Charles Darwin's theory of evolution. The second was the increased use of fieldwork by cultural anthropologists.

Darwin's publication of *The Origin of Species* (1859) and, several years later, *The Descent of Man* (1871) precipitated a period of upheaval and a "crisis of conscience." During this time, ethicists and other intellectuals were challenged to reexamine their deeply held assumptions about human culture and human nature.[14] According to Darwin, human instincts, including the moral sense, are nothing more than response structures that have in the past contributed to the survival of the species. The concept of the "good," instead of being something peculiar to human nature or part of our "divine" nature, is simply a means of the perpetuation of the species.[15] In this sense, Darwin's concept of morality is similar to that of contemporary sociobiologists who maintain that altruism is biologically based to ensure survival.

Connections

Is altruism based in selfishness? *See Chapter 1, page 18, and Chapter 7, pages 212–213.*

Social Darwinists, such as Herbert Spencer (1820–1903), embraced an ethics based on one universal moral principle: survival of the fittest. However, unlike Darwin, the social Darwinists expanded the idea of survival of the fittest from individuals to whole societies. Societal fitness was defined in terms of worldly success and progress, which in turn were linked to moral superiority. Much of what we attribute to Darwin, such as the idea of evolution as progress, came from Spencer and the social Darwinists. Although Darwin spoke of evolution as adaptation to changing environments rather than progress per se, belief in progress had become firmly entrenched in the Western psyche during the eighteenth-century Enlightenment. Rousseau's romantic notion of the "noble savage," the natural person unaffected by the restrictions of modern society, was never generally accepted and was easily usurped by the view of savages as a lower form of human life.

Connections

How did Rousseau's view of human nature influence his moral philosophy? *See Chapter 4, pages 123–124.*

According to Spencer, just as animals progress or evolve over time from lower life-forms, so too does humanity evolve culturally over time from the ignorant savage cultures to the higher, intelligent, and morally civilized Christians—what God (or nature) intended humans to be. He believed that as cultures progress they pass through intermediary stages on their way to higher, more evolved forms. Within a culture, those who were successful were better suited to survival—a belief that fostered a paternalistic and degrading attitude toward the poor and "undeveloped" Third World countries. We still find this in our foreign policy to bring "civilization" and democracy to tribal people in Afghanistan and elsewhere.

The assimilation of social Darwinism into the social sciences "scientifically" validated the prevailing Victorian worldview that the so-called savage was morally inferior to the civilized European. A linear model of cultural progress was developed, using modern "savages" to illustrate the prehistoric stages of human cultural development. Following is an excerpt from Spencer's *Principles of Ethics* (1897):

> For each kind and degree of social evolution determined by external conflict and internal friendship, there is an appropriate compromise between the moral code of enmity and the moral code of amity. . . . This compromise, vague, ambiguous, illogical, though it may be, is nevertheless for the time authoritative. . . . But such [inconsistent] moralities are, by their definitions, shown to belong to incomplete conduct; not to conduct that is fully evolved. We saw that the adjustments of acts to ends which, while constituting the external manifestations to life conducive to the continuance of life, have been rising to a certain ideal form now approached by the civilized man.[16]

Spencer's belief that evolution is synonymous with progress eventually won him a large popular following.

Even Charles Dickens (1812–1870), who championed the rights of the downtrodden workers in England during the Industrial Revolution, unquestioningly accepted the social Darwinian view of "savages" as morally inferior. During the mid-nineteenth century, adventurers would bring back "savages" from their travels to put on exhibit. After Dickens attended an exhibition of Zulus from Africa at a gallery in London, he wrote,

> I have not the least belief in the Noble Savage . . .
>
> He has no moral feelings of any kind, sort, or description; and his "mission" may be summed up as simply diabolical.[17]

Spencer's moral philosophy had a tremendous influence on philosophical thought during the late nineteenth and early twentieth centuries. Social Darwinism was used to justify the takeover and colonization of "primitive" societies by Europeans, as well as the privileged status of people with wealth and power, in the name of evolutionary progress. The ideas of social Darwinism are still evident in the moral philosophies of sociobiologists and the ethical egoism of American philosopher Ayn Rand.

Connections

What is Ayn Rand's view on the morality of capitalism? *See Chapter 7, pages 217-220.*

Exercises

1. Discuss Herbert Spencer's claim that civilization and moral progress go hand in hand. Are people from industrialized nations more moral than people from so-called Third World nations? Are humans as a species becoming more moral as we progress technologically? Support your answers using examples.

2. To what extent do the ideas of the social Darwinists still influence our thinking when it comes to social ethics and international policy? Identify examples of social Darwinism in your own thinking or that of others.

3. Social Darwinism has been used to morally justify competitive economic individualism as survival of the fittest. To what extent have the ideas of social Darwinism been used to support the view that those who are economically successful are morally better people than the poor? Support your answer.

Ruth Benedict: Cultural Relativism as a Protest against Social Darwinism

We recognize that morality differs in every society, and is a convenient term for socially approved habits.

—RUTH BENEDICT, "Anthropology and the Abnormal," p. 73

The modern version of cultural relativism emerged as a protest against social Darwinism and the imperialism that it supported. In the early twentieth century, several notable anthropologists and sociologists—including William Graham Sumner, Émile Durkheim, Franz Boas, and Ruth Benedict—spoke out against this degrading view of "primitive," simpler cultures.

In her landmark book *Patterns of Culture*, published in 1934, Ruth Benedict (1887–1948) uncovered the inconsistencies in the social Darwinists' claim that morality is found in a greater degree in civilized societies:

> Early anthropologists tried to arrange all traits of different cultures in an evolutionary sequence from the earliest forms to their final development in Western civilization. But there is no reason to suppose that by discussing Australian religion rather than our own we are uncovering primordial religion, or that by discussing Iroquois social organization we are returning to the mating habits of man's early ancestors.
>
> Since we are forced to believe that the race of man is one species, it follows that man everywhere has an equally long history behind him. Some primitive tribes may have held relatively closer to primordial forms of behavior than civilized man, but this can only be relative and our guesses are as likely to be wrong as right. There is no justification for identifying some one contemporary primitive custom with the original type of human behavior.

Robert Chanka of South Africa poses with his six wives and some of his twenty-six children.
Polygamy is legal in South Africa under certain conditions.
©ALEXANDER JOE/AFP/Getty Images

Discussion Questions

1. While acceptance for polygamy in the United States, at 17 percent as of 2017, is growing, the majority Americans still believe it is highly immoral. What are the moral issues, if any, involved in polygamy between consenting adults? Discuss whether these moral considerations transcend cultural boundaries.

2. Compare and contrast the issues involved in legalizing polygamy with those in legalizing same-sex marriage.

Although these anthropologists questioned the assumptions of the social Darwinists, at the same time they simply accepted at face value the stories being told about bloodthirsty practices such as cannibalism and bizarre sexual practices in certain cultures; many of these stories later turned out to be unsubstantiated or untrue.[18]

Like the social Darwinists, cultural relativists focus on the differences between cultures. Benedict, for example, rejected offhand the possibility of transcultural or universal moral standards altogether rather than look for a common moral sentiment or standard among all humans. She argued that morality in each culture cannot be evaluated by outside standards. Cultural customs cannot

Connections

What is the relationship between interpretation and analysis in the three-tier model of thinking? *See Chapter 2, pages 32-33.*

be evaluated internally by transcultural standards because such standards do not exist. There are no objective, transcultural moral standards or rational criteria to analyze the morality of a particular custom, such as cannibalism. Interpretation rather than analysis stands at the top of the "thinking" pyramid. Our culturally shaped interpretations or worldviews about what is right and wrong *are* our reality. (See reading from Benedict at end of this chapter.)

In other words, anthropologists such as Benedict and Sumner were not simply promoting sociological relativism. They were not just saying that cannibals believed that eating other humans was right: This is simply stating the obvious. Instead, the cultural relativists claimed that cannibalism was, in fact, morally right for cultures such as the Dobu of New Guinea, who apparently practiced cannibalism before the arrival of the Europeans. The popularity of cultural relativism was further promoted by the psychological theory of the time, which regarded morality as simply the internalization of cultural values.

The "right" way is the way which the ancestors used and which has been handed down. The tradition is its own warrant. . . . The notion of right is in the folkways, whatever is, is right. This is because they are traditional, and therefore contain in themselves the authority of the ancestral ghosts. When we come to the folkways we are at the end of our analysis.

—WILLIAM GRAHAM SUMNER, *Folkways* (1906)[19]

However, by advocating cultural relativism, these anthropologists ceased to be social scientists describing sociological phenomena and instead began to do exactly what they claimed to be avoiding—making value judgments about what is morally right and wrong. According to cultural relativists, a hypothetical kind-hearted Dobuan who tried to protect a stranger from her anthropophagous (man-eating) kinfolk was doing something that was *morally wrong*. She *ought not* to have protected the stranger.

Now, we may acknowledge that our kind and gentle Dobuan would have been regarded as deviant and perhaps mentally deranged in her own culture, but it is more difficult to argue that she was an immoral person. Indeed, today we generally regard a person who refuses to follow cultural mores that cause grave harm to others as highly moral. This is true not only when passing judgment on people from other cultures, but also when passing judgment on the behavior of people within our own culture.

Once we begin to examine cultural relativism, it becomes clear that the early advocates of this theory did not think through all the implications of their position. By advocating cultural relativism, anthropologists such as Benedict wanted to stop imperialist practices and replace them with greater respect for and tolerance of cultural differences.[20] If moral values are relative to each culture, then no culture's values can be superior to those of any other culture. And if no culture's values are superior they reasoned, then Western cultures have no justification for imposing their morality on other cultures. However, as we noted earlier, tolerance for cultural diversity that is not grounded in the universal principle of respect for human dignity legitimates turning a blind eye to cultural customs that violate basic human rights and dignity.

As caring people, we may sympathize with the intention of these anthropologists to promote tolerance and respect; however, this does not mean that their reasoning was correct. Their conclusion—that we should not impose our Western values on other cultures—does not logically follow from cultural relativism. The cultural relativists had no grounds to support the belief that *laissez-faire* ("live and let live") moral values are any better than those of the imperialists. Indeed, by opposing imperialism, they were going *against* the cultural mores of their own culture, and by doing so, they were encouraging immorality. To be consistent, they should have accepted, if not encouraged, imperialism and colonization as the morally correct behavior for Europeans at that time!

In summary, according to the cultural relativists, we cannot pass judgment on the moral values of other cultures because we have no valid grounds for criticizing the traditions of other cultures, no matter how despicable these traditions may appear to us. As cultural relativists, we can say that cannibalism is wrong for us as Americans or that slavery is no longer moral in the United States. But we cannot go beyond this to claim that cannibalism and slavery are wrong for cultures that condone these practices. We, as cultural relativists, may not like these practices, just as we may not like the fashion or art of another culture, but we cannot say they are morally wrong. Indeed, today, the use of workers in poorer nations as a source of cheap labor has been justified on the grounds that low pay for long hours and even child labor are traditions, and hence morally acceptable, in those cultures. British philosopher Mary Midgley argues that the idea that we can respect another culture without judging it is logically inconsistent since respect implies a positive judgment. She notes that placing a ban on moral judgment when it comes to other cultures leads to moral isolationism, an untenable position.

Exercises

*1. Do you agree with the cultural relativists that a person who deviates from cultural norms (such as our kind Dobuan) is immoral, but the conformist is, by definition, moral? Support your answer using examples from our culture and from your community service work.

2. Compare and contrast the theories of Benedict and Spencer. Does either theory present an adequate explanation of morality? Explain.

3. Democracy is regarded by many Americans as morally superior to other forms of government. If democracy is morally superior, does this justify trying to "export" democracy to countries such as Cuba and Iraq? Discuss also how both a social Darwinist and a cultural relativist would answer these questions.

Cultural Relativism and the Moral Community

Each group nourishes its own pride and vanity, boasts itself superior, exalts its own divinities, and looks with contempt on outsiders. Each group thinks its own folkways are the only right ones, and if it observes groups that have other folkways, these excite its scorn. Opprobrious epithets are derived from these differences. "Pig-eater," "cow-eater," "uncircumcised," "jabberers," are epithets of contempt.

—WILLIAM GRAHAM SUMNER, *Folkways* (1906), p. 13

Variations in cultural norms are sometimes due to differences in how cultures define their moral communities instead of differences in basic moral standards. The moral community is comprised of persons. **Persons** are beings who are worthy of respect because they have inherent moral value independent of their usefulness to anyone else. Cultural relativism, on the other hand, defines the moral community in *ethnocentric* terms. Someone has moral value only because his or her society grants this status. There is no source of moral value other than one's culture. Those who are granted moral status by their culture receive the protection and support of the community.

The Moral Community

If we consider the concept of moral community when examining the moral values and practices of another culture, we can find far more commonality among cultures. Among the Papuans of New Guinea, for example, a wife who came from within the group had full status; wives who had been captured during enemy raids did not come from within the group and, hence, were fair game for headhunters! And in Guantanamo Bay, Cuba, foreign detainees were subject to torture by water boarding, a practice that never would have been tolerated on American prisoners. Water boarding was not banned until 2009.

When violence does occur within the community, it must be justified. The bombing of "enemy" civilians of another culture, such as Afghanistan or Iraq, is referred to by the U.S. military as "collateral damage," a euphemism referring to unintended destruction of equipment and facilities as well, and is regarded with relative unconcern by many, though certainly not all, Americans. However, the same type of violent actions within the borders of our community, whether carried out by police officers or terrorists, such as the September 11, 2001, terrorist attacks on the World Trade Center, are met with unmitigated horror.

Now brotherhood in most of the myths I know of is confined to a bounded community. In bounded communities, aggression is projected outward.

For example, the ten commandments say, "Thou shalt not kill." Then the next chapter says, "Go into Canaan and kill everybody in it." That is a bounded field. The myths of participation and love pertain only to the in-group, and the out-group is the total other.

—Joseph Campbell, *The Power of Myth* (1988), p. 22

Some cultures are more inclusive and less hierarchical than others in their definition of moral community. The Dobuan and Papuans have a very exclusive definition of moral community. The Buddhist moral community, on the other hand, is inclusive and egalitarian. Because Buddhist ethics supports a universalist ethics rather than cultural relativism, all living beings are encompassed within their moral community—not simply members of their particular culture.

Many Native American cultures also include other humans and nonhuman animals in the moral community. The Pawnee Indians, for example, address "all of life as a 'thou'—the trees, the stones."[21] All beings are seen as objects of reverence and value. While the Pawnee recognize that it may be necessary to kill living beings for one's own survival, this must be done with respect and only when necessary. Other animals are not a resource for humans but co-dwellers.

Eagle Man (Ed McGaa) writes, in his book *Mother Earth Spirituality* (1990), about the Native American moral community:

> We, the American Indian, had a way of living that enabled us to live within the great, complete beauty that only the natural environment can provide. The Indian tribes had a common value system and a commonality of religion, without religious animosity. . . . Our four commandments from the Great Spirit are: (1) respect for Mother Earth, (2) respect for the Great Spirit, (3) respect for our fellow man and woman, and (4) respect for individual freedom (provided that individual freedom does not threaten the tribe or the people or Mother Earth) . . .

The moral community of a culture can be represented by using a mandala. **Mandala** is the ancient Sanskrit word for a circle that symbolizes the cosmic order.[22] The mandala includes within its borders all that is sacred or, in moral terms, all that has *intrinsic moral value*. When using a mandala to represent a culture's moral community, beings who have the greater status in that culture are placed toward the center of the mandala. As one moves further toward the edge of the mandala, one's moral value diminishes. Beings that are outside the moral community are placed outside the circle. Eagle Man includes all living beings and nature in the mandala; our mandala is less inclusive. Using a mandala, the moral community in the United States in 1800 might be represented as in Figure 6.1 on the following page.

Connections

How do utilitarians define moral community when it comes to nonhuman species? *See Chapter 8, pages 260-263.*

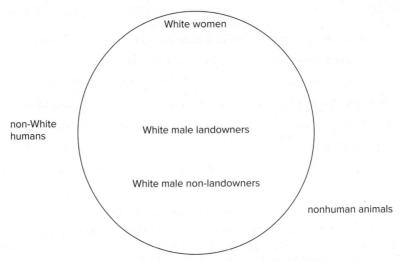

FIGURE 6.1   Mandala of the U.S. Moral Community in the Early 1800s

Cultural relativists such as Ruth Benedict were concerned about members of "primitive" cultures being exploited by more powerful cultures. However, not everyone living within a particular culture is a member of that culture's moral community. Exploitation can also occur within the culture.

Slavery and the Holocaust

Slavery was legal for more than two centuries in colonial America and the United States. Yet, as any historian can tell you, respect for human equality and a belief in justice *were* pre-Civil War American values. These values were even written into the U.S. Constitution. What has changed between now and then is *not* the basic moral principles but the definition of moral community. Slavery could only be morally justified by excluding the victims of slavery from the moral community. By excluding African Americans, the values of equality and justice did not apply to them. This definition of the moral community was reaffirmed by the U.S. Supreme Court in *Dred Scott v. Sanford* (1857):

> In the opinion of the court, the legislation and histories of the times, and the language used in the Declaration of Independence, show, that neither the class of persons that have been imported as slaves, nor their descendants, whether they had become free or not, were then acknowledged as part of the people, nor intended to be included in the general words used in the memorable instrument. . . .
>
> They had for more than a century before been regarded as beings of an inferior order; and altogether unfit to associate with the white race, either in social or political relations; and so far inferior that they had no rights which the white man was bound to respect; and that the negro might be lawfully reduced to slavery for his own benefit. . . .

This opinion was at that time fixed and universal in the civilized portion of the white race. It was regarded as an axiom in morals as well as in politics which no one thought of disputing, or supposed to be open to dispute. . . .

Now the right of property in a slave is distinctly and expressly affirmed in the Constitution. . . . He is himself property in the strictest sense of the term. And the Government in express terms is pledged to protect it in all future time, if the slave escapes from his owner.[23]

The "natural inferiority" of Africans was affirmed not only by popular opinion and the U.S. Supreme Court but also by the medical profession. Dr. William H. Holcombe of Virginia wrote, in the *Southern Literary Messenger*, in 1861: "The negro is not a white man with a black skin, but of a different species, . . . the hopeless physical and mental inferior organically constituted to be an agricultural laborer in tropical climates—a strong animal machine."[24] Women, likewise, because they were not regarded as fully rational, were relegated to the fringes of the U.S. moral community until 1920, when they were finally given the right to vote. Women, like Blacks and Hispanics, also earn significantly less than White males.

In Nazi Germany, the Jews were excluded from the moral community by Germany's supreme court and by public opinion. In 1936, the German supreme court ruled that "the Jew is only a rough copy of a human being, with human-like facial traits but nonetheless . . . lower than any animal . . . otherwise nothing. For all that bear a human face are not equal." The exclusion of the Jews from the moral community legitimized the Holocaust. Because Jews were outside the moral community, fundamental moral principles did not apply to them.

The cultural definition of moral community is fluid. For example, African Americans who were once outside the moral community of the United States are now inside. Unborn humans, who were once inside the moral community and protected by law, are now outside. Our animal companions and endangered species enjoy some protection from the moral community. Farm animals, insects, and most wild animals, on the other hand, are excluded from our culture's moral community and may be squashed, poisoned, shot, experimented upon, or raised in confining and cruel conditions without fear of censure from those at the center of our moral community.

Connections
How does cultural relativism influence women's moral development and sense of self-worth? *See Chapter 3, pages 96-97.*

Connections
How did the events of World War II contribute to our rethinking of the idea of moral community and human rights? *See Chapter 11, pages 357-359.*

Marginalized Groups

Just as some groups are outside the moral community, other groups may be relegated to the fringes or margins of the moral community. We refer to these groups as **marginalized**. It is not morally acceptable to kill or torture those who are marginalized, but they don't receive respect and legal protection or have access to the same opportunities as those who are closer to the center of the community.

For example, in the United States, African Americans receive harsher penalties and longer prison sentences than White males who commit the same crimes. Members of marginalized groups have also been used, without their

Between 1930 and 1953 the U.S. government conducted a study on syphilis using poor Black men as subjects. The study continued even after a cure for syphilis had been found.
Source: National Archives of Atlanta

consent, in medical experiments. Between 1930 and 1953, the U.S. Department of Health Services conducted a study on syphilis, known as the Tuskegee study, using—without their consent—poor Black men living in Macon County, Alabama, as subjects. Despite the discovery in the late 1940s that penicillin could cure syphilis, treatment was withheld from the nearly three hundred men participating in the study. As a result, many of the men died for the sake of scientific knowledge although their lives could have been saved. Medical experiments with contraception have also been conducted on poor Mexican American women without their knowledge or informed consent.[25]

Following the September 11 terrorist attacks in New York City, Arab Americans were detained and imprisoned without any actual charges brought against them. More recently, President Trump's ban on immigration from Muslim countries has raised fears among the Muslim American community that it will encourage discrimination and violence against Muslims in this country.

The cultural definition of moral community is, to a large extent, politically and economically motivated. Cultural relativism, in other words, supports a definition of the moral community that serves primarily to maintain the status quo. By doing so, cultural relativism protects the interests of those in power while morally sanctioning the marginalization and exploitation of other groups, thereby promoting ethnocentrism and legitimizing hatred and discrimination as morally acceptable.

During the mid-nineteenth century, thousands of Chinese immigrated to the western United States to work on the transcontinental railway and in the gold mines. Many employers preferred Chinese workers because they worked hard for lower wages and they refused to join unions. An anti-Chinese campaign, fueled by the new labor movement, quickly spread throughout the West and gave rise to demonstrations and violence. In 1879, the state of California adopted a provision to its constitution that forbade the employment of any "Chinese or Mongolian [in] any state, county, municipal, or other public work, except in punishment for crime." This provision was not repealed until 1952.

The Vicious Cycle

When cultural relativism defines the moral community in a hierarchical manner, it creates large groups of needy people who do not have full access to the opportunities and resources available to those who are closer to the center of the moral community. This, in turn, can lead to a vicious cycle, where those who are neediest come to be seen as unworthy, lazy, or bad and deserving of their degraded status. As such, they are regarded by those in the dominant position with suspicion and intolerance.

This attitude is evident today in the treatment of immigrants—legal or otherwise—from Mexico and Latin American. Gloria Anzaldua, author of *Borderlands/La Frontera: The New Mestiza*, writes:

> The U.S.-Mexican border *es una herida abierta* [is an open wound] where the Third World grates against the first and bleeds. And before a scab forms it hemorrhages again, the lifeblood of two worlds merging to form a third country—a border culture. Borders are set up to define the places that are safe and unsafe, to distinguish *us* from *them*. . . . A borderland is a vague and undetermined place created by the emotional residue of an unnatural boundary. It is in a constant state of transition. . . . Gringos in the U.S. Southwest consider the inhabitants of the borderlands transgressors, aliens—whether they possess documents or not . . . Do not enter, trespassers will be raped, maimed, strangled, gassed, shot. The only "legitimate" inhabitants are those in power, the whites and those who align themselves with whites. Tension grips the inhabitants of the borderlands like a virus. Ambivalence and unrest reside there and death is no stranger.[26]

If morality is synonymous with cultural norms, then the exclusion of people from the moral community should be fairly uncontroversial. Those in power should have no need to try to convince themselves and others that certain groups deserve a lower status. However, this is rarely the case. When a culture marginalizes or excludes a group of people from the moral community, the culture often feels compelled to justify its actions even to the point of engaging in blatant doublethink. Indeed, the group in power may even justify the exclusion of another group as being for their own benefit.

In 1830, with the encouragement of President Andrew Jackson, the U.S. Congress passed the Indian Removal Act. With the passage of this law, Native Americans became further marginalized. No longer was peaceful coexistence the official policy. Despite the sanction of the U.S. Congress, those in charge of the removal still felt compelled to morally justify their actions. The removal

Connections

How was John Locke's natural rights ethics used to justify the forced removal of the Native Americans from their land? *See Chapter 11, page 362.*

of the Indians from their homeland was justified by the European Americans as being in the Indians' best interests. Despite the fact that the Seminoles in Florida fought for seven years before finally giving up, the 1832 U.S. "treaty" that forced them off their homeland read as follows:

> The Seminole Indians [regard] with just respect the solicitude manifested by the President of the United States for the improvement of their condition, by recommending a removal to a country more suitable to their habits and wants than the one they at present occupy in the territory of Florida.[27]

Slavery was also defended by many prominent White Southerners as saving the slaves from "the horrible consequences of emancipation." Without slavery, it was argued, "the blacks would rapidly degenerate into a primitive barbarism" and the whole "fabric of civilization and liberty . . . would be completely demolished by the relentless fury of ignorant barbarians."[28] U.S. humanist Margaret Fuller wrote in 1843 regarding the doublethink involved in slavery:

Connections

What is doublethink and when are people most likely to use it? *See Chapter 2, pages 42–43.*

> Though the national independence be blurred by the servility of individuals; though freedom and equality have been proclaimed only to leave room for a monstrous display of slave dealing, and slave keeping; though the free American so often feels himself free, like the Roman, only to pamper his appetites and his indolence through the misery of his fellow beings, still it is not in vain, that the verbal statement has been made, "All men are born free and equal." There it stands, a golden certainty, wherein to encourage the good, to shame the bad.[29]

Under cultural relativism who is inside the moral community and who is marginalized can change over time. (Steve Kelley [1994]. By permission of Steve Kelley and Creators Syndicate, Inc.)

Fuller's observation is a good illustration that people, for the most part, *know* what is morally right. However, cultural norms and self-interest can modify how we apply moral knowledge in real-life situations. Martin Luther King Jr. once said that the "universe bends toward justice." King was a strong opponent of cultural relativism, and he believed that the call of justice in our hearts cannot be overridden by legal decrees or cultural norms. There are times in all of our lives when, upon reflection, we realize that we can do more toward making this a more compassionate and just world.

Exercises

1. How do you define the moral community? Draw a mandala of your moral community. Is it the same as the U.S. moral community? If not, how can you explain the discrepancy?

2. Make a list of the criteria that our culture uses for including or excluding humans and animals as well as the environment from the moral community. Discuss the extent to which these criteria reflect cultural norms. Do you consider these criteria acceptable? Explain.

3. Compare and contrast Ed McGaa's (Eagle Man) Native American concept of the moral community with that of European Americans. Discuss the implications of these different views on how we think about moral issues such as discrimination, terrorism, and climate change.

4. Thomas Jefferson wrote the following indictment against the king of England for encouraging slavery and the slave trade: "He has waged cruel war against human nature itself, violating its most sacred rights of life and liberty in the person of a distant people who never offended him, captivating and carrying them into slavery in another hemisphere, or to incur miserable death in their transportation thither."[30] Was Jefferson immoral for denouncing the cultural norms and laws of his time? Explain.

   On the other hand, Thomas Jefferson was a slaveowner himself. How did he justify this? Was he engaged in doublethink? If so, how is this discrepancy explained, if at all, by teachers in school and in history books?

5. In Northern India and in China, the birth of a female is often regarded as a tragedy. Many women undergo ultrasound or amniocentesis, so they can get an abortion if the fetus is female. In the United States, the majority of people consider amniocentesis for sex selection to be immoral. However, we generally have few qualms about using ultrasound or amniocentesis to detect Down syndrome or spina bifida in the fetus, so he or she can be aborted.

   Discuss selective abortion in light of cultural variations in definitions of moral community. How does the selective abortion of female infants in India and infants with birth defects in the United States affect the treatment of women and people with disabilities in these two cultures?

6. Discuss ways in which our moral community is politically motivated. In what ways do cultural definitions of where you fit in the moral community affect

your life the way you are treated, and the way you treat others? Use specific examples to support your answer.

*7. Which particular groups of people are most likely to need help from community service organizations in our culture? Is there any relationship between the populations most in need and their position on the mandala of the U.S. moral community? Relate your answer to the concept of ethnocentricity. Discuss how, if at all, your community service work influenced your concept of the moral community.

Cultural Relativism, Cross-Cultural Criticism, and Moral Progress

One of the first features which mark the distinction between a civilized, and a rude nation, is the value attached to human life, and the protection given it by the former. . . . Respect for human life, and vigilant protection of it, is a feature of civilization sadly absent in this country [the United States].

—FREDERICK DOUGLASS, "Contradictions in American Civilization" (1861)

The anthropologists who promoted cultural relativism in the late nineteenth and early twentieth centuries were concerned about Europeans and North Americans passing negative judgment on the moral values of "primitive" societies. However, cultural relativism also precludes non-European cultures from pointing out or defending ways in which they may be morally superior.

Are Some Cultures More Moral Than Others?

Connections

On what grounds does Gyges, in Plato's *Republic*, argue that people need society if they are to behave justly? *See Chapter 7, pages 209–210.*

Like most philosophers, Aristotle and Plato rejected cultural relativism. They argued that societies should be judged according to how well they live up to a certain transcultural moral ideal. In his *Republic*, Plato set forth a plan for a republic that he believed would be most conducive to the promotion of justice and virtue in its citizens. The structure of this republic, Plato maintained, is similar to that of the properly ordered person. Just as a good or just person promotes goodness and justice all around, so too does a just society promote justice and virtue in its individual citizens.[31] The ideal society would be ruled by philosopher-kings (and queens) who, because of their training in philosophy, would be more just and less open to false ideologies.

North African philosopher Ibn Khaldun (1332–1406) also rejected cultural relativism. In his book *The Muqaddimah*, Khaldun argued that nomadic cultures are morally superior to sedentary, urban cultures. The customs of nomadic cultures such as the Bedouins, he claimed, enhance good traits such as courage, cooperation, and striving for justice; the customs of sedentary and urban cultures encourage immorality. Sedentary people are more concerned with their own individual ends and the indulgence in worldly pleasures. This preoccupation, Ibn Khaldun suggested, leads to moral evils such as injustice, mutual aggression, greed, and lack of courage. Whether or not his interpretation is correct needs to be researched.

The association of social Darwinism with progress with European civilization has been used to justify the imposing of Western ways on the tribal people of Africa and another "undeveloped" countries. Indeed, some suggest that the rise of urban culture, which is relatively mobile and brings together people from diverse cultural backgrounds, encourages people to expand their concept of moral community. On the other hand, does the sedentary suburban lifestyle of many North Americans insulate us from diversity and make us more selfish and preoccupied with accumulating material goods, as Ibn Khaldun claimed it would?

Native American philosophers Ed "Eagle Man" McGas and John Fire Lame Deer likewise regard the European American lifestyle as morally unacceptable. They argue that the anthropocentric definition of moral community characteristic of Whites is destructive not just to the environment but to the humans who are part of this environment. This destructive attitude of Whites toward the environment, Lame Deer argues, is based upon the misconception that the earth, the wind, the rocks, and the water are dead or inert. For the Sioux, these elements are "very much alive," and worthy of moral respect.[32] We are all physical matter. Matter, in all its forms, has its own consciousness and life force.

A cultural relativist would simply dismiss what they say as being right only for them, but not for us, because there are no transcultural moral standards. Plato, Ibn Khaldun, Eagle Man, and John Fire Lame Deer, in contrast, claim that there *are* universal moral standards that we can use to pass judgment upon other cultures. Rather than dismissing a culture's values as relevant only to the people living within that culture, a universalist view of morality encourages us to listen to other points of view and to attempt to understand other people. We should also be willing to analyze and, if necessary, revise or reject our own cultural values in light of our new understanding.

Social Reform and the Rejection of Cultural Norms

Even more troubling to the cultural relativist than cross-cultural criticism is criticism of cultural norms from within that culture. Harriet Tubman was born in Bucktown, Maryland, around 1820. She served as a slave under several masters—some of whom beat the free-spirited girl several times a day. Despite her unhappy and abusive childhood, Tubman never gave up hope. In 1849, she escaped through the Underground Railroad, a network of antislavery activists who helped slaves escape to freedom in the northern states and in Canada. Tubman later became a "conductor" on the Underground Railroad, leading more than three hundred slaves, including her own parents, to their freedom.

Tubman was one of the thousands of fugitive slaves who sought sanctuary in another culture: Canada. Tubman rejected the United States' definition of moral community and instead regarded Canada's more inclusive moral community as superior. By making this judgment, she rejected the U.S. norm that she,

Connections

Why is getting our facts straight basic to good moral reasoning? *See Chapter 2, page 50.*

Connections

What is Social Darwinism? *See Chapter 6, pages 178-179.*

Child operatives in the spinning room of a Fall River, Massachusetts, mill, c. 1900.
(Photograph courtesy of the Fall River Historical Society.)
©Everett Historical/ Shutterstock

as a Black woman, did not have the same right to liberty as a White person. While some of us may celebrate Tubman as an American heroine, by rejecting U.S. cultural norms of her time and acting contrary to them, she would be censured as an immoral person by a cultural relativist.

The belief that there is a morality that stands above society and to which society is responsible has been a recurring theme throughout world history. Like Tubman, most social reformers, rather than urging people to be more culture maintaining, claim that cultural laws and norms are morally binding *only* when they respect and nurture human dignity. In doing so, social reformers maintain that they are not simply being arbitrary but that they are judging their culture in light of a transcultural standard of the ideal society. Injustice, social reformers argue, is wrong no matter what culture one lives in or what culture one was born in.

Immigrants, especially undocumented immigrants, are not the only people whose labor is exploited. Child labor used to be a common practice in the United States. In 1900, an estimated 25 percent of the mill workers in the New England textile mills were children 14 years and younger. While illegal or strictly regulated as in the United States and Canada, child labor is still prevalent in South Asia and sub-Saharan Africa, where almost one in every four children are engaged in work deemed by the United Nations to be harmful to their health and development including drug trafficking, armed conflict, slavery, sexual exploitation, and hazardous work.[33]

If morality is the same as cultural norms, then not only is the notion of moral progress meaningless, but social reformers such as Harriet Tubman and

César Chávez are nothing but common criminals. Most of us do distinguish between reformers and criminals, though, which demonstrates that, in practice, we do distinguish between cultural and moral norms.

Exercises

1. English psychologist Havelock Ellis (1859–1939) wrote: "It has always been found a terrible matter to war with the moral system of one's age; it will have its revenge, one way or another, from within or from without, whatever happens after." Think of a time when you took a moral stand against the norms of your peer group. Did the group try to get revenge on you? How did you respond?

2. Analyze Eagle Man's claim that we need to respect Mother Earth and all our fellow men and women, and to not possess more than we need, if we are to survive as a culture. Discuss what advice Eagle Man might give us regarding our moral responsibilities for preserving the environment and reducing global warming.

3. Child labor in factories is illegal in the United States. However, is it morally acceptable to purchase products made by factories in other countries that use child labor, as long as child labor is an acceptable practice in those countries? Support your answer. Discuss how a cultural relativist would answer this question.

4. In 1516, Sir Thomas More published a book entitled *Utopia*, which envisions an ideal society where everything is ordered for the best of humankind and where evils, such as poverty and bigotry, have been eliminated. Since then, several other books have been written about **utopias**—and anti-utopias—including Samuel Butler's *Erehwon* (1872), Charlotte Perkins Gilman's *Herland* (1915), Aldous Huxley's *Brave New World* (1932), B. F. Skinner's *Walden II* (1961), and Margaret Atwood's *The Handmaid's Tale* (1986).

   Discuss the ideas about utopia in light of one of these books or your own conception of an ideal society. Compare this ideal to our own culture.

5. In a democracy, the majority determines, for the most part, the moral norms that everyone is expected to follow. A democratic culture thus tends to reinforce an ethics of cultural relativism or conformity and the oppression of the individual conscience. In his book *On Liberty* (1859),[34] British utilitarian and libertarian John Stuart Mill (1806–1873), while not arguing that we should do away with democracy, nevertheless criticized it as being the "Tyranny of the Majority" and the "Tyranny of Custom." Discuss steps we might take, both as individuals and as a society, to make ourselves less vulnerable to majority opinion.

6. Amina Lawal, age thirty, became pregnant after having an affair with her neighbor Yahaya Mohammed, who had agreed to marry her. However, Mohammed reneged on his promise. Eight days after Lawal gave birth, the police arrested her for adultery, which was a capital crime in her home state of Katsina in Nigeria. Lawal was scheduled to be stoned to death as soon as her daughter Wasila was weaned. Typically, only the woman was sentenced to death by stoning.[35] In the end, the conviction was overturned, in part because of international outcry, as well as protests from some Nigerians.

On what grounds can we, as Americans, claim that the practice of stoning an adulteress is immoral? Discuss whether such claims can be reconciled with cultural relativism. If not, what criteria should we use in judging the morality of practices in other cultures? Discuss how Benedict might respond to this case.

The Holocaust and Disillusionment with Cultural Relativism

Postwar Sentiments

Cultural relativism fell out of favor with social scientists after World War II. Faced with the horrors of the Holocaust, it became harder and harder to maintain the belief that there are no standards of right and wrong outside of cultural norms. Anti-Semitism was a cultural norm supported by the majority of Germans before and during the war rather than a conspiracy of a few deranged and power-hungry men. This cultural perception is discussed in the following excerpt from Daniel Goldhagen's book, *Hitler's Willing Executioners* (1996):

> The men and women who became the Holocaust's perpetuators were shaped
> by and operated in a particular social and historical setting. They brought with
> them prior elaborate conceptions of the world, ones that were common to their
> society. . . . The Holocaust was the defining feature of German society during its
> Nazi period. . . . The program's first parts, namely the systematic exclusion of Jews
> from German economic and social life, were carried out in the open, under approv-
> ing eyes, and with the complicity of virtually all sectors of German society, from the
> legal, medical, and teaching professions, to the churches, both Catholic and Protes-
> tant, to the gamut of economic, social, and cultural groups and associations. . . .
>
> The killings [of the Jews] met with general understanding, if not approval. No
> other policy (of similar or greater scope) was carried out with more persistence of
> zeal, and with fewer difficulties, than the genocide, except perhaps the war itself.

Connections

What is the United Nations' "Universal Declaration of Human Rights" and why is it a rejection of cultural relativism? *See Chapter 11, page 357.*

Not only were the majority of Germans at that time anti-Semitic, but Jews were legally considered nonpersons (outside of the moral community) in Germany and therefore had no substantial rights. Thus, to take a stand against the Holocaust necessitated taking a stand against cultural relativism.

In 1945, the tribunal at the United Nations Nuremberg Trials put forth a list of universal standards of justice that established parameters on acceptable norms of civilized behavior. The tribunal maintained that these standards—which prohibited "crimes against humanity," "torture," "waging or preparing for an unjust war"—were not a cultural creation but universal moral standards and, as such, binding on all people everywhere. According to the charter, we each have an individual moral responsibility not to take refuge in any laws or customs of our culture that run contrary to universal moral standards. Between 1945 and 1949, almost two hundred war criminals were tried under this new charter.

Adolf Eichmann (1906-1962) in a bulletproof witness stand during his 1962 trial in Jerusalem for war crimes. Although Eichman issued orders as part of his job, he was never directly involved in the killing of any Jews.
©Bettmann/Getty Images

Discussion Questions

1. When asked if he ever questioned the orders of his superiors Eichman replied "Who am I to judge?" Discuss a time when you responded "Who am I to judge?" to avoid rocking the boat or going against the status quo.

2. Discuss how you might respond if your government asked you to order or to carry out acts that would bring about the suffering of others who are outside our moral community or living in a different culture. Use specific examples to illustrate your answer.

How can we reconcile these men's actions with the theory of cultural relativism? Hitler and the Nazis, rather than being deviants, had the support of the wider community. Indeed, as Goldhagen points out, what was perhaps most disconcerting about these war criminals, with a few exceptions, was their normalcy.

Political scientist Hannah Arendt refers to this cultural phenomenon, in her book about Adolf Eichmann, as the "banality of evil."[36] Like the slaveowners in the United States and the cavalry that hunted down and massacred thousands of Native Americans, the Nazis were, for the most part, "good" family men and upstanding members of their community. Although the official claim was that only "a relatively small percentage" of Germans had been Nazis or Nazi sympathizers, in fact, the exact opposite was the case.

Adolf Eichmann as the "Good" Citizen

Nazi Adolf Eichmann represents the quintessential cultural relativist. A medium-built, bespectacled bureaucrat, who worked as minister of transportation in Nazi Germany, his job was to arrange for the collection and deportation of all Jews. Following the war, Eichmann fled to Brazil with his family. In May 1960, he was abducted by representatives of the Israeli government and deported to Jerusalem, where he was charged with crimes against the Jews with intent to destroy the people. He was found guilty of these crimes and sentenced to death by hanging on May 31, 1961.

At his trial, Eichmann pleaded "not guilty in the sense of the indictment" to each of the counts brought against him. He had been a good, law-abiding citizen. In a police examination, he stated that he would have sent his own father to his death if that had been what the law required. Unlike with a common criminal, Eichmann's thinking and that of his society were in perfect harmony.

Eichmann recalled that he was horrified and repulsed by his first visit to one of these camps. He even told the SS commander about his feelings. Why then did he and other Nazi officials continue to follow orders? Members of extermination squads had quit their jobs without any serious consequences. At his trial, Eichmann said that, although he did initially have doubts about the extermination program, these doubts were put to rest when he realized that all his friends and professional colleagues supported the program. After all, he thought, "Who am I to judge?" Nobody, not even his pastor, ever reproached him for what he did in the performance of his duties.

As for the majority of his fellow countrymen, Eichmann's chief standard was the "good society," as he knew it. Arendt writes:

> His conscience was indeed set at rest when he saw the zeal and eagerness with which everyone in the "good society" reacted as he did. He did not need to "close his ears to the voice of conscience," as the judgment has it, not because he had none, but because his conscience spoke with a "respectable voice," with the voice of respectable society around him.[37]

If justice is a cultural creation, we then have no justifiable grounds for labeling Eichmann and the Nazi culture unjust or immoral. All we can say is that the Nazi culture was no better or no worse than our culture—just different.

Connections

What level of moral development does Eichmann exemplify? *See Chapter 3, pages 90–92.*

Connections

What is the role of moral sentiments in moral decision making? *See Chapter 3, pages 82–87.*

Exercises

1. Do you think it was morally acceptable for the United Nations to punish the Nazis for following the norms of their culture? Why or why not?

2. The Geneva Conventions contain guidelines for the humane treatment of prisoners of war. In a 2002 memo to then President George W. Bush, White House Chief Counsel Alberto Gonzales concluded that the Conventions do not apply to the prisoners taken in the war on terrorism. In 2009, President Obama issued a report closing the detention center at Guantanamo Bay and renewing the U.S. commitment to the Geneva Convention guidelines. As of 2017, Guantanamo Bay is still open. Should the United States be bound by international law and treaties, or should we only be bound to abide by international laws that are consistent with our current cultural values? Support your answer.

3. Following the sentencing of Adolf Eichmann, his defense lawyer, Dr. Servatius, responded: "The accused had carried out 'acts of state,' what happened to him might happen in the future to anyone; the whole civilized world faces this problem." Do you agree with Dr. Servatius? Could a similar Holocaust happen in this country? Support your answers.

4. Conflicts and civil wars in countries such as Syria, the Democratic Republic of the Congo, Chad, and South Sudan have been marked by grave human rights violations and atrocities, such as killings and rape, and have left millions of men, women, and children impoverished and homeless. Should the United Nations and other countries step in and help the refugees and work to bring an end to the conflicts? Or is it wrong for them to impose their moral values on other cultures by interfering with the internal affairs of a country? Support your answers.

*5. Discuss how acceptance of cultural relativism by most Americans allows, and perhaps even encourages, actions that are harmful to minority groups, such as Muslim Americans and Hispanics, under the guise of "the American way." Relate your answer to your community service work.

Critique of Cultural Relativism

> *Conventionality is not morality. . . . To attack the first is not to assail the last.*
> —CHARLOTTE BRONTË, *Jane Eyre* (1847), Preface

Connections

What is ethical skepticism? *See Chapter 4, page 121.*

1. *Cultural relativism is illogical.* Disagreement among cultures does not prove that objective, transcultural moral standards do not exist. To claim that they do *not* exist is to commit the fallacy of ignorance. At the most, we can adopt an initial position of ethical skepticism regarding the existence of objective

moral standards. Furthermore, by claiming that sociological relativism (what *is*) implies cultural relativism (what *ought* to be), cultural relativists are guilty of committing the naturalistic fallacy.

The assertion that moral values are created by consensus within a particular culture is also highly questionable. Indeed, it is even questionable whether the "primitive" cultures that anthropologists studied were really as simplistic as they were portrayed. Because visitors to foreign cultures generally talk primarily to people in positions of power, what is reported as cultural unanimity is often the values held by those in the dominant group. When viewing a culture from the eyes of those in power, we may come away with a one-dimensional view of the cultural values and remain unaware of the discontent of the people who are marginalized and often invisible to those passing through.

Connections

What is the fallacy of ignorance and the naturalistic fallacy? *See Chapter 2, pages 57–60.*

2. *Cultural relativism does not work in a pluralist society.* In today's world, it is much harder to accept the claim of anthropologists like Ruth Benedict that there is general agreement within each culture regarding moral values. In modern cultures, pluralism is generally an acknowledged fact. Almost all of us are members of several cultures. For example, I could be a member of the Cambodian American culture, the Roman Catholic culture, the Democratic Party, and my college culture. The definition of what constitutes a culture can vary from subculture to subculture and even from person to person. Because of this, cultural relativism is unworkable in a pluralistic society. Which values should we follow when the values of our various subcultures are in conflict? Cultural relativism, rather than offering moral guidance, provides no standard for deciding between conflicting moral values.

3. *Cultural relativism confuses custom with morality.* Most of us distinguish between moral values and nonmoral values or customs such as food preferences, religious rites, and preferences in fashion and music. By identifying morality with custom, cultural relativists include behavior in the moral realm that may be outside the scope of morality. A custom that is inconvenient or even offensive is not necessarily immoral. Nude bathing, cross-dressing, and the use of obscene language in our own society, for example, are not necessarily immoral even though they may offend some people and run contrary to the norms and even the law in some places.

Because cultural relativism does not need to offer any justification for imposing a particular cultural value on people—other than to say that it is the way things are done—it can become legalistic and oppressive, particularly during times of conflict or when a society feels itself threatened. Appealing to tradition to justify norms can lead to rigid conformity, a distrust of change, and a disdain for those who do not adhere to tradition. Conformity may be demanded not only in terms of avoiding criminal behavior but in dress, speech, and ideology as well.

4. *People act more morally when others are not around.* If culture is the ultimate source of moral values, then people would probably behave most morally when in a group of people, just as we tend to use better manners when we

are out with company than when we are home alone. However, research indicates the opposite. This suggests that the source of our moral guidance does not lie solely or even primarily in imposed cultural values.

Consider the case of Kitty Genovese (see page 123). Genovese was stabbed to death in front of her apartment. No one bothered to call the police. Many people interpreted the lack of action on the part of the bystanders as personal apathy and urban anonymity. However, a study in which emergencies were staged in various locations found that a person who is *alone* is much more likely to help the victim than someone who is part of a crowd of bystanders. Social groups, rather than encouraging us to behave morally, actually seem to inhibit helpful behavior. Our primary motivation for helping others, the researchers concluded, seems not to be social pressure or cultural norms but a sense of personal responsibility that tends to be diffused, rather than reinforced, when one is part of a crowd.

Even the best of people are not immune to the potentially "demoralizing" effects of being part of the crowd. As a young man, Gandhi secretly smoked, ate meat, and told lies when in the company of his boyhood friends—all actions he personally felt were immoral. He suffered tremendous feelings of guilt as a result of these incidents. The resulting resolutions he made about resisting such social pressure lasted for life.

Sometimes cultural norms, in the form of a role or a profession assigned to us by our community, can take us over. One of the most famous examples to illustrate the "antimoral" power that cultural norms regarding roles can have over us is the prison simulation experiment conducted at Stanford University in 1973 (see page 30).

5. *Cultural relativism does not correctly describe how we make moral judgments.* We do pass judgment on the "moral" norms of our own and other cultures. When we make a judgment, we do not do so by examining customs and laws or by checking the latest polls to see how the majority of people in that culture feel about a certain practice. Nor do we necessarily judge other cultures in light of our own norms. When we make these judgments, we generally do so by appealing to transcultural values such as justice and respect for human dignity rather than to cultural norms.

The explanation used by cultural relativists about how a moral sense develops does not fit with prevailing psychological theory on moral development. Around the age of three, children are already aware of the difference between a moral issue, such as stealing and lying, and a social custom, such as how to dress or eat. "Even with their limited conceptual powers," writes psychologist Tom Kitwood, "they can grasp the point that moral issues do not depend on the nature of social rules."[38] Only later, as people enter the conventional stage of moral development, do some people begin to confuse custom and morality.

6. *There are moral values that seem to exist in all or most known societies.* The degree of variance among moral values is not as extreme as cultural relativists claim. Many extremes of behavior—such as cannibalism, human

Connections
How does our conscience motivate us to come to the aid of those in distress? *See Chapter 3, pages 84–85.*

Connections
What did the Stanford Prison experiment find about the ease with which we adopt cultural roles? *See Chapter 2, page 30.*

Connections
What are the stages of moral development? *See Chapter 3, pages 90–94.*

sacrifice, and unrestricted sexual activity among children—that have been used to illustrate the irreconcilable differences between moral values in Western and "primitive" cultures have never been documented by reliable sources.[39] Indeed, some people, when they first come into prolonged contact with people from different cultures or subcultures, are surprised at the extent of shared moral values.

Connections

What are the basic moral principles most moral philosophers claim are universal? *See Chapter 8, pages 242-243, and Chapter 10, pages 314-316 & 331-335.*

There are norms, such as justice and parental duties to children, that are regarded as moral duties in every known culture. However, there are other norms, such as racism and sexism, that are also widespread—perhaps even universal. Yet these norms are generally acknowledged to be immoral and something we should strive to overcome, at least by those who are the victims of racism and sexism.

Although the presence of universal moral norms does not disprove cultural relativism, the cross-cultural agreement on certain moral values strengthens the case against this theory and places the burden of proof on the cultural relativists to explain how this has occurred.

7. *Cultural relativism is divisive and creates an us/them mentality.* As such, it legitimates the oppression and even the extermination of certain groups of people. The belief that people from other cultures do not have the same basic moral standards that *we* have, such as respect for human life and human rights, can lead to distrust. If morality is simply the creation of each culture, people from other cultures, such as Islamic cultures, may even have dangerous values. Thus, rather than encouraging tolerance, cultural relativism gives rise to distrust and "isms" such as nationalism, racism, sexism, and ethnocentrism.

Connections

What are some characteristics that are considered virtues in almost all cultures? *See Chapter 12, page 412-413.*

Because cultural relativism rules out the possibility of rational discussion between cultures, when cross-cultural values come into conflict and rhetoric or persuasion fails, groups may resort to either apathy and isolationism, when the other culture's values do not threaten theirs, or violence, when another culture's values or actions impinge on or threaten them. The latter happens on an international level, in the case of war, and on a national level, in the case of gang warfare and racial, gender, and ethnic violence.

As we noted earlier, almost all theories contain at least a grain of truth. Cultural relativism begins with the correct observation that our culture affects our interpretation of moral values and that these interpretations vary from culture to culture. However, from there, cultural relativism jumps to the unwarranted conclusion that morality equals custom.

Connections

How does a college education affect a young person's moral development? *See Chapter 3, page 93.*

Looking predominantly to our culture or to our peers for our moral values is a normal and healthy stage in a young person's moral development. Culture nurtures us and gives our lives significance within a historical context. As humans, we cannot exist outside a culture. Respect for and obedience to cultural authorities and laws are the mechanisms that bind us together as a society. However, as adults, we must move beyond dependence on others for our moral values.

Given our dependence on culture, is it really possible to step outside culture and look at our customs and norms impartially? There is little doubt that culture shapes the way we interpret the most basic moral principles. But we need to be discerning and to develop our analytical skills. Cultural relativism, when taken seriously, is a dangerous theory. By throwing out universal moral standards, cultural relativists also throw out the proverbial baby with the bathwater. In their well-meaning effort to debunk European and American claims of racial and moral superiority, they also throw out the possibility of common, transcultural moral standards, such as equality and respect for human dignity. The outcome has been the promotion of, not respect for cultural diversity and rational dialogue, but suspicion and intolerance.

Connections

Most American adults are at what stage of moral development? *See Chapter 3, pages 90–91.*

Humans are profoundly social animals. Like language, morality does not exist independently of culture. Just as all human languages share a common grammatical structure, so too, most moral philosophers believe, does morality share a common structure or foundation in all cultures. As with language, culture shapes how we express this common morality. Some cultures do a better job than others. Because of the role of culture in giving morality practical expression, it is important that we understand the norms of our culture and respect them to the extent that they do not conflict with the underlying moral foundation.

If we are to grow morally and make more satisfactory moral decisions in our lives, it is important that we should be willing to critically analyze our cultural norms in light of this universal, transcultural moral foundation. We will be studying this approach to morality as based on universal moral principles and concerns in the remaining chapters of this text.

Exercises

*1. Has your community service work made you more aware of the common values shared by all people? Or has it confirmed the cultural relativists' belief that people from various cultures are different when it comes to basic moral values? Explain using specific examples.

2. Just as the social Darwinists encouraged rumors of cannibalism to justify Western imperialism, societies often focus on differences (real or imaginary) between cultures to promote their political and military ends. Make a list of stereotypes that you've heard regarding the practices and moral values held by people of other cultures such as North Korea and Iran, and by different subcultures within our society, that differ sharply from those of your own culture or subculture. Are these stereotypes realistic?

3. Slogans are frequently used in times of war and social unrest to maintain loyalty to the culturally accepted ideology. For example, segregation was maintained with the slogan "separate but equal." Can you think of any slogans that are popular now that serve to keep us from examining certain inconsistencies in our own cultural norms?

Connections

What is the duty of reparation? *See Chapter 10, page 334.*

4. Reparation is a moral duty that requires us to make amends for past harms that we have caused others. Discuss how a cultural relativist might respond to requests from African Americans and Japanese Americans for the U.S. government to provide reparation for practices, such as slavery or internment, that were considered morally acceptable by the culture at the time. Are you satisfied with the response of the cultural relativist? Explain.

Summary

1. *Cultural relativism* is the metaethical theory that moral standards and values are created by groups of people or cultures and that morality is nothing more than socially approved customs.

2. Cultural relativism is *not* the same as *excusing* behavior.

3. Cultural relativism is *not* the same as *tolerance* for multicultural diversity.

4. *Sociological relativism* is the observation that there is disagreement among cultures regarding moral values. It is not a moral theory; it does not conclude that value systems are necessarily relative.

5. *Social Darwinists*, such as philosopher Herbert Spencer, claimed that people from "primitive" cultures were less morally developed than those from European cultures.

6. Anthropologists, such as Ruth Benedict and William Graham Sumner, disagreed with the social Darwinists, arguing instead that morality is relative to each culture.

7. Cultural relativists define the moral community in terms of cultural ideas regarding who has moral worth rather than in terms of transcultural moral standards such as dignity and human rights. Thus, cultural relativism can be used to justify the *marginalization* or exclusion of certain groups of people from the moral community.

8. The tribunal at the United Nations Nuremberg Trials declared that, rather than morality being relative to each culture, there are universal, transcultural moral standards. Several Nazi war criminals, including Adolf Eichmann, were tried and found guilty using these standards.

9. Most philosophers, including Aristotle, Plato, Ibn Khaldun, Eagle Man, and John Fire Lame Deer, claim that some cultures are more moral than others because they offer more opportunities for people to fulfill themselves.

10. According to cultural relativism, there is *no* such thing as *moral progress*. Social reformers who break laws and disregard social tradition are no better than common criminals.

11. Research has found that people tend to behave more morally when they are alone than when part of a group.

12. Cultural relativism does not work in a pluralistic society.

13. There are universal moral values that seem to exist in all or most known societies. These include a sense of moral community, provisions for mating and rearing of children, a taboo against incest, a sense of justice and fair division of labor, and limits on violence.

14. When conflicts exist between cultures, the only alternatives that cultural relativism provides for resolving these conflicts are isolationism and armed conflict.

 ## Anthropology and the Abnormal

Ruth Benedict

Modern social anthropology has become more and more a study of the varieties and common elements of cultural environment and the consequences of these in human behavior. For such a study of diverse social orders primitive peoples fortunately provide a laboratory not yet entirely vitiated by the spread of a standardized world-wide civilization. . . .

. . . [O]ne of the most striking facts that emerge from a study of widely varying cultures is the ease with which our abnormals function in other cultures. It does not matter what kind of "abnormality" we choose for illustration, those which indicate extreme instability, or those which are more in the nature of character traits like sadism or delusions of grandeur or of persecution, there are well-described cultures in which these abnormals function at ease and with honor, and apparently without danger or difficulty to the society. . . .

Every society, beginning with some slight inclination in one direction or another, carries its preference farther and farther, integrating itself more and more completely upon its chosen basis, and discarding those

Ruth Benedict, "Anthropology and the Abnormal," *The Journal of General Psychology* 10 (1934): 59–82. Notes have been omitted. Reprinted by permission of the publisher (Taylor & Francis Ltd, http://www.tanf.co.uk/journals).

types of behavior that are uncongenial. Most of those organizations of personality that seem to us most incontrovertibly abnormal have been used by different civilizations in the very foundations of their institutional life. Conversely the most valued traits of our normal individuals have been looked on in differently organized cultures as aberrant. Normality, in short, within a very wide range, is culturally defined. It is primarily a term for the socially elaborated segment of human behavior in any culture; and abnormality, a term for the segment that that particular civilization does not use. The very eyes with which we see the problem are conditioned by the long traditional habits of our own society.

It is a point that has been made more often in relation to ethics than in relation to psychiatry. We do not any longer make the mistake of deriving the morality of our own locality and decade directly from the inevitable constitution of human nature. We do not elevate it to the dignity of a first principle. We recognize that morality differs in every society, and is a convenient term for socially approved habits. Mankind has always preferred to say, "It is morally good," rather than "It is habitual," and the fact of this preference is matter enough for a critical science of ethics. But historically the two phrases are synonymous.

The concept of the normal is properly a variant of the concept of the good. It is that which society has approved. A normal action is one which falls well within the limits of expected behavior for a particular society. Its variability among different peoples is essentially a function of the variability of the behavior patterns that different societies have created for themselves, and can never be wholly divorced from a consideration of culturally institutionalized types of behavior.

Each culture is a more or less elaborate working-out of the potentialities of the segment it has chosen. In so far as a civilization is well integrated and consistent within itself, it will tend to carry farther and farther, according to its nature, its initial impulse toward a particular type of action, and from the point of view of any other culture those elaborations will include more and more extreme and aberrant traits.

Each of these traits, in proportion as it reinforces the chosen behavior patterns of that culture, is for that culture normal. Those individuals to whom it is congenial either congenitally, or as the result of childhood sets, are accorded prestige in that culture, and are not visited with the social contempt or disapproval which their traits could call down upon them in a society that was differently organized. On the other hand, those individuals whose characteristics are not congenial to the selected type of human behavior in that community are the deviants, no matter how valued their personality traits may be in a contrasted civilization.

The Dobuan who is not easily susceptible to fear of treachery, who enjoys work and likes to be helpful, is their neurotic and regarded as silly. On the Northwest Coast the person who finds it difficult to read life in terms of an insult contest will be the person upon whom fall all the difficulties of the culturally unprovided for. The person who does not find it easy to humiliate a neighbor, nor to see humiliation in his own experience, who is genial and loving, may, of course, find some unstandardized way of achieving satisfaction in his society, but not in the major patterned responses that his culture requires of him. If he is born to play an important role in a family with many hereditary privileges, he can succeed only by doing violence to his whole personality. If he does not succeed, he has betrayed his culture; that is, he is abnormal. . . .

A second reading is available online at www.mhhe.com/bossef17e. This reading is titled "Trying Out One's New Sword" by Mary Midgley. Go to the Web site and read the article before answering the following questions.

Discussion Questions

1. Analyze Ruth Benedict's argument that "morality differs in every society, and is a convenient term for socially approved habits." Discuss how Mary Midgley might respond to Benedict's claim.

2. Discuss Midgley's argument that cultural relativism creates "an isolating barrier between cultures." How might Benedict respond to Midgley's criticism?

3. Identify the conclusion and key premises in both Benedict's and Midgley's arguments. Which person makes the best argument? Support your position.

Notes

1. Herodotus, *The Histories*, trans. Aubrey de Selincourt (Harmondsworth, England: Penguin, 1972), pp. 219–220.
2. "Afghans Stone Women Protesting Sex Law," http://news.aol.com/article/afghans-stone-women-protesting-sex law/427974.
3. For example, headhunting was practiced in some areas of the Balkans in Europe, among the Jivaro of South America, and in some areas of New Guinea.
4. http://gallup.com/poll117328/marriage.aspv.
5. Myriam Francois, "Forget the Burkini Ban: France's Muslims Have Much Bigger Problems," *CNN.com*, September 11, 2016. See also Lila Abu-Lughod, *Do Muslim Women Need Saving?* (Cambridge, MA: Harvard University Press, 2013).
6. Emily Richmond, "Schools Are More Segregated Today Than Late 1960s," *The Atlantic*, June 11, 2002.
7. See Noam Chomsky, "Basic Principles," in *Chomsky: Selected Readings*, ed. J. P. B. Allen and Paul Van Buren (London: Oxford University Press, 1971), pp. 1–21.
8. Clyde Kluckhohn and Dorothea Leighton, *The Navaho* (Cambridge, MA: Harvard University Press, 1974), p. 296.
9. Geoffrey Gorer, "Man Has No 'Killer' Instinct," *New York Times Magazine*, November 26, 1966, p. 47.
10. Gontran de Poncins, *Kabloona* (New York: Reynal & Hitchcock, 1941).
11. Josefina Zoraida Vazquez and Lorenzo Meyer, *The United States and Mexico* (Chicago, IL: University of Chicago Press, 1985), p. 43.
12. "Changing Attitudes on Gay Marriage," Pew Research Center, "Changing Attitudes on Gay Marriage," June 26, 2017. http://www.pewforum.org/fact-sheet/changing-attitudes-on-gay-marriage/.
13. Charles Dickens, "The Noble Savage," in *Crowned Masterpieces*, vol. 4, ed. David J. Brewer (St. Louis, MO: Kaiser, 1902), pp. 1379, 1382.
14. For more on this topic, read Paul Lawrence Farber, *The Temptations of Evolutionary Ethics* (Berkeley: University of California Press, 1994).
15. Charles Darwin, *The Descent of Man, and Selection in Relation to Sex*, 2 vols. (London: Murray, 1871).
16. Herbert Spencer, *The Principles of Ethics* (1897), Vol. 1, pt. 1, secs. 51 and 52. For the complete text, go to http://oll.libertyfund.org/ToC/0155.php.
17. Dickens, "The Noble Savage," pp. 1379, 1382.
18. W. Arens, *The Man-Eating Myth: Anthropology and Anthropophagy* (New York: Oxford University Press, 1979).
19. William Graham Sumner, *Folkways* (Boston, MA: Ginn, 1906), p. 28.
20. Fred Voget, *A History of Ethnology* (New York: Holt, Rinehart, 1975), pp. 368–369.
21. Joseph Campbell, *The Power of Myth* (New York: Doubleday, 1988), p. 78.
22. Sanskrit is the ancient language of the Hindus.
23. *Dred Scott v. Sandford*, 19 Howard, 393 (1857), in *Documents of American History*, ed. Henry Steele Commager and Milton Cantor (Englewood Cliffs, NJ: Prentice-Hall, 1988), pp. 339–345.
24. William H. Holcombe, "Characteristics and Capabilities of the Negro Race," *Southern Literary Messenger* 33 (1986): 401–410.
25. Robert M. Veatch, "Experimental Pregnancy," *Hastings Center Report* (June 1971), pp. 2–3.
26. Gloria Anzaldua, *Borderlands/La Frontera: The New Mestiza* (San Francisco, CA: Aunt Lute Books, 1987), pp. 25–26.
27. See Jim Carnes, "Us and Them: A History of Intolerance in America," published by Teaching Tolerance, a project of the Southern Poverty Law Center, 1995, p. 16.
28. Excerpts from "A Pro-Slavery Argument," quoted in Arthur Young Lloyd, *The Slavery Controversy, 1831–1860* (Chapel Hill: University of North Carolina Press, 1939), p. 249.

29. Margaret Fuller, "The Great Lawsuit, Man versus Men, Woman versus Woman," *The Dial* 4, no. 1 (July 1843): 1-47.

30. A. A. Lipscomb and A. E. Bergh, eds., *The Writings of Thomas Jefferson* (Washington, DC: The Thomas Jefferson Memorial Association of the United States, 1903, 1917), pp. 1, 34.

31. Plato, *Republic* 2, pp. 368a–371e.

32. Richard Erdoes, *Lame Deer: Seeker of Visions* (New York: Simon & Schuster, 1976), p. 115.

33. UNICEF, "An Estimated 150 Children Worldwide Are Engaged in Child Labour," June 2016, http://data.unicef.org/topic/child-protection/child-labour/.

34. John Stuart Mill, *On Liberty* (Indianapolis, IN: Hackett, 1978).

35. Simon Robinson, "Casting Stones," *Time*, September 2, 2002.

36. Hannah Arendt, *Eichmann in Jerusalem: A Report on the Banality of Evil* (New York: Viking, 1963), p. 95.

37. Ibid., pp. 111–112.

38. Tom Kitwood, *Concern for Others: A New Psychology of Conscience and Morality* (London: Routledge & Kegan Paul, 1990), p. 102.

39. See Arens, *The Man-Eating Myth.* See also Ruth Benedict, *Patterns of Culture* (Boston, MA: Houghton Mifflin, 1934), p. 131. In this text, Benedict talks about the practice of cannibalism, which she never actually witnessed because it apparently had ended a few years before her arrival. In addition, in light of the startling disclosure by the Samoan girls (who were now older women) first interviewed by Margaret Mead for her book *Coming of Age in Samoa: A Psychological Study of Primitive Youth for Western Civilization* (1927) that they had invented the stories of sexual promiscuity among Samoan children to tease as well as please Dr. Mead, we should regard these stories as just that—stories—unless the events have actually been witnessed by other anthropologists or reliable sources.

SECTION III

Morality as Universal

Most moral philosophers maintain that moral principles are universally binding on all people regardless of their personal desires, culture, or religion. They argue that moral principles are discovered rather than created by humans.

This section begins in Chapter 7 by looking at ethical egoism. According to ethical egoists, the only moral principle is to do what is in our own best self-interest. Unlike ethical subjectivism, ethical egoism is based on a universal moral principle. We *ought* to do what benefits us even when we feel like engaging in self-destructive behavior.

Utilitarianism, in Chapter 8, expands the concept of interest or benefit to include the whole community. The principle of utility requires us to maximize pleasure and minimize pain for the greatest number rather than just seeking our own happiness.

Chapter 9 looks at natural law ethics. Natural law ethicists maintain that morality is grounded in unchanging natural or moral laws that are part of our rational nature and can be accessed through the use of reason.

Chapter 10 on deontology focuses on our duty rather than on the consequences of our actions. Duty, or doing what is right for its own sake, is the foundation of morality. Deontologists differ, however, regarding the source of duty (reason or intuition) and also on whether moral duties are absolutely binding.

Chapter 11 covers rights ethics. Natural rights ethicists claim that rights stem from our human nature and exist independently of our duties. Most rights ethics do not exist as a separate theory but as part of a broader moral theory such as ethical egoism, utilitarianism, or deontology.

The final chapter covers virtue ethics. Virtue ethics emphasizes right being over right action. Virtue ethics and theories of right action are not alternatives to ethical theories that stress right conduct; rather, they complement each other.

Instead of being mutually exclusive like ethical subjectivism and cultural relativism, universal theories generally focus on one particular aspect of morality rather than providing a comprehensive picture. Most of the moral philosophers in Section III include aspects of more than one of these theories in their moral philosophy.

Ethical Egoism
Morality Is Acting in Our Best Self-Interest

The achievement of his own happiness is man's highest moral purpose.
—AYN RAND, *The Virtue of Selfishness* (1964)

The individual is most likely to contribute to social betterment by

rationally pursuing his own best long-range interests.
—ROBERT G. OLSON, *The Morality of Self-Interest* (1965)

In the story of Gyges's ring in Plato's *Republic*, Glaucon tries to convince Socrates that it is better for people to do only that which benefits themselves. "Those who practice justice," Glaucon argues, "do it unwillingly because they lack the power to do injustice." To make his point, Glaucon tells the story of Gyges, a shepherd in the service of the ruler of Lydia. Gyges finds a gold ring in a chasm following a violent storm and earthquake. Before long, Gyges notices that, when he turns the setting of the ring so that it faces the inside of his hand, he becomes invisible to those around him. When Gyges realizes his power, he arranges to become a messenger to the king. When he arrives at the king's residence, he seduces the queen, kills the king, and takes over the empire.

From this, Glaucon concludes that it is more reasonable to be unjust—if we have the opportunity to do so without getting caught. Furthermore, if a just man and an unjust man both wore the same ring, Glaucon argues, their actions would be no different.

> Suppose now that there were two such magic rings, and the just put on one of them and the unjust the other; no man can be imagined to be of such an iron nature that he would stand fast in justice. No man would keep his hands off what was not his own when he could safely take what he liked out of the market, or go into houses and lie with any one at his pleasure; . . . and in all respects be like a God among men. Then the actions of the just would be as the actions of the unjust, they would both come at last to the same point.
>
> Indeed, Glaucon continues, the clever person, "while doing the greatest injustice, . . . has nevertheless provided himself with the greatest reputation for justice."[1]

What would you do if you had a ring that could make you invisible? Would you cheat on exams, spy on people, and steal with abandonment, as Gyges claims we would? In this chapter, we'll be studying two types of egoism: (1) psychological egoism, such as that advocated by Glaucon, which states we are biologically constituted so that we, by necessity, act in our own self-interests, and (2) ethical egoism which states that we *ought* to act in our best or rational self-interest even though we don't always do so. We'll also examine the real-life implications of ethical egoism and the laissez-faire capitalism, which is based on this moral theory.

What Is Ethical Egoism?

Like ethical subjectivism, most versions of egoism focus on isolated individuals who, like Gyges, are concerned only with their own interests. **Ethical egoism** differs from ethical subjectivism, however, because it is concerned with a *person's best self-interest*. Our best self-interests are those that are rational. The ethical egoist identifies happiness with the pursuit of rational self-interest. Ethical subjectivism, in contrast, asks only what people desire or feel is right for them.

Egoism is not the same as egotism. An **egotist** is a person who is arrogant, boastful, inconsiderate, and self-centered. Egotistical behavior is not necessarily in one's best self-interest because egotists tend to alienate others and, by doing so, limit their opportunities for happiness.

Connections

What are the underlying assumptions of ethical subjectivism? *See Chapter 4, page 121.*

Key Claims of Ethical Egoism

- Individual happiness is the greatest moral good.
- People achieve happiness by pursing their rational self-interests.
- People *ought to* pursue their rational self-interests.

Unlike ethical subjectivists, ethical egoists are not recommending that we mindlessly act out our desires, but instead that we rationally calculate which actions would most benefit us. What we feel is right for us is not always the same as what is, in fact, in our self-interest. Hanging out in bars, smoking cigarettes, or skipping classes may be things we want to do, but these activities, for the most part, are not in our rational self-interest. Sometimes, we must forgo our immediate desires to fulfill our long-term interests and achieve happiness.

Seeking our own interests does not necessarily entail ignoring the interests of others. Our long-term interests might best be served by allowing others to also pursue their interests. Helping others is often in our own self-interest because they will then be more likely to help us when we need them. In fact, sometimes the best way to get ahead is to do something for someone who is in a position to give us something we value in return.

Elements of ethical egoism are found in many ethical theories, including those of Plato, Aristotle, Herbert Spencer, Jeremy Bentham, John Stuart Mill, and David Hume. However, most moral philosophers, like Socrates, agree that personal happiness, while important, is only one of several goods by which to judge the morality of an action.

Epicurus: Egoism versus Hedonism

Egoism is not the same as hedonism. **Hedonism** is a philosophical doctrine that considers pleasure to be the *standard* of value. Whatever gives us pleasure becomes the guide to our actions. Philosophical hedonism takes many forms. The Cyrenaics, a philosophical school founded by Greek philosopher Aristippus of Cyrene (c. 435–360 B.C.E.), taught that pleasure is achieved by the immediate gratification of all our sensual desires.

Greek philosopher and ethical egoist Epicurus (341–270 B.C.E.) distinguished between the pleasures of this type of hedonism and ethical egoism. He argued that the concept of pleasure as the ultimate good is implanted in our mind by nature. As an ethical egoist, however, Epicurus is referring to rational pleasures, not the pleasures of debauchery and sadism.

Connections

What influence did Epicurus have on utilitarian theory? *See Chapter 8, pages 248-249.*

> When we say that pleasure is the goal we do not mean the pleasures of the dissipated and those which consist in the process of enjoyment . . . but freedom from pain in the body and from disturbance in the mind. For it is not drinking and continuous parties nor sexual pleasure nor enjoyment of fish and other delicacies of a wealthy table which produce the pleasant life, but sober reasoning which searches out the causes of every act of choice and refusal and which banishes the opinions that give rise to the greatest mental confusion.[2]

In summary, hedonism is concerned only with our immediate pleasures, whereas ethical egoism involves taking into consideration both the short-term and the long-term consequences of our actions. Rational or enlightened self-interest of the type that Epicurus supported involves prudence. Ethical egoists would avoid cheating on a test, even though it may help them in the short run, because it is more beneficial in the long run not to rely on cheating.

Exercises

1. Does the pursuit of our own self-interests lead to social order and harmony, or does it lead to social disharmony, aggression, and war? Support your answer using specific examples.

2. Imagine that you are short of cash to purchase the textbooks you need for the semester. As you're wondering whether to ask your parents for the money, you discover that a ring you bought at a thrift store, like Gyges's ring, can render you invisible if you turn the setting to face inside. Discuss whether it would be in your rational self-interest to steal the books.

*3. Nathaniel Hawthorne allegedly once said, "Happiness is as a butterfly which, when pursued, is always beyond our grasp but which, if you sit down quietly, may alight upon you." Discuss whether happiness comes from directly seeking it, or from pursuing other goals. If you are doing community service, relate your answer to your service.

---

*An asterisk indicates that the exercise is appropriate for students who are doing community service learning as part of the course.

4. Is pleasure sufficient to define what is in our own best self-interest? Identify other criteria you can use to determine whether an action is in your best self-interest. What is the relationship between your best self-interest and that of others? Explain, using specific examples.

5. Most superhero myths—such as Superman, Dr. Strange, Wonder Woman, and Batman—entail a normal person becoming invisible and being replaced with the persona of a superperson. Glaucon claimed that, if we could disguise our identity under a cloak and mask, we would use our superpowers for unjust ends rather than in the service of humanity. Do you agree? Support your answer. What would you do if you could become invisible or mask your identity, like the superheroes can?

Thomas Hobbes: Psychological Egoism

For every man by natural necessity desires that which is good for him.
—THOMAS HOBBES, *Philosophical Rudiments, English Works* (1839–1845), vol. 2, p. 25

Connections

What is the difference between a prescriptive and a descriptive statement? *See Chapter 2, pages 44–45.*

There are two main types of egoism: ethical egoism and psychological egoism. Ethical egoism is a normative or *prescriptive* theory about how things *ought* to be. We ought to act in the way that is in our own best self-interest. **Psychological egoism**, in contrast, is a *descriptive* theory about how things *are*.

Thomas Hobbes (1588–1679) was one of the first major philosophers to present a completely individualistic picture of human nature as basically egoist. Hobbes was born in England when the Protestant Reformation was in full swing. The wars and turbulent political atmosphere of Hobbes's early years convinced him that people form into societies only from fear of death and the need for security to pursue their interests.

According to Hobbes, people are basically selfish, aggressive, and quarrelsome. Without society, he argued, we would all live in a "state of nature" in which life would be "solitary, poor, nasty, brutish, and short."[3] People actually do live within a society and agree to obey certain rules, but this does not mean that we are no longer egoists by nature. Like Glaucon, Hobbes believed that we agree to abide by the rules of society, or to live under a "social contract," only because it benefits us (see the selection by Hobbes at the end of this chapter).

Hobbes denied that there is anything noble about so-called moral sentiments. We feel pity or sympathy for another person only because their misfortune is a reminder that the same thing could happen to us. Because we identify with people who are good, we feel much greater pity when a good person suffers misfortune than when an evil person suffers. Even great acts of charity and altruism, Hobbes argued, are performed only because we delight in demonstrating our powers and superiority by showing the world that we are more capable than those we serve. Is Hobbes's view of human nature as basically egoist correct?

According to sociobiologists such as E. O. Wilson, humans, like other animals, are genetically programmed to act in ways that further our own self-interest. In his book *On Human Nature*, Wilson claims that altruism is fundamentally

Scene from Lord of the Flies, *the movie based on a book by William Golding. The book chronicles the growing brutality and lawlessness of a group of British schoolboys stranded on a deserted island. Goldberg's portrayal of the boy's behavior exemplifies Hobbes' state of nature.*
©Photo 12/Alamy Stock Photo

selfish. Studies by sociobiologists have found that people prefer partners who are altruistic, thus, altruistic concern for others actually benefits us by enhancing our desirability as mates. Wilson writes:

> Can the cultural evolution of higher ethical values gain a direction and momentum of its own and completely replace genetic evolution? I think not. The genes hold culture on a leash. . . . Human behavior—like the deepest capacities for emotional response which drive and guide it—is the circuitous technique by which human genetic material has been and will be kept intact. Morality has no other demonstrable ultimate function.[4]

Psychological Egoism Explained

But what about people who take drugs, smoke cigarettes, and act in ways that undermine their relationships and their careers? A psychological egoist who is not so concerned with the perpetuation of the species may reply that taking drugs or smoking or being a jerk may have brought that particular person more immediate satisfaction than *not* engaging in these seemingly destructive actions. After all, drugs get us high, smoking is relaxing, and sabotaging relationships and careers gets us off the hook, thus freeing us up for other pursuits.

Other psychological egoists respond by using a weaker version of the theory. They argue that, although people may not always act in their own self-interest, they are always *motivated* to act in their own best interest. Epicurus argued that

Firefighters rescuing a survivor of the September 11, 2001, Twin Towers attack. Some people will rescue others despite considerable risk to their own lives.
©AF archive/Alamy Stock Photo

Discussion Questions

1. Were the rescuers heroes, or were they simply acting out of self-interest doing what brought them the most satisfaction? What about the people helping out in the photo who are civilians? Discuss what criteria you could use to distinguish between an act of selflessness and an act of self-interest.

2. Think of a time when you, or someone you know, engaged in what seemed to be an act of heroism or selflessness. Can the action also be explained as an example of psychological egoism? Explain.

---

people may fail to act in ways that benefit them not because of lack of motivation but because of error and ignorance. For example, a person who has been abused since childhood may not realize that abuse is not a normal part of an intimate relationship. Or a person may underestimate the pain that can accompany his or her actions. And most smokers started smoking as children, when they were not fully cognizant of the consequences of their actions.

Indeed, no matter what example we produce, the psychological egoist can always reply that the person must have acted as he or she did because it brought about more pleasure than pain. A person who commits suicide brings a painful existence to an end. A woman remains in an abusive relationship because the economic security outweighs the pain of the abuse. And so on.

The Limitations of Psychological Egoism

On the surface, it may appear that psychological egoism is an airtight theory, but the problem is that psychological egoists will not allow any explanations that do not fit into their theory. No matter what happens, they explain it as an example of egoism: People are always motivated by self-interest; therefore, whatever people do must have been motivated by self-interest. Such circular reasoning, or *begging the question*, adds nothing to our explanation of human motivation.

One of the requirements of any good scientific theory is that it must be **falsifiable**.[5] This means that there must be some type of evidence that could count against it. For example, the theory that the earth was flat could be, and was, disproved by explorers who sailed around the world and by observations of the shape of the earth's shadow on the moon during an eclipse. Psychological egoists, on the other hand, cannot devise any hypothetical situations that might disprove their theory.

Another problem with psychological egoism is that it is very difficult to know what actually motivates people. Our motives for performing an action and the consequences of that action are not always the same. People like Mother Teresa may derive great satisfaction from their altruistic actions, but this is not necessarily what motivates them to help others in the first place. It is even difficult to figure out our own motives sometimes! Consider how often you have replied, when asked why you did something, "I don't know."

Dan Stock, a thirty-eight-year-old policy analyst, was relaxing on an ocean beach in southern New England. He looked up and saw an older man and a child caught in a strong current. Stock ran into the water, followed by his Labrador retriever, Angus. Together they swam out and saved the drowning swimmers. Why did he risk his life? He did not risk his life to pass on his genes; the swimmers were complete strangers. When asked why he swam out into a dangerous current to save two drowning people, Stock replied that he didn't give it a second thought. It simply seemed to be the right thing to do. The people of Le Chambon, France, who provided refuge for Jews during the Nazi occupation of France in World War II (see page 41) also risked their lives to help strangers.

In cases such as these, psychological egoists claim that the real motive, even though it may be unconscious, is self-benefit. In the case of a martyr who gives his or her life to save others, the motive is either lasting recognition after death or ensuring a place in Heaven. But how do we know, for example, that this was Stock's motive? He is not religious. In addition, the argument that the real motive was unconscious commits the *fallacy of ignorance*. One cannot argue that one's conclusion is true simply because others cannot prove there are no unconscious egoist motives.

Also, sometimes we do struggle when our self-interest (or at least what appears to be in our self-interest) conflicts with what we believe to be the right thing to do. For example, you may be tempted to keep a wallet that you find—especially if it contains a lot of cash and you are a poor college student! But instead, with a sigh, you turn it in to the lost and found. No one sees you do this except the anonymous person at the counter. You receive no praise for your actions. One alternative explanation for returning the wallet might be that you are motivated by a sense of duty rather than pure self-interest.

Connections

What is the fallacy of begging the question? *See Chapter 2, pages 58-59.*

Connections

What is the relationship between stage of moral development and one's willingness to help someone in distress? *See Chapter 3, page 92.*

Egoism as a Prescriptive Theory

Asking why we behave as we *do* and asking how we *ought* to behave are two distinct questions. Unlike psychological egoism, which is a description of human behavior and motivation, ethical egoism is a prescriptive theory about what we ought to do. Ethical egoists argue that, although we may not always act out of self-interest, we *ought* to do so. Even if we agree that humans have a tendency to behave selfishly, this is *not* the same as saying that they *ought* to behave selfishly. To draw this conclusion is to commit the *fallacy of irrelevant conclusion*.

Although both Hobbes and Epicurus were psychological egoists, ethical egoists do not necessarily accept psychological egoism. Indeed, if we always acted in our own self-interest, there would be no need for moral theory because there would be no such thing as immoral behavior! It seems rather redundant to tell people that they ought to do what they are going to do anyway.

Connections

What is the fallacy of irrelevant conclusion? *See Chapter 2, page 60.*

Exercises

1. Think back to a time when you acted in a way that was not in your own self-interest. What motivated you to act this way? Why else might people act in ways that might not bring about the greatest pleasure for themselves?

2. Critically analyze the claim by psychological egoists that in a Hobbesian state of nature, like that in *Lord of the Flies*, we would all look out for only ourselves and life would be brutish and nasty. Use examples to illustrate your answer.

3. Discuss E. O. Wilson's claim that all our actions, including those such as doing community service and helping others, have as their ultimate function the perpetuation of the species. Can you think of an action, any action, that could not be explained as an example of psychological egoism?

4. During war and times of crisis, there are people who willingly sacrifice their lives to save others for a greater good. For example, on September 11, 2001, Todd Beamer and others on United Flight 93 overpowered the plane's hijackers and, in doing so, prevented the plane from crashing in Washington, D.C. Because of his heroic action, Beamer and the other forty-three passengers and crew members were killed when the plane crashed in a remote area of Pennsylvania. Discuss how Thomas Hobbes and E. O. Wilson might explain Beamer's actions. Are you satisfied with their explanation(s)? Support your answer.

*5. Discuss Hobbes's argument that all acts of charity are done simply to make us feel we are better than the people we are helping. Is your community service work motivated by a desire to feel superior? Explain.

*6. Is an act automatically egoist if a person gets pleasure out of it? Relate your answer to the concept of helper's high discussed in Chapter 3 and to your community service.

Ayn Rand: Objectivist Ethics and Rational Ethical Egoism

For centuries, the battle of morality was fought between those who claimed that your life belongs to God and those who claimed that it belongs to your neighbors . . . no one came to say that your life belongs to you and that the good is to live it.

—AYN RAND, *Atlas Shrugged* (1957)

The current popularity of ethical egoism has been fueled by the work of American novelist, screenwriter, and philosopher Ayn Rand (1905-1982). Rand defended a version of ethical egoism that she called "objectivist ethics."

Born in St. Petersburg (Leningrad), Russia in 1905, Rand immigrated to the United States in 1931. Her philosophy is in part an outgrowth of her experience living under both the Soviet and the U.S. systems of government. Rand became disillusioned with the demoralizing effects of collectivism and Soviet communism, and she concluded that ethical egoism, as exemplified by laissez-faire capitalism, is the only philosophy compatible with respect for the integrity and the reality of the individual human. To Rand, the United States was the "noblest, and, in its original founding principles, the *only* moral country in the history of the world."[6] She believed that we can best create an atmosphere where each individual can pursue his or her own interests by protecting people's individual liberty rights.

According to Rand, there is no source of values other than objective reality—hence, her term **objectivist ethics**. Like Hobbes and E. O. Wilson, Rand maintained that we value that which helps us survive, and that which helps us survive is what is in our own self-interest.

> Ethics is an *objective, metaphysical necessity of man's survival*—not by grace of the supernatural nor of your neighbors nor of your whims, but by the grace of reality and the nature of life.[7]

Rand adopted what first appears to be an Aristotelian view of human nature; she argued that reason sets us apart from all other species. Because reason is necessary for our survival, reason has moral value for humans. Therefore, we *ought* to act in a rational manner. According to Rand, to behave irrationally is to behave immorally.

However, at this point, Rand and Aristotle part ways. For Aristotle, humans are fundamentally social beings. Through our membership in a polis, our lives derive moral value and we can fulfill our nature as humans. "He who is unable to live in society, or who has no need because he is sufficient for himself," writes Aristotle in his *Politics*, "must be either a beast or a God."[8]

Rand, in contrast, regarded humans as fundamentally solitary individuals, each pursuing his or her own personal self-interest. Unlike Aristotle, who views the state, rather than the individual, as a self-sufficient whole, she argued that "there is no such entity as 'society,' . . . only individual men."[9] Her ideal society, or more accurately "collection of individual men," is an atomistic society where

Connections
What are the underlying assumptions of communism and capitalism and how do they differ? *See Chapter 7, pages 221-223.*

each of us must live and work only for ourselves and never for others. This type of society, she claimed, is the objectively real world—the only world in which we can prove our value and find rational happiness.

Rand's rational virtues, consequently, all involve the cultivation of individuality rather than social virtues. Her concept of rationality counsels us to:

1. *Be independent.* Live by the work of your own mind.
2. *Have integrity.* Don't sacrifice your convictions to the opinions of others.
3. *Be honest.* Don't fake reality.
4. *Be just.* Neither seek nor give that which is unearned or undeserved.

Rand assumed that any rational person would accept her list of virtues and what she called the supreme value of productive work.

In her novel *The Fountainhead*, Howard Roark is presented as her ideal of the moral person. Roark, a successful architect, lives his life entirely for himself. He asks nothing of other people and feels no obligation to help others.

Rationally self-interested people help others only if they will get something in return. Rand referred to voluntary cooperation as the *principle of trade* or justice. Doing something for someone else is morally justified *only* when we can expect to get something of similar value in exchange. Rand disagreed with sociobiologists that altruism can be compatible with our rational self-interests. Altruism, she argued, involves self-sacrifice or giving without expectation of return; therefore, altruism is immoral.

Christian ethics, in contrast, teaches us that selfishness and pride are the original sins and that altruism is a virtue. Rand turned this equation upside down. She maintained that centuries of being taught that we must live for others has eroded our sense of self-esteem and left us feeling guilty and full of self-hatred. For her, altruism is the equivalent of the Christian original sin, while selfishness is the greatest virtue. Altruism and compassion are vices because all altruism is based on self-sacrifice and demands by others to give them something that they have neither earned nor deserve. Altruists are willing to sacrifice their lives and interests to benefit others. This attitude not only turns the giver into an object; it also turns the receiver into a parasite. For this reason, Rand referred to an altruist as a "second-hander."

Connections

How would sociobiologists such as E. O. Wilson respond to Rand's claim that altruism is immoral and not in our best self-interests? *See Chapter 3, pages 75–76.*

> I have never known much good done by those who affected to trade for the public good. It is an affectation, indeed, not very common among merchants, and very few words need be employed in dissuading them from it.[10]
>
> —ADAM SMITH, *The Wealth of Nations* (1904)

Equally egregious, according to ethical egoists, is a situation where people are forced to turn over their money to help others. The Ayn Rand Center for Individual

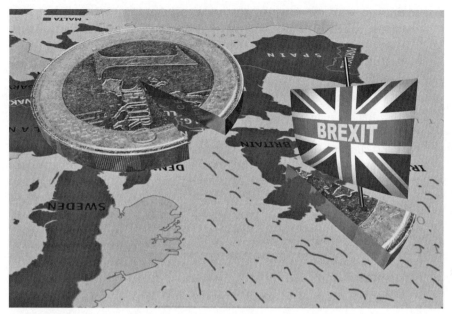

In 2016, Great Britain voted to withdraw from the European Union, thus freeing Britain from the trade restrictions placed on them as members of the European Union. The withdrawal, popularly known as Brexit, was hailed by advocates of Ayn Rand's philosophy as a victory for laissez-faire capitalism.[11]

©Kostasgr/Shutterstock

Rights opposed federal bailouts as stealing money from taxpayers and giving it to poorly run companies that now become parasites on the hard-working people of America. The cause of financial crises ethical egoists argue, is not capitalism and a free market system, but government intervention where the government overrides the participants' freedom to pursue their rational self-interests. To restore American prosperity, we need to return to a system where we are free to pursue our self-interests without interference from the government.

Rand was not merely claiming that pursuing our rational self-interest is synonymous with promoting the common good. She believed that people in general would be happier if we, as individuals, pursued our own self-interest instead of trying to help others. She advocated the importance of friendship and especially of love, regarding the latter relationship as one of the supreme values in life. She also argued that love was by its very nature a response to the lover's own most precious values, and, therefore, is necessarily selfish.

Exercises

1. Compare and contrast Rand's list of the four "rational virtues" with the version of egoism presented by Gyges. Discuss how each of them would answer the following questions: Why should we be independent and honest if we could

advance our self-interest by stealing someone else's ideas or property? Why should we be just if we can get away with being unjust? Support your answers.

*2. Do you agree with Rand that the principle of trade is the same as justice? Why or why not? Discuss how your life would be affected if all your interactions with other people were based on "trade." Discuss also how acting on this principle would affect your community service work.

*3. Discuss Rand's argument that the only good people can do for one another is "hands off." What effect would this principle have on people who depend on others, such as social service and government agencies, for services like social security, food stamps, or disaster relief? Would these people be better off, as Rand claimed, if we stopped giving them "hand-outs"? Support your answers.

4. Some people argue that President Trump's policy in dealing with other countries was inspired by Ayn Rand's novel *Atlas Shrugged*. Do you agree? Discuss how Ayn Rand might respond to Trump's "America First" policy when it comes to trade.[12]

Ethical Egoism and Laissez-Faire Capitalism

> *Productive work is the central purpose of rational man's life.*
> —AYN RAND, *The Virtue of Selfishness: A New Concept of Egoism* (1964), p. 27

Ayn Rand regarded the individual as the fundamental unit of economic activity. She also believed that the law of supply and demand is natural to human activity. From these two assumptions, she drew the conclusion that laissez-faire capitalism is the natural, and hence the best, economic system for human beings. **Laissez-faire capitalism** is an economic system based on individual freedom, the pursuit of rational and prudent self-interest, and minimal government interference.

Laissez-Faire Capitalism and a Free-Market Economy

Scottish economist and moral philosopher Adam Smith (1723–1790) laid out the foundations of laissez-faire capitalism in his book *Wealth of Nations*. The best society, he argued, is one where everyone is allowed the freedom to pursue their own self-interest in the marketplace. Smith's book, which was published in 1776, had a profound effect on the founding fathers of the United States.

> As every individual . . . endeavors as much as he can both to employ his capital in the support of domestic industry, and so to direct that industry that its produce may be of the greatest value; every individual necessarily labours to render the annual revenue of the society as great as he can. He generally, indeed, neither intends to promote the public interest, nor knows how much he is promoting it. . . . [H]e intends only his own gain, and he is in this, as in many other cases, led by an invisible hand to promote an end which was no part of his intention. . . . By pursuing his own interest he frequently promotes that of the society more than when he really intends to promote it.[13]

Laissez-faire capitalism views human nature as basically prudent and rationally self-interested. According to this theory, if everyone were allowed to pursue their own self-interests, the result would be the most efficient use of resources. In a free-market economy, consumers are free to spend their money in whatever manner brings them the greatest satisfaction. The capitalists, in turn, create jobs for workers by investing their money and energy in the production of goods that bring the greatest happiness to the consumer, thereby maximizing their own profits in the process. By acting selfishly, in other words, each person is actually benefiting others!

Rand and laissez-faire capitalists do not claim that we *always* act in a prudent and rationally self-interested manner. Ignorance and error, as Epicurus pointed out, can cloud our reasoning. Sometimes workers stay in jobs that don't make the best use of their talents, and consumers do not always spend their money in the most prudent manner.

There is no doubt that capitalism, as an economic system, has produced massive wealth and technological advancement. However, because capitalism is successful in raising the overall wealth and productivity, does that mean it is moral? Both Marxist and liberation ethicists argue that it is possible to have a successful economic system that raises the gross national product and productivity but that is nevertheless unjust.

Marxist Analysis of Laissez-Faire Capitalism

Marxists are among the most outspoken critics of capitalism and ethical egoism. Karl Marx did agree with the capitalists that people can find fulfillment in productive work; however, he also believed, like Aristotle, that we are primarily *socially* productive beings. The egoism of capitalism, therefore, was to Marx one of its greatest evils. Marxists claim that, rather than promoting the interests of the majority, capitalism benefits only a few at the expense of the many. Ethical egoism, therefore, is not a philosophy of "humans qua humans," as Rand claimed, but, according to Marxists, a philosophy of the elite.

Marx predicted that, with capitalism, the chasm between the rich and the poor would continue to grow. This trend has been occurring in the United States since 1970.[14]

The gap between rich and poor in the United States has been widening at an increased rate since the late 1990s, with the income of top earners remaining stable and that of others stagnating or even dropping. Indeed, the United States, along with Chile, Mexico, and Turkey, now has one of the highest levels of economic inequality in the world, according to a study by the Paris-based Organization for Economic Cooperation and Development.[15] Economic inequality is also increasing worldwide with the globalization of capitalism. Rather than seeing the growing income gap in this country as the result of greater concentration of income in the hands of the wealthiest few, many Americans blame their declining or stagnant earning power on "poor foreigners"—including illegal immigrant workers, outsourcing, and globalization.

The economic downturn that began in 2007 left more than five hundred thousand Americans homeless and millions more without jobs.
©McGraw-Hill Education/Christopher Kerrigan, photographer

Analyzing Images

1. According to Bureau of Labor Statistics, unemployment is significantly higher among Blacks, Hispanics, and young people. How might Rand explain this difference in rates of unemployment? Discuss what she would most likely say to the young man in the picture if she passes him on the street. How might you respond to Rand if you were the young man or a passerby?

2. Homelessness has risen among college students due in part to rising tuition and housing costs. Many of these homeless students keep their situation secret for fear of being stigmatized. You have just discovered that one of the students in your class is living out of her car. When you approach her about it, she becomes flustered and denies it. What should you do?.

Ethical egoists, like Rand, seem to assume that everyone is in a position to be a trader. Marxists, in contrast, point out that people's talents and their ability to trade skills and goods in a free-market economy vary enormously. Poverty, lack of access to resources, poor health, and social discrimination are only a few of the factors that place certain people at a distinct disadvantage. Women, in particular, have suffered in a capitalist system because much of women's labor, especially that which is based on caring and communal values, is unremunerated and undervalued. Patriarchal social structures also limit women's opportunities, especially women with young children, and access to resources and high-paying jobs.

The egoist's assumption that we are all in a position to act as traders, as we noted earlier, is questionable. Globally, as well as nationally, the playing field is very uneven. Wealthier nations can take advantage of their greater bargaining power and exploit labor in poorer nations by offering low wages and taking advantage of child labor. In the United States, large companies are doing more and more outsourcing to low-cost offshore locations, a trend President Trump would like to reverse.

The Globalization of Capitalism

According to ethical egoists, a global capitalist system will benefit both rich and poor nations as capital and trade flow from the richer nations to the poorer nations and back. Egoists believe that the wealth generated—in terms of industry, jobs, and education—will benefit the people of poorer nations by "trickling down" to them until they too will eventually be able to compete in the world market. However, the assurances of the ethical egoists have not been borne out. Rather than benefiting rich and poor nations alike, globalization has been accompanied by an increasing of the gap between the rich and poor nations.[16]

Liberation ethicists have become especially adamant in their denouncement of capitalism as immoral, exploitive, and a form of institutional violence: "The functioning of the [multinational] capitalist economy," writes liberation ethicist Gustavo Gutierrez, "leads simultaneously to the creation of greater wealth for the few and greater poverty for many."[17] To keep a stranglehold on the means of production, the wealthy would have to use not rational but irrational means such as force—police, military, and legal—to keep the poor from revolting.

The poor, the wretched of the earth . . . are calling into question first of all the economic, social, and political order that oppresses and marginalizes them, and of course the ideology that is brought to justify this domination.

—Gustavo Gutierrez, *The Power of the Poor in History* (1979), p. 191

Liberation ethicists note that a history of colonization has placed many people in the world at a great disadvantage "trading" in an international market. When colonizers come in and take over valuable resources and large tracts of land, the indigenous population is left with either impoverished land or no land at all. Meanwhile, technology and wealth remain concentrated in the hands of a few wealthy nations, while the people living in poorer areas of the world are becoming poorer and poorer. Because the capitalist goal is to maximize their profits, left to their own devices without government restrictions, they will continue to accumulate capital and economic advantage at the expense of the poor.

As the egoist predicts, the poor of the world, in order to advance their rational self-interests, will migrate, legally or illegally, to areas of the world that offer better opportunities and more financial security. The result has been a steady migration of impoverished people from Latin America and the poorer nations to the United States and other wealthy nations.

Both Marxists and liberation ethicists argue that the ethical egoism inherent in laissez-faire capitalism does not take seriously the dignity and integrity of each individual human, because the moral community includes only those humans ("traders") who have the ability and the opportunity to act in ways that promote their own self-interest. But what can a starving child trade with a capitalist in exchange for food and shelter? To respond to the plight of people who are starving by telling them to act in ways that promote their own self-interest is a meaningless gesture.

Rand argues that altruism is parasitic and degrading to the recipient. In contrast, both liberation ethicists and Marxists claim that it is the demands that the capitalists place on the workers that are cannibalistic rather than the demands of the world's poor for a fair share of the wealth. The capitalists, Marxists argue, did not get where they are by themselves but by using the labors of others for their own gain. Capitalism turns labor into a commodity—thereby reducing the workers to objects who must sell their labor to the capitalists to survive. Thus, workers become dispirited and alienated from the product of their labor. Nor are they receiving an equal share in the products of their labor. Instead, most of the money goes to the capitalists and wealthy shareholders.

Caribbean-born psychiatrist and political theorist Frantz Fanon (1925–1961) denounced the competitive individualism of ethical egoism as a tool of the oppressor to keep the workers oppressed. Because many workers do not have goods to trade on the economic market, they remain at a perpetual disadvantage, falling further and further behind. The workers, in turn, are blamed for their failure to compete on an even footing with those who oppress them. Furthermore, Fanon argued, ethical egoism's harsh indictment of altruism and communal self-interest prevents people who are oppressed from coming together and working as a group to overthrow their oppressors. He writes in his book *The Wretched of the Earth*:

A sweatshop in China that produces electronic parts. Much of the clothing we wear, as well as computers, iPhones and other electronics, are made in sweatshops in poorer countries such as China, India, Indonesia, and Haiti. Eighty-five percent of workers in Chinese sweat shops like the one pictured above are between the ages of 15 and 25. Many work twelve-hour days for as little as $8 a day.
©Mick Ryan/Cultura RF/Getty Images

Analyzing Images

1. Discuss how a laissez-faire capitalist, such as Ayn Rand, would respond to the growing reliance of wealthier countries, like the United States, on products produced in sweatshops overseas.

2. Just as Northerners supported slavery prior to the Civil War by buying cotton grown in the South, some argue that we are supporting sweatshops by purchasing cheap clothing and electronics made in Third world countries. Do we have a moral obligation to boycott, or at least avoid purchasing, these products; or, are we promoting the interests of those working in the factories by purchasing products made in sweatshops? Support your answer. Discuss how both Ayn Rand and a liberation ethicist might answer this question.

The colonialist bourgeoisie had hammered into the natives' mind the idea of a society of individuals where each person shuts himself up in his own subjectivity, . . . Now the native who has the opportunity to return to the people during the struggle for freedom will discover the falseness of this theory. The very forms of organization of the struggle will suggest to him a different vocabulary. Brother, sister, friend—these are words outlawed by the colonialist bourgeoisie, because for them my brother is my purse, my friend is part of my scheme for getting on.[18]

Fanon, instead of embracing the ethical egoists' motto "Look out for yourself," urged people to adopt a community-based ethics where "the interests of one will be the interests of all, for in concrete fact everyone will be discovered by the troops, everyone will be massacred—or everyone will be saved."

The only moral solution to the oppression of the poor, Marxists and liberation ethicists argue, is to renounce the ethical egoist ideology that underlies capitalism. It is unjust for people's share of societal goods to be directly dependent on their ability to compete in the capitalist marketplace. A more moral economic system, according to them, is one where people care for one another as a community.

From each according to his ability, to each according to his needs.

—KARL MARX

Individual versus Social Responsibility

Another criticism of laissez-faire capitalism is that a society based solely on trade undermines social values based on community. A transactional market economy, writes businessman and author George Soros:

> . . . is anything but a community. Everybody must look out for his or her own interests and moral scruples can become an encumbrance in a dog-eat-dog world. In a purely transactional society, people who are not weighted down by any consideration for others can move around more easily and are likely to come out ahead.[19]

Rand dismissed the Marxist critique of capitalism as an unrealistic longing for "a society in which man's existence will be automatically guaranteed him—that is, in which man will not have to bear responsibility for his own survival."[20] She argued that capitalism, by its very nature, creates optimal conditions for progress and growth by challenging people to do their best to further their lives. A socialist society, where rewards are not tied to our achievements, Rand maintained, will lead to stagnation rather than creating conditions for growth.

Connections

What is liberation ethics and why is it opposed capitalism? *See Chapter 11, pages 367-369.*

Both Rand's theory of ethical egoism and the critics of capitalism offer important insights. Rand emphasized the importance of individual responsibility; Marxists and liberation ethicists remind us of the importance of social responsibility. However, an adequate moral theory must consider and integrate both the individual and social aspects of morality. Although capitalists are not necessarily greedy or exploitive, an egoist ethics offers no reason or incentive for people not to pursue their own ends at the expense of others.

On the other hand, an ethical theory like Marxism, which for the most part ignores the individual, can just as surely create a sense of alienation by swallowing up individual interests and goals into the concept of the good of the community.

Exercises

1. Discuss the laissez-faire capitalist claim that people are essentially rational and prudent. What might keep people from being rational and prudent? Are people behaving immorally when they do not act in a prudent and rationally self-interested manner? Use examples to illustrate your answers.

2. In economics, the trickle-down theory is based on the assumption that the benefits of a policy that helps the capitalists will trickle down to the poorest of the poor; if the rich have more money to spend, they will presumably invest more in business, create more jobs, and sell more goods to maximize their profits. Has this policy worked? Why or why not?

3. According to the Bureau of Labor Statistics, young people, Blacks, and Hispanics have an unemployment rate that is significantly higher than that of the general population. Discuss how Ayn Rand might explain these differences in unemployment rates.

4. According to the Center for Immigration Studies, there are about 5 million illegal alien adults working in the United States, most for low wages. Discuss as well as evaluate what policy an ethical egoist might suggest regarding the status of illegal aliens who are currently living and working in the United States.

5. Discuss the Marxist analysis of Ayn Rand's position, particularly regarding the importance Rand placed on the protection of people's liberty rights and the freedom to pursue their own interests. Would Rand approve of the use of cheap labor by the multinational corporations in poorer nations? Why or why not? Discuss what solution she might propose for dealing with the problems of starvation and the plight of poorer nations in the world economy.

6. J. D. Sethi, an economic planner from New Delhi, India, points out that capitalist economics fails to take into consideration the basic human rights of all people. There are a "large number of Third World Nations" where the "people have been brutally exploited and denied minimum basic economic subsistence." As part of the solution to this problem, he suggests that all people be "guaranteed certain basic economic needs," including "education, primary health care, nutrition, family planning, and road and housing development," as well as jobs for "all people who are seeking jobs."[21]

   Discuss Sethi's claim that all people have basic rights that are independent of having to earn these rights. How might Rand respond to Sethi?

7. The oppression of women and minorities has resulted in more limited access to the free-market system than that enjoyed by White males. Government intervention in the form of affirmative action programs is intended to correct this

inequality. However, is affirmative action a morally acceptable solution? Support your answer.

Discuss how an ethical egoist might approach affirmative action and the problems of racism and sexism on your campus.

Ethical Egoism and the Moral Community

Many words have been granted me, and some are wise, and some are false, but only three are holy; "I will it!" Whatever road I take, the guiding star is within me; the guiding star and the lodestone which point the way. They point in but one direction. They point to me.

—Ayn Rand, *The Anthem* (1938), p. 109

Egoism, Self-Esteem, and Moral Development

According to developmental psychologists, most children are egoists: Their actions are, for the most part, motivated by self-interest. The egoism of the child provides the groundwork for building self-esteem and, as such, should be nurtured. Without first developing self-love, we cannot truly care for others. "To love is to value," Rand wrote. "Only a rationally selfish man, a man of *self-esteem*, is capable of love. . . . The man who does not value himself, cannot value anything or anyone."[22]

Connections

What is the first stage of moral development? See Chapter 3, page 90.

By pointing out the importance of self-love, Rand provided an important corrective to moral ideologies that glorify self-sacrifice and putting the needs of others first. However, by universalizing egoism as a moral principle—rather than seeing it as a stage in our moral development—we remain forever stunted at the preconventional level of moral reasoning trapped in our own self-interest and shut away from the richness of the wider moral community. Egoism and concern for our own well-being become integrated into the higher stages of moral development rather than being discarded when we move on to later stages. Egoism, in other words, is not the goal of morality, as ethical egoists claim; it is the seed from which our moral community grows to become more and more inclusive.

The moral community of ethical egoists is limited to themselves and those who can benefit them. Ethical egoism, rather than reaffirming the dignity of the human being, sees other people not as beings with intrinsic worth but as objects for one's own gratification and benefit.

Connections

Why does Rachels also reject ethical subjectivism? See Chapter 4, pages 134-135.

Philosopher James Rachels maintains that ethical egoism fails as a moral theory because it contains a logical contradiction in its definition of the moral community.[23] Ethical egoism claims to be the only moral theory that is compatible with respect for the integrity of individual humans, but in practice, Rachels argues it divides the world into two groups: myself and the others. My interests count more than those of other people. I am in the moral community, and others are outside it unless they have something they can "trade" with me.

Rachels asks, how can I justify placing my interests above those of others if everyone has equal moral worth? There is little doubt that by habitually putting others' needs before our own, as servile people do, we deny our own worth and consequently the principle of the dignity of all people. But by claiming that one person's interests (my own) are more important than those of others, ethical egoism is no better than racism or sexism or nationalism; each places the interests of certain groups of people above the interests of other groups. Thus, ethical egoism condones the very attitude it claims to oppose by requiring me to act as though my interests are more important than those of other people, thereby elevating one person (myself) over others. Rachels writes:

> [Consider] the starving people we could feed by giving up some of our luxuries. Then should we care about them? We care about ourselves, of course—if *we* were starving, we would go to almost any lengths to get food. But what is the difference between us and them? Does hunger affect them any less? Are they somehow less deserving than we? If we can find no relevant difference between us and them, then we must admit that if *our* need should be met, so should *theirs*.[24]

If we cannot justify our own preferential treatment, Rachels concludes, then ethical egoism is "unacceptably arbitrary."

Communitarianism

American philosopher and communitarian Hazel Barnes argued that egoism evades the "vision" of what it really means to be fully human, a concept that must include responsibility—our response to others as persons with moral value rather than objects that are merely means to our ends. By denying this, egoism deprives us of vast areas of human experience and growth.

> Any ethics, sooner or later makes some sort of appeal to the need and desirability of the expanded self. . . . I rejected [Rand's ethical egoism], not because it is self-centered or because it seeks self-aggrandizement. I criticize it for being selfish in the pejorative sense of restricting the horizons of the Self so as to leave the self-center, not enriched but impoverished, not blown up but withered and blighted.[25]

One of the challenges to ethical egoism in the United States comes from a philosophy known as **communitarianism**. While strands of communitarianism are found in many traditional moral philosophies, such as those of Aristotle and Confucius, modern communitarianism developed primarily as a response to the individualism of American liberalism. Libertarians, like ethical egoists, believe that the best society is one where people are free to pursue their rational self-interests. Communitarians, on the other hand, regard the democratic community as the basis of ethics. The human community—which encompasses community decisions, social conventions, and historic and religious traditions—rather than the individual, defines the moral community.

Connections

How does Aristotle define happiness or *eudaemonia*? *See Chapter 12, pages 396-397.*

> [A] consistently egoistic species would be either solitary or extinct.
>
> —MARY MIDGLEY, *Beast and Man: The Roots of Human Nature* (1980), p. 94

Connections

In what ways does cultural relativism legitimate marginalization of certain groups of people? *See Chapter 6, pages 185-186.*

By advocating community as an end in itself, however, communitarians run the risk of slipping into cultural relativism. As one critic writes, "one person's fond wish for community leads to another's fear of repression. Americans felt a strong sense of community when they put Japanese-Americans in concentration camps in the 1940's and persecuted suspected Communists in the 1950's."[26] Communitarian values based on consensus (popular appeal) have also be used to support slavery and antihomosexual legislation. Consensus, however, is irrelevant to the morality of slavery or equal rights. Instead, we need a moral theory that can take both individual dignity and the value of community into account.

Exercises

1. To what extent do you define your moral community in terms of how others can benefit you? Has your concept of the moral community changed since the beginning of the semester? If so, how?

*2. Does self-love require that you put your needs before those of others? Explain why or why not. What is the relationship, if any, between your feelings regarding your own self-worth and your consideration of the needs of others? Relate your answer to your community service.

3. Is communitarianism a viable alternative to ethical egoism? Do shared community values provide a better basis than individual rights for defining the moral community? Why or why not?

4. Discuss what policies an ethical egoist and a communitarian would be most likely to propose regarding the status of illegal immigrants in the United States. Which policy do you regard as most consistent with morality? Support your answer.

*5. Discuss how accepting ethical egoism would impact your doing community service. In particular, would it even be morally acceptable, according to an ethical egoist, to be doing the community service? Support your answer.

Self-Interest and Happiness

The task of ethics is to define man's proper code and values and thus to give him the means of achieving happiness.

—AYN RAND, *The Virtue of Selfishness* (1964), p. 33

Ayn Rand claimed that her moral theory is based on objective, discoverable facts about human nature and what makes humans happy. She also maintained that "the achievement of happiness is man's highest moral purpose":

Connections

How do utilitarians define happiness? *See Chapter 8, page 243.*

> Good is neither an attribute of "things in themselves" nor of man's emotional states, but an evaluation of the facts of reality by man's consciousness according to a rational standard of value. (Rational, in this context, means: derived from the facts of reality and validated by a process of reason.) The objective theory holds that the *good is an aspect of reality in relation to man*—and that it must be discovered, not invented, by man.[27]

Ethical egoism, as we noted earlier, assumes that human nature is such that we find happiness by pursuing our self-interests. However, if a life spent pursuing our personal self-interest does *not* lead to or maximize our happiness, then ethical egoism is a false theory. If it is correct, self-interested people—that is, people who value independent lifestyles, productive labor, and rationality—should be, in general, happier people. Altruistic and caring people, in contrast, should be unhappier about their lives.

Despite Rand's concern with objective reality, she never carried out any research about what sorts of pursuits make people happier. In fact, studies do not confirm Rand's apparently "objective" observations of what makes people happy. In the early 1980s, Dutch sociologist Ruut Veenhoven carried out a meta-study of 245 studies on happiness from all around the world.[28] "Happiness," for the purpose of his study, was defined as "the overall appreciation of life-as-a-whole." To his surprise, Veenhoven found that many commonly accepted ideas about happiness were not verified by actual studies.

Rand assumes that people who value independence and rationality and who live a productive lifestyle are, on the whole, happier. However, the prevalent belief in the Western world that hard work and productive labor are one of the most important contributing factors to happiness was not verified by the studies. "Recent studies in western nations," Veenhoven reports, "found no great differences in happiness between employed and unemployed people." Nor are people who work harder happier.

In addition, happiness levels are actually *relatively low* among people who place a high value on rationality or "*intellectual values* ('wisdom,' 'logic,' 'understanding')." The level of happiness "was also slightly lower among those who stressed *independence of others* ('individualism,' 'inner directedness,' 'freedom') and *self-control*. These negative correlations were most pronounced among males."[29] On the other hand, a person's happiness with his or her life as a whole was relatively high among those who gave a high ranking to "social values ('love,' 'sympathy,' 'friendship,' 'forgiveness,' 'tolerance,' 'group participation')." Happiness was also closely related to participation in volunteer organizations.

These findings are directly contrary to the claims made by ethical egoists regarding human nature. As such, these studies suggest that ethical egoism is an unacceptable theory because its basic premise regarding human nature appears to be incorrect.

Exercises

*1. Relate Veenhoven's findings regarding happiness to your own life. For example, does doing community service work make you feel happier? If so, why do you think this is the case?

2. In Leo Tolstoy's novel *The Death of Ivan Ilych*, Ivan Ilych has lived a comfortable and prosperous life. After completing law school, he "soon arranged as easy and agreeable a position for himself as he had at the School of Law. He performed his official tasks, made his career, and at the same time amused himself pleasantly and decorously. . . . The pleasures connected with his work were pleasures of ambition; his social pleasures were those of vanity."[30] His relations with his family likewise were based on tradeoffs and self-interest.

   In the end, his good life spent pursuing his own self-interest leads only to despair in the face of his impending death. As he lay in his bed dying, "the question suddenly occurred to him: 'What if my whole life has really been wrong?' . . . [He] began to pass his life in review in quite a new way. In the morning when he saw first his footman, then his wife, then his daughter, and then the doctor, their every word and movement confirmed to him the awful truth that had been revealed to him during the night. In them he saw himself—all that for which he had lived—and saw clearly that it was not real at all, but a terrible and huge deception which had hidden both life and death."[31]

   Discuss Tolstoy's message that a life spent pursuing one's own self-interest may be pleasant at the time but is not a life well spent. How would you feel about your life if you found out today that you had only a few months to live? What would you do differently if you had your life to live over?

Critique of Ethical Egoism

It is this realization that we are on a par with one another, that is the deepest reason why our morality must include some recognition of the needs of others and why then Ethical Egoism fails as a moral theory.

—JAMES RACHELS, *The Elements of Moral Philosophy* (1993)

Ethical egoism contains two important truths: (1) We all want to be happy, and (2) taking our interests seriously is important to our happiness. These truths have been mostly ignored in moral systems emphasizing self-sacrifice and altruism as the highest moral duties.

1. *Ethical egoism encourages the development of self-esteem.* One of the strengths of ethical egoism is that it encourages us to stand up for ourselves and not let other people take advantage of us. It also demands that we take responsibility for our actions and our lives. However, the simplicity of ethical egoism, appealing as it may be, is also one of its weaknesses. Are there really only two alternatives: selfishness or self-sacrifice? Is pursuit of our rational

self-interest the only or even the best path to happiness? Scientific studies suggest that it is neither. And even if pursuing our rational self-interest were the best means to individual happiness, does this, on its own, justify ethical egoism?

2. *Ethical egoism is self-defeating.* James Rachels argues that by having individual happiness as its only goal, ethical egoism becomes self-defeating. This phenomenon is known as the **hedonist paradox**. If we try to pursue only our own happiness, we are often left feeling frustrated and alienated. Individual happiness seems to be more often the by-product of other activities than a goal in itself. Indeed, as Veenhoven's study suggests, if we seek other goals in life—such as helping others, having relationships, or achieving wisdom— these activities often make us happy, even though we were not motivated by self-interest.

3. *Ethical egoism cannot be universalized.* If people want to maximize their self-interest, then it is not in their best interest to have ethical egoism universalized because their self-interest might conflict with someone else's. Thus, ethical egoism cannot consistently be promoted as a universal moral theory. Not all ethical egoists agree with this analysis. On the other hand, Ayn Rand maintained that the people who fail to pursue their self-interests interfere most with others' pursuit of their rational self-interests. While our self-interests may sometimes come into conflict, she argued, this creative tension is preferable to the demands placed on society by second-handers. Indeed, one of the basic tenets of laissez-faire capitalism is that competition encourages creative productivity.

4. *Ethical egoism provides no guidelines for resolving conflicts of interest between people.* Rand's assumption that there would be no clashes if people pursued their own rational self-interest and did not interfere with other people's right to pursue their self-interests is questionable. Protecting people's liberty rights—what Rand perceived to be the government's primary task—is insufficient to guarantee that everyone will, in fact, have the liberty to pursue their rational self-interests. In a world of limited resources and opportunities, people's self-interests sometimes come into conflict. When this happens, ethical egoism is unable to provide any moral guidelines for resolving the conflict.

5. *Ethical egoism is arbitrary.* While it may be that we cannot truly value others without first valuing ourselves, it does not follow from this that we should habitually put our interests above those of others. By doing so, the *ethical egoist* violates the principle that all people have equal dignity. James Rachels writes:

> [Ethical Egoism] advocates that each of us divides the world into two categories of people—ourselves and all the rest—and that we regard [our] interests of the first group as more important.... [But] what is the difference between myself and others that justifies placing myself in this special category? ... Failing an answer, it turns out that Ethical Egoism is an arbitrary doctrine, in the same way that racism is arbitrary.[32]

6. *Ethical egoism, like social Darwinism and ethical subjectivism, allows the powerful to exploit the weak.* Philosopher Mary Midgley criticizes Rand's philosophy as promoting an "extreme egoist individualism." She claims that Rand's philosophy is simply a rehashing of social Darwinism with its glorification of commercial freedom and elitism as "survival of the fittest." Midgley also argues that ethical egoism isolates the individual in a "fragmented, non-listening world" where morality is reduced to the private morality of ethical subjectivism thus giving the powerful permission to thrive and pursue their lifestyles at the expense of the weak.[33]

Ethical egoism, and the system of laissez-faire capitalism that it extols, may be attractive to those who are rich and have the power to pursue their own self-interest. The devastating effects of this ideology on the people and nations that are not in positions of economic power, however, are becoming more and more evident with the increasing accumulation of wealth and social goods in the hands of fewer and fewer people and the destruction of the environment in the name of economic progress.

No man is an island, entire of itself; every man is a piece of the continent, a part of the main; . . . any man's death diminishes me, because I am involved in mankind.

—JOHN DONNE, *Meditation XVII* (1623)

7. *Ethical egoism fails to take into account that we are social beings who exist only as part of a wider community.* We do not exist as isolated individuals who can act independently of social constraints. On the other hand, substituting communitarianism for ethical egoism is also problematic because basing morality on community well-being and consensus can lead to the exclusion of certain groups of socially unacceptable people from the moral community.

In Confucian ethics, virtue is associated with the well-being of the community rather than individual self-interest. Perfect virtue involves becoming free of egoism.[34] By this, Confucian ethics does not mean a life of self-sacrifice. There are times when self-denial may be called for, such as saving a drowning child without first negotiating to see what is in it for us. And it may sometimes be right to pursue our own self-interest. But, in general, the right path consists of choosing the medium between these two extremes.

The association of the moral life and happiness with seeking the mean is also found in Aristotle's philosophy. The idea that morality involves balancing our needs with those of others is also a central theme in Carol Gilligan's theory regarding moral development. Ethical egoism, in contrast, rejects any sort of compromise. Altruism and our own self-interest are seen as diametrically opposed: "There are two sides to every issue," wrote Rand. "One is right and the other is wrong, but the middle path is always evil."[35]

Connections

What is the Confucian doctrine of the mean? *See Chapter 12, pages 400-402.*

Connections

What is Gilligan's theory about the moral development of women? *See Chapter 3, page 95-96*

8. *Ethical egoism inhibits moral development.* Rand believed that capitalism would encourage people to be their moral best. However, studies have shown that this is not the case. A business education in the United States and the socialization process within U.S. business firms actually tend to inhibit and even decrease a person's level of moral reasoning rather than attract people of high moral integrity.[36] Indeed, people who use higher levels of moral reasoning have a poorer chance of rising to upper management positions in U.S. business firms.

9. *Ethical egoism is based on a false premise regarding the source of happiness.* Although Rand was vehemently opposed to cultural relativism, the high value she placed on productive work and rugged individualism as the keys to happiness seems to be based on Western capitalist norms rather than on a transcultural description of human nature. In fact, as we noted earlier, studies show that being involved in productive paid labor is not related to happiness. By extolling productiveness as one of the highest virtues, Rand appears to be promoting the values of American culture rather than a universal moral philosophy. Thus, her claim that we discover rather than invent the good is questionable.

In many Eastern philosophies, the moral life and the path to true happiness emphasize *overcoming* egoism and self-interest as a virtue. Moral maturity is viewed in terms of going beyond the self—the diffusing of *the one* or individual ego into *the One*, the I am into the I AM. According to these philosophies, we are all part of the same web of life rather than separate, isolated beings.

The task of ethics may take us beyond our self-centeredness, yet ethical egoism is an important reminder that the journey begins in the self. Only by first respecting ourselves and expecting the same from others can we eventually move beyond self-centeredness to genuine respect for others.

Exercises

*1. Critically analyze Rand's claim that there is no halfway point between self-interest and self-denial. Illustrate your answer with examples, including ones from your community service work.

2. Norwegian dramatist Henrik Ibsen wrote: "There is no way you can benefit society more than by coining the metal you know is yourself."[37] What do you think he meant by this? Relate your answer to exercise 2, page 232, on *The Death of Ivan Ilych*.

3. Evaluate Mary Midgley's argument that Rand's ethical egoism is simply a reworking of Spencer's theory of social Darwinism. Relate your answer to the spread of multinational corporations into non-Western nations.

4. English poet Samuel Coleridge (1772–1834) saw modern Western history primarily as a regression in egoism that leaves the "individual in a self-centered predicament." This, he regarded, not as a fulfillment of the human will as Rand

did, but as an intentional abandonment of the human will. Like the Eastern philosophers, he urged us not to deny the self but to go beyond our self-centeredness.[38] Do you agree? Discuss how Ayn Rand would most likely respond to Coleridge.

5. Critically analyze James Rachels' claim that ethical egoism fails as a moral theory since it cannot be universalized. Use specific examples to support your answer.

Summary

1. *Egoism* is concerned with what is in a person's rational self-interest. *Ethical subjectivism* is concerned with what people desire or feel is right for them.

2. *Hedonism* is the theory that happiness or pleasure is the standard for measuring the value of our actions. *Ethical egoism* is the theory that happiness is the purpose of ethics.

3. *Psychological egoism* is a descriptive theory. The first version of psychological egoism states that humans always *act* to further their own self-interest. The second states that humans are always *motivated* to act in their own self-interest. Glaucon in Plato's *Republic* and the philosophers Epicurus and Thomas Hobbes all argued that humans are basically psychological egoists.

4. Because psychological egoism will not admit any evidence against it, it fails the test of *falsifiability* and, therefore, is a pseudo-theory rather than a real theory.

5. Ethical egoism is a normative theory that states that we always *ought* to act in our own rational self-interest.

6. Many philosophers, including Aristotle, believe that happiness is an important value. However, they disagree with ethical egoists that it (a) is the only moral value and (b) can best be achieved through pursuing our individual self-interest.

7. Ayn Rand's version of ethical egoism is known as *objectivist ethics*. Objectivist ethics is based on the claim that right and wrong are naturalistic concepts based on objective reality and survival. Rand argues that humans are fundamentally solitary creatures, each pursuing our own rational self-interest. Productive work is the central interest of the rational person's life. The only proper relationship for people is that of traders, where each party benefits from the transaction.

8. The ethical egoist regards altruism as immoral because it involves self-sacrifice.

9. Ethical egoism supports an economy based on *laissez-faire capitalism*. Laissez-faire capitalism, as explained by Adam Smith, emphasizes the pursuit of rational and prudent self-interest, individual freedom, and minimal government interference.

10. Karl Marx and liberation philosophers such as Gustavo Gutierrez and Frantz Fanon all denounced laissez-faire capitalism as the unjust morality of the oppressor.

11. Ethical egoism reduces the moral community to the individual self.

12. Ruut Veenhoven, in his study of factors that contribute to happiness, found that people who valued rationality and independence were relatively unhappy; people who engaged in volunteer work and gave a high rating to social values were relatively happy. These findings are in direct contrast to the ethical egoist's claim of what contributes to human happiness.

13. According to developmental psychologists, egoism is a normal stage in a person's moral development. Most people move beyond egoism in their teens.

14. Most philosophers reject the ethical egoist's dichotomy between self-denial and self-interest. Confucian philosopher Mencius wrote that what is right is generally found in the medium between these two extremes. Some philosophers suggest that the path to true happiness entails going beyond egoism and realizing the interconnectedness of us all (the One).

 # Leviathan

Thomas Hobbes

Chapter 13

Of the Natural Condition of Mankind as Concerning Their Felicity and Misery

. . . Nature hath made men so equal, in the faculties of the body, and mind; as that though there be found one man sometimes manifestly stronger in body, or of quicker mind than another; yet when all is reckoned together, the difference between man, and man, is not so considerable . . .

. . . From this equality of ability, ariseth equality of hope in the attaining of our ends. And therefore if any two men desire the same thing, which nevertheless they cannot both enjoy, they become enemies; and in the way to their end, which is principally their own conservation, and sometimes their delectation only, endeavour to destroy, or subdue one another. . . .

Leviathan, edited by Michael Oakeshott (New York: Macmillan, 1947). Selections from chapters 13–15. Originally published 1651. (For an unabridged copy of these chapters and Hobbes's *Leviathan*, go to http://oregonstate.edu/instruct/phl302/texts/hobbes/leviathan-contents.html.)

Out of civil states, there is always war of every one against every one. Hereby it is manifest, that during the time men live without a common power to keep them all in awe, they are in that condition which is called war; and such a war, as is of every man, against every man. . . .

. . . In such condition, there is no place for industry; because the fruit thereof is uncertain: and consequently no culture of the earth; no navigation, nor use of the commodities that may be imported by sea; no commodious building; no instruments of moving, and removing, such things as require much force; no knowledge of the face of the earth; no account of time; no arts; no letters; no society; and which is worst of all, continual fear, and danger of violent death; and the life of man, solitary, poor, nasty, brutish, and short.

The passions that incline men to peace. The passions that incline men to peace, are fear of death; desire of such things as are necessary to commodious living; and a hope by their industry to obtain them. And reason suggesteth convenient articles of peace, upon which men may be drawn to agreement.

These articles, are they, which otherwise are called the Laws of Nature: . . .

Chapter 14

Of the First and Second Natural Laws, and of Contracts

Right of nature what. THE RIGHT OF NATURE, which writers commonly call *jus naturale*, is the liberty each man hath, to use his own power, as he will himself, for the preservation of his own nature; that is to say, of his own life; and consequently, of doing any thing, which in his own judgment, and reason, he shall conceive to be the aptest means thereunto.

Liberty what. BY LIBERTY, is understood, according to the proper signification of the word, the absence of external impediments: which impediments, may oft take away part of a man's power to do what he would; but cannot hinder him from using the power left him, according as his judgment, and reason shall dictate to him.

A law of nature what. Difference of right and law. A LAW OF NATURE, *lex naturalis*, is a precept or general rule, found out by reason, by which a man is forbidden to do that, which is destructive of his life, or taketh away the means of preserving the same; and to omit that, by which he thinketh it may be best preserved. For though they that speak of this subject, use to confound *jus*, and *lex*, *right* and *law*: yet they ought to be distinguished; because RIGHT, consisteth in liberty to do, or to forbear: whereas LAW, determineth, and bindeth to one of them; so that law, and right, differ as much, as obligation, and liberty; which in one and the same matter are inconsistent.

Naturally every man has right to every thing. The fundamental law of nature. . . . . [I]t is a precept, or general rule of reason, *that every man, ought to endeavour peace, as far as he has hope of obtaining it; and when he cannot obtain it, that he may seek, and use, all helps, and advantages of*

war. The first branch of which rule, containeth the first, and fundamental law of nature; which is, *to seek peace, and follow it.* The second, the sum of the right of nature; which is, *by all means we can, to defend ourselves.*

The second law of nature. From this fundamental law of nature, by which men are commanded to endeavour peace, is derived this second law; *that a man be willing, when others are so too, as far-forth, as for peace, and defence of himself he shall think it necessary, to lay down this right to all things; and be contented with so much liberty against other men, as he would allow other men against himself.* For as long as every man holdeth this right, of doing any thing he liketh; so long are all men in the condition of war. But if other men will not lay down their right, as well as he; then there is no reason for any one, to divest himself of his: for that were to expose himself to prey, which no man is bound to, rather than to dispose himself to peace. . . .

Chapter 15

Of Other Laws of Nature

The third law of nature, justice. From that law of nature, by which we are obliged to transfer to another, such rights, as being retained, hinder the peace of mankind, there followeth a third; which is this, *that men perform their covenants made:* without which, covenants are in vain, and but empty words; and the right of all men to all things remaining, we are still in the condition of war.

[*W*]hen a covenant is made, then to break it is *unjust:* and the definition of INJUSTICE, is no other than *the not performance of covenant.* And whatsoever is not unjust, is *just.* . . .

These dictates of reason, men used to call by the names of laws, but improperly: for they are but conclusions, or theorems concerning what conduceth to the conservation and defence of themselves; . . .

Discussion Questions

1. Analyze Hobbes's argument in the *Leviathan* that people behave morally only out of self-interest. Discuss how Ayn Rand might respond to Hobbes.

2. Discuss Hobbes's argument that all acts of charity are done simply to make us feel we are better than the people we are helping. Would Rand approve of charitable acts done to make us feel good about ourselves? Explain.

3. Discuss how Hobbes might respond to Rand's argument that if we lived in a perfectly laissez-faire society, each following our own self-interest and not hindering others from doing the same, conflicts between one person's self-interest and another's would not arise.

Notes

1. Plato, *Republic*, trans. G. M. A. Grube (Indianapolis, IN: Hackett, 1992), pp. 359b–361a.
2. Epicurus, "Letter to Menoeceus," *Hellenistic Philosophy*, pp. 62, 65.
3. Thomas Hobbes, *Leviathan* (New York: Macmillan, 1962), p. 100.
4. Edward O. Wilson, *On Human Nature* (Cambridge, MA: Harvard University Press, 1978), p. 167.
5. For more on this, see Karl Popper, *Conjectures and Refutations: The Crown of Scientific Knowledge* (London: Routledge & Kegan Paul, 1963).
6. Ayn Rand, *Philosophy: Who Needs It?* (New York: New American Library, 1984), p. 10.
7. Ayn Rand, *The Virtue of Selfishness* (New York: Penguin, 1964), p. 24.
8. Aristotle, *Politics* 1.2, 1252. In *The Basic Works of Aristotle*, ed. Richard McKeon (New York: Random House, 1941), pp. 27–29.
9. Ayn Rand, "Objectivist Ethics," in *The Virtue of Selfishness: A New Concept of Egoism* (New York: New American Library, 1964), p. 15.
10. Adam Smith, *The Wealth of Nations*, Bk. 2 (London: Everyman's Library, 1904), p. 400.
11. "The Brexit Is a Huge Victory for Freedom and Capitalism," https://www.reddit.com/r /Objectivism/comments/4pre9d/the_brexit_is_a_huge_victory_for_freedom_and/.
12. Raghu Krishnan, "Donald Trump's Policies Seem to Be Inspired by Ayn Rand's 'Atlas Shrugged'," *The Economic Times*, January 27, 2017.
13. Adam Smith, op. cit., Book IV, Ch. 2, p. 9.
14. Claire Groden, "The Gap between America's Richest and Poorest Continues to Grow," *Fortune*, February 28, 2016.
15. Organization for Economic Cooperation and Development (OECD), "Inequality and Income," May 2015, http://www.oecd.org/social/inequailty.htm.
16. Mike Collins, "The Pros and Cons of Globalization," *Forbes*, May 6, 2015, http://www.forbes .com/ sites/mikecollins/2015/05/06/the-pros-and-cons-of-globalization/.
17. Gustavo Gutierrez, *The Power of the Poor in History*, trans. Robert R. Barr (Maryknoll, NY: Orbis, 1983), p. 28.
18. Frantz Fanon, *The Wretched of the Earth*, trans. Constance Farrington (New York: Grove Press, 1963); quoted in *Beyond the Western Tradition: Readings in Moral and Political Philosophy*, ed. Daniel Bonevac, William Boon, and Stephen Phillips (Mountain View, CA: Mayfield, 1992), p. 50.
19. George Soros, *The Crisis of Global Capitalism* (New York: PublicAffairs, 1998), p. 75.
20. Ayn Rand, "The Divine Right of Stagnation," in *The Virtue of Selfishness*, (New York: New American Library, 1964), p. 143.

21. J. D. Sethi, "Human Rights and Development," *Human Rights Quarterly* 3, no. 3 (Summer 1981).

22. Rand, *The Virtue of Selfishness*, p. 35.

23. James Rachels, *The Elements of Moral Philosophy* (New York: Random House, 1986), pp. 76–78.

24. Rachels, *The Elements of Moral Philosophy*, p. 88.

25. Hazel F. Barnes, *An Existentialist Ethics* (New York: Knopf, 1967), p. 104.

26. Michael D'Antonio and Michael Krasny, "I or We," *Mother Jones* 19, no. 3 (May–June 1994): 1.

27. Ayn Rand, "What Is Capitalism?" in *Capitalism: The Unknown Ideal* (New York: New American Library, 1966), p. 30.

28. Ruut Veenhoven, *Conditions of Happiness* (Dordrecht, Netherlands: D. Reidel, 1984).

29. Ibid., p. 322.

30. Leo Tolstoy, *The Death of Ivan Ilych and Other Stories* (London: Oxford University Press, 1971), pp. 13, 29.

31. Ibid., p. 69.

32. Rachels, *Elements of Moral Philosophy*, 2nd ed., p. 88.

33. Mary Midgley, *Can't We Make Moral Judgements?* (New York: St. Martin's Press, 1993), Chapter 15.

34. From the *Analects of Confucianism*, discussed in *Beyond the Western Tradition*, ed. Daniel Bonevac, William Boon, and Stephen Phillips (Mountain View, CA: Mayfield, 1992), p. 259.

35. Ayn Rand, *Atlas Shrugged*, (New York: Random House, 1957), p. 978.

36. Lawrence A. Ponemon and David R. L. Gabhart, "Ethical Reasoning Research in the Accounting and Auditing Professions," in *Moral Development in the Professions: Psychology and Applied Ethics*, ed. James Rest and Darcia Narváez (Hillsdale, NJ: Erlbaum, 1994), pp. 117–118.

37. Quoted in *Webster's Treasury of Relevant Quotations*, ed. Edward R. Murphy (New York: Crown, 1978), p. 240.

38. Quoted from Samuel Taylor Coleridge, "Religious Musings," in *Coleridge and the Self: Romantic Egotism*, ed. Stephen Bygrave (New York: St. Martin's Press, 1986), p. 86.

CHAPTER 8

Utilitarianism
The Greatest Happiness Principle

Nature has placed mankind under the governance of two sovereign masters, pain and pleasure. It is for them alone to point out what we ought to do.
  —JEREMY BENTHAM, *Principles of Morals and Legislation* (1789)[1]

It is the business of the benevolent man to try to promote what is beneficial to the world and to eliminate what is harmful.
  —MO TZU, *Universal Love*, Pt. III, Sect. 16

Americans are evenly split over whether it is morally acceptable to use torture—also known as "enhanced interrogation techniques"— on a terrorist suspect to obtain information that might prevent a future terrorist attack.[2] The debate over the use of torture is based primarily on utilitarian thinking: that is, will torture result in more beneficial consequences and prevent more harm and suffering in the long run, than using other, less extreme, interrogation techniques?

Former president Barack Obama, who issued an executive order banning torture in 2009, opposed the use of torture. He disagrees that torture is the most effective means of interrogation in extreme cases. Obama also pointed out that allowing the use of torture has other harmful consequences. In addition to the suffering experienced by the detainee, it undermines the rule of law, alienates us from the rest of the world, and puts our own troops at risk for being tortured by enemy forces.

President Donald Trump, on the other hand, supports the use of torture on terrorist detainees, arguing that "torture absolutely works." His Defense Secretary James Mattis, in contrast, questions the effectiveness of torture and does not want it to be legal again. Trump agreed to defer to Mattis as the expert.[3]

Each of these three used utilitarian considerations in coming to their decision. Who is right and who is wrong? Does Mattis's greater experience as a military general put him in a better position to make a decision regarding the morality of torture? Where do you stand on the use of torture? If it could be shown that torture, in all likelihood, has prevented further terrorist attacks, would you be in favor of it? Or do other harmful consequences, such as the

241

effect on rule of law and our standing with other nations, outweigh this consideration? On the other hand, is torture inherently wrong no matter how many lives it may save?

In this chapter, we'll be studying utilitarian moral theory. We'll learn how to apply the principle of utility in developing and critiquing public policy as well as in making moral decisions in our own lives. Finally, we'll examine some of the strengths and the shortcomings of utilitarian theory.

Utilitarianism and the Principle of Utility

The Principles of Utilitarianism

Utilitarian ethics has had a profound influence during the past two centuries upon social reform and the shaping of public policy. Although there are various versions of utilitarianism, there are certain fundamental ideas common to all utilitarian theories. Most important, utilitarian theories are future looking or **consequentialist**—that is, the outcome or consequences of our actions are more important than our intentions.

Utilitarianism is oriented toward a particular goal: the greatest net happiness for all. Actions themselves are neither intrinsically right nor wrong. Instead, the rightness or wrongness of an action is determined solely by its consequences. If the consequences of a particular action or policy are, on the whole, beneficial and produce more good or happiness than harm, then that action or policy is morally acceptable. In other words, the ends justify the means.

The debate regarding genetically modified (GM) food is driven in large part by utilitarian concerns of risk/benefit. For example, Bt corn (corn genetically engineered with a gene from a bacterium that produces a pesticide that kills the European corn borer) produces a great crop yield (benefit), which in turn contributes to the happiness of people—especially those who are currently undernourished because there is not enough food to go around. On the other hand, Bt corn may be toxic to monarch butterflies (risk). There may also be risks to humans that we are currently unaware of that we need to take into consideration in our risk/benefit analysis. The bottom line for utilitarians is, do the benefits of GM food, such as Bt corn, outweigh the risks?[4]

According to utilitarians, the desire for happiness is universal, and humans intuitively recognize happiness as the greatest good. It is self-evident. While psychological egoists maintain that people are concerned only with their own interests or pleasures, most utilitarians believe that people are naturally sympathetic and concerned with promoting the happiness of others as well. This feeling of unity with our fellow creatures—what Chinese utilitarian Mo Tzu called "universal love"—is deeply rooted in our character. According to John Stuart Mill, the concern for universal happiness is so basic to the human character that a person "may be unable to conceive of the possibility of happiness to himself, consistently with conduct opposed to the general good."[5] What counts is not just our happiness but the happiness of the whole community of **sentient beings**—that is, beings capable of feeling pleasure and pain.

> The utilitarian standard of what is right in conduct is not the agent's own happiness, but that of all concerned. . . . In the golden rule of Jesus of Nazareth, we read the complete spirit of the ethics of utility.
>
> —JOHN STUART MILL, *Utilitarianism* (1863)[6]

To the question, What is it that makes people happy? utilitarians respond that *pleasure* makes humans and other sentient beings happy. *Pain* and privation of pleasure, on the other hand, cause unhappiness. Actions that produce the most pleasure or happiness are good; those that promote pain are bad. The only intrinsic good is pleasure; the only intrinsic evil is pain.

Happiness, however, cannot be implied simply from preferences or a majority vote, because people's choices are not always well-informed. The majority, either because of ignorance about an issue or because of irrational traditions and cultural norms, can be mistaken about the best action or the best social policy in terms of utility. Nor can sentiment alone provide a sufficient foundation for morality. British utilitarian Jeremy Bentham referred to unreflective sympathy as the "principle of caprice."[7] Sentiments such as sympathy are often based merely on subjective feelings of approval and disapproval without any rational grounds to support those feelings.

What we need instead, utilitarians maintain, is a rational principle to guide people's moral choices. This principle is the *principle of utility*, or the **greatest happiness principle**. It states:

> Actions are right in proportion as they tend to promote happiness, wrong as they tend to produce the reverse of happiness.[8]

Rather than relying upon our feelings of sympathy, utilitarians recommend that each person "test his particular feelings by reference to this general principle, and not the general principle by reference to his particular feeling."[9] If an action conforms to the principle of utility, it is morally right; if not, it is morally wrong. The principle of utility also requires that we be impartial; each person who will be affected by our decision should get equal consideration.

While most philosophers believe that intentions are important when judging the morality of an action, for utilitarians the sole criterion is the action's consequences. For example, in the case of Kitty Genovese, it would not have mattered whether someone called the police because the noise of her screaming was keeping the caller awake or whether the caller's motive stemmed from a sense of duty to help those in distress. What counts is that, by making the phone call, Genovese may have been saved from further pain.

Connections

What is the psychological egoist's view of human nature? *See Chapter 7, pages 212-213.*

Connections

How does utilitarianism differ from ethical egoism regarding the use of pleasure as a measure of good? *See Chapter 7, pages 210-211.*

Connections

What is the Kitty Genovese syndrome? *See Chapter 4, pages 127-129.*

The utilitarian emphasis on the consequences of our actions (or inaction) grounds it in reality rather than in abstract principles or subjective intentions. As such, utilitarian theory is an important corrective to the often-expressed excuses such as "I didn't intend any harm" or "Don't blame me; I'm not the one who did it."

Utilitarians, however, do not deny that intentions and moral character are important. They realize that people with good intentions and a virtuous character are more likely to act in ways that benefit others. Utilitarians such as Mill wrote of the importance of cultivating our natural "feeling of unity with our fellow creatures,"[10] what Australian utilitarian J. J. C. Smart referred to as an attitude of "generalized benevolence."[11]

Key Claims of Utilitarianism

- The desire for happiness is self-evident and universal.
- Pleasure brings about happiness; pain brings about unhappiness.
- People are naturally sympathetic and concerned with promoting the happiness of others.
- The rightness or wrongness of an action is determined solely by its consequences.
- An action is morally right to the extent that it promotes the happiness or pleasure of all those affected by it.
- An action is morally wrong to the extent that it increases unhappiness or pain.
- The moral community consists of all sentient beings.

Concern for All Sentient Beings

Connections

How does the utilitarian view of the moral value of other species differ from that of natural rights ethicists? *See Chapter 11, pages 381–389.*

The utilitarian's concern for the happiness of all sentient beings—regardless of their abilities, gender, social status, or even species—reflects the moral ideal of equality that was so important during the late eighteenth century. This ideal gave rise to both the American and French Revolutions. The utilitarians hoped that this moral ideal would someday be extended to all sentient beings—both human and nonhuman. Bentham wrote:

> The question is not, Can they *reason*? nor, Can they *talk*? but, Can they *suffer*?[12]

The principle of utility, or greatest happiness principle, utilitarians maintain, is fundamental not only to human nature but to all moral theories throughout the world. The utilitarian philosophy of Mo Tzu, for example, developed as a challenge to Confucianism and Taoism. We'll look at the utilitarianism of Mo Tzu later in this chapter. Buddhist ethics, although it places much more emphasis on character or virtue ethics, also contains a strong element of utilitarianism. In Buddhist ethics, *ahimsa*, or nonhurting, is regarded as an unchanging eternal law.

> And what, monks, is Right View? It is, monks, the knowledge of suffering, the knowledge
> of the origin of suffering, the knowledge of the cessation of suffering, and the knowledge
> of the way of practice leading to the cessation of suffering. This is called Right View.[13]
>
> —BUDDHA, "The Four Noble Truths"

Rule-Utilitarianism and Act-Utilitarianism

Utilitarian theory is sometimes broken down into act-utilitarianism and rule-utilitarianism. This distinction is the creation of modern philosophers, not one recognized by either Bentham or Mill. *Rule-utilitarians* are concerned with the morality of particular classes of actions, such as torturing or stealing. They maintain that the morality of an action depends on the consequences of following a rule about that class of actions, such as "Do not steal." In other words, we should, in any particular situation, follow the rule that, in general, brings about the greatest happiness for the greatest number.

Act-utilitarians are concerned only with the consequences of particular actions. No actions are inherently immoral. Universalizing moral rules against these actions fails to take into account that there may be situations, albeit rare, where lying, stealing, torturing, or assassination may be the best means to maximize happiness. Rather than following rules, the morality of each action should be judged on the basis of its utility rather than on the basis of general rules. Rule-utilitarians, in contrast, insist that we should follow a rule even when it is clear that, by doing so in a particular case, we will cause more pain than pleasure.

For example, regarding the use of torture on detainees who are suspected of terrorist activities, rule-utilitarians argue that we should obey the rule—embodied in the Geneva Convention and other laws—that prohibits torture, even if in a particular case we might gain valuable information through the use of torture. Act-utilitarians, on the other hand, argue that each case should be considered individually. If as a consequence of torturing a particular suspect, there is a reasonable probability that we might gain new information that could potentially save lives, then we *ought* to use torture.

Because obedience to rules is more important than utility, rule-utilitarians are not considered true utilitarians by some modern philosophers. Instead, they are regarded as, to use the words of J. J. C. Smart, "rule worshippers." In response, rule-utilitarians acknowledge that adopting a policy of always following the rules may not maximize utility in a particular case, but in the long run, it is the best way to achieve the goals of utilitarianism.

Rule-utilitarians make an important point. There is not always time, nor the foreknowledge and skill, to calculate all the possible consequences of an action. Furthermore, much of our moral knowledge is passed down in the form of general moral rules about the tendencies of certain classes of action to produce pleasure or pain. Therefore, following general rules can be expedient when we do not have time to calculate the resulting pain and pleasure of a particular action.

The United States has used unmanned drones to carry out assassinations—also known as "targeted killings"—in Pakistan, Afghanistan, Yemen, Libya, and Somalia. The drone attacks have killed several high-profile terrorist leaders, including American-born Anwar al-Awlaki. Hundreds of civilians have also been killed in these attacks. Drones are also used for surveillance in the United States as well as overseas.
©U.S. Air Force Photo/Lt. Col. Leslie Pratt

Discussion Questions

1. Discuss how a rule-utilitarian and an act-utilitarian might each respond to the use of unmanned drones to carry out assassinations. How about the use of drones for surveillance in the United States? Support your answers.

2. Defenders of the drone attacks argue that they have greatly weakened terrorist groups such as al-Qaeda and ISIL. Opponents disagree, arguing that the strikes, which have killed innocent civilians and children, are a violation of basic human rights and, as such, have become a recruiting tool for terrorist groups. Critically analyze both positions.

Exercises

1. In the past few decades, women have been applying to college at a significantly higher rate than men. To achieve gender balance, some liberal arts colleges are favoring male applicants, defending the practice on the grounds that colleges

where there is gender equity are more attractive to students. Discuss whether this admissions policy is justifiable in light of utilitarian theory.

*2. Discuss John Stuart Mill's claim that concern for our own happiness cannot be separated from a concern for the common good? Do you have a direct impulse to promote the common good? Or, do you only promote the common good when it is in your best self-interest to do so? Relate your answer to your community service work.

3. Marijuana is the most frequently used illegal drug in the United States, with about 30 percent of college students saying they use it.[14] Should marijuana for recreational use be legalized and, if so, under what circumstances? Support your answer citing research on the harms and benefits of marijuana and its legalization. Discuss how both an act-utilitarian and a rule-utilitarian would most likely approach this issue.

4. President Obama banned the use of torture stating that America had "lost its moral bearings" in allowing torture to be used on detainees at Guantanamo Bay.[15] Former vice president Dick Cheney disagrees. Cheney argues that the use of what he calls "harsh interrogation techniques" has been successful in extracting information from terrorist detainees to thwart future terrorist attacks. Is torture morally justified if it can prevent the death of hundreds of people? Or, is it always wrong? Support your answer. Discuss also how both an act-utilitarian and a rule-utilitarian might answer this question.

Jeremy Bentham: Utilitarianism and Social Reform

The interest of the community is one of the most general expressions that can occur in the phraseology of morals.

—JEREMY BENTHAM, *Principles of Morals and Legislation* (1789), Ch. 1

English jurist, philosopher, and social reformer Jeremy Bentham (1748–1832) promoted utilitarianism primarily as a tool of social reform. Although a lawyer by training, Bentham never actually practiced law. However, he remained interested in jurisprudence and legal reform throughout his life. Bentham's philosophy was deeply imbued with the ideals of equality and democracy. In particular, he called into question the old values that favored the status quo and justified inequality as part of God's natural order. The Industrial Revolution, coupled with the widespread political unrest that culminated in the American and French Revolutions, brought about tremendous changes in Western society during the late eighteenth and early nineteenth centuries.

The sudden surge in population growth in Europe during the late eighteenth century and the rise of the factory system in the mid-nineteenth century precipitated

*An asterisk indicates that the exercise is appropriate for students who are doing community service learning as part of the course.

Jeremy Bentham (1748-1832),
English jurist, philosopher, and
social reformer.
©Georgios Kollidas/Shutterstock

a shift from an agricultural and commercial society to a modern industrial society. People from the countryside flocked into the new industrial centers in search of jobs and a better life. The introduction of new technologies and the mechanization of the means of production left the workers increasingly dependent on their employers. The increasing dependence of the workers, in turn, led to the advent of child labor, widespread poverty among the working class, and the creation of vast urban slums. Bentham developed his utilitarian theory in response to the flagrant injustices of his time and the desperate needs of the poor and exploited workers. See the selection from Bentham's *An Introduction to the Principles of Morals and Legislation* (1789) at the end of this chapter.

Bentham's Utilitarian Theory

Bentham's moral theory was inspired in large part by the theories of Epicurus (341-270 B.C.E.) and David Hume (1711-1776). Epicurus believed that pleasure and pain were the measure of good and evil and that happiness could be best achieved by living a tranquil, pain-free life surrounded by friends. Both Hume and Epicurus claimed that certain traits are virtues because of their utility, or usefulness in promoting happiness. Bentham took Hume's ethics one step further by arguing that utility provides the *only* source of political obligation for the state. He believed that the principle of utility alone provides the test of what a law ought to be and which laws ought to be obeyed.

> It appears to be matter of fact, that the circumstance of utility, in all subjects, is a source of praise and approbation: that it is constantly appealed to in all moral decisions concerning the merit and demerit of actions: . . . and, in a word, that it is a foundation of the chief part of morals, which has a reference to mankind and our fellow-creatures.
>
> —DAVID HUME, *An Enquiry Concerning the Principles of Morals* (1751), p. 231

Bentham was concerned primarily with social reform. His objective was to devise a practical moral theory that could form a secure, scientific foundation for developing social policy and legislation and for critiquing the existing legal system. Many of the moral values espoused by the philosophers of that time he found to be too abstract to have much practical application for social reform. Bentham's theory also differs from the top-down approach that was used by the English government to formulate social policy. Utilitarian theory instead adopts a practical bottom-up approach—that is, it begins with the happiness of the people rather than imposing morality and social ideals upon them from above.

Like Epicurus, Bentham was convinced that only superstition (ignorance) and tradition prevented people from behaving rationally. Bentham was especially skeptical of the church and institutional Christianity; he regarded the Christian virtues of submissiveness, humility, and self-sacrifice—which were advocated (but rarely practiced) by those in power—as standing in the way of morality and social reform. Behaving in a certain way because of fear of "punishment at the hands of a splenetic and revengeful Deity," Bentham argued, is the "offspring of superstitious fancy."[16]

Connections

How do Bentham's views on social reform compare with those of cultural relativists? *See Chapter 6, pages 190-193.*

The Utilitarian Calculus

Bentham believed that the purpose of ethics is not only to tell us what our duties are but also to provide us with a test or criterion so that we can know these duties. To this end, he developed the **utilitarian calculus** (also known as the "calculus of pleasures" or the "hedonic calculus") as a means of determining which action, or policy, is morally preferable. He pointed out that this process of weighing costs and benefits need not be carried out before every moral judgment or legislative decision, but it should always be kept in mind.

Bentham came up with a list of seven factors that he believed should be considered when calculating the total amount of pleasure and pain caused by any action. The weight given to each of the factors would depend on the action or policy under consideration.

Connections

What are the basic tenets of hedonism? *See Chapter 7, page 211.*

**The Utilitarian Calculus: Seven Factors to
Take into Consideration in Determining
the Most Moral Action or Decision**

1. *Intensity:* Strength of the pleasure and pain. The greater the pleasure the higher the positive value; the greater the pain the more negative the value.

2. *Duration:* Length of time the pain and pleasure will last.

3. *Certainty:* Level of probability that the pleasure or pain will occur.

4. *Propinquity:* How near in time the pleasure or happiness will occur.

5. *Fecundity:* Extent to which the pleasure will produce more pleasure.

6. *Purity:* The pleasure does not cause pain at the same time.

7. *Extent:* The number of sentient beings affected by the action.

---

1. *Intensity involves the strength of the pain or pleasure.* The greater the intensity of the pleasure, the higher the positive value we assign to it. Conversely, the greater the intensity of the pain, the greater the negative value we give it. All else being equal, the act that produces the most pleasure is morally preferable.

2. *Duration refers to the length of time that the pleasure or pain lasts.* A pleasure of long duration is preferable to one of short duration, while a pain of short duration is better than one of longer duration. For example, the hour or so of pain we get from having a cavity filled by a dentist outweighs both the intensity and duration of pain we would have to suffer if we let the cavity go untreated.

3. *Certainty refers to the probability that the pleasure or pain will occur.* Physicians might choose a time-honored treatment over a new experimental treatment for a medical condition simply because they believe it is more likely that the old treatment will relieve the symptoms.

4. *Propinquity, or nearness in time, is related to certainty.* Generally, we can be more certain of immediate pleasures. Deferred pleasures, on the other hand, may be greater, if realized, but may never actually come to fruition.

5. *Fecundity means that the pleasure is productive of more pleasure,* rather like a stone thrown in the water and producing ripples. For example, a college education is, in general, more fecund than spending four years beach-combing.

6. *Purity entails pleasure that does not cause pain at the same time.* The less pain we cause in bringing about a pleasurable consequence, the better the action. If there will be a lot of pain, the dentist ought to use painkillers when drilling our teeth, even though she could achieve the same long-term results by drilling without Novocain.

7. *Extent refers to the number of sentient beings affected by the action.* In general, the more beings that experience pleasure or the fewer that experience pain as a consequence of the action, the higher the utility of the action.

The total happiness of the community is simply the sum of the interests of its several members. The higher the total pleasure, the greater the positive value. If the proposed policy has a higher positive than negative value, then it is a good policy. For example, imposing a mandatory curfew on campus may be inconvenient or cause pain to some people. But if it makes the campus more secure and increases the overall sense of well-being on campus, then it is morally justified. This type of cost-benefit analysis is also used by school districts in formulating policies for reducing school violence (pain) without unduly restricting students' freedom and autonomy (pleasure).

Although the utilitarian calculus looks relatively straightforward and works well in some cases, it can be confusing. For example, can pleasures and pains even be quantified? How do we assign a value to the pleasure of being in a relationship, or of overcoming a neurosis or phobia, or of enjoying good music? People also respond very differently to pain and pleasure. Should the pain of a hypochondriac, for example, count more than the pain of a stoic? In addition, should other factors, such as the quality of the pleasure, also be included in our calculations? Despite these problems and its lack of scientific accuracy, the utilitarian calculus is still very useful as a guideline.

Bentham was especially interested in applying his utilitarian calculus to the reform of the criminal justice system. He was opposed to the concept of retributive justice ("an eye for an eye") because punishment involves harming people without any increase in happiness as a result. As an alternative, Bentham proposed a prison system based on reform and rehabilitation.

Connections
Why did Immanuel Kant support capital punishment? *See Chapter 10, pages 341-343.*

Although his plan for a model prison was sanctioned by an act of Parliament, the failure of the English government to carry through the plan for a new prison further persuaded Bentham that the government did not have the welfare of the common people at heart. Despite this setback, Bentham's ideas have had a major impact on our current criminal justice system. Although modern prisons often fail to live up to their name as "correctional facilities," they are far more humane than the prisons of two hundred years ago.

Bentham's utilitarian theory, with its concerns for equality and impartiality, has also had a major influence on policymaking in the United States. As such, utilitarianism helps to compensate for the hierarchical definition of moral community that has plagued our Western concept of justice. Although the use of the death penalty has dropped dramatically since 2000, discrimination in giving the death penalty still exists. Studies show that our criminal justice system tends to be more sympathetic and lenient toward people who are closer to the center of the moral community, as defined by our culture. Over 34 percent of death row inmates who are executed are Black, though Blacks comprise only about 13 percent of the population in the United States. In addition, the odds of receiving the death penalty for murdering a White person are 3.5 times as high as those for murdering a Black person and over four times as high as those for murdering a Hispanic person.[17]

Bentham, ever true to his principle of utility and his concern for the well-being of the community, left his body for dissection to the Webb Street School of Anatomy—the first person ever to do so. His stuffed remains are still on display at University College at the University of London.

Exercises

1. Discuss Bentham's claim that punishment is an evil. Can punishment, including capital punishment, be justified on utilitarian grounds? Or, does punishment of criminals actually decrease the overall happiness of society, as Bentham maintains? What policy would a utilitarian most likely propose for dealing with potentially dangerous criminals?

2. Does an ethics dealing with societal issues require a different strategy than personal ethics? If so, how do the two strategies differ? On what grounds can you justify the differences?

3. Both ethical egoist Ayn Rand and utilitarian Jeremy Bentham regarded the Christian "virtue" of self-sacrifice as an obstacle to morality. However, both came to different conclusions about morality. Evaluate each of their positions and discuss how each might respond to the other's argument.

4. At one time, there were not enough kidney dialysis machines for everyone who needed them. One hospital in Seattle, Washington, used the utilitarian calculus to decide who would get dialysis. Age, health, involvement in community activities, the importance of a person's job to the community, and the number of dependents were just some of the factors taken into consideration in making a decision. Most of the patients who were denied kidney dialysis died as a result. Was this utilitarian solution the best way, from a moral point of view, for allocating kidney dialysis machines? Support your position.

5. Discuss the following case studies, using the utilitarian calculus:

    a. A group of women at Brown University were frustrated because they felt that the administration and the city police were not doing enough to prevent date rape on campus, so they decided to take the matter into their own hands. They wrote the names of men who had allegedly raped them on the wall of one of the ladies' rooms in a prominent building on campus. Use the utilitarian calculus to determine whether their action was morally justified. What other action, if any, might have produced a higher value?

    b. School-related stress among college students is a major source of unhappiness. Although a moderate level of stress can actually enhance our capacity to learn, both high and low levels of stress have been found to be damaging to the learning process and to students' general sense of well-being. Excessive stress—distress—can lead to panic, depression, and dropping out of school.[18] Teenagers who are highly stressed are also more likely to smoke, drink alcohol, and use illegal drugs.[19]

    Using the utilitarian calculus, draw up a proposal for your college or class that would address stress levels, thereby maximizing students' learning and sense of well-being.

c. Bruce, a senior accounting major and university basketball star, injured his knee in a game a few weeks before the end of the season. Bruce can play the last few games of the season if he is given a painkiller. If Bruce doesn't play, however, it is almost certain that the team will not win the final playoffs. On the other hand, if Bruce does play, he will probably cause permanent injury to his knee and walk with a limp for the rest of his life. Losing the playoffs may be costly to the university, which is already in serious financial trouble because of the state budget deficit; the opposing team's school is not in financial trouble. Bruce says he would rather not take the chance of permanently injuring his knee. Using the utilitarian calculus, decide whether Bruce has a moral obligation to play basketball.

d. Referring back to the opening scenario, use the utilitarian calculus to come up with a policy regarding the use of torture on suspected terrorists.

6. If you are still undecided about a major or future career path, carry out a utilitarian calculus to determine which major or career has the highest utility for you and others who will be affected by your choice. Are you satisfied with the results of the calculus? Discuss why or why not. If not, what other factors do you think should be included in making your decision?

*7. Using the utilitarian calculus, discuss whether community service should be mandated, either as part of the school curriculum or as part of a compulsory national service program.

John Stuart Mill: Reformulation of Utilitarianism

It is quite compatible with the principle of utility to recognize the fact that some kinds of pleasure are more desirable and more valuable than others.

—JOHN STUART MILL, *Utilitarianism* (1863), Ch. 2

The influence of Bentham on the philosophy of John Stuart Mill (1806–1873) can hardly be overestimated. Bentham's close friendship with the Mill family was a source of both intellectual inspiration and companionship. Mill was born in London in 1806, the eldest child of Harriet Burrow Mill and philosopher and journalist James Mill. Mill was educated at home, where he began learning Greek at age three. Bentham, who never married nor had any children of his own, became absorbed in the education of John Stuart. Before the age of fourteen, Mill rarely associated with children his own age—only with his family and his father's utilitarian friends, including Jeremy Bentham, who helped educate him to carry on the utilitarian tradition.

At the age of twenty, Mill had an emotional breakdown and sank into a deep depression that lasted for two years. He blamed the depression partially on the habit of analysis, which, he said, had a tendency to wear away at one's feelings. This depression helped free him from the hold that his father had on him.

Around 1830, Mill met and became a lifelong friend of Harriet Taylor, a liberal and highly educated woman. Although she was married, they became very close friends. They married in 1851 after the death of her husband.

Although Taylor never published under her own name, she had a tremendous influence on Mill's thinking and on his radical reformulation of Bentham's utilitarian theory. Mill wrote that he consulted her opinion on all of his works; he claimed that his well-known book *On Liberty* (1859) was a joint production.

When the East India Company went out of business in 1858, Mill accepted an invitation to run for Parliament. He served in Parliament until 1868.

Where Mill and Bentham Concurred

Although Mill held Bentham in great esteem, he came to recognize the inadequacies of Bentham's theory. Mill was also aware that Bentham's contributions to social ethics and legal reform were enormous. These contributions, Mill wrote in his biography of Bentham, should not be overlooked in our zeal to point out the deficiencies in his theory:

> [T]here is hardly anything positive in Bentham's philosophy which is not true . . . when his practical conclusions are erroneous, which in our opinion they are very often, it is not because the considerations which he urges are not rational and valid in themselves, but because some more important principle, which he did not perceive, supersedes those considerations, and turns the scales.[20]

Like Bentham, Mill was interested in political matters and social reform. Mill was an advocate of freedom of thought and expression, free trade, parliamentary reform, secret voting, equality for women and universal suffrage, annual elections, trade unions, and reform of land tenure.

Connections

How would modern care ethicists most likely respond to Mill's concerns about the treatment of women? *See Chapter 12, pages 406–410.*

Mill agreed with Bentham that superstition and tradition were serious impediments to the smooth, rational operation of society. In Mill's book *The Subjection of Women* (1869), he argued that traditional attitudes that oppress women prevent them from being as happy as they might otherwise be and also get in the way of women fully using their talents. "If there is anything vitally important to the happiness of human beings," Mill wrote, "it is that they should relish their habitual pursuit. This requisite of an enjoyable life is very imperfectly granted, or altogether denied to a large part of mankind."[21]

Like Bentham, Mill believed that education is an important tool for overcoming ignorance, one of the main causes of unhappiness. The primary role of education is to help both men and women become more rational and autonomous. Mill was, however, opposed to compulsory state schooling as a means of educating the public. On the other hand, he believed that the state should enforce universal education, whether it be carried out at home, in a school, or in the workplace.

Where Mill and Bentham Diverged

Despite Mill's admiration for Bentham, they disagreed on several counts. According to Bentham, equality is a moral ideal or prescription of how we ought to treat sentient beings. The happiness of any one individual is no more or less important than that of another. What is important, according to Bentham, is the quantity of pleasure, not its quality. The pleasure of playing darts is no different from the pleasure derived from writing a poem or listening to Beethoven. The pleasures of a pig should count no more or less than those of a human.

> It is better to be a human being dissatisfied than a pig satisfied; better to be Socrates dissatisfied than a fool satisfied.
>
> —John Stuart Mill, *Utilitarianism*, Ch. 2

Connections

According to Aristotle how do we cultivate the intellectual virtues? *See Chapter 12, page 395.*

Mill disagreed. He argued that some pleasures are more desirable than others. Mill maintained that human life is *qualitatively* better than the life of nonhuman animals. He believed that the primary means of ensuring happiness is to respect the dignity and personal autonomy of others. The freedom to make our own decisions, he argued, is basic to human happiness. A society that protects people's liberty and autonomy provides the best conditions for happiness to flourish.

Like Aristotle, Mill believed that the intellectual pleasures are superior to those of the body. The rational pleasures, even though they are less intense at times, are morally preferable to the simple pleasures of a pig, or those of the uneducated person or the fool. The pleasure of drinking beer or watching television, for example, is of a lower quality than that of spending the evening listening to a Beethoven concert or reading the poems of Elizabeth Barrett Browning. Mill supported this hierarchy of pleasures by claiming that people who had an opportunity to experience both the higher and the lower pleasures would prefer the higher (rational) pleasures. People persist in engaging in lower pleasures, he argued, only because of ignorance and superstition. (See the selection by Mill at the end of this chapter for his explanation of different kinds of pleasures.)

Mill also argued that to pursue happiness as our only goal is self-defeating. Pleasure is not the only criterion for judging the morality of an action. Instead, human dignity or integrity is morally good independent of the quantity of pleasure. By introducing the concept of the quality of pleasure and criteria other than pleasure, Mill moved away from being a strict utilitarian like Bentham.

Mill also rejected Bentham's concept of justice as impartiality being a first-order good. Impartiality demands that no one's happiness counts any more than the happiness of anyone else. Justice as impartiality can be used to defend the use of one person or a group of beings to maximize happiness for others. For example, justice as impartiality might permit the execution of an innocent person to restore harmony to a community disrupted by a particularly heinous crime. Instead of justice as impartiality, Mill advocated a concept of justice that focuses primarily on autonomy or self-determination. Justice as impartiality is good only if it first satisfies the needs of autonomy. The justice system in the United States, with its concern for protecting the rights of the accused, is closer to Mill's concept of justice.

A University of Georgia police officer asks a group of protestors to move their protest over the execution of Troy Davis to a free speech zone. At the time, free speech zones were limited to less than 1 percent of the campus. In 2015, the University of Georgia adopted a less restrictive free speech following a lawsuit from Young Americans for Liberty and Alliance Defending Freedom.[22]
©AP Photo/Athens-Banner Herald, David Mannin

Discussion Questions

1. Discuss how Mill would most likely respond to free speech zones and other restrictions on freedom of speech on college campuses.

2. Should any restrictions be placed on freedom of speech on college campuses and, if so, what should they be? Discuss how Mill might respond to these restrictions.

Connections

Why does W. D. Ross say the duty of nonmaleficence is a prima facie duty? *See Chapter 10, pages 331–332.*

The *principle of nonmaleficence*, or the "no harm" principle, was more important to Mill than the duty to directly maximize the overall happiness of the community. The "no harm" principle prohibits individuals or the government from interfering with another's actions except to prevent actions that will have harmful consequences. By "harm," Mill did not simply mean feeling offended or inconvenienced by someone else's actions. What he meant by "harm" included causing physical injury to others, unjustly encroaching on someone else's legitimate rights, the use of duplicity in dealing with others, taking unfair advantage of others, or selfishly failing to protect others from injury. Condemning or placing legal obstacles in the way of someone's pursuit of a particular lifestyle cannot be justified solely on the grounds that most people find the lifestyle offensive. Mill's "no harm" principle was used in the 1957 Wolfenden Report that led to the legalization in England of homosexual acts between consenting adults.

Mill was also opposed to censorship because of the human tendency to want to censure opinions that are at variance with those of the majority. He argued that censorship could lead to censoring truth, since humans are fallible. Even the smartest of us can make mistakes in judgment. We may believe that something is false and should be censored, but be mistaken in our belief. In addition, we need to have our facts correct in order to make the best decision regarding the consequences of certain actions. It is better that we have to filter out which information is false than to take a risk in censoring truth.

Like Bentham, Mill hoped that his ideas would be useful as guidelines for legislation and for the creation of a more tolerant society. Indeed, Mill's views on censorship continue to play a key role in the current debates over censorship of pornography and restrictions upon freedom of speech. For more on the application of utilitarian theory to issues in public policy, see pages 264–269.

Exercises

1. Mill said of his childhood: "I never was a boy; never played at cricket; it is better to let Nature have her way."[23] But if Nature had had her way, would he have become such an influential philosopher and social reformer? To what extent do parents have the right, or the moral obligation, to oversee and direct their children's lives if by doing so we can bring about greater utility or happiness for society? Support your argument.

2. Mill's distrust of state-run education is not without foundation. Studies have shown that public schooling, rather than counteracting superstition and tradition, actually reinforces prejudices such as racism and sexism and other attitudes associated with the status quo.[24] One study concluded that public schools, rather than being the proverbial melting pot or "great equalizer," actually close off some children's futures by perpetuating existing social inequalities.[25]

   Reflecting back upon your own schooling and college education, how, if at all, has it served to limit the development of your talents and your pursuit of happiness as a member of society, as well as your moral development? Discuss how a utilitarian might restructure our current education system to make it more rational, progressive, and less society maintaining.

3. Mill assumed that people who have experienced both higher and lower pleasures will prefer the former. However, is this true? Poor-quality novels sell more copies than the literary classics, despite children's exposure to the classics in school. And soap operas are a lot more popular than documentaries on public television. Discuss examples from your own life where, despite exposure to both higher and lower pleasures, you still preferred the lower pleasures. How might Mill respond to this phenomenon?

*4. Mill's reformulation of utilitarianism, like social Darwinism, has been used to morally justify a policy of cultural imperialism, where more educated Westerners could impose their pleasures and values on more "primitive cultures" under the guise of benefiting the people living in these cultures. Indeed, Mill himself was a supporter of British colonialism. Do you think this conclusion follows from the idea that the quality of some pleasures is greater than the quality of others? To what extent does this attitude lead to the neglect of the interests of certain groups of people in our own culture? Relate your answers to your community service work.

Mo Tzu: Utilitarianism as Universal Love

He should work to promote what is beneficial to the world, both directly and indirectly, and avoid what is of no benefit. Such is the way of the superior man.

—Mo Tzu, *Against Confucians*, Pt. I, Sect. 3926

Mo Tzu (c. 470–391 B.C.E.), also known as Mo Ti, lived in China during the period of the "hundred philosophers" (the late sixth to the early third century B.C.E.). This remarkably fertile period in Eastern thought was paralleled by the golden age of Greek philosophy in the West. Mo Tzu was born about 470 B.C.E., the same year that Socrates was born and nine years after the death of Confucius.

Connections

According to Confucianism, what are our most important duties? *See Chapter 10, pages 324–326.*

Confucianism and Taoism were the prevailing philosophies at the time. Mo Tzu regarded Confucians as uptight, pretentious, and characterized by mindless devotion to meaningless rituals. Mo Tzu advocated utilitarianism as an alternative to what he regarded as the passivity of Confucianism and Taoism. In Confucianism, virtue is associated with honoring tradition. Taoism, which emphasizes letting go and allowing virtue to flow naturally out of the Tao (the way the universe operates), is even more passive than Confucianism. Mo Tzu was as committed to peace and harmony as Confucianists and Taoists, but he did not believe that harmony came about from the unfolding of the natural order of things (the Tao) or from following tradition.

Despite Mo Tzu's dislike of Confucianism, he accepted a version of the Confucian principle of *jen*, or love, as the overriding moral principle. However, unlike Confucius, Mo Tzu believed that this principle should be applied equally and universally to all people.

Like Western utilitarians, Mo Tzu viewed morality pragmatically. The good society could best be achieved by actively seeking and promoting the good of the many. Mo Tzu taught that hate is the primary cause of pain in the world; universal love *(jen)* is the source of happiness and what is beneficial.

Mo Tzu was convinced that the ways of the people could be changed with the proper leadership by rulers who take delight in universal love and mutual benefit and strive to put these principles into practice. By using the standard of utility or universality, Mo Tzu believed, we can achieve a world of peace and harmony.

While Confucius emphasized filial loyalty, Mo Tzu argued that it is wrong to count the happiness of our family and friends as more important. According to Mo Tzu, we should give equal consideration to the happiness of all who will be affected by our actions, no matter what their social standing or relationship to us. Mo Tzu especially denounced the Chinese aristocrats' and feudal lords' luxurious lifestyles and wasteful spending on dances, elaborate funerals, and other rituals that added nothing to the material welfare of the nation or the common people. China's social order at that time was very hierarchical, so Mo Tzu's insistence on equality frequently met with ridicule.

Although Mo Tzu realized that people often act in harmful ways, he was also an optimist who believed that reform is possible. On a practical level, he argued, it is not enough to simply criticize people or practices; there is an element of chaos and selfishness in society and in humans that must first be overcome to achieve the good society. Therefore, he argued, we have a moral obligation to offer practical alternatives and to actively work for a better society. Any idea or principle that cannot be put into action is useless.

> Now if we seek to benefit the world by taking universality as our standard, those with sharp ears and clear eyes will see and hear for others, those with sturdy limbs will work for others, and those with a knowledge of the Way will endeavor to teach others. . . . When all these benefits may be secured merely by taking universality as our standard, I cannot understand how the men of the world can hear about this doctrine of universality and still criticize it![26]

Mo Tzu, like his contemporary Socrates, had a reputation for being confrontational when trying to get his message across. He spent his life moving from feudal court to feudal court. During his travels, he would engage rulers and other people he met along the way in philosophical discussion, all the time trying to convince them to live by seeking the good of the many. This did not sit well with those who benefited from the hierarchical ethics of Confucianism.

Not surprisingly, Mo Tzu's philosophy of equality irritated those in power, who eventually refused to listen to him. Mo Tzu responded by founding his own school to train people for the public life. During his life, he was popular with the common people and had about three hundred followers or disciples. Mo Tzu died in 391 B.C.E., and the Moism school of philosophy died out soon after his death. However, Mo Tzu's philosophy continues to exert an influence on Chinese thought to this day.

Connections

Would a feminist care ethicist be more likely to agree with Mo Tzu or with Confucius regarding the special importance of family and friends? *See Chapter 12, pages 407-409.*

Exercises

*1. What do you think Mo Tzu meant when he said that hate is the primary cause of harm in the world? Is universal love a realistic goal? Relate your answers to your community service work.

2. Mo Tzu emphasized the importance of actively working toward a better society rather than just talking about moral theory. Discuss a time when you were guilty of passivity regarding a social issue. How might you become a more active moral agent?

3. Confucius taught that our love should be strongest for our relatives and friends. Mo Tzu, in contrast, taught that universal love should not be partial or play favorites. Discuss these two competing concepts of moral obligation. Relate your answer to the concept of moral sensitivity in Chapter 3 as well as to Gilligan's care ethics. Support your answer using examples from your own life.

Utilitarianism and the Moral Community

[No] truth appears to me more evident, that beasts are endow'd with thought and reason as well as man.

—DAVID HUME, *A Treatise of Human Nature* (1730), p. 176

It is an implication of this principle of equality that our concern for others and our readiness to consider their interests ought not to depend on what they are or what abilities they possess.

—PETER SINGER, *Animal Liberation* (1990)

Utilitarian ethics calls into question the Western anthropocentric view of the moral community. Like many Eastern philosophies, utilitarianism extends the moral community to encompass all sentient beings. Because of their concern for equality, autonomy, and the happiness of all sentient beings, utilitarians have historically been in the forefront of movements for human equality and the welfare of nonhuman animals. Although in the last century we have come to accept (more or less) the ideal of human equality, the notion of equality among all sentient beings still seems absurd and counterintuitive to many Westerners. However, as utilitarian J. J. C. Smart notes, many of our "intuitive" moral concepts may be, in fact, nothing more than cultural norms or prejudices.[27]

Connections
Which model of rights—the self-assertion model or the interests model of rights—is most consistent with Mill's views? *See Chapter 11, pages 383-384.*

Australian utilitarian Peter Singer maintains that not to grant the same consideration to a nonhuman animal who has the same cognitive ability as a human is to engage in speciesism. Like racism and sexism, **speciesism** is a prejudice or bias against certain beings simply because of their membership in a particular group. Singer writes:

Racists violate the principle of equality by giving greater weight to the interests of members of their own race when there is a clash between their interests and the interests of those of another race. Sexists violate the principle of equality by favoring the interests of their own sex. Similarly speciesists allow the interests of their own species to override the greater interests of members of other species. The pattern is identical in each case.[28]

Our inclination to disregard the moral worth of other animals must be examined in light of the principle of utility and the ideal of equality rather than our particular cultural prejudices. Once we do so, most utilitarians maintain, we will find that these prejudices cannot be rationally justified but are merely the outgrowth of ignorance and tradition.

Not long ago, the concept of human equality seemed equally foolish to many people—including most philosophers. Slavery was regarded as morally acceptable for many centuries. The inferiority of women was also long accepted. When Mary Wollstonecraft published her *Vindication of the Rights of Woman* in 1792, most people ridiculed her views. One critic, Thomas Taylor, wrote in response to her tract that, if equality should apply to women, then why should it not be applied also to dogs, cats, horses, and other "brutes"? Because this, he suggested, was patently absurd, it would be ludicrous to extend equal rights to women. Taylor's response may seem ludicrous to us today, but at the time, it seemed to make good sense to most people.

The inclusion of the pleasure and pain of other animals in our utilitarian calculations, however, does not entail that nonhumans must be treated the same as humans. This conclusion would be as absurd as Taylor's argument that women should not be given the right to vote because, if so, the right to vote would have to be extended to all animals. Morally, there is no point in extending the right to vote or to attend public school to dogs and cats and horses because they have no interest in and would derive no pleasure or benefit from these activities. What gives a human pleasure and what gives a dog pleasure can be very different things. For example, a dog might get great pleasure out of agility training, but no pleasure out of a high school math class or great art. Children also have somewhat different preferences than adults. Similarly, it would be nonsensical to argue that, if women ought to be given free prenatal care, this right should also be extended to men. In other words, Taylor's argument against granting equal rights to women, because the same rights would then have to be extended to all animals, is based on a mistaken concept of equality as sameness. Following is another excerpt from Singer's *Animal Liberation*:

Connections

On what grounds do deontologists argue that nonhuman animals, unlike humans, lack intrinsic moral worth? *See Chapter 10, pages 315-317.*

> ... concern for the well-being of children growing up in America would require that we teach them to read; concern for the well-beings of pigs may require no more than that we leave them with other pigs in a place where there is adequate food and room to run freely. But the basic element—the taking into account of the interests of the being, whatever those interests may be—must according to the principle of equality, be extended to all beings, black or white, masculine or feminine, human or nonhuman.[29]

Although respecting the interests of other species does not entail treating them the same as humans, certain conclusions do follow if we accept the claim that the principle of utility should be extended to all sentient animals. For example, Singer concludes that, just as it is wrong for us to eat other humans, it is wrong to eat other animals because a vegetarian diet is equally nutritious for humans. He contends that it is particularly immoral to eat animals who are raised on farms where modern confinement techniques not only cause tremendous suffering to the animals but also frustrate their natural desires and instincts.

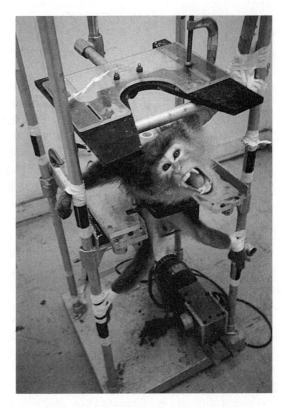

This photo, taken by PETA in 1981, led to the nation's first criminal conviction of an animal experimenter for cruelty to animals.
Image Courtesy of PETA, www.peta.org

Discussion Questions

1. Would it be morally preferable to use humans with severe cognitive deficits instead of healthy nonhuman primates in experiments like the one shown above? Support your answer. How would a utilitarian most likely answer this question? Support your answer.

2. Discuss whether you have a moral obligation to avoid, as much as possible, products that were developed using animal experimentation.

Connections

Do rights ethicists extend rights to nonhuman animals? *See Chapter 11, pages 383–384.*

Similarly, most medical experiments using sentient animals are immoral. Humans may benefit from this practice, but Singer argues that this does not in itself justify the suffering and death of millions of laboratory animals worldwide every year. Indeed over 100 million animals were used in experiments in 2016 with the United States using almost more than any other country, second only to China.[30] The use of animals in research has been on the decline since 1992, in part in response to protests but also because of the development of other techniques, such as computer simulation.

The use of nonhuman animals to benefit humans is often justified on the grounds that humans have a greater mental capacity. But not even Mill, who ranked human pleasure above the pleasures of other animals, would say that this alone justified the suffering of laboratory animals. If our concern is to benefit humans, then it could even be argued that it would be preferable to use brain-damaged humans rather than nonhuman animals because the results would be more accurate. Indeed, the use of certain "nonproductive" groups of humans, such as elderly people and children who are mentally retarded, has been justified by some researchers on utilitarian grounds.

Whenever experimenters claim that their experiments are important enough to justify the use of animals, we should ask them whether they would be prepared to use a brain-damaged human being at a similar mental level to the animals they are planning to use.

—PETER SINGER, *Animal Liberation* (1990), pp. 82–83

Although Singer argues for the inclusion of sentient nonhuman animals in our moral community, he cautions us not to interpret this as implying that all lives have equal worth. Like Mill, Singer believes that certain qualities, such as self-awareness and the capacity for abstract thought, are higher pleasures and should be given greater consideration. This, however, does not justify speciesism; nor does it justify the degradation of humans who lack these capabilities because sentience, or the capacity for pain and pleasure, is the foundational criterion for inclusion in the moral community.

The principle of utility demands that we do not take refuge in religious and cultural traditions but instead examine our actions and decisions in light of the actual consequences. This entails overcoming our ignorance regarding the extent to which our lifestyle is built upon the suffering of other people or animals and the destruction of the environment. We also need to ask if economic progress contributes to greater happiness for society in general. Does economic progress lead to greater happiness for society in general? Or, does it increase the happiness of the few at the expense of the many—including the millions of other species that share this planet with humans? Utilitarian theory also requires that we consider both the short-term and long-term consequences of our actions on the environment, not only for humans but for all sentient beings.

Exercises

1. Adam Smith in 1776 (see pages 220–221) argued that laissez-faire capitalism is the best way of promoting the public good and interests of everyone in society. Do you agree? Is capitalism consistent with the utilitarian view of the moral community? Support your answers.

2. Critically analyze Singer's claim that most humans are speciesists. If you are a speciesist, on what grounds do you morally justify it?

3. Although we no longer capture and put humans from other cultures on display, it is still considered morally acceptable to place nonhuman animals in zoos for educational purposes. Can this practice be morally justified?

4. While many, if not most, Americans think it's wrong to cause pain to other animals, 96 percent of Americans, according to a 2016 National Harris Poll, are meat-eaters.[31] Does a lack of malicious intent morally justify actions that indirectly harm other animals? Support your answers.

5. How does your lifestyle contribute to the suffering of other human and nonhuman sentient beings, as well as to global warming and the destruction of the environment? Discuss steps you could take to make your lifestyle more in accord with the requirements of the principle of utility.

The Principle of Utility in Public Policy

Utilitarianism is particularly useful in the formulation of public policy. Utilitarian theory is also used by colleges to develop policies around issues like AIDS testing, free speech zones, and the distribution of goods such as scholarships. In this section, we'll look briefly at three public policy issues in light of the principle of utility: voluntary euthanasia, military conscription, and taxing fattening, nonnutritious food.

Euthanasia: Is Death Always a Harm?

One of the issues currently facing us is the formulation of a social policy regarding the moral permissibility of actively bringing about one's own death or that of another sentient being.

Planned death is a rational system that honors self-determination and extracts from a purposeful, unavoidable death the maximum benefit for the subject, the subject's next of kin, and for all of humanity.

—Jack Kevorkian, "Medicide: The Goodness of Planned Death,"

Free Inquiry (Fall 1991), p. 15

Many people regard it as morally acceptable, and perhaps even obligatory, to euthanize an animal companion that is old and in pain; yet some of the same people think that it is wrong to do the same for their ailing parents or grandparents. They may support this discrepancy by arguing that the killing of a nonhuman animal—as long as it is done in a quick and painless manner—is not as immoral as killing a human. Religious ethicists also argue that the taking of human life, which is created in the divine image, is a sin against God.

Utilitarians disagree. Utilitarians do not believe in the sanctity or intrinsic worth of life. The worth of a particular life depends only on the degree to which the pleasures of that life outweigh the pain of continued existence. Singer writes:

> [O]nce we realize that the fact that a being is a member of our own species is not in itself enough to make it always wrong to kill that being, we may come to reconsider our policy of preserving human lives at all cost, even when there is no prospect of a meaningful life or of existence without terrible pain.[32]

In his essay "Of Suicide," David Hume supports the moral permissibility of suicide on the grounds of utility and autonomy. Thus, Hume would support voluntary **euthanasia**, especially when the pain in a person's life outweighs the pleasure that he or she derives from living. Hume, like the utilitarians, rejected the anthropocentric view that human life has a special sacred value that the lives of other beings lack. "The life of man," he wrote, "is of no greater importance to the universe than that of an oyster."[33] A time may come when we are no longer productive members of society, and our life no longer brings us any happiness. The removal of misery is a good consequence even if suicide is an unfortunate means to that end.

Connections
On what grounds does Hume maintain that moral sentiments are more important than reason? *See Chapter 12, page 404.*

I am not obliged to do a small good to society at the expense of a great harm to myself: when then should I prolong a miserable existence, because of some frivolous advantage which the public may perhaps receive from me?

—David Hume, "Of Suicide"[34]

Some ethicists oppose the deliberate ending of human life on the grounds that, unlike killing animals who, they claim, lack a concept of the future, suicide thwarts humans' future aspirations. However, this argument does not make sense to a utilitarian because death marks the end of sentient existence. At the point of death, there no longer exists a being who can suffer from the pain of having had his or her aspirations thwarted. Also, some people, such as those who are suffering from terminal illnesses, have no future aspirations except to be relieved of their suffering. Death represents the fulfillment, rather than the thwarting, of future aspirations in these cases. When there is great suffering and the person desires death, death may be less of an evil than that person's continued existence. If this is the case, killing oneself or another person may be the most beneficent act.

But what about the pain to those left behind? The distress brought on by the loss of a loved one, however, is only relevant when the deceased person is a member of a family or community who would be pained by his or her loss. Indeed, if the harm to a person's family and community is increased by the continued existence of a person, that person may even have a moral obligation to commit suicide, as in the case of the elderly Eskimos (see page 173).

Connections

What is the position of natural law ethicists on the morality of euthanasia? *See Chapter 9, pages 298-299.*

On the other hand, utilitarians do not support euthanasia as a blanket public policy. Most humans have an understanding of and fear their impending death. Simply the awareness that they, too, may be put to death when they are no longer "useful" to society could cause great suffering and anxiety. According to John Stuart Mill, security and a safe environment are "the most indispensable of all necessaries after physical nutriment."[35] For this reason, utility may require a social policy that protects human lives, even though these lives may not be valued by others. Among the Kabloona Eskimos, the elderly father had a say not only about the timing of his death but also about the manner in which he would die. Feeling safe and secure entails that a person's autonomy be respected in issues of life and death: People should have some choice in the time and manner of their death.

Military Conscription: Should National Service Be Mandatory?

Many people believe that a well-trained military is necessary to ensure a secure and safe environment. Currently, the United States relies on a voluntary military force. However, would military conscription—or a draft—promote greater happiness for the community?

Those who oppose conscription claim that it lowers the quality and motivation of the military—thus putting our country at greater risk for harm. There are also fewer combat casualties when the army is volunteer rather than conscript.[36] Opponents also argue that conscription violates our liberty rights. Therefore, there have to be good reasons, in terms of benefiting the greatest number affected by the policy, for overriding our liberty rights. They also note that conscription, at least as it has been practiced in the past, places a greater burden on poor, uneducated people while college students get deferments. Thus, at least as conscription was instituted in the past, it violates the principle of impartiality that was so important to Jeremy Bentham.

Those who favor conscription, in addition to regarding it as a responsibility incurred because of our membership in the political community, point out that although it may restrict our liberties, this is offset by the necessity in times of crisis to go to war to protect these liberties that are essential for our happiness. In addition, research has found that democracies with a conscripted army are more reluctant to fight an unpopular war where the harms of going to war may outweigh the benefits. Thus, a conscripted army acts as a check against an overzealous administration and Defense Department. Indeed, both Mill and Bentham expressed concern that government did not always have the happiness of the people at heart.

Unlike Mill and Bentham, utilitarian Mo Tzu was a pacifist, believing that promoting the ideal of universal love would prevent war. Therefore, he would have been opposed to conscription. Both Mill and Bentham, on the other hand, believed that war may be justified under limited circumstances. However, since war clearly brings about great harm, it is best to try to avoid it. In his *Principles of International Law*, Bentham listed the principle causes of war along with "means of prevention" for each cause. Although we do not know how Bentham felt about universal military conscription, Mill in his essay *On Liberty* (1859) supported it, although under what circumstances is unclear.

War is mischief upon the largest scale.

—JEREMY BENTHAM, "Of War," in *Principles of International Law* (c. 1789)

The Universal National Service Act (H.R. 163), which was introduced in Congress in 2002, was reintroduced in Congress in 2003 in response to the strain being placed on the professional military by the war in Iraq and the war on terrorism. The act was revised and reintroduced again in 2005, 2006, 2007, 2010, 2011, and 2013.

If passed, the act would reinstate conscription making it "the obligation of every U.S. citizen [male and female], and every other person residing in the United States, between the ages of eighteen and twenty-five to perform a two-year period of national service, unless exempted, either through military service of through civilian service in a federal, state, or local government program or with a community-based agency or entity engaged in meeting human, educational, environment, or public safety needs. . . ." Harlem Congressman Charles Rangel (D), who introduced the 2013 bill, argues that many of the recruits in our current "all volunteer" army are from urban centers with high unemployment and from economically depressed small towns who are driven to enlist for economic reasons. Many of these volunteers are forced to do multiple tours of duty. Requiring national military service would reduce the burden on this segment of the population.

Would Mill and Bentham approve of this act? Utilitarianism requires that we base our calculation of the utility of a particular policy on up-to-date facts, and an assessment of the potential consequences of the policy given the existing social and international conditions. The question is not whether conscription is a good general rule, but whether it would be the best public policy for the United States now in the early twenty-first century.

Taxing Fattening, Nonnutritious Foods: Should Government Tax Lifestyle Choices

Obesity rates have risen dramatically in the past thirty years, especially among children. "Obesity" is defined as having a body mass index (BMI) of 30 or more. Almost 20 percent of American children and teens, ages 2 to 19, are now obese. Most of these children will be obese as adults.[37]

Obesity is associated with type 2 diabetes, stroke, certain types of cancer, osteoarthritis, and bone and joint problems. The costs associated with obesity are estimated to add over 140 billion a year to health care costs in the United States.[38]

Michele Obama working with students in the "Let's Move" Program. The former first lady plays an active role in the fight against childhood obesity by encouraging young people to exercise more and eat healthier food.
©AP Photo/Carolyn Kaster

Congress, so far, has stayed away from introducing measures to curb obesity, such as taxing sugary and fatty foods. At the state level, David Paterson, former governor of New York, proposed a "fat tax" that would apply to fattening drinks such as soda pop with little or no nutritional value. Lawmakers have estimated that a 10 percent "fat tax" could add about 450 million dollars a year, money that could defray the health care costs associated with obesity.[39]

Arguments for a "fat tax" are: (1) it encourages people to reduce their consumption of fatty foods and eat healthier, (2) it would raise money for the government to offset the medial expenses associated with obesity, and (3) it would lower health costs. Arguments against a "fat tax" are: (1) it is discriminatory toward obese people, (2) it punishes companies that produce products that people enjoy but are deemed unhealthy by the state, (3) it would pose a burden on all taxpayers who already pay enough taxes, (4) it unfairly penalizes poor people who are most likely to purchase less expensive, fattening foods in order to stretch their food budgets, and (5) it puts what should be personal responsibility for our eating habits into the hands of the government. The "nays" won and the tax was never implemented.

Would a utilitarian approve of taxing fattening foods? Both Bentham and Mill believed in the use of legislation to maximize the utility or happiness of society. The state, both maintained, has a duty not to let people suffer. While

Bentham believed that all people seek to maximize pleasure and minimize pain, he was aware that people, because of ignorance and tradition, may engage in behavior that is harmful to themselves and others. Mill also supported government taxation on substances such as alcohol, if the tax could be justified on utilitarian grounds.

On the other hand, even if the benefits of a "fat tax" are greater than the harms, does such taxation justify the restrictions on our individual freedoms? As we noted earlier, the obesity rates have increased dramatically in the United States. The question remains: Is legislation and the taxing of fattening foods the best solution to the problem from a utilitarian point of view?

Exercises

1. Is it morally acceptable to euthanize people who have terminal illnesses and who want to end their lives? Why or why not?

2. Billions of dollars are spent each year on intensive and often futile treatments for people in their last months of life. Indeed, up to one-third of Medicare expenditures occur in the last year of life.[40] Does the financial burden on the family and on society justify withholding of costly treatment or even euthanasia of terminally ill people, with or without their consent? Discuss how a utilitarian might respond to this question.

3. Select one of the following public policy issues: capital punishment, legalization of recreational marijuana, or censorship of online pornography. Research the issue, including the arguments for and against each position on the policy. Discuss what a utilitarian would most likely propose regarding particular policy. Discuss also whether there are factors other than those used by utilitarians that you should be considered and why these factors are morally relevant.

4. According to the Centers for Disease Control, there are more than 1.1 million people in the United States who are HIV positive. Half of new cases are among young people between the ages of thirteen and twenty-four, the majority of whom do not know that they are infected.[41] While college students are somewhat less likely than the average people their age to be infected, AIDS is still a concern since many students engage in risky sexual behavior.

   Based on a recommendation from the Centers for Disease Control (CDC), the government advises that all people between the ages of thirteen and sixty-four be tested. Your college is considering a policy requiring all entering students to be tested for HIV. Discuss how utilitarians might respond to this policy.

5. During World War II, Nazi scientists used concentration camp inmates as subjects in several experiments. For example, to learn more about how long downed German pilots could survive immersion in the frigid North Sea, three hundred camp inmates were forced to suffer submersion in tanks of ice cold water for long periods of time. Many of them died during the experiments.

Discuss whether the medical data—data that could potentially save hundreds of future lives—should be available to scientists and physicians. How would a utilitarian most likely respond to this issue?

6. Peter Singer agrees that "there is nothing wrong with a society in which children are bred for spare parts on a massive scale."[42] Critically analyze his position. Discuss also how an ethical egoist and another utilitarian, such as John Stuart Mill, might respond to Singer.

7. Most experts agree that global warming is primarily the result of human activities. Do we have a moral obligation to refrain from activities, such as driving a vehicle that gets low gas mileage or living a lifestyle based on overconsumption, that contribute to global warming? Discuss what type of public policy a utilitarian might suggest regarding this question.

8. Prior to his imprisonment in 1999 for murder, Dr. Jack Kevorkian assisted in more than forty suicides. Most, but not all, of his patients suffered from terminal illnesses. Judith Curren, a forty-two-year-old mother of two young children whom Kevorkian assisted to commit suicide did not have a terminal illness. She was suffering from obesity, depression, alleged spousal abuse, and possibly chronic fatigue syndrome as well. Is suicide justified in cases where a person does not have a terminal illness but just finds life burdensome and devoid of pleasure? Explain. How would a utilitarian respond to this question?

Critique of Utilitarianism

1. *The utilitarian insistence on equality and impartiality is both one of utilitarianism's greatest strengths as well as one of its weaknesses.* Justice as impartiality presumes that people living in a community share a common conception of the good. However, deontologist John Rawls criticizes Bentham's utilitarian theory for its failure "to take seriously the distinction between persons."[43] Different people, he notes, have different needs and different projects or goals. The capitalist's idea of happiness, for example, is not the same as that of the religious contemplative. What gives one person great pleasure—such as improving the schools, setting aside public parks or building a new bowling alley—may not bring another person pleasure at all. In addition, there are other good things, such as friendship and aesthetic enjoyment, that bring us happiness.

Connections

According to ethical egoist Ayn Rand, what brings people happiness? *See Chapter 7, pages 230-231.*

Justice, Rawls argues, also requires that we treat people fairly and in proportion to both their needs and their merits; a person who has worked hard deserves a raise or promotion because he or she has done a good job. Utilitarians, on the other hand, are not concerned with what a person deserves but with whether rewarding a person produces the most utility.

2. *Utilitarianism can violate the principle of retributive justice, which requires that people be treated fairly and that any penalties be proportional to the misdeed.* Utilitarian theory can be used to justify severe penalties for relatively minor crimes in order to maximize the total happiness of the community. For example, in an episode of *Star Trek: The Next Generation*, the crew of the starship *Enterprise* was

visiting a planet that appeared to be a blissful utopia reminiscent of the Garden of Eden. That is, until Wesley Crusher, the teenage son of the *Enterprise* physician, breaks a law by accidentally falling into a municipal flower garden. As a result of his misdeed, Wesley is sentenced to death by the planet's authorities. While harsh penalties may have been successful in maintaining the community's peaceful and happy existence, the question still remains: Are they morally justified? Many of us, like the crew of the *Enterprise*, would say no, because such penalties are unfair and undeserved, no matter how much they benefit the larger community.

Similarly, racial and ethnic profiling—especially young men from Muslim countries—at airports may make sense to a utilitarian. By only targeting a population from which most terrorists have come, as President Trump wanted to do in his 2017 ban on people coming into the United States from certain predominantly Muslim countries, racial profiling saves money and time by not having to vet people—such as elderly, white women—who are statistically very unlikely to be a terrorist threat. On the other hand, the vast majority of Muslims from the Middle East are peace-loving and not a threat to anyone. To subject only them to extensive security checks, many would argue, is unfair and undeserved, no matter how much it may benefit the community.

3. *In their concern for maximizing the happiness of the greatest number, utilitarians fail to give sufficient attention to the integrity of the individual.* Most moral philosophers believe that integrity and personal responsibility need to be taken into consideration when determining the rightness or wrongness of an action. Utilitarianism sometimes requires us to act in ways that violate our integrity and our conscience. Actions do not just happen as part of a wider context of the general good: Each of us is responsible for what we do as individuals. For example, executing an innocent person simply to bring about peace in a community involves using people as a means to a greater social good and for this reason is morally questionable. It would also, in all likelihood, cause pain—in the form of guilt—to the person carrying out the killing, as happened in the case of Raskolonikov, in Dostoyevsky's *Crime and Punishment*, after he murdered a wealthy but stingy woman in order to redistribute her wealth to those in need.

4. *Utilitarianism does not give sufficient attention to the role of moral sentiments.* According to utilitarians such as Bentham, feelings such as guilt or regret are morally relevant only if they are based on certain characteristics of the situation that tend to promote pleasure and diminish pain. However, most people believe that moral sentiments do matter. Utilitarianism, by telling us to ignore or try to overcome feelings of moral repugnance toward certain actions, alienates us not only from personal responsibility for our actions but also from our moral sentiments and conscience.

Conscience is more than a calculator of the common good. If someone refuses to kill an innocent person, even to preserve social order, it still seems incorrect to say that he or she is responsible for the deaths that may result, just as it seems morally appropriate that a person would feel guilty for participating in the killing of an innocent person.

Connections

What are the different kinds of moral sentiments? *See Chapter 3, pages 82-87.*

5. *Utilitarianism may impose an impossible standard by requiring that we act in ways that maximize happiness.* Although we may agree that it is good to act in ways that promote happiness and to avoid acting in ways that cause pain to others, to expect people to *always* act in ways that maximize happiness for the greatest number imposes too great a burden on people. If we took the principle of utility seriously, some critics claim, we would be obliged to spend all of our spare time benefiting the community by performing community service, caring for poor children, and helping others. This would leave us no time to pursue our own plans or to do things we enjoy such as watching television, playing with our happy and well-fed children, or taking a nice bubble bath.

Mill responded that this criticism is based on a misinterpretation of utilitarian theory. The purpose of utilitarian ethics, he pointed out, is the "multiplication of happiness" rather than the maximization of happiness in all cases. To expect people to always act to maximize happiness for the greatest number is simply unrealistic. He also contended that taking care of ourselves and those close to us contributes to maximizing the common good. He wrote:

> It is a misapprehension of the utilitarian mode of thought, to conceive it as imply-ing that people should fix their minds upon so wide a generality as the world, or society at large. The great majority of good actions are intended not for the benefit of the world, but for that of individuals, of which the good of the world is made up; and the thoughts of the most virtuous man need not on these occasions travel beyond the particular persons concerned, except so far as is necessary to assure himself that in benefiting them he is not violating the rights, that is, the legitimate and authorized expectations of any one else.[44]

6. *If people do not have intrinsic moral value, they can be used as a means only.* One of the weaknesses of Bentham's strict utilitarianism is that, if the sole goal of morality is to maximize the total utility of the community, there are times when the happiness of society can be increased by scapegoating or pun-ishing an innocent person. However, doing this involves ignoring a person's liberty rights in order to maximize utility—a conclusion that Mill, in his refor-mulation of Bentham's theory, found objectionable.

Strict utilitarians respond to this criticism by pointing out that, in almost all cases, scapegoating is wrong because, in real life, lies are often found out. When this happens, it does great damage to people's sense of security and trust. Also, our faith in the criminal justice system will be undermined if it is discov-ered that the system is punishing people who are known to be innocent.

7. *Utilitarianism has been accused of committing the naturalistic fallacy.* Util-itarianism has been criticized for defining the good with a physical or psycho-logical quality like pleasure. According to G. E. Moore, by doing this, utilitarians commit the *naturalistic fallacy*. Moore claimed that the "good" is not based on any observations about the world but is instead intuitively known or self-evident. Goodness is a nonnatural, intuitive quality or entity that is unanalyzable and indefinable. Therefore, he argued, we cannot go from an observation about what is (we seek pleasure and avoid pain) to a statement

Connections

What is the naturalistic fallacy? *See Chapter 2, pages 61-62.*

about what *ought to be* (we ought to maximize pleasure and minimize pain). Moore's allegation that utilitarian theory is flawed because it is based on the naturalistic fallacy is one of the primary reasons that utilitarianism fell into disfavor with modern philosophers.

Some more recent thinkers—including Ayn Rand, E. O. Wilson, and Mary Warnock—question Moore's criticism of utilitarian theory. Like Hume, they argue that what *is* must be taken into account when formulating a moral theory. Warnock writes: "For is it not a fact that some types of behaviour tend to do good, and others do harm? And how in the end, if not on the basis of this fact, can we make sense of discriminating some actions as right in morals, and others as wrong?"[45]

8. *The primary weakness of utilitarianism is not its claim that consequences are important but its claim that only consequences matter.* It is not that utilitarian theory is wrong but that it is incomplete. The appealing *simplicity* of utilitarianism, which is one of its most attractive features, is also one of its weaknesses. While utilitarian considerations are certainly important, most moral philosophers think there are other factors that need to be taken into consideration, such as fairness, autonomy, and respect for human dignity.

9. *Utilitarianism challenges our anthropocentric view of the moral community.* One of the greatest strengths of utilitarian theory, is that it challenges us to rethink our traditional notions about moral community, in particular our anthropocentrism and disregard for the well-being of sentient nonhuman animals. It reminds us that tradition alone cannot serve as a foundation for morality. By questioning traditional philosophical notions of moral community, utilitarian theory demands that we either justify them or discard them.

10. *Utilitarianism offers helpful guidelines for making moral decisions.* Despite its limitations, utilitarian theory offers some important insights into the nature of morality and provides helpful guidelines for applied ethics. Utilitarian theory is a reminder that any moral theory that does not take happiness and consequences into account should be regarded with suspicion. The purpose of morality is not to make our lives more tedious or to make us feel more guilt- ridden but to improve the quality of our lives by promoting ideals and behavior that provide optimal conditions for us to flourish both as individuals and as a community.

[A]ll ethical doctrines worth our attention take consequences into account in judging rightness. One which did not would simply be irrational, crazy.[46]

— John Rawls, *A Theory of Justice* (1971)

11. *Utilitarian theory serves as a reminder that we should be ready to provide good reasons for our moral decisions.* Although nonutilitarians may regard other moral concerns as more fundamental than the principle of utility, we need to consider the consequences of our decisions. Even G. E. Moore, who was one

of the most celebrated critics of utilitarian theory, wholeheartedly agreed with the utilitarians that consequences must be taken into consideration:

> All moral laws, I wish to shew, are merely statements that certain kinds of actions will have good effects. The very opposite of this view has been generally prevalent in Ethics. . . . It has been characteristic of certain schools of moralists, as of moral common sense, to declare that the end will never justify the means. What I wish first to point out is that "right" does and can mean nothing but "cause of a good result," and is thus identical with "useful": whence it follows that the end always will justify the means, and that no action which is not justified by its results can be right.[47]

Most people draw from several moral theories when making moral decisions. While some of these theories may be incompatible, such as cultural relativism and utilitarianism, the theories in this text that regard morality as universal complement each other and enrich one's moral life. Utilitarianism is one of these enriching theories. We will be learning more about utilitarian theory and its contribution to moral philosophy in the following chapters.

Exercises

1. Tying rewards to individual merit puts tremendous pressure on people to achieve, often at the expense of others. Is our emphasis on individual merit as one of the criteria for giving out rewards—such as income, grades, and social recognition—simply a bias of our capitalist system, where people are expected to compete with one another for a share of social goods? Is there another system that might be preferable in terms of maximizing the overall happiness of the community? Support your answers.

2. Using Bentham's concept of justice as impartiality, discuss how students' work should be evaluated and graded in college.

3. Discuss how a utilitarian might respond to the following policies regarding criminal justice: (a) criminal charges of assault for people who are HIV-positive who knowingly pass on the infection during sexual intercourse, (b) a mandatory prison sentence for driving under the influence of alcohol, or (c) chemical castration of pedophiles and repeat sexual offenders. What do you think of these policies and why? Relate your answers to the different strengths and weaknesses of utilitarianism.

4. Have you ever had to choose between your personal integrity and utility? If so, explain how you made your decision regarding the most moral course of action. How would a utilitarian most likely regard the morality of your solution? Were you satisfied with your decision? Why or why not?

Summary

1. Utilitarianism is a *consequentialist* theory. An action is right or wrong depending on the consequences of that action. The happiness of the community is the proper goal of our actions.

2. The *principle of utility*, also known as the *greatest happiness principle*, states that "actions are right in proportion as they tend to promote happiness, wrong as they tend to produce the reverse of happiness."

3. Happiness is identified with *pleasure*, unhappiness, with *pain*. The only intrinsic good, therefore, is pleasure.

4. The principle of utility applies to all *sentient beings*, not just to humans. Sentient beings are those capable of experiencing pleasure and pain.

5. British philosopher Jeremy Bentham advocated utilitarianism primarily as a tool of social reform. Bentham argued that all pleasures are equal.

6. Bentham came up with a *utilitarian calculus*, which included seven factors that he said should be taken into account in calculating the total amount of pleasure and pain produced by an action. These seven factors are intensity, duration, certainty, propinquity, fecundity, purity, and extent.

7. John Stuart Mill disagreed with Bentham that all pleasures are equal. He claimed that the pleasures of being a human are of a superior quality to the pleasures of being a nonhuman animal because the pleasures of the intellect are superior to the pleasures of the body.

8. Mill believed that protecting people's autonomy or *liberty rights* is the best way of maximizing happiness in a society.

9. Mill's "no harm" principle, also known as the principle of *nonmaleficence*, prohibits individuals and governments from interfering with someone's actions except to prevent harm.

10. Chinese philosopher Mo Tzu promoted utilitarianism as an alternative to Confucianism and Taoism. He taught that hate is the primary cause of harm in the world and universal love is the source of happiness.

11. *Rule-utilitarianism* states that we should follow the rule that, in general, brings about the greatest happiness for the greatest number. *Act-utilitarianism* states that the morality of each action should be judged by its utility.

12. Utilitarians include all sentient beings in their moral community. Australian utilitarian Peter Singer argues that not granting the same consideration to a nonhuman animal that we would to a human with the same cognitive ability is to engage in *speciesism*.

13. Utilitarian theory plays an important role in the formulation of public policy around issues such as stem cell research.

14. Because human life does not have intrinsic worth, death is not always a harm. When the suffering of a life outweighs its pleasure, death may be morally permissible.

15. The utilitarian concept of justice as *impartiality* fails to take into account the importance of individual integrity and personal responsibility.

16. British philosopher G. E. Moore argues that utilitarianism is flawed because it commits the *naturalistic fallacy* by going from a statement about what *is* (pleasure and pain) to a statement about what *ought to be* (principle of utility).

17. Utilitarianism, with its emphasis on the importance of consequences and happiness, is a useful and powerful moral theory. It is currently making a comeback among philosophers and social policymakers.

 ## An Introduction to the Principles of Morals and Legislation

Jeremy Bentham

I. Nature has placed mankind under the governance of two sovereign masters, *pain* and *pleasure*. It is for them alone to point out what we ought to do, as well as to determine what we shall do. On the one hand the standard of right and wrong, on the other the chain of causes and effects, are fastened to their throne. They govern us in all we do, in all we say, in all we think: every effort we can make to throw off our subjection, will serve but to demonstrate and confirm it. In words a man may pretend to abjure their empire: but in reality he will remain subject to it all the while. The *principle of utility* recognises this subjection, and assumes it for the foundation of that system, the object of which is to rear the fabric of felicity by the hands of reason and of law. Systems which attempt to question it, deal in sounds instead of sense, in caprice instead of reason, in darkness instead of light. . . .

An Introduction to the Principles of Morals and Legislation (London: Clarendon Press, 1907). Some notes have been omitted. (The complete book is available online at www.econlib.org/library/Bentham/bnthPml.html.)

*The principle here in question may be taken for an act of the mind; a sentiment; a sentiment of approbation; a sentiment that, when applied to an action, approves of its utility, as that quality of it by which the measure of approbation or disapprobation bestowed upon it ought to be governed.

II. . . . By the principle* of utility is meant that principle which approves or disapproves of every action whatsoever, according to the tendency which it appears to have to augment or diminish the happiness of the party whose interest is in question: or, what is the same thing in other words, to promote or to oppose that happiness. I say of every action whatsoever; and therefore not only of every action of a private individual, but of every measure of government.

III. By utility is meant that property in any object, whereby it tends to produce benefit, advantage, pleasure, good, or happiness, (all this in the present case comes to the same thing) or (what comes again to the same thing) to prevent the happening of mischief, pain, evil, or unhappiness to the party whose interest is considered: if that party be the community in general, then the happiness of the community: if a particular individual, then the happiness of that individual.

IV. The interest of the community is one of the most general expressions that can occur in the phraseology of morals: no wonder that the meaning of it is often lost. When it has a meaning, it is this. The community is a fictitious *body*, composed of the individual persons who are considered as constituting as it were its *members*. The interest of the community then is, what?—the sum of the interests of the several members who compose it.

V. It is in vain to talk of the interest of the community, without understanding what is the interest of the individual. A thing is said to promote the interest, or to be *for* the interest, of an individual, when it tends to add to the sum total of his pleasures: or, what comes to the same thing, to diminish the sum total of his pains.

VI. An action then may be said to be conformable to the principle of utility, or, for shortness sake, to utility, (meaning with respect to the community at large) when the tendency it has to augment the happiness of the community is greater than any it has to diminish it. . . .

. . . Pleasures then, and the avoidance of pains, are the *ends* which the legislator has in view: it behoves him therefore to understand their *value*. Pleasures and pains are the *instruments* he has to work with: it behoves him therefore to understand their force, which is again, in other words, their value.

 ## Utilitarianism

John Stuart Mill

. . . The creed which accepts as the foundation of morals, Utility, or the Greatest Happiness Principle, holds that actions are right in proportion as they tend to promote happiness, wrong as they tend to produce the reverse of happiness. By happiness is intended pleasure, and the absence of pain; by unhappiness, pain, and the privation of pleasure. . . . [P]leasure, and freedom from pain, are the only things desirable as ends; and that all desirable things (which are as numerous in the utilitarian as in any other scheme) are desirable either for the pleasure inherent in themselves, or as means to the promotion of pleasure and the prevention of pain.

. . . It is quite compatible with the principle of utility to recognise the fact, that some *kinds* of pleasure are more desirable and more valuable than others. It would be

absurd that while, in estimating all other things, quality is considered as well as quantity, the estimation of pleasures should be supposed to depend on quantity alone.

If I am asked, what I mean by difference of quality in pleasures, or what makes one pleasure more valuable than another, merely as a pleasure, except its being greater in amount, there is but one possible answer. Of two pleasures, if there be one to which all or almost all who have experience of both give a decided preference, irrespective of any feeling of moral obligation to prefer it, that is the more desirable pleasure. . . .

. . . Few human creatures would consent to be changed into any of the lower animals, for a promise of the fullest allowance of a beast's pleasures; no intelligent human being would consent to be a fool, no instructed person would be an ignoramus, no person of feeling and conscience would be selfish and base, even though they should be persuaded that the fool, the dunce, or the rascal is better satisfied with his lot than they are with theirs. . . .

Utilitarianism (London, 1863). Originally published in three installments in *Fraser's* magazine, 1861. (The complete book is available online at http://etext.library .adelaide.edu.au/m/mill/john_stuart/m645u/.)

... According to the Greatest Happiness Principle, as above explained, the ultimate end, with reference to and for the sake of which all other things are desirable (whether we are considering our own good or that of other people), is an existence exempt as far as possible from pain, and as rich as possible in enjoyments, both in point of quantity and quality; the test of quality, and the rule for measuring it against quantity, being the preference felt by those who in their opportunities of experience . . .

. . . [T]he happiness which forms the utilitarian standard of what is right in conduct, is not the agent's own happiness, but that of all concerned. As between his own happiness and that of others, utilitarianism requires him to be as strictly impartial as a disinterested and benevolent spectator. In the golden rule of Jesus of Nazareth, we read the complete spirit of the ethics of utility. To do as you would be done by, and to love your neighbor as yourself, constitute the ideal perfection of utilitarian morality. As the means of making the nearest approach to this ideal, utility would enjoin, first, that laws and social arrangements should place the happiness, or (as speaking practically it may be called) the interest, of every individual, as nearly as possible in harmony with the interest of the whole; and secondly, that education and opinion, which have so vast a power over human character, should so use that power as to establish in the mind of every individual an indissoluble association between his own happiness and the good of the whole. . . .

Discussion Questions

1. According to Bentham, how do superstition and tradition interfere with maximizing pleasure for the greatest number in society? Discuss what solutions or policies utilitarians, such as Bentham or Mill, might suggest for overcoming these two obstacles.

2. Analyze Mill's argument that human pleasures, especially those of educated humans, have great moral value. Discuss the implications of Mill's position for a policy regarding public funding for special education programs for children with cognitive disabilities. Would the money be better spent on programs for the brightest and most gifted children? Discuss how both Mill and Bentham might answer this question.

Notes

1. Jeremy Bentham, *Principles of Morals and Legislation* (London: Clarendon Press, 1907), p. 1. (This edition is a reprint of Bentham's new edition of the book, published in 1823.)
2. Somini Sengupta, "Torture Can Be Useful, Nearly Half of Americans in Poll Say," *The New York Times*, December 5, 2016.
3. Oliver Darcy, "TRUMP: Secretary of Defense James Mattis Authorized to 'Override' Me on Torture," *Business Insider*, January 7, 2017.
4. For more information on Bt corn production go to Ohio State University College of Food Agriculture, & Environmental Sciences, "Handy Bt Trait Table for U.S. Corn Production for 2017,"

http://agcrops-cms.cfaes.ohio-state.edu/newsletter/corn-newsletter/2017-3/handy-bt-trait
-table-us-corn-production-updated-2017.

5. John Stuart Mill, "Utilitarianism," in *Utilitarianism*, ed. Mary Warnock (New York: Meridian, 1962).

6. Ibid., p. 268.

7. Bentham, *Principles*, p. 50.

8. Mill, "Utilitarianism," p. 257.

9. J. J. C. Smart and Bernard Williams, *Utilitarianism, For and Against* (Cambridge, England: Cambridge University Press, 1973).

10. Warnock, ed., *Utilitarianism*, (New York: Meridian, 1962) pp. 26–27.

11. Smart and Williams, *Utilitarianism, For and Against*, p. 7.

12. Jeremy Bentham, *Introduction to the Principles of Morals and Legislation* (London: Free Press, 1970), chapter 17.

13. "The Four Noble Truths," in *Thus Have I Heard: The Long Discourses of the Buddha—Dīgha Nikāya,* trans. Maurice Walshe (Boston, MA: Wisdom, 1987), pp. 346–347.

14. For latest statistics, go to National Institute on Drug Abuse at https://www.drugabuse.gov.

15. David Gardner, "U.S. Lost Its Moral Bearing over Torture Says Obama—and Warns Bush Officials Could be Charged," *Daily Mail* (UK), April 21, 2009.

16. Bentham, *Principles*, p. 41.

17. "Facts about the Death Penalty," Death Penalty Information Center, Washington, DC, February 2, 2017.

18. Neal A. Whitman, David C. Spendlove, and Claire H. Clark, *Student Stress: Effects and Solutions* (Washington, DC: ASHE-ERIC Higher Ed. Research Report No. 2, 1984), p. 2.

19. "Facts on Stress," *The Washington Post*, January 23, 2007, www.washingtonpost.com.

20. John Stuart Mill, "Bentham," in *Utilitarianism*, ed. Mary Warnock (New York: Meridian, 1962), p. 98.

21. John Stuart Mill, *The Subjugation of Women* (Cambridge, MA: MIT Press, 1869/1970), p. 100.

22. To read the new policy on free speech zones go to: University of Georgia, "Policy on Freedom of Expression," February 20, 2015, http://www.adfmedia.org/files/YALUGpolicy.pdf.

23. Warnock, *Utilitarianism*, p. 10.

24. For example, see Judith Boss and Katherine Wurtz, "Is Mandatory Schooling Inherently Unjust?" *The Educational Forum* 58, no. 3 (1994): 264–275; G. L. Brandt, *The Realization of Anti-Racist Teaching* (Philadelphia, PA: Hemisphere, 1986); Barbara Kantrowitz, B. Rosado, and L. Rosado, "Falling Further Behind: A Generation of Hispanics Isn't Making the Grade," *Newsweek*, August 19, 1991, p. 60; and M. Sadker and D. Sadker, "Sexism in the Classroom," *Vocational Educational Journal* 60 (1985): 30–32; Laurie Cooper Stoll, *Race and Gender in the Classroom* (Lanham, MD: Rowman & Littlefield, 2013).

25. Sadker and Sadker, "Sexism," p. 30.

26. Mo Tzu, "Universal Love," in *Mo Tzu: Basic Writings*, trans. Burton Watson (New York: Columbia University Press, 1963).

27. Smart and Williams, *Utilitarianism*.

28. Peter Singer, *Animal Liberation* (New York: Random House, 1990), p. 9.

29. Ibid., p. 9.

30. RSPCA, "The Use of Animals in Research and Testing," 2016, www.rspca.org.uk /laboratorynimals.

31. The Vegetarian Resource Center, "How Many Adults in the U.S. Are Vegetarian and Vegan?" Poll conducted by Harris Poll, 2016, http://www.vrg.org/nutshell/Polls /2016-adults-veg.htm.

32. Singer, *Animal Liberation*, p. 19.

33. David Hume, "Of Suicide," in *Of the Standard of Taste and Other Essays*, ed. John Lenz (Indianapolis, IN: Bobbs-Merrill, 1965), p. 158.

34. Ibid.

35. Mill, "Utilitarianism," p. 308.

36. Joseph Paul Vasquez III, "Shouldering the Soldiering: Democracy, Conscription, and Military Casualties," *Journal of Conflict Resolution* 49, no. 6 (December 2005): 849–873.

37. Centers for Disease Control and Prevention, "Childhood Obesity Facts," 2014, http://www .cdc.gov/healthyyouth/obesity/facts.htm.
38. Centers for Disease Control, "Adult Obesity Causes and Consequences," 2016, www.cdc.gov /obesity/adult/causes.html.
39. Al Van Abbema, "Fat Food Tax to Pay for Health Care? A Modest Proposal–Pros and Cons," 2009, http//:ezinearticles.com/?Fat-Food-Tax-to-Pay-For-Health-Care?-A Modest Proposal.
40. Christopher Hogan, June Lunney, Jon Gael, and Joanne Lynn, "Medicare Beneficiaries' Costs of Care in the Last Year of Life," *Health Affairs* 20, no. 4 (July 2001): 188–195.
41. Scott D. Rhodes, "HIV/AIDS on College Campuses," *The Charlotte Post Online*, December 23, 2005, pp. 4–5, www.thecharlottepost.com/09_14_health.html.
42. Quoted in Marvin Olasky, "Blue-State Philosopher," *World Magazine*, November 29, 2004.
43. John Rawls, *A Theory of Justice* (Cambridge, MA: Belknap Press, 1971), p. 187.
44. Mill, "Utilitarianism," p. 270.
45. Warnock, *Utilitarianism*, p. 31
46. Rawls, *Theory of Justice*, p. 30.
47. G. E. Moore, Prinicipia Ethica (1903), chapter 4, para. 80.

CHAPTER 9

Natural Law Theory
Morality Is Part of Rational Nature

There is in fact a true law—namely right reason—which is in accordance with nature, applies to all men and is unchangeable and eternal. By its commands this law summons men to the performance of their duties; by its prohibitions it restrains them from doing wrong.
  —MARCUS TULLIUS CICERO, *The Republic* (51 B.C.E.)

Human law has the aspect of law to the extent to which it is in accord with the correct norm; and from this viewpoint it is evidently derived from the eternal law.
  —THOMAS AQUINAS, *The Summa Theologica*, Bk. I, Pt. II, Qu. 93, Art. 3

What Is Natural Law Ethics?

In 1997, in one of the most controversial birth announcements in history, Ian Wilmut of Roslin Institute in Scotland announced to the world the birth of the first mammal, a lamb named Dolly, cloned from an adult cell. The announcement of Dolly's birth set off a flurry of debate over the morality of cloning and genetic engineering. The completion of the human genome project six years later raised further questions about the morality of using genetic engineering in humans. In 2012, fertility specialists in the United States revealed that they had created thirty healthy babies who had been genetically altered. Since then technologies, such as in vitro gametogenesis (IVG), have been developed that allow scientists to create embryos from stem cells. CRISPR/Cas9, another new technology, enables scientists to edit the genome for desirable traits. These developments have left many ethicists fearful about the ethical ramifications of these recent developments and their use in large-scale embryo farming and the creation of designer babies.[1]

Most people oppose the use of genetic engineering in humans for enhancement. But what about using it to correct devastating genetic defects such as Tay-Sachs disease or to make humans more resistant to disease? Or, is genetic engineering for any reason immoral because it involves tampering with our human nature?

In this chapter, we'll be studying natural law theory, which maintains that moral—or natural—law is grounded in rational human nature, and the implications of the theory for issues such as genetic engineering and environmental ethics. We will also look at just war theory, which grew out of natural law theory.

> There are some general principles in the holy books of all religions that teach love,
> charity, liberty, justice and equality for all the human family, there are many grand and
> beautiful passages, the golden rule has been echoed and re-echoed around the world.
>
> —Elizabeth Cady Stanton, *The Woman's Bible* (1895), Pt. 1, p. 13

Natural Law and Reason

According to **natural law theory**, morality is universal and grounded in rational nature. Natural law does not mean laws of physics, but laws of rational human nature, which, unlike the fixed laws of physical nature, are free and autonomous. Natural or moral law is unchanging and eternal. Natural law is also universally knowable to humans through reason. As such, it is universally binding on all humans.

Morality is reason put into action. One of the roles of reason is to keep our emotions or passions in check. Aristotle's Doctrine of the Mean was put forth as a method for using reason to find the mean between excess and deficiency. For Aristotle, we function best as humans and are happiest when we are perfecting our human capacities, reason being the highest and most important of these capacities.

Connections

What is Aristotle's Doctrine of the Means? *See Chapter 12, pages 400-402.*

Fundamental Goods

Natural law is **teleological**—that is, it is grounded in a specific view of the purpose or goal of the natural order. Natural law is based on the presumption that humans possess a common rational human nature and, therefore, share common goals. Aristotle, whose ethics is discussed in greater depth in Chapter 11 on Virtue Ethics, also believed that everything has a goal for which it is aimed. The goal for humans is *eudaimonia* or happiness. The four fundamental goods that promote this goal are life, procreation, knowledge, and society. An action is right if it brings about or promotes one of these fundamental goods.

The guidelines contained in natural law are very general, unlike normative moral rules that have more specific guidelines for action such as "do not steal." For Thomas Aquinas (c.1225–1274), the basic principle of natural law is "do good and avoid evil." The Golden rule of Judeo-Christian religion is another example of a principle of natural law. Because the moral guidelines contained in natural law are very general, we need to use our reason in deriving normative rules, such as "do not steal" from natural law.

Human Laws

Human or manmade laws are binding only if they are just and consistent with natural law. Aquinas wrote in his *Summa Theologica*: "Human law has the aspect of law to the extent to which it is in accord with the correct norm, and from this viewpoint it is evidently derived from the eternal law." The United Nations Nuremberg Charter is based on natural law theory. According to the charter, rulers and citizens—regardless of their particular religious affiliation or lack thereof—are responsible "under God and [natural] law." Natural law, the charter continues, includes prohibitions against "crimes against humanity," "torture," and "waging or preparing for an unjust war." Each person has an individual responsibility not to take refuge in the (human) laws or customs of their culture.

Because our ultimate responsibility is to a universal moral code, people such as Adolf Eichmann, can be tried under international law when cultural laws are contrary to natural law. Indeed, civil disobedience may be appropriate under certain circumstances. We'll be examining the criteria for civil disobedience later in this chapter.

As we noted earlier, natural law ethics is teleological. Both Christian and Jewish natural law ethics look toward a messianic age when the human law will be in perfect harmony with natural law. When this happens, true peace and justice will be realized, and "the lion shall lie down with the lamb."

Natural Law Ethics and Religion

Although a belief in God is not essential for one to be a natural law ethicist, natural law ethics is often associated with religion. For example, natural law ethics is at the heart of Catholic moral theory. However, unlike divine command theory, natural law ethics does not depend on the existence of a personal god. Both Aristotle and Roman philosopher Cicero (106–43 B.C.E.) believed that natural law exists as part of the natural order. Cicero wrote in his *Republic and the Laws*:

Connections
What are the basic claims of divine command theory? *See Chapter 5, page 144.*

> There is one, single, justice. It binds together human society and has been established by one single law. That law is right reason in commanding and forbidding. A man who does not acknowledge this law is unjust, whether it has been written down or not.

Variations of natural law theory are found in moral philosophies throughout the world. African philosopher Kwame Gyekye is a member of the Akan tribe in Ghana. Akan moral philosophy is a blend of natural law ethics and utilitarian ethics (which we'll study in the next chapter). Gyekye rejects the claim of divine command theorists that something is good *because* God loves it or approves of it. In response to Socrates's question in Plato's *Euthyphro* "Do the gods love holiness [the good] because it is holy [good], or is it holy [good] because the gods love it?" Gyekye writes:

> [The] response of the Akan moral thinker would be that God approves of the good because it is good. The reason is, if something is good because God approves of it, how would that good thing be known to them? How would they know what God approves of in a nonrevealed religion? On the contrary, their ascription of moral

Connections

How do divine
command the-
orists interpret
the story of
Abraham and
Isaac? *See
Chapter 5,
pages
143-144.*

attributes to God and the sanction that he is believed to apply . . . in the event of a
breach of the moral law clearly suggest the Akan conviction that God approves of
the good because it is good and eschews the evil because it is evil.[2]

Natural law ethicist and Jewish scholar Lippman Bodoff interprets the story of
Abraham and Isaac as a conflict between blind obedience (divine command theory)
and moral choice (natural law theory). He argues that God, rather than expecting
blind obedience, was "testing Abraham to see if he would remain loyal to God's
moral law . . . even when divinely commanded to break it." Abraham was also testing
this "new" God to see if God was worthy of worship. A God who was worthy of
worship would not allow Abraham to kill his son because this was contrary to moral
(natural) law. In the end, both Abraham and God passed the test.

Exercises

1. Aldous Huxley, in his futuristic dystopian novel *Brave New World* (1932), envisioned world where humans are engineered by the government to fit into certain
   useful categories through the manipulation and conditioning of embryos and
   fetuses. In this efficient but joyless world, happiness is found only through the
   use of the soul-numbing drug Soma. Discuss Huxley's concerns about embry-
   onic engineering for "desirable" traits in light of the current proposed use of
   genetic engineering for enhancement.

2. Discuss Aristotle's claim that we can discern, through the use of reason, the
   fundamental goods for humans. Do you agree with his list of the fundamental
   goods? Why or why not? If not, what do you think are the fundamental goods
   and on what basis do you think this?

3. Should Eichmann have been punished for obeying the laws of his country?
   Support your answer. Discuss how both a natural law ethicist and a cultural
   relativist would answer this question.

4. Compare and contrast the Bodoff's explanation of the Abraham and Isaac story
   with that of a divine command theorist. Which explanation do you find most
   compelling and why?

Thomas Aquinas: Catholic Natural Law Ethics

Catholic theologian and philosopher Thomas Aquinas (c. 1225-1274) was profoundly influenced by Aristotle, whom he referred to simply as "The Philosopher." Like Aristotle, Aquinas believed that we function best as humans when
we are perfecting our human capacities, reason being the highest and most
important of these capacities. Although Christian morality is based primarily
on the Bible and Church tradition rather than reason alone, Aquinas pointed
out that reason has been given to humans by God and, as such, offers a vehicle
for discerning natural or moral law.

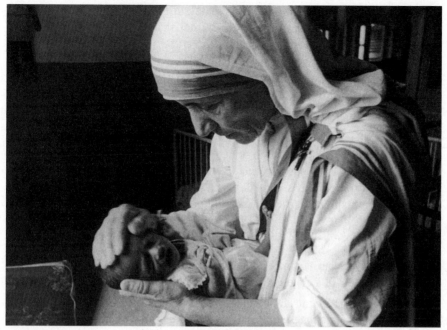

Mother Teresa (1910-1997) ministering to the poor in Calcutta, India. Catholic natural law ethics states that all humans have intrinsic moral value and that we have a moral obligation to help the poor. In 2016, Mother Teresa was canonized by the Catholic Church as St. Teresa of Calcutta.
©Photo by Keystone-France/Getty Images

Key Claims of Natural Law Theory

- Morality is found in unchanging principles of moral (natural) law in nature.
- Natural law is universal and applies to all humans at all times.
- Humans can access natural law through the use of reason.
- Manmade laws are authoritative only if they are just and consistent with the principles of natural law.

Because moral law is embedded in human reason, our actions do not depend on our perception of God's will or commands at any particular moment. Therefore, to the question "Is morality relative to religion?" Aquinas would answer, "No." Natural law is universal and applies to all rational beings. Religious people and atheists alike are all bound by the same moral principles.

Protestant Rejection of Catholic Natural Law Ethics

While natural law theory has become a mainstay of Catholic ethics, Protestants are less likely to adopt a natural law approach with what they perceive as the elevation of reason over faith. Many Protestant churches see human reason as fallen and, consequently, fallible. Therefore, we cannot rely on human reason alone for moral guidance.

In addition, Protestant theologians maintain that natural law ethics places too much emphasis on human autonomy rather than our relationship with and dependence on a living God for guidance. Natural law ethics, they argue, also ignores the redemptive act of Christ's sacrifice on the cross, which weakens the determinative quality of natural law ethics.

The Four Types of Laws

According to Aquinas, God as the most perfect and rational being furnishes the end toward which the universe is directed. The moral or natural law is our human way of participating in and actively working toward that vision.

In his hierarchy of laws, Aquinas recognized four types. Eternal law is the highest law; human law is the least binding on us:

1. *Eternal law* is the uncreated reason of God that guides the universe as it moves toward a particular goal or end.

2. *Divine law* directs humans and other creatures to their supernatural end, which consists of a vision of God and eternal blessedness.

3. *Natural law*, or moral law, is the special way that rational creatures, such as humans, participate in eternal law and are thereby directed toward their earthly happiness.

4. *Human law* is at the bottom of the hierarchy of laws; it is law, such as legislation or cultural norms, that is derived by humans from natural law.

Because the application of natural law can change as we humans progress toward our natural or divine end, it is incumbent upon us to use reason to decide how to apply these general guidelines in a specific situation and at specific times in our history. Both Christian and Jewish natural law ethics look toward a messianic age when human law will be in perfect harmony with natural law. When this happens, true peace and justice will finally be realized, and "the lion shall lie down with the lamb."

Even though we as humans may not have direct access to eternal law, because the universe was created by a rational God we can rely on natural law to participate in eternal law. Natural law, however, is not dependent on a belief in God. Natural law, because it is accessible to all rational beings, Catholic or atheist, provides a universal morality for all humans and is binding on all humans.

Connections

What is the position of deontologist Immanuel Kant on the morality of capital punishment?" *See Chapter 10, pages 341-342.*

The Catholic Natural Law Concept of Human Rights

The Roman Catholic view of human rights is based on natural law theory. The belief in our duty to respect the intrinsic world of all humans—even those who are not rational or sentient—has made Catholic ethicists adamant in the opposition to both abortion and euthanasia, as well as stem cell research. Pope Francis and the American Catholic Church have also taken a stand against capital punishment on the grounds that "it involves the deliberate infliction of evil on another."

The classic expression of the Roman Catholic doctrine on human rights is contained in Pope John XXIII's 1963 encyclical "Pacem in Terris," which affirms the equality of all humans "by reason of their natural dignity." Furthermore, the rights that stem from natural law should be protected by human law and special programs to ensure the rights of "the less fortunate members of the community [who are] less able to defend their rights."[3] The encyclical states:

> Any human society, if it is to be well-ordered and productive, must lay down as a foundation this principle, namely, that every human being is a person, that is, his nature is endowed with intelligence and free will. By virtue of this, he has rights and duties, flowing directly and simultaneously from his very nature. These rights are therefore universal, inviolable and inalienable.[4]

The Catholic Church is still in the process of assimilating human rights theory. Although the church has been a powerful force in the international fight for equal human rights, it has been accused of ignoring human rights in its own Canon of Law by excluding women and gay men from ordained ministry and by forbidding men who are ordained the right to marry and restricting their rights to freedom of expression. The church has responded to these accusations by stating that "the principles which rightly apply to human societies in general do not apply to the church because of its divine institution, its supernatural end, its specific objectives and practice, and its dependence on Scripture for its basic norms and structure."[5] However, this raises the question of whether God would require immoral means—in this case, the denial of basic rights—to achieve a divine end. Indeed, some catholic ethicists argue that the denial of these rights is inconsistent with natural law theory.

Principle of Double Effect

Natural law is not authoritarian. It requires that we use our reason to discern the purpose of things and actions in the universe and act accordingly. Natural law also makes allowances for different understandings of how it applies in specific situations, such as restrictions placed on the priesthood.

In some situations, it is unclear what is right and wrong. In this case, we may apply to the **principle of double effect**, which states that an action that causes a serious harm may be permissible if that harm is an unintended side effect of bringing about a particular good. Aquinas used the example of self-defense to illustrate this principle. While it is wrong to take an innocent life, killing in self-defense may be justified if it is the only means of saving one's life and if only as much violence is used as is necessary to save one's life. In this case, the death of the person threatening our life is not intended, and should be avoided if at all possible, but is an unfortunate side effect of preserving our own life. This principle allows a pregnant woman, whose life is at stake, to get a hysterectomy or chemotherapy if that is the only way to save her life, even though it may result in the unintended death of her unborn child. The principle of double effect has also been used to justify the unintentional killing of civilians in wartime.

While natural law ethicists oppose euthanasia, they may allow the use of morphine for a dying patient who is in terrible pain. While the morphine may shorten the person's life, unlike active euthanasia, this is an unintended side effect of alleviating the pain.

We'll be looking more at the application of natural law ethics to contemporary moral issues on page 298.

To summarize, natural law ethicists, such as Aquinas, answer no to the question: "Is morality relative to religion?" Natural law is universal and applies to all rational beings: God and humans, religious people and atheists alike are all bound by the same moral principles. We act morally for the same reasons that God does.

Exercises

1. While Catholic natural law theorists believe we can rely on reason for moral guidance, Protestants generally regard human reason as fallible. Critically analyze the two positions. If not reason, how else might we discern what is moral and immoral? Support your answer.

2. Pope Francis and the American Catholic Church oppose capital punishment on the grounds that "it involves the deliberate infliction of evil on another." Support for capital punishment is dropping, although the majority of Americans still support it. While American Catholics are less likely that Protestants and people who are unaffiliated to support capital punishment, a 2015 Pew Research survey found that 53 percent of Catholics still support it.[6] Why do you think this is so? If not their religion, where else might they be getting their moral guidance? Discuss also whether capital punishment is consistent with natural law theory.

3. Relate the principle of double effect to the assassination of terrorist leaders such as Osama bin Laden.

Just War Theory

Natural law theory has had a major impact on our thinking about the morality of war and the conditions that justify war. According to natural law ethicists' **just war theory**, a war cannot be morally justified simply on the grounds of a divine command or cultural relativism. Instead, it must meet certain conditions that are consistent with natural law.

Conditions for a War to Be Just

In his *Summa Theologica*, Thomas Aquinas lists several conditions that must be met for a war to be just.[7] This list has been refined and expanded by contemporary natural law theorists (see box on page 289).[8] The purpose of these conditions is to ensure that war is humanely conducted and is ultimately directed toward the establishment of lasting peace and justice. Natural law theory and the conditions for a just war have been codified by the United Nations in documents such as the Geneva Conventions and the Nuremberg Charter.

An Afghan town destroyed by a military air strike. As of 2017, more than thirty thousand civilians, including children, have been killed or have died as a direct result of the war.[9]

©specnaz-s/iStock/Getty Images Plus

Discussion Questions

1. Is the U.S. war against Afghanistan justified under the just law theory? Relate your answer to conditions for a war to be just, described below.

2. Discuss what you would do if you were a military pilot and you were asked to drop a bomb on a village, knowing that it would most likely result in civilian deaths but might also bring about the death of an al-Qaeda leader. Discuss also how both a utilitarian and a natural law ethicist might answer this question.

Just War Theory

Jus ad bellum (conditions that should be met before going to war)

1. War must be declared and waged by a legitimate authority.
2. There must be a just cause for going to war.
3. War must be the last resort.
4. There must be a reasonable prospect of success.
5. The violence used must be proportional to the wrong being resisted.

Jus in bello (conditions that should be met for a war to be conducted justly)

1. Noncombatants should not be intentionally targeted.
2. The tactics used must be in proportion to the injury being redressed.
3. Prisoners of war must be treated humanely, that is, given "benevolent quarantine."

Shortcomings of Just War Theory

One of the weaknesses of just war theory is that, while the rules and conditions of a just war may seem to be reasonable in theory, it can be difficult to determine if they are being satisfied in an actual situation. For example, what is meant by a legitimate authority? Does it have to be the government of a sovereign nation, or can it be an organization such as al-Qaeda or the rebel American colonists who declared war against Britain?

Also, what constitutes a just cause? Does the fear that another nation might have weapons of mass destruction justify a preemptive strike? When is declaration of war justified as the last resort, and how do we determine if a tactic is proportional? Furthermore, how are we to define "prisoner of war"? If terrorist groups are not legitimate authorities, does that give the United States the right to relegate captured terrorist suspects to the category of "enemy combatants" who do not have the same rights as prisoners of war?

The biggest weakness of just war theory is its vagueness that leaves it open to many, sometimes conflicting, interpretations. The Vatican, under Pope Francis, recently rejected just war theory as outdated stating that it has "too often been used to justify violent conflicts and the global church must consider Jesus's teaching on nonviolence."[10]

Exercises

1. Discuss the war against terrorism in the context of both the divine command theory and just war theory. Discuss whether launching missiles at suspected terrorist strongholds in Afghanistan, Iraq, and Pakistan, even though it has resulted in thousands of civilian deaths, is justified under just war theory.

2. Was the United States justified in dropping the two atomic bombs on Japan in World War II? Given the destructive power of modern weapons, how much loss of civilian life is acceptable as "collateral damage"?

Henry David Thoreau: Natural Law Theory and Civil Disobedience

If the law is of such a nature that it requires you to be an agent of injustice to another, then I say, break the law.

—HENRY DAVID THOREAU, "Civil Disobedience" (1849)

Henry David Thoreau (1817–1862), American author, abolitionist, and naturalist, was a champion of environmentalism, human rights, and civil disobedience. He preferred the simple life and lived on and off in a cabin on Walden Pond for several years. He refused to pay the local poll taxes because of his opposition to the Mexican–American War and slavery. As a result, he spent a night in jail.

Civil disobedience tends to most effective when combined with peaceful legal protests. Shane Red Hawk, of the Sioux tribe of South Dakota, along with other tribal leaders led a protest in Washington DC in April 2014 against the Keystone XI Pipeline. While this was for the most part a legal protest, some of the protestors choose to engage in peaceful civil disobedience. Several hundred people were also arrested in a protest involving civil disobedience the previous month.
©Jim Lo Scalzo/Epa/REX/Shutterstock

Thoreau's essay on "Civil Disobedience," excerpts from which can be found at the end of this chapter, called for individuals to resist an unjust government. His actions and his writings on civil disobedience had a profound influence on Martin Luther King, Jr. and Gandhi, and have laid the groundwork for carrying out acts of civil disobedience.

When Is Civil Disobedience Morally Justified?

Members of animal liberation groups break into laboratories to set the animals free; antiabortionists block women from entering Planned Parenthood clinics; before the legalization of abortion, women formed cooperatives to assist other women in getting abortions; workers stage illegal strikes to protest unfair working conditions; during the Vietnam War, college students openly burned their draft cards to protest the war; churches give sanctuary to illegal immigrants who fear deportation; and climate change protesters disrupt fossil fuel mining operations and the building of the Keystone Pipeline. Are these people justified, on the grounds of a higher moral law, in breaking the law of the land?

Natural law ethicists answer with a qualified yes. According to natural law theory, a person is justified in breaking a human law if the law they are breaking

Connections

Do nonhuman animals have rights we ought to respect? *See Chapter 11, pages 383-384.*

conflicts with natural law and if breaking the unjust human law does not create more harm than obeying it would cause. A law may be unjust because it has one of the following characteristics:

Connections

Under what conditions are slavery and the degradation of women morally acceptable to a cultural relativist? *See Chapter 6, pages 184-185.*

1. *It is degrading to humans.* The laws that permitted slavery and segregation in the United States and laws that allow men in Afghanistan to demand sex from their wives are degrading to humans.

2. *It is discriminatory.* Laws that apply to one group of people but not to another may also be unjust. For example, the Fourteenth Amendment to the U.S. Constitution gave all men, but not women, the right to vote. The laws that supported the caste system in India were also unjust because they were discriminatory.

3. *It is enacted by an authority that is not truly representative.* The cry "no taxation without representation," which sparked the American Revolution, was a protest over this type of unjust law.

4. *It is unjustly applied.* Search and seizure laws in this and other countries, for example, are intended to protect citizens from dangerous people; however, these laws are sometimes unjustly applied to harass or punish political dissenters or other controversial figures.

Natural Law Is Higher than Human Law

Because natural law is higher than human law, when human laws or cultural norms conflict with natural law or any of the higher laws, civil disobedience may be not only morally acceptable but morally required. **Civil disobedience** involves the refusal to obey certain government or human laws for the purpose of trying to bring about a change in legislation or government policy.

[Human] laws can be unjust because they are contrary to the divine good, for example, the laws of tyrants which promote idolatry or whatever else is against divine law. In no way is it permissible to observe them.

—THOMAS AQUINAS, *The Summa Theologica*[11]

Most people who break laws are not engaged in civil disobedience because most criminals are not interested in social reform. A person may break a law simply because it is an inconvenience to obey it—we exceed the speed limit, drive through red lights, and lie about our age at the local bar.

Some people break a law with good intentions; yet, their interpretation or application of natural law may be called into question. Most Roman Catholic theologians, for example, believe that natural law prohibits suicide. If this is the case, then what Dr. Kevorkian did in assisting terminally ill people end

A civil dissident blocking tanks during protest in Tiananmen Square in Beijing China, 1989. Over three hundred demonstrators were killed during the protest against China's totalitarian government.
©Bettmann/Getty Images

their lives was morally wrong. However, both Kevorkian and these theologians agree that we have a higher moral duty to respect and treat other humans with dignity. In other words, they agree on the general content of moral or natural law. What they disagree on is the *application* of this higher law in a specific context. The morality of homosexuality and same-sex marriage is another issue that is debated among natural law ethicists. In cases such as these, it may sometimes be difficult to decide who is mistaken, particularly because our idea of morality is so bound up with our cultural norms and subjective feelings rather than with reason.

Henry David Thoreau's Four Criteria for Protesting an Unfair Law

Another consideration is the best way to protest an unfair law. We may agree on the content of natural law and its application to a particular situation, but we can still disagree about how to protest an unjust human law. Henry David Thoreau (1817–1862) believed that petitions to elected representatives and other indirect democratic processes may be insufficient to bring about social change.

Thoreau's essay on "Civil Disobedience" (1849) continues to be one of the prominent works in the field. Excerpts from his essay are included at the end

Connections

How would a cultural relativist respond to Thoreau's essay regarding civil disobedience?
See Chapter 6, pages 191–192.

of this chapter. (To read "Civil Disobedience" in its entirety online, go to http://eserver.org/thoreau/civil.html.)

When breaking an unjust human law, Thoreau wrote, we must do so in a way that is consistent with moral law. First, *only moral and nonviolent means should be used to achieve our goals.* These methods include boycotting, illegal picketing and blocking traffic, nonviolent resistance, and nonpayment of taxes. Second, *an effort should first be made to bring about change through legal means.* Most people who engage in civil disobedience continue to try to change the unjust law through legal means as well. Third, people engaging in civil disobedience must be *open and public about their actions.* If no one knows we are breaking the law, then it is unlikely that our actions will have much impact on lawmakers! Finally, dissidents must be *willing to accept the consequences of their actions*—such as prison sentences, fines, deportation, loss of a job, or social disapproval. When Thoreau refused to pay his taxes, as a protest against the evils of slavery, the authorities threw him in jail.

Criteria for Civil Disobedience

1. Only moral and nonviolent means are used to achieve our goals.
2. An effort is first made to bring about a change through legal means.
3. The actions are open and public.
4. Dissidents are willing to accept the consequences of their actions.

Army Spc. Mark Wilkerson's actions are an example of civil disobedience. Wilkerson first tried legal means to protest his involvement in what he regarded as an unjust war in Iraq by applying for conscientious objector status. After he was denied this status, he went AWOL for more than a year before deciding to turn his protest into an act of civil disobedience by turning himself in to military authorities and accepting the consequences of his actions. Wilkerson also issued a public statement to the press regarding his reasons for refusing to fight in the war in an effort to bring about change in the government's policy.[12]

> I am not willing to kill or be killed for something I don't believe in. My morals said going to Iraq was not the right thing to do. I was not going to live a life of violence.
>
> —ARMY SPC. MARK WILKERSON, taped statement at Fort Hood, Texas

Martin Luther King Jr.

Although not all natural law ethicists regard God as the source of natural or moral law, some of the most courageous acts of civil disobedience have been spearheaded by men and women of deep religious convictions. During the Montgomery boycotts in 1955 and 1956, civil rights leader and natural law ethicist Dr. Martin Luther King Jr. called for civil disobedience of the local segregation laws. King was born in 1929 in Atlanta, Georgia, the grandson of a sharecropper. Despite the constant oppression of racism and segregation, his father, a respected Baptist minister, and his mother, Alberta King, taught their three children that they could overcome the humiliation of segregation. King agreed with Saint Augustine's statement that "an unjust law is not law at all." In his letter from a Birmingham jail, King explained that if our conscience tells us a law is unjust, being willing to go to prison for our belief shows the highest respect for the law and encourages others to be just.[13]

The life and writings of Indian philosopher Mohandas Gandhi had a profound influence on King. Like King, Gandhi believed in a higher moral law against which human laws could be judged. Gandhi used the term *Satyagraha* to describe civil disobedience based on passive resistance and noncooperation. *Satyagraha* embodies deep respect and love for *all* living beings, even oppressors.

Martin Luther King Jr. (1929–1968) delivering his famous "I have a dream" speech in Washington, DC, 1963. In 1964, King received the Nobel Peace Prize for his work in civil rights and racial equality.
©Bettmann/Getty Images

Discussion Questions

1. When King was told by some of his colleagues that it was not the right time to engage in civil disobedience, he explained that the advice to "wait" until the time was right are the words of the oppressor, and that the right time to fight is now. Discuss.

2. Think of an issue about which you feel strongly such as abortion, same-sex marriage, transgender bathrooms, or Trump's proposal to ban people from coming into the United States from certain Muslim-majority countries. If you disagree with the current law or policy, are you morally obligated to try to change it? If so, discuss what actions you would take and why.

King became one of the driving forces behind the civil rights movement in the 1950s and 1960s. Beginning with the bus boycott in Montgomery, he and other civil rights leaders such as Rosa Parks deliberately violated southern segregation laws as a means of protesting injustice. Because of his protest, King, like Thoreau, was arrested and sent to jail. In 1964, King won the Nobel Peace Prize (the youngest person ever to do so) for his role in leading nonviolent demonstrations. King's antiestablishment teachings made him the target of violence from White racists. In 1968, he was assassinated in Memphis, Tennessee, where he had gone to speak out on behalf of striking sanitation workers.

Feminist Civil Disobedience

Natural law ethicists who engage in civil disobedience often come into conflict with the law because of their rejection of cultural relativism and their belief in a higher moral law. The early feminists in the United States used civil disobedience, based on natural law theory, to protest human laws that denied women certain basic rights. Many early feminists were jailed as a result of their civil disobedience. Susan B. Anthony was arrested in 1872 for registering and voting in an election, a right enjoyed only by men at the time. During her trial, she urged all women to refuse to accept unjust laws that discriminate against women.

> I shall earnestly and persistently continue to urge all women to the practical recognition of the old revolutionary maxim, that "Resistance to tyranny is obedience to God."
>
> —Susan B. Anthony (1881)[14]

Exercises

1. List some examples of unjust laws. Explain why they are unjust.

2. Discuss the following case studies. Which are examples of civil disobedience? If they are not examples of civil disobedience, explain why and

discuss what type of civil disobedience a person could engage in to protest the law.

a. Mary Beth believes it is unfair that faculty and staff have better parking facilities on campus than commuter students. She frequently has to park in a commuter lot that is almost a half mile from her classes. Meanwhile, there are plenty of empty spots in the faculty lots. The other day, while cutting through one of the faculty lots on her way to class, she noticed that one of the cars was unlocked. A parking decal was on the dashboard. Mary Beth checked to make sure that no one was around, and then she took the decal and placed it on the windshield of her own car.

b. University Church in the Chicago area gives sanctuary, in defiance of federal law, to illegal immigrants resisting deportation.

c. Brice is opposed to animal testing. Last night, he and two of his friends broke into the laboratory in the pharmacology building on campus. They released the lab animals and then destroyed the laboratory equipment used for animal experimentation. The next morning they turned themselves in to the campus police.

d. In 1995, Timothy McVeigh blew up the Oklahoma City Federal Building, killing 168 people. McVeigh carried out the bombing as a protest against the government's killing of eighty Branch Davidians near Waco, Texas.

e. Native American activists Russell Means and Dennis Banks organized a nonviolent demonstration in Washington, DC in 1972 to protest the broken promises made to Native Americans by the U.S. Bureau of Indian Affairs and to lobby for reforms within the Bureau of Indian Affairs.

f. When the demonstration in Washington (described in "e") did not yield satisfactory results, Means and Banks led about five hundred Native Americans in a six-day takeover of the Bureau of Indian Affairs.

g. During the Vietnam War, many Americans who were opposed to the war emigrated to Canada to avoid the draft.

h. The notorious pirate Anne Bonny was born in Ireland in 1700 as the illegitimate daughter of a wealthy lawyer and a servant. Because of the scandal of adultery, her family was forced to move to South Carolina. Here, Anne entered a life of piracy by dressing up as a man because women were then not allowed to be crew members on ships.

3. Discuss how a cultural relativist would respond to the civil disobedience of people such as Martin Luther King Jr., Susan B. Anthony, and Gandhi.

4. Are we morally required to take action against an unjust law? Does the democratic process encourage compromise on social issues? Use specific examples of what you consider to be an unjust law or policy to illustrate your answer.

*5. Would you be more likely to engage in civil disobedience since becoming involved in community service? Discuss.

---

*An asterisk indicates that the exercise is appropriate for students who are doing community service learning as part of the course.

Natural Law Theory and Contemporary Moral Issues

Because life is good and has intrinsic moral value, natural law ethicists oppose abortion (except to save the life of the mother), capital punishment, active euthanasia, and unjust wars. On the other hand, because natural law is based on very general principles, it is open to interpretation, especially in issues such as contraception and homosexuality, where human life is not at stake. New medical technologies also present a challenge for natural law theorists.

Connections

Why was Gutierrez critical of laissez-faire capitalism? *See Chapter 11, pages 367–368.*

Despite disagreement on how to interpret natural law in certain situations, natural law ethicists, because of their belief that natural or moral law is higher than human law, have been active not only in protesting unjust laws but in working for social justice. The focus on the intrinsic worth of all humans has motivated proponents of natural law ethics, such as Mother Teresa, Martin Luther King, Jr., Elizabeth Cady Stanton, and Gustavo Gutierrez, to work tirelessly in helping the poor and seeking social justice. This focus is currently being expanded to the worth of all living beings and the environment.

In the following section, we will look at three issues—euthanasia, environmental ethics, and genetic engineering and cloning—in light of natural law ethics.

Euthanasia

Natural law health care ethics requires that we honor the dignity of each person from conception to death. *Active euthanasia* is wrong because it involves the direct and intentional killing of a person. The position of natural law ethicists is reflected in the American Medical Association's stand against active euthanasia. People who are dying deserve to be treated with compassion and respect.

Connections

How does the utilitarian view on euthanasia differ from that of natural law ethicists?" *See Chapter 8, pages 264–266.*

But what about passive euthanasia? *Passive euthanasia* is defined as withholding life support or medical treatment. Natural law ethicists reject passive euthanasia of a person who is not dying, such as the withholding of needed medical care for a newborn with Down's Syndrome or in the case of some of Kevorkian's patients who had debilitating conditions that were not fatal. However, if a person is dying and further therapeutic interventions are likely to be futile, in that they cause more harm than benefit, then it is morally acceptable, according to natural law ethicists, to withhold treatment. Similarly, hydration and medically assisted nutrition are optional if these interventions cannot be reasonably expected to prolong life and will be excessively burdensome to the dying person.

Catholic health care avoids the use of futile or burdensome technology that offers no reasonable benefit to patient or resident.

—U.S. Conference of Catholic Bishops, "Ethical and Religious Directives for Catholic Health Care Services," 2001–2012.

The use of morphine or other pain-suppressing medicines is also permissible under the principle of double effect, even though it may shorten the life of the person. In these cases, the intended side effect is easing the pain of the suffering person, while hastening death is an unintended side effect. Organ donation, in the case of someone who is dying or is brain dead, is also morally permissible as long as the benefit to the recipient is proportionate to the harm done to the donor.

Another consideration in making health care decisions is that we be responsible stewards of available health care resources. This notion of being responsible stewards is echoed in natural law theorists' concern for the environment.

Environmental Ethics

Thoreau was one of the forerunners of the environmental movement in the United States. Thoreau rejected the idea that we need to look beyond nature to find a "higher reality." He insisted instead that moral meaning resides in the natural world. Rather than humans being above or outside of nature, he believed in the harmonious interdependence of all of nature (including humans). Because of this interdependence, we should be respectful toward all of nature and cautious in tampering with nature.

> Every creature is better alive than dead, men and moose and pine trees, and he who
>
> understands it aright will rather preserve its life than destroy it.
>
> —HENRY DAVID THOREAU, *The Maine Woods*, 1864.

Like Thoreau, many native American tribes regard nature as having intrinsic moral worth. In 2012, the Lakota people and the Black Hills Sioux Nation Treaty Nation sent a message to former president Obama and Congress asking them to forbid construction of the Transcanada Keystone pipeline out of concern for the negative impact on the ecosystem and the Lakota way of life. The pipeline, they stated "would violate the traditional law, the natural law. . .and the sovereignty of the Great Sioux Nation."[15]

While Thoreau has had a profound influence on the environmental movement, because of anthropocentric focus of much Western thinking and the belief that the Earth and its resources belong to humans, most natural law ethicists have not been as quick to become involved in the environmental movement as they might be. Religious teachings in particular have been used to reinforce the privileged status of humans. Aquinas, for example, simply accepted Aristotle's teaching that only humans have intrinsic moral worth. It should be noted, however, that not all Catholic natural law ethicists accept Aquinas's view of nonhuman nature.

Over the past several decades, there has been an increasing focus among natural law ethicists on the moral value of nonhuman nature and our obligation

Connections

On what grounds do some native Americans claim that Christianity has permitted the exploitation of nature by humans? *See Chapter 5, pages 155–156.*

Polluting the air is immoral because it damages the environment and harms humans and animals by causing respiratory problems and cancer.
©Design Pics/Kelly Redinger

to treat nature with respect. Natural law ethicists point to the creation story in the *Bible* in which God views all of creation, including the natural world, as good (Genesis 1:10). In light of this, the passage where God gives humans dominion over all creatures (Genesis 1:26) is seen as a call to stewardship, rather than domination.

Some natural law ethicists, both religious and nonreligious, regard the environmental problems we are currently facing, including climate change, as the results of our poor stewardship. Exploitation of the environment for selfish gain or lavish lifestyles violates our responsibility to care for nature. Stewardship requires not only conservation of nature but making sure that our lifestyle does not use up so many resources that it affects those living in poorer nations.

St. Francis of Assisi (1450–1517), like Thoreau, has been influential in the modern environmental movement, particularly among Catholic natural law theorists. Francis of Assisi believed that nature is inherently good and that God communicates to humans through nature. Consequently, it is a sin to destroy nature. Pope John Paul II in his 1990 World Day of Peace Message stated:

> [W]orld peace is threatened not only by the arms race, regional conflict and continued injustices among peoples and nations, but also be a lack of *due respect for nature*, by the plundering of natural resources and by a progressive decline in the quality of life . . .
>
> [No] peaceful society can afford to neglect either respect for life or the fact that there is an integrity to creation. . . . When the ecological crisis is set within the

broader context of *the search for peace* within society, we can understand better the importance of giving attention to what the earth and its atmosphere are telling us: namely, that there is an order in the universe which must be respected, and that the human person . . . has a grave responsibility to preserve the order for the well-being of future generation. . . .

[Saint Francis of Assisi] offers Christians an example of genuine and deep respect for the integrity of creation . . . It is my hope that the inspiration of Saint Francis will help us to keep ever alive a sense of "fraternity" with all those good and beautiful things which Almighty God has created.

Natural law ethics offers a powerful incentive for treating the environment with respect. The growing concern of natural law ethicists for the well-being of the environment is a hopeful sign that we may be able to stop or reverse some of the environmental damage caused by humans.

Cloning as a Fertility Treatment

When most people hear the word *clone*, they think of movies such as Star's War's "Attack of the Clones" with armies of clones trying take over the world. This concern may not be farfetched. The U.S. Defense Advanced Research Projects Agency is allegedly working on genetically engineering super soldiers who will be capable of superhuman feats and can regrow lost limbs as well as go days without sleep. These super soldiers would then be cloned for use in combat.

Most people, including natural law theorists, find the idea of cloning an army of "superhumans" repugnant. But what about a situation where a married couple is infertile and cannot have children naturally? It is estimated that 10 percent of couples who want a child are infertile. Cloning would allow them to have a child who is genetically related to at least one of them. Furthermore, identical twins are, in a sense, clones of one another, so it wouldn't be the only situation where two people in a family share the same genetic code.

Natural law theorists oppose cloning as a reproduction option, even in cases of infertility. As for the argument that natural twins are "clones," natural law ethicists point out that identical twins occur as a result of a natural process—the splitting of the zygote into two individuals within the mother's womb or fallopian tubes. Natural twins also carry the elements of the genetic codes of two parents—a man and a woman. *Cloning*, in contrast, produces identical individuals through asexual reproduction, either by embryo splitting or nuclei transfer. Asexual reproduction violates natural law because it breaks down the natural structure of the family as mother, father, and child(ren).

Cloning, in other words, runs counter to "the procreative teleology of sexuality" by breaking the connection between sex and procreation. A child, according to Catholic natural law ethicists, has "a right to be conceived." Children who are clones, like the "superhumans" described above, are "made" rather than begotten as nature intended. As such, clones are not valued for their intrinsic world as humans but as mere instruments to benefit others. No longer are two parents—a man and a woman—necessary to produce a children. Cloning is the ultimate one-parent family, since men are no longer needed in the reproductive process. It is, to use the words of bioethicist Leon Kass, the "ultimate narcissistic self-recreation."[16]

In addition, natural law ethicists argue, cloning violates human dignity in a way that natural twining does not because cloning reduces people to their genetic codes. It treats people as a means only—commodities—rather than beings with intrinsic moral value. Because cloning involves the destruction of surplus embryos, it also meets the same objections as abortion. However, technology in the future may be able to clone an egg or cell without destroying surplus embryos or donating the surplus embryos to other women who are infertile and would like a child.

In the following section, we will be looking at some of the strengths and weaknesses of natural law theory.

Exercises

1. Natural law ethicists opposed active euthanasia. However, what about cases where the debilitating pain of a dying person cannot be controlled by medication? Discuss whether active euthanasia in these cases might be compatible with respect for the dignity of the person. Relate your answer to the quote on page 298 from the "Ethical and Religious Directives for Catholic Health Care Services."

2. $55 billion is spent on doctors and hospital care during the last two months of life. Twenty to thirty percent of these costs, the majority of which are covered by the federal government through programs such as Medicare, have "no meaningful impact" on the patients' life.[17] Discuss what advice a natural law ethicist might give to a dying patient who is considering expensive medical care that, in all likelihood, would have "no meaningful impact" on his or her life.

3. Examine your lifestyle and future plans in light of its effect on the environment.

4. Critically analyze the natural law claim that a child "has a right to be conceived." What is the basis of this right? Does this right supersede parents' rights, if there is such a right, to have a child who is related to at least one of them? Critically analyze the basis of both these supposed rights.

5. There are examples of cloning in nature. Many plants as well as amoebas, sea anemone, and even armadillos are able to clone themselves. Does this add weight to the counterargument that cloning is a natural process? Explain.

6. Select a contemporary moral issue, other than the three discussed in this section, and examine the issue in light of natural law ethics. Do you agree with the position that a natural law ethicist would most likely take on the issue? If not, explain why not.

Critique of Natural Law Theory

1. *Not all people agree on what is morally required.* Because the basic principles of natural law are so general, it is open to divergent interpretations. This problem is further compounded by the fact that humans are not perfectly rational. Because we have imperfect reason and are subject to error, different people may interpret natural law and its application differently.

2. *Natural law theory is based on a dualistic worldview.* Natural law assumes that humans are a special creation who have incorporeal souls and, hence, are free and autonomous. As such, humans are qualitatively different from other purely physical animals. However, not only is human reason imperfect, reason is found throughout the animal kingdom to various degrees. In addition, reason can also be programmed into artificial intelligence. On the other hand, there is currently a shift in natural law ethics away from the Aristotelian view that only humans have moral value to a more holistic view of the environment and all species as having moral worth.

3. *Because natural law theory is teleological, the end or fundamental good toward which it is aimed can sometimes become more important than respect for individual rights and dignity.* For example, some natural law ethicists argue that both homosexuality and the use of birth control are immoral because they do not further the end of procreation. On the other hand, because natural law is teleological, its application can change. For example, a normative rule prohibiting artificial birth control may have been the fulfillment of natural law at one time (promoting the survival of the human species), but the present human condition may now require that this rule be rescinded. Indeed, the appropriateness of a rule against contraception is an issue that is currently the subject of much debate among Catholic natural law ethicists.

4. *There is disagreement among natural law theorists on the list of fundamental goods.* It is assumed that we intuitively know what the fundamental goods are. However, not everyone agrees about what they are. Aquinas, as we noted earlier, believed procreation to be a fundamental good. For other people, procreation is not a fundamental good and indeed may be regarded as something to be avoided, given overpopulation. Other natural law ethicists have a different list of fundamental goods. Thomas Hobbes maintained that self-preservation is a fundamental good and that the laws of nature direct us to this good.[18] Others hold goods such as friendship, fulfillment through work, and self-preservation to be more fundamental. Indeed, given the variability of human interests and goals, is agreement on a list of fundamental goods even possible?

5. *Natural law theory commits the naturalist fallacy.* Even if there are fundamental goods common to all humans that we can agree on, natural law theorists are committing the naturalistic fallacy in deriving what we *ought* to do from what *is*. For example, the fact that cloning is unnatural in humans does not mean that we ought not to do it. We need reasons other than the unnaturalness of the technology.

Exercises

1. What do you consider to be the two or three most fundamental goods or goals of human existence? Working in small groups, compare and contrast your list with those of others in your group. How do differences in what you regard as fundamental goods affect your position and those of others in your group on specific moral issues such as same-sex marriage, war, and gender roles?

2. Some people claim that we should keep our religious morality and public morality separate. For example, a Catholic politician may believe that abortion or active euthanasia is immoral, but this does not necessarily mean, the argument goes, that these practices should be illegal or are wrong for non-Catholics. Does this argument make sense if natural or moral law is universally binding upon everyone? If one's religious morality does not apply in public life, then is it really morality at all? Discuss.

Summary

1. *Natural law theory* states that morality is independent of religion and God's commands, and grounded in rational nature. We can discern natural law through the use of reason.

2. Natural law is *teleological* and oriented toward a specific purpose of the natural order. There are certain fundamental goods that promote this goal.

3. The United Nations Nuremberg Charter is based on natural law theory.

4. Thomas Aquinas lists four types of laws: *eternal, divine, natural* (moral), and *human* (legal laws and cultural norms).

5. The natural law theory of Aquinas has had a major influence on modern Catholic teaching.

6. *The principle of double effect* states that an action which causes serious harm may be permissible if that harm is an unintended side effect.

7. *Just war theory* lists five conditions that a war or a declaration of war must meet in order to be considered just.

8. If a human law is unjust and conflicts with moral (natural law), we may have a moral obligation to engage in *civil disobedience.*

9. Henry David Thoreau listed four criteria that must be met for engaging in civil disobedience.

10. Martin Luther King, Jr. was a natural law ethicist and civil rights activist who engaged in civil disobedience in order to call attention to racial injustices.

11. Natural law ethicists oppose active euthanasia because it involves the intentional killing of a person.

12. Natural law ethicists are active in the environmental movement because of the belief that nature is good and that humans are called upon to be stewards of the environment.

13. Cloning is immoral because it is unnatural and breaks down the traditional family structure.

 ## The Summa Theologica

Thomas Aquinas

Whether There Is an Eternal Law?

. . . A law is nothing else but a dictate of practical reason emanating from the ruler who governs a perfect community. Now it is evident, granted that the world is ruled by Divine Providence, . . . that the whole community of the universe is governed by Divine Reason.

Now among all others, the rational creature is subject to Divine Providence in the most excellent way, in so far as it partakes of a share of providence, by being provident both for itself and for others. Wherefore it has a share of the Eternal Reason, whereby it has a natural inclination to its proper act and end: and this participation of the eternal law in the rational creature is called the natural law. . . . [T]he light of natural reason, whereby we discern what is good and what is evil, which is the function of the natural law, is nothing else than an imprint on us of the Divine light. It is therefore evident that the natural law is nothing else than the rational creature's participation of the eternal law. . . .

"Natural Law," *The Summa Theologica*, Vol. II, translated by the Fathers of the English Dominican Province (Westminster, MD: Christian Classic, 1911), pp. 90–108. (The complete *Summa Theologica* is available online at www.ccel.org.ccel/aquinas/summar.toc.html.)

Whether an Effect of Law Is to Make Men Good?

. . . A law is nothing else than a dictate of reason in the ruler by whom his subjects are governed. Now the virtue of any subordinate thing consists in its being well subordinated to that by which it is regulated: thus we see that the virtue of the irascible and concupiscible faculties consists in their being obedient to reason; and accordingly *the virtue of every subject consists in his being well subjected to his ruler,* as the Philosopher [Aristotle] says (*Polit.* i). But every law aims at being obeyed by those who are subject to it. Consequently it is evident that the proper effect of law is to lead its subjects to their proper virtue: and since virtue is *that which makes its subject good,* it follows that the proper effect of law is to make those to whom it is given, good, either simply or in some particular respect. . . .

. . . Since then every man is a part of the state, it is impossible that a man be good, unless he be well proportionate to the common good: nor can the whole be well consistent unless its parts be proportionate to it. Consequently the common good of the state cannot flourish, unless the citizens be virtuous, at least those whose business it is to govern. But it is enough for the good of the community, that the other citizens be so far virtuous that they obey the commands of their rulers. . . .

. . . A tyrannical law, through not being according to reason, is not a law, absolutely speaking, but rather a perversion of law; and yet in so far as it is something in the nature of a law, it aims at the citizens' being good. For all it has in the nature of a law consists in its being an ordinance made by a superior to his subjects, and aims at being obeyed by them, which is to make them good, not simply, but with respect to that particular government. . . .

Whether the Natural Law Contains Several Precepts, or One Only?

. . . Now a certain order is to be found in those things that are apprehended universally. . . . [T]he first principle in the practical reason is one founded on the notion of good, viz., that *good is that which all things seek after.* Hence this is the first precept of law, that *good is to be done and pursued, and evil is to be avoided.* All other precepts of the natural law are based upon this: so that whatever the practical reason naturally apprehends as man's good (or evil) belongs to the precepts of the natural law as something to be done or avoided.

Since, however, good has the nature of an end, and evil, the nature of a contrary, hence it is that all those things to which man has a natural inclination, are naturally apprehended by reason as being good, and consequently as objects of pursuit, and their contraries as evil, and objects of avoidance. . . . [T]here is in man an inclination to good, according to the nature of his reason, which nature is proper to him: thus man has a natural inclination to know the truth about God, and to live in society: and in this respect, whatever pertains to this inclination belongs to the natural law; for instance, to shun ignorance, to avoid offending those among whom one has to live, and other such things regarding the above inclination. . . .

Whether the Natural Law Is the Same in All Men?

. . . [T]he natural law, as to general principles, is the same for all, both as to rectitude and as to knowledge. But as to certain matters of detail, which are conclusions, as it were, of those general principles, it is the same for all in the majority of cases, both as to rectitude and as to knowledge; and yet in some few cases it may fail, both as to rectitude, by reason of certain obstacles (just as natures subject to generation and corruption fail in some few cases on account of some obstacle), and as to knowledge, since in some the reason is perverted by passion, or evil habit, or an evil disposition of nature; . . .

 ## On the Duty of Civil Disobedience

Henry David Thoreau

How does it become a man to behave toward the American government today? I answer, that he cannot without disgrace be associated with it. I cannot for an instant recognize

---

[1849, original title: Resistance to Civil Government]

that political organization as my government which is the *slave's* government also.

All men recognize the right of revolution; that is, the right to refuse allegiance to, and to resist the government, when its tyranny or its inefficiency a regret and unendurable. But almost all say that such is not the case now.

But such was the case, they think, in the Revolution of '75. If one were to tell me that this was a bad government because it taxed certain foreign commodities brought to its ports, it is most probable that I should not make an ado about it, for I can do without them. All machines have their friction; and possibly this does enough good to counterbalance the evil. At any rate, it is a great evil to make a stir about it. But when the friction comes to have its machine, and oppression and robbery are organized, I say, let us not have such a machine any longer. In other words, when a sixth of the population of a nation which has undertaken to be the refuge of liberty are slaves, and a whole country is unjustly overrun and conquered by a foreign army, and subjected to military law, I think that it is not too soon for honest men to rebel and revolutionize. . . .

It is not a man's duty, as a matter of course, to devote himself to the eradication of any, even to most enormous wrong; he may still properly have other concerns to engage him; but it is his duty, at least, to wash his hands of it, and, if he gives it no thought longer, not to give it practically his support. If I devote myself to other pursuits and contemplations, I must first see, at least, that I do not pursue them sitting upon another man's shoulders. . . .

Unjust laws exist: shall we be content to obey them, or shall we endeavor to amend them, and obey them until we have succeeded, or shall we transgress them at once? Men, generally, under such a government as this, think that they ought to wait until they have persuaded the majority to alter them. They think that, if they should resist, the remedy would be worse than the evil. But it is the fault of the government itself that the remedy is worse than the evil. It makes it worse. . . .

If the injustice is part of the necessary friction of the machine of government, let it go, let it go: perchance it will wear smooth–certainly the machine will wear out. If the injustice has a

spring, or a pulley, or a rope, or a crank, exclusively for itself, then perhaps you may consider whether the remedy will not be worse than the evil; but if it is of such a nature that it requires you to be the agent of injustice to another, then I say, break the law. Let your life be a counter-friction to stop the machine. What I have to do is to see, at any rate, that I do not lend myself to the wrong which I condemn.

As for adopting the ways of the State has provided for remedying the evil, I know not of such ways. They take too much time, and a man's life will be gone. . . .

I do not hesitate to say, that those who call themselves Abolitionists should at once effectually withdraw their support, both in person and property, from the government of Massachusetts, and not wait till they constitute a majority of one, before they suffer the right to prevail through them. I think that it is enough if they have God on their side, without waiting for that other one. Moreover, any man more right than his neighbors constitutes a majority of one already. . . .

Under a government which imprisons unjustly, the true place for a just man is also a prison.

There will never be a really free and enlightened State until the State comes to recognize the individual as a higher and independent power, from which all its own power and authority are derived, and treats him accordingly. I please myself with imagining a State at last which can afford to be just to all men, and to treat the individual with respect as a neighbor; which even would not think it inconsistent with its own repose if a few were to live aloof from it, not meddling with it, nor embraced by it, who fulfilled all the duties of neighbors and fellow men. A State which bore this kind of fruit, and suffered it to drop off as fast as it ripened, would prepare the way for a still more perfect and glorious State, which I have also imagined, but not yet anywhere seen.

Discussion Questions

1. Analyze Aquinas's argument that there is a higher law than human law. If there is a higher moral law, is it necessary to bring in a God to explain or validate this higher law? Discuss how both Aquinas and Thoreau might answer this question.

2. Working in small groups, discuss whether there are any injustices in our country today that call us to resist the government and engage in civil disobedience. Discuss how you might carry out the civil disobedience in a manner that is consistent with the four criteria for civil disobedience (page 294).

3. Choose a current moral issue and discuss how both Aquinas and Thoreau might respond to it.

Notes

1. Ed Gent, "Designer Babies Dilemma in Sharp Focus with Moving Fertility Tech," January 19, 2017, http://singularityhub.com/2017/01/19/designer-babies-dilemma-in-sharp-focus-with-fast-moving-ferility-tech. See also Ekaterina Pesheva, "The Promise and Peril of Emerging Reproductive Technologies," Harvard Medical School, January 11, 2017, https://hms/harvard.edu/news/promise-and-peril.

2. Kwame Gyekye, *An Essay on African Philosophical Thought: The Akan Conceptual Scheme* (New York: Cambridge University Press, 1987).

3. Pope John Paul XXIII, "Pacem in Terris" (New York: American Press, 1963), para. 56, 79.

4. Pope John Paul XXIII, "Pacem in Terris," para. 9.

5. John P. Langan, "Human Rights in Roman Catholicism," in *Human Rights in Religious Tradition*, ed. Arlene Swidler (New York: Pilgrim Press, 1982), p. 38.

6. Michael Lipka, "Some Major U.S. Religious Groups Differ from Their Members on the Death Penalty," July 13, 2015, http://www.pewresearch.org/fact-tank/2015/07/13/some-major-religions-differ-from-their-members-on-the-death-penalty.

7. Thomas Aquinas, *The Summa Theologica*, P. II, question 40, first article.

8. For more on just war theory, see Michael Walzer, *Just and Unjust Wars* (New York: Basic Books, 1977); and C. A. J. Coady, "War and Terrorism," in *A Companion to Applied Ethics*, ed. R.G. Frey and Christopher Health Wellman (Oxford, UK: Blackwell, 2003), pp. 254–263.

9. Mark Lander, "The Afghan War and the Evolution of Obama," *The New York Times*, January 1, 2017.

10. Joshua J. McElwee, "Vatican Conference Rejects 'Outdated' Just War Theory," *National Catholic Reporter* vol. 52, no. 15 (May 6-19, 2016): 1.

11. Thomas Aquinas, *The Summa Theologica* 1, pt. 1.2, question 96, answer 4.

12. Angela K. Brown, "AWOL Soldier to Surrender," DenverPost.com, August 31, 2006.

13. "Letter from a Birmingham Jail," *Where Do We Go from Here? Chaos or Community?* (New York: HarperCollins, 1965, 1991).

14. Elizabeth Cady Stanton, Susan B. Anthony, and Matilda Joslyn Gage, eds., *History of Women Suffrage*, vol. 2 (New York: Fowler & Wells, 1881) p. 689.

15. Deborah LaVallie, "Tribes Look at Keystone," *The Tribal Independence*, March 9, 2012.

16. Leon Kass, "The Wisdom of Repugnance: Why We Should Ban the Cloning of Humans," *The New Republic* 216, no. 22 (1997): pp. 17-26. Note: Although Kass is not strictly a natural law theorist, he does adopt their position on cloning.

17. "The Cost of Dying—End-of-Life Care," *CBS News*, August 8, 2010.

18. Thomas Hobbes, *Leviathan*, chapter 15.

CHAPTER 10

Deontology
The Ethics of Duty

Two things fill the mind with ever new and increasing admiration
and awe, the oftener and more steadily we reflect on them: the
starry heavens above and the moral law within.
    —IMMANUEL KANT, *Critique of Practical Reason*[1]

Look to your own duty; do not tremble before it.
    —*Bhagavad Gita*[2]

You are a physician at a college health center. One of your patients, Eric, a 27-year-old graduate student, comes to you complaining of pain when he urinates. Tests reveal that he has gonorrhea. When you tell him the results of the tests, he pleads with you not to tell his wife about his condition since he is worried that she'll leave him if she finds out he has been unfaithful. His wife is a senior at the same college and also one of your patients. Eric swears that he loves his wife and that this was a one-night stand and that he will never be unfaithful again. He asks you to tell his wife, should she ask you, that he is taking antibiotics for a urinary tract infection. What should you do?

A study at a major hospital revealed that the majority of doctors were willing to use deception in a case such as this and would back up the husband's story.[3] However, is this lie morally justified? While a utilitarian might say "yes," if the benefits of lying outweigh the harm (possible breakup of marriage) of telling the truth, most deontologists would say that we have a duty to tell the truth in cases like this and that lying is wrong.

In this chapter we'll be studying deontology, which regards duty, rather than consequences, as the foundation of morality. We'll also develop strategies for making moral decisions in our lives when these duties come into conflict as in the above case.

Deontology and Duty

Deontology is one of the most popular approaches to ethics. Deontological theories regard duty as the basis of morality. The word **deontology** comes from the Greek word *deon*, meaning "duty" or "that which is obligatory." Moral duties are not the same as legal duties or cultural norms. A moral duty is transcultural and universally binding. If a cultural norm or law conflicts with a moral duty, then the moral duty should take precedence over the legal duty.

There are strong strands of deontology in both Confucian and Hindu ethics and in many Western ethical theories. The high standards of moral excellence put forth by deontologists have also inspired psychologists, such as Lawrence Kohlberg, to study moral development and to map the transition to postconventional moral reasoning, as exemplified in deontological ethics.

For deontologists, the moral law is not defined in terms of consequences or whether it promotes some particular goal as it is in ethical egoism and utilitarian theory. Instead, the moral law is an end in itself. Moral duty requires the recognition of and submission to moral laws or rules. Immanuel Kant taught that we should act purely out of good will, not because of rewards or punishment or other consequences. Hindu ethics, in the *Bhagavad Gita*, also teaches that righteous living (dharma) requires discipline and acting out of a sense of duty rather than out of concern for the consequences of our actions:

> Be intent on action, not on the fruits of action;
> Avoid attraction to the fruits
> and attachment to inaction!
> Perform actions, firm in discipline,
> relinquishing attachment;
> be impartial to failure and success—
> this equanimity is called discipline.

With the exception of Kant, who argued that moral duties are absolute, most deontologists regard moral duties as *prima facie*. An **absolute duty** is one that is always morally binding regardless of the circumstances. There are no exceptions. For example, Kant regarded the duty not to lie as an absolute duty.

A **prima facie duty**, on the other hand, is morally binding *unless* it conflicts with a more pressing moral duty. The duty not to lie, for example, may conflict with the duty to prevent someone's death. In this case, a prima facie deontologist may decide that the duty to prevent someone's death overrides the duty not to lie. Whether or not lying is morally justified in order to save our patient's marriage (in the introductory scenario) is a more controversial question and would require an in-depth analysis of the other duties and rights at stake in this case.

Connections

What is the relationship between a moral duty and a moral right? See Chapter 11, pages 360–361.

Duties can also be positive or negative. A **positive duty** entails actively doing something, such as extending a helping hand or returning a favor. A **negative duty**, on the other hand, requires us to restrain ourselves from doing something, such as stealing, cheating on a test, or beating up a motorist who cuts us off in traffic. Most duties have both negative and positive elements. The duty of nonmaleficence or "do no harm," for example, is usually a negative duty. We should refrain from harming others, even when we feel a desire to do so. Nonmaleficence, however, can also be a positive duty when it requires us to actively do something to stop or remove a harm, such as calling the police when we see someone being assaulted. Nonmaleficence as a positive duty also involves taking action to prevent future harms, such as warning employees about risks in the workplace or strapping young children into car seats.

Although deontologists agree that duty is the basis of morality, they differ in their views regarding the source of moral duty. Kant maintained that moral duty can only be grounded in reason. Sir W. David Ross, on the other hand, claims that moral duties are self-evident: We know what they are through intuition. Ross writes in his book *The Right and the Good*:

> [T]he moral order . . . is as much part of the fundamental nature of the universe as is the spatial or numerical structure expressed in the axioms of geometry or arithmetics. In both cases we are dealing with propositions that cannot be proved, but that just as certainly need no proof. . . .
>
> We have no more direct way of access to the facts about rightness and goodness and about what things are right or good, than by thinking about them; the moral convictions of thoughtful and well-educated people are the data of ethics just as sense-perceptions are the data of a natural science. . . . The verdicts of the moral consciousness of the best people are the foundation on which we must build.[4]

Deontology is often presented as diametrically opposed to utilitarian theory, but this is misleading. Utilitarians also regard duty as important. "It is part of the notion of Duty in every one of its forms," wrote John Stuart Mill, "that a person may rightfully be compelled to fulfill it."[5] For a utilitarian, however, our only duties are to maximize happiness (duty of beneficence) and to minimize pain (duty of nonmaleficence) for the greatest number. Deontologists, on the other hand, recognize additional duties. They also emphasize duty for duty's sake rather than because of its consequences.

Deontologists have been accused of being nothing more than rule-utilitarians. Rule-utilitarians and deontologists both believe that rules should be universal; however, the reasoning behind the formulation of the rules is different. The rule-utilitarian asks which rules, in general, bring about the best consequences. Deontologists, in contrast, ask whether a rule, such as "do not lie," is logically consistent. In other words, would a rational person wish that this rule be made a universal moral law?

Deontologists take into consideration more than just happiness when deciding which rules should be universalized. Kant, for example, acknowledged that we have a duty to assure our own happiness because "discontent with one's state, in a press of cares and amidst unsatisfied want, might easily become a great temptation to the transgression of duty." However, unlike the utilitarians, Kant and other deontologists considered the pursuit of happiness an indirect duty because we already have in us "the strongest and deepest inclination towards happiness."[6]

Connections

What is the principle of utility? *See Chapter 8, pages 242-244.*

Connections

What is the difference between a rule utilitarian and an act utilitarian? *See Chapter 8, pages 245-246.*

Exercises

1. When making moral decisions, do you act purely from a sense of duty? Discuss other considerations, such as fear of punishment or peer pressure, that motivate you to behave morally. Use specific examples to illustrate your answer.

2. Discuss whether a person's intentions are relevant to doing good. Are being virtuous and acting out of a sense of duty more important than doing good because of the consequences? Support your answer.

3. Adolf Eichmann had never himself killed or even given an order to kill a Jew or any other human being. Although he had been fully informed about the mass killings of Jews, his response was that this had nothing to do with his job. Nevertheless, the court found him guilty, ruling that "the legal and moral responsibility of him who delivers the victim to his death is, in our opinion no smaller and may even be greater than the liability of him who does the victim to death."[7] Discuss whether the ruling was morally justified.

4. Discuss whether industries that create products, such as cigarettes or assault rifles, that harm consumers should be held morally responsible for the harms they directly or indirectly cause. Discuss also if retailers, such as Wal-Mart or the Gap, as well as we consumers have a negative duty to avoid products created by these industries.

Immanuel Kant: The Categorical Imperative

Act only on that maxim through which you can at the same time will that it should become a universal law.

—IMMANUEL KANT, *Fundamental Principles of the Metaphysics of Morals* (1785), p. 421

Duty and the moral *ought* emerged as a dominant theme during the seventeenth and eighteenth centuries in Western philosophy. This period, known as the *Enlightenment*, was equaled only by the fifth and fourth centuries B.C.E., which witnessed the golden age of ancient Greek philosophy and the birth of Confucianism and Moism in China and of Buddhism in India.

Connections

What, according to Plato, is the ideal type of society for promoting virtue and justice in its citizens? *See Chapter 6, page 190.*

The Enlightenment gave rise to some of the most influential philosophy in Western history, including the deontology of Immanuel Kant (1724–1804) and the rights ethics of John Locke (1632–1704) and Thomas Jefferson (1743–1826). The rise of science and technology during this period reinforced the ancient Greek belief in the fundamental rational nature of humans and the potential of reason to solve all our problems. The concern with the public sphere that was so central to the philosophy of Plato and Aristotle was gradually replaced with an emphasis on autonomy and the dignity of the individual. The individual life, independent of the community, became a value in and of itself.

The Life of Immanuel Kant

Immanuel Kant was perhaps the greatest and most influential of the Enlightenment ethicists. He was born in 1724 in Königsberg, Prussia, the son of a saddler. His mother, a devout Pietist (a Lutheran sect), was remarkable for her good character and natural intelligence and had a great influence upon her son's development.

In 1755, Kant got a job as privatdozent at the University of Königsberg; this licensed him to give lectures. As a lecturer, he was playful, witty, and entertaining. To his many friends, he was a role model and an inspiration. In 1770, after years of trying to procure a permanent teaching position, Kant was finally appointed Professor of Logic and Metaphysics. His first great work in philosophy, *Critique of Pure Reason*, was not published until 1781, when Kant was in his late fifties. It was followed, by several other great works.

Kant's most notable trait, it was said, was his sincerity and his devotion to the concept of moral duty. During his later years, Kant gained fame as a sort of oracle. People would come from all around to Königsberg to consult him on all sorts of issues, including the lawfulness of vaccinations. Kant died in 1804, having spent his entire life in Königsberg.

The Ought Quality of Morality

In his early writings, Kant acknowledged the role of a natural moral sense or feeling of concern for others. However, as he became more involved in the critical, analytical philosophy that dominated continental Enlightenment philosophy, he moved away from his earlier position to draw a sharp distinction between reason and feelings.

Kant believed that most people already *knew* right from wrong. Like Aristotle, he used the everyday experience of morality, along with the tentative presumption that our ordinary knowledge of morality is legitimate, as his starting point. In doing so, Kant took care not to confuse morality with cultural relativism, which he strongly opposed. What interested him about our ordinary knowledge of morality were the very general moral principles that transcend cultural particulars.

Kant believed that the problem most people have is not in *knowing* what is morally right but in *doing* it. His primary concern was not to produce a list of duties but to establish a metaphysical groundwork or foundation for ethics that would explain, once and for all, why we *ought* to behave morally (see the selection by Kant at the end of this chapter). To accomplish this, he first asked: What gives morality its imperative or *ought* quality? What is the supreme principle of morality that provides a solid foundation for moral judgment?

Only reason, Kant concluded, can provide a sound foundation for the universality of morality. Empirical data and feelings, though not irrelevant, are insufficient to provide the foundation for moral law. He wanted to keep morality free from the taint of self-interest and external considerations (heteronomy). If there

Connections

What is the role of empirical propositions in a moral argument? *See Chapter 2, pages 49-50.*

is a moral law and if it is to be morally binding, then it must be logically compelling. As a rational being, I can only will what is not logically contradictory; this includes not making an exception of myself. If a particular action is right or wrong, it must always be so. Otherwise, we are being logically inconsistent.

Because the formulation of general moral principles cannot be derived from empirical experience, Kant concluded that moral knowledge must be a priori. An **a priori proposition** is one that we can know to be true prior to or without reference to actual experience. He referred to the a priori aspect of morality as the metaphysical foundation of morality.

Carrying this line of thinking one step farther, Kant argued that reason requires not only that moral duties be universal but also that they be *absolutely* binding. There can be no exceptions. For example, we should *never* lie, even in a situation where lying might have beneficial consequences, such as lying to a potential murderer in order to save someone's life.

Kant's Categorical Imperative

Unlike **hypothetical imperatives**, which tell us we ought do something *if* we desire to achieve a certain result—such as telling a lie to save a life—moral obligations are categorical, or unconditionally binding upon us. A **categorical imperative** states that we ought to do something regardless of the consequences.

The categorical imperative is also a formal principle—that is, it lacks a specific content. It has been compared to the Tao, or the Way, in Eastern philosophy. Kant came up with two formulations of the categorical imperative. The first formulation states:

> Act only on that maxim through which you can at the same time will that it should become a universal law.

Kant thought that all rational beings would agree with this formulation of the categorical imperative, even though there may be disagreement about the particular details of moral behavior. To illustrate what he meant by this, he drew an analogy between ethics and mathematics. To someone unskilled in mathematics, the three triangles at the top of page 315 all look different, just as at first glance different ethical systems can appear to be unrelated. However, through the application of reason, we can discover formal principles that govern all triangles. Similarly, by the use of reason, Kant argued, we would all come up with the categorical imperative as the foundation of morality.

As a formal principle, the categorical imperative provides a framework for deriving moral maxims or laws, such as "do not lie" or "honor your parents," that can be applied in specific situations. When deciding whether a particular rule or maxim is moral, we need only ask ourselves whether what we are proposing has the formal character of law—that is, would we as a rational person will that it be a universal law? To illustrate his point, Kant considered a maxim that would allow us to make "lying promises," promises that we do not intend

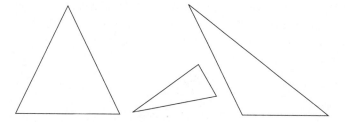

to keep. In answer to the question "Does a lying promise accord with duty?" Kant wrote:

> I have then to ask myself "Should I really be content that my maxim (the maxim of getting out of a difficulty by a false promise) should hold as a universal law (one valid both for myself and others)? And could I really say to myself that every one may make a false promise if he finds himself in a difficulty from which he can extricate himself in no other way?" I then become aware at once that I can indeed will to lie, but I can by no means will a universal law of lying; for by such a law there could properly be no promises at all . . . and consequently my maxim, as soon as it was made a universal law, would be bound to annul itself.[8]

Reason as the Foundation of Morality

Because reason, according to Kant, provides the foundation of morality, morality would not exist in the world without rationality. This makes humans, and other rational beings, very special beings. Whereas rational beings have free will, Kant maintained that everything else in nature operates according to physical laws. Furthermore, because autonomy is essential for dignity, only rational beings have intrinsic moral worth. As beings with intrinsic worth, rational beings can never be treated as expendable but must be respected with dignity as ends in themselves. This society of all rational beings, according to Kant, constitutes the "kingdom of ends." This ideal is summed up in the second formulation of the categorical imperative (also known as the practical imperative):

> So act as to treat humanity, whether in thine own person or in that of any other, in every case as an end in itself, never as a means only.

We have a duty to always respect people as ends in themselves; Kant was not implying by this that we could *never* treat another person as a means, however. Obviously, this would be impossible. We use our teachers as a means of furthering our education; we use bus drivers as a means of getting to school or to work; we use doctors as a means of healing our bodies. Kant was saying that we cannot treat a person *only* as a means. In other words, we cannot simply dispose of a person once we no longer need their services in the way we discard a pen or a tongue depressor once it is no longer of use to us. Even though we may no longer have any use for these people, we still have a moral obligation to continue to treat them with respect and dignity.

Connections

What is an autonomous moral agent and how does it differ from a heteronomous moral agent? *See Chapter 1, page 12.*

For many young people the Internet and other forms of social media, such as mobile phones and iPads, are an integral way in which they conduct their personal lives. Even when in the same room with other people, they may communicate with each other using social media rather than talking face to face.
©Michael Hitoshi/Getty Images

Discussion Questions

1. Is social media "depersonalizing" our interaction with other people and contributing to anxiety and social isolation? One study found that "people are meaner online that in 'real life'," a phenomenon researchers blamed on anonymity and invisibility.[9] Thinking about your own use of social media, are you less likely to regard the person you are communicating with as a person with intrinsic moral worth, than you would if you were interacting with that person face-to-face? Given this phenomenon of depersonalization, discuss whether you have a moral obligation to limit your use of social media and/or to engage in more face-to-face contact.

2. Relate your answer to the previous questions to Kant's categorical imperative. Discuss what Kant, were he alive today, might think the moral issues involved in the use of social media and what suggestions he might have for how and when to use it.

In line with this honesty requires not just raw truth, but also stating the truth in a way that respects the dignity of people as ends in themselves. Telling someone who asks you how she looks that she is ugly shows a lack of respect for her as a person. On the other hand, people deserve an honest answer. People who have lied, Kant claimed, no matter how well intentioned ("I didn't want to hurt her feelings"), have failed in their duty to the other person because the lie restricts their autonomy. To lie to other rational beings such as the wife in the opening scenario, is to offer them a profound insult regarding their ability to make decisions about their own life or their ability to handle the truth.

Deontology, with its emphasis on the intrinsic worth of rational beings, has been regarded as an important corrective to strict utilitarian theory where an individual may be sacrificed for the greater good of the community. On the other hand, Kant defined the moral community more narrowly than utilitarians. Utilitarians include all sentient beings, whereas Kant insisted that only rational beings are worthy of moral respect.

So far as animals are concerned we have no direct duties. Animals are not self-conscious and are there merely as a means to an end. That end is man.

—IMMANUEL KANT, "Duties Towards Animals and Spirits" (1779)

Even though nonhuman animals lack intrinsic worth, according to Kant, he argued that cruelty to nonhuman animals is morally wrong except when such cruelty directly benefits humans, such as in science experiments. In other circumstances, cruelty to nonhuman animals is wrong because it often spills over into an attitude of meanness and hardness in our dealings with other humans.

Exercises

1. Apply the categorical imperative to the following scenarios:

   a. Your roommate Beth has been depressed lately. She's not keeping up with her studies and has even talked about committing suicide. One evening, she agrees to go to a party with you. As you're ready to leave, she asks you how she looks. She looks pretty awful. Her mascara is smeared, her hair is unkempt, and her clothes are dirty and unsuitable for the occasion. How do you answer her question?

   b. Your best friend Grace just got engaged to Bob. Grace can only say how wonderful Bob is, but you have reason to believe otherwise. Every so often, she turns up in class with a black eye. When you ask what happened, she says she fell. Recently, you learned from a sorority sister, whom Bob had dated before he met Grace, that Bob physically abused her, and in fact, she had to be hospitalized after one particularly brutal attack. Grace asks you to be her maid of honor at the wedding. What do you say?

2. Compare Kant's description of the categorical imperative to the Eastern notion of the Way. How are the two concepts similar? How do they differ? Discuss the strengths and weaknesses of each approach.

3. Discuss whether the use of torture on terrorist suspects who in all likelihood have information that endangers the American public, violates Kant's categorical imperative, which prohibits using a person as a means only. Discuss also how a utilitarian would answer this question and how Kant might respond to their argument.

4. Are you satisfied with Kant's definition of personhood and moral community? What criteria should we use to determine whether another being (say, an alien from another planet) is rational or has self-consciousness? Using Kant's definition of personhood, discuss whether it would be morally permissible: a) to use human embryos in stem cell research, b) to breed children in order to use their organs as spare parts, or c) euthanize elderly people with dementia who are no longer rational. Discuss also how Kant would respond to utilitarian Peter Singer's support of these policies.

The Good Will and Proper Self-Esteem

We cannot think of anything in the world or outside of it that could be purely good—

something that is good in itself, without qualification—except a good will.

—IMMANUEL KANT, *Fundamental Principles of the Metaphysic of Morals* (1785), p. 393

Kant's Concept of the Good Will

The duty to improve ourselves as moral people is important in virtually every ethical system. In Confucian and Buddhist ethics, continuous self-improvement through right living and right thinking is the only way to reach moral excellence. For Kant, the development of the good will and proper self-esteem is the only way to ensure that we will consistently do our duty.

Connections

What is the role of the good will in virtue ethics? *See Chapter 12, page 423.*

As autonomous and rational beings, we have the ability to use our reason to discern what is right and wrong without needing to rely on outside authorities. A person of **good will** always acts out of a sense of duty and a reverence for the moral law without regard for consequences or immediate inclinations. As autonomous beings, people of good will are free from external pressures. They are lawgivers unto themselves; that is, they impose the moral law upon themselves. Kant, however, was not suggesting that morality is relative or subjective. Instead, he believed that all rational beings would arrive at the same conclusions regarding what is right and wrong.

A person of good will can be depended on to do what is right, even when other motives are absent. An action that is done out of sympathy or because

Immanuel Kant (1724-1804), German philosopher. Kant (seated second from the left) is shown enjoying dinner with his friends. Kant was said to be witty and entertaining as well as a role model and inspiration to his many friends.
©INTERFOTO/Alamy Stock Photo

one enjoys helping others, rather than out of a sense of duty, may be praiseworthy; however, according to Kant, such an action has no moral worth. It is easy to help others who may someday return the favor or to feel compassion for those who are like us. Acting out of duty and the good will, on the other hand, involves the intention to do what is right, regardless of our feelings or any rewards. Cultivating the good will is also at the heart of Christian ethics. Jesus taught:

> If you love those who love you, what credit is that to you? Even sinners love those who love them. If you do good to those who do good to you, what credit is that to you? For even sinners do the same. And if you lend to those from whom you hope to receive, what credit is that to you? Even sinners lend to sinners, to receive as much again. But love your enemies, and do good, and lend, expecting nothing in return. (Luke 6:32-35)

The term *duty*, unfortunately, has a negative connotation for many people. Indeed, Kant has often been interpreted as promoting a sort of joyless duty. However, he was not suggesting that we ought not to feel sympathy for others or receive joy from helping others or from personal friendships. Kant believed that friendship is important as a means of connecting with others. Friendship also contributes to the development of our moral character by inspiring virtues such as compassion, wisdom, generosity, and happiness—virtues that make it easier for us to act in accordance with the good will. Indeed, Kant was described by his friends and students as a man of great feeling and compassion. "How often he moved us to tears," wrote one of his friends.

> How often he agitated our hearts, how often he lifted our minds and feelings from the fetters of selfish eudaemonism [inner happiness] to the higher consciousness of freedom, to unconditional obedience to the law of reason, to the exaltation of unselfish duty![10]

Virtues like compassion may make it easier for us to do our duty and, for this reason, are important to cultivate; for Kant, however, it is the good will that *motivates* us to do our duty. The sentiments that might accompany a moral action are not what make the action moral, because we have a moral duty to help others even when we do not feel sympathy for them or get no joy out of helping them. If we separate our motivations, it is the sense of duty, rather than immediate inclination, that gives an action its moral worth. However, Kant did not believe that we should not act unless our motives are pure.

Cultivating the Good Will

By forming friendships and exhibiting respect for others we nurture the good will. Community service can help to develop the good will. For example, an ethics student chose to do community service work with Habitat for Humanity (a nonprofit organization that builds homes for low-income families), not out of good will, but primarily out of self-interest. "I chose to do this work," he wrote, "because I very much enjoy working outdoors and also enjoy framing houses." At the beginning of the semester, this student was at the lower level of conventional reasoning. By the end of the semester, though, he had entered the postconventional level that exemplifies Kant's principled reasoning. As expected, his motivation for volunteering changed as he progressed in his moral development. At the conclusion of his journal, he wrote:

Connections

What are the conventional and postconventional stages of moral development? *See Chapter 3, page 91.*

> It seems to be pure caring which fuels the desire to give to others, and it seems to be a very moral thing to do. . . . I initially began this volunteer work because it was required for this class; but I noticed that the people [who worked on the project with him] did not need a class to make them come out and build this house.[11]

By caring for others as beings with intrinsic moral value (what the student calls "pure caring," as opposed to sentimental caring), the student volunteer strengthened his own good will. By the end of the semester, he was more autonomous. He continued to volunteer even after the semester was over because it was the right thing to do rather than because of extrinsic incentives.

Cultivating the good will and a sense of duty is an important corrective to our "feel good" approach to morality. For most of us, obstacles and subjective limitations, such as self-interest and pleasure, can at times take priority over the good will. A perfectly good will such as the will of God, on the other hand, has no obstacles to overcome; it acts purely out of the good will. For the perfectly good will, Kant writes, "there are no imperatives. 'I ought' is here out of place, because 'I will' is already of itself necessarily in harmony with the law."[12] Here, there is no distinction between reason and inclination. The perfectly good will always acts in accordance with the "ought." The concepts of duty and moral obligation are irrelevant because these come into play only when reason and inclination are in conflict. The moral life of the imperfect being, in contrast, is one of continual struggle between moral duty (reason) and desire.

The Duty of Self-Improvement

The cultivation of a good will involves the recognition that as rational beings, we have just as much moral value as anyone else. Kant believed that our primary moral duty is self-respect and the development of proper self-esteem. We have a duty to treat ourselves with respect, just as we have a moral duty to treat others with respect.

> The greatest love I can have for another is to love him as myself. I cannot love another more than I love myself. . . . Our duties towards ourselves [therefore] constitute the supreme condition and the principle of all morality. . . . He who transgresses against himself loses his manliness and becomes incapable of doing his duty toward his fellows.
>
> —IMMANUEL KANT, "Duties to Oneself"[13]

Kant was highly critical of moral philosophies that teach a person "should give a thought to himself only after he has completely fulfilled his duty towards others."[14]

> No one can demand of me that I should humiliate myself and value myself less than others; but we all have the right to demand of a man that he should not think himself superior. Moral self-esteem, however, which is grounded in the worth of humanity, should not be derived from comparison with others, but from comparison with the moral law.[15]

Kant was not advocating ethical egoism, though. Self-respect is not the same as putting our own interests first, but neither do people with self-respect value themselves less than others. Instead, self-respect stems from our sense of moral duty and, as such, is the basis of our respect for others.

The importance of proper self-esteem in our moral development has been verified by psychological studies. Studies of well-being show a high correlation between positive self-esteem and high esteem for others. Young people with high self-esteem also have more friends, are better able to resist harmful peer pressure, are less sensitive to criticism or to what people think, have fewer mental health problems, are better informed, . . . and are more apt to be assertive and get their needs met."[16]

Proper self-respect, besides being related to respect for others, makes one less dependent on the opinions and reactions of others. People who have high self-esteem receive more respect from others and are less vulnerable to being exploited by

Connections
What are the basic tenets of ethical egoism? *See Chapter 7, page 210.*

others.[17] People with low self-esteem, on the other hand, "are especially vulnerable to developing stress disorders [such as] underachievement at school, depression, irritability, anxiety, fatigue, nightmares, hyperactivity, aggressive behavior, withdrawal from others, nervous laughter, body aches and emotional tension."[18]

When one is doubtful about one's worth, it is easy to use another's actions and reactions to define oneself.

—VIRGINIA SATIR, *The New Peoplemaking* (1988)

Deontologists maintain that self-esteem is a meaningless concept unless it is grounded in the cultivation of good will. Promoting self-esteem as an end in itself has become a driving force in parenting and education. To build self-esteem, children are routinely praised with such phrases as "you're the best," "you're the smartest," and "you are exactly what God intends you to be." According to educational psychologist William Damon, emphasizing self-esteem as an end in itself, independently of a person's character or actions, does not develop self-esteem but instead engenders distrust of adults and a false self-image:

> Even though these white lies are intended to help rather than to deceive, children can and do see through them. If repeated often enough, these deceptions will undermine the child's trust in the adult's veracity. Even more dangerous, perhaps, children may actually internalize these empty phrases and dissociate their feelings of self-worth from any conduct that they are personally responsible for.[19]

Self-esteem that is not founded upon the development of moral character and good will encourages self-deception, egoism, and narcissism. In 1993, eight students from Lakewood High School in California were taken into custody for raping and molesting girls as young as ten years old. The boys belonged to a gang in which they won points through sexual conquest. Their activities were well-known around the school and were even accepted as normal by some school authorities and members of the community: "Boys will be boys." When the boys were interviewed on *Dateline* one of them responded with pride, "I'm definitely comfortable with myself and my self-esteem." When asked if he liked himself, one of the other boys answered, "Yeah, why wouldn't I? I mean, what's not to like about me."[20]

Key Claims of Deontology

- Duty is the basis of morality.
- Moral principles are universal.
- Reason is important in discerning and applying moral principles.
- Persons cannot be used as a means only.
- The moral community consists of all rational beings.

Proper self-esteem is not the result of empty praise or membership in a gang. According to Kant, we have a duty to use our freedom responsibly. People who rely on the flattery of others to inflate their self-esteem are not autonomous moral agents. True self-respect does not depend on outward achievements or the praise of others but comes from having a good will and living a principled life. Like happiness, proper self-esteem cannot be pursued as an end in itself. It is developed by seeking and living the good life.

The development of proper self-esteem is critical to our growth as autonomous moral reasoners. In Carol Gilligan's scheme of moral development, to make the transition from the conventional stage of moral development (where others' needs come before our own) to the postconventional stage (where we are able to balance our needs with those of others), we must first realize that we have equal moral worth. Only by saying no to exploitation and subservience can we fulfill our moral duty to ourselves and to others.

Connections

What are Gilligan's stages of moral development? *See Chapter 3, page 95.*

Exercises

*1. What motivates you to engage in good actions? What happens when you lack the inclination to do good? Illustrate your answers with examples from your life. If you are doing community service, relate your answer to your work.

*2. Some college courses require students to do community service. Are the teachers and students in these cases using the people they are serving as a means only—that is to fulfill a class requirement and to promote the students' moral development? Discuss how Kant would respond to this question and to the practice of a college's requirement of community service.

3. In the Dr. Seuss book *Horton Hatches the Egg*, Horton promises to help Lazy Mayzie by sitting on her egg. When he made the promise, he didn't realize that Lazy Mayzie was going to be gone for weeks. Discuss whether the fact that she "tricked" him into sitting on her egg excuses him from responsibility for caring for the egg. Relate your answer to a similar experience in your own life.

4. Read about the life of a moral reformer, such as Martin Luther King, Jr., or examine the life of your own moral hero. What motivated this person to continue even when the cause seemed hopeless? Was it reason or sentiment—or both? Explain.

5. Do you agree that we have a duty to develop proper self-esteem? Do you treat yourself with self-respect? Explain. Discuss how self-respect, or the lack of it, affects your treatment of other people.

*An asterisk indicates that the exercise is appropriate for students who are doing community service learning as part of the course.

Confucius: Duty and the Community

The cultivation of the person depends upon setting the mind in the right.

—CONFUCIUS, in *The Commentary of Tseng*[21]

Confucian moral philosophy emphasizes our duties, as a member of a family and the community. Confucius (551-479 B.C.E) is said to be the first professional teacher in China, and he began what would become a tradition of wandering scholars in China. He traveled from province to province with his pupils, teaching and trying to influence the rulers. Confucius became the most revered philosopher in China and radically changed Chinese philosophy by focusing on our duties to humanity rather than on spiritual concerns.

Like Bentham and Mo Tzu, Confucius was interested in promoting a moral system that could be used to formulate public policy and to provide people with a stable and harmonious social order. Unlike Mo Tzu and the utilitarians, though, Confucius believed that the only way to put society back on the right path was to instill in people a respect for duty as set forth in the tradition of the ancient sages. He believed that the duties prescribed by the ancient sages were universal and binding upon all people. He also believed, like Kant, that these duties could be known through the use of reason.

In Confucianism, *yi*, or righteousness, demands that we do what is right simply because it is our moral duty. Moral knowledge—knowledge of our duties—is possible because our minds are united with the universe. To do our moral duty is to act in accord with the universal principle—the *Tao*, also known as *the Way*. The Way, writes neo-Confucian philosopher Chi Hsi (1130-1200), is "the principle that nourishes and develops all things."[22] The Way is part of our nature, just as Kant regarded moral law as being within each of us.

> "Is there a single word which can be a guide to conduct throughout one's life?"
> The Master said, "It is perhaps the word 'shu.' Do not impose on others what you yourself do not desire."[23]

Connections

What are communitarian ethics? *See Chapter 7, pages 229-230.*

While Western deontologists tend to focus on the individual, Confucian deontology emphasizes communitarian values and duties over individual autonomy. There are five duties of universal obligation; these include the duty between ruler and citizen as well as duties between different members of the family. According to Confucius, the moral qualities or virtues by which these duties are "carried out are three . . . Wisdom, compassion and courage. These are the three universally recognized moral qualities of man."[24] See the reading from the *Analects of Confucius* at the end of this chapter.

The Confucian emphasis on communitarian duties, however, does not entail ignoring our own moral development. The duty of self-cultivation is important because it makes us better citizens and members of the community. Self-cultivation involves developing our mental abilities; as well as avoiding activities, such as drunkenness and debauchery, that cloud our reason.

Self-cultivation and social duty are not considered to be at odds but are simply different aspects of the whole or the Tao. Because duty is associated with the Way,

*A polar bear clings to a melting iceberg. The effects of greenhouse emissions from industrial-
ized countries such as China and the United States, have contributed to global warming
throughout the world. The green Confucian movement, with its emphasis on our duty to act in
harmony with nature, has been active in promoting solutions to global warming.*
©Geostock/Getty Images

or Tao, by doing our duty we can achieve inner harmony and inner peace as well
as world peace. According to Confucius, only by cultivating a sense of duty and
harmony within ourselves can we hope to achieve peace in our family, in our society,
and in the world at large. People who neglect self-cultivation will not have a mind
that is in harmony and equilibrium. People who lack inner harmony are more likely
to make mistakes in their viewpoints, and this can lead to harm and disruption of
the harmony of the community.[25] Only those who honor the duty of fidelity and
maintain harmony within their families are suitable to be leaders of the state.

He who is in harmony with Nature hits the mark without effort and apprehends the

truth without thinking

—*The Analects of Confucius*

The Confucian emphasis on universal harmony includes the duty to act in
harmony with nature. This ideal has inspired the environmental movement in
Asia, including China, the world's largest emitter of greenhouse gases. Pan Yue,
China's vice minister for environmental protection from 2008 to 2015, has called
on traditional Chinese religions such as Confucianism, which promotes the idea
of humans and nature as being one, to promote environmental awareness and

ecological sustainability. For example, the green Confucian movement is concerned with global warming and rationally developing and conserving resources. In addition, the United Nations Kyoto Protocol for reducing CO_2 emissions was first proposed by the Japanese, a country where Confucianism and Buddhism are the two official state religions.

Exercises

1. In the *Analects* (see reading at end of chapter), Confucius argued that communitarian duties are more important than pursuing our individual self-interest. Ayn Rand, in contrast, thought that the best way to achieve a stable society and individual happiness was by putting our self-interest above communitarian values. Using examples from your own experience, discuss which argument is stronger.

2. The Confucian and the Buddhist approaches to world peace require both self-awareness and social awareness. Can people who are not at peace with themselves, their family, and their community still effectively promote world peace? Or, does world peace begin with self-cultivation? Support your answers. Discuss how both Confucius and Kant would answer these questions and why.

3. The duty of filial piety is also found in the biblical commandment requiring us to honor our parents. Does the duty of filial piety entail doing everything our parents tell us to do? How should we respond to abusive parents or to parents whose plans for our future conflict with our own? Relate your answer to the Confucian duty of self-cultivation and the duty of filial piety.

4. Discuss what Confucius would most likely think of the practice of American companies laying off American workers and outsourcing services and manufacturing to "third-world" countries. Discuss also what his position might be on our government's obligation, if any, to illegal immigrants working in the United States.

Is the Duty Not to Lie Absolute?

To be truthful (honest) in all deliberations, therefore, is a sacred and absolutely commanding decree of reason, limited by no expediency.

—IMMANUEL KANT, *Critique of Practical Reason* (1788)

A person of good will, according to Kant, always does his or her duty no matter what the consequences. Kant assumed that moral maxims regarding our duties, such as "keep your promises" and "do not lie," would never conflict with one another because they are based on reason. In his *Critique of Practical Reason* (1788), Kant adopted an absolutist position when it came to lying. He used the following example to illustrate his point that moral duties, such as the duty not to lie, are absolute:

> After you have honestly answered the murderer's question as to whether his intended victim is at home, it may be that he has slipped out so that he does not

come in the way of the murderer, and thus that the murder may not be committed. But if you had lied and said he was not at home when he had really gone out without your knowing it, and if the murderer had then met him as he went away and murdered him, you might justly be accused as the cause of his death. For if you had told the truth as far as you knew it, perhaps the murderer might have been apprehended by the neighbors while he searched that house and thus the deed might have been prevented. Therefore, whoever tells a lie, however well intentioned he might be, must answer for the consequences, however unforeseeable they were, and pay the penalty for them.[26]

According to Kant, not even the most altruistic intentions justify neglecting our duty not to lie, even a lie to save someone's life. In the above scenario if the murderer had found and killed his victim because of your honesty, you are not responsible for the death of the victim. Your only moral duty in this case was not to lie. The murderer bears full responsibility for his actions.

Confucius said: "I do not see what use a man can be put to, whose word cannot be trusted."

—*The Analects of Confucius*, 2.22

Confucius maintained that lying by leaders or public officials is particularly egregious since it demonstrates a lack of sincerity or trustworthiness. When subjects are lied to by their government, it erodes the bond between citizens and the government and damages people's trust in their country's leadership.

Sissela Bok: The Duty Not to Lie Is Prima Facie

But what about cases where it is almost certain that a lie will save many lives? Deontologist Sissela Bok, in her book *Lying*, suggests that although lying is generally wrong, there may be rare cases where the duty to lie conflicts with the more important duty to protect innocent human life. She defines a *lie* as "any intentionally deceptive message which is stated"[27] to distinguish lying as a moral action from unintentionally misleading someone because of ignorance of the truth or withholding the truth.

Bok discusses the case of vessels used to smuggle Jewish refugees out of Nazi-occupied areas as an example of a moral dilemma or a situation when lying might be morally required. A patrolling Nazi boat that happened to pass these vessels would call out and ask the captain of the vessel whether there were any Jews on board. If the captain responded no, the Nazis would let the vessel go on its way. If the captain said yes or refused to answer, the Nazis would board the vessel and shoot the Jews. Would it still be our moral duty, in this case, to tell the truth?

Connections

What are five steps for resolving a moral dilemma? *See Chapter 2, page 66.*

Kant would probably say yes. Bok disagrees. She asks: Is not preventing murder more important than telling the truth? By telling the truth, don't we bear at least some of the responsibility for the resulting deaths? Bok writes regarding Kant's position:

> "[I]t is a very narrow view of responsibility which does not also take some blame for a disaster one could easily have averted, no matter how much others are also to blame. A world where it is improper even to tell a lie to a murderer pursuing an innocent victim is not a world that many would find safe to inhabit."[28]

Although lying may be morally regrettable, Bok concludes that in some circumstances lying may be the only way to avert danger. In these cases, lying may be morally justified.

Bok is aware that most people lie too much and far too easily. As a deontologist, she acknowledges that we have a duty not to lie. On the other hand, unlike Kant, she also recognizes the importance of looking at consequences. However, she rejects utilitarianism as too simplistic to deal with complex situations when the outcome of one's actions is uncertain. She argues that we ought not to lie even if, by doing so, the net benefit will be the same as that brought about by not lying because lying restricts the autonomy of the person, such as Eric's wife in the opening scenario, who is the target of the lie. By lying, the liar gains power over the person he or she duped. Indeed, Bok maintains that deception may well outrank force as a means of getting people to acquiesce.

Excuses

Because we have a duty not to lie, we need to justify those times when we do lie. In her examination of the excuses we use, Bok notes that paternalism is one of the most common: the claim by the liars that they are benefiting the person they are duping. Parents, doctors, politicians, and other people in positions of power may be tempted to use this excuse to justify their lies, but in almost all cases, Bok notes, this claim stems from a failure to respect the dignity and intrinsic worth of other people whom liars regard as lower than themselves.

Another common excuse is that the lie is being told in the name of a higher good, as in the Milgram study. In this study, subjects were led to believe that they were delivering actual shocks to the learner. This, however, involved treating a person as a means in the name of the higher good—in this case, increasing our knowledge about human behavior. While a utilitarian might approve of this approach, treating a person who is a research subject as a means only is immoral because it violates the categorical imperative. Many parents lie to their young children about Santa Claus being real rather than a fantasy figure, excusing the lie on the grounds that it stimulates children's imagination. In fact, there is no connection between children's belief in Santa as a real person and their "fantasy

Connections

How did Milgram justify lying to the subjects and how did the subjects respond when they found they had been duped? *See Chapter 2, pages 30-31.*

scores," which measure a child's ability to engage in make-believe.[29] Indeed, by telling children Santa is a real person, parents may actually be negating the benefits of the use of the Santa Claus story in stimulating children's imagination.

People may also justify their lies on the grounds that the other person lied to them first. However, this in no way justifies lowering ourselves to lie. To do so is a violation of our own dignity as well as that of the other person. Bok also rejects the excuse that it is okay to lie to someone simply because he or she is our enemy. Lying to an enemy in wartime incurs the risk of increasing hostility. It also damages the trust of one's compatriots because lying to the enemy necessarily involves deceiving the general public. Therefore, even during wartime, lies are not justified except in situations of clear crisis.

Three Criteria

When deciding whether lying is morally justified in a particular case, Bok suggests that we use the following criteria: First, we should *look for another alternative to deception.* For example, will telling the truth work? If so, we ought to tell the truth. Second, we should *ask ourselves whether the lie can pass the test of publicity* by examining the lie from the viewpoint of others. Moral justification must be capable of being made public and accepted by reasonable persons. Finally, we should *engage in personal soul-searching.* Would we like to be lied to in this situation? If we would not like to be the person being duped, then we ought not do it to someone else.

Kant believed that, for moral duties to be universal, they have to be absolute; however, does this necessarily follow? Bok, like other deontologists, agrees with Kant that moral rules such as "do not lie" should be universal rather than relative to an individual or a culture. Everything being equal, we expect everyone to abide by this rule. If there were no rule against lying, society as we know it would soon come to a grinding halt. But would we also want to make the rule "do not lie" absolute—that is, binding in *every* case? Like Bok, most deontologists say no. They disagree with Kant that accepting a moral rule as universally valid entails going the extra step to claim that it must also be absolutely binding—that there can never be any exceptions. By doing this, critics claim, Kant has committed the fallacy of accident.

Connections

Why are absolutists most likely to commit the fallacy of accident? *See Chapter 2, page 57.*

Bok's Three Criteria for Deciding Whether a Particular Lie Is Justified

1. Is there a workable alternative to deception?
2. Does the lie pass the test of publicity: that is, would lying in this case be acceptable to reasonable people?
3. Would we like to be lied to in this situation?

Exercises

1. Using Bok's list of criteria, discuss whether the deception in each of the following case studies is morally justified:

    a. It is said that what matters most in Japan is not that everything is always perfect but that everything always *appears* to be perfect. Well-attended funerals and weddings are important to a family's honor, and some people are willing to pay "convenience agencies" anywhere between $200 and $1,500 for fake friends, family, and colleagues. The "guests" are briefed about what to say to bolster the image of the family. Young men who want to impress a woman friend with their bravery might also hire a punk to hassle them, so they can step in and challenge the punk, who then runs away. In Tokyo, one of the most densely populated places on earth, these deceptions are rarely discovered. Are these types of deceptions, undertaken to avoid shame or social stigma, morally justified?

    b. According to former abortion rights advocate and abortion clinic director Dr. Bernard Nathanson, the number of maternal deaths due to illegal abortions was intentionally exaggerated to gain public support for the legalization of abortion. "I confess that I knew the figures were totally false," he later wrote. "But in the 'morality' of our revolution, it was a useful figure, widely accepted."[30] Are lies like these justified if they are for the "greater good"? Support your answer.

    c. Government agencies will only approve a new drug after clinical trials have shown that subjects receiving the drug do significantly better than those receiving a placebo—an inert treatment such as a sugar pill. This process involves randomly dividing subjects into two groups. One group receives the treatment drug and the other a placebo. Neither knows which they are getting. Subjects receiving the placebo often improve because of their expectation that they are getting the drug. Using Bok's three criteria, discuss whether the practice of using placebos in medical research is morally justified.

       Many physicians also use placebos. For example, they may give a sugar pill to a woman suffering from headaches that the physician believes are psychosomatic. Discuss whether this practice is morally justified.

    d. Police sometimes use entrapment to catch criminals. In Atlantic City, New Jersey, the mugging of tourists returning from the casinos has become such a problem that the police have established an antimugging decoy squad. A police officer pretending to be a drunk and disorderly tourist is dropped off in a neighborhood where there have been recent muggings. As a result of the efforts of this decoy squad, muggings have dropped significantly. Is the deception justified? Why or why not?

2. Discuss the Stanley Milgram experiment in light of Bok's three criteria. How would you have responded to being lied to had you been a subject in the experiment?

Prima Facie Deontology

[N]o act is ever, in virtue of falling under some general description, necessarily right . . .

[because] moral acts . . . have different characteristics that tend to make them at the

same time prima facie right and prima facie wrong; there is probably no act, for

instance, which does good to anyone without doing harm to someone else, and vice

versa.

—W. D. Ross, *The Right and the Good* (1930), Ch. 2

Kant thought it would be possible to derive absolute moral maxims from his categorical imperative, but in fact, the application of the categorical imperative is not as easy as it first appears. One of the weaknesses of Kant's theory is that it does not give actual guidelines about how to word moral maxims. Instead of "do not lie," how about "do not lie except to save someone's life"? However, this wording is still too narrow; there may be other situations where lying is morally justified. To list all of these situations would be tedious, if not impossible. Furthermore, in the vast majority of situations, the maxim "do not lie" is a good moral rule.

W. D. Ross's Seven Prima Facie Duties

Most deontologists overcome this difficulty by saying that moral duties, while universal, are prima facie—a term popularized among moral philosophers by Scottish deontologist W. D. Ross (1877-1971). **Prima facie duties** are moral duties that may on occasion be overridden by stronger moral claims. Kant argued that duties are absolute because they are derived from reason, and it is therefore logically inconceivable for duties to conflict. Ross turned Kant's argument around. He argued that, by making a moral rule such as "do not lie" absolutely binding, the rule destroys itself because there are times when lying may be the right course of action.[31] From a logical point of view, duties cannot be absolute because there are situations where they may come into conflict. Because duties are context-bound, circumstances will affect which moral duties are most important in any given situation.

Ross pointed out that there are times when the *ought* or good and what is right are not the same. In other words, we may acknowledge that we *ought* not to lie, but situations may occur when it is *right* to lie. If lying seems the only way to save someone's life it would be the right thing to do, even though in principle we ought not to lie. Recognizing the *ought* as having universal validity does not necessarily entail that these principles are absolute or always the right ones to follow in every situation.

Ross identified seven prima facie duties, which he claimed we intuitively know (Table 10.1). These include the future-looking utilitarian duties of non-maleficence (minimize pain) and beneficence (increase happiness). These two duties are summarized in the Confucian duty of *jen* (humaneness). Ross also

TABLE 10.1   Ross's Seven Prima Facie Duties

Future-Looking Duties
>   **Beneficence** (the duty to do good acts and to promote happiness)
>   **Nonmaleficence** (the duty to do no harm and to prevent harm)

Duties Based on Past Obligations
>   **Fidelity** (duties arising from past commitments and promises)
>   **Reparation** (duties that stem from past harms we caused others)
>   **Gratitude** (duties based on past favors and unearned services)

Ongoing Duties
>   **Self-improvement** (the duty to improve our knowledge and virtue)
>   **Justice** (the duty to give each person equal consideration)

recognized two ongoing prima facie duties and three that stem from past actions or commitments. By "duties," Ross does not mean motivation but a duty to perform a certain action. We do not have a duty to feel grateful or to regret past harms that we have caused. Our duty is to perform certain actions—such as keeping promises and repaying favors—irrespective of our motives.

Although Ross agreed with the utilitarians that consequences matter when applying moral principles, like Bok he rejected the most basic assumption of utilitarian theory that only pleasure has intrinsic value. Ross argued instead that "no amount of pleasure equals the smallest amount of virtue." Utilitarian theory, he claimed, does not do full justice to the highly personal character of duty that Kant captured in his concept of the good will. Ross also found utilitarian theory inadequate because, by focusing only on future consequences, it neglects the past as well as ongoing duties. For example, a utilitarian may urge us to keep a promise, not because we made a past commitment to someone, but because by not keeping our promise we may damage future trust. Deontologists, on the other hand, believe that past actions do create moral obligations independently of any possible future consequences.

Connections

What is the greatest happiness principle? *See Chapter 8, page 243.*

The future-looking duties of nonmaleficence and beneficence have already been discussed in depth in the previous chapter on utilitarian theory. Following are discussions of the two ongoing duties and the three duties based on past obligations.

Self-Improvement

Self-improvement is the first of Ross's ongoing prima facie duties. By self-improvement, deontologists do not mean getting a new wardrobe or job training. **Self-improvement** as a moral duty entails constantly striving to improve our knowledge (wisdom) and our virtue.

The duty of self-improvement is important in virtually every ethical system. For both Confucius and Kant, self-improvement and the development of proper self-esteem are essential to the cultivation of the good will. The Hindu and

Buddhist concept of karma likewise involves the duty to cultivate within our-selves "peacefulness, self-control, austerity, purity, tolerance, honesty, knowledge, wisdom and religiousness." In Buddhist ethics, continuous self-improvement through right living and right thinking is the only way to reach moral excellence and enlightenment. Self-improvement does not end in this lifetime. Buddhists believe that we are repeatedly reincarnated until we reach moral enlightenment. Even the utilitarians believe that self-improvement, although not a direct duty, is important because a person with a benevolent and virtuous disposition is more likely to act in ways that benefit others.

Justice

The ongoing duty of **justice**, like self-improvement, is recognized by just about every moral system. A sense of justice emerges in children, regardless of their culture, at a very young age. Because justice is regarded by many philosophers as the most important duty of all, it will be discussed in greater detail in the following section.

Fidelity

Fidelity, the first of the three duties based on past obligations, stems from past commitments we have made. We keep promises, not because we are thinking of beneficial future consequences, but because of our past action in making the promise. Like promises, some commitments are voluntary, such as wedding vows or commitments to our friends, college, or career. For instance, a firefighter has a duty to attempt to save someone caught in a burning building, whereas we do not because we have not made a commitment to that profession.

The duty of fidelity can also stem from involuntary commitments. The duty of filial piety, for example, is very important in Confucian deontology. Yet most of us did not have a choice about who our parents would be or in what country we would live. Nevertheless, we still have a commitment to care for our elderly parents and to be loyal to our country (within the limits of moral decency).

When people do not keep their commitments, we may feel resentment and a sense of betrayal. Those who have a strong sense of fidelity to their past commitments are people whom we can trust. They remain loyal even when they are tempted to stray or to divulge secrets.

Fidelity that is not grounded in reason can lead us astray. People like Eichmann were willing to participate in the murder of thousands of Jews in the name of fidelity to their country. Gang members steal, maim, and kill, all in the name of loyalty to their gang. And suicide bombers kill civilians and themselves out of loyalty to a national or religious ideal. Because blind loyalty can be such a powerful sentiment, very few individuals will engage in whis-tle-blowing by informing on coworkers or friends who are engaged in immoral activities. Those who do blow the whistle often do so at considerable personal risk, including the risk of being ostracized by their coworkers and friends.

Connections

What virtues are considered most import-ant in Bud-dhism and in Confucian-ism? *See Chap-ter 12, page 412.*

Connections

What is the difference between resentment and moral out-rage and why are both con-sidered moral sentiments? *See Chapter 3, pages 84–86.*

When Linda Almonte, a division vice president at JPMorgan Chase, told her boss about possible fraud she had found in a major deal she was working on, instead of praising her, he fired her. "Employees get fired all the time for blowing the whistle," says Dana Gold, a fellow at the Government Accountability Project that advocates for whistleblowers. "Its a predicable phenomenon."[32]

Reparation

The duty of **reparation** is also based on past actions. Reparation requires that we make up for past harms that we have caused others. These harms may have been direct or indirect, individual or collective, intentional or unintentional. Reparation requires acknowledging our wrongdoing and taking action to compensate the person or persons we have harmed. Unlike retribution, which requires punishment for past wrongdoing, reparation serves to reestablish balance between people by having the wrongdoer make some sort of restitution to the harmed party. Automobile insurance companies, for example, act as our agents in making reparation to other people we have harmed by our careless driving. Some judges sentence minor offenders to do community service as a way of repaying the community for the harm they have caused to the people of the community.

The extent of reparation owed depends on the magnitude of the harm and the degree of our willing participation in bringing about the harm. For a small harm, a simple apology will generally suffice. Greater harms, such as causing someone grave bodily or mental injury or centuries of oppression visited upon a certain class of people, demand more extensive restitution. Almost fifty years following the incarceration during World War II of 120,000 people of Japanese ancestry living in the United States, Congress passed the Civil Liberties Act of 1988, better known as the Japanese American Redress Bill. The bill acknowledged that "a grave injustice was done" and mandated that Congress pay each victim of internment $20,000 in reparations.

In 2009 the U.S. Senate passed a resolution apologizing for slavery and racial discrimination. However, the resolution contained a disclaimer stating that it says nothing about supporting or authorizing reparation. In 2016, a group of leading human rights lawyers affiliated with the United Nations came out with a statement saying the history of slavery and racial discrimination against African Americans justifies the United States government paying reparations. The recommendation is not legally binding on the United States.[33] So far no reparations have been offered.

Connections
How does cultural relativism contribute to our tendency to marginalize certain groups of people? *See Chapter 6, pages 185–186.*

Gratitude

Gratitude is the third duty that is based on past actions. Our sense of gratitude is evoked when we receive gifts or unearned favors and services from others. Like reparation, gratitude is linked to the duty of justice. The demand for fair exchange or expressing gratitude for favors done is one of the first ways a child learns the duty of justice.

Gratitude is morally admirable in virtually every culture. Many psychologists and sociologists regard gratitude as an inborn emotional response. Sociologist Georg Simmel maintained that gratitude is the fundamental bond that forms and holds societies together.[34] The Roman statesman and philosopher Cicero called gratitude "the mother of all virtue." Not to show gratitude or to return a favor begrudgingly is seen as a great insult and an indication of a mean personality. The Omaha Indians of North America said of the ungrateful person: "He does not appreciate the gift. He has no manners."

While most Western deontologists maintain that we have duties only to other rational beings, some see gratitude as having more global implications. Ecologist and environmental philosopher Thomas Berry wrote in his book *The Dream of Earth*:

> If the earth does grow inhospitable toward human presence, it is primarily because we have lost our sense of courtesy toward the earth and its inhabitants, our sense of gratitude, our willingness to recognize the sacred character of habitat, our capacity for the awesome, for the numinous quality of every earthly reality.[35]

Gratitude stems from a natural impulse to maintain proper balance and equality. Ross maintained that gratitude is not merely a matter of sentiment but requires the use of our reason to know when it is morally appropriate. When the giver and the receiver are of equal status, the receiver is in a position to express gratitude in a way that re-creates and affirms the importance of balance in the relationship. It also serves to deepen the commitment to a relationship. The exchange of gifts as a means of strengthening relationships is probably most obvious among family, lovers, and close friends.

Give as much as you receive and all is for the best.

—MAORI (New Zealand) proverb

However, giving to another person who has less power and who is not able to return the favor can also be a means of dehumanizing and gaining power over the weaker person by creating in that person an ongoing sense of gratitude and obligation. Indeed, the charge of ingratitude is one of the most frequent accusations made by the rich against the poor.

Conflicting Duties

Any of these seven duties can come into conflict with another. Whenever we have a conflict or moral dilemma, we must carefully weigh each duty, decide which are the most compelling in that particular situation, and try to arrive at a resolution that honors as many of the duties as possible. Because moral duties are prima facie, they can come into conflict in a particular situation. We may promise our patient not to tell anyone that he is being treated for gonorrhea. However, this promise may conflict with the duty of nonmaleficence if we later discover that he has passed the infection on to his wife and possibly to other partners as well. When faced with a moral dilemma, we have to decide which of the competing moral duties is the most compelling under those particular circumstances.

Although Ross admitted that his list of prima facie duties may be incomplete, he also believed that all reflective, rational people would agree that these are moral duties. "There is nothing arbitrary about these prima facie duties," he wrote. "Each rests on a definite circumstance which cannot seriously be held to be without moral significance."[36]

Exercises

1. Discuss whether moral duties are prima facie or absolute. Does the concept of duties as prima facie weaken the moral law, as Kant feared it would? Support your answer.

2. Discuss whether the U.S. government, as well as corporations that have benefited from past slavery and racial discrimination, have a duty of reparation toward the descendants of slaves.

3. Working in small groups, select one of the case studies from exercise 1, page 330. When deciding if lying was morally justified in this case, were there other morally relevant considerations besides the consequences? If so, what were these considerations? Were they based on past or present duties? Which of the duties conflicted? How did you resolve the conflict? Was your solution the same as that of other people in your group? If not, were some of the solutions better than others? Support your answers.

4. Do you agree with Ross that all rational people would agree with his list of prima facie duties? Are there any other duties you would add to his list or any that you would remove? Explain.

5. Going back to the scenario at the beginning of the chapter, identify which moral duties are in conflict in this case. If the wife came to visit you and you found out that she was pregnant (given that gonorrhea can cause complications during pregnancy), would this alter your initial decision about how to respond to the husband's request? If so, explain why. Discuss how a deontologist would have most likely handled this situation.

6. In Edward Westermarck's book *The Origin and Development of the Moral Ideas* (vol. 2, p. 158), he argues that gratitude is only for equals. Those with less power do not owe the duty of gratitude to those who have much more than they do. Do you agree with him? Do people being served by social service agencies owe gratitude to those who support these services through their taxes, charitable donations, or volunteer work? Relate your answer to the victims of hurricanes such as Katrina and other natural or manmade disasters.

7. Using the steps outlined in Chapter 2, pages 66–67 for resolving moral dilemmas, try to resolve the following moral dilemmas or one of the dilemmas listed

at the end of that section, taking into consideration the different prima facie moral duties.

a. Rose and Joe have been living together in a monogamous relationship for the past two years—since the beginning of their sophomore year at college. They both agreed, at the time they moved in together, that either could leave the relationship at any time. However, Rose unexpectedly became pregnant. Because she is opposed to abortion, she has resigned herself to having the baby. When Rose is six months pregnant, Joe decides to leave. He leaves a short note saying, "It was fun while it lasted, but it's time for me to move on." What should Rose do?

b. You are a rookie police officer. You have been asked to serve as an under-cover agent to catch drug dealers on campus. This involves posing as a col-lege student. Should you accept the assignment?

c. Imagine that you are a college librarian who is approached by a federal agent with a search warrant for a student's records. Under the USA Patriot Act, the FBI can get a search warrant for a person's library records, even if they do not have probable cause to believe that this person has committed a crime.[37] You know that this student, who was born in Iran and moved here as a young child, is writing a paper on terrorism for his political science class. You believe that this student is kind and trustworthy and has no connection with any terrorist group. What should you do?

d. Pedro has been working for you for several years as a foreman on your ranch. He is an excellent worker and is well liked. Pedro has been living in the United States for thirty years and has a wife and three children, one of whom is valedictorian of her high school class. You find out by accident that Pedro came to the United States from Guatemala as an eleven-year-old with his illegal-immigrant parents. Pedro's wife, you discover, is also an illegal immigrant. However, their children, because they were born in the United States, are American citizens. Referring to Ross's list of moral duties, dis-cuss whether you should report Pedro and his wife to the immigration authorities.

The Duty of Justice

Justice is the first virtue of social institutions, as truth is of systems of thought.

—JOHN RAWLS, *A Theory of Justice* (1971), p. 3

The duty of justice is regarded by many philosophers as our most important duty as members of our community. The ongoing duty of justice requires that we give each person equal consideration. Because laws and social institutions are generally the agencies for balancing conflicting interests, the issue of justice is closely tied in with that of the good society. However, legal justice is not always consistent with moral justice. Not all laws are just, nor are all demands for justice addressed by laws. The duty of justice is generally subdivided by philosophers into two types: distributive and retributive justice.

Distributive Justice

Distributive justice refers to the fair distribution of benefits and burdens in a society. Benefits include education, highways, housing, economic opportunities, and police and fire protection. Taxes, jury duty, and military conscription are examples of shared burdens. Distributive justice presupposes that (1) there are conflicts of interest and (2) people have competing claims for certain limited or scarce societal goods.

For example, there are not enough well-paying jobs, college scholarships, or affordable housing. Therefore, the distribution of these goods is an issue of justice. Because there is a limited amount of money available for college scholarships, if you get a scholarship, someone else will be denied one. When there is not enough of something to satisfy everyone, how should the goods be distributed?

Distributive justice requires impartiality: treating equals equally and unequals in proportion to their individual differences. Because circumstances are rarely equal, disagreements frequently arise in the actual application of this principle. Simply giving everyone an equal share is not necessarily just, because not everyone shares the same concept of the good life nor does everyone have the same needs. If we gave everyone a small scholarship to go to college, for example, that would be unjust to those who want to go to college but need more than a small scholarship. It would also be a waste of money for those who have no desire to go to college or are multi-millionaires.

Connections

According to Marxists, why is Marxism a more just economic system than capitalism? *See Chapter 7, pages 221–222.*

Marxist philosophers emphasize need as the key criterion in distributive justice. They claim that the economic arrangements of the capitalist system are unjust because many people's basic needs go unmet while the capitalists continue to control more and more of the society's resources, including college degrees.

Aristotle, on the other hand, maintained that justice does not necessarily entail that everyone should get the same share of society's resources. He was opposed to democracy, preferring instead an oligarchy or an elitist political system based on merit (meritocracy). Those who have contributed most to the community, he argued, deserve the most in return.[38]

Most moral philosophers believe that both need and merit should be taken into consideration. The issue of merit or achievement is particularly relevant for the distribution of goods such as scholarships, rewards for achievement, and skilled jobs. People who have worked hard deserve a raise or a promotion simply because they have done a good job, regardless of their need for additional income. Awarding high-paying jobs and college scholarships solely on the basis of merit, on the other hand, is considered unjust by some philosophers because not all of us have the same opportunities to achieve educational and professional goals. They reject Aristotle's elitist concept of justice, pointing out that past injustices and economic disadvantages have limited the opportunities of marginalized groups of people.

In a just society, we all deserve a fair opportunity to pursue our goals. To create fair opportunities, affirmative action programs have been established to compensate disadvantaged people for past deprivations. Some people are opposed to affirmative action; they claim that it can create resentment among White men, lower the quality of work, and turn minorities and women into "petitioners for favors."[39] Even though the U.S. Supreme Court has upheld the right of colleges to consider race in admissions, several colleges and state high-er-education systems, including Michigan, Texas, Washington, Connecticut, Arizona, Nebraska, New Hampshire, and California, have banned affirmative action in admissions. As a result, there has been a 35 percent drop in enrollment of underrepresented minorities at many competitive colleges.[40] The question remains, if not through affirmative action, how can we best distribute fair opportunities in college admissions to groups of people who have been disadvantaged?

John Rawls: A Theory of Justice

Deontologist John Rawls (1921–2002) in his book *A Theory of Justice* argued that justice demands not only impartiality but treating people fairly and in pro-portion to their needs as well as their merits. There are inequalities of birth and natural endowment (what Rawls called the *natural lottery*) and historical circum-stances that are undeserved but create disadvantages for certain people. People who have lower than average intelligence, or who are not born into wealth, are systematically excluded from enjoying the opportunities that others take for granted. Simply redistributing the wealth through welfare and charity does not solve the root problem, as long as the underlying conditions that disadvantage certain people still exist.

Rawls's solution to this problem was to found justice upon a social contract. To establish a social contract that is unbiased and based on impartiality, he uses a conceptual device that he termed the *veil of ignorance.* Under the **veil of igno-rance**, each person is ignorant of the advantages and disadvantages—including, for example, economic standing, gender, intelligence, health, place of birth—that he or she will receive in this life. This prevents people from promoting principles of justice that are biased in their favor. Rawls wrote:

> In justice as fairness the original position of equality corresponds to the state of nature in the traditional theory of the social contract. This original position . . . is understood as a purely hypothetical situation characterized so as to lead to a certain conception of justice. Among the essential features of this situation is that no one knows his place in society, his class position or social status, nor does any know his fortune in the distribution of natural assets and ability, his intelligence, strength, and the like. . . . The principles of justice are chosen behind a veil of ignorance. This ensures that no one is advantaged or disadvantaged in the choice of principles by the outcome of natural chance or the contingency of social circum-stances. Since all are similarly situated and no one is able to design principles to favor his particular circumstances, the principles of justice are the result of a fair agreement or bargain.[41]

Demonstrators face off with riot police during a Vietnam War protest in Washington, DC, May 21, 1972. One hundred and seventy-three of the demonstrators were arrested during a violent confrontation with the police.
©Archive Photos/Stringer/Getty Images

Discussion Questions

Connections

What is the utilitarian position on military conscription? *See Chapter 8, pages 266-267.*

1. In addition to the belief that war against the Vietnamese was an unjust war, many of the demonstrators were protesting the injustice of the military draft system which gave deferments to college students, thus placing an unfair burden on economically disadvantaged youth. Applying Rawls' second principle of justice, critically evaluate this argument. Discuss what position Aristotle would most likely take on this issue.

2. What other prima facie moral duties, such as fidelity to one's country and nonmaleficence, are involved in serving in the military? Explain. Using the 5-step method for solving a moral dilemma on page 68, discuss what you would do if you were conscripted to serve in a war that you believed to be unjust.

Under these conditions of impartiality, Rawls argues that all rational people would agree upon the following two *principles of justice:*

First: Each person is to have an equal right to the most extensive basic liberty compatible with a similar liberty for others.

Second: Social and economic inequalities are to be arranged so that they are both (a) reasonably expected to be to everyone's advantage, and (b) attached to positions and offices open to all.[42]

Using these two principles, Rawls suggests that the primary social goods be distributed equally. **Primary social goods** include social goods, such as housing, food, police protection, and education, that are necessary to pursue our liberty rights and our concept of the good life. Nonessential goods, on the other hand, do not need to be distributed equally as long as the inequalities are still consistent with the rights of others to pursue their liberty and enjoy fair opportunity.

One of the problems with Rawls's theory is determining what constitutes a natural disadvantage: Aren't almost all of our abilities and disabilities, at least to some extent, a result of the "natural lottery"? For example, it has been documented that taller people and more attractive people have an advantage in the job market. Studies also show that oldest and only children tend to be more highly motivated as adults and make better leaders. Most presidents of the United States have been either an oldest child or oldest son. Should appearance or birth order be considered undeserved disadvantages that create a right to some form of public assistance or affirmative action in hiring?

Rawls's assumption that all rational people would, under the veil of ignorance, agree upon these two principles has also been called into question. Some people might be willing to take greater risks, and others might prefer a less egalitarian distribution of social goods. Despite these criticisms, Rawls's theory of justice has provided a powerful tool for reforming social institutions and has been used to develop policy in areas such as health care reform, education, and the economy.

Retributive Justice

Retributive justice, the second type of justice, involves punishment for wrongdoing. Punishment for a crime, according to most deontologists, is our duty because the moral order requires that the guilty should suffer in proportion to the magnitude of their crime. Retributive justice, according to Kant, belongs to the judicial or penal system, rather than private judgment.

Retributive justice is not the same as revenge, which is based on sentiment rather than reason. Nor should it be based on utilitarian calculations of the consequences of punishment in specific cases. Kant writes:

> The penal law [retributive justice] is a categorical imperative; and woe to him who creeps through the serpent-windings of utilitarianism to discover some advantage that may discharge him from the justice of punishment. . . .

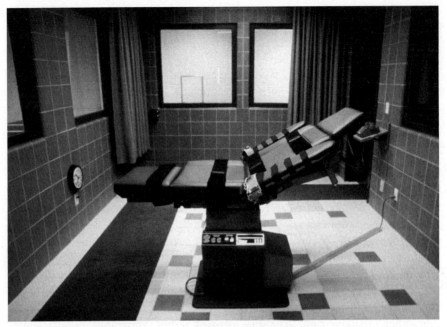

China, Iran, Saudi Arabia, Iraq, and the United States have the highest death penalty rates in the world. The United States is the only Western democracy with the death penalty. The use of the death penalty in the United States has been on the decline since 1999.
©Scott Olson/Getty Images

Discussion Questions

1. Kant supported the death penalty on the grounds that it was the only way to satisfy the requirement of retributive justice as well as to affirm the murderer's dignity by acknowledging his responsibility for his crime. Utilitarian Jeremy Bentham, in contrast, opposed the death penalty because, he argued, the deliberate infliction of suffering on a person who has committed an evil only adds more suffering and evil to the world. Discuss and debate both positions on the issue.

2. Criminal defense attorney Clarence Darrow (1857–1938) was an opponent of the death penalty. He believed that human behavior is determined by our environment and circumstances. Since it is out of our control, it does not deserve to be punished. Discuss Darrow's position in light of the discussion on determinism and moral responsibility on page 80. Discuss also how Kant would respond to Darrow's position.

It is the principle of equality, by which the pointer of the scale of justice is made to incline no more to the one side than the other. It may be rendered by saying that the undeserved evil which any one commits on another, is to be regarded as perpetrated on himself. Hence it may be said: "If you slander another, you slander yourself . . . if you strike another, you strike yourself; if you kill another, you kill yourself." This is the right of retaliation (jus talionis); and properly understood, it is the only principle which in regulating a public court, as distinguished from mere private judgment, can definitely assign both the quality and quantity of a just penalty.[43]

Unlike Kant, some moral philosophers regard retributive justice as neither rational nor self-evident. Utilitarians oppose retribution because it involves the deliberate infliction of pain and deprivation. Punishment can only be morally justified, according to utilitarians, on the grounds of the future-looking duties of beneficence and nonmaleficence. Thus, punishment should be used only when the beneficial effects of it outweigh the evil of inflicting pain on a sentient being.

The impersonal demands of retributive justice can also come into conflict with care ethics and the moral principle of ahimsa (nonviolence). In addition, a justice system based on punishment has been criticized for simply increasing violence in the world and in the heart of the wrongdoer rather than restoring justice. Jesus, in particular, spoke out against retributive justice (*lex talionis*).

Connections

What does it mean to practice ahimsa? *See Chapter 3, pages 82-83.*

> You have heard that it was said "An eye for an eye and a tooth for a tooth." But I say to you, Do not resist one who is evil. But if anyone strikes you on the right cheek, turn to him the other also.
>
> —MATTHEW 5:38-39

Retributive justice remains one of the most controversial moral duties. Kant's notion of harming another person as a means of showing respect for that person seems odd to some people. Most people feel guilty when they do wrong, yet guilt does not entail an expectation of punishment. Indeed, fear of punishment will often lead to deception regarding our wrongdoing rather than accepting blame. Also, the negative response of most wrongdoers to punishment, including increased resentment and lowered self-esteem, should cause us to reexamine the belief that retributive justice is a moral duty.

Exercises

1. Discuss Kant's claim that retributive justice is a moral duty. Does retributive justice justify capital punishment, or should there be limits on retribution? Support your answer.

2. Justice Antonio Scalia opposed affirmative action in the 2008 *Fisher v. The University of Texas at Austin* case, arguing that "really competent blacks would win admission without special considerations . . . to get them into the University of Texas where they do not do well, as opposed to having them go to a less-advanced school, a slower track school where they do well." Critically analyze Scalia's position. In particular, does it meet the requirements of the duty of distributive justice? Explain.

3. How should income be distributed? Is it fair that people who have been working at a job the longest, yet no longer have dependent children, get paid more than younger workers who usually have greater needs—such as a family to support and a mortgage to pay? Discuss how we should balance merit and need in distributing economic resources.

4. Rawls considers disabilities as part of the "natural lottery." But our talents and abilities are also part of the natural lottery. Discuss how, if at all, these factors should be taken into consideration in distributing societal good. Relate your answer to your own life circumstances.

5. Some nations have natural advantages over others. Discuss whether having a natural advantage creates in wealthy nations a duty of justice to share their wealth with nations that are at a natural disadvantage.

6. Certain groups of people, such as Native Americans and African Americans in the United States, have been severely disadvantaged in the past by social institutions that discriminated against them. Discuss whether society has a moral duty to redistribute social goods through programs such as affirmative action to groups of people whose ancestors have been gravely disadvantaged in the past. Discuss your answer in light of Rawls's two principles of justice.

7. To what extent is it morally permissible for a society to use coercion to force people to share the societal burdens? As taxpayers, should we be held responsible for supplying the needs of others—through welfare and disability programs—who are not working or who cannot support themselves? Support your answers.

Critique of Deontology

1. *Western deontologists have been accused of promoting an abstract moral philosophy that sacrifices community in the name of individual autonomy.* Kant's assumption that people are basically autonomous, private units who are free to carry out the moral law fails to take into consideration that we are all part of a wider social network of relationships.

German philosopher Georg Hegel (1770–1831) questioned Kant's belief that individual autonomy and rationality are possible prior to membership in an ethical community. He argued that our sense of self cannot exist outside of personal interaction and community. Like Confucius, Hegel believed that the unhappiness of one is the unhappiness of us all. Hegel compared modern society to a zoo filled with animals, each in its own cage with no community spirit. Indeed, Kant's emphasis on individualism has been suggested as a contributing

Connections

What do feminist care ethicists mean when they say "caring is a active virtue"? *See Chapter 12, pages 408–409.*

factor to our modern-day sense of alienation and a society where many of us live isolated lives.

   2. *Deontologists tend to focus too much on justice and abstract principles and ignore moral sentiments such as caring.* The deontologists' concern with justice and abstract principles of duty has been criticized by feminist care ethicists such as Carol Gilligan and Nel Noddings as a distinctively male approach that ignores caring relationships. Although studies have shown that deontology is not a distinctly male approach, feminist care ethicists nevertheless raise an important point. Practical morality is constructed dialectically through interaction with others, not merely by an autonomous examination of the dictates of our reason. By reducing morality to one component—moral judgment—deontology fails to take into account the influence of relationships and the role of moral sensitivity in informing our moral values. Knowing what is right on the level of reason does not necessarily mean that we will do what is right. Reason alone, without the ability to sympathize with others, seems unable to produce the categorical imperative. Abstract rational principles, care ethicists argue, are insufficient to motivate us or provide us with concrete guides to action. History has, time and again, shown how easy it is for us to set aside these abstract formal principles and slip back into dogmatism, violence, and intolerance.

> While an ethic of justice proceeds from the premise of equality—that everyone should be treated the same—an ethic of care rests on the premise of nonviolence—that no one should be hurt.
>
> —Carol Gilligan, *In a Different Voice* (1982)

   Nietzsche likewise accused Kant's moral rationalism of being hostile to life by its rejection of the natural passions and instincts of life.[44] Nietzsche argued that true morality is dominated by an instinct for life, not abstract reason. Nietzsche wrote:

> [Virtue] must be our own invention, our most necessary self-expression. . . . The fundamental laws of self-preservation and growth demand the opposite—that everyone invent his own virtue, his own categorical imperative. A people perishes when it confuses its duty with duty in general.[45]

   Nietzsche's criticism, however, is partly based on a misperception of the concept of duty. Kant and other deontologists such as Confucius and Ross did not believe that doing one's duty is antithetical to personal growth and relationships or to the expression of our natural passions and instincts. They were aware that the love of humanity in general is not a good substitute for particular friendships and relationships. There is no logical contradiction involved, for example, in universalizing a maxim that states: "In life-threatening situations, we should first, all other things being equal, try to save ourselves and those who

Connections

Why did Nietzsche regard the ubermensch to be a paradigm of the virtuous person? *See Chapter 12, pages 414–415.*

are members of our immediate family." In fact, rational people would hardly be willing to universalize a maxim that states: "I ought to do, or be willing to do, for anyone what I do for my family and friends." In other words, a justice-based ethics, as Gilligan refers to deontology, and a care-based ethics are not necessarily incompatible with each other.

3. *Deontology may be compatible with consequentialist theories.* Most deontologists believe that consequences, though not as important as duty, should be taken into consideration. Kant's denial that consequences are morally relevant has been criticized by utilitarians as well as other deontologists. Indeed, utilitarian John Stuart Mill pointed out that the categorical imperative, by its very nature, requires that we take consequences into account when adopting moral rules. According to Mill, rational people would not universalize a moral rule that would harm, rather than benefit, the moral community:

> When Kant propounds as the fundamental principle of morals, "So act, that the rule of conduct might be adopted as a law by all rational beings," he virtually acknowledges that the interest of mankind collectively . . . must be in the mind of the agent when conscientiously deciding on the morality of the act. Otherwise he uses words without a meaning; . . . To give any meaning to Kant's principle, the sense put upon it must be, that we ought to shape our conduct by a rule which all rational beings might adopt with benefit to their collective interests.[46]

Despite its shortcomings, the strengths and richness of deontology far outshine its weaknesses. In any case, it would be a mistake to consider any philosophical theory, or even any scientific theory, as a finished or complete statement about a particular phenomenon. One of the characteristics of a good theory is that it is open-ended and generates further thought. In this respect, deontology has made important contributions to the study of ethics.

Although Kant's moral philosophy, because of its formal character and lack of specificity, suffered a serious decline in popularity among philosophers during the first half of the twentieth century, it is now making a comeback. Few philosophers accept Kant's moral philosophy in its entirety; still, Kantian deontology is one of the most, if not *the* most, influential and fertile moral philosophies in modern history. Kant's thinking has had a major influence on modern European and American moral philosophers such as Sissela Bok, John Rawls, and W. D. Ross; it has also left its mark on philosophers around the world. Deontology, with its emphasis on the dignity of the individual, has also had a major influence on the development of rights ethics in both Western and non-Western philosophies.

Exercises

1. Read the following quote from André Gide's novel *The Immoralist*:

   "If there's one thing I detest it's a man of principles," [Michel said].

   "You're right," Menalque answered, laughing, "he is the most detestable kind of person in the world. You can't expect any kind of sincerity from him, for he only does what his principles have ordered him to do, or else he considers what he does as a transgression."

Are people of principle detestable, as Michel and Menalque claim? Or are they the best and sincerest of people, as Kant claimed? Support your answer.

2. Evaluate the claim of care ethicists that deontology fails to take into consideration the role of sentiments in making moral decisions. Discuss ways in which deontology might be integrated with care ethics.

3. Nietzsche claimed that Kant's approach to moral education, with its emphasis on duty, promotes a boring herd morality. Nietzsche wrote: "'What is the task of all higher education?' To turn men into machines. 'What are the means?' Man must learn to be bored. 'How is that accomplished?' By means of the concept of duty . . . 'Who is the perfect man?' The civil servant. 'Which philosophy offers the highest formula for the civil servant?' Kant's."[47] Critically analyze Nietzsche's claim that a deontological approach to moral education turns people into machines.

Summary

1. *Deontology* is a popular approach to ethics in world philosophies and religions.

2. According to deontologists, for an action to have moral worth, it must be done from a sense of *duty*.

3. Deontologists disagree about the ultimate source of moral duties—whether it is reason or intuition.

4. The difference between utilitarianism and deontology is, in part, one of emphasis; utilitarians regard consequences, rather than duty, as most important for morality.

5. Confucian deontology emphasizes community responsibility over individual autonomy.

6. Duty and the *ought* were important themes in seventeenth- and eighteenth-century European Enlightenment ethics.

7. Immanuel Kant is the most influential Western deontologist. Kant wanted to establish a groundwork or foundation for morality that would explain why we ought to behave morally. He claimed that reason provides the foundation of morality.

8. A *hypothetical imperative* tells us that we ought to do something if we want to achieve a certain result. A *categorical imperative* states that we ought to do something regardless of the consequences.

9. Kant's categorical imperative states that we should be willing to universalize moral maxims and that we should never treat a person only as a means to an end.

10. Kant's categorical imperative is a *formal principle*—that is, it lacks specific content.

11. According to Kant, only rational beings are able to act freely or autonomously. Therefore, only rational beings such as humans have intrinsic moral worth. Nonhuman animals are not part of the moral community or kingdom-of-ends.

12. A person of *good will* acts out of an autonomous sense of duty. This sense of duty, according to Kant, stems from reason.

13. One of our primary moral duties is the development of self-respect or proper self-esteem.

14. Kant claimed that moral duties are *absolute* duties and that there are no exceptions to this rule.

15. Sissela Bok and W. D. Ross claim that moral duties are prima facie. A *prima facie duty* is a moral duty that may be overridden on occasion by stronger moral claims.

16. Bok argues that it may be permissible, under certain circumstances, to break a moral rule such as "do not lie."

17. Ross lists seven prima facie duties: *Beneficence* and *nonmaleficence* are future-oriented duties; *fidelity, reparation,* and *gratitude* are duties based on past actions; *self-improvement* and *justice* are ongoing duties.

18. There are two types of justice: retributive justice and distributive justice. *Retributive justice* requires punishment for wrongdoing. *Distributive justice* is concerned with the fair distribution of social goods.

19. John Rawls maintains that distributive justice should be based on impartiality and fairness.

20. Georg Hegel rejected Kantian deontology as focusing too much on individual autonomy and ignoring the importance of community.

21. Feminist care ethicists criticize moral theories such as deontology that privilege reason.

 # The Analects of Confucius

James Legge, Translator

Book I

CHAP. IV. The philosopher Tsang said, I daily examine myself on three points:—whether, in transacting business for others, I may have been not faithful;—whether, in intercourse with friends, I may have been not sincere;—whether I may have not mastered and practised the instructions of my teacher.

CHAP. VIII. 1. The Master said, "If the scholar be not grave, he will not call forth any veneration, and his learning will not be solid. 2. Hold faithfulness and sincerity as first principles. 3. Have no friends not equal to yourself. 4. When you have faults, do not fear to abandon them."

Reprinted From Legge, James. *The Chinese Classics (Confucian Analects)* (Urbana, Illinois: Project Gutenberg). Retrieved May 22, 2017, from http://www.gutenberg.org/ebooks/3330?msg=welcome_stranger.

Book II

CHAP. I. The Master said, "He who exercises government by means of his virtue may be compared to the north polar star, which keeps its place and all the stars turn towards it."

CHAP. III. 1. The Master said, "If the people be led by laws, and uniformity sought to be given them by punishments, they will try to avoid the punishment, but have no sense of shame. 2. If they be led by virtue, and uniformity sought to be given them by the rules of propriety, they will have the sense of shame, and moreover will become good."

Book IV

CHAP. II. The Master said, "Those who are without virtue cannot abide long either in a condition of poverty and hardship, or in a condition of enjoyment. The virtuous rest in virtue; the wise desire virtue."

CHAP. V. 1. The Master said, "Riches and honours are what men desire. If it cannot be obtained in the proper way, they should not be held. Poverty and meanness are what men dislike. If it cannot be avoided in the proper way, they should not be avoided. 2. If a superior man abandons virtue, how can he fulfil the requirements of that name? 3. The superior man does not, even for the space of a single meal, act contrary to virtue. In moments of haste, he cleaves to it. In seasons of danger, he cleaves to it."

Book V

CHAP. XV. The Master said of Tsze-ch'an that he had four of the characteristics of a superior man: -- in his conduct of himself, he was humble; in serving his superiors, he was respectful; in nourishing the people, he was kind; in ordering the people, he was just.

Book XII

CHAP. X. 1. Tsze-chang having asked how virtue was to be exalted, and delusions to be discovered, the Master said, "Hold faithfulness and sincerity as first principles, and be moving continually to what is right; -- this is the way to exalt one's virtue. 2. You love a man and wish him to live; you hate him and wish him to die. Having wished him to live, you also wish him to die. This is a case of delusion. 3. It may not be on account of him being rich, yet you come to make a difference."

Book XVI

CHAP. X. Confucius said, "The superior man has nine things which are subjects with him of thoughtful consideration. In regard to the use of his eyes, he is anxious to see clearly. In regard to the use of his ears, he is anxious to hear distinctly. In regard to his countenance, he is anxious that it should be benign. In regard to his demeanor, he is anxious that it should be respectful. In regard to his speech, he is anxious that it should be sincere. In regard to his doing of business, he is anxious that it should be reverently careful. In regard to what he doubts about, he is anxious to question others. When he is angry, he thinks of the difficulties (his anger may involve him in). When he sees gain to be got, he thinks of righteousness."

Fundamental Principles of the Metaphysic of Ethics

Immanuel Kant

Nothing can possibly be conceived in the world, or even out of it, which can be called good without qualification, except a Good Will. Intelligence, wit, judgment, and the other *talents* of the mind, however they may be named, or courage, resolution, perseverance, as qualities of temperament, are undoubtedly good and desirable in many respects; but these gifts of nature may also become extremely bad and mischievous if the will which is to make use of them, and which, therefore, constitutes what is called *character*, is not good. . . .

To be beneficent when we can is a duty; and besides this, there are many minds so sympathetically constituted that, without any other motive of vanity or self-interest, they find a pleasure in spreading joy around them, and can take delight in the satisfaction of others so far as it is their own work. But I maintain that in such a case an action of this kind, however proper, however amiable it may be, has nevertheless no true moral worth, but is on a level with other inclinations, e.g. the inclination to honour, which, if it is happily directed to that which is in fact of public utility and accordant with duty, and consequently honourable, deserves praise and encouragement, but not esteem. For the maxim lacks the moral import, namely, that such actions be done *from duty*, not from inclination. . . .

. . . [A]n action done from duty derives its moral worth, *not from the purpose* which is to be attained by it, but from the maxim

by which it is determined, and therefore does not depend on the realization of the object of the action, but merely on the *principle of volition* by which the action has taken place, without regard to any object of desire. . . . It cannot lie anywhere but in the *principle of the will* without regard to the ends which can be attained by the action. . . .

. . . *Duty is the necessity of acting from respect for the law.* I may have *inclination* for an object as the effect of my proposed action, but I cannot have *respect* for it, just for this reason, that it is an effect and not an energy of will. . . . The pre-eminent good which we call moral can therefore consist in nothing else than *the conception of law* in itself, *which certainly is only possible in a rational being,* in so far as this conception, and not the expected effect, determines the will. This is a good which is already present in the person who acts accordingly, and we have not to wait for it to appear first in the result.

But what sort of law can that be, the conception of which must determine the will, even without paying any regard to the effect expected from it, in order that this will may be called good absolutely and without qualification? As I have deprived the will of every impulse which could arise to it from obedience to any law, there remains nothing but the universal conformity of its actions to law in general, which alone is to serve the will as a principle, *i.e.* I am never to act otherwise than so *that I could also will that my maxim should become a universal law.* . . . The common reason of men in its practical judgments perfectly coincides with this, and always has in view the principle here suggested. . . .

From what has been said, it is clear that all moral conceptions have their seat and origin

Fundamental Principles of the Metaphysic of Ethics, translated by Thomas Kingsmill Abbott (London: Longman's, Green and Co., Ltd., 1873), pp. 30–39, 44–59, and 71. Notes have been omitted. (To read Kant's book online, go to www.bartleby.com/32/601.html.)

completely *à priori* in the reason, and that, moreover, in the commonest reason just as truly as in that which is in the highest degree speculative; that they cannot be obtained by abstraction from any empirical, and therefore merely contingent knowledge; that it is just this purity of their origin that makes them worthy to serve as our supreme practical principle, . . .

. . . [T]here is an imperative which commands a certain conduct immediately, without having as its condition any other purpose to be attained by it. This imperative is Categorical. It concerns not the matter of the action, or its intended result, but its form and the principle of which it is itself a result; and what is essentially good in it consists in the mental disposition, let the consequence be what it may. This imperative may be called that of Morality. . . .

. . . [W]hen I conceive a categorical imperative I know at once what it contains. For as the imperative contains besides the law only the necessity that the maxims shall conform to this law, while the law contains no conditions restricting it, there remains nothing but the general statement that the maxim of the action should conform to a universal law, and it is this conformity alone that the imperative properly represents as necessary.

There is therefore but one categorical imperative, namely this: *Act only on that maxim whereby thou canst at the same time will that it should become a universal law.*

Now if all imperatives of duty can be deduced from this one imperative as from their principle, then, although it should remain undecided whether what is called duty is not merely a vain notion, yet at least we shall be able to show what we understand by it and what this notion means. . . .

If then there is a supreme practical principle or, in respect of the human will, a categorical imperative, it must be one which, being drawn from the conception of that which is necessarily an end for every one because it is *an end in itself,* constitutes an *objective* principle of will, and can therefore serve as a universal practical law. The foundation of this principle is: *rational nature exists as an end in itself.* Man necessarily conceives his own existence as being so: so far then this is a *subjective* principle of human actions. But every other rational being regards its existence similarly, just on the same rational principle that holds for me: so that it is at the same time an objective principle, from which as a supreme practical law all laws of the will must be capable of being deduced. Accordingly the practical imperative will be as follows: *So act as to threat humanity, whether in thine own person or in that of any other, in every case as an end withal, never as means only.*

Discussion Questions

1. Analyze Kant's argument in his reading that reason provides the foundation of morality. Do you agree with Kant that all rational people would concur with the categorical imperative? Is it logically necessary, as Kant claimed, that all moral imperatives be categorically (universally) binding? Support your answers. Discuss also how Confucius might answer these questions.

2. Kant tends to focus on the individual while Confucius focuses on the community. Discuss whether their two approaches are in conflict or whether they complement each other. Support your answer using specific examples.

Notes

1. Immanuel Kant, *Critique of Practical Reason*, trans. T. K. Abbott (London: Longmans, Green, 1909), p. 260.
2. *Bhagavad Gita*, ch. 2. v. 31, in *A Sourcebook in Asian Philosophy*, ed. John M. Koller and Patricia Koller (New York: Macmillan, 1991).
3. *Providence Journal*, May 6, 1989, p. 1. See also Steven Novella, "The Ethics of Deception in Medicine," *Science-Based Medicine*, January 23, 2008.
4. W. D. Ross, *The Right and the Good* (Oxford: Oxford University Press, 1930), p. 41.
5. John Stuart Mill, "Utilitarianism," in *Utilitarianism and Other Writings*, ed. Mary Warnock (New York: Meridian, 1962), p. 304.
6. Immanuel Kant, *The Moral Law: Groundwork of the Metaphysic of Morals*, trans. H. J. Paton (London: Routledge & Kegan Paul, 1991), p. 64.
7. Hannah Arendt, *Eichmann in Jerusalem: A Report on the Banality of Evil* (New York: Penguin, 1976), p. 193.
8. Kant, *The Moral Law*, p. 68.
9. Melinda Wenner Moyer, "Rudeness on the Internet," *Scientific American*, August 20, 2012.
10. As quoted by Lewis White Beck in his "Foreword" to Immanuel Kant's *Lectures on Ethics* (Indianapolis, IN: Hackett, 1775–1780/1963), p. ix.
11. Quoted in Judith A. Boss, "Volunteer Community Service Work and Its Effect on the Moral Development of Ethics Students," thesis, University of Rhode Island (M.S.1991), p. 77.
12. Kant, *The Moral Law*, p. 39.
13. Immanuel Kant, "Duties to Oneself," in *Lectures on Ethics* (Indianapolis: Hackett, 1775–1780/1963), p. 118.
14. Ibid., p. 117.
15. Immanuel Kant, "Proper Self-Respect," in *Lectures on Ethics*, p. 127.
16. M. McLaughlin, "Embedded Identities: Enabling Balance in Urban Contexts," in *Identity and Inner-City Youth: Beyond Ethnicity and Gender*, ed. S. B. Heath and W. W. McLaughlin (New York: Teacher's College Press, 1993), p. 54; and Ashley L. Merianos et al., "The Impact of Self-Esteem and Social Support on College Students' Mental Health," *American Journal of Health Studies*, vol. 2, no. 1 (2013): 27–34.
17. Norman M. Bradburn, *The Structure of Psychological Well-Being* (Chicago, IL: Aldine, 1969), p. 144.
18. Allen N. Mendler, *Smiling at Yourself: Educating Young Children about Stress and Self-Esteem* (Santa Cruz, CA: Network, 1990), p. xvi.
19. William Damon, *Greater Expectations* (New York: Free Press, 1995), p. 73.
20. Joan Didion, "Trouble in Lakewood," *New Yorker*, July 26, 1993, p. 50.
21. *The Commentary of Tseng*, as quoted in *A Sourcebook in Asian Philosophy*, ed. John M. Koller and Patricia Koller (New York: Macmillan, 1991), p. 3.
22. Chi Hsi, "Selected Writings," in *Sourcebook in Asian Philosophy*, ed. Koller and Koller, p. 548.
23. Chan Wing-tsit, *A Source Book in Chinese Philosophy* (Princeton, NJ: Princeton University Press, 1963), bk. 3:1.
24. Confucius, as quoted in Ben Raeburn, *Treasury for the Free World* (Freeport, NY: Books for Libraries, 1946).
25. Chu Hsi, "Selected Writings," pp. 542–543.
26. Immanuel Kant, *Critique of Practical Reason and Other Writings in Moral Philosophy*, trans. Lewis White Beck (Chicago, IL: University of Chicago Press, 1949), p. 348.
27. Sissela Bok, *Lying* (New York: Pantheon Books, 1978), p. 14.
28. Ibid., p. 44.
29. Judith Boss, "Is Santa Corrupting Our Children's Morals?" *Free Inquiry*, vol. 11, no. 4 (Fall 1991): 24–27.
30. Bernard N. Nathanson and Richard N. Ostling, *Aborting America* (Garden City, NY: Doubleday, 1979), p. 193.
31. W. D. Ross, *Kant's Ethical Theory* (Oxford, England: Clarendon Press, 1954).

32. "J. P. Morgan Chase Whistleblower 'Essentially Suicide' to Stand Up to Bank," *HuffPost Business*, May 7, 2012, www.huffingtonpost.com/2012/05/07/linda-almonte-jpmorgan-chase-whistleblower.
33. Ishaan Tharoor, "U.S. Owes Black People Reparations for a History of 'Racial Terrorism' says U.N. Panel," *Washington Post*, September 27, 2016.
34. Georg Simmel, "Faithfulness and Gratitude," in *The Sociology of Georg Simmel*, ed. and trans. Kurt H. Wolff (New York: Free Press of Glencoe, 1964), pp. 379–395.
35. Thomas Berry, *The Dream of Earth* (San Francisco, CA: Sierra Club Books, 1988), p. 2.
36. W. D. Ross, *The Right and the Good* (Oxford, England: Clarendon Press, 1930), p. 19.
37. Martin Kasindorf, "FBI's Reading List Worries Librarians," *USA Today*, December 16, 2002, www.usatoday.com/news/nation/2002-12-16-librarians_usat_x.htm.
38. Aristotle, *Politics* 3.9. In *The Politics of Aristotle*, trans. Ernest Barker (New York: Oxford University Press, 1958).
39. Lisa H. Newton, "Reverse Discrimination as Unjustified," *Ethics* 83 (July 1973).
40. Scott Jaschik, "The Impact of a Ban on Affirmative Action," *Inside Higher Education*, January 14, 2009.
41. John Rawls, *A Theory of Justice* (Cambridge, MA: Belknap Press of Harvard University Press, 1971), p. 12.
42. John Rawls, *A Theory of Justice* (Cambridge, MA: Belknap Press of Harvard University Press, 1971).
43. Immanuel Kant, "The Right of Punishment," in *The Metaphysic of Morals* (1785).
44. Friedrich Nietzsche, "Twilight of the Idols," in *The Portable Nietzsche*, ed. and trans. Walter Kaufman (New York: Penguin, 1982), pp. 489–490.
45. Friedrich Nietzsche, "On the Future of Education," Lecture series given at the Museum at Basel, Switzerland, 1872.
46. John Stuart Mill, "Utilitarianism," Chapter 5.
47. Friedrich Nietzsche, "The Future of Education," Lecture series given at the Museum of Basel, Switzerland, 1872.

CHAPTER 11

Rights Ethics

*We hold these truths to be self-evident, that all men are created
equal, that they are endowed by their Creator with certain
inalienable Rights, that among these are Life, Liberty and the
Pursuit of Happiness.*
　　　—United States Declaration of Independence (July 4, 1776)

*. . . all acts and duties which follow from the rights of others are
the most important of the duties we have towards others. . . . There
is nothing in the world so sacred, as the rights of others.*
　　　—IMMANUEL KANT, "Duties Dictated by Justice"[1]

Nadya Suleman captured international media attention when she gave birth to
octuplets in 2009 using an assisted reproductive technology known as in vitro
fertilization (IVF). However, public reaction quickly turned negative when it
was discovered that Suleman, dubbed "Octomom" by the press, not only was
jobless and living on public assistance, but she had six other children, all under
the age of seven. Like the octuplets, the six older children were conceived
through IVF. Many people criticized Suleman's decision saying she did not have
a moral right to have more children if she was unable to support them. The
physician who implanted the six embryos (two of the embryos split into twins)
also came under criticism.

Suleman defends her right to have as many children as she wants, and says
that she is being singled out for criticism because she is a single mom. She also
maintains that she can support her family and signed a contract for a reality
show, a move that has brought further criticism down on her for violating the
children's right to privacy. Suleman still relies on some public assistance to
support her family.

Do women have a right to have as many children as they want? Do children
have a right to a decent life and, if so, how should this right be recognized?
Should people who cannot support a child have the right to have children?
While we generally draw the line at physical abuse and abandonment, what
about parents who are deemed to be inadequate or inattentive parents? If we
are not willing to restrict people's right to bear children, does the state then
have a duty to provide public assistance to the children whose parents cannot
support them? Where do parents' rights end and the state's duties begin?

In this chapter, we'll be studying rights ethics. Rights ethicists regard civil liberties and entitlements to basic social goods as the foundation of morality. We'll also examine the basis of these rights and look at the relationship between rights and duties.

The Emergence of Rights Ethics in Modern Society

Human rights is not a new concept; however, the articulation of human rights by philosophers is a relatively recent development. **Rights ethics** states that our entitlements as members of society are the foundation of ethics. With the exception of natural rights ethics, rights ethics does not exist as a separate theory but as part of broader moral theories such as deontology, utilitarianism, and natural law ethics. Even where rights have not been explicitly discussed in traditional writings, such as in Buddhist philosophy, the assumption of rights is embedded in the concepts of duty and respect for the dignity of people.

The Divine Right to Rule

Before the eighteenth century, the focus of moral theory was primarily on duty— duty to the king, to God, to the state, to the church, and to the moral law. The language of rights in Western philosophy emerged mainly in the context of the growing confrontation with the idea of absolute sovereignty. Monarchs [it's a more gender-neutral term] had previously claimed to have the divine right to rule. Now, their subjects were claiming that they also had rights that the sovereigns were bound to respect. This dissatisfaction culminated in the U.S. Declaration of Independence (1776) and the French Declaration of the Rights of Man and Citizen (1789).

The American Bill of Rights* (the first ten amendments to the U.S. Constitution) expands on the rights outlined in the Declaration of Independence. The first amendment states:

> Congress shall make no law respecting an establishment of religion, or prohibiting the free exercise thereof; or abridging the freedom of speech, or of the press; or the right of the people peaceably to assemble, and to petition the Government for a redress of grievances.

Cultural relativists claim that the moral rights outlined in these documents did not exist before the acceptance of these documents by their respective societies. Rights ethicists disagree; they claim that the documents did not create these rights. Instead, the writers of these documents were demanding that certain God-given rights formerly denied by society be recognized.

In theory, these documents recognized the equal rights of all humans, but this was not the case in actual practice. In the United States, the existence of slavery

Connections

According to cultural relativists, what is the source of rights, if any, for a particular group of people such as women and blacks? *See Chapter 6, pages 187–188.*

*To read the complete Bill of Rights, go to www.archives.gov/founding-docs/bill-of-rights-transcript.html

and the denial of certain basic rights to women, such as the right to vote and the right of married women to own property, precipitated a second rights movement.

The Women's Rights Movement

Many of the people who were involved in the abolitionist movement, such as Elizabeth Cady Stanton (1815–1902) and Frederick Douglass (1817–1895), were also involved in the women's rights movement. Stanton attended Troy Female Seminary in New York, one of the first academies to offer women a quality education. There, she studied logic, physiology, and natural law ethics. In 1840, she and her new husband, journalist Henry Stanton—also an abolitionist and women's rights activist—attended a global antislavery conference in London. However, she was excluded from participation in the conference because of her gender. Here she met Lucretia Mott. Together, they began making plans for the first women's rights convention, which was held in Seneca Falls, New York, in 1848.

Stanton and Mott were the driving forces behind the writing of the "Declaration of Sentiments and Resolutions of the First Woman's Rights Convention."[2] In her address to the convention, Stanton referred to the principles and guaranteed rights that were put forth in the U.S. Declaration of Independence and Bill of Rights.

> [W]e are assembled to protest against a form of government existing without the consent of the governed—to declare our right to be free as man is free. . . . The world has never yet seen a truly great and virtuous nation, because in the degradation of woman the very fountains of life are poisoned at their source.

Signing of the Declaration of Independence, 1776. The Declaration of Independence and the Bill of Rights were grounded in a belief in natural rights.
©John Parrot/Stocktrek Images/Getty Images

Stanton believed that suffrage, or the right to vote, was part of a greater issue. As president of the National Woman's Suffrage Association, she opposed the Fourteenth Amendment to the U.S. Constitution, which granted the vote to all male citizens (regardless of race) aged twenty-one years of age and older, because of its exclusion of women. She also protested the sexual abuse of women and championed coeducation and the concept of men and women taking equal responsibility for the care of their children. It was not until 1920, long after the deaths of Stanton and Susan B. Anthony, and long after many other Western nations had granted women the right to vote, that women were finally given the right to vote in the United States.

World War II

World War II gave rise to a renewed interest in rights ethics. The atrocities of the Holocaust brought to light the weaknesses and dangers of cultural relativism—in this case, the cultural relativism that had tried to justify the horrors of the Nazi regime. If rights are the creation of society, as cultural relativists claim, then rights can be removed by societal laws, as happened in the 1936 German supreme court ruling that deprived Jews of most of their rights. The subsequent dehumanization and persecution of the Jews lead to a call by the international community for the recognition of fundamental human rights.

Connections

How did the cultural relativist's definition of the moral community permit and even condone atrocities such as slavery and the holocaust? *See Chapter 6, pages 184-185.*

Human Rights

In 1948, the United Nations issued the Universal Declaration of Human Rights (available online at http://www.un.org/en/udhrbook/pdf/udhr_booklet_ en_web.pdf). According to it, human rights are not simply a Western creation but belong to all people everywhere. The Universal Declaration was followed by the push for decolonization in Asia and Africa and the challenge for Westerners to overcome Eurocentric thinking. International pressure from government groups and organizations such as Amnesty International has also been put on countries that engage in gross human rights violations, such as torture and genocide.

In India, under Gandhi's leadership, rights ethics emerged as a direct challenge to the unequal privileges of the caste system. Gandhi wrote:

> Men are equal. For, though they are not of the same age, same height, the same skin and the same intellect, these inequalities are temporary and superficial, the soul that is hidden beneath this early crust is one and the same for all men and women belonging to all climes. . . . The word "inequality" has a bad odour to it, and it has led to arrogance and inhumanities, both in East and West.[3]

With the strong emphasis of Buddhist ethics on the dignity of all beings, modern Buddhist ethicists have also become some of the leading advocates of rights ethics, promoting not only human rights but also the rights of nonhuman animals and the environment.

Moral versus Legal Rights

Much of the current debate over rights in the United States focuses on constitutional rights; however, moral and legal rights can conflict. Because laws are not the source of fundamental moral rights, it is possible to have a legal or constitutional right that violates a moral right. The fact that women did not have the legal right to vote in this country until 1920 did not mean that there was no moral basis for the demand that women be given voting rights; the fact that women now have the legal right to abortion likewise does not necessarily mean that the right to abortion is a moral right.

We also have certain legal rights, such as the right to operate a motor vehicle, that are neither moral rights nor do they violate any moral rights. Similarly, not all moral rights are legal rights. We have a moral right, but not a legal right, to fidelity from our spouses or significant others. We also have a moral, but not a legal, right not to be deceived by our family and friends.

Furthermore, there are legal rights that may or may not be moral rights. For example, even though it is legal, some people question the moral right of women to carry pregnancies of more than three fetuses, as in the case of Nadya Suleman, when doing so puts the babies at risk of lifelong disabilities.

The legal rights of which [a person] is deprived, may be rights which *ought* not to have belonged to him; in other words, the law which confers these rights, may be a bad law.

—JOHN STUART MILL, *Utilitarianism* (1863), Ch. 5

Connections

How do cultural relativists view social reformers? *See Chapter 6, pages 191–193.*

Cultural relativists maintain that there is no distinction between moral and legal rights. Moral rights do not exist independent of legal rights. Rights ethicists disagree. They maintain that the position of the cultural relativists is counterintuitive. For example, in the U.S. Supreme Court *Dred Scott v. Sanford* decision of 1856, the court ruled that "the right of property in a slave is distinctly and expressly affirmed in the Constitution." If moral rights were the same as legal rights, this ruling should have settled the slavery issue once and for all. However, the claim that slavery violated the rights of African Americans continued to be presented by abolitionists despite this court ruling. Other public protests that occur when certain rights—such as freedom of speech—are withdrawn or violated by the government also suggest that our legal rights are based on independent, nonlegal rights. For example, the American Civil Liberties Union argues that the USA Patriot Act unjustly infringes on citizens' right to privacy as well as detainees' right to a fair trial.

Some cultures deny certain groups of people the same rights that are enjoyed by those in power, but this does not mean that these cultures do not accept, at least in theory, a moral standard of human equality. Rights ethicists John Locke and Thomas Jefferson recognized, in theory, the moral equality of all humans. Yet at the time, equal rights were legally extended only to White male landowners. Indeed, Jefferson himself was a slaveholder.

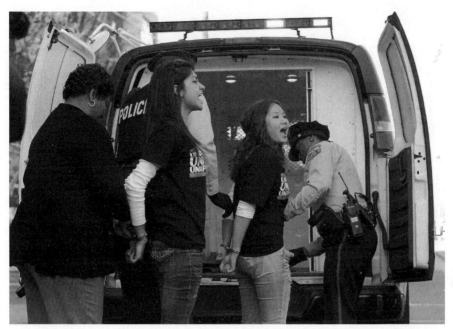

Tania Chairez, 19, a student at the University of Pennsylvania, and Jessica Hyejin Lee, 20, a junior at Bryn Mawr College, were both arrested at an immigrant-rights rally. Both Chairez and Lee are illegal immigrants who came to this country with their parents as young children.
©AP Photo/Alex Brandon

Even cultures that torture and deny basic rights to certain groups of people still generally recognize the basic moral standard of human equality. In response to the cultural relativists' claim that the concept of human rights is a Western cultural norm, it is interesting that it was the powerful Western nations, not the non-Western nations, that were the most reluctant to endorse the United Nations' Universal Declaration of Human Rights.

Discussion Questions

1. While illegal immigrants such as Chairez and Lee do not have a legal right to a college education in many states in the United States, do they have a moral right to a college education and to job opportunities enjoyed by American citizens? Support your answer. Discuss how a cultural relativist and a rights ethicist would answer this question.

2. The DREAM Act (acronym for Development, Relief, and Education for Alien Minors Act) was first proposed in 2001 and reintroduced in 2017 but has not, as yet, passed Congress. If passed, it would allow young people who are illegal immigrants to remain in the United States if they meet certain criteria such as coming to this country before the age of sixteen and having graduated from a U.S. high school or earned a GED or served in the military. Critically analyze the pros and cons of the DREAM Act. Discuss what position a rights ethicist would most likely take on the act.

Disability rights aren't just civil rights to be enforced here at home. They are universal rights to be recognized and promoted around the world.

—BARACK OBAMA, *White House Speech*, July 24, 2009

Exercises

1. Bring in newspaper or magazine articles that pertain to rights. Discuss the nature of the particular rights that are in question.

2. Most people believe that we do not have a moral right to use racist and sexist terms that demean other people. However, does this imply that derogatory language and activities should also be illegal? How about professors or speakers who use language that demeans or offends students? Should universities have the ability to restrict speech on campus? Support your answers.

*3. Does the issue of rights ever arise in the course of your community service work? If so, what are these rights? Are the people who claim that they have, or should have, these rights able to exercise them? If not, why not?

John Locke: Natural Rights Ethics

The state of nature has a law of nature to govern it, . . . that being all equal and independent, no one ought to harm another in his life, health, liberty, or possession. . . . And that all men may be restrained from invading others' rights, . . .

—JOHN LOCKE, *Second Treatise on Civil Government* (1690), Ch. 2, Sect. 6–7

Rights are generally seen as either (1) derived from duties or (2) natural and existing independently. If rights are derived from duty, there are no rights apart from duties. If a person has a right, then we have a duty or obligation to honor that right. On the other hand, if rights are natural and independent of duties, then government merely has to protect people's freedom to exercise their rights; it does not have a duty to provide people with the means to achieve these rights. The philosophical doctrine of natural rights first appeared in Western philosophy in the seventeenth century as a demand for equality for all people.

Connections

What are the key claims of natural law theory? *See Chapter 9, pages 282-283.*

Natural rights ethicists argue that all humans have rights apart from their membership in a civil society or political state. Rights are *self-evident* and God-given and exist independently of and prior to any duties we may have. These rights stem from our human nature. We do not have to qualify to have rights, nor do we earn them. The claim of equality is not something we invent or determine by

---

*An asterisk indicates that the exercise is appropriate for students who are doing community service learning as part of the course.

law; it is self-evident, even though humans are unequal in terms of physical, mental, and social characteristics. Rights are also *inalienable;* they cannot be taken away. Because only humans have rights, according to most natural rights ethicists, the term *natural rights* is often used synonymously with the term *human rights.*

Key Claims of Natural Rights Ethics

- Natural rights stem from our human nature, which is a special creation of God.
- All and only humans have rights.
- Rights are self-evident and inalienable.
- We do not have to qualify for or earn these rights.
- Rights exist independently of and prior to duties.

John Locke's Concept of Natural Rights

John Locke and Thomas Hobbes are two of the most prominent natural rights ethicists. According to them, the primary purpose of government is to protect humans in the exercise of their equal rights. Although we might possess perfect freedom in the state of nature, our enjoyment of it is very uncertain. The **state of nature** is the condition in which people lived before the formation of the state or government. Because all societies have at least a rudimentary form of government, it is uncertain whether people ever lived in a state of nature.

Hobbes argued that, in this state of nature (whether real or hypothetical), there would be "continual fear, and danger of violent death; and the life of man, solitary, poor, nasty, brutish, and short." In the state of nature, people are egoists, each asserting their rights without concern for others. People enter into a social contract so that everyone might better preserve their own rights. According to Hobbes, subjects have no natural rights against the sovereign except self-preservation. Locke, on the other hand, expanded the concept of natural rights to include the rights to life, liberty, and property. Locke's concept of rights has had the greatest influence on American political theory.

John Locke (1632–1704) was born in Somerset, England, and raised in a liberal Puritan family. He was appointed Reader in Censor of Moral Philosophy at Oxford in 1664. In 1665, Locke entered the diplomatic service. He was later appointed Lord Chancellor by the Earl of Shaftesbury. Shaftesbury was later involved in a plot against King James II and was forced to flee to Holland. Locke, worried about his own safety, also took refuge in Holland, living there under an assumed name. He did not return to England until shortly after the revolution in 1688. Back in England, Locke continued his writing. His treatises on civil government, education, and religion were immensely popular.

While Thomas Hobbes was horrified by the idea of citizens rebelling against their sovereign, Locke thought that we should resist a government that misuses its power to deny our natural rights. Because government arises from a social contract among people and because people have equal rights, Locke believed

Connections

What are Hobbes' three laws of nature? *See Chapter 7, pages 237-238.*

Connections

Why did Hobbes believe that abiding by the rules of society was important? *See Chapter 7, pages 212-213.*

that the best form of government for protecting our natural rights is a democracy. In his *Two Treatises of Civil Government*, published in 1690 (see selection at end of chapter), Locke attacks the idea of the divine right of kings.

Locke was especially concerned that government respect what he believed to be our natural right to own property. The right to own property, however, is conditional upon our use and enjoyment of it. By mixing our labor with the land and using the fruits of our labor, it becomes our property. According to Locke, God gave the world to humans as a resource; the vast wilderness of the earth was created by God for humans to subdue and turn into provisions to support human life. Locke's religious views were reinforced by the Enlightenment concept of nature that depicted the world as a giant machine without any life or inherent value of its own. Nature has only instrumental value defined in terms of human desires. Land that was left in a wild state or allowed to revert to its natural uncultivated state was, in Locke's mind, "spoilage" or "waste land." Only by being mixed with human labor do natural resources acquire value. Locke was particularly contemptuous of the "several nations of the [Native] Americans" that did nothing to "improve" the land.[4]

Locke was convinced that, even if every man had as much property as he could make use of and even if the population of the earth was doubled, there would still be more than enough land for everyone. For those who could not find sufficient land in England or Europe, he suggested "let him plant in some inland, vacant places of America."[5] Because many Native Americans did not cultivate their land but left it in a "wasteful state of wilderness," the European settlers, according to Locke, could rightfully take possession of it. By the mid-1700s, English colonists controlled most of the Southeast, usurping Indian lands and even selling the Indians into slavery. As the United States grew, the demand for land, especially by plantation owners, increased. In 1830, Congress passed the Indian Removal Act that resulted in tens of thousands of Native Americans being forcibly removed from their land and homes by U.S. federal troops and resettled on a reservation in Oklahoma.

Locke was aware that some people might try to take possession of more property than they could use, thus letting some of it go to waste. Because the law of nature is unwritten and indeterminate, it is easy for people in the state of nature to misapply it when there is no established judge. Therefore, civil laws are needed to determine and to protect property rights.

Locke's political theory was formulated at a time of political unrest. His doctrine of natural rights, with its belief that there are certain inalienable human rights that all societies and people are bound to respect, found expression in both the French and American Revolutions. The doctrine had a profound influence on the thinking of Thomas Jefferson, who was only twenty-six when he wrote the first draft of the Declaration of Independence. The influence of natural rights ethics in the United States is especially evident by the way that rights are usually discussed without any reference to duty.

Ayn Rand

Ayn Rand was one of the foremost contemporary defenders of natural rights ethics. According to her, the doctrine of natural rights created the possibility of free societies. The United States is the first free society founded upon natural rights ethics. Only through capitalism, Rand argued, can individual rights and a free society be sustained. "Those who advocate laissez-faire capitalism," she wrote, "are the only advocates of man's rights."[6] The sole purpose of government is the protection of our individual rights. Our ability to choose how to use our property and our choice of a career or where to sell our goods or labor are regarded by Rand as intimately related to our freedom to pursue the good life. Inadequate resources may limit our freedom and our ability to achieve our concept of the good life, but according to her, this cannot be used as a general objection to free enterprise. She wrote:

Connections

How does Rand use ethical egoism to support laissez-faire capitalism? *See Chapter 7, pages 220-221.*

> The most profoundly revolutionary achievement of the United States of America was the *subordination* of society to *moral* law.
>
> The principle of man's individual rights represented the extension of morality into the social system—as a limitation on the power of the state, as man's protection against the brute force of the collective, as the subordination of *might* to *right*. The United States was the first *moral* society in history.[7]

According to Rand, moral rights define and protect our freedoms without imposing obligations on anyone else. For example, the right to property does not entail an obligation to provide people with property; the right to life does not entail an obligation to provide people with the necessities of life. Rand believed that the people who use violence to deprive others of their rights are only a small minority. The harm that these criminals have done in our free society is infinitesimal compared to the horrors perpetuated by governments that believe they have the right to restrict people's liberties in the name of the social good.

The doctrine of natural rights has come under criticism. One of its weaknesses is its lack of grounding in reason and experience. Locke believed that "natural reason" and "revelation" alike "give us an account of those grants God made of the world to Adam and to Noah."[8] However, there is considerable disagreement over exactly what these natural rights are, and there is no way of resolving the disagreement. Just as kings claimed that they had a divine right to rule, the dogmatic claim that rights are natural or self-evident leaves us no room for a rational justification for these rights. Also, because natural rights exist independently of and prior to duty, natural rights ethics has been accused of promoting ethical egoism by allowing the strong to pursue their interests and rights at the expense of those of who have less power. For example, it has been argued that even though illegal immigrants may have a right to a college education, the state does not have a duty to provide such an education.

Connections

What is a marginalized group? *See Chapter 6, pages 185-186.*

Annette Baier argues that the **liberalism** supported by natural rights ethics does not take into account the limitations placed upon marginalized groups by traditional societal roles. Although voluntary agreement is the paradigm of moral obligation in liberal morality, women and children are excluded from entering into voluntary trade agreements if they accept their traditional roles.

This situation creates what Baier calls an internal contradiction in liberals' moral beliefs regarding equal human rights. This contradiction, she notes, does

The Trail of Tears, painted by Robert Lindneux, 1942, depicts the suffering of the Cherokee people during their forced removal in 1838 from their lands in the Southeast to Oklahoma. An estimated four thousand Native Americans died during the perilous journey. Locke's natural rights ethics was used to justify the takeover of Native Americans' lands by European settlers.

not "vanish once women have equal legal rights with men, as long as they are still expected to take responsibility for any child they conceive voluntarily or nonvoluntarily, . . ."[9] This failure to acknowledge and take into account the limitations that society places on certain groups of people is one of the major weaknesses of natural rights ethics, particularly in a capitalist society.

Exercises

1. Working in small groups, make a list of the rights that you regard as self-evident. If there is disagreement, discuss how might you resolve it.

2. Discuss whether the use of theology and the claim that God endowed humans with special rights is adequate as a foundation for moral rights. If not, what justifications do you use to support your claim that there are certain moral rights?

*3. Relate Locke's belief that we have a right to take over land that is not being used productively to the current policy of eminent domain, which allows the government to seize people's property for economic development. Do you support this policy? Explain.

4. Locke was writing at a time when the human population of the world was one-tenth of what it is now. Would Locke agree that our current capitalist system of ownership is consistent with natural moral rights? Explain.

5. If our legal rights regarding property ownership are inconsistent with certain moral rights, should the laws regulating property ownership in this country be changed? If so, what changes would you make? What changes, if any, might Locke make? Support your answers.

6. According to Locke, Native Americans had no claim on the land, with the exception of the land that they were cultivating at the time. Do you agree? Why or why not? Discuss Locke's viewpoint in light of current developments such as the wish of Native Americans to build casinos on their reservation land as well as the U.S. government's action in taking over undeveloped land belonging to Native Americans for mining, oil, and natural gas exploration.

7. To what extent has Locke's attitude toward property influenced our attitude toward the wilderness and land? Do you agree with his view of the wilderness? Support your answers.

8. Critically analyze Rand's claim that laissez-faire capitalism is the only system that can protect our individual freedoms. How would Locke most likely respond to Rand's position? Create a dialogue between Rand and Locke.

9. In *Kelo v. City of New London* (2005), the U.S. Supreme Court extended the power of eminent domain to permit local governments to seize property for "private economic development." Imagine that your city government is about to use its power of eminent domain to appropriate your apartment building for a shopping mall. Some of the long-term residents are upset and want to stage a sit-in to prevent the wrecking equipment from tearing down the building. They ask you to join them. What should you do and why?

The Marxist Critique of Natural Rights Ethics

Karl Marx

Karl Marx (1818–1883) was one of the most influential critics of natural rights ethics. Marx was born in Prussia (now part of Germany). As a young man, he studied law, his father's profession, but he soon decided that he was more interested in philosophy; he completed a PhD in philosophy at the age of twenty-three. Marx was opposed to the more traditional theoretical approach to philosophy. The role of the philosopher, he believed, is not simply to interpret the world but to change it. He initially intended to become a university teacher but abandoned the idea to become the editor of a radical newspaper.

In 1843, Marx and his wife moved to Paris, where Marx joined the Communist League. In Paris, Marx began his lifelong friendship with Friedrich Engels, the son of a wealthy German textile manufacturer. In 1848, he and Engels published the *Communist Manifesto*. Because of Marx's radical ideas, he found himself unwelcome on the Continent. So in 1849, he and his family settled permanently in London, where he lived in poverty, choosing to devote his energies to fighting for the rights of the downtrodden working class (proletariat).

Connections

Why did Rand believe that laissez-faire capitalism is the best economic system? *See Chapter 7, pages 220–221.*

Marx rejected the doctrine of natural rights as a bourgeois invention. He believed that the plight of the workers in capitalist countries such as England was due, in part, to the acceptance of natural rights ethics. Marx argued that the list of so-called natural rights is historically conceived to justify certain economic and political systems. For example, Locke's "natural right to own property" (including slaves) serves to protect the holdings of those in power—the landowning bourgeois—rather than the majority of people who cannot afford to exercise their "natural" right to own property. The right to own property, in turn, justifies free-market capitalism and ethical egoism, by legitimating the increasing accumulation of property in the hands of the few.

For example, the 2016 U.S. Census reports that almost two-thirds of Americans "own" their own home. In fact, it is a mortgage company or a large bank that actually owns the houses in the majority of these cases. About a million families lost their homes to foreclosure in 2016. In addition, home ownership among young people is down nearly ten points lower than it was a decade ago, in part because of the burden of high student loans.[10]

Unlike Locke and Rand, Marx argued that rights do not exist as an abstraction but as part of our membership in a civil society. A right that can only be exercised if we have the power to assert ourselves is a "meaningless mockery" to those who lack social and political power. Rights are not based on self-assertion, Marx maintained; rather, rights are demands that create duties for society to provide its members with certain social goods.

Natural rights ethicists believe that government exists to protect our rights. However, Marx argued that in a capitalist society government exists to protect the individual rights of property owners and those in power at the expense of the majority who do not own property. Humans, Marx believed, are naturally cooperative, but the institution of private property and the class system created by it prevent humans from being free to exercise their potential. In particular, Marx believed that productive property, such as factories, businesses, and mines, should be publicly owned rather than privately controlled by capitalists.

Marx argued that rights should not just be based on our ability to assert them, but rather on our interests and needs as members of a civil society. For example, if a person has a right to an education, then the state has a corresponding duty to provide this education. Indeed, one of the ten points of Marx's 1883 *Communist Manifesto* was the establishment of "free education for all children in public schools." In contrast, with the self-assertion model adopted by natural rights ethicists, only those who could assert their rights by having the means to pay for productive property or an education would be entitled to own a factory or business or to receive an education.

True equality and freedom, according to Marx, entail communal ownership of the means of production rather than individual ownership. Marx was not suggesting the type of communism in the old Soviet Union, where the government merely took over the role of oppressor. Instead, Marx had in mind a stateless society where the people were truly in charge. Whether or not this sort of utopia is possible, given the realities of human nature, is still under debate.

Although Marx was not opposed to violent revolution to overthrow the capitalist economy, he envisioned the possibility of a nonviolent revolution in more democratic countries such as the United States and Britain.

Gustavo Gutierrez and Liberation Ethics

Many contemporary rights movements, such as that led by Peruvian **liberation ethicist** and social activist Gustavo Gutierrez (born 1928) accept Marx's criticism of natural rights ethics. A mestizo (part Quechuan Indian), Gutierrez was born among the oppressed in Lima, Peru. After considering a career in medicine, he found his real interest in the priesthood. In 1955, he completed a master's degree in philosophy and psychology at Catholic University in Louvain, Belgium. He also studied theology in France and Rome.

After almost a decade, Gutierrez returned to Peru and found that his theological education did not fit with the social reality of poverty in Latin America. He began to formulate his own theology, based on his involvement with the people of Rimac, a slum in Lima. Gutierrez also grew increasingly dissatisfied with the official position of the church in Latin America. He believed that the church should rethink its position on contraception, the ordination of women, the economic structure in Latin America, and, as a pacifist, the gospel's understanding of violence. Although Gutierrez is a world-renowned writer, public speaker, and social activist, he prefers to remain among the poor in the slums of Lima. In 2016, he received the *Pacem in Terris* Award for his work.

Gutierrez is critical of laissez-faire capitalism, with its focus on liberty rights and its presumption that a democracy will ensure human rights. Systems of democracy based on liberalism, he notes, do not protect the rights of the poor. Instead, the right to private ownership has been granted at the expense of the rights of the poor. Liberal democracy claims to promote equal rights but "is only for the middle class and actually only enhances the flexibility with which the prevailing system exercises its domination over the popular masses."[11]

This alternative language [of "rights of the poor"] represents a critical approach to the laissez-faire liberal doctrine to the effect that our society enjoys an equality that in fact does not exist.

—GUSTAVO GUTIERREZ, *The Power of the Poor in History* (1979), p. 87

While natural rights ethicists claim that capitalism is a natural economic system, Gutierrez, like Marx, argues that any attempt to separate the ideology of natural rights ethics—and the capitalist system that it supports—from its roots is to ignore historical reality. Like the aristocracy they replaced, the capitalist bourgeoisie claimed to have an absolute and inalienable right to control the economy—an economy that Gutierrez describes as "based on private enterprise—and on the vicious exploitation of workers (in Europe) and the poor (in colonial and neocolonial lands)."[12] While globalization of capitalism has created wealth for a small percentage of people in developing nations, it also has contributed to pollution, global warming, environmental degradation, population displacement, and unemployment, thus leaving millions in poverty and the gap between the rich and poor an ever widening chasm.[13]

Gutierrez instead envisions a society founded upon a theology of liberation. Natural rights ethics is based on self-assertion. Gutierrez turns this upside down. A society where the rights and dignity of everyone are respected, he argues, must start from the "underside of history" by defending the rights of those who have been oppressed and plundered by the world. True democracy, according to him, cannot be imposed upon a culture but must instead be preceded by the development of a just economic system. Gutierrez writes:

> Defending human rights means above all defending the rights of the poor. It is
> a prophetic theme, and one deeply rooted in the tradition of the church. And it
> must be kept in mind in order to avoid falling into the liberal focus with regard to
> human rights. The liberal approach presupposes, for example, a social equality that
> simply does not exist in Latin American societies.[14]

Insensitivity to the historical and social contexts in which moral rights are exercised can lead to misunderstandings or even the belief that people from other cultures are morally stunted. This assumption, Gutierrez points out, has often been used to justify imposing Western notions of moral rights on other nations.

Makeshift slums in front of a backdrop of wealth and luxury in New Delhi, India. With the introduction of Western capitalism and outsourcing of information technology, India has become one of the international centers for telephone marketing and customer service.
©Dr. Parvinder Sethi

Discussion Questions

1. Gutierrez is critical of the assumption that democracy can protect our human rights. Discuss whether the rights of the people living in the slums in New Delhi are being violated by the multinational corporations who move their operations there in order to take advantage of the large potential workforce and cheap labor.

2. Think of a time when you called customer service and got a representative in another county. How did you react and what was the basis of your reaction? Relate your answer to the concept of rights and moral community. Discuss also what Gutierrez might think of our growing dependence on workers in Third World countries for information technology and customer service.

Respecting cultural diversity, however, does not imply that we must fall back into cultural relativism or refrain from ever criticizing other cultures. In fact, Marxists and liberation ethicists are highly critical of cultures where the rights of the poor and powerless are not taken seriously. Instead, we must take care not to simply accept the interpretations of those in power.

Exercises

1. Discuss Marx's criticism of natural rights as a political weapon for justifying the privileges of the economic and political elite. Discuss how Rand might respond to Marx's criticisms of natural rights ethics.

2. Marx believed that, if property were communally owned, criminals would disappear. Under true communism, he argued, there would be no need for the powerful military and police forces that are typical in capitalist societies. Rand, on the other hand, believed that putting control of property in the hands of the government or collective would do more damage than that done by criminals. Critically analyze their respective positions.

3. Are laissez-faire capitalism and communism the only alternative systems for protecting human rights? Discuss what type of society might be best for optimizing human rights and freedom while nurturing community and interdependence. What concept of moral rights did you use to come up with your ideal society? Discuss how Marx, Gutierrez, Locke, and Rand might each respond to your ideal.

4. Many college students use their credit cards to pay their college tuition, a practice that can cost students several thousand dollars more in interest than a student loan does. Because of the high interest costs, some colleges do not allow students to use credit cards to pay for their tuition. Is this fair or is it a violation of students' rights? Discuss how Marx might respond to the issue of rising tuition costs.

5. In Gutierrez's book *The Power of the Poor in History*, he argues that a prophetic interpretation of the Bible, rather than Locke's individualistic interpretation, provides the best foundation for a rights ethics that is consistent with justice and respect for human dignity. Do you agree? Discuss how Locke and Marx would respond to Gutierrez.

Rights and Duties

The right of every man to life is correlative with the duty to preserve it; his right to a decent standard of living, with the duty of living it becomingly; and his right to investigate the truth freely, with the duty of pursuing it even more completely and profoundly.

—POPE JOHN XXIII, "Pacem in Terris" (1963)

Connections

What are the key claims of deontology? *See Chapter 10, page 322.*

Utilitarianism, deontological theories, natural law ethics, and Buddhist ethics all base rights on duty. Although moral rights imply a corresponding duty, not all duties have a corresponding right. Because moral duty is a broader concept, rights ethics is sometimes included as a branch of deontology. According to duty-based rights ethics, rights are not granted but are rather something to which we are entitled. Others have a *duty* to honor our rights. For example, if we have a right to health care, then the state has a duty to provide it. In contrast, natural rights ethicists argue that our possession of a right does not create a duty on the part of others to honor or fulfill that right.

Philosophical concepts do not exist in a vacuum but have real-life consequences. Basing rights on the power to assert ourselves or the presence of an agent who will act on our behalf allows us to disregard the rights of those who lack the political power or force of law to exercise their moral claims. The U.S. Supreme Court in *Johnson v. McIntosh* (1823) and subsequent cases ruled that Native Americans, in accordance with treaties, have a right to certain lands; however, they have no legal means for asserting that right in order to regain that land. So, practically speaking, this natural right is useless.

On the other hand, if rights are derived from duty, then we are under an obligation to make sure that rights are honored. Our failure to discharge this obligation or duty becomes a violation of a person's right. If you have a duty of reparation, then I have a right to restitution from you. If we both have a right to basic health care, then the community has a moral duty to provide us with it, regardless of our ability to pay or purchase health insurance. If you have the right not to be harmed, society has a duty to provide security in the form of police protection.

Connections

What is the principle of utility, or the "greatest happiness principle"? *See Chapter 8, page 243.*

Rights and the Utilitarian Duties

Jeremy Bentham attacked the notion of natural rights as "rhetorical nonsense— nonsense upon stilts." According to him, rights are neither natural nor inalienable. Instead, rights are derived from the principle of utility and are therefore calculable and changing, depending on the interests and needs of those involved.

Legislators, not individuals, must determine what rights are appropriate for producing the greatest happiness of the greatest number. Without government to curtail selfishness, he argued, any talk of rights makes no sense. All rights stem from the laws of society and, therefore, cannot be inalienable. "There is no right," Bentham argued, "that, when the abolition of it is advantageous to society, should not be abolished."[15]

John Stuart Mill likewise believed that rights exist only within a social context and are derived from the principle of utility. We have a right to walk the streets without fear of being molested or robbed because society has a duty of nonmaleficence to protect us from harm by providing police protection.

> When we call anything a person's rights, we mean that he has a valid claim on society to protect him in the possession of it, either by the force of law, or by that of education and opinion. . . .
>
> To have a right, then, is, I conceive, to have something which society ought to defend me in the possession of. If the objector goes on to ask, why it ought? I can give him no other reason than general utility.[16]

Unlike Bentham, who argued that there are no absolute and inalienable rights, Mill believed that the right of individual liberty is absolutely binding on society. People should be free to pursue their own plans as long as they do not harm anyone else. The only time our liberty can be curtailed is when we are using it to interfere with another person's liberty or rights.

One of the difficulties with using the principle of utility, at least as formulated by Bentham, as the sole basis of rights is there is no right to life—what many consider to be the most basic right—independent of utility. If it would benefit society to deprive certain people of their lives—such as killing children with disabilities—then, according to the principle of utility, we ought to do so. Individual rights, in other words, cannot be reduced to utility since the greatest good for the greatest number is not necessarily good for the individual.

Connections

Why did Mill believe that freedom is essential for humans' happiness? *See Chapter 8, pages 254-255.*

Rights and Human Dignity

According to Kant, the basis of rights is not the principle of utility but the categorical imperative. "Respect for the rights of others," he wrote, "is rooted in principle." Because the categorical imperative requires that we treat other persons with dignity, one of our chief duties is respect for the rights of others. Rights protect our status as persons. The categorical imperative does not create any specific rights but rather the formal right to be treated with respect. Our equal right to be treated with dignity is the strongest claim we can assert; it does not need to be justified. According to Kant:

Connections

What is the categorical imperative and what is it based on? *See Chapter 10, pages 314-315.*

> It is our duty to regard [others] as sacred and to respect and maintain them as such. . . . Woe unto him who trespasses upon the right of another and tramples it underfoot! His right should be his security; it should be stronger than any shield or fortress.[17]

Kant also argued that we all have an equal right to share in the goods provided us by nature. God provides the bounty of nature, but dividing up the goods has been left to humans. The duty of justice requires each of us to make sure that others receive an equal share and that we each restrict our own consumption. Those of us who have a greater share of the world's wealth, Kant says, have a duty to be charitable and to share our wealth with those who are poor.

The connection of duty to rights is particularly strong in liberation ethics, as is the demand for equal rights for those who are currently being oppressed. In liberation theology, the right to own land is limited by the landowners' duty to share with the poor. The Torah or Old Testament, for example, requires landowners to leave portions of their fields and vineyards for the poor, so they will not go hungry.[18] Likewise, a person has a right to food stamps because the state has a duty of distributive justice to ensure that citizens have certain social goods that are essential to a life of dignity.

Prima Facie Rights and Duties

The concept of moral duties is generally considered to be broader than that of rights. Moral rights imply a corresponding duty, but not all duties have a corresponding right. The duty of beneficence, which entails doing good merely for the sake of good, does not imply that others have a right to our kindness and services. However, once you make a commitment to perform certain acts of beneficence, such as serving at a soup kitchen on a particular day, the people you are working with now have a right, based on your duty of fidelity, to expect your services on that day.

Like duties, most rights are prima facie rather than absolute and can be overridden in a particular case by a more compelling right or duty. For example, we do not have an absolute right to freedom of speech or to own property. The duty of nonmaleficence is more compelling than the freedom to yell "Fire!" in a crowded theater. And our right to own property is limited by the duty of justice.

When Cultures Clash

Divergent interpretations and ordering of rights and duties can lead to conflict when two cultures come together. In the West, we regard liberty rights as more compelling than duties of fidelity stemming from our membership in a community or family. Confucian deontologists, on the other hand, regard parents' rights to filial loyalty from their children to be more important than the children's individual liberty rights.

This clash between the Western emphasis on individual liberty rights and other cultures' emphasis on communal rights can be a source of misunderstanding. Unlike in the United States, which has an individualist, top-down approach to business negotiation, in many Asian and African nations communal and family input is critical. In Nigeria, for example, extended families are given great power in negotiating a business deal and the words of the elders are usually decisive, in both local and foreign negotiations.[19]

The diversity among cultures has led some people to conclude that the concept of rights is culturally relative and a Western invention. Cultural relativists point out that some non-Western nations have cultural customs that do not respect women, children, and certain groups. These are their values, and repulsive though they may seem to us, we should not interfere with them. A case in point is the custom of female circumcision (also known as genital mutilation), which is practiced in more than twenty African countries and some parts of Asia. Many Western nations find this practice barbaric and oppressive to women, yet a majority of the women in these cultures see it as a rite of passage into womanhood. Most ethicists disagree with the cultural relativists, however. They argue that the duty to respect the dignity of all humans may require us to interfere when the rights that affirm that dignity are being seriously violated.

Human rights violations can be particularly egregious during times of war because of our tendency to identify morality with our own cultural norms and to dehumanize "the enemy," including civilians. According to the United Nations, victims of armed conflict are more likely to be civilians than soldiers. Rape has been used as a weapon of war as well as spoils of war. Hundreds of thousands of women and girls have been raped during the past twenty-five years in the wars in Africa, Syria, and Yugoslavia.[20]

Respecting human rights on an international level involves respecting cultural diversity and national self-determination. On the other hand, respect for the equal rights of all people also involves a duty to protest cultural practices that trample upon the most basic human rights of certain groups of people, thereby depriving them of their dignity.

Connections

What is the difference between sociological relativism and cultural relativism? *See Chapter 6, pages 172-173.*

Connections

How do cultural relativists define moral community? *See Chapter 6, pages 182-186.*

Exercises

1. Discuss whether the various natural human rights—such as the right of self-preservation and the right to life, liberty, property, and happiness—are always consistent with the duty to respect human dignity. Use specific examples to support your answer.

2. Do people have the right to have as many children as they want, as in the case of Nadya Suleman described in the opening scenario of the chapter? Or do people have a duty to limit the number of children they have based on their ability to support those children? At the opposite end of the spectrum, do governments have the right to limit family size to two children as in China and do people have a duty to respect the government mandate? Support your answers.

3. Outright bans or strict controls on handguns exist in only a handful of U.S. cities. Do we have a *moral* right to own handguns? Does the legal or constitutional right to own a handgun conflict with any moral rights or duties? If so, what are these rights and duties? Are they more compelling than the right to own a handgun? Support your answers.

4. Young adults are the group least likely to vote. In the 2008 presidential election, only 50% of people between eighteen and twenty-nine voted, compared to almost 60 percent of the general population.[21] In our democracy voting is seen as a right, not a duty, whereas in many democracies voting is a duty and is mandatory. Should voting be mandatory in the United States? Do we as citizens have a duty to vote in presidential elections? Support your answers.

5. The United States is the only Western democracy that uses the death penalty. Although the majority of Americans[22] support capital punishment, the Catholic Church, the European Union, and the United Nations all regard it as a serious violation of human rights. The Universal Declaration of Human Rights, Article 3, states that "everyone has a right to life."

   Discuss the claim that capital punishment violates basic rights. Is the cultural belief that the duty of retributive justice overrides the right to life in capital cases sufficient to justify the use of capital punishment in the United States? Support your answer.

6. Pope Francis issued a statement rejecting the just war theory, saying that it has "too often been used to justify violent conflicts." Discuss his concern in light of what is happening now in Syria and other current wars.

Liberty (Negative) Rights and Welfare (Positive) Rights

No one can compel me to be happy in accordance with his conception of the welfare of others, for each may seek his happiness in whatever way he sees fit, so long as he does not infringe upon the freedom of others to pursue a similar end which can be reconciled with the freedom of everyone else within a workable general law—i.e. he must accord to others the same right as he enjoys himself.

—IMMANUEL KANT, "On the Relationship of Theory to Practice in Political Right" (1792)

Just as there are different categories of duties, moral rights can be divided into liberty rights and welfare rights. **Welfare** or **positive rights** entail the right to receive certain social goods such as adequate nutrition, housing, education, and police and fire protection. **Liberty** or **negative rights** entail the right to be left alone to pursue our legitimate interests without interference from the government or other people. Our **legitimate interests** are those that do not violate other people's similar and equal interests. A misogynist, for example, may have an interest in keeping women out of the workplace, but this does not give him the right to discriminate in hiring because that would violate women's right to equal opportunity. Parents may have an interest in having a night on the town, but they do not have the right to do so if this violates their young children's right to security and reliable supervision.

Legitimate Interests

Libertarians oppose political restrictions on individual freedom. According to them, respect for other people entails allowing them the freedom to develop and exercise the capacities that are necessary for them to pursue their own concept of the good. This includes freedom of speech, religion, and privacy, as well as freedom from coercive interference from the government. Consequently, most libertarians—such as Locke, Rand, and Mill—believe in minimal government. The freedom to choose or to discover the life that is best for us is basic to the exercise of our autonomy. This freedom is limited only by an appeal to our sense of reason and fairness.

Connections

According to utilitarians, what is the primary purpose of government? *See Chapter 8, page 249.*

Former Harvard philosopher and libertarian Robert Nozick (1939–2002) wrote:

> Our main conclusions about the state are that a minimal state, limited to the narrow functions of protection against force, theft, fraud, enforcement of contracts, and so on, is justified; that any more extensive state will violate a person's rights not to be forced to do certain things, and is unjustified.[23]

In his later life, Nozick recanted the libertarian position because of its implications for the weakest members of society. In a libertarian state with minimal government, the poor, the infirm, and the elderly may starve amidst wealth and plenty since in such a state the starving have no positive or welfare rights to food or other forms of government assistance.

Buddhist ethics interprets legitimate interests in a more communal fashion. Our economic freedoms, including our choice of a career, are subject to restrictions imposed upon us by right livelihood. Rather than simply considering the interests of the individual, the restrictions entailed by the concept of right livelihood serve to protect the integrity of the entire moral community.

Liberty (Negative) Rights

According to utilitarians, liberty rights stem from the principle of utility. Our legitimate interests include anything that tends to increase (or at least not to decrease) pleasure for the greatest number. For a Kantian deontologist, however, our liberty rights are circumscribed by the categorical imperative, which prohibits us from treating another person only as a means no matter how many other people will benefit. Consider the example of a Peeping Tom on campus who gets great pleasure from secretly watching women undress in their dormitory rooms. Deontologists would argue that this sort of pleasurable peeping at someone without their permission is not a legitimate interest. It is wrong for a Peeping Tom to use these women only as a means *even if* the women do not know what is happening and *even if* neither their happiness nor their freedom is affected by the action of the Peeping Tom. Liberty rights place limitations on how we may treat another person *independently* of the consequences. In other words, would-be Peeping Toms have a duty to respect the privacy rights of women, independently of the consequences of doing so.

> Each person is to have an equal right to the most extensive liberty compatible with
>
> a similar liberty for others.
>
> —JOHN RAWLS, *A Theory of Justice* (1971), p. 60

Our liberty rights are also limited by our duty to treat ourselves with respect. We do not have the right to do anything that could infringe upon our own legitimate interests. According to Kant, as humans, our primary interest is the exercise of our rationality and autonomy. Suicide is an abomination because it involves the misuse of freedom of action to destroy oneself and one's freedom: "If I kill myself," Kant wrote, "I use my powers to deprive myself of the faculty of using them. That freedom, the principle of the highest order of life, should annul itself and abrogate the use of itself conflicts with the fullest use of freedom."[24] My life may seem worthless to me or I may be a burden to others, but this is not a sufficient reason for me to bring about my demise.

> When . . . disappointments and hopeless misery have quite taken away the taste
> for life; when a wretched man, strong in soul and more angered at his fate than
> faint-hearted or cast down, longs for death and still preserves his life without loving
> it—not from inclination or fear but from duty; then indeed his maxim has a moral
> content.[25]

In the United States, we tend to place more importance on liberty rights than on welfare rights, although there have been more restrictions on people's liberty rights since the terrorist attacks of September 11, 2001. Ayn Rand's rational egoism represents the extreme libertarian position, where liberty rights are the only type of rights we are bound to respect. Our choice of a career and how to use our property are carefully protected rights. Our emphasis on liberty rights at the expense of welfare rights, however, tends to seriously handicap those who are unable to assert their liberty rights either because of natural disadvantages or because of traditional roles that limit their options. Simply granting access to certain social goods, such as jobs and education, will not ensure that people will be able to pursue their legitimate interests.

Welfare (Positive) Rights

Welfare or positive rights are important because, without a minimal standard of living, we cannot pursue our legitimate interests. Because we cannot pursue these legitimate interests without certain social goods such as housing, food, and education, society has a duty to provide and protect these conditions. Gustavo Gutierrez believes that, when working toward the liberation of the poor, it is more important to focus on welfare rights than on liberty rights. When people finally have these rights, he argues, the other liberty rights will follow. In most countries, for example, health care is regarded as a welfare right, and society has a duty to provide its citizens with adequate health care.

In the United States, on the other hand, many, though not all, people regard health care as a privilege. The only duty the government has in this regard is to protect citizens' liberty to seek or purchase health care. The American belief is that, when people are free, we can acquire these goods on our own. Libertarians, in particular, object to anything more than a very limited concept of welfare rights because welfare rights require that someone else, whether another individual or the government, supply us with social goods. Jobs, schools, subsidized housing, and medical technology do not occur naturally but are goods and services produced either directly or through taxation. This, Ayn Rand argued, turns those who are forced to give up part of their income to pay taxes to provide the goods and services for others into slave labor. For example, Rand would argue that forcing taxpayers to support Suleman's octuplets is a violation of our rights.

Connections

Why did Ayn Rand oppose welfare rights and other government "handouts"? *See Chapter 7, pages 218-219.*

Massachusetts in 2003 became the first state to allow same-sex marriage. It is now legal in all 50 states.
©Justin Sullivan/Getty Images

Discussion Questions

1. Is marriage a moral right? If not, why not? If it is, what is the basis of the right? Discuss how both a utilitarian and John Rawls might answer this question.

2. Although same-sex marriage is now legal in the United States, several clergy have refused to perform same-sex marriages. They argue that it is a violation of their principles since marriage is a sacred covenant between a man and a woman. Some of these clergy have been fined and even served jail time for their refusal. Do these clergy have a moral right to refuse to perform same-sex marriages? Support your answer.

If some men are entitled by right to the products of the work of others, it means that those others are deprived of rights and condemned to slave labor.

Any alleged "right" of one man, which necessitates the violation of the rights of another, is not and cannot be a right.

—AYN RAND, "Man's Rights" (1963)[26]

John Rawls, like Locke and Rand, believed that the best society places a premium on noninterference and freedoms such as freedom of speech, freedom of the press, and the freedom to pursue one's concept of the good. However, Rawls departs from a strict libertarian model in regard to claims over property and other social goods that are necessary for people to pursue their own interests or their concept of the good. According to Rawls, differences in wealth are permissible only if they serve to benefit the least well-off in society. Justice requires that those who fared poorly in the natural lottery be entitled to the same as those who fared well. We do not have an absolute right to goods that others desperately need but are merely a surplus for us.

Rawls' attempt to resolve the apparent conflict between our liberty rights and the demands of those who are disadvantaged for the products of our labor has been fruitful in formulating policies regarding both political and economic rights. For example, Rawls's model was used to generate a health care policy for the United States to provide state-funded medical care (Medicaid) for those who could not afford it and yet allow others the liberty to purchase the best medical care they could afford.

One of the problems in formulating public policies regarding the distribution of social goods is defining what counts as welfare or positive rights. Do we have a right to free or affordable medical care? If so, do we have a welfare right only to minimal medical care or to the best medical care available? Do we also have a right to a college education? If so, does this mean that we have a right to free tuition if we cannot afford to pay for it ourselves? Do we have a right to a happy childhood? Do we have a right to marry whomever we want, as long as we are both adults and capable of giving our informed consent?

The extent and limits of our liberty rights can be just as ambiguous. Do we have a right to work in an obscenity-free environment? Or does freedom of speech entail that our coworkers have a right to use obscene language in the workplace? Does freedom of the press extend to publishing or broadcasting racist and sexist material?

Former United Nations ambassador Jeane Kirkpatrick (1926–2006) believed that the rhetoric of rights has gotten out of hand. She compared our practice of issuing endless declarations of human rights to writing "a letter to Santa Claus." People now have "rights" to such things as "full development of personality," to "peace," to a "new economic order." The assumption that rights are natural and do not have to be justified has contributed to this problem. The list of rights, Kirkpatrick wrote, "can multiply indefinitely because no clear standard informs them, and no great reflection produced them."[27] She pointed out that, when people lack the ability to assert these ideal rights or to fulfill their life goals, they complain that someone or the government must be depriving them of their rights. Kirkpatrick argued that having an interest in achieving a goal is not the same as having a right to that goal and that what is needed instead is a discussion of liberty and welfare rights within a realistic social setting instead of a utopian context.

Exercises

1. Which of the rights listed in the United Nation's Universal Declaration of Human Rights (see http://www.un.org/en/udhrbook/pdf/udhr_booklet_en_web .pdf) are liberty (negative) rights and which are welfare (positive) rights? Make a list of the rights that you think are most important and a list of those that you consider least important. Which type of rights—liberty or welfare—occurs most in each list?

2. Libertarians believe that the power of the government should be limited. In which of the following cases, in your view, would it be morally acceptable for the government to limit our liberty? Support your answers.

    a. Military conscription for men and women ages 18–45

    b. Forcing the homeless into shelters when the temperature drops well below freezing

    c. Mandatory steroid and drug testing for college athletes

    d. Mandatory AIDS testing for medical workers

    e. Prohibiting people under twenty-one from purchasing alcohol

    f. Smoking bans in public places, such as parks, streets, and beaches

3. In his book *On Liberty*, John Stuart Mill argued that "liberty of the press [was] one of the securities against corrupt tyrannical government," including the "tyranny of the majority" in democratic countries. The current definition of

"terrorism" allows the FBI to investigate online discussion boards that are used by groups that they suspect might have anti-American or terrorist connections. Discuss whether John Stuart Mill would regard this as an infringement on the "freedom of the press."

4. There are over 20 million pornographic Web sites, and 25 percent of all search engine requests are for pornography. Pornography is a multibillion dollar enterprise. In a typical week, 40 million Americans visit porn sites on a regular basis, with 70 percent of men between the ages of 18 and 24 viewing these sites in a typical month.[28] Should freedom of speech extend to the Internet and, if so, should there be limitations on this freedom? Support your answer.

5. In 1991, a student was expelled from Brown University for shouting racist, homophobic, and anti-Semitic epithets outside a campus dormitory. The student was drunk at the time. This was the second time he had been found guilty of violating school rules against engaging in "abusive, threatening or demeaning actions based on race, religion, gender, handicap, ethnicity, national origin, or sexual orientation." President Gregorian of Brown University assured the press that the university would never expel anyone for exercising freedom of speech. However, he defended the university's action in this case by arguing that, although the university's code of conduct does not limit free *speech*, it does prohibit *actions* that show "flagrant disregard for the well-being of others."

   Do you agree with Gregorian? When, if ever, does speech become action? Discuss how you would have handled the situation if you had been president.

6. Following the September 11th terrorist attacks, more than one thousand Arab American men were arrested and imprisoned, some for months without a hearing, for unrelated minor infractions. Many were not even told why they were being detained. Discuss whether restricting the rights of certain groups of people in times of crisis is morally justified and, if so, on what grounds.

7. Lawyer Alan Dershowitz argues that political correctness on college campuses is a serious threat to intellectual freedom and promotes intolerance. He notes that the P.C. movement contains two contradictory tenets: "(1) the demand for 'greater diversity' among students and faculty members; and (2) the need for 'speech codes,' so that racist, sexist and homophobic ideas, attitudes and language do not 'offend' sensitive students." Do you agree with Dershowitz? Discuss how Mill might respond to Dershowitz's argument.

8. In the United States, people have a legal right not to know about their AIDS status. In some states, even convicted child molesters and rapists have a legal right to privacy regarding their AIDS status. In Canada, in contrast, people do not have a legal right not to know their AIDS status, and they can be held criminally liable if they have unprotected sex and do not tell their partners they are infected with the AIDS virus.

   Discuss the two policies in light of liberty and welfare rights. Do victims of sexual assault or partners of people who may be at risk for AIDS have a moral right to know the AIDS status of their assailant or sexual partner? Or are the privacy rights of people who may be infected with the AIDS virus more compelling? Support your answers.

9. Do you agree with Jeane Kirkpatrick's criticism of the current proliferation of rights declarations? Discuss how Kirkpatrick might respond to the list of rights in The Universal Declaration of Human Rights. How can we determine when the claim to a particular right is a reasonable expectation? Support your answer using specific examples.

Rights and the Moral Community

As we noted earlier, possession of rights has been interpreted as stemming from either (a) the power of self-assertion or (b) the interests of beings who may or may not be moral agents. These two models are based on two different paradigms that often come into conflict in discussions over who has what rights and what it means to be the bearer of certain rights.

Connections
On what grounds do utilitarians argue that nonhuman animals are part of the moral community? *See Chapter 8, pages 260-263.*

Traditional natural rights ethics supports a model of rights based on self-assertion. According to this model, the only beings who have rights are those who can make and defend moral claims. Humans, it is argued, have a capacity for rationality and autonomy. Nonhuman animals, on the other hand, lack this capacity for moral choice and self-assertion. Therefore, only humans are members of the moral community.

The Self-Assertion Model of Rights

Philosopher Mary Anne Warren supports the self-assertion model of rights for beings who are persons. She defines a *person* as someone who possesses at least some of the following attributes: consciousness and the capacity to feel pain, reason (the developed capacity to solve new and relatively complex problems), self-motivated activity, the capacity to communicate on indefinitely many possible topics, and the presence of self-concepts and self-awareness.[29]

According to Warren, some humans, such as fetuses, newborns, the comatose, and those who are severely mentally retarded, are not persons and, therefore, are not the bearers of rights. An infant may have rights but only indirectly because of the rights of the parents; however, an unwanted infant has no right to life because the right to life in this case is dependent on the child being wanted by a person. Similarly, animal companions such as dogs and cats may have indirect rights that other nonhuman animals lack because their humans have property rights regarding them that we are bound to respect.

[W]hen an unwanted or defective infant is born into a society which cannot afford and/or is not willing to care for it, then its destruction is permissible.

—MARY ANNE WARREN (1973)[30]

One of the problems with the self-assertion model is that it excludes non-rational humans as well as nonhuman animals. Yet, we generally recognize and protect the rights of small children and humans with severe brain damage, despite the fact that they are not generally recognized as capable of moral judgment and, in some cases, have no potential for rationality.

Another problem with the self-assertion model is its assumption that self-assertion of rights depends on rational thought. Yet many nonhuman animals, as well as infants, respond with indignation when their interests or needs are ignored or thwarted, even though they may lack the power to make others acknowledge their rights.

Connections

What is the fallacy of ignorance? *See Chapter 2, page 58.*

Also, using the possession of reason as a necessary criterion to be a bearer of rights does not succeed in creating a clear line between humans and other animals. The claim that other animals lack free will and self-consciousness because we cannot prove that they have these faculties is based on the *fallacy of ignorance* rather than any actual proof. Furthermore, if other animals are incapable of relatively complex reason, there would be no point in using nonhuman animals in learning experiments.

The Interests Model of Rights

An alternative model is based upon the principle of equal consideration of interests. According to this model, the existence of interests is based on our capacity for suffering and pleasure and our concept of the good life. Infants have a right to a secure and safe environment because it is in their interests. The interests model starts with the presumption of moral equality. The principle of equality among humans, as we have already noted, is not based on an empirical description of the actual equality but on a moral ideal of equal concern for others regardless of their social and political power or their particular abilities.

The self-assertion model, in contrast, limits "equal" respect to only those humans who have the power to demand respect from others. By doing so, the self-assertion model sets up a contradiction between the principle of equal respect and its claim that rights are based on self-assertion. To make equality of rights based on the possession of rationality and the power of self-assertion is a denial of equal human rights.

Pros and Cons of the Two Models

Both the self-assertion model and the interests model have shortcomings. The self-assertion model fails to take into account the social context in which people assert their rights. Those with social and political power are able to assert their rights at the expense of those who are weaker. The inability of certain groups to assert their rights leads to their further degradation. The interests model, on the other hand, allows the weak and those unwilling to assert themselves to fulfill their interests at the expense of those who work hard.

Most of us believe that people who work hard should be rewarded for their effort, but most of us also believe that those who, through no fault of their own, are unable to pursue their interests have a right to some help. Much of public policy consists of determining what constitutes a legitimate interest and when this interest becomes a claim upon others.

Rights and Nonhuman Animals

Discussions of equality and rights in traditional Western moral philosophy have generally been limited to questions of human equality. The battle for equal rights for all groups of humans during the various civil rights movements fueled a demand for respect for the rights of nonhuman animals as well. Many people who were engaged in human rights movements, such as Mohandas Gandhi, Mary Wollstonecraft, Susan B. Anthony, Elizabeth Cady Stanton, and Horace Greeley, later became involved in the animal rights movement. The early feminists regarded animals as the next logical step, after acquiring rights for women and other humans, and were at the forefront of the antivivisection movement. If we are to take the concept of equal interests seriously, then it must be extended not just to humans but to all sentient beings.

The animals of the world exist for their own reasons. They were not made for humans any more than black people were made for white, or women created for men.

—ALICE WALKER, Foreword to Marjorie Spiegel's *The Dreaded Comparison* (1989)

The moral equality of all sentient beings, however, does not entail that humans and nonhuman animals have the same rights. Different species have different interests. There are distinctly human rights, such as the right to religious freedom and the right to a formal education, that other animals lack because they have no interest in either organized religion or formal schooling. Different people also have different interests. For example, men do not have a right to a routine mammography. Able-bodied humans do not have a right to collect disability payments.

On the other hand, all sentient beings have an interest in not being tortured, not because they are capable of rational thought but because they have the capacity to feel pain. Philosopher James Rachels writes:

> While it is generally acknowledged by philosophers that liberty and freedom from coercion are essential if we humans are to develop and lead the types of lives where we can exercise our powers as rational agents, it is also true that liberty is necessary for many non-human animals if they are to live the sorts of lives, and thrive, in ways that are natural to them.[31]

The right of nonhuman animals to have enough space in which to pursue their interests is recognized and minimally respected in the Animal Welfare Act and its amendments. The Animal Welfare Act (1966) also expects experimenters to respect animals' interests in health care, proper nutrition, and a clean living space; however, the act does not recognize their liberty rights or their right to life. John Rawls points out that our current discussions of justice are limited because they fail to "embrace all moral relationships . . . and [they] leave out of account how we are to conduct ourselves toward animals and the rest of nature."[32] He suggests that, to devise a correct description of our relations to animals and the environment, we will have to "work out a world view that is suited for this purpose."[33]

Gandhi was adamantly opposed to the exploitation of nonhuman animals. Like the Buddhists, his moral philosophy centered on the interconnectedness of all life and the importance of extending moral respect to all living beings if we are to have a peaceful world. Because we are all interconnected, in Buddhism there is a strong emphasis on welfare rights and the correlative duty to provide care for everyone. Nagarjuna, in the *Friendly Epistle and Jewel Rosary of Royal Advice*, for example, recommends not only the total care of all citizens and travelers passing through but also that "a special custodian be appointed to provide food, water, sugar and piles of grain to all anthills, caring also for dogs and birds."[34]

Tom Regan, in his book *The Case for Animal Rights* argues that it is not merely an act of kindness or beneficence to treat animals with respect. Animals who have desires and interests, an emotional life, and a psycho-physical identity over time are what Regan calls "subjects-of-life." Subjects-of-life can be either moral agents or moral patients. *Moral agents* include those who can be held morally accountable. Moral patients include human infants, people who are mentally disabled, and most mammals. Both moral agents and moral patients, as beings that are subjects-of-life, have inherent value and a right to respectful treatment. As humans, we have a right to defend ourselves against animals that pose innocent threats, such as those that are carriers of diseases harmful to humans; however, we cannot override other animals' rights simply for our own pleasure or to make a profit. The goal of wildlife management, Regan argues, is to defend animals' rights by providing them with the opportunity to live their own lives free of human predation and exploitation.

Connections

What is anthropocentrism? *See Chapter 1, page 17.*

The idea of extending equal treatment to all living beings runs contrary to the beliefs of John Locke, who based his natural rights ethics on the presumption that humans are a special and unique creation of God. He argues that to base rights on equal consideration of the interests of all living beings, rather than on the so-called special nature of humans, is to deny the natural order of creation. This anthropocentric, theologically based worldview of humans not only disallows the possibility of nonhuman beings having rights but grants humans the inalienable right to exploit nonhuman animals and the environment with impunity.

Buddhism and Rights Ethics

Buddhists have been very active in many of the contemporary rights movements. The principle of human rights can be found in Buddha's teachings on the "Holy Community" (*Aryasamgha*). Unlike natural rights ethics, Buddhist ethics is not founded upon a theological worldview that places humans below God but above nonhuman animals. Instead, the reality of human interdependence with all other beings is at the heart of Buddhist rights ethics. Our most important duty is not to harm living beings (ahimsa). All living beings, not just humans, have a correlative right not to be harmed. The right to be treated with respect and not to be harmed extends not just to humans and other animals but to all of nature.

Buddhism affirms the absolute worth of the individual being; at the same time, it regards the individual in relation to the good of the whole. The concepts of equality and moral rights are meaningful only to the extent that they belong to the greater realm of existence. Events, and hence rights, originate in relationship. Consequently, we have a duty to affirm and respect the rights and dignity of others. To see ourselves as isolated individuals is to fragment or truncate ourselves. To be true to the self is to extend beyond oneself. Each event in our lives—each life process—is "virtually dependent on or related to all the elements present within the surroundings. . . . In other words, each individual is responsible for maintaining an extensive concern for everything that lies in his or her path of experience."[35]

Because morality demands that we continually expand our moral community, it does not make sense in Buddhist ethics to speak of rights from a strictly human point of view. Relationship involves all living beings and all of nature. Western natural rights ethics, in contrast, allows us to devalue nonhumans and to regard nature purely objectively and to continue to exploit it.

[W]hat we call "rights" inheres not only in people but equally in all sentient beings, as well as in nature itself.

—TAITETSU UNNO, "Personal Rights and Contemporary Buddhism" (1988), p. 137

Contemporary Buddhist ethicists regard the egoism of the self-assertion model of natural rights ethics as destructive to individual self-realization and to community. Our Western economy, based on an individualistic concept of natural human rights, where there is no correlative duty to act compassionately and to avoid harming others, has created a world where danger and inequality abound. Buddhist ethicists maintain that we cannot solve worldwide problems of human misery and environmental destruction while permitting an individualism that allows people the right to freely pursue their own concept of the good life at the expense of other human and nonhuman beings.

The Buddhist concept of right livelihood also involves avoiding occupations that harm others, such as the military or working for a company that exploits human labor or creates products that harm humans or other beings. In this sense, Buddhist ethics offers an alternative communal vision of rights that may have even greater relevance for today's world than it did in Buddha's time.

Exercises

*1. Which model of rights—the self-assertion model or the interests model—is most prevalent in our society? Use examples, including those from your community service work, to support your answer.

2. Critically analyze the position that our interest in a minimum standard of living or in good health constitutes a claim on society to provide these. Does society have an obligation only to make it easier for us to assert these rights, or does it have an actual obligation to provide certain social goods such as housing and health care? Support your answer.

3. Tom Regan argues that other animals have a right not to be eaten by us, used in experiments, or caged in zoos. Discuss his position in light of the self-assertion model and the interests model of rights. If we accept the self-assertion model, which states that only moral agents have rights, would this justify the use of infants and brain-damaged adults as well as nonhuman animals in medical experiments? Defend your position.

4. Using the three-tier model of reasoning from Chapter 2, pages 31–34, analyze Locke's, Warren's, Buddha's, and Regan's worldviews regarding the proper place of humans in the natural order. Which interpretation is most consistent with your experience? How does this worldview affect your thinking on the rights of nonrational humans and nonhuman animals? Explain.

5. Examine your college major and your future career plans in light of the Buddhist concept of right livelihood and in light of the libertarian concept of laissez-faire capitalism. Which approach do you think is most consistent with the demands of Kant's categorical imperative? Explain.

6. Buddhist ethicists see rights in relation to our membership in the global community. How should we, as members of a wealthy nation, balance our rights with the rights of survival of people in poorer nations? Discuss your answer in light of your own lifestyle and our national policy.

Critique of Rights Ethics

Rights are an important component of any moral philosophy. Although few philosophers deny that rights are meaningful, the origin and nature of rights have been the focus of considerable debate. Natural rights ethics in particular has had a tremendous influence on modern Western culture.

1. *The theological basis of natural rights ethics, which privileges humans as a special creation, is difficult to justify.* The reduction of nonhuman animals and the environment to the status of resources for humans has had devastating effects on our environment. Furthermore, the claim of natural rights ethicists that rights are based upon the principle of equality has led animal rights advocates to question why this principle should not also be extended to nonhuman animals. The extension of rights to all humans and even to nonhumans has been a difficult endeavor, but one that has been very fruitful in calling our attention to the dignity of those who are different from us.

2. *The belief of natural rights ethicists that rights are self-evident is problematic.* Marxists have called into question the "natural" and "inalienable" right to own property. They argue that rights are historically conceived and often work to benefit those in power. The doctrine that rights are self-evident and do not need to be justified has also led to a proliferation of demands for certain rights. Without any criteria for justifying rights, there is no way to decide which of these rights should be taken seriously and which are frivolous. For this reason, most philosophers argue that rights are derived from duties and, in particular, from the fundamental duty of respect for the dignity of others.

3. *The separation between liberty and welfare rights is not clear-cut.* Most rights ethicists distinguish between liberty and welfare rights. However, the libertarian assertion that liberty rights do not involve imposing upon the rights of others, as do welfare rights, ignores the need for the legal and social structures—including the police, the military, and the courts—that are necessary to protect these liberty rights, such as the right to own property. In other words, the self-assertion model favored by libertarians actually depends on a welfare right to be protected by an extensive and expensive legal and police system.

4. *Not all people are equally capable of asserting their rights.* The philosophical belief that all people are created equal has too often been treated as a description rather than as a moral ideal. Basing rights on self-assertion favors those who have access to political and social power at the expense of those who lack this power. The interests model, on the other hand, tends to favor those who are weak—whether because of the natural lottery, restrictive social roles, or just plain laziness—at the expense of those who show initiative.

5. *Rights protect our dignity as persons.* Rights ethics is mainly problematic if it is used as a complete explanation of ethics; however, it is an important component of an ethics theory. The concept of rights focuses our attention on the claim that others must be treated with respect in a way that talk of duties alone does not. If we do not have rights, then all our claims to be treated with respect simply amount to requests for favors and privileges. If there are no rights, then we need to make a case for having our freedom or enjoying the same opportunities that others in our society enjoy.

Exercises

1. Critically evaluate the rationale behind the claim that only humans have moral rights.

2. Make a list of six to eight moral rights. Which two of these rights do you consider to be most important and why? What is the source of these rights? Are these rights self-evident or do they come from society or elsewhere? Discuss also whether your exercise of these rights is based on your interests or on your ability to assert them.

3. Referring to the rights you listed in exercise 2, do these rights exist independently of duties or are they derived from duties? Explain. Discuss ways in which these rights protect your dignity and your ability to pursue your interests and life goals.

Summary

1. The articulation of rights ethics in Western philosophy emerged during the period of Enlightenment as a protest against the concept of absolute sovereignty. This dissatisfaction culminated in 1789 with the French Declaration of the Rights of Man and Citizen and the U.S. Bill of Rights.

2. Slavery and the denial of certain basic rights to women led to a renewed interest in rights ethics in the United States in the mid-1800s.

3. Interest in human rights was renewed following World War II and the Holocaust. In 1948, the United Nations issued the Universal Declaration of Human Rights, which is based on a natural law theory interpretation of human rights.

4. Moral rights are not the same as legal rights.

5. According to natural rights ethicists, such as Hobbes, Locke, and Jefferson, rights are self-evident and inalienable and exist independently of and prior to duty. They stem from our human nature, which is created in the image of God. All and only humans have rights. For this reason, natural rights are often referred to as human rights.

6. According to natural rights ethicists, all humans are created equal. This is known as the principle of equality.

7. Thomas Hobbes and John Locke were two of the leading rights ethicists of the Enlightenment. Thomas Jefferson was especially influenced by the philosophy of John Locke.

8. Hobbes and Locke maintained that people lived in an unpleasant *state of nature* before the formation of government. The primary purpose of government is to protect people's equal rights.

9. Locke stated that we have a natural right to own property. By mixing our labor with the land, it becomes our property.

10. Ayn Rand argued that a laissez-faire capitalist society is the only type that can protect people's natural rights.

11. Both Locke and Rand were libertarians. A *libertarian* places more value on liberty rights. A strict libertarian is opposed to placing any social or political restraints upon individual freedom.

12. Karl Marx was opposed to any conception of rights that existed independently of the duty of justice. He argued that the list of so-called natural rights was historically conceived to justify certain economic and political systems and to protect the landowning bourgeois.

13. *Liberation ethicist* Gustavo Gutierrez argues that the right to private ownership has been won at the expense of the rights of the poor.

14. Marx and Gutierrez argue that rights must be considered within a historical context.

15. Most philosophers maintain that rights are derived from duty. Because moral duty is a broader concept, rights ethics is sometimes included as a branch of deontology.

16. Jeremy Bentham thought that any talk of natural rights existing independently of the laws of society was nonsense.

17. John Stuart Mill argued that moral rights exist only within a social context and are derived from the principle of utility. Mill also believed that liberty rights are more important than welfare rights.

18. According to Immanuel Kant, rights stem from the categorical imperative and from our duty to respect the dignity of all people.

19. Most philosophers consider rights to be prima facie rather than absolute.

20. There are two basic types of moral rights: *Liberty* or *negative rights* entail the right to be left alone to pursue our *legitimate interests* (interests that do not violate others' similar and equal interests). *Welfare* or *positive rights* entail the right to receive our proper share of certain goods.

21. John Rawls attempts to resolve the conflict between liberty rights and welfare rights through the application of his principles of justice.

22. Only those in the moral community possess rights. The possession of rights has been interpreted as stemming from either (a) the power of self-assertion or (b) the interests of beings. Most natural rights ethicists believe that rights are based on self-assertion.

23. Mary Anne Warren supports the self-assertion model of rights. The only beings who have rights, she maintains, are those who meet certain criteria that include consciousness, reason, self-motivation, the ability to communicate, and self-awareness.

24. The interests model is based on the principle of equality. Tom Regan argues that the principle of equality also applies to nonhuman beings that are the subjects-of-life with their own desires and interests.

25. Buddhist rights ethics is based on our interdependence with all living beings and our duty not to harm other living beings (ahimsa).

Two Treatises of Civil Government

John Locke

Of the State of Nature

... 4. To understand political power aright, and derive it from its original, we must consider what estate all men are naturally in, and that is, a state of perfect freedom to order their actions, and dispose of their possessions and persons as they think fit, within the bounds of the law of Nature, without asking leave or depending upon the will of any other man.

A state also of equality, wherein all the power and jurisdiction is reciprocal, no one having more than another, there being nothing more evident than that creatures of the same species and rank, promiscuously born to all the same advantages of Nature, and the use of the same faculties, should also be equal one amongst another, without subordination or subjection, ...

6. But though this be a state of liberty, yet it is not a state of license; though man in that state have an uncontrollable liberty to dispose of his person or possessions, yet he has not liberty to destroy himself, or so much as any creature in his possession, but where some nobler use than its bare preservation calls for it. The state of nature has a law of nature to govern it, which obliges everyone; and reason, which is that law, teaches all mankind who will but consult it, that, being all equal and independent, no one ought to harm another in his life, health, liberty, or possessions. For men being all the workmanship of one omnipotent and infinitely wise Maker— ... they are His property, ...

Of Property

... 25. God, who hath given the world to men in common, hath also given them reason to make use of it to the best advantage of life and convenience. The earth and all that is therein is given to men for the support and comfort of their being. And though all the fruits it naturally produces, and beasts it feeds, belong to mankind in common, as they are produced by the spontaneous hand of Nature, and nobody has originally a private domination exclusive of the rest of mankind in any of them, as they are thus in their natural state, yet being given for the use of men, there must of necessity be a means to appropriate them some way or other before they can be of any use, or at all beneficial, to any particular men. ...

26. Though the earth and all inferior creatures be common to all men, yet every man has a "property" in his own "person." This nobody has any right to but himself. The "labour" of his body and the "work" of his hands, we may say, are properly his. Whatsoever, then, he removes out of the state that Nature hath provided and left it in, he hath mixed his labour with it, and joined to it something that is his own, and thereby makes it his property. It being by him removed from the common state nature placed it in, it hath by this labour something annexed to it that excludes the common right of other men. ...

Of the Beginning of Political Societies

95. Men being, as has been said, by nature all free, equal, and independent, no one can be put out of this estate and subjected to the political power of another without his own consent, which is done by agreeing with other men, to join and unite into a community for their comfortable, safe, and peaceable living, one amongst another, in a secure enjoyment of their properties, and

a greater security against any that are not of it. This any number of men may do, because it injures not the freedom of the rest; they are left, as they were, in the liberty of the state of Nature. When any number of men have so consented to make one community or government, they are thereby presently incorporated, and make one body politic, wherein the majority have a right to act and conclude the rest. . . .

99. Whosoever, therefore, out of a state of Nature unite into a community, must be understood to give up all the power necessary to the ends for which they unite into society to the majority of the community, unless they expressly agreed in any number

greater than the majority. And this is done by barely agreeing to unite into one political society, which is all the compact that is, or needs be, between the individuals that enter into or make up a commonwealth. And thus, that which begins and actually constitutes any political society is nothing but the consent of any number of freemen capable of majority, to unite and incorporate into such a society. And this is that, and that only, which did or could give beginning to any lawful government in the world. . . .

"Natural Rights," from *Two Treatises of Civil Government* (London: A & J Churchill, 1698). Notes have been omitted.

Discussion Questions

1. Relate the provisions in Articles 25 and 29 of the Universal Declaration of Human Rights (available online at http://www.un.org/en/udhrbook/pdf/udhr_booklet_en_web.pdf) to the current discussion on entitlements, such as health care and education.

2. Critically analyze Locke's argument that there is a natural, God-given right to own property. Does the belief that such rights are natural, rather than derived from duty, work to benefit those who have the least power in our society? Or does it further empower those who are already privileged? Support your answers.

3. Discuss whether Locke's position on rights is consistent with that of the Universal Declaration of Human Rights.

Notes

1. Immanuel Kant, "Duties Dictated by Justice," in *Lectures on Ethics* (Indianapolis: Hackett, 1775–1780/1963), p. 211.
2. Elizabeth Cady Stanton, Susan B. Anthony, and Matilda Joslyn Gage, eds., *History of Woman Suffrage* (New York: Fowler & Wells, 1881), pp. 1, 70–73.
3. Mohandas K. Gandhi, quoted in Anand T. Hingorani, *Gandhi for the 21st Century, Vol. 11: None High, None Low* (Mumbai, India: Bhavans, 1975), p. 2.
4. John Locke, "On Property," in *Two Treatises of Government* (1690), sect. 41.
5. Ibid., sect. 36.
6. Ayn Rand, *The Virtue of Selfishness* (New York: New American Library, 1961), p. 117.
7. Rand, *The Virtue of Selfishness*, p. 93.

8. Locke, "On Property", sect. 25.

9. Annette Baier, "Trust and Antitrust," *Ethics* 96 (January 1986): 247.

10. U.S. Census Bureau News, "Housing Vacancies and Homeownership," 2016, www.census .gov/housing/. See also http://realtormag.realtor.org/daily-news/2016/04/29/home-ownership-rate-nears-record-lows.

11. Gustavo Gutierrez, *The Power of the Poor in History*, trans. Robert R. Barr (Maryknoll, NY: Orbis Books, 1983), p. 87.

12. Ibid., p. 176.

13. "Inside Gate, India, India's Good Life; Outside Gate, The Servants' Slums," *New York Times*, June 9, 2009, p. 1.

14. Gutierrez, *The Power of the Poor in History*, p. 211.

15. Jeremy Bentham, "Anarchical Fallacies," in *Society, Law, and Morality*, ed. Frederick A. Olafson (Englewood Cliffs, NJ: Prentice-Hall, 1961), p. 347.

16. John Stuart Mill, "Utilitarianism," in *Utilitarianism*, ed. Mary Warnock (New York: Meridian, 1962), p. 309.

17. Immanuel Kant, *Lectures on Ethics*, trans. Louis Infield (New York: Harper & Row, 1963), p. 193.

18. For example, see Leviticus 14: 9–10 and Deuteronomy 24: 19–20.

19. Samuel A. Spralls III, Patrick Okonkwo, and Obasi H. Akan, "A Traveler to Distant Places Should Make No Enemies: Toward Understanding Nigerian Negotiating Style," *Journal of Applied Business and Economics*, 12, no. 3 (2011): 11–25.

20. United Nations, "Background Report Information on Sexual Violence Used as a Tool of War," March 14, 2013.

21. See http://www.civicyouth.org for a further breakdown of these statistics.

22. Gallup Poll, "Death Penalty," May 3–6, 2012.

23. Robert Nozick, *Anarchy, State and Utopia* (New York: Basic Books, 1974), p. ix.

24. Kant, "Duties to Oneself," in *Lectures on Ethics* (Indianapolis: Hackett, 1775–1780/1963), p. 123.

25. Immanuel Kant, *The Moral Law: Groundwork of the Metaphysic of Morals*, trans. H. J. Paton (London: Routledge & Kegan Paul, 1991), p. 63.

26. Ayn Rand, "Man's Rights," in *The Virtue of Selfishness: A New Concept of Egoism* (New York: New American Library, 1964), p. 113.

27. Jeane J. Kirkpatrick, "Human Rights and Foreign Policy," in *Human Rights and American Foreign Policy*, ed. Fred F. Baumann (Gambier, OH: Kenyon College, Public Affairs Conference Center, 1982), p. 9.

28. "The Stats on Internet Pornography," January 4, 2013, www.dailyinfographics.com/the-stats-on-internet-pornography.

29. Mary Anne Warren, "On the Moral and Legal Status of Abortion," *Monist* 57, no. 1 (January 1973).

30. Ibid.

31. James Rachels, "Do Animals Have a Right to Liberty?" in *Animal Rights and Human Obligations*, ed. Tom Regan and Peter Singer (Englewood Cliffs, NJ: Prentice-Hall, 1976).

32. John Rawls, *A Theory of Justice* (Cambridge, MA: Harvard University Press, 1971), p. 17.

33. Ibid., p. 512.

34. Robert A. F. Thurman, "Social and Cultural Rights in Buddhism," in *Human Rights and the World's Religions*, ed. Leroy Rouner (Notre Dame, IN: University of Notre Dame Press, 1988), pp. 157–158.

35. Kenneth K. Inada, "The Buddhist Perspective on Human Rights," in *Human Rights in Religious Tradition*, ed. Arlene Swidler (New York: Pilgrim Press, 1982), p. 38.

CHAPTER 12

Virtue Ethics and the Good Life

*Ethics is sometimes described as the theory of virtue. . . . A man
who complies with coercive laws is not necessarily virtuous. To be
virtuous man must, to be sure, respect the law and be punctilious
in his observance of human rights; but virtue goes beyond this, to
the disposition from which the action . . . arises.*
— IMMANUEL KANT, "Introductory Observations,"
Lectures on Ethics

*The rule of virtue can be compared to the Pole Star which commands
the homage of the multitude of Stars without leaving its place.*
— CONFUCIUS, *The Analects*[1]

More high schools and colleges now require community service for graduation.
Some states have introduced bills that would mandate community service for
students at state colleges and universities. These statewide initiatives have generally met with resistance. Adria, a single mother, is already struggling to balance work, family, and college. She says that the community service requirement,
on top of a full course load and having to work twenty hours a week to support
herself and her child, is too great a burden and unfairly discriminates against
nontraditional students. Adria also maintains that forcing students to do community service violates the volunteer quality of community service. While she
agrees that we should give back to the community, she argues that it should be
because we choose to out of a sense of good will, not because we are forced to.
She maintains that students may be turned off by community service if they are
being coerced into doing it, and thus may be less motivated to perform it in the
future.

Proponents of mandatory community service disagree with Adria. They
point out that community service combined with a program of service learning
promotes a sense of empathy and civic responsibility as well as the moral
development of students. It is through habituation, the repeated performance
of good works, that we become more virtuous. They also note that part of the
mission of colleges is to produce a well-rounded student, not to just pass on
academic information. This task should include the moral and character
development of students.

Is promoting the development of virtue in students part of the mandate of colleges? Can, or should, colleges impose personal and moral growth on students? In addition, does mandating community service entail using the recipients of the community service as a means only? Indeed, can we be compelled to be virtuous, or does the desire to be virtuous have to come from within us, as Adria claims?

In this chapter, we'll be studying virtue ethics and the importance of a virtuous character. We'll also look at the relationship between character and action. Finally, we'll examine the role of moral education in shaping our character and behavior.

Virtue Ethics and Character

Virtue ethics emphasizes *right being* over *right action*. According to virtue ethics, the sort of person we are constitutes the heart of our moral life. More important than the rules or principles we follow is our character. A person of virtuous character can be depended upon to do the right thing. Virtue ethics is not an alternative to ethical theories that stress right conduct, such as utilitarianism and deontological theories. Rather, virtue ethics and theories of right action complement each other.

Buddhism, Taoism, feminist care ethics, and the moral philosophies of David Hume, Aristotle, and Jesus are often classified as virtue ethics. Confucian ethics has strong traditions of both virtue ethics and deontology. Many of the ancient Greek ethicists also focused mainly on virtue and character rather than on duty and principles.

We are not concerned to know what goodness is, but how we are to become good men, for this alone gives the study [of ethics] its practical value.

—ARISTOTLE, *Nicomachean Ethics*, Bk. 2, Ch. 2

What Is a Virtue?

A moral **virtue** is an admirable character trait or disposition to habitually act in a manner that benefits oneself and others. The actions of virtuous people stem from a respect and concern for the well-being of themselves and others. The virtue of *jen* in Confucianism, for example, is translated as benevolence, love, affection, compassion, altruism, or perfect virtue. In Hinduism, the four cardinal virtues are nonviolence, truth, purity, and self-control, and in Christianity the seven main virtues are faith, hope, charity, fortitude, justice, prudence, and temperance.[2] However, virtue is more than simply a collection of disparate personality traits. Virtue is an overarching quality of goodness or excellence that gives unity and integrity to a person's character and, in turn, his or her actions.

A **vice**, in contrast, is a character trait or disposition to act in a manner that harms oneself and/or others. Vices stand in our way of achieving happiness and the good life. Ill will, anger, uncontrolled sexual desire, sloth, restlessness, and worry are considered in Buddhist ethics to be vices or undesirable character traits. These traits stand in the way of enlightenment and moral perfection.

Not all beneficial traits are moral virtues. Traits such as health and intelligence are beneficial, but they are not what we would consider moral virtues. What distinguishes moral virtues from other beneficial characteristics, according to most philosophers, is the will—the faculty that allows us to make rational choices. We do not decide to be intelligent or healthy in the same sense that we choose to be courageous or generous.

Aristotle divided the virtues into two broad categories: intellectual and moral. The intellectual virtues, he claimed, are based on excellence in reasoning skill and include wisdom and prudence. The moral virtues include courage, temperance, liberality, generosity, magnificence, proper pride, gentleness, truthfulness, justice, patience, friendliness, modesty, and wittiness.

According to Aristotle, the intellectual virtues are cultivated through growth and experience, and the moral virtues are cultivated through habit and action. Wisdom is the most important virtue because it is the one that makes all other virtues (intellectual and moral) possible. (See Table 12.1 on page 401.) However, wisdom alone is not sufficient for moral virtue; practice or habituation is also necessary:

> [T]he moral virtues we do acquire by first exercising them. The same is true of the arts and crafts in general. The craftsman has to learn how to make things, but he learns in the process of making them. . . . By a similar process we become just by performing just actions, temperate by performing temperate actions, brave by performing brave actions.[3]

Deontologist W. D. Ross likewise lists "self-improvement," or the development of a virtuous character, as one of his seven prima facie duties. Indeed, Ross is often considered an Aristotelian in his approach to ethics.[4]

Aristotle distinguished between moral virtues and natural virtues. Traits such as gentleness, friendliness, courage, and loyalty in a cat or a dog, or in a child, are natural virtues rather than moral virtues because they presumably do not involve the will. In other words, Aristotle would say that Angus, my friend Dan's dog who helped to rescue some drowning swimmers, was simply doing what came naturally to him as a Labrador retriever. In contrast, Aristotle would probably argue that Dan's courageous actions, even though they may have seemed spontaneous, were the outcome of years of cultivating the virtue of courage until it became a habitual response to seeing others in danger.

One of the trademarks of virtuous people is that they not only act on principle, but they give us an example to follow: They are our heroes. Persons of character such as Harriet Tubman, Buddha, Jesus, Elizabeth Cady Stanton, Socrates, and Martin Luther King Jr. do not merely give us principles to follow. More important, they give us an example to follow by acting as role models. Virtuous people can be counted on to act in a manner that benefits others. They

Connections

How does striving toward enlightenment or self-realization benefit us and others? See *Chapter 1, pages 13–14.*

Connections

Why were Dan Stock's actions seemingly inconsistent with psychological egoism? See *Chapter 7, page 215.*

also show a willingness to perform *supererogatory* actions—going beyond what is required by everyday morality. Vicious people, on the other hand, only perform beneficial actions when it benefits them.

People tend to emulate those who are at a higher stage of moral development. Because of this, a highly virtuous person in a leadership role can have a morally uplifting effect upon the whole community. In the French village of Le Chambon, for example, thirty-five hundred villagers rescued more than six thousand Jews, mostly children, from the Nazis. The leader of the community was André Trocme, a local pastor who advocated nonviolent resistance to the Nazis and universal love and compassion for all people. Similarly, when Gandhi, who believed in respect for all life, insisted on using only nonviolent resistance in India's fight for independence from Britain, the people of India rallied behind him.

Because virtuous people, such as Gandhi and André Trocme, tend to act in ways that benefit others, developing a virtuous character plays a role in utilitarian theory. Mill wrote:

> There is nothing which makes [the virtuous person] so much a blessing to [other members of society], as the cultivation of disinterested love of virtue. And consequently, . . . [utilitarianism] enjoins and requires the cultivation of the love of virtue up to the greatest strength possible, as being above all things important to the general happiness.[5]

Connections

How do gains in moral development affect our real life behavior? *See Chapter 3, page 92.*

Virtue, Happiness, and Human Nature

Virtue ethics is based upon certain assumptions about human nature. Most virtue ethicists believe that virtue is important for achieving not only moral well-being but also happiness and inner harmony. Aristotle referred to this sense of psychological well-being as **eudaemonia**. Eudaemonia is a condition of the soul or psyche; it is the good that humans seek by nature and that arises from the fulfillment of our function as humans. Eudaemonia is similar to Eastern and modern Western concepts such as enlightenment, nirvana, self-actualization, and proper self-esteem.[6]

People who are virtuous enjoy being so. By being virtuous, we are truest to ourselves. Therefore, virtue is essential to inner harmony and contentment. "There is no greater joy for me," Confucian philosopher Mencius taught, "than to find, on self-examination, that I am true to myself. Try your best to treat others as you would wish to be treated yourself, and you will find that this is the shortest way to benevolence."[7] Westerners will recognize this as the Golden Rule; in Chinese ethics, it is known as the **principle of reciprocity**.

In modern Western philosophy, with our emphasis on disembodied reason, we tend to lose sight of the connection between virtue and happiness. However, there is scientific support for the claim that there is an intimate connection between happiness and leading a virtuous life. As we noted in Chapter 7, Veenhoven's review of studies on factors that contribute to happiness found that happiness levels are highest among people who value inner peace, love, sympathy, friendship, forgiveness, and tolerance—all traits that most philosophers consider virtues.[8]

Most (if not all) moral philosophies that stress right action also recognize the role of virtue in bringing about right actions. A courageous and compassionate person is more likely to come to someone else's rescue. An honest and loyal person is more likely to carry out the duty of fidelity; a generous person is more likely to act justly than someone who is stingy; and a compassionate person is more likely to refrain from harming others. However, although virtue involves right action, it is not reducible to actions.

The Role of Intention

An action may be morally good because it has a certain quality, such as being beneficial; however, this in itself does not make it a virtuous act. For example, a wealthy person may give a million dollars to a charity simply because she wants the tax deduction or a building named after her. Although the act itself is good in terms of its consequences, we would probably hesitate to say that she is virtuous for doing it. The actions of a virtuous person stem from an underlying disposition of concern for the well-being of others and themselves, or what Aristotle called "a certain frame of mind." A poor widow may give her last coin to the needy out of compassion. Although the consequences of her action are not nearly as far-reaching as those of the wealthy patroness, most people would agree that the widow is the more virtuous of the two.

While utilitarians maintain that the disposition of a person is irrelevant to the goodness of an action, they recognize the importance of virtue since a virtuous person is more likely to perform beneficial acts and abstain from harming others. Being virtuous not only brings the virtuous person pleasure but also contributes to the happiness of others. For this reason, we ought to cultivate a virtuous and benevolent disposition. According to Mill, it is through the cultivation of our natural feelings of benevolence that we generate the "most passionate love of virtue, and the sternest self-control. . . . A person whose desires and impulses are his own—are the expression of his own nature, as it has been developed and modified by his own culture—is said to have character."[9]

Connections
What, according to utilitarians, makes an action morally praiseworthy? *See Chapter 8, pages 242–243.*

Cultivating the Good Will

Simply refraining from harming others is not enough to make us virtuous. It is also necessary to actively cultivate a *good will*. Performing morally good actions is the means by which our natural predisposition and energies are developed into virtues. According to Mill, reflection, which includes moral analysis, provides the bridge that connects action and the cultivation of a virtuous disposition. Our actions test our old habits and call upon us to reflect on our past actions and to reevaluate ourselves and our choices. Reflection, which is grounded in moral values, in turn generates a habitual moral response.

Connections

What is the connection between proper self-esteem and cultivating the good will? *See Chapter 10, pages 318-323.*

Although Kant's moral philosophy focuses primarily on duty, a virtuous character, as embodied in the good will, was very important to him. Indeed, his *Groundwork* of the Metaphysic of Morals opens with a statement not about duty, but about the importance of the good will. A person of good will has good intentions. A virtuous disposition, according to Kant, helps us in our struggle against unruly impulses and obstacles that stand in the way of doing our duty. The more virtuous the person, the easier this struggle will be.

Exercises

1. What is your greatest virtue? If you cannot think of any, ask your friends, family, or classmates who know you what your virtues are.

2. What is happiness? Are virtuous people, such as your hero, happier than vicious people? Are you happier when you are being virtuous? Do you agree with Mill that most people desire virtue and the absence of vice? Relate your answers to the concept of conscience discussed in Chapter 3 and to Gyges' claim in Chapter 7 that the unjust person is happiest.

3. Think of a time when you were asked to help somebody in need, but you didn't feel like doing it. What did you do? Discuss whether it is hypocritical or virtuous for you to do good deeds, such as community service, even though you don't want to and you don't feel any good will toward the person or people you are helping.

4. How would you answer the question: "Do I really have to be good in my heart or do I just have to act good?" Discuss how important being a person of good will, or cultivating the good will, is to your self-concept. Be specific.

*5. Community service in conjunction with an opportunity to reflect on the service provides an excellent opportunity, according to developmental psychologists, to develop virtue and moral character. Discuss ways in which your community service has made you a more virtuous person.

Aristotle: Reason and Virtue

The Importance of Reason for Aristotle

Western philosophy has long considered reason to be more important than sentiment or emotions. "Moral" sentiments such as sympathy have at times been dismissed as residual instincts belonging to our lower or animal nature. Aristotle

---

*An asterisk indicates that the exercise is appropriate for students who are doing community service learning as part of the course.

regarded humans as basically rational beings who must strive to control their nonrational nature. He argued that the nonrational part "from which spring the appetites and desires" participates in reason in a subordinate role.

Aristotle believed that all life has a function that is peculiar to its particular life form. The function peculiar to human life is the exercise of reason.[10] Virtue involves living according to reason. According to Aristotle, virtue is essential if we are to achieve the good life. Only by living in accord with reason, which is our human function, can we achieve happiness (eudaemonia) and inner harmony. (See the selection from Aristotle's *Nicomachean Ethics* at the end of this chapter.)

According to Aristotle, immorality results from a disordered psyche. Virtue serves as a correction to our passions by helping us resist our impulses and passions that interfere with us living the life of reason: the good life. For example, the virtue of courage is a corrective to the emotion of fear. Temperance is a corrective to the temptation to overindulge or to seek immediate pleasure. Aristotle, however, did not want to see passion eliminated; he recognized that emotion is a component of moral goodness. Although our emotions and passions should always be subject to the control of reason, this is not the same as saying that emotions are bad and should be eliminated. Rather, he was saying that emotions such as fear or boldness and anger or pity are appropriate at times, but only when they are under the control of reason.

> **Connections**
> What is the role of habituation in achieving virtue? *See Chapter 3, pages 79-80.*

Aquinas: Reason and Faith

Natural law ethicist Thomas Aquinas was influenced by Aristotle. Like Aristotle, Aquinas saw virtue and reason as correctives to our passions or the animal side of our nature. Aquinas, however, added a new dimension to Aristotelian ethics—that of human sinfulness. He argued that reason alone is not enough to keep humans on the right path. Without God's help, we will succumb to weakness and temptation. For Aquinas, supreme happiness and virtue come from knowing God and through communication with God. Therefore, faith in God was the most important virtue to Aquinas, and pride the greatest vice:

> **Connections**
> Why is reason important in Aquinas's natural law theory? *See Chapter 9, page 282.*

> It is impossible for man's happiness to consist in a created good, for happiness is the perfect good which wholly brings desire to rest . . . nothing can bring the will of man to rest except the universal good. This is not found in any created thing but only in God, for all creatures have good by participation. Hence only God can satisfy the will of man. . . . Therefore, man's happiness consists in God alone. . . . Ultimate and perfect happiness can only be in the vision of the divine essence.[11]

Exercises

1. Aristotle regarded the godly life of contemplation as one of pure happiness. In Buddhist ethics, contemplation is seen as an essential ingredient on the path

to both happiness and the life of virtue. What does the term *contemplation* mean to you? Discuss what role, if any, it plays in your moral life.

2. Discuss the following quotes in light of Aquinas's belief that humans are sinful by nature and Mencius's belief that humans are good by nature.

a. "Scratch a saint, a villain bleeds; beneath each white man, Jim Crow dwells; behind every gentile, an anti-Semite lurks."[12]

b. "All men have a mind which cannot bear to see the sufferings of others."[13]

*3. The emphasis that Aquinas and other natural law ethicists place on faith as the highest virtue has had a profound influence on the Christian concept of service and the good person. Discuss the following prayer from Mother Teresa in the context of your community service work.

The fruit of SILENCE is Prayer
The fruit of PRAYER is Faith
The fruit of FAITH is Love
The fruit of LOVE is Service
The fruit of SERVICE is Peace[14]

Aristotle and Confucius: The Doctrine of the Mean

Perfect is the virtue that accords with the Constant Mean!

—CONFUCIUS, *The Analects*

According to the **doctrine of the mean**, virtues generally entail moderation or seeking the middle path. This doctrine is found in both Eastern and Western philosophies. Buddhist ethics denounces the extremes of excessive indulgence and self-mortification or self-denial. For Buddha, the path of liberation—the life of virtue and inner tranquillity—entailed taking the middle path, also known as the noble path. In Islam, balance or moderation is considered a virtue as well. The Qur'an (25:63–67) states: "And the servants of (God) Most Gracious are those who . . . are not extravagant and not niggardly, but hold a just (balance) between those (extremes)." In feminist care ethics, which we'll study later in this chapter, mature care ethics involves striking a balance between egoism (putting our own needs first) and self-sacrifice. The most thorough explanations of the doctrine of the mean, however, are found in the writings of Aristotle and Confucius. Confucius wrote:

Before the feelings of pleasure, anger, sorrow, and joy are aroused it is called equilibrium (*chung*, centrality, mean). When these feelings are aroused and each and all attain due measure and degree, it is called harmony. Equilibrium is the great foundation of the world, and harmony is its universal path. . . .

The superior man exemplifies the Mean (*chung-yung*). The inferior man acts contrary to the Mean.[15]

TABLE 12.1   Aristotle's Doctrine of the Mean

DEFICIT (VICE)	MEAN (VIRTUE)	EXCESS (VICE)
Cowardice	Courage	Foolhardiness
Inhibition	Temperance	Overindulgence/intemperance
Miserliness	Liberality	Prodigality/extravagance
Shabbiness	Magnificence	Bad taste/vulgarity
Lack of ambition	Proper pride	Ambitiousness
Poor-spiritedness	Gentleness	Irascibility
Peevishness	Friendliness	Obsequiousness/flattery
Maliciousness	Righteous indignation	Envy
Sarcasm	Truthfulness	Boastfulness
Boorishness	Wittiness	Buffoonery
Shamelessness	Modesty	Shamefacedness

According to Aristotle and Confucius, most virtues entail finding the mean between excess and deficiency. Some character traits or dispositions, however, are good or evil in themselves. For example, both men believed that ignorance and malice are always vices, and wisdom is always a virtue. In Buddhist ethics, the virtue of *ahimsa*, or nonharming, which is reflected in a person's respect for all living beings, is good in itself. For Confucians, "absolute sincerity" is always a virtue and is the highest virtue that we can cultivate. "Only those who are absolutely sincere," Confucius wrote, "can fully develop their nature."

Most moral qualities, however, can be destroyed by deficiency or excess, just as physical health can be damaged by eating too much or too little food. Similarly, some people take virtues to such an extreme that they are no longer virtues but vices. Most of us, for example, have fallen prey to a very "honest" person who delights in "telling it like it is," much to the discomfort of his or her audience.

The doctrine of the mean should not be misinterpreted as advising us to be wishy-washy or to compromise our moral standards. Aristotle and Confucius were not suggesting that we seek a consensus or take a moderate position. Most moral reformers have taken positions that differed sharply from the status quo. The abolitionists as well as the early feminists, for example, were considered extremists and fanatics. The doctrine of the mean is meant to apply to virtues, not to our positions on moral issues. Aristotle was not referring to being lukewarm or a fence-straddler but to seeking *what is reasonable* (see Table 12.1). Aristotle wrote:

> It is the nature of such things to be destroyed by defect and excess . . . ; both excessive and defective exercise destroys the strength, and similarly drink or food

Connections

What types of resistance do fence-straddlers tend to use? *See Chapter 2, pages 41–42.*

which is above or below a certain amount destroys the health . . . So too is it, then in the case of temperance and courage and the other virtues. For the man who flies from and fears everything and does not stand his ground against anything becomes a coward, and the man who fears nothing at all but goes to meet every danger becomes rash; . . . courage, then, [is] destroyed by excess and defect, and preserved by the mean.[16]

Along similar lines, for Confucius the mean is whatever is consistent with harmony and equilibrium, or the Way (Tao).

The mean is to some extent dependent on the individual person as well as his or her culture. The mean in Confucian ethics entails doing what is proper to one's station in life—be it ruler, servant, or parent. Confucius pointed out that, when traveling the Way, we must start from the nearest point. This point will be lower for some people than for others. Courage, for example, which is the mean between cowardice and foolhardiness, is not the same for all people. A person who is struggling to overcome agoraphobia would be showing courage just by going outside. With repeated practice, the virtue of courage will become strengthened, until the former agoraphobic will actually enjoy going outside for walks and meeting new people. On the other hand, for a very sociable person, going outside for a walk and meeting new people are not acts of courage. Courage for this person would involve a willingness to take a different sort of risk—perhaps giving up a home and financial security and moving to another area of the world to devote one's life to people who are impoverished. On the other hand, if people get too carried away, they might go to the opposite extreme and become foolhardy, giving away all their material goods and thus placing an undue burden on their children and on society to support them in their old age.

Another vice that we must beware of is trying to be perfect. For example, in Hindu spiritual communes (ashrams), there is a vice known as scrupulosity: People become so self-absorbed in their attempt to achieve perfection that they are no longer able to relate well to others, instead adopting a holier-than-thou attitude. Demanding perfection of ourselves can also lead to procrastination or doing nothing. To achieve perfection, people must seek the middle path between scrupulosity and apathy.

Connections

What, according to utilitarians, brings people the greatest happiness? *See Chapter 8, page 243.*

How do we know when we have found the mean? There are no formulas for deciding what is virtuous for a particular person in a particular situation. Aristotle offers the following practical advice: "(1) Keep away from that extreme which is more opposed to the mean . . . (2) Note the errors into which we personally are most liable to fall . . . (3) Always be particularly on your guard against pleasure and pleasant things."[17]

By living according to the doctrine of the mean, Aristotle and Confucius both believed, we can find the greatest happiness and inner harmony. To do this, it is important to be aware of the tendencies of your personality so that, if necessary, you can habituate yourself to compensate for them. This involves noticing how you respond to others.

Exercises

1. Is your greatest virtue, as described in exercise 1, page 398, a mean between deficit and excess? If so, what are the corresponding deficits and excesses?

2. Confucius compared the virtuous person to an archer who is able to hit the bull's eye. How do you correct yourself when you begin to slip toward one of the two extremes? Does it get easier to achieve the mean with practice? Use specific examples to illustrate your answer.

3. Martin Luther King Jr. wrote that "many people fear nothing more terribly than to take a position which stands out sharply and clearly from prevailing opinion." Discuss the differences between this type of conformity and acting in accordance with the doctrine of the mean.

David Hume: Sentiment and Virtue

No quality of human nature is more remarkable both in itself and its human conse-
quences, than the propensity we have to sympathize with others.

—DAVID HUME, *A Treatise on Human Nature* (1740)[18]

Aristotle distinguished between reason and sentiment in the virtuous disposition. This division is generally one of emphasis rather than an either/or situation. Eastern philosophers tend to regard sentiment as more important. Chinese philosopher Lin Yutang (1895–1976), for example, believed that sentiment is more important than reason.

While most Western philosophers emphasize reason over sentiment, others, such as David Hume and Nel Noddings, believe that sympathy and caring are the most important virtues. According to them, moral sentiments like compassion and sympathy are forms of knowledge regarding moral standards that should be taken seriously. **Sympathy** forms the heart of our conscience. Sympathy involves both feeling pleased by another's accomplishments and feeling indignation at another's injury or misfortune. Sympathy joins us to others, breaking down barriers. In Confucian ethics, caring in the context of the traditional family is extremely important. It is absurd, Mencius argued, to claim that one ought to save a stranger rather than one's child; our special obligations to those we have a relationship with goes beyond our abstract obligations to one another as humans.

David Hume (1711–1776) also disagreed with the rationalists regarding the role of reason in willing actions. He was described by one of his acquaintances as "one of the sweetest tempered Men & the most Benevolent that was born. . . . There was a simplicity & pleasantness of Manners about him that were delightful in Society."[19] His kindness and cheerful philosophical attitude earned him the nickname "Saint David" in Scotland.

Connections

What is the difference between sympathy and compassion? *See Chapter 3, pages 82–83.*

The Importance of Sentiment

Unlike Kant and Aristotle, Hume argued that reason or reflection can only tell us *what* is right or wrong. Reason, however, cannot *move* us to act virtuously. Instead, it is sentiment that moves us to act virtuously. According to Hume, sympathy is the greatest virtue, and cruelty, or the lack of sympathy, is the greatest vice. His claim is not without empirical support. In a study of people who rescued Jews during World War II, most rescuers reported that they rarely engaged in reflection before acting.[20] They reported that they acted instead from a sense of care and sympathy.

When Hume spoke of moral sentiments, he was not talking about irrational desires or the whims of ethical subjectivism. Moral sentiments are a form of knowledge and can be as difficult to discern and to master as logic. Moral sentiments, he wrote, "are so rooted in our constitution and temper, that without confounding the human mind by disease or madness, 'tis impossible to extirpate and destroy them."[21] Although sentiments are more important than reason for motivating us to do good, reason should not be dismissed. Rather, Hume argued, reason and sentiment work in conjunction to affirm each other:

> There has been controversy started of late . . . concerning the general foundation of morals, whether they be derived from REASON or SENTIMENT;
>
> [It is true that] reason and sentiment concur in almost all moral determinations and conclusions. . . . But though reason, when fully assisted and improved, be sufficient to instruct us in the pernicious or useful tendency of qualities and action; it is not sufficient alone to produce any moral blame or approbation. . . . It is a requisite that a sentiment should here display itself, in order to give a preference to the useful above the pernicious tendencies. This sentiment can be no other than a feeling for the happiness of mankind (sympathy) and a resentment for their misery (anti-cruelty). . . . Here reason instructs us in the several tendencies of action, and humanity (sympathy) makes a distinction in favor of those which are useful and beneficial.[22]

Sympathy as a Virtue

Sympathy opens us up to others by breaking down the us/them mentality that acts as a barrier to expanding our moral community. For example, in community service, volunteers often initially see the people they are working with as the other—as disadvantaged and needy, with problems that must be fixed. This attitude stems from a lack of sympathy. Without sympathy or compassion, doing community service can be divisive and demeaning to others, despite our best intentions. "When you give somebody a thing without giving yourself," Philip Hallie writes, "you degrade both parties by making the receiver utterly passive and by making yourself a benefactor standing there to receive thanks—and even sometimes obedience—as a repayment."[23]

Connections

How does cultural relativism contribute to an us/them mentality? *See Chapter 6, page 200.*

Sympathy involves being in a relationship in a way that reason does not. The sympathetic person sees service as a mutual process where all parties are engaged. Sympathy as a virtue entails listening to the people we are serving rather than defining their problems ourselves and imposing our ready-made

> **Key Claims of Virtue Ethics**
>
> - Right being, or the type of person we are, is more important than right action.
> - A virtue is a character trait or disposition to habitually act in a manner that benefits oneself and others.
> - A virtuous person, as a person of good will, is more likely to do what is right.
> - Virtue contributes to our moral well-being as well as our happiness.
> - In general, virtue entails hitting the mean between excess and deficit.

solutions on them. Sympathy opens up our hearts to hear the stories of those we are serving. By allowing them also to serve us, we can learn from their experiences and their strengths.

The importance of moral sentiment is also found in Plato's dialogue "Euthyphro." (See pages 161–162.) Socrates happens to run into Euthyphro near the courthouse where Socrates is to be tried for blasphemy and corrupting the youth of Athens. Socrates asks Euthyphro what brings him to the courthouse. Euthyphro replies that he is prosecuting his elderly father for murder. Socrates then proceeds to question Euthyphro about the propriety of a son prosecuting his father when the victim is a stranger:

> Good heavens! Certainly, Euthyphro, most men would not know how they could do this and be right. . . . Is then the man your father killed one of your relatives? Or is that obvious, for you would not prosecute your father for the murder of a stranger.
>
> It is ridiculous, Socrates [Euthyphro replies], for you to think that it makes any difference whether the victim is a stranger or a relative. One should only watch whether the killer acted justly or not.[24]

Had Euthyphro acted virtuously, Socrates asked, in bringing his own father to trial? Justice and reason demand that everyone be treated equally, but caring requires also that our moral decisions be made in the context of relationships.

Exercises

1. Do you agree with Hume that we are motivated to act by sentiment or do you agree with Aristotle and Kant that reason motivates us? Think back to a key event that changed the way you acted toward a particular person or group of people. Did this event involve rational arguments regarding which action was right? Or were you moved to change the way you acted more from a feeling of sympathy for the other person(s)? Explain.

*2. Discuss the quotation from Philip Hallie on page 404. Is service without sympathy degrading to both parties? Relate your answer to your own community service work. Discuss how, if at all, your involvement in community service has enhanced your sympathy for others.

3. Would a virtuous person, as Euthyphro claimed, treat his or her friends and relatives just like everyone else? In his book *1984*, George Orwell envisioned a society where children are praised for informing on their parents' illegal thoughts and activities. Are these children behaving in a morally virtuous way? Why or why not? Is whistle-blowing always wrong? Would it make a difference if the person they informed on was not a friend or family member? Support your answers.

Nel Noddings: Feminist Care Ethics

> *The caring for self, for the ethical self, can emerge only from a caring for others.*
> —NEL NODDINGS, *Caring: A Feminine Approach to Ethics*
> *and Moral Education* (1984), p. 14

There are several approaches to **feminist ethics**, including maternal ethics, lesbian ethics, care ethics, and ecofeminism. Each of these approaches strives to create a nonsexist, gender-equal ethics. They also take into account the importance of moral sentiment in women's moral reasoning.

Feminist Approaches to Ethics

Western ethical theory has been faulted by feminists for valuing traditional masculine traits and virtues such as reason, independence, individual achievement, and

Dr. Jack Kevorkian (1928–2011) with his "suicide machine." Kevorkian, an advocate of euthanasia, assisted in 130 deaths. In 1999, he was arrested and convicted of second-degree murder and sentenced to ten to twenty-five years in prison.
©AP Photo/Richard Sheinwald

Discussion Questions

1. Kevorkian maintained that his actions in helping sick and dying people commit suicide, or "die with dignity," were acts of mercy. Feminist Susan Wolf disagrees.[25] She argues that the traditional view of women as self-sacrificing puts pressure on them to request euthanasia once they become a burden to others. In line with this, she points out that the great majority of Kevorkian's "clients" were women and were suffering from less severe conditions than his male clients. Critically analyze both positions. Discuss how a feminist care ethicist might respond to the debate.

2. Hospice opposes active euthanasia. They believe that patients request euthanasia because they are not getting the palliative care they need to live their last days in relative comfort and dignity. Is an ethics of care and caring-for adequate for dealing across-the-board with patients who request euthanasia? Support your answer using specific examples.

---

autonomy over traditional feminine virtues such as sympathy, interdependence, community, and peace. Most modern feminist ethicists believe that these gender differences are a combination of nature and nurture.[26] In addition, feminist ethicists maintain that the issues that arise in the "private world" of home and family have been too often dismissed by traditional ethicists as boring and morally uninteresting.

Feminist Ethics is an attempt to revise, reformulate, or rethink those aspects of traditional western ethics that depreciate or devalue women's moral experience.

—ROSEMARY TONG, "FEMINIST ETHICS"

Feminist care ethics was developed primarily from Carol Gilligan's study of women's moral development in which she found that women tend to be more focused on relationships, while men are more likely to refer to abstract principles and reason in making moral judgments. **Care ethics** emphasizes the virtue of caring within the context of actual relationships over considerations of abstract duties and universal moral principles. Care ethics is concerned with more than just the private realm of family and personal relationships, however. It's also meant to be taken seriously in discussing social issues and formulating social policy.[27]

While care ethicists do not reject the use of principles altogether, they believe that it is care, not rational calculations or an abstract sense of duty, that creates moral obligation. Practical morality is constructed through interaction with others, not merely by the dictates of reason.

Care ethicists maintain that rather than just motivating us, moral sentiments such as compassion and sympathy have a cognitive function and are forms of knowledge. Care ethics, they argue, offers better guidance in many practical situations and social issues such as abortion, war, physician-assisted suicide, and same-sex marriage. For example, care ethics plays a central role in the opposition of the hospice movement to euthanasia and hospice's belief that we should put our efforts into providing a more caring and supportive environment for those who are dying.

Caring as an Active Virtue

Care ethicist Nel Noddings maintains that morality is an "active virtue" that requires two feelings: (1) the sentiment of natural caring and (2) love, which is our response to the remembrance of caring.[28] Like Aristotle and Kant, Noddings agrees that "I want" and "I ought" are more in harmony in the morally virtuous person. However, at this point, feminist care ethics departs from the ethics of Aristotle and Kant, who regarded humans to be at their best when exercising their rational faculty. Noddings claims that we are at our moral best when we are "caring and being cared for."[29] It is care, not rational calculations or an abstract sense of duty, that creates moral obligations.

Caring becomes the basis of moral action because, in caring for someone, a person thereby makes a commitment to act on behalf of the one who is cared for. An ethics of care requires that we give of ourselves in the context of relationship, not simply out of an abstract sense of duty.

Care ethicists, however, do not advocate an ethics of self-sacrifice—which typifies many women at Gilligan's conventional stage of moral reasoning—where we put the needs of others before our own. Just as proper self-esteem is at the heart of Kant's moral person, so too is proper self-care important to care ethicists. True caring and self-respect can develop only in a relationship.

Some care ethicists, including Noddings, believe that the care perspective is "characteristically and essentially feminine."[30] There is evidence, however, that the preference for sentiment over reason cuts across gender lines. Hallie, in his study of the people of Le Chambon, noted that compassion and sympathy were more important in motivating them to help the Jews than abstract principles. In Sam and Pearl Oliner's study of people who rescued Jews during World War II, they also found that "the language of care dominated. Pity, compassion, concern, and affection made up the vocabulary of 76% of the rescuers and 67% of the rescued survivors."[31]

An inclination to care, however, is not always enough. When our personal inclination to care is lacking, our commitment to an ideal or principle motivates us to do what is right. "When we turn our attention to the 'ones cared-for' we are engrossed with them," Noddings writes. "This caring is often filled with joy, but when it is not, when we do not feel like caring for the other, we must have recourse to our commitment to the ethical ideal of caring."[32] At this point, care ethicists and deontologists find common ground. A person of good will—a

Connections

What is the role of social dissonance in pushing a woman beyond Gilligan's self-sacrificing, conventional stage of moral development? *See Chapter 3, pages 97-98.*

person who is truly virtuous and caring—can be counted on to act out of a sense of duty even when the emotional inclination to do so is lacking.

Defining the Moral Community

Like most Western ethicists, Noddings includes only humans in the moral community because, according to her, only humans are capable of being in a reciprocal relationship. Caring-for is only morally relevant in situations where the other being in the relationship is also capable of caring-for as well as being cared-for. Noddings acknowledges that the feelings we experience in our relationships with other animals are very much like those experienced in relationships with other humans; nevertheless, she concludes that " . . . it seems obvious that they cannot be the ones-caring in relation to humans. . . . We do not have a sense of the animal-as-subject as we do of a human as subject."[33] Because care is limited to human relationships, nonhuman animals can be used in ways that benefit humans.

Care ethics has been criticized as too narrowly defining our moral obligations to others and as being inadequate for dealing with situations that do not involve reciprocal relationships. Feminist ethicists are understandably concerned about women buying into the traditional morality that emphasizes self-sacrifice, yet Noddings's claim that caring-for is morally called for only when there is the possibility or expectation of being cared-for in return smacks of Ayn Rand's rational egoism rather than genuine virtue.

"[L]oving perception" of the nonhuman natural world is an attempt to understand what it means for humans to care about the nonhuman world.

—KAREN J. WARREN, "The Power and the Promise of Ecological Feminism" (1990)

Ecofeminist Karen Warren expands care ethics to include all living creatures and all of nature.[34] Care, according to her, is not limited by the ability of the recipient to reciprocate. The virtue of sympathy or care joins us to others and breaks down barriers, not just between humans, but between humans and the rest of the natural world. Warren maintains that one of the goals of feminism is the liberation of nature as well as women by erasing oppressive categories based on superiority and privilege, and "the creation of a world in which difference does not breed domination."[35] To do this, we need to cultivate what philosopher Marilyn Frye refers to as the "loving eye" of care ethics rather than the "arrogant eye" of an ethics based on domination and conquest.[36]

Care Ethics and the Duty of Justice

By focusing on caring and downplaying concerns about justice, care ethics has been charged with fostering injustice by reinforcing traditional patterns of

Connections

Why, according to Kant, is a person of good will more likely to act out of a sense of duty? *See Chapter 10, pages 321–323.*

Connections

What did Kant teach regarding our moral duty to nonhuman animals? *See Chapter 10, page 317.*

inequality in the family as well as patterns of paternalistic relationships where caring for the "other" is based on assumed inequality. The separation of justice from care raises the question of whether a person can authentically care for another in a situation where one is in an economically and socially subordinate position.

For example, caring was used as a justification for colonialism since it, or so the argument went, spiritually benefited and promoted the welfare of those being colonized. The fact that colonization primarily furthered the economic interests of the colonizer was disregarded. Because the cultures being colonized had a lower economic standard of living to start with, as long as the colonizer did not further lower their standard of living, these economic discrepancies were simply accepted as the status quo rather than being viewed as unjust.

Connections

How was social Darwinism used to justify colonialism? *See Chapter 6, pages 176-177.*

In her work on the role of care ethics in colonialism, Uma Narayan argues that the claims of justice may be a *precondition* for caring. She writes: "Social relationships of domination often operate so as to make many who have power unable to genuinely care about the marginalized and powerless."[37] Struggles for greater justice have the potential to foster the cultivation of caring since justice requires that we see others in relationship as equal individuals with their own needs and dignity, rather than adopting a paternalistic attitude toward others.

In a similar manner, justice unbalanced by a sense of care, can be just as inadequate. In her book *Dead Man Walking*, Helen Prejean enjoins her readers to see death row prisoners through sympathetic eyes. She claims that one reason people favor the death penalty is that we don't identify with the condemned persons; we don't see them as humans like us. Before we can discuss the morality of capital punishment, we first have to see those who are condemned from a care perspective as well, rather than from a purely justice perspective.

[A complete ethics of care] does not recommend that we discard categories of obligation, but that we make room for an ethic of love and trust, including an account of human bonding and friendship.

—ANNETTE BAIER, "What Do Women Want in a Moral Theory?"[38]

Although the language of care ethics tended to dominate, most of the rescuers in the Oliners' study also mentioned deontological principles such as equity and fairness as well as a concern for human rights.[39] Carol Gilligan also came to realize that rather than providing alternative accounts of morality, the care perspective and the justice perspective work best in conjunction with each other.

Exercises

1. Mary Wollstonecraft and John Stuart Mill believed that gender roles and the differences in men's and women's morality are the result of culture and oppression. Others argue that the differences are primarily innate or the combination of heredity and culture. Make a list of virtues that you associate with men and a list of virtues you associate with women. Working in small groups, discuss the sources of these gender differences. Support your answers.

2. Feminist theologian Mary Daly contends that the Madonna, who is presented as the ideal woman by the church, demeans women by portraying the ideal as passive and only in relation to men (son and father).[40] Discuss whether feminist care ethics is compatible with Christian ethics.

3. Imagine that you are a nurse. Your patient, who is dying of cancer, tells you that she feels her life is no longer worth living and pleads with you to end her life. While you care deeply about this patient, her request conflicts with your professional ethics and your duty not to harm patients. Discuss how you might balance these concerns in resolving this moral dilemma.

4. Discuss how a feminist care ethicist, such as Noddings, might approach issues in environmental ethics such as global warming and the destruction of rain forests for agriculture. Is care ethics adequate for dealing with these issues? Support your answer.

5. Do you agree with Karen Warren and Marilyn Frye that sexism and the domination of women are linked to the domination of nature? Relate Frye's concept of the loving eye to your own lifestyle and your sense of who you are vis-à-vis other people and nature.

6. Feminist ethicist Sara Ruddick contrasts maternal thinking with military thinking. She writes: "The analytic fictions of just-war theory require a closure of moral issues final enough to justify killing and 'enemies' abstract enough to be killable. . . . Maternal attentive love, restrained and clear-sighted, is ill adapted to intrusive, let alone murderous, judgments of others' lives."[41] Discuss her claim that "maternal practice is a 'natural resource' for peace politics." Discuss also what criteria a care ethicist might propose for a just war theory (see page 289).

Is Virtue Relative to Culture, Social Status, and Gender?

There is no doubt that people disagree about which virtues are more important. Aristotle, Confucius, and Plato regarded wisdom as the highest virtue. Aquinas claimed that faith is the highest virtue, while Hume and Noddings think that sympathy is the highest. But do their differences go deeper than one of priorities? Although sympathy is the highest virtue for Noddings,

Hume, and Buddha, none of them deny the importance of cultivating wisdom and discernment. Nor did Aristotle deny the role of sentiments in morality. Though the lists of virtues vary somewhat, there is much overlap. In Plato's virtue ethics, for example, there are four cardinal virtues: wisdom, courage, temperance, and justice. In Confucianism, there are three: wisdom, courage, and *jen* (love); in Islam, the four virtues are wisdom, courage, charity, and justice.

Most people, in other words, seem to agree about what is a virtue and what is a vice. According to a Gallup poll, almost all parents want to bring up their children to be honest, kind, and empathetic. However, are these simply American virtues, as some cultural relativists claim? Also, are there some virtues that are peculiar to women and other characteristics that are virtues only for men? Noddings and Gilligan claim that men and women tend to place higher values on a different set of virtues. Men, they maintain, emphasize traits such as courage, assertiveness, and fairness. Women are more concerned with virtues related to caring, such as compassion, forgiveness, gentleness, and loyalty.[42]

Connections

What, according to Rand, are the four rational virtues? *See Chapter 7, page 218.*

There is also no shortage of examples of cultural differences. In some cultures, courage in battle is the most important virtue for a man; women, in contrast, are praised for being gentle, peaceful, and even submissive. In Buddhist cultures such as Tibet, a peaceful disposition is considered a virtue in both men and women. In addition, there are instances in which what one culture regards as a virtue another regards as a vice. Some cultures regard cooperation as a virtue; in the United States, a competitive spirit and hard work are virtues. Aristotle, on the other hand, had only scorn for the "commercial virtues." Some Christian ethicists stress self-sacrificing humility as the greatest virtue, yet Nietzsche and Rand regarded this type of humility as a vice.

Is Virtue Culturally Relative?

Philosopher Robert Solomon argues that virtue is culturally relative and that the virtues listed by Aristotle were simply those of the Greek aristocracy:

> The question, "What is the good life and how should I live?" is very much an open question, and no single set of virtues, ambitions, or accomplishments provides the answer for everyone. . . . We would like to think of what Aristotle called the good life as a single universal goal, common to ancient Greeks, medieval Chinese, and modern Americans, but we are aware of cultural differences, and the legitimacy of these differences, in a way that Aristotle was not.[43]

Connections

What is the difference between sociological relativism and cultural relativism? *See Chapter 6, pages 172-175.*

But is Aristotle's list of virtues really as culture-bound as Solomon claims? Aristotle taught that friendliness, sympathy, benevolence, and honesty are important virtues because without these virtues we tend to alienate our friends and family. Because humans are social animals, no one can achieve the good life without friends and family. Is this simply a cultural norm of the ancient Greek aristocracy? Confucius also thought that the social virtues and family ties were very important.

Although different cultures and groups of people may emphasize different virtues (sociological relativism), this does not mean that virtue is culturally relative in the sense that the concept of virtue is a cultural creation. Indeed, what is most striking are the similarities among the various lists of virtues rather than the differences. For example, anthropologist Clyde Kluckhohn noted that, among the Navaho, the primary virtues are generosity, loyalty, self-control, peacefulness, amity, courteousness, and honesty.[44] These virtues are not seen as peculiar to the Navaho but are regarded by them as desirable for all humans and as universal as the air we breathe. The Egyptian text *The Instruction of Ptahhotep*, written more than four thousand years ago, states that the following virtues should be practiced toward everyone: self-control, moderation, kindness, generosity, justice, truthfulness, and discretion. The Swahili proverbs teach that a virtuous person is kind, cautious (prudent), patient, courageous, self-controlled, humble (in the Kantian sense), honest, fair, responsible, respectful, and cooperative.[45] Thus, although the relative importance of different virtues may vary from culture to culture, the list of what are considered virtues and what are considered vices seems to be transcultural.

Furthermore, something that may at first appear to be a basic difference may turn out to be merely a difference in how a specific virtue is expressed within a cultural context. Courage in a warrior culture, for example, means putting up a good fight and willingness to die in battle. Courage in a pacifist culture is expressed differently—perhaps as nonviolent resistance and the willingness to stand up to one's oppressors without retaliating or using violence in return. However, in both the warrior culture and the pacifist culture, courage involves avoiding cowardliness yet not going to the other extreme of being foolhardy.

Certain basic virtues, as Aristotle noted, seem to be necessary for our well-being as humans and for the achievement of the good life, no matter who we are or where we live. To make an analogy, different cultures have very different dietary habits. Even within a culture individuals have distinct dietary needs: Growing children need more protein and carbohydrates, women need more iron and calcium than men, and men need more calories than women. The basic nutritional needs of humans are universal, however. The dietary habits of different cultures can be judged in light of these universal standards. We all need vitamin C or we will get scurvy, whether we live in Iceland or Fiji. The calorie requirements of women, assuming similar activity levels, are roughly the same no matter where they live. Just as different cultures emphasize different virtues, the foods used as sources of vitamin C and caloric intake can vary greatly.

Similarly, those basic virtues that are conducive to the good life are the same for all humans because we share the same basic nature. Indeed, Chinese philosopher Lin Yutang remarked that what some cultures perceive as virtues are actually vices when examined in light of the concept of the good life: "The three great American vices seem to be efficiency, punctuality, and the desire for achievement and success. They are the things," he wrote, "that make the

Connections

How did Plato answer the question: "Are some cultures more moral than others?" *See Chapter 6, page 190.*

American so unhappy and nervous."[46] Cultures that do not encourage or nurture good character or that label vices as virtues—just as some junk food companies advertise their food as "nutritious"—do not provide an environment that is conducive to the good life.

Nietzsche and the Übermensch

Nietzsche was an outspoken critic of cultural relativism. He maintained that certain character traits are destructive while other traits enhance our growth. He was especially critical of the traditional bourgeois Christian morality that, he claimed, forms the basis of modern Western morality. This morality, which extols meekness, unconditional forgiveness, self-sacrifice, and equality as virtues, he argued, is destructive to individual integrity and growth.

Self-effacing humility and meekness play no role as virtues in the life of Nietzsche's **Übermensch**, or "superhuman," just as they play no part in the life of Aristotle's virtuous person or the Confucian superior man. Nor was this type of humility, according to Nietzsche, part of the teachings of Jesus. Indeed, Nietzsche apparently admired Jesus as an example of an Übermensch. Nietzsche also believed that "the last Christian died on the cross" and that modern Christian morality bears little resemblance to that promoted by Jesus.

Connections

Why did Nietzsche argue that an "instinct for life" is more important than moral duty? *See Chapter 10, page 345.*

The Übermensch is a person of integrity and self-mastery who is able to rise above the morality of the crowd and exercise the "will to power," which entails self-mastery and human nobility. Nietzsche's concept of will to power has often been misinterpreted as the will to dominate and subjugate others. However, truly strong or virtuous people, according to him, are not cruel, nor do they desire to subjugate others. Indeed, Nietzsche's last act before collapsing and dying months later without ever fully recovering consciousness was to embrace a horse that was being flogged by its owner.

By the will to power, Nietzsche meant "the will to grow, spread, seize, become predominant"[47] that is found in all living beings. In his book *The Dawn*, Nietzsche lists "*The good four. Honest* with ourselves and whatever is friend to us; *courageous* toward the enemy; *generous* toward the vanquished; *polite*—always: that is how the four cardinal virtues want us."[48] Weak people, in contrast, make humility, self-sacrifice, and equality into virtues because they lack the courage, power, and personal resolve to live the life of a great person.

Not everyone agrees with Nietzsche that moral virtues are a manifestation of the will to power. On the other hand, self-effacing humility and self-sacrifice do not, for the most part, lead to a happy and fulfilling life—at least not in this life. Battered women, for example, are often advised to try to be more humble, agreeable, and submissive[49] and to forgive their batterers. Ironically, the very women who hold highly traditional moral views and who try hardest to please are the most likely to be abused by their husbands and partners.[50] Because humility, self-sacrifice, unconditional forgiveness, and the other so-called Christian virtues can harm women and perpetuate domestic violence, these can hardly be considered moral virtues. Humility, expressed through meekness and a willingness to sacrifice oneself for others, may be a religious or cultural virtue, but it cannot be considered a moral virtue. Like junk food that is bad for our bodies, virtues that impede our growth as humans are junk virtues. A culture that promotes junk virtues as true virtues is destructive to the development of moral character.

Connections
Why did Gilligan reject self-sacrifice as the highest stage of moral development in women? *See Chapter 3, pages 96–97.*

Buddhist and Hindu Virtue Ethics

There are strong strands of virtue ethics in both Buddhist and Hindu ethics. Buddhist ethics, rather than focusing on self-sacrifice, is directed toward self-realization or Nirvana and the extinction of suffering. According to Buddha, the normal human condition is accompanied by suffering. In addition to ignorance and irrationality, two major causes of suffering are the moral vices of greed and hatred. To overcome suffering, we need to cultivate wisdom as well as the virtues of giving and love.[51] Buddhist scriptures teach:

> A man who, although he has learned to abstain from overt immoral acts, still persists in nursing ill-will harms himself. . . . With his malevolent mind a man will be burned up. Therefore you should strive to think of all that lives with friendliness and compassion and not with ill-will and a desire to hurt.[52]

Hindu ethics, as taught in the "Path of Devotion," likewise holds that enlightenment and moral perfection are achieved by the use of reason. The good life is lived according to the dictates of the mind. The desires are part of our lower nature, and when these are not under the control of the mind, they can lead us astray.

According to Krishna, who is an incarnation of the God Vishnu, the enlightened person refrains from hurting himself and others and seeks through reason to cultivate a virtuous character. The perfect person:

> feels hatred for no contingent being . . . is friendly, . . . content and ever integrated. . . . fearless and pure in heart, steadfast in the exercise of wisdom, open-handed and restrained . . . none hurting, truthful, from anger free . . . at peace, averse to calumny, compassionate to all beings, free from nagging greed, gentle, modest, never fickle, ardent, patient, enduring, pure, not treacherous nor arrogant,—such is the man who is born to inherit a godly destiny.[53]

The Development of Virtue

A virtuous character does not develop in isolation but in community. We do not become more virtuous by merely reflecting on or intellectualizing virtues but by *living* a virtuous life. A good society provides an environment where virtues are encouraged and where people can thrive and develop to their fullest potential.

The "virtues" of independence and economic success that we emphasize in the United States—especially for men—might not be moral virtues at all because, in general, they do not benefit, but rather harm the individual. When teachers, parents, and child-development specialists in Japan and the United States were asked to name the most important things that preschool children should learn, the first choice of those from Japan was sympathy and a concern for others, followed by cooperation. Americans, on the other hand, thought self-reliance was the most important value; sympathy was rarely mentioned.[54]

One might argue that Americans have pushed self-reliance to such an extreme that it has now become a vice. On the other hand, cooperation as a virtue can also be carried to an extreme when it becomes transformed into mindless conformity. What we need to do, most virtue ethicists argue, is seek the mean between these extremes.

Exercises

1. Robert Solomon maintains that virtues are culturally relative. Do you agree with him that the virtues listed by Aristotle are peculiar to the Greek aristocracy? Compare this list to those that you and your classmates made in response to exercise 1 on page 398 in this chapter.

2. Joyce Trebilcot, in her article "Two Forms of Androgynism," argues that, instead of seeing virtues in terms of gender, people should be allowed to develop their own character and virtues free from the limitations of gender roles and perhaps even cultural expectations.[55] Do you agree? Is this even possible? Explain.

3. Professional codes of ethics and institutional mission statements frequently include a list of virtues that members of the profession or institution are expected to follow. Discuss the concept of virtue in relation to the particular profession or lifestyle to which you aspire.

4. Critically analyze Nietzsche's claim that virtue is the manifestation of the will to power. Discuss the will to power in your own life and its connection to virtue.

5. Discuss what Nietzsche would have thought of people such as Trocme (the French pastor at Le Chambon), Martin Luther King Jr., and Mother Teresa—all of whom based their work on Christianity.

6. Discuss Lin Yutang's claim that some of the American cultural virtues are not virtues but traits that actually harm us. Relate your answer to your own experience.

7. Both Hindu and Buddhist virtue ethics include the idea of reincarnation; we should cultivate a virtuous character lest we end up in a subsequent incarnation in the shoes of someone or something we harmed, whether intentionally or through ignorance on our part. Would you be more virtuous if you believed in reincarnation? Discuss how a belief in reincarnation might influence your cultivation of a virtuous character.

Moral Integrity and the Unity of Virtue

[V]irtue in a man will be the disposition which (a) makes him a good man, and (b) enables him to perform his function well.

—ARISTOTLE, *Nicomachean Ethics*, Bk. 2, Ch. 6

According to Aristotle, virtue is a unifying concept rather than simply a collection of different personality traits. We speak of a good person as being virtuous in a general sense. Virtue, in other words, is the *disposition* that predisposes us to act in a manner that benefits ourselves and others. In the Gospel of Luke, Jesus compares the virtuous person to a tree or a grapevine that bears good fruit. We know good people by the fruit they bear:

> For no good tree bears bad fruit, nor again does a bad tree bear good fruit; for each tree is known by its own fruit. For figs are not gathered from thorns, nor are grapes picked from a bramble bush. The good man out of the good treasure of his heart produces good, and the evil man out of the evil treasure of his heart produces evil; for out of the abundance of the heart his mouth speaks.[56]

The concept of virtue as a unifying principle in the human psyche, rather than a collection of discrete personality traits, is found in both Eastern and Western virtue ethics. Virtue, according to Confucian ethics, stems from an all-pervading unity.[57] Lao Tzu, founder of Taoism, spoke of the Tao as the cosmic unity that underlies all phenomena and shapes and informs our moral character.

Without this underlying "all-pervading unity" or good will, otherwise virtuous traits, such as truthfulness and loyalty, can become harmful on their own. True compassion as a virtue, for example, stems from who we are as a person; it comes from what Kant calls the good will. To be compassionate simply for the sake of being compassionate is merely role-playing and, as such, is perverse. The truthfulness of a braggart and the loyalty of gang members are not virtues because these are not expressions of the good will; they only seem to be virtues if we take a piecemeal approach. The good life entails cultivating all the virtues; it involves living a life of integrity.

Virtuous people have a well-developed moral character, one of the four components of moral behavior discussed in Chapter 3. Virtue is integral to their self-concept. They do not behave begrudgingly, nor do they do what is right because of fear of punishment. Like André Trocme, who led the villagers of Le Chambon in rescuing Jews during World War II, virtuous people do not just happen to act in a way that is good. They act virtuously because doing so is integral to who they are.

According to psychologists Anne Colby and William Damon, people with a high level of moral commitment carry out their commitments in a spontaneous manner by force of habit.[58] Virtuous people enjoy being virtuous; they do not need to struggle to overcome temptation or make sacrifices to be virtuous.

Connections

What are some of the types of immature defense mechanisms? *See Chapter 2, pages 38-42.*

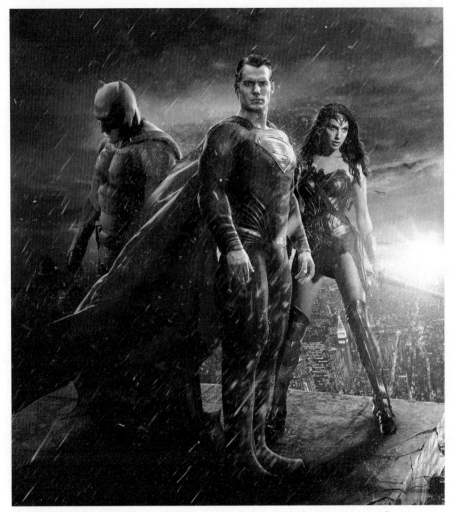

Superheroes use their superpowers for the public good. As such they serve as paradigms of virtuous people.
©Warner Bros/DC Comics/Kobal/REX/Shutterstock

What is extraordinary about highly moral people is that they apply this habitual moral mode to the furthest reaches of their social visions. Their moral sensibilities are quickly engaged by any number of observations or incidents.[59]

People who are morally virtuous are not as likely as people with weak characters to mindlessly follow authority or to do things under social pressure. Rather than keeping their innermost self intact by use of immature defense mechanisms and resistance, virtuous people organize their innermost self based on integrity. People of integrity, such as Elizabeth Cady Stanton and other moral reformers, have the strength of character to stand by their principles even if they are unpopular.

The cultivation of virtue and the good will is a lifelong process. Very few people ever attain a level of moral development where they no longer struggle against temptation. According to Aristotle, for those who constantly strive to be virtuous, being a virtuous person gradually becomes much easier and more pleasurable. To determine whether we are virtuous people, Aristotle suggests that all we must do is ask ourselves whether we find pleasure in acting virtuously.

Exercises

1. Jesus taught that virtue can lead only to good actions. Do you agree with him? Support your answer.

2. Virtues help to shape our aspirations for what sort of person we want to be. Discuss how cultivating a virtuous disposition may help you achieve your goals. Discuss also how being virtuous defines who you are. Explain using specific examples from your own life.

3. Describe someone—a parent, teacher, public figure, or fictional character—who is a personal hero to you. What characteristics make this person your hero? Relate these characteristics to those described as virtues by virtue ethicists.

4. Discuss whether or not you have a moral obligation to use your talents and special gifts for the betterment of mankind and the world. Use specific examples to illustrate your answer.

*5. Can practicing good actions, even though your motives may be morally questionable, help you become a more virtuous person? Relate your answer to the opening scenario in this chapter as well as to your community service.

Virtue and Moral Education

The sages, also have first devoted themselves to study, and thus know the truth. The common people, also have knowledge of [good] from birth. . . . Study and self-control should follow the lead of intuitive knowledge.

—*The Philosophy of Wang Yang Ming*[60]

Questions regarding the basic nature of humans, the influence of reason and sentiment on moral behavior and character, and the role of God in human virtue all contribute to the formulation of our ideas regarding moral education and the cultivation of a virtuous character. If people are basically depraved, then more effort must go into this process. Aquinas, for example, believed that people are basically evil and that a rigorous program of moral education is needed to correct this natural tendency. Moral education, according to this view of human nature, is not so much a matter of cultivating children's natural moral sense as

Connections

What was Rousseau's "Law of the Heart"? *See Chapter 4, page 123.*

of imposing morality upon them—a view complete opposite to that of Rousseau.

Are People Basically Good?

Lao Tzu, like Rousseau, regarded people as basically good. The Tao, he maintained, not only shapes our character but provides us with ethical principles. We have only to lose ourselves in the Tao just as a fish loses itself in water. Cultivating virtue involves letting go and letting the guiding principles flow naturally out of the Tao. However, Lao Tsu did not advocate apathy and shutting ourselves off from the world. Moral education instead involves being open to others and affirming their natural goodness.

Confucian philosopher Mencius also believed that human nature is originally virtuous. Benevolence and righteousness are internal, not things imposed on us from the outside. According to him, virtue is intimately tied in with sincerity and being true to oneself. Thus, the process of becoming a virtuous person depends on "setting the mind in the right."[61] The content person, Mencius taught, is one who "reveres virtue and delights in rightness." Unless our mind is in the right, there will be neither inner harmony nor harmony in the household.

> The Way of greater learning lies in keeping one's inborn luminous Virtue unobscured.
>
> —*The Greater Learning*[62]

Chinese philosopher Wang Yang Ming likewise taught that virtue is innate. However, he took a more active approach to moral education than did either the Taoists or Mencius. He emphasized the importance of moral education as a means of developing the goodness inherent in our natures. He believed that the teacher should be "indefatigable and energetic in his efforts to guard this knowledge of the good."[63] Moral education also involves practice.

Like Wang Yang Ming, Aristotle emphasized the importance of practice in the development of virtue. While Aristotle believed that we have a natural inclination to be virtuous, he also believed that moral virtue is the outcome of habit rather than simply a product of our natural endowments. Consequently, it is not enough to simply nurture our natural inclinations. We acquire virtue primarily through repetition or habituation. Because humans are social as well as rational beings, becoming virtuous involves both the cultivation of reason and proper socialization. We do not become just simply by believing in the principle of justice. We become just or unjust in the course of our dealings with others. It is our duty, therefore, to practice the various virtues so that we will become proficient.

The Importance of Moral Education

According to Aristotle, it is generally easier for people to be virtuous if their early childhood education reinforced virtuous behavior; however, it is never too late to habituate ourselves to being virtuous by constant practice of moral actions. Practicing any art or craft, Aristotle reminds us, is initially burdensome. Just as a novice artisan or musician finds practice tedious at first, so too practicing virtue may be onerous to the novice.

We need to work at it to become a virtuous person. We cannot just say, "I am who I am—take me as I am." Indeed, many students, when they first begin their community service, complain that it is too much work. The more we practice and the better we become at something, however, and the more we will enjoy it. Just as continuous practice on a musical instrument makes it easier, and more enjoyable, for us to play that instrument well, so too does constantly performing good actions make it easier for us to be virtuous people. There is not "the smallest likelihood of a man's becoming good," Aristotle counseled, by any other means than by "repeated performances" of virtuous actions.

Connections

What are the three factors that contribute to the development of our conscience? *See Chapter 3, pages 75-79.*

The moral virtues . . . full development in us is due to habit.

—ARISTOTLE, *Nicomachean Ethics*, Bk. 2

Because the formation of good habits is so important, moral education should start at an early age. The Oliners, in their study of people who rescued Jews from the Nazis, found that virtue education during childhood had a significant effect on the rescuers' later behavior. The rescuers' commitment to "actively protect or enhance the well-being of others," they noted, "did not emerge suddenly under the threat of Nazi brutality." The development of a virtuous character as well as a sense of moral duty had been instilled in them since childhood: Seventy percent of rescuers in the Oliners' study, as compared to 56 percent of nonrescuers, stated that their parents emphasized the development of virtues such as honesty, respect, compassion, generosity, helpfulness, expansiveness, and hospitality.[64] Rescuers were also more than twice as likely to state that their parents taught them that moral values applied universally to all humans. The following are typical of the comments of rescuers regarding their childhood moral education:

> I learned to be good to one's neighbor—to be responsible, concerned, and considerate. To work—and work hard. But also to help—to the point of leaving one's work to help one's neighbor. . . .
>
> [My father] taught me to love my neighbor—to consider him my equal whatever his nationality or religion. He taught me especially to be tolerant.[65]

College student helping out in a soup kitchen. According to the Corporation for National and Community Service, about 30 percent of college students engage in community service—a rate higher than that of the general public.
©Ariel Skelley/Getty Images

Discussion Questions

1. Community service is encouraged but not required at some colleges. Should community service be required for graduation? Working in small groups, develop a community service policy for your college.

2. If you are doing community service as part of your academic program, discuss how, if at all, it has influenced your career, life goals, and moral development. Be specific.

Like Aristotle and the Confucian philosophers, Buddhists also emphasize the importance of cultivating virtue. However, according to Buddhists, moral education involves changing our way of thinking more than practicing virtuous acts. While Aristotle believed that a change of heart usually follows a change of actions, Buddhists maintain that the change of heart comes first. We need to give up the illusion that we are a separate reality. Buddhist scriptures state:

> . . . you should strive to think of all that lives with friendliness and compassion, and not with ill-will and a desire to hurt. For whatever a man thinks about continually, to that his mind becomes inclined by habit of force. Abandoning what is unwholesome, you therefore ought to ponder what is wholesome; for that will bring you advantages in this world and help you to win the highest goal.[66]

Even those ethicists who believe that humans are naturally good maintain that moral education is important in becoming a virtuous person. This requires both practicing virtuous behavior and cultivating the good will.

Exercises

1. Do you agree with Mencius and Lao Tzu that people are naturally good or with Wang Yang Ming and Aristotle that virtue is not inborn but must be developed through habituation? Support your answer.

*2. Referring back to the opening scenario, evaluate the arguments presented for and against mandating community service in college.

*3. Courts sometimes assign people who have been convicted of minor crimes to do community service work. Although we may agree that practice is important in the development of a virtuous character, is it morally acceptable for the courts to use the people at a community service site to develop offenders' moral virtues? Support your answer.

4. To what extent has the college experience made you a more virtuous (or more vicious) person? Explain using specific examples. Discuss how a Buddhist ethicist might answer this question.

Critique of Virtue Ethics

1. *The primary criticism of virtue ethics is that it is incomplete.* Virtue ethics has been criticized for its lack of emphasis on actions. This criticism is partly based on a misinterpretation of the concept of virtue. Virtue ethicists do not mean virtue to imply a list of character traits but rather a unity of character. A virtuous person is motivated to help others by participating in community service and by striving for reform. As both Mill and Kant pointed out, virtuous people are more likely than others to do what is right.

2. *Virtue alone does not offer sufficient guidance for making moral decisions in the real world.* Virtue may be adequate for the saint, but most of us also need formal moral guidelines. It has been suggested that, developmentally, virtue ethics is associated with a high level of autonomous moral reasoning. Indeed, according to Kant, to a person of perfectly good will, the concept of duty no longer applies.

Most virtue ethics do not toss out abstract principles regarding duties and rights but rather give them a personal face. Nor does virtue ethics, in any form, entail discarding reason and relying on our "good" feelings. In the virtuous person, reason and feeling are logically connected; they complement and confirm each other. In Confucian ethics, for example, the concept of *jen* (love) is complemented by that of *yi*, which means righteousness or justice.

Virtue ethicists, in other words, are not suggesting that we ignore moral principles: They are saying that virtue is more fundamental than duty because virtue enables us to recognize and carry out our duty.

3. *Virtue ethics, and in particular feminist care ethics, does not pay enough attention to considerations of justice and impartiality.* One of the primary criticisms of care ethics is that, in seeing a sense of duty as a sort of backup when caring is weak, it makes our concerns regarding justice less important. In addition, by portraying caring as the primary virtue or moral concern of women, it can inadvertently reinforce gender stereotypes and gender inequality.

4. *Virtue ethics goes beyond pure duty and rights-based ethics by challenging us to rise above ordinary moral demands.* Philosopher Christina Sommers argues that individuals are transferring too much responsibility for the well-being of others onto institutions and professionals. She argues that these solutions are incomplete and that what is needed instead is the virtuous individual. In her essay "Where Have All the Good Deeds Gone?" she uses the example of Miss Pickins to illustrate her point:

> For the past seven years Miss Pickins, who is ninety-one, has lived in Miller House [a home for the elderly]. Last year her doctor ordered her to stop smoking. This upset a daily routine she had enjoyed—coffee and cigarettes in the lounge downstairs with the men. She became depressed, lost interest in leaving her room, and now spends most of her time there alone. The woman who runs the home made Miss Pickins keep the sound of her radio so low that she cannot hear it. . . .
>
> Simone de Beauvoir has said, "By the fate it allots to its members who can no longer work, society gives itself away." Who is to blame for the fate that has been allotted to Miss Pickins . . . ? A few concerned neighbors could transform the residence into a much happier place. But that is not going to happen.[67]

5. *The development of a virtuous character is essential to the concept of the good life and the good society.* Ralph Waldo Emerson once said, "Character is higher than intellect." When people give a higher priority to becoming the most virtuous and caring people that they can be, then people like Miss Pickins will at last be able to look forward to a better and happier life.

While virtue ethics does not stand on its own as an independent moral theory, nor do most virtue ethics intend to, virtue ethics offers an important corrective to a morality based on abstract moral principles and rights.

Exercises

*1. Do you agree with Christina Sommers that a virtuous disposition, more than just a sense of duty, is what motivates us to help people like Miss Pickins? Why or why not? If everyone, or at least more people, were virtuous, how would this affect your community service or the need for your services? Use specific examples to illustrate your answer.

*2. Discuss how the college experience could be restructured to encourage the development of virtue in students and the rest of the college community.

Summary

1. Virtue ethics emphasizes character or *right being* over right action.

2. A *virtue* is an admirable character trait or disposition to act in a manner that benefits oneself and others. A *vice* is a character trait or disposition to act in a manner that harms oneself and others.

3. Not all virtues are moral virtues. There are also intellectual virtues and natural virtues.

4. According to Greek virtue ethicists, virtue is essential to the achievement of *eudaemonia*, or psychological well-being and inner harmony.

5. Both deontological theories and utilitarian theories recognize the importance of virtue. Kant, for example, believed that we have a moral obligation to cultivate the good will; and Mill, to cultivate a benevolent disposition.

6. Aristotle divides the human psyche into the rational and nonrational elements. In a virtuous person, reason is in charge of the nonrational elements. Therefore, wisdom is the greatest virtue and ignorance is the greatest vice.

7. Aquinas regarded reason as the most important human faculty. However, he thought that we could not be virtuous without God's help. Therefore, faith is the greatest virtue and pride is the greatest vice.

8. The *doctrine of the mean* states that virtue, in general, entails moderation or seeking the middle path. This doctrine is found in philosophies throughout the world.

9. David Hume argued that sentiment is more important than reason for motivating us to do what is right. Hume regarded *sympathy* as the highest virtue and cruelty as the greatest vice.

10. Feminist care ethicists, such as Nel Noddings and Carol Gilligan, argue that caring and relationship form the basis of morality.

11. Although different cultures may regard certain virtues as more or less important than others, the concept of virtue and the list of basic virtues seem to be transcultural.

12. Virtue is a unifying concept rather than a collection of personality traits. A virtuous person has integrity.

13. Friedrich Nietzsche's concept of the virtuous person is the *Übermensch* ("superhuman"). The Übermensch is motivated by the "will to power."

14. Buddhist virtue ethicists believe that cultivating virtuous thought is more important than practicing virtuous actions.

15. Some virtue ethicists, such as Lao Tzu and Mencius, regard people as basically good. Therefore, becoming virtuous entails simply letting go and flowing with the Tao. Other virtue ethicists, such as Aristotle and Wang Yang Ming, believe that a virtuous character results from practice and habituation.

Nicomachean Ethics

Aristotle

Book I

Chapter 1

Every art and every inquiry, and similarly every action and pursuit, is thought to aim at some good; and for this reason the good has rightly been declared to be that at which all things aim. . . .

Now such a thing happiness, above all else, is held to be; for this we choose always for itself and never for the sake of something else, but honour, pleasure, reason, and every virtue we choose indeed for themselves (for if nothing resulted from them we should still choose each of them), but we choose them also for the sake of happiness, judging that by means of them we shall be happy. Happiness, on the other hand, no one chooses for the sake of these, nor, in general, for anything other than itself. . . .

Presumably, however, to say that happiness is the chief good seems a platitude, and a clearer account of what it is is still desired. This might perhaps be given, if we could first ascertain the function of man. . . . Life seems to be common even to plants, but we are seeking what is peculiar to man. Let us exclude, therefore, the life of nutrition and growth. Next there would be a life of perception, but it also seems to be common even to the horse, the ox, and every animal. There remains, then, an active life of the element that has a rational principle; . . .

. . . [I]f this is the case, [and we state the function of man to be a certain kind of life,

and this to be an activity or actions of the soul implying a rational principle, and the function of a good man to be the good and noble performance of these, and if any action is well performed when it is performed in accordance with the appropriate excellence: if this is the case,] human good turns out to be activity of soul in accordance with virtue, and if there are more than one virtue, in accordance with the best and most complete. . . .

Book II

Chapter 1

Virtue, then, being of two kinds, intellectual and moral, intellectual virtue in the main owes both its birth and its growth to teaching (for which reason it requires experience and time), while moral virtue comes about as a result of habit, whence also its name *ethike* is one that is formed by a slight variation from the word *ethos* (habit). From this it is also plain that none of the moral virtues arises in us by nature; for nothing that exists by nature can form a habit contrary to its nature. . . .

Chapter 5

Next we must consider what virtue is. Since things that are found in the soul are of three kinds—passions, faculties, states of character, virtue must be one of these. . . .

Now neither the virtues nor the vices are *passions*, because we are not called good or bad on the ground of our passions, but are so called on the ground of our virtues and our vices, and because we are neither praised nor blamed for our passions (for the man who feels fear or anger is not praised, nor is the man who simply feels anger blamed, but the man who feels it in a certain way), but for our virtues and our vices we *are* praised or blamed.

Nicomachean Ethics from Richard McKeon, ed., *The Basic Works of Aristotle* (New York: Random House, 1941). Copy of an earlier translation by Benjamin Jowett (1817-1893). From Books I, II. Notes have been omitted. (To read the complete *Nicomachean Ethics* online, go to http://etext.library.adelaide.edu.au/mirror/ classics.mit.edu/aristotle/nicomachean.)

Again, we feel anger and fear without choice, but the virtues are modes of choice or involve choice. Further, in respect of the passions we are said to be moved, but in respect of the virtues and the vices we are said not to be moved but to be disposed in a particular way.

For these reasons also they are not *faculties;* for we are neither called good nor bad, nor praised nor blamed, for the simple capacity of feeling the passions; again, we have the faculties by nature, but we are not made good or bad by nature; . . .

If, then, the virtues are neither passions nor faculties, all that remains is that they should be *states of character.* . . .

Chapter 6

We must, however, not only describe virtue as a state of character, but also say what sort of state it is. We may remark, then, that every virtue or excellence both brings into good condition the thing of which it is the excellence and makes the work of that thing be done well; . . . Therefore, if this is true in every case, the virtue of man also will be the state of character which makes a man good and which makes him do his own work well.

Virtue, then, is a state of character concerned with choice, lying in a mean, i. e. the mean relative to us, this being determined by a rational principle, and by that principle by which the man of practical wisdom would determine it. Now it is a mean between two vices, that which depends on excess and that which depends on defect; and again it is a mean because the vices respectively fall short of or exceed what is right in both passions and actions, while virtue both finds and chooses that which is intermediate.

Discussion Questions

1. Analyze Aristotle's argument that virtue and the good life require living a life according to reason with our sentiments under the control of our reason. Do you agree with Aristotle? Support your answer.

2. Discuss Aristotle's claim that most, but not all, virtues lie in the mean. Use specific examples to illustrate your answer.

3. Discuss Noddings' argument, found on pages 411–412, that ethical caring is limited by the possibility of reciprocity in caring. Discuss, in light of her argument, whether we have a moral obligation to care for small children or people who are severely disabled mentally and, as such, are not capable of "caring for others" in a reciprocal relationship. Discuss also how Aristotle might respond to Nodding's position.

Notes

1. *Confucian Analects*, bk. 4:4, in *The Chinese Classics*, ed. and trans. James Legge (Shanghai, China: Chinese Book Co., 1891).
2. "Various Systems of Virtue Categorized by Number," www.virtuescience.com/virtuenumbers.html.

3. Aristotle, *Nicomachean Ethics*, bk. II, ch. 1. From Richard McKeon, ed., *The Basic Works of Aristotle* (New York: Random House, 1941).

4. *Encyclopedia of Philosophy*, s.v. "Ross, William David."

5. John Stuart Mill, *Utilitarianism* (1861), ch. 4.

6. Norman M. Bradburn, *The Structure of Psychological Well-Being* (Chicago, IL: Aldine, 1969), p. 224.

7. "Book of Mencius," bk. 7A, pt. 1, ch. 9, v. 3. in *The Chinese Classics*, trans. James Legge.

8. Ruut Veenhoven, *Conditions of Happiness* (Dordrecht, Netherlands: D. Reidel, 1984).

9. John Stuart Mill, "On Liberty," in *Utilitarianism and Other Writings*, ed. Mary Warnock (New York: Meridian, 1962), p. 189.

10. J. A. K. Thomson, trans., *The Ethics of Aristotle* (Baltimore, MD: Penguin, 1953), pp. 38–39.

11. Thomas Aquinas, *The Summa Theologica*, Part I of the second part, question 2, article 8.

12. Harold M. Schulweis, in the "Foreword" of Samuel P. Oliner and Pearl M. Oliner, *The Altruistic Personality: Rescuers of Jews in Nazi Europe* (New York: Free Press, 1988), p. xii.

13. "Book of Mencius," bk. 2, A6, pt. 1, ch. 6, v.3.

14. Mother Teresa, *A Simple Path* (New York: Ballantine Books, 1995).

15. Confucius, "Doctrine of the Mean (*chung-yung*)."

16. http://etext.library.adelaide.edu.au/mirror/classics.mit.edu/Aristotle/nicomachean.2.ii.html.

17. Aristotle, *Nicomachean Ethics* 2:9., trans. H. Rackman (Cambridge, MA: Harvard University Press, 1975).

18. David Hume, *A Treatise on Human Nature*, ed. L. A. Selby-Bigge (Oxford, England: Clarendon Press, 1740/1978), p. 367.

19. Quoted in Ben Ami Scharfstein, *The Philosophers: Their Lives and the Nature of Their Thought* (New York: Oxford University Press, 1980), p. 196.

20. Oliner and Oliner, *The Altruistic Personality*, p. 169.

21. Hume, A *Treatise*, p. 474.

22. David Hume, "An Enquiry Concerning the Principles of Morals," in *Hume's Ethical Writings*, ed. Alasdair MacIntyre (New York: Collier, 1965), pp. 24–26.

23. Philip Hallie, *Lest Innocent Blood Be Shed* (New York: Harper & Row, 1985), p. 72.

24. Plato, "Euthyphro," in *Five Dialogues*, trans. G. M. A. Grube (Indianapolis, IN: Hackett, 1981), pp. 4b–e.

25. Susan M. Wolf, "Gender, Feminism, and Death: Physician-Assisted Suicide and Euthanasia," in *Feminism and Bioethics*, ed. Susan M. Wolf (New York: Oxford University Press, 1996), pp. 282–317.

26. Rosemary Tong, "Feminist Ethics," *Stanford Encyclopedia of Philosophy*, http://plato.stanford.edu/entries/feminism-ethics.

27. Virginia Held. "The Meshing of Care and Justice." *Hypatia* 10, no. 2 (1995): 128–132.

28. Nel Noddings, *Caring: A Feminine Approach to Ethics and Moral Education* (Berkeley: University of California Press, 1984), p. 79.

29. Ibid., p. 80.

30. Noddings, *Caring*, p. 8.

31. Oliner and Oliner, *The Altruistic Personality*, p. 168.

32. Noddings, *Caring*, p. 15.

33. Ibid., p. 148.

34. Karen J. Warren, "The Power and Promise of Ecological Feminism," in *Environmental Ethics*, ed. Susan J. Armstrong and Richard G. Botzler (New York: McGraw-Hill, 1993), pp. 434–444.

35. Ibid., p. 444.

36. Marilyn Frye, "In and Out of Harm's Way: Arrogance and Love," in *The Politics of Reality* (Trumansburg, NY: Crossing Press, 1983), pp. 75–76.

37. Uma Narayan, "Colonialism and Its Others: Considerations on Rights and Care Discourses," *Hypatia* 10, no. 2 (1995): 140.

38. Annette Baier, "What Do Women Want in a Moral Theory?" in *Principles of Biomedical Ethics*, 5th ed. Tom Beauchamp and James Childress, ed. (New York: Oxford University Press, 2001), p. 371.

39. Oliner and Oliner, *The Altruistic Personality*, p. 163.

40. Mary Daly, *The Church and the Second Sex* (Boston, MA: Beacon Press, 1985).

41. Sara Ruddick, "Mothers and Men's Wars," from *Maternal Thinking: Toward a Politics of Peace* (Boston, MA: Beacon Press, 1989), pp. 141-159.

42. See Carol Gilligan, "Concepts of the Self and Morality," *Harvard Educational Review* (November 1977): 481-517; Nancy Chodorow, *The Reproduction of Mothers: Psychoanalysis and the Sociology of Gender* (Los Angeles: University of California Press, 1978); and Caroline Whitbeck, "The Maternal Instinct," in *Mothering: Essays in Feminist Theory*, ed. Joyce Trebilcot (Totowa, NJ: Rowman and Allanheld, 1984).

43. Robert C. Solomon, *Ethics: A Short Introduction* (Dubuque, IA: Brown, 1993), pp. 107, 126-127.

44. Clyde Kluckhohn and Dorothea Leighton, *The Navaho* (Cambridge, MA: Harvard University Press, 1974), pp. 296-299.

45. Albert Scheven, *Swahili Proverbs* (Lanham, MD: University Press of America, 1981); quoted in *Beyond the Western Tradition: Readings* in *Moral and Political Philosophy*, ed. Daniel Bonevac, William Boon, and Stephen Phillips (Mountain View, CA: Mayfield, 1992), pp. 65-68.

46. Lin Yutang, *The Importance of Living* (New York: Reynal & Hitchcock, 1937), p. 162.

47. Friedrich Nietzsche, *Beyond Good and Evil*, from *The Portable Nietzsche*, trans. Walter Kaufmann (New York: Viking Penguin, 1982).

48. Friedrich Nietzsche, *The Dawn*, from *The Portable Nietzsche*, trans. Walter Kaufmann.

49. James M. Alsdurf and Phyllis Alsdurf, "A Pastoral Response," in *Abuse and Religion*, ed. Anne L. Horton and Judith A. Williamson (Lexington, MA: Heath, 1988).

50. Claudio Bepko, "Disorders of Power: Women and Addiction in the Family," in *Women in Families*, ed. Monica McGoldrick, Carol Anderson, and Froma Walsh (New York: Norton, 1989), p. 412.

51. See Damien Keown, *The Nature of Buddhist Ethics* (London: Macmillan Press, 1992).

52. *Buddhist Scriptures*, trans. Edward Conze (New York: Penguin, 1959), p. 109.

53. *Bhagavad Gita*, with commentary by R. C. Zaehner (Oxford, England: Clarendon Press, 1969), pp. 447-448.

54. Joseph Tobin, David Wu, and Dana Davidson, *Preschool in Three Cultures: Japan, China and the United States* (New Haven, CT: Yale University Press, 1989), p. 190.

55. Joyce Trebilcot, "Two Forms of Androgynism," *Journal of Social Philosophy* 8, no. 1 (January 1977): 4-8.

56. Luke 7:43-45, in *The New Oxford Annotated Bible* (New York: Oxford University Press, 1977).

57. *Confucian Analects*, bk. 4:15 p. 1-2.

58. Anne Colby and William Damon, *Some Do Care: Contemporary Lives of Moral Commitment* (New York: Free Press, 1992).

59. William Damon, *Greater Expectations* (New York: Free Press, 1995), p. 158.

60. *The Philosophy of Wang Yang Ming*, trans. Frederick Goodrich Henke (Carbondale, IL: Open Court, 1916); quoted in Bonevac, Boon, and Phillips, *Beyond the Western Tradition*, p. 330.

61. From *Tseng Tzu*, ch. 6, p. 428.

62. From the Confucian text *The Greater Learning*, in *A Sourcebook in Asian Philosophy*, ed. John M. Koller and Patricia Koller (New York: Macmillan, 1991), p. 424.

63. Wang Yang Ming, quoted in Bonevac, Boon, and Phillips, *Beyond the Western Tradition*, p. 330.

64. Oliner and Oliner, *The Altruistic Personality*, pp. 166-170.

65. Ibid., pp. 166-167.

66. *Buddhist Scriptures*, trans. Edward Conze (New York: Penguin, 1959), p. 109.

67. Christina Sommers, "Where Have All the Good Deeds Gone?" *Hastings Center Report*, August 1982.

Applying Moral Theory
in Real Life

The unexamined life is not worth living.

Know thyself.

—PLATO/SOCRATES

Most people have no problem knowing what is morally right and wrong in the majority of situations. But when there is a conflict between moral demands, the differing moral theories can leave us feeling confused about how to go about making a moral decision. Which theory, or theories, do we turn to for guidance?

The relativist moral theories obviously won't do. Ethical subjectivism legitimates acting on cruel personal whims while cultural relativism can legitimate oppressive cultural customs. Some people look to religion, rather than personal or cultural values, for moral guidance. Divine command theory and religious ethics that are dependent on or relative to particular religious beliefs offer even less guidance since they tend to fall prey to the same problems that plague the other forms of ethical relativism.

As people mature in their moral reasoning, they look to universal moral principles and sentiments, rather than relativist theories, for moral guidance. According to developmental psychologists, people at the higher stages of moral reasoning tend to make more satisfactory moral decisions and are better at resolving moral dilemmas.

Utilitarianism, one of the first universal moral theories we studied, has proven to be useful in evaluating and developing public policy. However, it risks neglecting personal integrity in seeking the greatest good for the community. Ethical egoism, on the other hand, focuses too much on the individual to the neglect of the community and social good.

Natural law theory claims that morality is universal and part of the natural order and that we can discern what is moral through the use of reason. Although some natural law theorists claim God as the ultimate source of morality, others regard the moral law as part of our rational nature.

Kantian deontology, while offering a strong foundation for ethics in the form of the categorical imperative, tends to be too demanding. It also ignores consequences in making moral decisions. Prima facie deontology provides a corrective to the rigidity of Kantian deontology and, at the same time, recognizes future-looking duties. However, neither form of deontology adequately addresses the issue of moral rights. Rights ethics, on the other hand, without being tied to deontology, allows the strong to assert their rights at the expense of the weak.

Finally, virtue ethics points out the importance of a virtuous character in morality and the importance of seeking the mean. However, except for persons at the higher stages of moral development, character does not, on its own provide adequate guidelines for making moral decisions in everyday life, especially ones involving issues of justice.

While all the moral theories we studied have a different focus, there is a great deal of overlap between the universal moral theories. They all claim that moral principles should be applied universally and impartially. They all require that we treat persons with respect—whether person be defined as all sentient beings or, more narrowly, as only rational beings. And, all the universal moral theories promote self-improvement in virtue and wisdom.

As stated in Chapter 1, theories, by their nature, tend to oversimplify. They are like telescopes. They zoom in on certain key points rather than elucidating the total extent of thinking about ethics. Because we cannot see and measure morality in the same sense that we can see objects in the physical world, to arrive at moral truths we must rely on other faculties, such as intuition, reason, and sentiment—if, in fact, we will ever be able to discern the nature of moral truth. This puts us in a position similar to the blind men trying to describe the elephant. The Buddha told the following story when he heard that some holy men were quarreling over their beliefs:

> Once a king invited all the blind men to his palace. Then he asked his servant to bring an elephant. The servant did so and said, "An elephant is like this," and told each blind man to feel a different part of the animal. Then the king came and asked the blind men what an elephant was like.
>
> Those who had felt the head said, "Sire, the elephant is like a jar." Those who had felt the ear said, "It is like a winnowing basket." The tusk was likened to a post, the trunk to a plow's pole, the body to a granary, the foot to the base of a column, the rump to a mortar, the tail to a pestle, and the tuft of the tail to a broom. Then they started to quarrel. "I'm right. You are wrong." And this led to fighting.
>
> The Buddha said that those who insist that what they believe is right and everyone else is wrong are like the blind men who thought that a part of the elephant was the whole.[1]

Each of the blind men correctly described a part of the elephant, but they mistook the part for the whole. In a similar manner, because morality covers such a broad scope of issues, different philosophers tend to focus on different aspects of morality. Problems arise when they claim that their insight is the whole picture—that morality is merely consequences or merely duty or merely having good intentions. Morality is not a simple concept that can be captured in a nice tidy theory; it is a multifaceted phenomenon.

W. D. Ross likened moral decision making to the artistic process. According to Ross, there is no set formula for determining which action we should take in a moral dilemma. The general duties themselves may be self-evident, but judgments about our duties in a particular case are not. Consequently, we need to use reason and creativity to make judgments about our duty in that situation. Ross believed that this lack of clarity is due to the nature of moral decision making, which, he claimed, is more like creating a work of art than solving a mathematical problem: The finished paintings might look very different, but we are all painting from the same palette. Universal moral principles, like the artist's palette, provide the form rather than the specific content of our final decision. Ross believed that, to demand ethicists provide us with pre-determined moral decisions is as unreasonable as artists demanding that their mentors tell them exactly how their finished works should look.

Like any creative undertaking, moral decision making requires the proper tools and expertise in reasoning; however, it also demands that we personally enter into the process. The sort of moral decisions we make says as much about the kind of people we are as it does about the universal moral principles themselves. Thus, in making satisfactory and well-informed moral decisions in your life, it is important to know yourself and to constantly strive to overcome immature defense mechanisms and narrow-mindedness in order to become a more virtuous and wise person.

Note

1. Quoted in Catherine Hewitt, *Buddhism* (New York: Thompson, 1995), p. 21.

Glossary

a priori proposition A statement that we can know to be true without reference to or prior to any experience.

absolute duty A duty that is always morally binding without exception regardless of the particular circumstances.

absolutist A person who believes that moral principles are morally binding regardless of the particular circumstances.

abusive fallacy A fallacy that occurs when a person disagrees with someone else's conclusion, but instead of addressing the argument, the person attacks the character of the person who made the argument.

active euthanasia The direct and intentional killing of a person.

ad hominem fallacy An argument directed against a person. The abusive fallacy and the circumstantial fallacy are both ad hominem fallacies.

agape Unconditional love.

ahimsa The Buddhist principle of nonhurting.

analysis The process of critically examining our worldview using reason and logic.

anthropocentrism The belief that human beings are the central or most significant entity of the universe.

appeal to force A fallacy that occurs when a person uses or threatens to use physical, psychological, or legal force in an attempt to coerce another person to accept a conclusion.

appeal to inappropriate authority A fallacy that occurs when someone appeals to an expert or authority in a field other than the one under debate.

appeal to tradition A fallacy that occurs when someone argues that a practice or attitude is morally acceptable because it is a tradition or cultural norm.

argument A type of reasoning composed of two or more propositions, one of which is claimed to follow logically from or be supported by the others.

autonomous moral agent A self-determining person who looks to his or her own reason for moral guidance.

begging the question This fallacy, also known as circular reasoning, occurs when the premise and conclusion are actually different wordings of the same proposition.

behaviorism The psychological theory that our behavior, including our moral behavior, is a product of our environment and our culture.

biological altruism Inborn cooperative behavior.

care ethics A type of feminist ethics that emphasizes the virtue of caring within the context of actualrelationships over considerations of abstract duties.

categorical imperative A term introduced by Immanuel Kant to describe a moral injunction that is unconditionally binding upon us.

circumstantial fallacy A fallacy that occurs when someone argues that another person should accept a certain position because of his or her special circumstances, such as lifestyle or membership in a particular group based on characteristics such as race, ethnicity, gender, nationality, or religion.

civil disobedience The refusal, on moral grounds, to obey certain government laws, for the purpose of trying to bring about a change in legislation or government policy.

civil religion A set of institutionalized beliefs, symbols, and rituals that provide a religious dimension to a nation's collective life.

cloning Production of identical individuals through asexual reproduction, either by embryo splitting or transfer of nuclei.

cognitive dissonance Psychological conflict resulting from incongruous beliefs and attitudes held simultaneously and when the current means of resolving the conflict is shown to be inadequate. See also *ontological shock.*

cognitive theory The metaethical theory that moral statements can be either true or false.

communitarianism The theory that community is the basis of ethics.

compassion An active form of sympathy involving praxis or social action.

conclusion A proposition that is affirmed or denied on the basis of other propositions in an argument.

conscience An inner sense of right and wrong.

consequentialism The ethical theory that the consequences of our actions are more important than our intentions.

433

cultural relativism A type of ethical relativism that maintains that morality is created collectively by groups of humans and that morality therefore differs from culture to culture.

cynicism Distrust in others' motives and disbelief in the possibility of knowing the truth.

deductive argument An argument where the conclusion *necessarily* follows from the premise *if* the premise is true and the reasoning process is valid.

defense mechanisms Psychological methods, which humans usually learn at an early age, for coping with difficult situations.

deontology The ethical theory that duty is the basis of morality.

descriptive ethics A branch of sociology that describes the moral beliefs of a given society without passing judgment on them.

descriptive statement A statement that tells us what is. Most scientific statements are descriptive.

determinism The theory that all events, including human actions, are governed by causal laws.

distributive justice The duty to distribute the benefits and burdens of a society in a fair manner.

divine command theory A type of ethical relativism that states that morality is relative to or dependent on God's will.

doctrine of the mean The doctrine that moral virtues, in general, entail moderation or seeking the middle path.

doublethink Simultaneously holding two contradictory views and believing both to be true.

duty That which is morally obligatory.

egotist A person who is arrogant, boastful, and self-centered.

emotivism The moral theory that moral statements are neither true nor false but simply expressions of feeling.

empiricism The theory that all, or at least most, human knowledge comes to us through the five senses.

enlightenment See *self-realization*.

epigenetic rules Innate patterns that guide the behavior and thought of humans and other animals.

epistemological privilege A theory that privileges the insight of people who are socially and economically disadvantaged.

epistemology The branch of philosophy that is concerned with the study of knowledge.

ethical egoism The metaethical theory that every person should do what is in his or her best self-interest.

ethical relativism The theory that morality is created by people and that moral systems can be different for different people.

ethical skepticism The theory that it is difficult, if not impossible, to know whether moral truths exist or the nature of these truths.

ethical subjectivism A type of ethical relativism that claims that morality is relative to each individual person.

ethics A branch of philosophy involving the study of the fundamental principles and concepts regarding right and wrong conduct.

eudaemonia Aristotle's term for the happiness that humans by nature seek and that arises from the fulfillment of our function as humans.

euthanasia The act of painlessly bringing about the death of a person who is suffering from a terminal or incurable disease or condition.

existentialism The philosophical theory that humans are defined only by their freedom.

fallacy of accident A fallacy that occurs when someone applies a rule that is generally accepted as valid to a particular case where exceptional or accidental circumstances render the rule inappropriate.

fallacy of equivocation A type of fallacy where the meaning of an ambiguous term shifts during the course of the argument.

fallacy of ignorance A fallacy committed whenever someone argues that a conclusion is true simply on the grounds that it has not been proved false or that it is false simply because it has not been proved true.

fallacy of irrelevant conclusion A fallacy committed when a person uses premises to support or reject a conclusion other than the one at which the premises are directed.

falsifiable The requirement that a theory must be falsifiable means that there must be some evidence or argument that could count against it. A theory that will not admit any evidence against it is known as a pseudo-theory.

feminist ethics The rethinking of traditional ethics to create a nonsexist, gender-equal ethics that takes into account the importance of moral sentiment in women's moral reasoning.

fidelity A moral duty of loyalty that stems from a commitment made in the past.

good will A will that always acts from a sense of duty and reverence for moral law, without regard for consequences or for immediate inclinations.

gratitude A moral duty that stems from past favors or unearned services received.

greatest happiness principle The utilitarian principle that actions are right in proportion to how much they tend to promote happiness and wrong when they tend to produce unhappiness. This is also known as the principle of utility.

guilt A moral sentiment that results from the violation of a moral norm.

habituation A term used by Aristotle to describe the regular practice of virtuous behavior, much as one practices the piano or any other skill, until it becomes second nature.

hasty generalization A fallacy that occurs when someone uses only unusual or atypical cases to support a conclusion.

hedonism A philosophical doctrine that considers pleasure to be the standard of moral value.

hedonist paradox The observation that the pursuit of our own happiness as our only goal is self-defeating.

helper's high The moral sentiment or positive affect we experience when helping others.

heteronomous moral agent Someone who looks to others for moral guidance.

hypothetical imperative A moral injunction that tells us we ought to do something *if* we desire to achieve a certain result—such as telling a lie to save a life. Moral obligations, in contrast, are categorical or unconditionally binding upon us.

individual relativism See *ethical subjectivism.*

inductive argument An argument where the conclusion *probably* follows from the premise but we can't be 100 percent sure.

informal fallacy An argument that is psychologically or emotionally persuasive but logically incorrect.

intuition Immediate or self-evident knowledge.

just war theory A list of conditions in natural law theory to ensure that war is humanely conducted and directed toward the establishment of lasting peace.

justice The moral duty to give each person equal consideration.

karma In Eastern philosophy, the universal moral force that holds us responsible for the consequences of our actions in this lifetime as well as in future lifetimes.

laissez-faire capitalism An economic system based on the pursuit of rational and prudent self-interest, individual freedom, and minimal government interference.

legitimate interests In rights ethics, interests that do not prevent others from pursuing similar and equally important interests.

liberalism The theory that opposes social and legal constraints upon individual freedoms. The term *libertarian* is sometimes used synonymously with the term *liberal.*

liberation ethics The ethical theory based on social and political reform and a demand for respect of the dignity and rights of all people.

libertarian A person who is opposed to any social or political restraints upon individual freedom. See *liberalism.*

liberty or negative right The right to be left alone to pursue our legitimate interests without interference from the government or from others.

logic The study of correct and incorrect reasoning.

mandala The ancient Sanskrit word for a circle that symbolizes the cosmic order.

marginalization The act of relegating beings or groups to the fringes or margins of the moral community.

metaethics The subdivision of ethics concerned with appraising the logical foundations and internal consistencies of ethical systems. Also called *metaethical theory* or *theoretical ethics.*

metaphysical dualism The theory that reality is composed of two substances: material bodies and nonmaterial mind or spirit.

metaphysical materialism The theory that reality consists of only one substance: material (physical) bodies.

metaphysics The branch of philosophy concerned with the study of the nature of reality, including what it means to be human.

metta The term for universal compassion in Buddhist ethics.

moral agents Those beings who can be held morally responsible for their actions.

moral character One of James Rest's four components of moral behavior. The integration of moral reasoning, moral sensitivity, and moral motivation into one's personality.

moral community All beings who have moral worth in themselves and, as such, deserve the respect of the community.

moral dilemma A situation where there is a conflict between moral values; no matter what solution is chosen, it will involve doing something wrong in order to do what is right.

moral indignation The anger or moral outrage that some people feel at the sight of others being harmed.

moral minimalism The belief that morality only consists of certain minimal moral requirements, such as not torturing or murdering innocent people.

moral motivation One of James Rest's four components of moral behavior. The placing of moral values above competing nonmoral values.

moral reasoning One of James Rest's four components of moral behavior. The application of logical analysis to moral issues. Lawrence Kohlberg emphasizes moral reasoning in his theory of moral development.

moral sensitivity One of James Rest's four components of moral behavior: The awareness of how our actions affect other people.

moral sentiments Emotions that move us to feel moral approval or disapproval.

moral tragedy This occurs when people fail to take appropriate moral action and instead make decisions that they later come to regret.

natural law theory The theory that morality is grounded in unchanging natural or moral laws that are part of our rational nature and can be accessed through the use of reason.

natural rights ethics The theory that moral rights stem from our human nature, which is a special creation of God.

naturalistic fallacy The logical mistake (according to some moral philosophers) of drawing a conclusion about what *ought* to be from premises about what *is.*

negative duty A moral duty to restrain ourselves from doing something.

negative right *See* liberty right.

noncognitive theories Metaethical theories that claim there are no moral truths.

nonmaleficence The moral principle that we should do no harm.

normative ethics A subdivision of ethics that gives us practical guidelines or behavioral norms.

objectivist ethics A term used by Ayn Rand to describe her version of ethical egoism.

ontological shock An event that shakes our worldview, and our very being, to the core. Ontological shock leads to cognitive dissonance.

ontology The study of being or the nature of being.

opinion A statement that is based only on feeling rather than on fact.

pacifism The belief that the right to life is an absolute right.

passive euthanasia Withholding life support or medical treatment.

persons Beings who are worthy of respect as valuable in themselves rather than because of their usefulness or value to others. Members of the moral community.

philosophy Literally, the "love of wisdom"; the systematic and critical search for truth and meaning in our lives.

popular appeal A fallacy that occurs when someone appeals to popular opinion or the opinion of the majority to gain support for a conclusion. Popular appeal can take different forms; the first is known as the band-wagon approach, and the second is snob appeal.

positive duty A moral duty to actively perform a particular action.

positive right *See* welfare right.

positivism The philosophical theory that all genuine human knowledge is based upon scientific observation.

praxis The practice of a particular art or skill. In ethics, praxis entails informed social action.

premise A proposition that supports or gives reasons for accepting the conclusion in an argument.

prescriptive statement A statement dealing with values or what *ought* to be. Moral statements are prescriptive.

prima facie duty A duty that is morally binding unless it conflicts with a more pressing moral duty.

primary social goods Goods, such as food, housing, police protection, and education, that are necessary for us to pursue our liberty rights and our concept of the good life.

principle of double effect The principle that an action which causes a serious harm may be permissible if that harm is an unintended side effect of bringing about a particular good.

principle of reciprocity The moral principle in Confucian ethics that states that we have a moral duty to treat others as we would wish to be treated ourselves.

proposition In logic, a statement that expresses a complete thought. A proposition can be either true or false.

psychological egoism The descriptive theory that humans are basically egoists who always act in their own self-interests.

rationalism The theory that most human knowledge comes to us through reason rather than through the physical senses.

rationalization In philosophy, the use of rhetorical devices, fallacies, and resistance in arguments rather than reason and logical analysis.

reason Understanding the connection between the general and the particular.

relativist theories Metaethical theories that claim that there are no universal moral principles or values and that morality is instead created or invented by humans.

religion An institutionalized set of beliefs about a transcendent god(s).

reparation A moral duty that requires us to make amends for past harms we have caused others.

resentment The anger or moral outrage a person feels when personally injured by another.

resistance The use of immature defense mechanisms—such as isolation, rationalization, doubt and indecision, denial, repression, and displacement—as a means of preventing our worldview from being analyzed.

ressentiment Deep-seated resentment, frustration, and hostility accompanied by a sense of being powerless to express these feelings directly.

retributive justice A duty that requires punishment in proportion to wrongdoing.

rhetoric A means of defending a particular worldview rather than analyzing it. Unlike a logical argument, rhetoric uses only statements that support a particular opinion and disregards any statements that do not support this opinion.

rights ethics The ethical theory that people's entitlements as members of society are the basis of ethics.

self-actualization See *self-realization.*

self-improvement The moral duty to improve our knowledge and our virtue.

self-realization The process of devoting one's life to self-cultivation and the search for ultimate values. A life lived in harmony with one's ultimate nature.

sentient beings Beings with the capacity to experience pain and pleasure.

shame A feeling that occurs as a result of a social blunder or violation of a social norm. Unlike true guilt, which is a moral sentiment, shame is governed by external sanctions.

skepticism Maintaining a doubtful, yet open and questioning, attitude toward statements that are claimed to be true.

sociobiology The branch of biology that applies evolutionary theory to the social sciences.

sociological relativism The observation that there is disagreement among cultures regarding moral values. Unlike cultural relativism, sociological relativism is neither an argument nor a moral theory. It is merely a descriptive statement about societies.

sociopath A person who lacks a conscience or sense of moral responsibility.

Socratic method A technique developed by Socrates, using a question-and-answer format to break down resistance, thereby forcing people to critically analyze their preconceived notions.

speciesism A term coined by utilitarian Peter Singer to describe prejudice or bias against a particular being simply because of its membership in a particular species.

spirituality An inner attitude of reverence or deep respect for the ultimate moral worth or sacredness of oneself and others.

state of nature The hypothetical condition in which people lived before the formation of the state or governments.

superego Freud's concept of conscience; the superego develops as a reaction formation against our childhood Oedipus complex.

supererogatory Moral actions that are above and beyond what is normally expected of an individual.

sympathy A moral sentiment that involves the ability to imagine the feelings of others.

teleological A theory that is based upon a specific view of the purpose or goal of the natural order. Natural law theory and utilitarianism are teleological theories.

theoretical ethics See *metaethics.*

Übermensch In Friedrich Nietzsche's philosophy, a superhuman or free-spirited person who is able to rise above the herd morality of the crowds and exercise his or her will to power.

universalist theories Metaethical theories that claim there are objective, universal moral principles and values that are true for all humans.

utilitarian calculus A process of weighing costs and benefits to determine which action is morally preferable.

utilitarianism The metaethical theory that actions producing the most pleasure are good and those that promote pain are bad.

utopia An ideal society.

values clarification Ethics education based on nonjudgmental and nondirective discussion of moral issues.

veil of ignorance A conceptual device used by John Rawls to establish a social contract that is unbiased and based upon impartiality.

vice A character defect or disposition to act in a manner that harms oneself and others.

virtue An admirable character trait or disposition to habitually act in a manner that benefits oneself and others.

virtue ethics The ethical theory concerned primarily with character and the type of people we should be rather than with our actions.

welfare or positive right The right to receive primary social goods such as adequate nutrition, housing, education, and police and fire protection.

worldview The combined interpretations of our experiences.

Index

Information presented in figures and tables is indicated by *f* and *t*.